dig infinity!

dig infinity!

the life and art of Lord Buckley

oliver trager

welcome rain publishers
new york

DIG INFINITY: The Life and Art of Lord Buckley

Direct any inquiries to:
Welcome Rain Publishers LLC
23 West 26th Street
New York, NY 10010

Library of Congress Cataloging-in-Publication Data
Trager, Oliver.
Dig infinity : the life and art of Lord Buckley / Oliver Trager.
p. cm.
Includes index.
ISBN 1-56649-157-6
1. Lord Buckley. 2. Entertainers—United States—Biography. I. Title.
PN2287.L637T732001
791'.092—dc21
[B] 2001026125

Printed in the United States of America
Text design by Cindy LaBreacht

First Edition: April 2002
1 3 5 7 9 10 8 6 4 2
A Black Market Book

for elaine and cole

for my mother and father

for all members of the royal court:
past, present, and future

"Laughter truly is religious. It gives off vibrations from the subconscious. It swings its sounds from the subconscious. When a person is laughing he's illuminated the full beauty of a human being. And the womanhood, when she's happy and laughing, is OOOOOOOOOOOOH—mother magnate. Many times when you find yourself laughing you say, 'Oh I wish John were here, he'd love this.' You're thinking love, you're vibrating love. It's a prayer."

—Lord Buckley, 1959

"A true researcher proceeds amongst riddles."

—Jan Potocki: *The Manuscript Found in Saragossa*

CONtents

author's note on concept and format

In that Lord Buckley's unorthodox legacy does not lend itself to conventional biographical treatment, the parameters of the genre have been manipulated to more adequately reflect the subject's life and work. Therefore, *Dig Infinity!* unfolds on several levels simultaneously: biography, oral history, autobiography, scrapbook, anthology, and critique.

Different typeface styles and margin sizes are employed to delineate the correct voice for each ingredient in this literary gumbo.

The traditional biographical overview and integrating commentary will appear in this 9-point Helvetica.

The oral history from the many witnesses in the book as well as Lord Buckley's own autobiographical and philosphical musings will appear in this 9-point Times Europa. Additionally, album liner notes and previously published memories appear in this same style.

The material is arranged chronologically and thematically according to either the era in which each contributor first encountered Lord Buckley or when a specific topic arises about which they comment. *Each participant is first introduced by a brief description of their life and their connection with Buckley in this 9- point Times Europa italic.*

Imagine, if you will, an all-night bull session in the smoky atmosphere in the dressing room of a Greenwich Village jazz club. Some witnesses drop by to throw in their two cents when a salient topic arises or stay the duration, acting as a chorus to the verbal jam. Should the reader become confused as to the identity of a witness, an alphabetized "Cast of Characters" is available for quick reference at the end of the manuscript.

> Lord Buckley's carefully transcribed monologues, appearing in either full or excerpted form, are available in this 9-point Times Europa but printed within the confines of this narrower margin. This has been done both to distinguish it from the rest of the text and to enhance its sometimes difficult readability. Though Buckley's work obviously comes off better on recording than on the printed page, those with a good eye and ear for its particular and peculiar cadences can derive an excellent notion of its inner rhythms and nuances. Just take a deep breath and *blow!*

The scrapbook element of this biographical collage reprints articles, reviews, and obituaries drawn from the press. These inclusions appear in this 9-point Courier Bold to best invoke the stylistic spirit of newsprint.

Let the Great Lord Buckley Renaissance commence!

INTRODUCTION

Floating through some inverse abysm of time and space, your subconscious mind encounters the fantastic cast of characters from the absurdist theater of the sublime and ridiculous, the sacred and profane—a cartoon cornucopia from the mind/tongue of the human experience: Alvar Núñez Cabeza de Vaca (The Gasser) leads a charge of bug-eyed conquistadores to the Fountain of Youth, Old Ebeneezer Scrooge counts his barley, Willie the Shake plays strip poker with Cleopatra and Marilyn Monroe, James Dean and the Marquis de Sade plan an escape route off Devil's Island, Abe Lincoln and Hezikiah Jones harmonize on a few choruses of "On the Sunny Side of the Street," Nero and Julius Caesar pitch their next B-movie to Governor Slugwell on a runaway train to Flip Manor while Commander Abba-Dabba-Foo rides his own railroad through Einstein's Playground (that's the Milky Way for all you double-square octagon heads) hoping to catch The Nazz's last set at the Club DeLisa.

If you know something's happening but not sure quite what, let me hip thee: It's Lord Buckley, Jack.

Lord Who?

Lord Buckley: the white, six-and-a-half-foot-tall, ex-lumberjack cat who invoked both the manners of English aristocracy and the street language of black America.

Lord Buckley: the hemp-headed hipster who worked the Walkathons and tent shows of the Depression.

Lord Buckley: the picaresque pill-popping darling of Al Capone.

Lord Buckley: the stand-up comic who could celebrate Jesus Christ *and* the Marquis de Sade in the course of a single gig.

Lord Buckley: the jazz philosopher who jammed with Charlie Parker.

Lord Buckley: the gallivanting guru who appeared in a Marilyn Monroe flick.

Lord Buckley: the Scotch-swigging shaman who swung light-years ahead of the Summer of Love.

Lord Buckley: the flim-flamming/huckster/con man/drifter/grifter who streaked at a Frank Sinatra concert, started his own bebop church, and threw a lifelong Mardi Gras.

Lord Buckley: America's great neglected verbalist visionary who is about to put his whammy on you . . . yes, you!

Lord who?

Before Cool (b.c.) there was Lord Buckley: the original viper, the Hall of Fame Hipster, the baddest Beatnik, the first flower child, the premier rapper. Lord Buckley, best known for his "hipsemantic" retellings of Bible stories, Shakespeare soliloquies, and modern poetry in the 1950s.

Lord who?

Fast-forward from his humble, turn-of-the-cenutry roots in Tuolumne, California (a tough mining and lumber town in the foothills of the Sierra Nevada, where he sang on street corners busking for small change from assorted roughnecks), to the 1930s, 1940s, and beyond. His scattershot career carried him from the dance marathons and Capone's murkiest Windy City dives to tours with Woody Herman, Gene Krupa, Ed Sullivan's U.S.O. troupe, bebop's first stages, and vaudeville's last. Somewhere along the way, Buckley (as true to the tradition of jazz royalty as Duke Ellington, Count Basie, and King Oliver) had become a Lord, creating a kingdom in miniature, replete with his own peculiar sense of protocol and a lifestyle that might make even de Sade blush.

Lord who? Lord Buckley, that's who!

Me? I first got bit by the Lord Buckley bug in the fall of 1976—fresh from a cross-country hitchhiking and freight-train-hopping adventure, chasing the ghosts of Kerouac and Cassady to Alaska and back. I was open for any- and everything.

Returning as a sophomore to Bennington College in Vermont, I fell in with a severely funky, nonmatriculating crowd centered on a mercurial, middle-aged gadfly by the name of Harold L. "Doc" Humes. You can read more about Doc in this book, but the spell he cast on an upper-middle-class, uptown nineteen-year-old trying-to-be-hippie kid was enormous. With his long silver mane and nonstop rap flowing, he resembled some pixie-dusted incarnation of Ernest Hemingway on acid.

While most of his persona was, in retrospect, an ecstatic, hyperbolic verbal plume of wildly entertaining (if sometimes a little scary) self-aggrandizement, his credentials were anything but. Novelist, inventor, Marshall Planner, *Paris Review* cofounder, cosmologist, conspiracy theorist—he certainly came on as someone who had been there, done that, flapped it, dapped it, and bapped it in spades. Naturally, he was *way* more interesting than anything my college professors at the time were offering at premium tuition prices.

Not only had Doc known Lord Buckley back in the day, but he was riding shotgun when the cabaret card brouhaha brought an end first to His Lordship's last gig . . . and then his life.

One of Doc's acolytes was a fellow by the name of Mark Miller who kind of took care of the old guy. One afternoon Mark brought an LP over to my dorm room. He was pretty mysterious about it as I recall—wouldn't even if drop it on the turntable until we were psychically lubricated with nature's combustible best.

The album was *The Best of Lord Buckley* and, as I studied the psychedelic cover and read the liner notes, I had no idea what to expect when the needle finally touched down on vinyl . . . or suspect that I was about to begin bushwhacking an underground byway of the mind in search of the seven-ply source of the sound I was about to hear.

In deference to our state of mind, I think the first piece he played me was "Jonah and the Whale," which, because it treated ganja with sympathy and humor, immediately won me over—even if I wasn't quite sure what it was I was hearing. So rhythmically encoded was the slang, so rapid-fire was the delivery, so steeped in lush, cartoonish imagery that Buckley's word pictures seemed to float across the inner screen of my skull. Even as hip as I thought I was, the language was a foreign one to my ears. Yet I found myself belly laughing at the pure joy of the storyteller's art and craft.

Next up was "The Nazz," Lord Buckley's hepster retelling of three miracles in the life of Jesus Christ. And like all true believers, I felt as if I had just stumbled on the Dead Sea Scrolls of the New Apocalypse.

No, I didn't then and there foresake my sanity and all my worldly goods to follow the Buckley muse to each corner of the lower forty-eight, points upward and beyond—that wouldn't come till much later. Rather, he became another piece of my incubating perception of the great weird world underground railroad—an irregular line that includes stops at each subterranean station of that ever-lovin' cross and pickin' up various and sundry passengers on its horizon-to-horizon trek: Bird & Diz, Sun Ra & Moondog, Partch & Pynchon, Coltrane & Soul Train, Dylan & The Dead, Smiths Patti & Harry, Kurosawa & Keaton, Stengel & Berra.

Over the next few years I slowly began collecting Buckley's out-of-print LPs in used-record stores, plumbing the album sleeves for any clues—more missing pieces of a puzzle wrapped within a mystery coiling inside a conspiracy and sandwiched between an enigma with a schmear.

In the summer of 1985, while pretending to do some research for my father in the reading room of the Main Branch of the New York Public Library, I hit the microfilm machines during some downtime hoping to come across the few scraps of Buckley ephemera I knew must be there waiting for me. These turned out to be his *New York Times* obit, Albert Goldman's *Life* magazine article, and little bits o' this 'n' that.

Devouring these morsels of information like they were long-lost parts of an ancient map to El Dorado, I sat at my table in some kind of warm, ecstatic glow. The late-afternoon light was pouring through those famous library windows and bathed me with a vision I have yet to shake. I saw my life's work unfolding before me—a golden road of unlimited devotion. I knew then and there which book I was put on this here Earth to write. Definitely one of those moments when the angels blew God's trombones like the Basie band and beckoned with perfumed whispers: "Be there or be square!"

I went home that night and filled my journal page with names—names of anybody and everybody who might have anything to do with telling Lord Buckley's story. Yes! It was going to be an oral history, at least partially. After all, since Buckley was one of those characters people tell such great stories about, why not find these people, record their tales, and share them with whomever might listen. I figured there must be *somebody* out there who dug Lord B as much as me. Maybe even a couple of somebodys.

But like the hardworking slacker that I was, I promptly dropped the list and my little stash from the library into a folder, which I stuck in my file cabinet and proceeded to forget.

When I got together with my wife, Elaine, about five years later, I played her some Buckley, capping off the little wax-spinning session with his "Bad-Rapping of the Marquis de Sade." I told her a bit about Buckley, showed her the library clips, and must have seemed pretty enthusiastic, because (against what now must be her better judgment) she encouraged me to pursue my idea.

It was then that I began making my first few, fitful stabs at contacting Lord Buckley's friends and associates, most of whom seemed touched and happy that a younger person still cared. I got busy. One contact led to another and then another and then another. My trips to library became more frequent and fruitful.

At some point, I'm not sure when or where or how, I sensed that I had embarked on what Native Americans might call a "vision quest." Like a Jew wandering in the desert of the obtuse monocultural homogeny that seems to engulf our sweet jumpin' little green sphere as somebody's idea of the millennium turns a page, I felt as if I was spreading Lord Buckley's gospel, Johnny Appleseed–style, for one reason and one reason only: to help people laugh before they get killed.

You know, the Grateful Dead took their name from a cycle of folktales that essentially recast the venerable story of the Good Samaritan: a lone traveler encounters a group of people arguing over a corpse. Apparently, the deceased left a heap of debt and none of the townsfolk is flush enough to spring for even the most modest burial. After the traveler pays for the proper internment, he encounters a dangerous crisis and is saved at the last moment by someone who later reveals himself to be the spirit of the person he had buried.

In so many ways, those of us in the Buckley omniverse who have been keeping his legacy alive are participants in a living myth, giving the man a proper burial before sending his ever-lovin' spirit into the folds of the living sky. Lord Buckley died a martyr's death precisely at the point in mid-twentieth-century social, cultural, and political history when his gifts and vision would have not only gained him the type of recognition he so richly deserved but consequently impacted the national zeitgeist as well. Yet his artistic contribution and uniquely American life remain criminally neglected, relegated to something far less than footnote to a footnote to a footnote status. Until now.

For the new Princes and Princesses just arriving at the Castle doors, proceed with caution. Listen not for a traditional punch line (there are none), but for the buoyant, earthy soul of the man and his sermons. For Royal Court dignitaries and jestors returning to the Church of the Living Swing, welcome back. And for all "People Worshipers" everywhere: DIG INFINITY!

For more about His Lordship visit Lord Buckley Online:
http://www.industrialhaiku.com/Lord_Buckley_Online.html.

PROLOGUE

presenting lord buckley

Ed Sullivan

America's preeminent impresario, Ed Sullivan was one of Lord Buckley's closest friends. Buckley toured with Sullivan's U.S.O. troupe during World War II and appeared on his television program many times in the 1940s and 1950s. His brief inclusions here and at the conclusion of this book are drawn from his TV show and his syndicated column as it appeared in the November 14, 1960, edition of the New York Daily News.

I would like you to meet a significant figure in American entertainment. His Lordship, Dick Buckley . . . Buckley, come out here!

Lord Buckley

Lord Buckley's personal reminiscences, commentary, and material laced throughout this book are drawn from newspaper and magazine articles, liner notes, officially released recordings, unreleased recordings, his September 1959 interview with Bill Butler on KPFA-FM in Berkeley, California, and his August 1960 interview with Studs Terkel on Chicago's WFMT-FM.

I'm a people worshiper. I think people should worship people. I really do.

I went out looking for God the other day and I couldn't pin him. So I figured if I couldn't find him I'd look for his stash: his Great Lake of Love that holds the whole world in gear. And when I finally found it I had the great pleasure of finding that people were the guardians of it. Dig that. So, with my two times two is four, I figured that if people were guarding the stash of love known as God then, when people swing in beauty, they become little Gods and Goddesses. And I know a couple of them myself personally and I know you do too.

I think people should worship people. I like to worship something I can see . . . something I can get my hands on . . . get my brains on. I don't know about that *Gee-Ho-Vah* cat—I can't reach him.

I don't know. It seems every time I found myself in a bind nothing mystic came to help me. Some man or some woman stepped up there and said, "We'll help you. We'll do this, we'll do that." That's the way it looks to me.

So recently, on the San Berdoo Freeway, I got hung up in an old junker car going to Las Vegas, Nevada. Right in the middle of the freeway during the rush hour it conked out. It was a madhouse—like having lunch in the middle of the

Indianapolis Speedway. About three days went by and finally along came God. There were two of them: a big God and a little God. And they didn't know me from a "from-a." But they pushed and they pulled and they tugged and they twisted and they yanked and they gave me every possible assistance in the world and finally got me on my way. I haven't seen them since.

I hope I haven't offended your religious beliefs but I think people should worship people. I really do. I really do.

Studs Terkel

Studs Terkel is America's preeminent oral historian of the workingman. His August 1960 radio interview with Lord Buckley on Chicago's WFMT revealed both men at their finest.

The voice you hear, that greeting, that salutation is that of His Highness Lord Richard Buckley, referred to by his followers as "His Hipness."

Now perhaps if, during this program, you might have a difficult time understanding all that His Highness has to offer, just remember what he has to say does make sense in its own strange and unique way.

Steve Ben Israel

New York actor/director/stand-up philosopher Steve Ben Israel was an early member of the Living Theater with Julian Beck. Steve has crafted a neglected body of work that includes a "Hip Gahn"–inspired piece, "The Spinning Wheel, Baby." His latest séance to contact the living, Non-Violent Executions, *is a one-man show combining humor, poetry, stories of rare poignancy, and virtuosic acting to pierce the slick armor masquerading as sense in our time.*

I'm in my '49 Buick on the Shore Parkway in Brooklyn. I turn on the radio and listen to Symphony Sid and all of a sudden I'm hearing "Jonah and the Whale." And I can't believe it and I know I'm on the right station even though I was expecting to hear jazz. And I listen to it and just can't believe it. It was like I'd landed from another planet and said: "There's somebody from my hometown!"

I go off the Shore Parkway. I find a telephone booth. I know Sid's number because Sid took requests. I call the number and Sid answers: "Yeah? Who? What? Hello? What is it? What is it?"

I said, "Sid, what was that?"

"What was what?"

I said, "Sid! What was that 'Jonah and the Whale'?"

"That was Lord Buckley. I gotta go."

"Sid, where do you get it?"

"Colony Record Store. I gotta go."

"Where's that?"

"Fifty-first Street."

"Thanks a lot, Sid."

. . . brrrrrpppp—right off to the Colony Record Store. They have one copy left. I play it all night. Half of it I don't get. I just don't get it. I'm too young. What was it? 1959? '60? I'm twenty-one, twenty-two. I'm getting some of it. But there's so much goin' on here that I have to listen to it over and over and over and over to get the language. Some of it I just didn't get . . . didn't get it at all.

I used to carry the album around with me like that character in *The Connection* who carries around the Charlie Parker record, shows up at people's pads, plugs the Victrola into the lightbulb, plays a Charlie Parker tune and then splits. I carried this record around wherever I went and made a complete nuisance of myself like I discovered gold. "Tutankhamen?! Yeah I know but I got this Lord Buckley thing."

Wherever I went I played it. Over and over and over. It was getting all beat up and scratched. I have this image of about eight of us hunched over the little soundbox like from an Eric Drucker painting listening to "The Nazz."

I was doing my own work based on that same impulse and trying to discover myself.

1 birth of the cool

Lord Buckley

I had a very auspicious beginning. I was attended by a midwife and, because I was very slippery, they made a grab for me and missed, and I hit the john—BOOM! They fished me out and wiped me off. I don't think it's harmed me any.

Family legend, half truth, personal myth, apocrypha, misconception, and mystery seem to have tailed Lord Buckley from his birth. One thing for which there is no doubt: the place of his birth in Tuolumne, California, in the high foothills of the Golden State's Sierra Madre is one of the most spectacularly beautiful locales on Earth. At the end of a county road on the rising western slopes of the Sierras sits the sleepy town of Tuolumne. The few homes and stores scattered haphazardly around in what now passes for downtown are the only testament to the hamlet's legacy as a nexus of what was California's once-thriving mining and lumber industries. The lush evergreen forests and the mountains above them surround the town like some verdant Vatican of the upper altitudes. Those trees and the gold nestled deep beneath them brought thousands of hearty souls seeking their fortunes in the mid- to late nineteenth century.

Gold! That precious commodity that men and women crave with a passion unlike any other. Its lure drew the Spanish conquistadores across an unknown and terrifying ocean. It propelled nations in a worldwide scramble to find and claim it. At various times and places during the nineteenth century hundreds, then thousands, and finally hundreds of thousands of men and women abandoned their homes and loved ones in their pursuit of the glittering ore. Gold! The stuff of which dreams are made, the loose change of Kings . . . and Lords.

California's gold rush brought an influx of prospectors, merchants, adventurers, and others to the area's newly discovered gold fields. The discovery of gold at Sutter's Mill early in 1848 drew more than forty thousand prospectors to California within two years. A ribbon of four hundred miles of nearby streams and rivers was rich with the yellow stuff. It bled from the surrounding mountains into an area stretching from the Trinity River in the north to the Tuolumne River in the south.

Word of the discovery shot around the world. The size and worth of the find, as reported, staggered the imagination. Soon miners, tradesmen, farmers, and "argonauts" of every description hurried to the Sierra Nevada mining fields, and many of them extracted hundreds of dollars' worth of dust and nuggets from the Earth daily.

Thus began the gold rush of 1849. Some ninety thousand prospectors journeyed by land across a continent or by sea around South America. Mexicans, Chileans, Germans, Frenchmen, Englishmen, Irishmen, Italians, Portuguese, Swedes, Norwegians, Poles, Chinese, Australians, and Hawaiians raced to California to seek their prize, creating a boiling mass of people of all nations. By the end of the year California had achieved a sufficient population to apply for admission as a state in the Union.

Although few of them struck it rich, their presence was an important stimulus to the region's economic and cultural growth. Agriculture, commerce, transportation, and industry grew rapidly to meet the needs of the settlers. Mining of other rare minerals in the area soon became big business as corporations replaced the individual prospector.

Among the later pioneers in the early 1860s, after the gold plunder had all but ceased, were Henery and Eliza Bone of Cornwall, England. Eliza is remembered as a loving but fiercely devout religious woman who may have passed on her strong beliefs to her children and grandchildren. As the dire economics in Europe and the promise of America's fortune forced the great migration to United States' shores, the Bones found themselves first on a boat sailing across the Atlantic Ocean and then traversing a vast continent. Not long after disembarking in Seattle, Eliza bore a daughter, Annie Laurie Bone, on May 24, 1863, at Pleasant Flat near Iowa Hill in Placer County, California, not far from Lake Tahoe.

The trail stops briefly after that. There is no indication or record of where the family settled or what they did. But in the mid-1880s Annie Laurie married one Robert Liddell at Iowa Hill. The couple had two children, Elsie Olivia, in 1885, and a son, Robert, in 1887.

But things did not work out for Annie Laurie and Robert. They divorced not long after the birth of their son, a relatively rare occurrence in those days.

A strong, good-looking woman, Annie Laurie was courted by several suitors, including a wealthy San Franciscan. But not being in love, she spurned their proposals.

William Buckley, a handsome lad born on December 19, 1863, and hailing from Manchester, England, had also made the grueling voyage across surf and turf to seek his reward in the Golden State.

According to family legend, William Buckley was the oldest of fourteen children whose wealthy father, James Buckley, owned a racetrack in Manchester. At age twenty-eight he rejected his stern upbringing and stowed away on a ship to America. Though he was eventually found out, he finished the trek around Cape Horn, the ship finally docking in the wide-open city of San Francisco.

There are two versions of how William and Annie Laurie met. In the first, William ventured to Iowa Hill where he encountered the mother of two, began to court the woman, and soon won her heart before the two were married July 7, 1892.

The second explanation has an impoverished Annie Laurie working as a laundress in San Francisco and sending all her savings home to her mother, who was caring for the two toddlers in Iowa Hill. A chance meeting between the two at the city's wharves initiated a magical romance.

After marrying, the couple moved to Auburn, California, near Iowa Hill, where William was able to land a high-ranking job at the local mine. The two also ran a boardinghouse for miners—Annie Laurie laundered their apparel and prepared lunches to feed them during their long, thankless underground shifts.

According to Elaine Thomasen, Lord Buckley's first cousin and family historian, who bases her research on family journals, ephemera, and a great memory: "Will

Buckley was superintendent at Pioneer Mine, Iowa Hill. Annie owned and ran a boardinghouse and hotel at nearby Damascus known as Big Dipper Mine. She had hired help to do the work and cooking, including Chinese. They met, fell in love, and were married at Auburn, California, by Justice of the Peace Charles McKelvy. 'It was the happiest day of my life,' writes Annie. The honeymoon was in San Francisco for two weeks. They were in clover during this time. William adopted Laurie's two children."

Though William was away from home much of the time, working in the Auburn mine or following the seasonal opportunities in the lumber camps and work in the many other mines in the region, they seemed to have had no trouble amassing a sizable brood. By 1901 the loving relationship had produced four more children (Mabel, Lester, James, and Ben), all born at Iowa Hill.

A major family crisis occurred when the hotel burned down at Damascus in 1904. The Buckleys moved to the Mother Lode town of Tuolumne in 1904 and it was there that Helen Byrl, known as Nell, was born that same year.

Tuolumne was an industrial nexus where companies in both the mining and lumber business had set up shop. William secured work at Tuolumne's Confidence Mine, but he periodically still had to travel in order to gain employment, such as in the Nevada gold fields. Sometimes he would be gone for as long as two years at a stretch. Though he sent all of his savings to his family, Annie Laurie fell back on her experience as a laundress, accommodating the many laborers eking out a subsistence existence in town.

Tuolumne was a typical turn-of-the-century boomtown where the lure of riches collided with the abject poverty of the region. The hamlet boasted dozens of bars and brothels to satisfy the considerable appetites of the men doomed to toil in its raw environs. The hardscrabble townsfolk lived from pillar to post, always just getting by in the harsh, often unforgiving surroundings in pursuit of the American Dream.

On Thursday April 5, 1906, Richard Myrle Buckley, reportedly weighing in at an unbelievable twelve pounds, filled out the Buckley clan just before the great San Francisco Earthquake two weeks later. Contrary to local legend, the baby's immense size at birth probably had nothing to do with the dramatic shift in the San Andreas Fault, though some claimed it was the planet's delayed reaction to his arrival.

A final story concerning Buckley's birth concerns Annie Laurie's personal heroics. According to family legend, the winter of 1906 had been a particularly brutal one. In fact, there was still snow on the ground when Annie Laurie felt the onset of labor. With William away working, she bundled up her entire family and led them to the local doctor to deliver the baby, a month shy of her forty-fourth birthday.

Buckley's unusual middle name is probably worthy of note here. Pronounced and sometimes misreported as Merle (or even Muriel), Myrle seems to be a name of unknown family origin, probably picked by Annie Laurie simply to rhyme with Nell's middle name, Byrl.

One of the many tall tales often repeated about Lord Buckley, that he was of Native American heritage, has *no* validity. But there are several notions as to how this rumor came into being. There is some indication that the place of his birth was at Miwok Village, a local Native American trading post. The local Native American women could have been equally or more adept at the art of assisting childbirth than the town doctor, and Annie Laurie could well have decided to employ them for the task.

However, the most reliable sources stand by the accepted family history that Richard, like all of his siblings, was born at home with the aid of a midwife. Later in her life Annie Laurie was married to a man of Native American descent, a fellow named Al Harlan, so this is another possible source for the confusion in lineage. Additionally, Annie Laurie's maiden name, Bone, has an elemental quality that may also have contributed to confusing the tale of correct ethnic descent.

On a different tack, Lord Buckley may have just enjoyed putting people on with the story, or perhaps it was a falsehood repeated so often that it passed into the realm of acceptance. Certainly it has added to the Lord Buckley mystique.

Less frequently it has been posited that the Buckleys were of Scandinavian heritage, again incorrectly derived from the immigration of laborers from those countries to the Great Plains and Northwest at the turn of the century.

Marie Rozier

A Tuolumne, California, native for all of her ninety-something years, the late Marie Rozier saw her hometown go from the rough-and-ready hub of California's mining and lumber industry to the sleepy hamlet it has remained since the 1960s, when the fortunes of those two industries dwindled. She was Lord Buckley's oldest known surviving friend.

Tuolumne was a rough town back when I was young. The lumber business and the mining were both going on back then. The logging started around the turn of the century and the mining started much earlier than that. The town was made up of lumberjacks and miners and they fought all night. There was a lot of hard drinking in the many saloons in town. There were ranches scattered all through the Sierras back then so the cattle drives would bring the cowboys through town.

There were about two thousand permanent residents back when the mill was in operation. We had a real good lumber setup here then. The Piney Mill and Box factory had a mill in the woods. There were two main camps every year with about 250 men working in each camp. Almost every man I knew worked in the logging camp in the woods: pulp timber, setting chokers, working in the commissary.

The logging still goes on but the mills closed down in 1960 or '61. Eventually it burned down. Whether it was arson or not we don't know.

The Buckleys were a prominent family in Tuolumne. There's quite a few Buckley headstones up in the cemetery.

I remember when Dick Buckley was born and I remember that he was quite a character. We all lived in the same little town and all played together and grew up together. They lived on Birch Street. Nellie Buckley was his sister and they were a very close, big family. His older brothers were even taller than him. His father worked in the mines.

He entertained everybody but we all entertained each other. You *had* to back then because there was no TV or radio or movies. Everybody worked and life was hard but we all helped each other out.

Dick Buckley always talked a lot. He was a very energetic person. Like me he didn't have much formal education because there were only eight grades in the local school. But he used to write. He liked to write wild stories about his family.

By all accounts the Buckleys were a wild and rambunctious crew, with each kid bringing up the next. Mabel did much of the child rearing but got married and left home at a fairly young age.

Nell took Richard under her wing and the two often busked for small change, singing on the streets of Tuolumne for passing miners, lumberjacks, cowboys, and Chinese laborers. The young performers often had to compete with one of the town's biggest draws—the savage dog and coyote fights staged at the local saloons. With a mostly absentee father, the children had to fend for and amuse themselves. As a result, they indulged themselves in elaborate spells of make-believe and fantasy.

Tragedy struck the Buckleys on October 1, 1909, when Annie Laurie's eldest son, Robert Lidell, was killed in a mining accident at the tender age of twenty-one. According to the death certificate, the accident occurred at the New Albany Mine and an inquest was held that very day. The certificate further indicates that he was unmarried, had taken the last name Buckley, and was buried at Carter's Cemetery on October 4.

An apocryphal tale that seems to have some basis in truth is that the young man was decapitated on the mine elevator as it was taking him and his fellow miners to the surface after a hard day's work. Someone cracked a joke and Robert supposedly reared his head back in laughter into a passing beam. The story has transmuted somewhat over time. The incorrect version has his younger brother Richard (the future Lord Buckley) as the teller of the joke. As Richard was just three years old when Robert was killed, this aspect of the story is one of the earliest examples of exaggeration of the Buckley myth.

Though his appearances in the household were intermittent, William Buckley is recalled by surviving family members as a strict disciplinarian. In an interview near the end of his life Lord Buckley remembered that his father was once determined to make a cabinetmaker out of him. As Lord Buckley mentioned decades later: "But when I became so bored that I fell asleep at the workbench and cut the end off of one of my fingers, he gave up his crusade."

In 1915 William Buckley came home for the last time—stricken with miner's consumption, the most common ailment and leading cause of death for those working in the dark dungeons of the Earth. During his final weeks, young Dickie clung to his father—he wanted to sleep right next to him on the porch in the cool air where the doctor had William sleep. William's death on September 16 of that year was a typically difficult one and left the family practically destitute. His grave can also be found in Carter's Cemetery in Tuolumne.

Fortunately, the surviving sons were old enough to have commenced working as miners and lumberjacks, so the money they earned continued to help make ends meet. Despite the hardships, the earliest photo of Richard Buckley was taken as part of a family portrait when he was still a child, and it shows a cherubic yet distinctive young boy dressed in a clean, dark Boy Scout suit. No one in the photo looks particularly happy and, as it was taken shortly after William's death, their grieving seems plain enough.

One of the earliest indications of Richard's independence occurred in 1916 when he was ten years old. Invited by friends in the Bay Area to attend the San Francisco Exposition, Annie Laurie brought along her youngest. But it was easy to get lost in the throngs milling around the exposition grounds and young Richard did just that. However, when Richard was located, it was Annie Laurie who was shocked to discover that the boy seemed totally nonplussed by the ordeal.

The burden of raising the large family fell even harder on Annie Laurie's shoulders. But nothing could ever stop her from fulfilling her duties . . . or from shooting mountain lions out her back door. She remained the family matriarch until her death in 1953.

Elaine Thomasen

Lord Buckley's cousin is his oldest surviving relative and also happens to be a fine watercolorist, gentle raconteur, and, most important, a passionate family historian.

Annie Laurie was Richard "Lord" Buckley's mother. He just adored her and she just loved him.

Annie Laurie was so quick-witted. Everyone who met her just loved her. She had people come to see her from miles and miles around. She used to have what I call "Annie-isms." She would say, "And now you can stew in your own juice." I'd hear her talk to her children and say this. "You made a mistake, learn from it and never repeat it." "Don't be misled by a pretty or handsome face." "Pretty is as pretty does." "Judge people by their actions and not their words." "I live in the far, far west where men are men and women are glad of it." If they had a snowstorm in Tuolumne or the weather was bad, she would say, "Well, it snowed like mischief you have never seen." She had a dear, dear way of talking. They just popped off the top of her head—she was just so completely original.

I just loved her. I felt so close to Annie Laurie because she was so giving and so loving. I loved her values in life. She didn't value monetary things. She valued the gifts of love and the gift of being kind to others and the gift of helping people. She was just a wonderful, wonderful person. I think that all rubbed off on Lord Buckley. He's his mother's own child, really. They were very much alike. I think he was her favorite. She loved all children dearly, but he just entertained her lavishly and entertained the neighbors when they would come in.

He was entertaining, I think from age two or three—just almost right from the very beginning. He did pantomimes. Oh, he'd imitate and mimic the neighbors when they'd come in. And Annie would get a big kick out of it, but she told him he'd have to be careful, she didn't want him to get into trouble. He was very precocious, very talented and gifted. And the seventh son of a seventh son—so that has some bearing, I'm told.

I think he was seeking a deep meaning in life as a young child. And he was a prolific reader. After his father died, he would spend more time with his cousins than his own family. His cousins, Ann and Matt Thomas, were studying Christian Science at the time and to him that was something that had a deeper meaning. But I think from that he became interested in other religions and I think he was trying to seek that deeper meaning through other religions. I think Hinduism and Buddhism enter into that somewhere. But he still had that basic stuff from Christian Science that he just loved.

Annie Laurie's laundry provided a steady stream of characters. But the meager income afforded by such a business prompted a move to the big city of Stockton, California, then just a cowtown lying on the northern edge of the San Joaquin Valley, just about halfway between Tuolumne and San Francisco.

The older boys took jobs as apprentices in a local manufacturing company, and things took a positive turn when a chance encounter brought Annie Laurie together with Al Harlan, an old suitor of reported American Indian heritage. Harlan, a colorful but dependable Tuolumne native whose wild and wonderful yarns probably had an influence on Richard, also evidently cast a spell on Annie Laurie, as the two married around 1918. Harlan was in the ice business and took on an apprentice: twelve-year-old Richard.

It is unclear what schooling the Buckley children had or what their churchgoing habits, if any, were. Some have suggested that the children's formal education, such as it was, in a one-room schoolhouse in Tuolumne, could not have gone past the eighth grade at the very most. But Mrs. Thomasen found that while this was probably true for the older children, Nell and Ben graduated from high school in Stockton, California—suggesting that Dick may have followed their example, since he was younger than them. That Lord Buckley, at least in the latter part of his life, seemed so aware of the world and its disciplines is another reason to think that his education reached into the secondary level. Mrs. Thomasen also notes that the teachers in the area were excellent, dedicated, principled ladies. "By fourth grade," Mrs. Thomasen writes, "students were well educated in the practical sense. Most studied history, biography, geology, and astronomy at home, none of these being taught at that time in the mountain schools."

Mrs. Thomasen also believes it possible that their grandmother, Eliza Bone, with her strong religious beliefs, may well have had an influence in their Bible studies. It is safe to assume that the comings and goings of the family, the continuous scraping for money, a supportive community, the antic storytelling of Annie Laurie and Al Harlan, and maybe the odd Paul Bunyan story or two all contributed to Richard's later artistic instincts and social interests.

When he became old enough, Dick worked in the logging camps as a tree-topper. He got the job after another tree-topper had fallen to his death. Tree-topping, a harrowing endeavor, consisted of climbing to the summit of a tree, sawing off its top, and securing long ropes near its pinnacle, which men on the ground would pull to guide its falling path after it had been cut through at the bottom. At any rate, the lumber chief, an uncle of Buckley's known as "The Bull of the Woods," offered an extra ten dollars a day to anybody who would take over the tree-topping job until they hired a new man. Despite the obvious dangers, Dick quickly snapped up the job—ten dollars a day was a small fortune in the early 1920s. It is said that he climbed a tree and did a fine job not only in executing this difficult task but also in spitting tobacco juice on anybody he could hit from his lofty perch.

Richard Clayton, another surviving Buckley relative, remembers the teenage Dick Buckley with a guitar or ukulele frequently in hand and as a young man who "liked to sing and dance and have a good time."

Taken as a whole, with his natural curiosity, the desperation of Tuolumne, the economic and cultural limitations of the region, and the move to Stockton, it is natural that Dick would have taken the first chance he had to shake the dust off his heels and move on.

Lord Buckley

Man, this village was so small I had to leave there because there wasn't even enough room for me to change my mind.

Though the most sublime fruits of his creative journey were realized decades later, the seeds of Lord's Buckley's future aesthetic can easily be found in his roots. His British heritage, the family's magnanimous personalities, his mother's way with words and philosophy, the economic desperation of his childhood and adolescence, his hometown's inherent frontier toughness, Christian Science, the necessity of entertainment in the hard-edged community, and the barrelhouse atmosphere of early-twentieth-century Tuolumne all contributed in luring Dick Buckley to a life on the stage and informed his artifice.

The region had long since lost its luster by the time Buckley turned twenty in 1926. Around this time he set off to meet his brother Lester to work as a roughneck in the Texas oilfields. But he never made it. By his own account, Buckley met a traveling musician in a Galveston, Texas, boardinghouse who dared the young Californian into performing with him. Buckley took his dare and hit the road with this mysterious figure soon after, allegedly touring the western tent shows of the era.

While there is no surviving evidence of Buckley's tenure with or exposure to the tent and medicine shows of the mid- to late 1920s and early 1930s other than the illusory accounts of others, it is likely that he had at least some exposure to this virtually extinct realm of the American performance experience. Spawned in the southern United States during the early nineteenth century, vestiges of this crazy culture can still be found at country fairs across the United States or even on any given summer afternoon at Coney Island. The tent show comedian and straight man, who engaged each other in witty slapstick repartee, were commonly known on the circuit as "Mr. Tambo" and "Mr. Bones." Nearly a century later the "Tambo and Bones" formula would evolve into "Amos 'n' Andy," one of the best-known comedic teams in popular culture and a model for some of Dick Buckley's earliest (and latest) popular performances.

At a strapping six foot three, 185 pounds, Dick had a magnificent broad-shouldered, deep-chested physique that he had developed in his hardworking lumberjacking youth. It was during his early career that he realized he could astound audiences with his acrobatic abilities and freakish physical feats such as standing somersaults or taking a step back and executing an Olympian broad jump that would send him sailing out over the heads of the astonished patrons for a center-aisle landing. It was with similar abandon that Dick left home . . . and he never looked back.

Lord Buckley

Well I got into show business . . . I was on my way to Mexico to join my brother in an oil campaign. I got as far as Galveston, Texas, and met with a long, angular Texan in a boardinghouse playing guitar.

And the first date I ever played in my life and the first theater I was ever in in my life was the Million Dollar Aztec Theater in San Antonio. The manager of the theater, Mr. Epstein, he says, "Gentlemen, I'm paying you but I want to tell you, you are the *lousiest* act I ever played in my life."

And he was right! He was right.

2 they shoot horses, don't they?

Lord Buckley

I had a good act with Red Skelton in the Walkathons and all that sort of thing. It was a tremendous, powerful psychological dramatic show event of salesmanship. And, contrary to what people thought, it was very healthy for all the participants.

When Carl Sandburg described Chicago as the "city of the big shoulders," he forgot to mention the strong arms. Certainly the Windy City in the Roaring Twenties and Depressed Thirties was just that: a brawling, corrupt, iron-fisted town.

How Buckley wound up in Chicago in the mid-1930s seems lost to history. There is speculation that he was based back in California as some type of burlesque or café entertainer and word-of-mouth evidence that he was briefly betrothed.

But once relocated to Chicago, Buckley (with a natural comic bent) gravitated toward the theater, interspersing appearances at nightclubs in gangster-ruled speakeasies with an extended session as a saucy comic and notoriously successful nonstop-talking master of ceremonies at a particular then-current craze in the history of American popular culture: the dance marathon or the Walkathon. Though times were tough for most, Buckley is said to have been earning hundreds of dollars a month and usually spending them even faster.

Several years after he left Tuolumne, Dick came to visit his family during the Depression in a Cadillac limousine with a chauffeur, wide wheels, and a convertible top. Dick claimed he was making eight hundred dollars a week and his cousin, Richard Clayton, remembers him sharing that money with his family. Clayton also remembers that Dick sent all of his old clothes home to Annie Laurie to distribute to the family.

Walkathons and dance marathons were twenty-four-hour-a-day endurance contests in which couples walked or danced until they dropped, usually several weeks, sometimes even months, after they started. (For the last word on this vital aspect of Depression-era Americana, check out *Dance Marathons* by Carol Martin.)

Beginning as part of the dance craze of the teens and twenties, the Walkathons became, when the Depression hit, a popular entertainment and cultural performance that gave the moral, social, and economic crises of the time an expressive form. During this period of rapidly changing social dance styles, dancing and self-expression became synonymous as dance competitions became part of the local homemade happenings. People danced nonstop to set new hourly records, and their endeavors were reported in newspapers across the country.

The fad manifested a potent form of drama. Between the two world wars the Walkathons were a phenomenon in which working-class people engaged in emblematic struggles for survival. Battling to outlast other contestants, the dancers hoped to become notable. There was crippling exhaustion and anguish among the contenders, but ultimately it was the coupling of authentic pain with staged displays that made dance marathons a national craze.

Within the well-controlled space of theater, the participants revealed actual life's unpredictability and inconsistencies, and indeed, the frightful aspects of Social Darwinism. In this grotesque theatrical setting a horrifying metaphor was revealed: the ailing nation grappling with difficult times. In some respects the raw, rebellious nature and quality of the events could be viewed as the era's equivalent of punk rock: a youth culture's desperate attempt at social resuscitation through extraordinarily harsh means.

By the early 1930s these competitions kicked into a new phase of marathon in which people danced and rested for a specified amount of time. However, it was soon discovered that the spectators' interest could last longer than the dancers' feet. Promoters began to change the rules so the show could last longer. In the Walkathons, dancing and walking alternated in a contest of continual motion. This meant the event could last longer since *moving* came to mean a sluggish shift of weight as the show wore on into weeks and months.

Walkathons also featured elimination contests designed to close the show with a full house. Instead of two or three couples fading on the dance floor until all but one

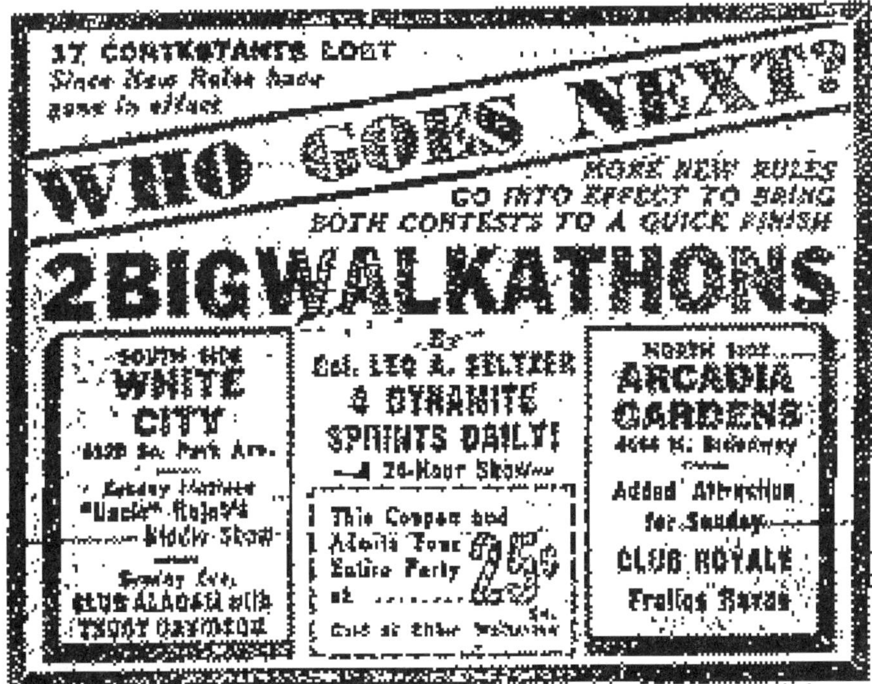

Chicago newspaper ad from a 1935 Walkathon where Buckley worked as an MC.
Author's Collection.

dropped, Walkathon promoters brought the show to a close by staging sprints, "zombie treadmills," and special stunts like running while chained to your partner. One fall and the contestants were eliminated. The heyday of the Walkathon was from 1932 to 1936. Shows continued after this date, even after World War II, but these postwar events were really the last spasms of a dying phenomenon. Eventually, led by maverick entrepreneur Leo Seltzer, the Walkathon would mutate into the Roller Derby, a step-cousin of professional wrestling. And today's "reality television" shows such as *Survivor* can rightly be seen as a modern manifestation of the Walkathon, complete with its endurance contest, elimination bouts, and, naturally, social drama.

Promoters pushed these fly-by-night, seat-of-the-pants operations across the country, primarily in the industrial Midwest in small towns like Muskegon, Michigan, and Kankakee, Illinois, as well as the big cities like Chicago and Kansas City. The fad was so popular that, at its height, it employed twenty thousand people: contestants, promoters, floor judges, trainers, nurses, cooks, janitors, cashiers, ticket-takers, publicity agents, musicians, lawyers, and, of course, emcees.

Dick Buckley was, along with Red Skelton with whom he was paired early on, the best of the Walkathon comic emcees, becoming something of a legend in that exotic world. Buckley was in such high demand that it is rumored that he was once kidnapped by a rival Walkathon outfit.

Buckley worked ten hours a day—without a stage, without a set, without a curtain or a spotlight or a stooge or an orchestra, without a script or a prompter or sound effects or any precedents whatsoever. It was while working under these demanding conditions that he learned how to utterly transfix an audience.

Larry Storch

Best known as the irascible but lovable Corporal Randolph T. Agarn on the TV sitcom F-Troop, *Larry Storch has had a varied and notable career in show business. Breaking in as a stand-up comedian the late 1940s, Storch was a frequent movie and television performer. Voice-over artist and mimic extraordinaire, Storch met Lord Buckley in the late 1940s and was a member of His Lordship's Royal Court in the 1950s.*

He and Red Skelton used to work the dance marathons and tent shows back in the thirties. I once heard a story that Lord Buckley even swung by a rope from one end of the arena to another with a basket of eggs. He held onto the rope with one arm and, if you can imagine this, threw raw eggs at the audience with the other, swinging back and forth above them.

Ten hours of entertaining, seven days a week, made staggering demands upon comic inventiveness. To keep the Walkathon patrons from boredom, Buckley told jokes, made faces, did imitations, took pratfalls, crawled under seats, kissed ladies, climbed chandeliers, sat on laps, walked on all fours, imitated drunks, recited poetry, performed card tricks, and rode a tricycle around the edge of the balcony—whatever it took to keep the show rolling.

A photo of Buckley from this era displays a striking but harried young man, khaki shirt unbuttoned at the collar and cigarette in hand, holding a microphone and spewing forth God-knows-what spiel to keep the throngs on their toes.

Buckley's involvement with the Walkathons garnered him his first documented press. At the height of the craze, *Billboard* ran a special section in its weekly pages called "Endurance Shows" that covered the various aspects of the social phenomenon and included advertisements that may have lured the twenty-eight-year-old Dick Buckley into its ranks:

ATTENTION EMSEES
Am adding two capable Men of proved
ability to my staff of Emsees,
with following qualifications:
After Midnight and Afternoon Man who
can produce clean Blackouts and Bits
—"no smut."
Also a No. 1 Straight Man
who can sell contestants
and show my way
No collect wires. Give full particulars,
including salary, in first letter

Under the headline "Seltzer Chi Setting Fast Pace" in the January 19, 1935, edition of *Billboard,* the following notice appeared covering two Chicago Walkathons:

Business at Leo A. Seltzer's Walkathons continues to be way above normal and both the Arcadia Gardens and the Coliseum shows are playing to fine audiences. The present standing at Arcadia Gardens is 20 couples and two solos, and the setup here has been strengthened by the acquisition of Dick Buckley as emsee, replacing Red Skelton. Buckley is pleasing the North Side crowds, as is Erskine Tate and his 11-piece orchestra.

The February 2, 1935, *Billboard* continued its coverage of the Chicago show:

Bobby Reed has proved a surprise in the emcee work and is handling broadcasts and doing straights, in addition to working in comedy stints with Dick Buckley.

Four days later, the *Chicago American,* which had been following the local Walkathons, first mentioned Buckley with an intriguing notice, which raises more questions than it answers:

Dick Buckley, the "spontaneous" comedian brought to Chicago from Hollywood by Leo A. Seltzer, is creating laughter galore for spectators at the walkathon now in progress at the Arcadia.

> Following a successful appearance in a comedy movie short and several engagements in California night clubs, Buckley journeyed to Chicago to accept the duties of chief funmaker for Seltzer's North Side walkathon.

One wonders what the comedy short in question was and if it is still in existence or relegated to the celluloid trash heap.

A little more than a week later, a dashing photo of a mustachioed Buckley wearing a jacket and tie looking every bit the leading man appeared in the *Chicago American* with the following caption: "Of the many masters of ceremonies employed to furnish continuous laughter at Leo A. Seltzer's 'Walkathon' now in progress at the Arcadia, Dick Buckley is generally conceded to be one of the most popular. Dick's ready wit has placed him high in the esteem of walkathon fans."

That the Walkathons acted as a safe "crossover" forum is evidenced by notices such as the following from the February 19, 1935, *Chicago American,* which serves as the first indication of Buckley's exposure to black culture:

> A new feature has made its appearances at Leo A. Seltzer's Arcadia Walkathon. Each Sunday night hereafter will be known as "Harlem Night," with Erskine Tate and his orchestra providing both the background and the principals for what is promised as the fastest colored revue ever to invade the North Side.
>
> Acts from the major colored cafes and those featuring colored talent will augment Tate and his entertaining organization each Sunday evening as long as the endurance continues.

Erskine Tate was an accomplished violinist, banjoist, arranger, and bandleader when he appeared as part of the established Walkathon entertainment, but on the downside of his career. Born in Memphis, Tennessee, in 1895, he was most prominent in the decade after World War I when he worked as a sideman in Louis Armstrong's performing and recording bands of the mid-1920s before becoming the bandleader at Chicago's Vendome Theatre.

Newspaper ads publicizing the Walkathon spectacles did their share of both reporting and sensationalizing the scene, life-and-death-style, with large type declaring "Who Goes Next?" or doing their best to lure spectators with kiddie shows, nightly sprints, a frolics revue, huge floor shows, a St. Patrick's Day gala celebration, public dancing, dance classes, and twenty-five-cent coupons, natch. One advertisement even invited customers to "Bring Your Beds—Stay as Long as You Like."

The Walkathons had something for everyone—nightclub, flophouse, community center, school, day-care center, and town square rolled into one. And Seltzer and his promoters were not above offering more risqué fare with late-night acts that included an act billed as "Zorine and Her Eight Nudist Dancers," who would leave their usual haunt at Colosimo's, Chicago's then-self-proclaimed oldest café on Wabash Avenue, to "perform" at the Walkathons, where they appeared in several of their dance creations—most likely a form of burlesque. Seltzer's genius can be glimpsed in his uncanny decision to follow Zorine with an Easter Sunday fashion parade later in the week.

A larger, more prominent photo of Buckley appeared in the *Chicago American* on the funnyman's twenty-ninth birthday, April 5, 1935. Under the banner "HE HOLDS LAUGHS!" a clean-shaven, more zany-looking Buckley is pictured holding another comic in his arms while striking a pose worthy of Fred Astaire. The caption reads: "Dick Buckley, master of ceremonies of Leo A. Seltzer's Arcadia 'Walkathon,' holds an armful of laughs in Chaz Chase, famous musical comedy dancer and comedian. Chaz was a recent visitor at Seltzer's North Side 'Walkathon' and, for laughs, ended up in the not-too-steady arms of Comedy-Master Buckley."

Buckley seems to have worked his way up in Seltzer's show to the post of assistant emcee, but it wasn't until the June 1, 1935, *Billboard* hit the streets that any substantial mention of the rising star was made under the headline "Seltzer Chicago Shows Setting Long-Hour and Fine-Biz Records":

Coming into the homestretch both of Col. Leo A. Seltzer's Walkathons here are shattering all records for duration and attendance.

The Arcadia Gardens Event reached a climax Sunday morning at 2 o'clock when a record 3,991 hours was passed. A jammed house was on hand to fittingly celebrate the occasion by contributing to the terrific din which was reminiscent of a New Year's Eve Party. Seltzer's talent-studded staff of emcees, including Dick Buckley, Eddie Snyder, Chic Snyder, Rajah Bergman, Frankie Belasco et. Al, led the festivities at a lively pace, while the popular Erskine Tate Orchestra contributed excellent music.

With only three couples and two solos remaining of an original entry of 89 couples, there seems no doubt that the finish is close at hand. However, the closing days are giving the spectators the biggest thrill of all, with each added hour setting a new record.

Later in the month Buckley had moved on to a Cleveland Walkathon where Red Skelton's wife, Edna, was working as a nurse.

Buckley stayed with the Cleveland show through mid-July, when local authorities closed it. Moving on to the East Coast, *Billboard*'s August 3, 1935, issue found Buckley at a Secaucus, New Jersey, show:

The Mishkind and Rubin marathon dance derby here is past its 1,700th hr. with seven couples still plodding the boards. Bob Lee and Dick Buckley joined the show about two weeks ago and are pleasing the fans. The nightly feature is Bob Lee's human derby and it has proved a good method of eliminating contestants.

Perhaps the most interesting (and potentially incriminating) *Billboard* notice concerning Buckley ran in the August 31, 1935, edition in the "Staff Briefs" column:

Dick Buckley recently had a letter from a friend in Frisco which, according to word from Bob Lee, in New York, disclosed that he had sent Dick money to join him in a new club venture in Reno. Upon investigation it appears that similar occurrences have several times taken place recently, and in all instances, it has been shown that Dick was in some other part of the country than where money was sent. Someone is using Dick's name, and promoters are warned to be careful of phony wires, etc.

A final, undated *Chicago American* clip has Buckley blazing off into the same western sunset from which he mysteriously appeared:

Followers of Leo A. Seltzer's Walkathons at the Coliseum and Arcadia Gardens may see their oft-repeated predictions come true when Dick Buckley, Eddie Snyder and "Rajah" Bergman, Seltzer's aces of comedy and song, leave Chicago Sunday night for screen tests in Hollywood.

Movieland scouts, impressed by their performances at the Walkathons have taken an option on their services.

Despite the hefty financial rewards, the Walkathons were not a glamorous gig. It was not simply that hard times lay upon the land. The promoters who put on Walkathons had long shown a tendency to leave town while under the influence of heavy gate receipts. No one knew how to cope with the unscrupulous, mercenary situation until Edna Skelton came into the picture. A sometime Walkathon contestant herself, she licked the problem by stipulating that unless she was employed as head cashier, right in the ticket booth, her talented husband, and his coworkers, would not perform. In this way she froze Skelton's fee (and Buckley's when Red and Dick worked the same Walkathon) before the promoter ever saw dime one of the scratch.

But such examples of comradeship between the two men were rare, as Dick and Red had a somewhat competitive relationship. Skelton was a very serious young man, dead-set on success and all its trappings. Buckley, as one can well imagine, was somewhat more free-spirited. So Skelton would get more than a little irked when Buckley goofed on him, playing little pranks like hiding his props or interrupting the act with his own brand of one-upmanship. When Red was the recipient of a well-timed hotfoot, he knew who the culprit was. Even twenty-five years later, Skelton was still known to diss Buckley, remembering all too well the antagonism that lay between them.

Even so, Buckley and Skelton worked the Walkathon circuit, drifting from Chicago to Kansas City, Atlantic City, St. Louis, Columbus, Minneapolis. It was a wretched life.

Skelton once said that during this period, "I'd lie in bed and cry. Edna would reach over and put the blanket around my shoulders and pat my cheek and keep saying, 'Go to sleep, honey. You got to get your rest. Go to sleep.'"

Roger Bergman, another famed emcee from the Walkathon era, was known as "The Rajah" because he played the part of a Indian rajah in so many acts. Possibly it was this type of moniker and persona transformation that may have led Dick to consider adopting an alternative handle and accompanying act.

Despite its obvious shortcomings, Buckley was still a player in the human misery racket well into the late 1930s. According to his Social Security number application dated January 20, 1937, Richard Myrle Buckley of 4652 Hazel, Chicago, Illinois, was still employed by Seltzer's Coliseum Walkathon of 1439 South Wabash Avenue.

The last endurance show notices appearing in *Billboard* found Buckley finishing out the Secaucus show in mid-October 1935. By the end of the year, however, Dick seemed to be edging out of the Walkathon netherworld. According to the December 14, 1935, *Billboard:*

Bob Lee writes he is doing well in New York City as booker and agent. He recently sold Dick Buckley to the Congress Café for 10 weeks, followed by the Brown Derby, Boston, on an indefinite run. Bob says Walkathon emsees have something on the ball entirely lacking in the average night-club emsee and that Dick is a good bet to go places.

Anita O'Day

One of the most unique vocal talents ever to hit the jazz scene, Anita O'Day was a star with Stan Kenton's fabled big bands during the height of the Swing Era. She first crossed paths with Dick Buckley at the Chicago Walkathons during the 1930s. Those wild days are documented in her 1981 autobiography, High Times Hard Times, *and appear here with the permission of Limelight Editions.*

As soon as I saw the ad for the Arcadia Gardens contest, I rushed to sign up. What did I have to lose? Plenty, though I couldn't foresee it. I goofed, but I can't say I regret it. Because I met and worked with Dick Buckley, the chief emcee, and Red Skelton, the Midnight Maniac.

Both were highly talented in totally different ways just as they were completely different human beings. Skelton was so success-oriented that nobody interested him unless they were of some immediate use to him. Edna Stillwell, his ex-contestant wife, was a gifted comedy creator who was always busy developing new characters and material for him. Red learned Edna's routines, performed them over and over until he perfected them and then cherished them. He used them in Walkathons, nightclubs, vaudeville, adapted them for radio and when he got to be a big TV star, he was still doing some of the same bits. He was like a singer who learned the melody and never varied his performance once the song had been mastered. I absorbed a lot watching him, and I don't feel I'm detracting from his stature when I say that, skilled as his timing and slapstick clowning were, I never felt that he had a natural creative genius.

Skelton wanted great commercial success so badly I think he'd have climbed a ladder of razor blades barefoot to get to the top. Acclaim and money were his gods. If he was also an artist, it was in spite of himself. And I happen to think that as a pantomimist he brought his work to the level of art. But he was a hard person to feel close to. I think that's why very few of the Walkathoners felt he was one of us.

The self-ordained Lord Buckley, in contrast, viewed all people as princes and princesses, lords and ladies, counts and countesses. The athletically inclined Buckley would climb the high skeletal structure above the contest floor and clown around, half-stoned, with slips and starts that would have spelled curtains for him if he'd made a miscue. You could only conclude that someone was watching over him. For that I was eventually thankful, because Dick Buckley was rhythmical and he took a special interest in my singing.

Unlike Skelton, Buckley performed for the joy of creating. If it hadn't been a Walkathon, it could have been for a small crowd on a street corner or for his own amusement alone in his room. He was so much his own man, nobody, but nobody could control him. Bread? It was something to spend, a convenience, but not a necessity, not important enough to lead to compromise.

Mel Welles

Actor, director, and writer Mel Welles is a key figure in the legacy of Lord Buckley. In the 1950s Welles collaborated with Buckley on several of His Lordship's most famous pieces, including "Gettysburg Address."

You've got to remember that he was a comic at dance marathons. If you've seen the picture *They Shoot Horses, Don't They?* you know that would drive someone to drink. It was a world where not only did the desperate side of people reveal itself so boldly but the exploiters stripped them of their dignity as well.

Steve Allen

Comedian, writer, actor, pianist, composer, and poet, the late Steve Allen was a cornerstone figure in mid- and late-twentieth-century American culture and entertainment. Lord Buckley appeared on the Allen-hosted Tonight Show *in 1955.*

It makes sense that Buckley and Skelton were partners back then. They were different comics who shared a certain dynamic and spirit. Part of it was that the audio systems in those days, if they existed, were so lousy that a Wally Cox couldn't have made it in the business at all, or even a Bob Newhart. Those comics couldn't work until there were good P.A. systems. But the older guys could dominate an audience because they *had* to.

In 1936 the only mention of Buckley in the pages of *Billboard* was in a weekly ad that (with the exception of shifting management) read as follows:

Season's Greetings
from
"California's Chatterbox"
DICK BUCKLEY
M. C.
Direction: B. BERNARDI, 85 Riverside Drive, New York

Billboard ad circa 1935

Concurrent with his participation in the Walkathon craze, Buckley gravitated increasingly to Chicago's nefarious nocturnal speakeasies.

Jim Burns

Jim Burns is a British writer whose notes on Lord Buckley appeared in various publications. His witness in this book is excerpted from "The Hip Messiah," his August 12, 1963, article in The Guardian *and his September 1970 article in* Jazz Monthly.

According to some reports Buckley was active in nightclubs as long ago as the Twenties, a not at all doubtful suggestion when one considers that poetry readings and similar activities were not unknown in Chicago clubs during that period. There was a flourishing bohemian café life—and it is reasonable to assume that someone like Buckley would have a ready-made audience available for this kind of "in" humor. I don't want to get involved in any long and detailed discussion of bohemian life in Chicago but it is worth recommending Kenneth Rexroth's *An Autobiographical Novel* for its fascinating description of activities there. It isn't irrelevant to mention this book because it's reasonable to presume that Buckley's social attitudes were more than probably colored by his experiences early in his life. Buckley doesn't seem to have been obviously active during the Thirties and I would guess that the break-up of the free-and-easy radical bohemianism of the Twenties left him high and dry and without an audience. To generalize, one can see a whole tradition of American dissent falling apart around 1930 (Rexroth uses the Sacco-Venzetti execution of 1927 as a convenient marker), with the result that Communist domination during the Thirties meant that much social comment was strait-jacketed to the partyline. Buckley clearly would not fit into this context.

No one symbolized Prohibition Chicago better than Alphonse Capone. His name is synonymous worldwide with Public Enemy Number One. By instinct Capone was a heartless, mindless murderer. The gun, young Capone believed, solved all. Yet by the time he was twenty-six Capone had transformed himself from a heartless killer into a shrewd executive, bossing an enormous payroll and charged with keeping the criminal rewards flowing. At that tender age he had become the most powerful crime boss of the time, and he could—and did—boast that he "owned" Chicago.

At the zenith of its power the Capone organization numbered more than one thousand members, most of them experienced gunmen. But this represented only a portion of Capone's power base. Not only did "Scarface Al" own the police, but he had aldermen, state's attorneys, mayors, legislators, congressmen, and even governors in his back (and front) pockets. With influence like that, Capone took on the character of a public utility by limiting his gang's activities mainly to rackets that enjoyed strong public support: booze, gambling, and prostitution.

The center of these pursuits was in the speakeasies under Capone's thumb. Some of these (the Sundodger, the Roamer Inn, Chez Paree, Planet Mars, and the Ball of

Fire) were establishments to which a dapper Dick Buckley was no stranger. Buckley won the affection of the Mob by ridiculing the audience members in the city's murkiest dives, and eventually, behind Capone's bankroll, he opened his own posh nightspot, Chez Buckley. Hiring every top jazzman of the day, Dick took his act home with him as well, presiding over parties that lasted for days and developing a lifestyle that might conservatively be described as libertine.

Reportedly, Capone once stated uncategorically that Dick Buckley was "the only man who can make me laugh."

Charles Tacot

Charles Tacot was Lord Buckley's road manager for a stint in the 1950s. For many years his liner notes to the famed Elektra recording The Best of Lord Buckley *provided virtually the only information available on His Lordship.*

The "blast 'em and insult 'em" school of comedians so popular today was actually started by Buckley when, back in the twenties, he became the pet of one of the big Chicago gangsters, who set him up in a nightclub because he liked the way Dick put on the suckers. Of course, Dick had the protection of the gangland element during that period, and possibly he never got over it. He carried a bit of it with him always. He never really expected retribution to come or be paid. Dick always figured he would get away with it, and he usually did. It seemed predestined that Dick could never really become successful during his lifetime. He used up all his luck just staying alive.

Buckley's life was exactly like his act. In other words he lived his life in bits. When he would do something it had a beginning, a middle and a climactic end. To him, performing in front of you or me was just as important as it was in front of a thousand people. So he lived his life that way.

When he was working in Chicago during the thirties, Al Capone's guy came up to him and said, "Boss thinks you're great. What do you want?"

Buckley says, "I want a club—Chez Buckley."

This is the middle of Prohibition but the guy says, "Okay, ya got it."

So Buckley supervises the doing of this club and they open it up. On opening night he realizes he doesn't have any material because he's a winger. He wings it. And he finally comes out on the dance floor and says, "My Lords and Ladies of the Royal Court, I must beg your help here."

And he goes over to each gangster's wife and takes their mink coat. "May I? I'll bring it right back." He piles them all on the fuckin' dance floor and pulls out a can of lighter fluid and he squirts it on the coats. Nobody believes it, of course. They don't know what he's going to do while he says: "When is flame not a flame either in the heat or in the cold? And when is what you see not what you see but what you think you see?" He's doing all this double-talk and making them all sit still. After a few minutes the lighter fluid starts to evaporate and becomes flammable, he whips out a match, lights it, says, "Here it is!" He hits the pile of coats with it and: "Pow!"

First it has a sort of blue flame about a foot off the furs and then it settles down in there and starts to burn. The flame gets a little yellowish and it becomes obvious that it really is burning and these chicks are sitting around watching their fur coats go up in smoke.

Buckley at this point is standing at the bar next to the stage. He used to do a jump act where he would jump four feet right up in the air. Straight up. He jumped straight up: Boom!—onto the bar and starts tap dancing down the bar as these fuckin' furs all burnt. And he gets to the end of the bar and the bartender says, "Jesus, I don't know if I want to be around here when Al stops laughing." Because Al Capone was laughing at that moment.

Buckley said, "You know man, you're right."

And he jumped down, ran out of the front door and caught the next train to New York.

Well, it turned out that Al Capone bought all the coats and thought it was wonderful. He knew the guy. What the fuck were a bunch of fur coats to him. It was the funniest thing that ever happened. Buckley hadn't waited and that was the end of Chez Buckley.

But everything in his life was that way. He would blow anything for a laugh. He was a man who played with his life that way. It was brilliant and unrecognized except for show business people.

Adam Keefe

The late Adam Keefe was one of the hot young stand-up comics of the late 1950s and early 1960s. Appearing frequently at various New York City venues and as a regular on The Ed Sullivan Show, *Keefe was an orbiting member of Lord Buckley's floating Royal Court.*

One of the great stories I heard was when Buckley was working a club in Chicago called the Suzy Q. He hired an open-backed hearse and was lying in an open coffin in the back of the hearse. There was a big sign on the side of the hearse that said: "The Body Comes Alive at the Suzy Q" and he's lying there in the coffin smoking a joint riding around Chicago.

Buckley's proclivity to take the antics home with him for extended, ecstatic celebrations began around this time. For instance, it was not uncommon for the host to lock the window securely, build a roaring fire in the fireplace, and, when his inebriated guests began to show signs of heat prostration, gently suggest that they disrobe, even initiating the process himself to aid his manipulations.

After the Walkathons and the repeal of Prohibition, Buckley continued to work the taprooms of Chicago. But, unable to garner the paydays he was accustomed to, he also turned to vaudeville, burlesque, and the hotel lounge circuit as familiar and profitable alternatives.

As an extension of his lumberjack build and Walkathon routines, Buckley continued to employ the use of acrobatic moves in his nightclub act.

Pud Brown

The late clarinetist and saxophonist Pud Brown was devoted to music for seventy of his seventy-nine years, starting out in his family's band at the age of five. Twenty-seven of his most fruitful years in jazz were spent in California where he was a featured soloist in Jack Teagarden's band. He went to New Orleans in 1975 for a two-week gig and never left.

He did all these acrobatic things like jumping over tables. He was an ad-libber. I heard that he once got run out of a club because he pulled his thing out and slapped it on a table. He got into porn a little bit maybe. I think that kind of thing stopped him from being really big.

George Greif

A legendary mover and shaker in show biz, George Greif began his career managing Lord Buckley. He went on to handle a diverse crew that included Billy Eckstine, José Feliciano, the New Christy Minstrels, Elsa Lanchester, and the Crusaders. His encounter with George Harrison in the 1970s helped inspire the tune "Crackerbox Palace," in which he and Lord Buckley are referenced in the lyrics.

I first met Lord Buckley in the late 1940s or 1950. Our meeting took place in the Essex House in New York and he did something that totally freaked me out. We were in the bedroom and the window was wide open and he leaped across the beds and it looked like he was headed right out the window. But he landed in the space between the bed and the window. He was always looking to shock you. I wouldn't say he was an acrobat but he had very good physical abilities. He was a very strong guy.

Milt Holland

It was while playing traps in a Chicago speakeasy that drummer Milt Holland first caught Dick Buckley's act. According to Holland, Buckley had come to the nightspot with a bizarre entourage that included a seven-foot giant named "Junior," a gorgeous strawberry blonde, and a huge Russian wolfhound.

Buckley sat down in the middle of the floor and everybody's out there laughing, smoking, nobody paying any attention, and he'd just stare each person down. And finally they all got quiet. And then he simply started swearing at each person. "You son-of-a-bitch. You bastard!" It got quieter. Couple of snickers here and there. Anyway, he went around the room like that and then he said, "Now Junior will jump through that hole in the door. Give me a drum roll!" So I gave them a drum roll, and, sure enough, Junior jumps headfirst through this little porthole that led to the kitchen. And we hear this crashing and these horrible noises. Then everybody's laughing and Buckley and his entourage walk out. That was the end of their act.

Anita O'Day

I became a protegee of Buckley.

The Planet Mars, at 1117 Wilson Avenue, had a regular show, as regular as any show laid out and emceed by Dick Buckley could be, because Dick was an anarchist at heart. If, five minutes on stage, he decided the audience was square, he'd boom out, "That's all, folks. The show has been concluded."

Dick was always in trouble because he refused to play Casper Milquetoast with the bosses. The owners could work him over, give him his lumps, but he still ran things his way. The only way they could have controlled Dick would have been to kill him. A couple of them wanted to, but they weren't about to do that because wherever he played, he did business.

At the Planet Mars, Dick's acrobatics were even wilder than they had been at the Arcadia Gardens. The stage was slightly elevated and tables were scattered around the room. Dick would be up there on stage sipping gin, smoking tea or popping pills as casually as if he were in the privacy of his home. In the midst of a low-key bit, he'd let out a war whoop, sprint to the edge of the stage and leap into space, barely clearing the heads of the customers with his arms and legs as he sailed beyond the tables.

There were all kinds of wild scenes at the Planet Mars which made me feel if I could keep my cool there, I could perform anywhere.

The cast never knew what to expect. Once, when everything was quiet, the audience heard a shriek. Suddenly, Al Lyons dashed through the crowd, wearing only a red cap with a tassel and a pair of shorts. A couple of seconds later, Dick sprinted after him with a long loaf of Italian bread sticking out of his pants like a huge penis. Seconds later, Dick's Great Dane, with a pet monkey on its back, bounded out, pursuing Dick. It was just an Olsen and Johnson kind of thing, but naturally, with Dick, it had to have a sexual connotation.

Dick wanted nothing written down. Even the most far-out comics had routines at that time. I remember Bill Dohler, who played alto sax and loved jazz, telling Dick how much he admired his comic improvising. "But everybody has a certain underlying form to work from," he said. "Even the great masters have to have that."

"Not I," Dick announced, drawing himself to his full six feet two inches. Dick was the forefather of Professor Irwin Corey, Lenny Bruce and such Chicago improvisers as Mike Nichols, Elaine May and Shelley Berman who made it big twenty-five years later.

I admired Dick because he was, like, the *action*. And my aim had always been to be where it was. I suppose to most people these were just dull little taverns, but I came from a very dumb, one-room-and-kitchenette scene so the taverns seemed glamorous to me.

On the other hand, Dick always lived in spacious quarters supplied to him by a real estate man who was a Buckley fan. He got Dick a series of apartments where all Dick's friends were welcome at any time of the day or night. If, temporarily, you didn't have a pad, you could sleep there as long as floor space remained. What's more, Dick supplied all the food and other goodies to keep the party going from morning to night.

His first wife, as far I know, was Angel Rice, but she soon cut out after he took up with a tall blonde with a lovely complexion whom everybody called Peaches. Now Dick and Peaches generally received in the nude. Friends were free to bring their friends, too. Often they'd bring along somebody who was semi-legitimate, only to be met at the door by a stark naked Peaches. I knew her quite well, but I don't believe I ever saw her except in the buff.

Guests were also invited to leave their clothing by the door. But those of us who didn't want to shed our clothes didn't have to. Whatever way you chose to play, it was all right with Dick. That was your game.

Eventually, he elevated himself to Lord Buckley, but at this time he was playing a Greek king or a Roman emperor and he modeled life in the apartment on their customs. For instance, when he'd be lying on the couch, he'd signal Peaches, who'd immediately fetch a bowl which he'd urinate into.

One thing I want to make clear. This was no sex orgy. Dick just felt it created a free atmosphere in which he'd tell stories, play good music, whatever.

Those of us who got to know Buckley found that nothing was sacred where his perverted sense of humor was concerned. He was truly the first of the insult-type comics—before people like Don Rickles and the late Lenny Bruce—although I think Buckley's subjects were often too strong for audiences then.

Lord Buckley

A little truth. Truth is strange to the ears. Even wild truth: things that happen that supercede and carry on beyond the parallel of practiced credulity.

3 in a mist

Lord Buckley

One time in Chicago I isolated myself to the point that I lost my love and my contact to the people that I loved. I couldn't get to them. They didn't know that.

I loved them but I suddenly backed away. I broke all those love strands and I tightened up. And I had money in my pocket. I had wheels—a long set of wheels.

I had to go somewhere. I didn't want to go anywhere. I didn't want to go. I didn't want to see anyone I knew, anyone I ever knew, I didn't want to meet anyone new. I wanted to be alone.

Buckley's movements in the late 1930s and early 1940s are not easy to trace chronologically.

Portland, Oregon, was one town where Dick Buckley at least temporarily set up shop. Some recall a stint on local radio there during the medium's golden age, but when old Portlanders get together and tell Buckley stories, they all mention his blue gigs at the Midnight Club, an after-hours bootleg joint on Second and Everett near the city's fish market. They also recall the dapper sporting man tooling around town in an expensive raccoon coat and an even snappier set of wheels.

Buckley's weird sense of humor is also recalled. One of his favorite pranks was to coax an unsuspecting friend up to his hotel room where, in the dim blue light, a woman's head could be faintly discerned sleeping on the pillow. When he saw that curiosity was getting the best of his chum, Buckley would flick on the ceiling light to reveal a store mannequin as his bedmate.

Another similar, often-told Buckley tale from the early 1940s and beyond involved him inviting a lady friend to step into her birthday suit in the middle of one of his round-the-clock shindigs. He would then turn the light switch on and off very quickly creating a strobe effect while she took Chaplinesque steps around the room much to the delight of his other guests.

But Chicago was his primary base and its jazz the music he was associating himself with for much of that time.

Despite its place as the hotbed of jazz activity in the 1920s and 1930s, black Chicago musicians held an ambivalent attitude toward their white counterparts, colored by the history of American race relations and professional competition. This was echoed in the ambiguity in white attitudes toward South Side black players. The complexity of these perceptions was perhaps most dramatically personified by jazz clarinetist/soprano saxophonist Mezz Mezzrow, whose memoir, *Really the Blues,* articulated an extreme primitivist position that toppled into a kind of reverse racism of its own.

Ultimately Mezzrow and Buckley can be seen as embodying the major attitudes described in Norman Mailer's essay "The White Negro." According to Mailer, "hipsters" expressed their alienation from a war-torn, materialistic world in a mystic religion that focused on "The Negro," who appeared to offer a model for finding physical pleasure and musical expressiveness in the midst of despair. Mezzrow, a white man who insisted on being regarded as black, was debatably the most outspoken example of a historical phenomenon that stretched back through vaudeville and minstrelsy to the nineteenth century. As Mezzrow himself put it: "They were my kind of people. And I was going to learn their music and play it the rest of my days. I was going to be a musician, a Negro musician, hipping the world about the blues the way only Negroes can. I didn't know how the hell I was going to do it, but I was straight on what I had to do."

Albert Goldman

Though the late Albert Goldman's "pathographies" of Elvis Presley and John Lennon may have been justifiably castigated, his neojournalistic account of Lenny Bruce (Ladies and Gentlemen, Lenny Bruce) *and writings on Lord Buckley rate highly. His testimony in this study is drawn from his 1969* Life *magazine article, his 1982 article in* High Times, *and a chapter from his book* Freak Show.

In the 1930s, if you dug jazz, black talk and the ghetto lifestyle—especially flip attitudes toward work, sex and dope—you were a hipster: a viper. But in that the whole idea of the hipster was a black conception, a white hipster was a contradiction in terms. If a white man embraced the hipster identity, he would have to become, to a greater or lesser degree, a black man. The greatest of the white hipsters, Mezz Mezzrow, actually made the switch and insisted on being treated as a black man. The white jazz musician compromised: copying the lingo and the lifestyle, mimicking the music but never cutting off his retreat to the white world.

Perhaps the most vulnerable of hipsters was the white comic. He couldn't hide behind the abstractions of music or function only in a world of friends and acquaintances who were color blind. After years of hanging around the same jazz joints with musicians and sharing reefers with them in men's rooms at the price of their ridicule, it was the most natural thing in the world for a comic like Dick Buckley to drift into their lingo on stage and come on like a verbal jazzman whose larynx was his axe.

Yet for a white man to walk out onto a public stage, even today, and uncork that genie in the bottle—that crazy nigger-talkin', dope-smokin', juice-slashin' *jive* that was the core of the old underground jazz life—is to invite violent reactions from both whites and blacks. This is why it took even so bold a performer as Lord Buckley years to bring his act out of the closet; why he suffered a martyr's fate for doing in public what lots of white Americans have always done in private: pretending that the fairies have granted your three hip wishes and now you're (1) black; (2) high; (3) holding a horn that you're blowin' like Hell! Isn't

Scorsese's crappy *New York, New York* a Panavision monument to that classic American fantasy!

One of the earliest records of Buckley's formal association with jazz comes from Milt Hinton, bassist, photographer, and Cab Calloway big-band alumnus, who remembers Dick Buckley entertaining the crowd at Chicago's Hotel Sherman with an audience-participatory hat-snatching act between sets when the Calloway troupe performed there on successive New Year's Eves in 1939, 1940, and 1941. In between, Buckley was beginning to carve out as a name for himself as a comic/emcee on the vaudeville circuit.

Studs Terkel

I remember Dick Buckley at the Rialto Theater in Chicago, playing straight man to the top bananas of the times, two clowns known as Charlie Country and Kenny Brenner.

He was a boozer. He got into a lot of brawls . . . he was Dick Buckley. And then something happened: the transformation. I don't know if AA played a role or what made him change.

Indeed, Buckley often mixed it up in fisticuffs and enjoyed showing off the tooth marks on his paw where some less fortunate rounder's puss had left its dental imprint.

Lord Buckley

I was drinking the good juice. Suddenly I decided I would go to the Club DeLisa. I didn't want to go to the Club DeLisa. But I had to go somewhere.

In the late 1930s Dick Buckley began frequenting Chicago's Club DeLisa, a club known for its spectacular variety entertainments. Some allege that he became one of the few white performers to appear on the Club DeLisa's storied stage. Either way, he gained vital exposure to black performance—experience he began to use to his own ends a decade later. An examination of the club's history and its artistic, social, and economic milieu may shed some light on the formation of Buckley's ideas and performance style.

Loosely modeled on the Cotton Club in New York City, the Club DeLisa was an important institution on Chicago's South Side from 1933 to 1958. But unlike its New York cousin, the Club DeLisa nurtured a mixed, "black and tan" clientele. The Club DeLisa featured variety shows with singers, comedians, music for dancing, and choreographed dance numbers.

The DeLisa was designed with spectacular entertainment in mind. The dance floor in front of the bandstand could be raised hydraulically for shows. The house was lit by dim red fluorescent lights, and the stage had multicolored theatrical lighting that illuminated the female dancers dressed in two-piece outfits, often with a Caribbean flavor, cutting the rug. The DeLisa's band played four sets a night and all night on Sunday, beginning at 5 p.m. and culminating in a 6:30 a.m. Monday-morning "breakfast dance," which musicians and dancers from other clubs would attend. The basement was the scene of illegal Monday-morning blackjack, poker, and dice games played by pimps, hustlers, "sporting men," and squares.

The DeLisa's program changed each month. Among the monthly show titles advertised in the early 1940s in the local black newspaper, the *Chicago Defender,* were "Music Hall Revue," "Show-Boat Flotsam," "Dude Ranch Revue," "Early Fall Caper," "Romance and Rhythm," "Bronzeville Holiday," "Bag O' Tricks," and "Copper-Cabana Revue."

Lady Elizabeth Buckley

Certainly there would have been no Royal Court without Lady Elizabeth Buckley. It was while holding court with Lord Buckley that her unique "Ballet for Living" set the upbeat tone for all *that transpired. "Ballet for Living" is a form of choreography blending bebop and Balanchine that Lady Buckley practiced and perfected her entire life. The woman who reared His Lordship's two youngest children was also responsible for inspiring him to experiment with "hipsemantic" interpretations of the classics. Sadly, her passing in 1996 did not allow her to enjoy a greater recognition of her husband's legacy.*

The joining of the working class of America—the white and the black—took place, strangely enough, in nightclubs. And that's when jazz was born. The beautiful Duke Ellington with his beautiful "Sophisticated Lady" came forward. I wished that I had lived in that era because they seemed so *there.*

The Club DeLisa must have had a profound effect on Buckley. The tent show circuit, Walkathon palaces, Capone's speakeasies, and other venues provided a precedent for the experience. But the large scale of the Club DeLisa shows—the size of the club, the diversity of its audience, the number of performers, the variety of acts, the elaborate staging, lighting, and costumes, and the fame of some of the performers and audience members was extraordinary. In time its visual, verbal, and theatrical elements were to figure significantly in Buckley's own presentations.

Mort Fega

Late-night radio "communicaster" Mort Fega spread the gospel of jazz and Lord Buckley on New York City's WEVD during the 1950s and 1960s on his late-night, all-night, every-night program. Although they only became acquainted late in His Lordship's life, Fega was invited by Lady Buckley to eulogize her husband at his memorial service.

A lot of people mistook Buckley's fondness for the black dialect as a parody. In fact, it was a token of esteem. I've often made the comment that if there was some magic elixir which would permit a white person to become black, that it is my considered opinion that Buckley probably would have been first on line for the dosage. If anyone was the personification of the freewheeling, easygoing lifestyle of jazz, it was Buckley. He was the embodiment.

Charles "Tubby" Boots

The late Miami Beach showman Tubby Boots left his Baltimore, Maryland, home at the age of twelve for the quixotic world of Lord Buckley and the Royal Court in New York City in the late 1940s. When Buckley relocated in Southern California several years later, Boots joined him and was a collaborator on several of His Lordship's hippest hip classics. After that the amiable comedian displayed his versatility in theaters, clubs, and concerts, on television, and on cruise ships around the world. In the Royal Court of Lord Buckley, Tubby was known by a variety of monikers, including "Prince Booth" and "Princess Lily."

One time he was talking with the singer Ruth Brown and he said, "You know, Lady Brown, I understand what you're going through because I am a believer."

And she said to Buckley, "No, you don't know what I'm going through. You've never been refused service at a restaurant. You've never had to go to a bathroom that said 'Blacks Only.' You have to be black to understand. You sympathize but you don't understand."

And he said, "You know, you're right." And Buckley always remembered that.

H. L. "Doc" Humes

Novelist, Paris Review *cofounder, inventor, street-corner philosopher, and concerned citizen Harold Louis "Doc" Humes brought Lord Buckley to New York City for the ill-fated Jazz Gallery gig in October 1960 and to contribute to the soundtrack for a never-completed and now-lost film,* Don Peyote, *which Humes was producing. After Buckley was prevented from performing, Humes valiantly championed His Lordship's cause by forming the Citizen's Emergency Committee, a loose-knit group of the city's artistic and political intelligentsia, to fight the cabaret card laws. Doc passed away in September 1992 shortly after this interview was conducted. Some of Doc's testimony is also drawn from an article he published in* Swank *magazine.*

He was part of that West Coast thing and he didn't come East very often which is why nobody knew him in the East. They knew him by his records and stuff like that but very few people actually knew him. Some people even thought he was black. That was a source of great amusement to Buckley. He had story after story after story to tell, as you can well imagine, of people meeting him who were surprised that he was an ofay.

Buckley was by no means confined to Chicago venues during this period. In the fall of 1941 he had at least a short residency in *Fun for the Money,* an apparently unsuccessful Hollywood stab at staging a New York–style vaudeville revue. It opened at the Hollywood Playhouse on September 1. According to the program (featuring a photo of a tweed-clad Dick Buckley brushing his chin mischievously while playfully mugging for the camera), the thirty-five-year-old entertainer had small supporting roles in several skits with titles like "It's Fun for the Money Tonight," "Lost in a Crowd," "I've Got a New Rhythm for Old Shoes," "A Word to Mr. Jones," and "All I Wanna Do Is

Dance." More significantly, Buckley was given his own solo slot near the end of Act One, though there is little evidence hinting at what exactly constituted his act.

Reviews of the show were few and sketchy. Harrison Carroll of the *Los Angeles Herald and Express* filed the following notice—mentioning "Dick Buckley (best in his Englishman monologue)"—in the September 2, 1941, edition:

Real coin has been poured into the production of Fun for the Money, the new revue which opened last night at the Hollywood Playhouse. Very few Broadway musicals are as lavishly costumed as this potpourri of songs, dances and sketches that George Shafer offers as his bid for a Los Angeles-born show to match the big-time offerings of New York . . . Fun for the Money is what the title promises but it could have been more.

Charlie Barnet

A colorful character in his own right, Charlie Barnet spurned his privileged upbringing for the music and tenor saxophone he loved. Among the first white bandleaders to showcase black stars, Barnet's 1939 recording of "Cherokee" helped lay the groundwork for the emerging bebop revolution. His autobiography, Those Swinging Years, *is a rich read from which the following reminiscence is excerpted.*

One incident stands out in my memory of an unfortunate trip to California. I used to go over to a club called Slapsie Maxie's. We finished at 1:30 and the club had a show that went on at 2:00 a.m. You could drink all the drinks at your table at that time, but you couldn't order more. So I would call, order some drinks, and get there just in time for the show. Now Slapsie Maxie's was owned by [former prizefighter] Maxie Rosenbloom and some other Jewish gentlemen. On this particular night they were auditioning a guy by the name of Lord Buckley. Nobody knew anything about him and when he was introduced there was just a smattering of applause. Comedy was the motif of the club and comedians like Ben Blue, Sammy Lewis, and Cully Richards appeared there. Buckley was a big, overbearing man who looked and acted very British, although he did not affect the accent. He proceeded to deliver a half-hour dissertation on what a great man Adolf Hitler was. The predominantly Jewish audience was waiting for the punch line of the year, but it never came. There was a big silence as Buckley concluded with some particularly extravagant praise of Hitler and left the stage. Then all hell broke loose. They picked him up and threw him out on the street. That was my first contact with Lord Buckley.

A rare, atmospheric photo of Dick Buckley from this era is one of those noirish, spotlit jobs featuring an elongated shadow cast behind the subject. The dark, pinstripe-suited performer, cigarette confidently in hand and fedora perched just so, stares menacingly at the camera, looking more like one of Capone's goons than a nightclub comic. Indeed, at this point in his career, he was probably a little bit of both.

As the big-band blast of bass, saxophone, and drum swept across the country, Dick Buckley found himself at the vanguard of the big-band scene in the late 1930s and early 1940s. The music of the big bands throbbed in hotel ballrooms, nightclubs, and movie theaters, and on the radio in millions of homes. Their music quickly spread from coast to coast as names like Benny Goodman, Woody Herman, Gene Krupa, Louis Armstrong, Fletcher Henderson, Duke Ellington, Count Basie, Tommy Dorsey, and Glenn Miller became celebrated in even the most remote burgs.

It was while touring with the Herman (as a temporary replacement for a singer) and Krupa troupes that Buckley cut his jazz teeth as a comic emcee. But it was a grueling life.

In the early 1940s a few key events transpired that indirectly contributed to the circumstances associated with Buckley's early demise in 1960.

In 1941, while on tour with the Krupa band in Reno, Dick tied one on and was arrested for public drunkenness—an infraction for which he apparently plead guilty and paid a small fine before being released.

During World War II, Buckley hooked up with Ed Sullivan's U.S.O. troupe, which toured military bases and arms factories entertaining troops and arms factory laborers throughout North America. One stop even included Alaska. While visiting his home base of Chicago in 1943, Dick got popped with an unspecified amount of marijuana, a serious charge even then. But he was not convicted this time because, as the story goes, Sullivan pulled some strings with the director of the F.B.I., his buddy J. Edgar Hoover, who encouraged local authorities to back off on the charge. Additionally, an unspecified charge stemming from a visit to Indianapolis around this time came back to haunt Buckley in his end days.

These busts, a couple of angry husbands, and several other extroverted antics (including the infamous ill-fated late-night car trip on Chicago's State Street trolley tracks he later recounted in the uproarious bit "My Own Railroad") prompted those close to Buckley to suggest he seek residence in another town.

Berle Adams

Berle Adams has been in show business for well over half a century. Starting out as an office boy at the General Artists' Corporation, a talent agency in Chicago, Adams went on to manage Louis Jordan and his Tympany Five, cofound and become president of Mercury Records, and act as executive vice president of MCA, Inc. In the 1940s he was a partner with Bookie Levin of Mutual Entertainment Agency, agents for Dick Buckley. His particular episodes with Buckley recounted here took place in 1943 and 1944.

Dick was unpredictable even in those days. These were his big drinking and womanizing days. Many clubs wouldn't bring him back, especially hotels, because it was precarious to have him work—they didn't know what was going to happen next.

He wanted to play the Chase Hotel in St. Louis, which was a very important date. So Bookie Levin, who was very close to Dick and always anxious to keep him working, booked him. Bookie did a fabulous job for him. Bookie asked me to intercede because Harold Koplar, who bought the talent and who was the son of the owner, and I were quite friendly and Bookie thought I could convince Harold to forgive Dick for whatever he did the last time he was there. So I worked the thing out for him.

The first week was terrific. The second week I received a call from Koplar: "Get that madman out of my hotel!"

I said, "What did he do?"

"He tried to set fire to the hotel!"

I said, "Come on Harold, you're exaggerating."

He said, "Call him! Find out!"

So I called Dick. I said, "Dick, what the hell happened?"

He said, "Well, after the show, a couple of babes followed me up to the room. I wanted to get rid of them because I had my eyes on somebody else and I couldn't get them out of the room. So I lit a match and threw it in the wastebasket that was full of paper and hollered: 'Fire!' How was I supposed to know the drapes were going to catch on fire?"

Another factor contributing to Buckley's exodus from Chicago may have been the birth of his first-known progeny. Frederick Buckley was born out of wedlock to Paula Banks in 1937, but beyond that little has been revealed about Buckley's relationship with her. It is also unclear exactly where the child was born, where he was raised, or whether Buckley even knew that he had fathered a child until Fred came forward in the mid-1950s and forged an apparently warm but short-lived bond with his father.

The circumstances surrounding Buckley's liaison with Paula Banks bring up the general question of his relationship with women, how many times he actually married, and what exactly the results of these unions were. Buckley was allegedly married six times, and there is indication that as early as 1928 he was betrothed to a wealthy Seattle, Washington, woman several years his senior by the name of Emerald Botting. Presumably, the rigors and temptations of show business contributed to the marriage's early demise, as they would to at least several others.

Along with Anita O'Day's recollections of Peaches and Angel Rice, a Jewell Lange, Joanna Daum, and an unnamed women of Russian heritage are remembered by Buckley's friends as at least temporary legal mates. While the marriage to Daum was annulled, the others presumably ended in divorce. Some suggest that a couple of these marriages might have been shotgun affairs, from which Buckley somehow later extricated himself. Other speculation centers on the notion that his heavy drinking may have led to ceremonies, which may have been only dimly recalled on the rocky morning after. At any rate, the open and itinerant nature of the biz was not conducive to domestic serenity.

Larry Storch

Once in Washington, D.C., he was nailed by the house detective in a hotel room with a young girl, whiskey, and some reefers. He was brought in front of the judge first thing in the morning and Buckley, with the lungs of an animal, just put his head back and roared up at the ceiling, "Oh God! The whole world has turned against me!"

The judge saw what he was in for, pounded his gavel, and dismissed the case, telling the bailiff, "Get this guy out of here. I never want to see him again. Let someone else handle this case."

One of the stories told about Buckley from this era concerned the night that he was doing a show and saw a beautiful woman from the stage. He stopped his act abruptly and said, "Your grace, your beauty, your magnificence, my God, aren't you a spectacle!"

She looked at him shyly but it didn't matter: Buckley was zeroing in on his prey. He looked at her and said, "I have a present for you." He opened up his jacket, handed her a piece of lettuce, and went back into his act.

But he couldn't continue. "Oh! What is it about you? Your face? Your eyes? The sound of your voice? The way you sit there?" Then he said, "I have another present for you." And he opened up his jacket, took out a slice of tomato, and gave it to her.

He went back into his act, started performing, but stopped again and said, "I can't stand it anymore! I must have you, every inch of you: your beauty, your your your . . . *everything.* Will you please make mad and passionate love to me right here in front of the whole audience?"

The beauty demurred: "Noooo."

Stunned, Buckley looked inquisitively into the audience and complained, "Isn't that just like a woman. You buy 'em dinner . . ."

Tubby Boots

Buckley rarely talked about his past. But he once told me a story about a time he was hanging with some musicians when he was living in Chicago. This was when he was drinking heavily in the early 1940s and he loved to party. So he's telling these musicians, "Man, you know my wife cooks so fine. You would not believe how my wife cooks. She is the greatest cook in the world. Now when we finish the gig tonight, we all gonna go over to my place and I'm gonna get her to burn some food for us. So we all gonna go over to my place."

So they finished the gig and Buckley and all these musicians hop into the car—about six or seven of them. And they drive over to Buckley's house and he ain't stopping: "Man, this bitch can cook. You never had food like this . . ."

Well they open up the door, walk in and here's his wife on the couch giving head to some musician. Buckley didn't bat an eye. She never stopped. The musician was ready to go. The other musicians were behind Buckley watching this whole scene. And Buckley turned around to them and said: "But she is a good cook."

Certainly Dick Buckley was a man of large, spontaneous appetites, and sex was probably at or near the top of his list of favorite pursuits. Being a handsome stage performer didn't hurt matters either. And if Chicago was getting a mite too small for his indulgences and ever-suspect reputation, then perhaps another district was in order. New York City, with its looser mores, was a natural place for Buckley to further sample the fruits of indiscretion.

Larry Storch

Another night, on his wedding night, before he married Elizabeth, he was married to another girl, a very pretty, redheaded lady. And at the Astor Hotel in New York City, now long-demolished, he walked in with his bride after their wedding. This was to be their wedding night.

It was quite late and two Marines were in the lobby. They had just come back from Guadalcanal and were donned in metal so you know how far back it goes. He looked at them and said, "You are two of the biggest shitheads I've ever seen in my life!"

They turned around. There's nobody in the hall except them. They said, "You mean to tell me . . . are you talking to us?"

He said, "Nobody else but. There's no one else in here, is there? Biggest shitheads I've ever seen in my life!"

Well they beat the tar out of him, knocked some of the teeth out of his head. Later on, after I heard the story, I said to him, "Richard, why in God's name did you do that?"

All he said was, "I wanted to see the looks on their faces."

George Greif

Once he told me that he had a brand new Cadillac. He had hired a chauffeur, they were driving along Ocean Avenue in Palm Beach, Florida, when he said, "Turn left and drive into the ocean." So the chauffeur drove into the water, pulled back out and drove back onto Ocean Avenue. When they were back on the road, the chauffeur asked, "Why did you do that?" And Buckley said, "I always wondered what it would be like to go to sea in a Cadillac."

Lord Buckley

First of all, I must say that the vibrations from the men are great and powerful and beautiful and the inspiration from the lovely ladies *magnificent*. Every time I see so many lovely girls like this it always brings to my mind's eye that I am the happiest fellow in the world.

But what *cuts* me to the *quick* is when I *think* of all the lovely ladies . . . in the hands of *amateurs*.

4 amos 'n' andy

Lord Buckley

I went through the various scenes and movements of show business and trios and singles and finally I achieved a thing called "mass pantomimtism" which is the art of voice projection through people. It's employed and controlled by a thing called "staccato control," which is a system of piercing touch, a lightning touch preceded by a very strong sound.

While working the Walkathons, touring the movie-house vaudeville circuit of the 1930s, and just playing around with friends, Buckley developed and perfected a four-way act that he used for the rest of his career.

Anita O'Day

He developed the "Amos 'n' Andy" bit which became his best routine at home, using his naked friends.

The bit, commonly called "Amos 'n' Andy," "The Four Chairs," or simply "The Chairs," involved four audience members being called on stage to sit in chairs and soundlessly gesticulate while Buckley, seated behind them, spontaneously supplied their voices. The supplied sound consisted of black vernacular grafted from the characters on the popular radio show: Amos, Andy, Kingfish, Lightnin', Madame Queen, and Sapphire. Drawing on the news of the day or his own particular whims, Buckley's "Amos 'n' Andy" ad-lib combined with his Svengali-like audience manipulations made him a favored attraction.

The popular culture produced two distinct versions of "Amos 'n' Andy", one the logical outgrowth of the other. The original version of the team was the brainchild of white comedians Charles Correll and Freeman Gosden, who played the characters—both on stage and on radio—in blackface. *The Amos 'n' Andy Show* was one of radio's first wildly successful programs, showing what could be achieved by this infant medium. Starting up in 1929 as a fifteen-minute broadcast, the radio show lasted (in reruns) into the mid-1960s, clocking in over thirty-five years on the ether. It was radio's first national success, and the magnitude of that achievement is best described by George Burns: "Gracie and I knew that vaudeville was finished when theaters began advertising that their shows would be halted for fifteen minutes so that the audience could listen to Amos 'n' Andy. And when the Amos 'n' Andy program came on, the vaudeville would stop, they would bring a radio onstage, and the audience would sit there watching the radio."

Most Baby Boomers are familiar with the later incarnation of Amos 'n' Andy as a television show broadcast in the early to mid-1950s and the first with an all Black cast. It was among the first shows to go into syndication but was finally canceled in 1964 after many civil rights organizations protested what they felt were its negative stereotyping.

The basic scenario of Buckley's "Amos 'n' Andy" routine is a simple one: Andy and Kingfish (played by two of the men) recount a recent binge while Madame Queen and Amos (played by a woman and the remaining, usually most glamorous, man) create love sparks resulting in the pair kissing, much to the delight of the studio audience. In the earlier two instances, DeFore and Derek are engaged to play the leading man and seducer. In later appearances in the mid- and late 1950s, Buckley tapped Sullivan himself to play the part of the great seducer . . . much to Ed's obvious enjoyment.

Typically Buckley would begin the exercise by plunking goofy-looking hats on his participants, sitting his stooges in chairs on stage in front of him while he kneeled behind them, jive-singing a rousing send-up of "On the Sunny Side of the Street" in his best Louis Armstrong growl. Upon the fanfare's conclusion he would then inform the audience of what they were about to witness with the following embellished explanation: "Ladies and gentlemen. Through the lovely lady and three gentlemen seated upon the chairs, through these four charming people I will *pro*ject four different and distinct voices. *Each* and every one of them will be given an *in*dividual voice to pantomime. They, themselves, will not say word one. But when they hear the voice allotted to them they will move their lips, eyebrows, nose, facial muscles, jaws, and whatnot in a pantomimic manner thereby simulating actual speech."

During this spiel Buckley continually moved his hands across the backs of his subjects as if to acclimate them to his touch. He would then demonstrate the technique on each participant separately and ensure their understanding of the bit before setting the imaginary (and somewhat debauched) scene—amazingly slipping in a drug reference under the radar in one of the 1949 appearances: "The time, the summertime. Yes, the beautiful, warm, golden summertime of Southern California. They're seated in a *lovely* Spanish garden in the fabulous San Fernando Valley and it's sundown in San Fernando and the moon—catch that beautiful Southern California moonlight shining right down in their eyes. They're relaxed. They've had a double shot of tequila apiece and a very new California drink called a 'Benzedrine Float.' They are looking up into the moonlight and Andrew is talking."

He would then begin supplying the voices and playing his quartet like marionettes. In the later 1949 Sullivan appearance, a sense of the bit can be gleaned from this excerpted sample:

Kingfish: Well, tomorrow's another day, my dear boy, don't forget that. Every time the year rolls round you can't tell who's going to pick up on the crowd.

Amos: Yeah, you got somethin' there.

Madame Queen: I'm hip, he's got somethin' there. He's comin' on with the come on.

Amos: You ain't lyin', baby! You talkin' straight. Ain't nothin' I like better than a hip chick.

Madame Queen: I'm hip yo' hip, too, Daddy.

Amos: I'm hip yo' hip I'm hip!
Kingfish: Hip hip . . .
All: Hooray!

Later in the bit, Amos begins his seduction of Madame Queen:

Madame Queen: I've never seen such a gorgeous night in all my life. Stars in the sky certainly do make a girl feel romantic in this here kind of weather, I swear.
Amos: Baby, you know, you is a pretty little chick. You know that, Sugar?
Madame Queen: Is I, Daddy?
Kingfish: That's what the man said.
Andy: Uhh-huh!
Amos: You know, you is sittin' beside one of the greatest lovers in the New-Nited-States of America, baby?
Madame Queen: Is that the truth?
Amos: That's the truth and furthermore—
Madame Queen: What's that, you little rascal?
Amos: I'm going to give you the most wild, supersonic kiss that you ever received in your born days. I'm gonna out-Gable Gable.
Madame Queen: Well come on, Daddy, I'm ready.
Amos: Well here I come, baby!
Buckley: Take over my boy!

At this point, the man was on his own to fulfill the oral, nonverbal obligations of the ad-lib.

Buckley had the act down pat by World War II, and he regularly broke it out to crack up the troops while touring with Ed Sullivan's U.S.O. outfit. Sullivan enjoyed the act (and Buckley's friendship) so much that he had the comic appear on his television show semiannually from 1949 through 1959.

Tubby Boots

Ed Sullivan was the last person in the world you'd think would love Buckley. Buckley had the same beliefs at the end of his life that he had when he met Sullivan in the early 1940s. You wouldn't think that they would be that close. It's the amazement at the differences of the people. But people didn't know what Sullivan felt because Sullivan never told them. Sullivan was like Buckley because they both thought about and felt alike about the same things. Sullivan might not have bought into His Lordship and all the Royal Court crap but he still felt strongly about equality. He always put black artists and people from all races on his television show. He wanted something to appeal to everyone. He was very forward-thinking in that regard.

Buckley died owing Sullivan three hundred thousand dollars. Nobody could get ten cents out of Ed Sullivan. But Sullivan loved him and called him "Your

Lordship." Sullivan was the squarest man in the world. And Buckley didn't take money from Sullivan because Sullivan had money. He genuinely saw Sullivan as a human being and as a person that people couldn't see in him. He only took from people he loved. He took for his family, which was the Royal Court. It was like a father of a family looking after everybody. If one had it, they all had—sharing what they had among the flock.

Every week for twenty-three years columnist-turned-TV-host Ed Sullivan promised his audience "a reeallly big SHEW tonight" and he delivered every week, packing his hour with the hottest singers of the day—from pop to rock to opera—plus dancers, comedians, circus acts, and even dramatic recitations.

Sullivan's show premiered June 20, 1948, as *Toast of the Town;* the name was changed to *The Ed Sullivan Show* on September 18, 1955. The hour-long variety show ran Sunday nights on CBS until June 6, 1971, and both bandleader Roy Bloch and the June Taylor Dancers stayed with Sullivan as regulars.

Jerry Lewis and Dean Martin made their television debuts on that first show and split their pay of $200, part of the $375 allotted for talent that night. Among others making their U.S. network television debuts on the show were Charles Laughton, Bob Hope, Lena Horne, Dinah Shore, Eddie Fisher, the Beatles, and Walt Disney. Disney's own show, which premiered in 1954 on ABC, eventually surpassed Sullivan's as the longest-running prime-time network show.

Most people viewing Sullivan's showcase on the black-and-white TV sets of the era saw comedians Carol Burnett, Alan King, Jackie Mason, Joan Rivers, Will Jordan, and Dick Buckley, whose four-way "Amos 'n' Andy" bit became a Sullivan show perennial.

The routine demonstrates Buckley's earliest recorded use of black dialect in his act. It is interesting that he copied the popular radio program in which white performers like himself and his audience participants portrayed stereotypical black characters.

Surviving kinescopes of Buckley's television appearances have preserved a glimpse of this very important, though badly dated, aspect of his performance. In early 1949 Buckley made his first appearance on Sullivan's *Toast of the Town* television show. As he would on virtually all of his TV appearances with Sullivan, Buckley performed the "Amos 'n' Andy" bit with a quartet of celebrities gathered in the theater. This time they included golf's first woman superstar Babe Didrickson Zaharias and actors Dan DeFore (later of TV's *Hazel* fame), John Howard, and Frankie Albertson.

Berle Adams

He wasn't doing any of his hip material back then. The only hip he was doing was coming out of these "Amos 'n' Andy" characters. He would mask behind them and so it wasn't Dick Buckley. But through the voices of these characters he could use innuendo and get across the things he wanted to. The people he got from the audience were fantastic. Nobody got insulted no matter what he said, even when the material was a little blue.

It wasn't generally perceived as offensive for a white person to perform using the black idiom in those days. That was a much different period. *Amos 'n' Andy* was the outstanding radio show of the time. Everybody stopped and remained at home just to hear *Amos 'n' Andy*. It was accepted that a white person could play a black. Absolutely. He never got any playback on that. It was all fun.

There were a lot of great black comics back then who Dick might have learned from. Spo-Dee-O-Dee—Sam Theard—was one of them. He worked for me. He was one of the Apollo Theater's house comics in New York. The Apollo Theater had three or four house comics. If the management, Mr. Schiffman, didn't like the comic that came with the show, he would have one of his house comics perform instead. And Sam was one of them. Spo-Dee-O-Dee.

Later in 1949 Buckley was on the Sullivan show again with actor John Derek, baseball stars Phil Rizzuto and Gene Hermanski, and Hermanski's fiancée, Phyllis, acting as his "Amos 'n' Andy" puppets.

Comparing these first two extant outings of Buckley's Amos 'n' Andy is interesting because they are word-for-word and gesture-for-gesture doppelgangers. Regardless of this static quality, they provide a valuable glimpse at this rock-steady component of Buckley's presentation.

Larry Storch

I never saw him write anything down. You know he was able to pick four people out of an audience and do an entire routine with them. He would walk out into an audience and pick out four people. But it would take him fifteen minutes. He would walk up and down the aisle and it was absolutely hypnotic. Finally, he would settle on one and say, "You! Up on the stage immediately! And don't you dare dally for fear of my wrath! You don't want to make me angry! You know my temper, you've heard of it haven't you?! Up on stage!"

And by God, they would get up out of their seats and go right up onto the stage. I saw old people hobble up. I mean a woman would throw away her cane or crutches and, by God, they would make it up on stage.

When the selection process was completed, Buckley would then seat them on stools in front of him. He would tap each one on the back and tell them to move their lips and suddenly here "vas un olt Chewish man" and Buckley would tap someone else on the back and they'd move their lips and out would come Louis Armstrong's voice and it was absolutely hysterical.

And Buckley, of course, would make it all up on the moment. He would ad-lib whatever he wanted to do. It was the damndest sight you ever saw.

Red Rodney

One of the first of the first and best of the best, the late Red Rodney was among the most important bebop trumpeters after Dizzy Gillespie and Miles Davis. On the road since he was fifteen years old, his collaborations and friendship with Charlie Parker were vividly portrayed in Clint Eastwood's 1988 film Bird. *Right up until the end, Rodney was still fiercely dedicated to the music, touring, and hard blowing.*

He did a four-way audience-participatory bit when I first met him. He got hipper later and I think that hurt him professionally. The only one that liked him was Ed Sullivan who kept having him on to the end. No matter what he did Sullivan always hired him. Sullivan was a loyal man: if he liked you he kept hiring you.

I loved Buckley's hip stuff but when he started doing it, his career was going downhill: he wasn't working at all and having bad times.

By the mid-1940s the days of vaudeville and burlesque were on the wane. Buckley had, by this point, risen to the top of the heap, working the circuit with some of the era's biggest names.

Before the radio and the video and the movies, vaudeville was *the* American form of popular entertainment. Dancers, singers, magicians, comedians, animal handlers, acrobats, contortionists, and many ukulele strummers filled theaters across the land. From the 1880s through the 1930s the country watched the headliners doing their turns: Weber & Fields, Burns & Allen, Bert Lahr, Bert Williams, Ethel Barrymore, Ethel Waters, the Nicholas Brothers, and other sibling teams. And there were lesser-known curiosities like A. Robins, the Banana Man, who silently filled the stage with furniture from the innards of his black cloak; the potentate whose act consisted of spouting astounding quantities of liquid onto a fire; the "regurgitator" who swallowed a baby shark; and don't forget the spoon players or that the often-lame closing act on the bill was called "playing to the haircuts" by vaudeville insiders because that's what the hapless last onstage hack could see heading up the aisles and out the theater doors while he performed.

The elements that merged in American vaudeville were as intrinsic to the cultural sustenance of the country as apple pie. It brightened the lot of immigrants weaned on English music halls, the Yiddish theater, minstrelsy, the commedia dell'arte, and burlesque. Like the audience, the acts came from the working class. And like other American institutions of the time, vaudeville consigned blacks to stereotypical racial roles—Sambo characters—which held back many but from which some managed to emerge as stars.

Because he was a rising star in the country's top venues during the form's dying days, Buckley's legacy in the oeuvre is surprisingly, if repetitively, well documented, eased by *Billboard*'s weekly performers' "route" listings during the last years of World War II. Another feature of Buckley's reviews throughout his career was their occasional inaccuracy as to his nationality, often identifying him as an Englishman, hinting at the persona he was then projecting from center stage.

Typically, a show (including a film, a live band, a comic, dancers, and perhaps a novelty act) would roll into town on a Friday and stay for a week before moving on. Thus Buckley was presenting his "Amos 'n' Andy" bit on some of the country's more noted venues.

A scan through the newspapers of the era is at once a charming stroll down memory lane and a sobering reminder of the harsh reality of World War II. Not only are the hard-news pages filled with the latest dispatches from both fronts (and the odd baseball pennant race), but entertainment sections featured notices of newsreels with the latest, breaking developments: "Yanks in Germany! 1st Army Crosses Nazi Frontier!," "Siegfried Line Battle! First Combat Films of Battle for Germany!," and "Invasion of Palau! U.S. Forces Capture Peleliu!"

In the days before CNN (or even Walter Cronkite, for that matter), the local theater served as an important link to world events. It was in this grim environment that vaudeville's last stages provided some solace for a nervous nation. From mid-July of 1943 though early 1945, Buckley shared the stage and the circuit with scores of stars, rising stars, soon-to-bes, has-beens, wannabes, and never-would-bes including Henny Youngman, tap dancers Lathrop and Lee, Harry James, Tommy Dorsey, Earl Hines, Lionel Hampton, Cab Calloway and his Cotton Club Orchestra, Count Basie, Hal McIntyre and his Orchestra, The Iwanos, Paul Robeson, and Gene Baylos.

Additionally, some of the films featured during his weekly runs crisscrossing the circuit included both the great and the totally forgettable reels of the era: *Roger Touhy, Gangster*, *Frontier Badman*, *Laura*, *Double Indemnity*, *Bride by Mistake*, *Arsenic and Old Lace*, *Meet Miss Bobby Sox*, *I Escaped from the Gestapo*, *Cabin in the Sky*, *The Song of Bernadette*, *Jane Eyre*, *Gangway for Tomorrow*, *The Fighting Seabees*, *Marriage Is a Private Affair*, and *The Great McGinty*.

Some of the more amusing audience draws involved stunts such as Frank Sinatra singing contests.

During a three-day July 1943 stint at the Paramount in Springfield, Massachusetts (that included a special midnight show for war and defense workers), Buckley received glowing reviews in the local papers where he was advertised as "Broadway's Favorite" on the bottom of a bill topped by the Tommy Tucker Orchestra. Buckley's bit went over big-time in Springfield, where he even made headlines in the July 20 *Springfield Daily News:* "Paramount Has Smart Show Headed by Tommy Tucker and Band—Versatile Orchestra Mixes Ballads with Jive and Humor; Ventriloquist Dick Buckley Clicks." The reviewer was no less enthusiastic in appraising the presentation:

> For unusual humor, Dick Buckley and his not so dumb dummies from the audience had the audience in an uproar with his ventriloquist's take-off of characters from Amos and Andy.

The *Springfield Union* was even more over-the-top in its review that same day:

> Our laurels go to Dick Buckley, introduced by Tommy as an Englishman with an American sense of humor. Buckley has a sophisticated approach in his timing and a change of pace that is both individual and entertaining and his comedy is exceptionally good. He gets four stooges on the stage, uniformed service men, and puts on a four part monolog with his stooges acting as his Charlie McCarthys and it lays 'em in the aisles. His last stunt, a hat trick is one of the funniest bits of burlesque we have seen in many a day.

With Judy Garland and Van Heflin starring in *Presenting Lily Mars* on the big screen, Richard Buckley appeared next in a large revue on the stage of Washington, D.C.'s, Loew's Capitol and received the following notice in the July 25, 1943, *Washington Post:*

Richard Buckley is master of ceremonies and has a couple of audience-participation acts in which he takes stooges from the house. He doesn't lure them up there, he orders them and makes them like it.

Buckley then settled in for a monthlong run at New York City's Strand Theatre before moving on for a week in Bean Town.

The ads in the Boston papers made special note of "Dick Buckley & Co.—*New! Different! The Audience Makes The Fun!"* The review in the *Boston Daily Globe* of September 3, 1943, at Boston's RKO Theatre virtually ignored the featured act of Jerry Colonna, focusing on "English" comedian Buckley.

Rounding out the year with appearances at Pittsburgh's Stanley Theater, the Radisson in Minneapolis, the Oriental in Chicago, and the Palace in Cleveland, Buckley continued his swing through the Midwest in the beginning of 1944 with a week at the Albee Theatre in Cincinnati. This was followed by week at the Michigan Theatre in downtown Detroit before a monthlong run at the Glass Hat—a New York City nightclub nestled in the catacombs of the Belmont-Plaza Hotel.

When he hit Philadelphia in early March, advertisements for his show at the Earle Theatre played up the performer's linguistic flexibility: "Dick Buckley 'Accent On Comedy'." As Mildred Martin pointed out in her March 3, 1944, review of the show for the *Philadelphia Inquirer:*

Everything from hisses to kisses went at the Earle yesterday . . . The kisses were enthusiastically delivered by a sailor from Brooklyn to a blushing brunette, two of four volunteers from the other side of the footlights who assisted Dick Buckley in his side-splitting act involving funny hats, monkeyshiners on the mike and a knack for making people look pleasantly silly.

He was back in New York for a two-week run at the Loew's State in mid-April. Paul Ross reviewed the show for *Billboard:*

Last section of the bill was consumed by Dick Buckley, a newcomer to these parts. He's a tall, British-looking and acting guy who's strongly reminiscent of George Sanders, of the movies. Uses a good idea in audience participations which, however, takes too much time being readied, at least the way he does it. Gimmick involves pulling four people from their tables to be stooges, with Buckley sitting back of them, voice-throwing and making them move their lips in pretended talk and sings.

As worked at the opener, the stint drew amused laughs and a good hand. Buckley followed with another participation stunt using hats, which was the best thing he showed. Closed with an imitation of an old man which ran things right into the ground.

After an apparently slow spring and early summer, Buckley took the stage of New York's Strand Theatre at Broadway and Forty-seventh Street for a three-week August residency and garnered the following notice from *Billboard*'s Larry Nixon:

Dick Buckley clicked for constant laughs. His audience participation routine with four from the cash customers ranks pantomiming while he did his standard Amos and Andy bit brought plenty of laughs and again screams, but more for the way the job was done than for excellence of material. Bobby soxers in house laughed so much the comic went off to weak hand.

After a gig at the Steel Pier in Atlantic City, New Jersey, Buckley headed west. Opening for Woody Herman at the RKO Palace, Buckley garnered the following notice in Peter Bellamy's October 7, 1944, review in the *Cleveland News:*

Comedian on the bill, and his act is unique in vaudeville, is Dick Buckley, who as usual stops the show . . . The man has rare originality and talent for producing laughter.

Back at the RKO in Boston later in the month, Buckley was opening for Perry Como, then a young singing sensation making his first appearance in The Hub. While the review in the October 27, 1944, *Boston Daily Globe* soft-peddled Como's act and

Cleveland newspaper ad from Buckley's 1944 vaudeville days. Author's Collection.

was somewhat dismissive of Buckley's shtick as well ("turns members of the audience into human dummies and specializes in polished insults"), the *Boston Herald* led off its report of the affair with two paragraphs on Buckley, all but burying Como.

After return stops to Philly's Earle Theatre and Cleveland's Palace, Buckley closed his fall tour in early December with a memorable week at Chicago's palatial Oriental, where he shared the bill with, according to the ads in the Windy City papers, "Your Ace Drummer Man GENE KRUPA and his Sensational Orchestra That Swings with Strings."

Kicking off 1945 at the Center Theater in Norfolk, Virginia, Buckley was next spotted at the Adams Theater in Newark, New Jersey, in mid-February opening for Woody Herman, whose big band then included tenor saxaphonist Flip Phillips and bassist Chubby Jackson.

It was at this time that the extensive *Billboard* "routes" listing was de-emphasized and truncated, making precise chronicling of the balance of Buckley's vaudeville itinerary next to impossible.

Tubby Boots

He was like a father figure to me.

I met Buckley when I was seven years old when I was working at the Hippodrome in Baltimore, Maryland, and I was in awe of him. I saw his act every time he would come back to play the theater. I would take that week off from school and we became very good friends.

I would sit in the theater all day and watch the shows. I'd stay out of school for the whole week—my mother would pack me a lunch—she knew what I was doing because I wanted to learn about show business.

Buckley would do his hat-switching act. Every other show he would get me up to do it with him. I'd hang out with him backstage, we'd go out for lunch or dinner, he'd sneak me back into the theater and I'd watch the whole stage show again.

I started working nightclubs in Baltimore when I was eleven. I weighed 250 pounds and passed myself off as twenty-one.

I got arrested in a strip joint and the police said: "We're not going to throw you in jail but you're not going to work this town again—you're too notorious." So they actually put me on a train and said: "Where you wanna ticket to?"

I said, "New York."

And they put me on a train when I was twelve. I didn't run away—I was forced to leave. So when I got to New York I called Buckley and, pretending to sob, said, "My mama died in a car crash . . . my father was with her . . ."

Unbeknownst to me, he called my mother and told her, "He's with me."

So he got me a job at the Three Deuces, passing me off as twenty-one.

In 1946 Buckley set up shop for a run as the house comic and emcee at the Loew's State Theater on Broadway between Forty-sixth and Forty-seventh Streets for his last documented appearance on the vaudeville circuit. Along with screenings of the grade-

C *Boy's Ranch,* Dick was sharing stage duties with songstress Dale Belmont, Charles "Dizzy" Smith's big band, and the gravity-defying tap-dance duo, the Nicholas Brothers.

There was also an extended stay at the Strand Theatre in Times Square around this time. Milt Hinton, a Swing Street regular by then, remembers encountering Buckley on his way to work one evening. The performer was strutting down Broadway with a woman on his arm, dressed to the nines in a spanking-new tuxedo missing only one minor accessory . . . the pants.

Buddy Jones

Buddy Jones was a seventeen-year-old tuba player when he had his life altered forever by meeting Charlie Parker in Kansas City. Since that fateful meeting in 1942, Jones has played bass with the likes of Lennie Tristano, Buddy De Franco, Charlie Ventura, and Joe Venuti. He joined the Jack Sterling Morning Show *on CBS radio in 1952 and was a regular there for twelve years. These days he can be found lugging his ax around Carmel, California.*

There is the story about his last chance on Broadway at the old Loew's Theater. They had stage shows in the movie theaters back then. They were going to take one last shot with Lord Buckley as the headliner at one of the shows. They had had some success and every week they would change the shows. It was kind of a throwback to the glory days of vaudeville.

The week they were going to have Lord Buckley they told him, "Buckley, I'm telling you: if you mess up this time you're never going to get work on Broadway again. This is a big opportunity. We know you're a character. Just don't mess up this time. This is your last chance on Broadway."

Here was a chance for him to really make a comeback. It was quite a good gig headlining a theater on Broadway. And so, on opening night, he comes walking out on stage stoned out of his mind. He was really very drunk. It was his little inside joke. It was his last chance on Broadway and he better be right, so he just got terribly drunk.

He walked out right up to the front of the stage, looked up and grinned at everybody and fell unconscious into the drums in the orchestra pit making a terrible noise. He cut himself and was bleeding. They had to carry him out on a stretcher and that was his last chance.

He knew it was all a joke anyway: that you had to play the game and that talent doesn't count. He wasn't into that, you know. Making fun of it was the kind of joke he did just for himself.

Fayard Nicholas

Fayard and Harold Nicholas were the Nicholas Brothers, the dynamic tap-dancing duo that redefined and reinvigorated the genre. They toured with and befriended Lord Buckley in the 1940s. From the 1930s through the 1950s the Nicholas Brothers were, with the exception of Fred Astaire and Bill "Bojangles" Robinson, the most famous dancers in America.

Buckley was the wildest. Oh my goodness. He would walk on his hands while telling jokes on stage. He would say, "I just got back from Hollywood," and he'd stick his tongue out and roll it back into his mouth. Everybody knew what he meant . . . 'nuff said.

He was doing his "Amos 'n' Andy" bit then but I didn't like his use of the black voice. Sometimes I'd go in the wings and look at different acts but when he, or any other white comedian, would do that, I'd leave. But I never told anybody what they should do and it didn't stop us from being friends and hanging out with each other.

We would do four or five shows a day. Some theaters, like the Chicago Theater, we did eight shows a day. It was hard work but a lot of fun. We were young and ambitious so we did these shows. But we got tired and often slept between sets. We worked from 9 a.m. until 12 midnight but instead of going home to bed in our hotel room, we'd go out to some after-hours spot and hang out having a ball. We'd get to our hotel about six or seven o'clock in the morning but we'd have to get up and do the nine o'clock show and so we didn't get to sleep at all.

Harold Nicholas

Dick was one really happy crazy guy. He was very open. In fact, he was married when we were with him and I guess he was teaching his wife to be like him.

When we were on the road, in Boston and in Chicago, he'd invite us up to his hotel room. He would always want people around because he talked a lot. He was always performing. Women were always attracted to him because of his spiel.

He used the black voice in his act but that was never a problem for me because I knew he was straight himself. He was just doing that for the audience. He wasn't racist at all.

Lord Buckley

And this magnificent band, this magnificent spirit of the rhythm and flow in freshness and power and surge and inspiration and charge, by gad, is the new church. So this is a chapel. Are you there?

Buckley often relied on the old "Human Pyramid" routine, which was a sister piece to his "Amos 'n' Andy." Choosing ten people from the audience with much ado, he would have them form a pyramid with the four largest men on their hands and knees supporting lighter rows of three, two, and one—the one at the top usually being a small woman or a child. With the monumental task finally complete, Buckley would gasp, "I know how to get them up . . . but I haven't figured out how to get them down!"

With that he would exit stage right and let gravity play its natural role in uproariously toppling the human colossus.

The itinerant nature of the entertainment world makes Buckley's domiciles difficult to pin down at this time. Some old friends recall a basement palace in Greenwich Village.

Mel Welles

I first met him in the early 1940s when he had an apartment in Greenwich Village sort of below street level. There was a skylight under the grate of the street that was filled with multicolored whiskey bottles that street people had dropped in.

Conte Candoli (jazz trumpeter and alumnus of Woody Herman's Thundering Herd) remembers Buckley's penthouse digs at the Forrest Hotel on Forty-ninth Street near Broadway in late 1940s. And many Fifty-second Street habitués took part in Buckley's marathon bull sessions outside the Brill Building, the last true home of Tin Pan Alley, where an embryonic version of the Royal Court would be in session for hours.

But if the "Amos 'n' Andy" bit would at least partially butter his bread for the remainder of his life, there is no doubt that it was beginning to wear thin as Buckley's main gig by the time the Axis nations were waving their white flags.

Harry "The Hipster" Gibson

Along with Lord Buckley, Slim Gaillard, Babs Gonzalez, and a handful of others, the late Harry "The Hipster" Gibson was one of the early performance practitioners of the hipsemantic. The Hipster's memories appearing in this book were drawn from the liner notes of his 1986 Progressive label LP, Everybody's Crazy but Me, *and from an interview conducted by California writer Kirk Silsbee. Harry first met Lord Buckley in 1941 at the Three Deuces, a nightclub on New York City's Fifty-second Street. His Lordship christened Harry "The Prince of Hip."*

Buckley was workin' the Palace Theatre then and he was good. He was so good that they kept bringing him back. In those days, you worked two weeks and then the next act comes in. They'd have a couple of acts booked, they have 'em signed, so they have to come in no matter what. Buckley did so great at the Palace that a couple or two or three acts later, that makes it about three or four months, you dig, they want Buckley back again, so they book Buckley back into the Palace Theatre. He is the biggest cat in vaudeville with his Amos 'n' Andy thing. It was so big they hadda call him back, you dig. He is one of the biggest guys in vaudeville at that time. He mighta been the biggest cat in vaudeville. He was a big-time vaudeville act and gettin' big-time money.

One of the biggest programs on CBS was *The Coca-Cola Bottling Program.* It was a big concert orchestra. I'm still playin' in The Deuces and Leon and Eddie's, and all of a sudden my agent Ernie Anderson says, "Hey, I got a gig for you. How would you like to work at CBS?"

Wow, CBS was the biggest broadcast thing out of New York. This is a big concert band, right, and the only thing they want for me is when the jazz chorus comes along for the piano player, I'll blow the jazz part. All I have to do is read the chart. It's gotta be a forty-piece band, it could have been more.

The piano player ain't got nothin' but a boop and then he got a twelve-bar rest, another bop-a-doop-boop: there ain't nothin' there. Then all of a sudden *ZOOP!* Ninety-two-bar rest. Jazz piano eight bars—boop—and I'm off with a 132-bar rest . . . I look up and I got a couple a hundred bars rest. I'm still sittin' there and I gotta go to the john. I go out the door, I go to the john and who do you think walks in the door but Buckley. He says, "Hey, what are you doin' here, man?"

"I'm drug. This is a drag-ass job," I said. "Goddamn, I'm playin' with this fuckin' band next door, they give me two hundred and goddamn knows how many bars rests, I don't get to play nothin' but eight bars every now and then, what the fuck . . . " I was drug.

He says, "Hey, cool it man." You know Buckley. "What you need is a little medicine. You gotta cool down now, you know. And it just happens that I have a beautiful little joint here and I think we oughta smoke it." Boom, he lights up and I light up there and I'm talkin' and we're smokin' and I'm tellin' him how bad this band was! I'm complainin' to Buckley about it: "What am I doin' here? I'm a jazz piano player." Just for the money, this is the best bread I ever made in my life. I'm complainin': "Aw man, what a drag." And, of course, we're lightin' up, he's got a joint, man, and we're smokin' back and forth.

And Buckley said: "Well, what do you mean, you think you've got it bad, look what I have to do. I'm up on the stage, I gotta talk to these squares in front of me."

I said, "I just wanna blow piano, I don't want to sit in back of a piano and listen to these guys rehearse. Man, they're goin' on and on with the rehearsal and the singer and whole thing."

Buckley said, "Yeah, I'm hip, I know what you're talkin' about, Hipster, a piano player like you . . ."

"Yeah, what am I doin' up here, just tryin' to make money or somethin'?"

We're gettin' into the thing and he's got a little taste, he's got a flask, now *he* don't drink, but he carries a flask for his *friends.* See, he's always got a little somethin' to help, he says, "Just in case somebody might have a heart attack or somethin' . . . I always keep it hid, I make sure I got the demon rum right in my hand, for emergencies . . . ya dig."

"Man," I said, "this ain't music, this is just piecework." I'm high, Jack, boom, I'm bombed out.

He said, "Well, you know, kid, why don't you just quit?"

I said, "You know, you're right. What am I doin' here? Let's go, man." Boom! We walk outta the joint. I said, "Which way you goin'?" He said, "I'm goin' back to the Palace." "I'm goin' with you."

So we go back to the Palace. In the meantime, he's complainin' about *his* job. We're getting bombed, he's got another joint—boom—we're smokin', I'm backstage with him. He gets out on stage—boom—goes into his act. Buckley's act was he walked out on stage with a cigarette, he's smokin' a cigarette like a stick o' grass. And he's talkin', he's gettin' these people up there to this Amos 'n' Andy thing. And he gets up there, he's got his cigarette. I'm there, I'm wavin' and he's lookin' at me like "Oh man, what a drag. Look at what I'm doin'." All of a sudden he gets in back and says, "Hold everything, I want you people to stay, I gotta go talk to the man!"

What the deal was, he wanted to go out in the alley and get a little high. He ain't in the mood to do his thing, he's gotta get a little higher, so we go out in the alley, he looks at me and he said, "I gotta do this *four times a day!*"

"Yeah," I said. "Oh man, I don't believe that—that's slave labor!"

Buckley said, "Yeah man, what am I doin', I can't go back there!"

And I said, "You don't want that gig! Tell 'em to go fuck off!"

So he goes, "I'm gonna go in and tell 'em to fuck off!"

His eyes bug out when he get angry. You know what that cat looks like, he got that big mustache and his hair standin' on end. And he's lookin' at me, "Come on, Hipster, let's split!"

We go walkin' out of there. I go, "What about those people up there?" He goes, "Fuck those people on stage, I can't go back there!"

Both of us walked out of our gigs on the *SAME DAY!* We're walkin' down the alley, we're goin' past the front of the joint. And, as we go past the front, I said, "Man, you left them guys up there!" He says, "Go ahead and see if them cats are still up there." So I walked in the door—boom—I look up and there they all are. I come back, "Yeah, they're all on stage."

And we walkin' down the street, we ain't that far from the White Rose Tavern so we go in for some free lunch. I go up and order a boilermaker because Dick Buckley *ain't* drinkin' you know. Boom—he goes up for the free lunch, comes back from the counter and puts those big fat sandwiches in front of us. He says, "Man, I ain't gonna do that shit no more, no how, no way!" Boom—we start eatin' and the people were still up on the stage waitin' for Buckley to get *back!*

That was the end! He says, "Hey Hipster, this is the end of vaudeville and I just killed it. So let's forget about it. I'll go into the nightclub business like you."

Lord Buckley

To the people who don't know, to be cool means to believe. To stay cool is to have the sweet fragments of serenity rock your wig away.

5 the hipsemantic

Lord Buckley

All the swingers and all the goers and all the divinities of the high rhythm of the sweet jump of the flash of the sound of life itself into the language of the people . . . may I say, beloveds.

World War II profoundly altered the fabric and beat of American life. Those changes were reflected with pointed acuteness by jazz (and specifically bebop) more than perhaps any other American art form. In its way, bop successfully broached the issue of race, which remained on the back burner until the thousands of returning black servicemen who helped preserve democracy demanded a small taste of the same.

Charles Tacot

Lord Buckley wound up meaning more to the language from the standpoint of bringing hip jargon into respectability than he did as a comic. He did more for the English language in bringing the black idiom into favor than anyone else before him.

Albert Goldman

Imitation being the highest form of flattery, Richard Buckley soon took to impersonating Negroes on stage, though never in blackface. Standing before his audience in a tuxedo and pith helmet, with his lobster eyes and imperious waxed mustache giving him the look of an apoplectic English lord, he would open his thin waspy lips and out would pour the thickest, blackest, funkiest stream of slum ghetto jive talk ever heard on the American stage. What made the act even more bizarre was the use to which he put this low-down gutter language. He could get so far into his black bag that not only did he convince you of his essential negritude, he did something more remarkable. He got down to that black bedrock where Negro speech and Negro music are one and the same thing: where jive and jazz, salt and sass come welling out of the ground in a pungently mixed stream. Patterning his words and sounds into powerfully propulsive licks and riffs, Lord Buckley proved himself to be the first and only successful jazz comic in the history of American show business.

The idea of an aristocratic gent doing dialect wasn't new. George A. Moore was a vaudevillian who performed black dialect while wearing a top hat and tails. Buckley may have seen the man work, since Moore (who died in December 1940) began his career in Chicago and toured the circuits regularly. But what Buckley did with the idea was startling and new, both in his concepts and in his swinging delivery.

David Amram

Composer, musician, conductor, author, and farmer, David Amram has lived for music since his first jam session in the early 1940s. He associated and worked with many bebop and Beat Generation artists, including Dizzy Gillespie, Jack Kerouac, Charles Mingus, Oscar Pettiford, and Bob Dylan, to name just a very few. Amram accompanied Lord Buckley on piano the night before His Lordship's death. His 1980 composition "Ode to Lord Buckley" stands as both a testament to that evening and an homage to Buckley's talents.

Lord Buckley realized that people such as Charlie Parker and Dizzy Gillespie were bona fide twentieth-century geniuses of music. Dizzy, God bless him, was an encyclopedia of world rhythms and the whole impact of pan-African music as it spread all over the world, influencing all cultures and psychology. Charlie Parker, when I met him in early 1952, knew a whole lot about painting, poetry, writing, the Koran, and different kinds of music. He could have been a sociologist or an ambassador.

These were incredibly brilliant people who advanced the horizons for all of us, and Lord Buckley was a part of that era and a part of that ethos. And, like Charlie Parker, Dizzy and other masters at that time, he worked small clubs that never held more than a few hundred people for the majority of his lifetime. And yet Lord Buckley was a kind of hero. People would come from hundreds of miles to see him. He was legendary to musicians.

I began seeing Lord Buckley at a distance from time to time when he was performing at local clubs before I went in the Army in 1952 or was there at my gigs in New York when I played with Oscar Pettiford's band and with Mingus between 1955 to 1958. He'd always be there with other people and would kind of say "Hi." But I never really had a chance to speak to him at any great length because there were always a lot of people around him doing the same thing. I was a lot younger and really didn't feel I had any right to come over and barge in. But we used to talk a little, and he communicated like musicians do: nonverbally. He was always warm.

Bebop's kaleidoscopic verve delivered a haymaker to American culture and sealed black America's contribution to the twentieth-century arts with a level of mastery and seriousness never heard before. Charlie Parker's "Now's the Time" served as a battle cry and affirmation of the new music's artistic and political integrity. It seemed to say: "We are here and we demand to be heard!" Or as a later generation would say: "Say it loud, I'm black and I'm proud!" Similarly, Lord Buckley's appreciation of what he called the "American Beauty Negro" anticipated the notion of "Black is beautiful" popularly and politically expounded a generation later.

Richmond Shepard

Actor, stand-up mime, director, and producer, Richmond Shepard has worked on both coasts in venues ranging from the hip clubs of 1950s Los Angeles to the avant-garde of New York's Living Theater. He met Buckley while doing a stint at the Club Renaissance, a fabled Los Angeles hangout. In 1983, along with actor John Sinclair, he wrote and produced Lord Buckley's Finest Hour, *a one-man show based on Buckley's life and routines.*

The only thing "American Beauty" we ever heard of was the American Beauty Rose, which was a very popular, very beautiful red flower. And when he introduced his dialect by saying "I fell in love with the dialect of the American Beauty Negro," it was, at that time, shocking to some and very gratifying to everyone else. This was a time before there were any blacks on television, I mean, none! The whole situation has changed a lot since the midsixties. So, anybody who actually heard him discuss the "American Beauty Negro" and shared his admiration of this dialect and these people and words with such beauty would say: "Go ahead, Buckley, swing, let's hear some more!"

In 1946, the year after the end of World War II, bebop achieved a sudden, dramatic breakthrough. Large eastern and midwestern cities now boasted smart clubs. There was the Argyle Lounge in Chicago, El Sino in Detroit, others in Boston, Philadelphia, Washington, Cleveland, St. Louis, Kansas City, Milwaukee, and Minneapolis. The jazz musician, particularly the saxophone player, had surfaced as the culture hero of the new generation, the way that guitar heroes emerged in the 1960s. Small combos and bands led by veterans of the jazz wars were being booked out over the lounge circuit for real money.

The hub of the new music was New York City's Fifty-second Street, the tidal pool of modern jazz. On a given night as many as a dozen top-shelf combos would be playing "The Street," as it was known by its regulars. It was not uncommon for a club to feature a house comic among other variety acts to spice things up between sets, and all through the 1940s Dick Buckley was a common sight on the bandstand.

"Grampa" Al Lewis

Best known as "Grampa" on the 1960s television show The Munsters, *Al Lewis's career harks back to the early 1920s when he broke into show business as a circus barker. Since then he has run his own medicine show and performed in vaudeville, radio, theater, movies, and television. He has also scouted high school basketball talent from coast to coast and run for governor of New York State in 1998 as a Green Party candidate. Some of his most cherished credits aside from* The Munsters *include* Car 54 Where Are You? *and the Jonathan Demme film* Married to the Mob. *For many years, when not working on a film, Lewis could be found holding court at Grampa's, his Italian restaurant in Greenwich Village, or holding forth on his weekly WBAI-Pacifica radio program.*

I think I first saw Lord Buckley in Frisco sometime in the forties. I also saw him perform in New York City at the Savannah Club or the Kentucky Club, a high-class female impersonators' club.

He was very inventive, creative, free-form. He came out of the stream-of-consciousness tradition. Lord Buckley was the intellectual. The pendulum swung completely the other way with Lord Buckley. Back then when you went into a nightclub—what we used to call a sawdust-on-the-floor bucket-of-blood nightclub—whereas on the one hand you saw B. S. Pulley with the most outrageous dirty act, on the other hand (the intellectual end) was the off-the-wall tilting-at-windmills Lord Buckley.

Before stepping into the Onyx, Jimmy Ryan's, the Three Deuces, or any one of the neighborhood's famous haunts, a patron might be greeted at the entrance to the basement club by Pee Wee Marquette, the three-foot, nine-inch doorman decked in a zoot suit and loud tie, smoking a torpedo-sized cigar. As the band finished its set with a cymbal-crashing crescendo and the audience freshened their drinks at the bar, Buckley might hop on stage and extol the performers with salutations before embarking on a mission of whimsy befitting his new role as a verbal jazz ambassador.

Garry Goodrow

A veteran of both above- and underground theater in America, Gary Goodrow's credits include The Connection, *Shirley Clarke's influential 1960 film (drawn from the Living Theater's legendary stage production), and involvement in The Committee, an important West Coast improv troupe.*

The only time I ever saw Lord Buckley perform on stage was at a birthday party for Charlie Parker that was held in Birdland. I'm not sure of the year—I do know I was in my teens. All my jazz idols were there, including Dizzy, who was busily racing all over the room, providing lots of laughs. When Buckley took the stage with his booming voice, jive talk, and Shakespearean diction, he began with a long (and funny) denunciation of St. Patrick's Cathedral. Although he kept me laughing, I was mystified at first: what in the hell was he getting at? By the end of his five minutes it was quite clear. His last line, delivered with arms outstretched and face tilted upward like Henry V calling the troops to glory, was, "There are only two cathedrals in New York City—the Palace Theatre and Birdland!"

David Amram

For many of us, he was a combination of Walt Whitman, Charlie Parker, Baudelaire, and Laurence Olivier.

Like Whitman, Lord Buckley was always lyric and grandiose. He reminded me of Charlie Parker as he created new stories out of thousands of unique patterns with spontaneous flights of fancy and one-time-only improvisations drawn from the moment. He seemed to relive Baudelaire's spirit as a mad, burning passionate poet, always romantic and worldly, in spite of the overwhelming setbacks that would have destroyed almost anyone else. Like Olivier, he could create and become any number of unforgettable human beings and make you remember them forever. Lord Buckley was much more than his defined role as a comedian and entertainer. He was a visionary and a true American original who influenced a whole generation. All who heard him recognized him as an underground genius of spontaneous American poetry and humor. He captured the great joy and the great melancholy of the 1940s and 1950s.

Robin Williams

The preeminent comic of our times, Robin Williams continues to expand the boundaries of his art. His astute insights into Lord Buckley's contribution underline His Lordship's impact on succeeding generations of performers.

The first time I *really* heard Lord Buckley, I thought to myself, "*This* is amazing."

It's got layers on it. You can take it on the comic layer and you just can keep getting deeper and deeper with it. The musical layer, the literary layer—it's full of literary references.

It's so hard to hear his stuff without hearing his voice. It's an instrument. Somewhere between a sax and a bass is Buckley.

Hearing his work is like hearing the great jazz riffs—they are full entities unto themselves.

There are places in his work where he could improvise. They might have been improvised to begin with but most of them are translations. They are literally like translated texts.

Decades before the academy discovered that African American patois was a legitimate, even artful form of language, Dick Buckley was embracing it, whether it was through his vaudevillian stage bits or the wild stories he told backstage to anyone who would listen—and most of them, once collared by Dick, had to. The use of the black idiom and, when creatively appropriate, a British accent gave rise to the two most common misconceptions about Buckley: that he was black or British. Though he was neither, what controversy still exists around him arises from the misaimed criticism he attracted due to his use of African American vernacular. Clearer heads would realize that he celebrated the dialect as one of the most lively variations of English ever devised, and he regularly paid homage to its roots and beauty.

Red Rodney

There was an improvisatory element to his work that was similar to what we were experimenting with in bebop. He was around jazz because we were very bohemian and, of course, *he* was very bohemian. He catered to those tastes. He had great jazz instincts but I don't know if he knew very much about jazz. If you played jazz and you were his friend, you were the greatest. But I don't think he knew anything of substance about the music.

The most impressive feature of Buckley's work was the way he patterned music into language and vice versa. His instinctive feel for the way words blur into chant and song was ripe with passion. Buckley was always passionate, always hot with that dangerous old-time gospel jazz beat. And like all jazzmen, his goal was transcendence.

Buckley forged the fractured fragments of the disunited bopster nation into powerful paeans to the hip life. He viewed this squalid, sordid, shadow world as Melville saw the Whale, Joyce saw Odysseus, Pynchon saw Orpheus, or Wagner saw a Valkyrie: the stuff of epic song. Never mind that the song wasn't always in tune and that some of the notes remain a little corny; Buckley pulled it off with the power and depth of his soul. His magnetic stage presence sucked up his audience with the authority of a beatific bard. During this period Buckley spawned the whole tradition of the modern comic, rocker, and rapper—possessed by the Spirit like stump preachers and revivalists who are the remote ancestors of rock 'n' roll.

It wasn't only the text of Buckley's routines that were spoken in his "American Beauty Negro" vocabulary and syntax. He also delivered them in a combination jazz and gospel rhythm that was rapid and upbeat, about as close to music as the spoken word can get. He sometimes invented his own words and often punctuated his rolling sentences with a one-syllable bleat that sounded like a trombone note. He still had a strong, pleasant emcee's baritone that had the urgency and ebullience of someone who's just settled a great score.

In this regard Buckley can be viewed as a kind of stepping-stone between his scat-singing contemporaries and today's rap raconteurs. Scat singing, that wordless vocalese mimicking the wailing instrumental solo, may have started with Louis Armstrong who, when he dropped his lyric sheets during the recording of "Heebie Jeebies," vocally improvised over the chord changes, but the bebop 1940s raised the art to a level of lunacy and expertise.

Bebop anthems like "Oo-Bop-She-Bam" were the scattergun vowel howls that exploded from that region between beret and goatee along the Fifty-second Street clubs. Masters like Eddie Jefferson, Slim Gaillard, King Pleasure, Leo Watson, Babs Gonzales, Joe Carroll, and Jon Hendricks were the musical grandpappies of its diluted modern expression.

Operating so far to the left of Louis Armstrong that he passed as a weirdo, Slim Gaillard stands as one of jazz's premier comedian-eccentrics, the hepcat as novelty artist to end all novelty artists. Slim laughed in rhythm, barked in rhythm, clucked like a chicken in rhythm. Like Buckley, he made up his own language and proceeded to adapt it to Spanish, Hebrew, and Arabic. Story has it that he was so fond of the suffix -rooney (as in "You got the federation blues-o-rooney") that when he was introduced to Mickey Rooney he asked what his last name was.

Gaillard began recording his musical version of jive, liberally mixed with nonsense syllables. Two of his better-known efforts were "Cement Mixer (Puttie-Puttie)" and "A-Reet-a-Voutee." And for an insider's insider demo of the language and its uproarious powers, Babs Gonzales's hipper-than-hip reminiscence of old jazz pianist Clyde Hart's funeral is an absolute must.

There is little difference between Gaillard's "vouteroonie" and the hippity-hop quick-mix raps of Grandmaster Flash, Kurtis Blow, or Ice T. It has been the hipster's vernacular for at least half a century, and Lord Buckley's place in this lineage should not be overlooked.

Buddy Jones

Buckley was like a jazz scat singer. I don't know why he didn't actually do some of that as such but you could just hear him scat sing and he always seemed like he was a musician to me. When I talked to him about music it wasn't like talking to a nonmusician. He had the soul of a jazz musician. I'm sure in some way he had a lot of knowledge of the music because he always had some of us old-time jazz musicians with him socially and in his business. As a matter of fact, that's who he hung out with more than comedians or people in other parts of the entertainment business.

Comedian is not the word to describe him. He didn't come out and use words and have these routines like the other comedians at that time. He would play to the house and be able to go out and wing it. He improvised as jazz musicians did. He was thinking in musical terms, I'm sure of that. It was the sound he had and the timing.

Jon Hendricks

When Jon Hendricks takes off on one of his scat solos, fasten your seat belt! The man who defined, redefined, and redesigned vocalese for nearly half a century encountered Lord Buckley during the 1950s.

Lord Buckley and his wife were giving a party in Chicago. We [the famed vocal trio Lambert, Hendricks and Ross] had just opened in town and so he invited us. But when we walked in there was no place to sit because everybody in Chicago was there. Buckley was sitting on a kind of lounge chair and he said, "Here, Prince, sit here," and he patted his knee.

I said, "Okay," and I sat on his knee. That way he had his face right in my ear.

He said, "You've got their ear now, tell them the truth."

That was about the best thing anybody ever said to me because that's what I have always tried to do. It showed me that he had tremendous insight and was very aware of what we were up to. He was probably the hippest guy I ever met.

He was experimenting with scat and improvising on historical reportage. He was a historian but not an academic. He was a poet. He was talking about historical things but the way jazz musicians might have spoken about them. He spoke the language.

Laughter and jazz go hand in hand. You never saw a good jazz show without a good comedian and all good comedians are jazz fans without exception because they're doing the same thing: they're taking life and improvising on it. They're taking choruses on life. They take sixteen bars.

Buckley's use of the black idiom was not offensive. Show business was never like that. These methods of judgment were never a part of show business. I've been in show business since I was seven years old and I never heard about that kind of reaction.

Everybody in show business was all one family. In show business you were exempt from the racism of the rest of society. Once you were in show business you just didn't act like that because you wouldn't last ten minutes. Nobody behaved in that kind of racist way. Everybody loved one another. Everybody helped everybody out. Nobody thought like that. The only people who thought like that were people not in the business. Blacks not only didn't resent Lord Buckley, they liked anyone who knew their language to speak it with authority. So we all dug him.

Dizzy Gillespie

A twentieth-century treasure, trumpeter John Birks "Dizzy" Gillespie spearheaded two major American musical movements: bebop and cubop. Diz ran with Buckley in the mid-1940s, and his reminiscences were gathered by Cleveland radio producer David C. Barnett in 1990.

I knew Lord Buckley and his wife. What I liked about him is the way he could recite. He'd say, "They get on magnabuttasitemin youmakcattabare wa! Shay matso laidoh metro see nothing but a: 'bow boom! Bit dee set doh mo yo la her get that zoon do dum bin do bare, oh!'" He was doing rap and scat before anybody. Yeah, Lord Buckley was like that. He could recite that rap. I don't know if it was off the top of his head or not. These young kids. There wasn't no problem with Buckley being white. Anybody can do like that, talk like that. More power to them. There was none of that, no. Not that I know of, I never heard nobody say a thing across the line with him.

The emerging African American culture of the 1940s in which Buckley had immersed himself was a veritable "underground" culture. Blacks traditionally nurtured a private but collective oral culture, one they often could not "write down," but one they created, crafted, shared with each other, and preserved for subsequent generations out loud, but outside the hearing of the white people who enslaved them and discriminated against them. It was in this isolated and protected black social enclave that African American vernacular was engendered and thrived.

But charting with any scholarly precision this complex and marvelous process is extraordinarily difficult, if not impossible, to achieve precisely because the process was surreptitious. Nevertheless, and quite uncannily, what was essentially an isolated, southern, rural phenomenon migrated north and west with the ex-slaves, underwent various sets of transformations in urban settings, became transformed again and again as blacks continued to migrate throughout the country, and eventually emerged as a national black culture. And of the cultural forms that emerged from their complicated historical process, only black music making was as integral to the culture of

African Americans as has been the fine art of storytelling—forms that Dick Buckley was absorbing with passion and respect.

In this regard, Buckley can be seen as a kind of throwback to and extension of West Africa's "griots"—traveling musician/historians who have been described as "walking libraries with knowledge of the past, present and future of our people" by Musa Suso, a modern griot. Traditionally, a griot undergoes a lengthy apprenticeship (usually under the direction of a family member) in a laborious process that involves committing extensive oral histories to memory and learning to master the traditional musical instruments involved. Traveling griot families are still welcomed into villages as "keepers of the tradition," prized for their ability to provide details of a particular village's history and/or family lineage. And like traveling jazz and blues bands (as well as performers of Buckley's ilk), griots have been viewed with ambivalence among society's upper stratum while being embraced by common folks.

Dick Gregory

Comedian, political activist, assassination theorist, health visionary, and freedom fighter, Dick Gregory's career perfectly mirrors the social metamorphosis of the mid- to late twentieth century.

Lord Buckley's use of the African American idiom was brilliant. It wouldn't take nothing to do that now but imagine the guts and integrity it took for him to do it in his time. "Political Correctness" notwithstanding, I think his material would go over big now because America, despite its many problems, is more mature than it was then.

Mose Allison

Master jazz/blues pianist and vocalist, Mose Allison encountered Lord Buckley in 1960. His witness here comes courtesy of Cleveland radio journalist David C. Barnett.

Can a black man fly an airplane? Can Leontyne Price sing Wagner? Everything dies hard; you know, there's still some pockets of resentment but I don't think anybody takes that seriously.

I never had any problems with black musicians or anything like that resenting what I do. I had more trouble with white Ivy Leaguers and people who consider themselves as specialists, experts or something. I'm sure there's been some resentment. But, you know, I gave up worrying about that more than thirty years ago.

The new bop underground needed new linguistics. To *broom* meant to travel by air; the hipster figure of speech referred to the witch's favored conveyance. Money was *gold. Eyes* meant willingness or enthusiasm. A *pad* was an apartment. Old jazzmen's expressions were stale and dated the speaker. As root ideas they gave way to verbal improvisations, in the same way that old tunes served as armatures for bop compositions, the way that "Cherokee" was devised from "I Got Rhythm."

Etymology remained reasonably straightforward. The intent was always the same: to exclude the uninitiated, to confound the square, to strengthen the inner community. *Out of this world* became *gone*—shorter and more allusive. *Blow your top* became *flip your wig,* leading to *flipped, flipped out, wigged, wig, and wiggy. Knocked out* yielded *gassed,* as in an old-fashioned nitrous-oxide-equipped dentist's chair. The verb *gas* gave the noun *gas,* a delightful experience. *Cool* and *dig* served as verbs, adverbs, adjectives and nouns. Hipsters invented such portmanteau words as *chinchy* (cheap *and* stingy). *Like* (still overused in the mother tongue) as adjective, adverb, verb, preposition, and conjunction, began to appear in every third sentence. Sometimes, it stood alone, like a sentence in itself, followed by an implied exclamation point or question mark, or merely a dash and a raised eyebrow. If you were *hip,* you *dug.* The *put-down* became the *put-on,* a highly developed art, often so subtle that the victim was unaware that he was being put anywhere.

Like the new music, the new linguistics revolved around fixed points and established ideas. Like the music, it was a language in motion, subtly changing from day to day, with ever-fresh coinages and connotations subject to common concepts and needs. Spoken quickly and inflected, it was nearly incomprehensible dialect. Linguistically, as well as musically, the boppers had closed the door. The idea was to be on the inside looking out. That was the reason for all those heavily smoked sunglasses, defiantly worn in the darkest nightclub.

Dick Buckley may have been influenced by *The Original Handbook of Harlem Jive,* a slightly fanciful lexicon of the new argot compiled and published by Dan Burley, a hep columnist with the *Amsterdam News.* The slender volume contained parodies including the soliloquy from *Hamlet* from which Buckley could have developed his own hipsemantic take. Buckley may also have been familiar with the *Hipster's Dictionary*—a similar book written by Cab Calloway, the flamboyant bandleader, composer, and lexicographer—as a sort of *Webster's* in hip.

Lord Buckley

I've heard competent and respected musicians say that this is the only jazz . . . it should be done, it's stuff that should be done with music because it has the jazz rhythm. It has the flexibility.

With the new sounds and language came new mores. If the new language was exotic, by contrast, behavior had become curiously circumspect. Loud voices were frowned down, as were hurried, headlong (frantic) actions. This detail of improper etiquette was explored at length by Buckley's friend and cohort Harry "The Hipster" Gibson in his recording "Frantic Ferdinand the F-F-Freak." Dress tended to become neater and more conservative. The handshake gave way to "the dap"—elaborate palm swiping and finger popping—a still-evolving folk form that can be viewed on just about any inner-city street corner.

The life of a jazzman, which Buckley lived—the hours they worked, the large amount of time they spent in rootless transit—set them apart from the workaday world. Jazz had always been antiestablishment, and jazzmen remained painfully beholden to their equivocal place in the entertainment world. Now came the hipsters in revolt against the jazz establishment itself, and Buckley embraced their energy wholeheartedly. To the hedonistic concepts of life prevalent among Swingmen, the new lifestyle added a social awareness. The two-party system of government with cardboard candidates was a "hype"; it's legal system a "scam." The "system" was seen as a labyrinthine leviathan designed to oppress. World War II was a grotesque side show staged by sick old men who had succeeded in turning America into a gulag.

Phil Schaap

Jazz archivist, historian, and celebrant, Phil Schaap has been the voice of New York City jazz radio for three decades as heard on WKCR (the home of FM). Phil can be heard each weekday morning from eight-twenty to nine-thirty with his outstanding Charlie Parker program Bird Flight.

It seems to me that the situation that Lord Buckley's in are word pictures of a scene that is *his* scene. That he sees the pictures as having to do with jazz, is one of many of the period. But you see some blendability between jazz and spontaneous wordcraft. That's his scene. He's not unique to that scene. Kerouac, for instance, wanted to do it. Lord Buckley's scene predates and postdates the Beatnik world. It was really a unique period of American humor. The original minstrels were whites using black slang. "Jump Jim Crow" was an 1840s performance hit by a white minstrel in blackface which we have this term to this day rooted in that.

So who were the beatniks, why did they dig jazz, and how did they use it? The beatniks were renegades. They felt, I'm speaking broadly, the determination by American society that it was going to homogenize America as a postscript to World War II and as a summary statement to the New Deal was stupid. And they said so. They felt that an avenue of expression, of individuality, was clear in jazz, perhaps even clearest in jazz. And they realized that any antimainstream statement could be best explained in jazz because here was a music rooted in the African American tradition, an American tradition, their second-class status was throughout the history of music making. Yet, here were these first-class artists getting to the root of things in a very spiritual, soulful way largely through music—meaning instrumental music, but occasionally through words. That was inviting to beatniks, plus the music was still popular.

The beatnik movement was operational before rock and roll had finalized the demise of jazz as a pop music. The success of rock and roll illustrated the demise of jazz as pop music. There wasn't any real battle, so to speak.

Beatniks, as opposed to their descendants, the hippies and those kind of people, embraced jazz as their soundtrack music as opposed to progressive rock for lack of a real descriptive term of the sixties. And this was the blend. They heard a message in the music.

Now, getting back to Lord Buckley's use of black slang as a performance artist, they used *a* message. I don't know what the message would be. This is one artist feeling one component of jazz and displaying it. Plus, there were a great number of jazz artists who, in their day-to-day displays of lifestyle, were creating the beatnik life culture. These were not necessarily black musicians at this time. There was a whole huge outcropping of jazz being commercially viable which was known as "cool jazz," right at the dawn of the beatnik scene. And, on the West Coast, it was well represented by record companies, nightclubs and artists who were largely white. They spoke the lingo. They created new terms that were largely employed by beatniks. And their records, which had the reflectiveness of Lester Young's breakthroughs, were more popular records. If you want the racist angle, that would still be important to me at this late date. Anybody can say any word. You can't copyright a word, can you?

So somebody says a word and somebody else wants to use the word. That's cool as long as you don't quote it as your own invention and using it as text—that would be plagiarism. Using words isn't.

Turning the coin over, the beatnik culture, perceived as largely a white culture, was not embraced by the hard-core black musicians. They didn't act as beatniks supposedly did. Jack Kerouac's or Lord Buckley's approach to where the world really stood was meaningless to a large slice of black hipsters. It was just a whole different world, yet there was common ground.

Lord Buckley was a white person who understood the message of jazz. He understood its potential as a blend of spoken word and music. Music is background, prerecorded and live performed, doubly spontaneous, and this is an ongoing concept. Perhaps more in the central focus than it was anytime. He was devout and zany which are both illustrations of bebop and beatnik heart, so that was his scene.

The whole jazz business culture is completely misunderstood by today's audiences. They haven't got a clue what going to a jazz club in 1956 meant. They would not recognize it. Birdland didn't have all-jazz. They had comedians. Variety in the Ed Sullivan or vaudeville or circus sense was a component of every Fifty-second Street club.

After the clubs closed on The Street, Buckley hung out with the musicians at the Stage Door Delicatessen on Sixth Avenue around the corner from Fifty-second Street, eating skyscraper sandwiches. According to *Bird,* Ross Russell's fanciful biography of Charlie Parker, one of the regulars who held court there was a drummer known only as Mouse who liked to invent an imaginary dialogue in which Churchill, Stalin, Hitler, Franklin D. Roosevelt, Haile Selassie, and Mussolini took part. Mouse turned the heads of state into real "heads." Liberally supplied with reefer, he summoned them to an imaginary summit conference to moderate their differences. In this relaxed environment, Mouse would describe the statesmen as they chummily discussed the ways and means of ending the war.

The evolving language of the hipsters came to Buckley naturally. It was what the jazz musician had always spoken, though constantly updated, like musical ideas. *Cool, dig, solid, gone, drag* were new and useful words. Laden with encoded meaning, they expressed much quickly, and Buckley had much in common with its most admired practitioners, particularly Lester "Pres" Young, the "President" of the tenor saxophone and original hip verbalist.

In fact, very little about Lester Young was unoriginal. In his cornerstone essay, "Pres," jazz critic Whitney Balliett wrote: "Eccentrics flourish in crowded, ordered places, and Young spent his life on buses and trains, in hotel rooms and dressing rooms, in automobiles and on bandstands." No doubt the same could be said to have contributed to Buckley's mercurial persona.

Though there was no known meeting between the two, Lester Young and Buckley shared similar entertainment roots, having cut their teeth in the traveling tent shows of the 1920s. Unlike Buckley, Pres was extremely aloof and wary, though both men spoke a personally coded language. Lester had the curious habit of calling fellow musicians "Lady," and was responsible for hanging the tag "Lady Day" on his musical soulmate Billie Holliday. Additionally, Pres was fond of addressing women as "Duchess." Coincidentally or not, Buckley would confer both titles upon many members of the female gender in the glory days of his Royal Court.

Much of Young's language has vanished, but here's a sampling: *Bing and Bob* were the police. A *hat* was a woman, and a *homburg* and a *Mexican hat* were types of women. An attractive young girl was a *poundcake. Startled doe, two o'clock* meant that a pretty girl with doelike eyes was in the right side of the audience. *Can Madam burn?* meant *Can your wife cook?* A *gray boy* was a white man. *I feel a draft* meant that he sensed a bigot nearby. People *whispering on* or *bussing on* him were talking behind his back. A *zoomer* was a sponger, and a *needle dancer* was a heroin addict. A *tribe* was a band, and a *molly trolley* was a rehearsal. *Have another helping,* said to a colleague on the bandstand, meant *Take another chorus.*

While any personal association between Buckley and Lester Young is sketchy, His Lordship and Charlie Parker are often recalled as partying partners. Perhaps not so coincidentally, Bird was fond of putting on the aristocratic airs of English nobility, accent included.

Red Rodney

Buckley and Bird were friends. I think I introduced them because I had known Buckley for a long time. When I got together with Charlie Parker and started playing on Fifty-second Street in those groups, Buckley came to see me and I introduced him to both Bird and Dizzy. They took to him immediately. Everybody liked him. He was a very nice man. A bit crazy but in a nice way—he was a lovely guy.

He never made it to England but he spoke like a Britisher. He called everyone "Your Lordship" and "Your Ladyship" even before he was Lord Buckley. He used the British accent but he used the black voice as well. I used to be so embarrassed when he would do that. I don't know if Bird and Diz regarded it kindly, but they regarded him kindly and he was not a bigoted man, not at all. So I think what he did was okay. Today it would certainly not be acceptable at all the way he did it. It would be socially and politically unacceptable even though he was sympathetic to civil-rights issues. He wasn't making fun of anybody when he was doing the black voice. It was just part of his act and it was part of the humor in his act . . . the bit I didn't like so much.

Garry Goodrow

The next time I saw Lord Buckley was a couple of years later. A musician friend of mine invited me to smoke some opium. He took me to an apartment building somewhere in Midtown, where we rode the elevator to the top floor, then went up some stairs to the penthouse (at least that's how I remember it). On the stairs, I could hear old-fashioned, tinny music playing and the sound of dancing feet. My friend didn't knock, just opened the door. There in the living room were Buckley, another, rather elderly man, and a woman. They were all three naked, except for straw hats, tap shoes, and canes, and they were performing old vaudeville tap routines, music provided by a stack of scratchy 78s. They all tipped their boaters to us, and I thought I was in heaven.

Lord Buckley

Ladies and gentlemen, the only person who is ever actually qualified to make a great, strong, profound remark en masse is a person who has made *every* mother mistake in the world. Not once but *many* times.

6 lord and lady

Lord Buckley

I forgot to tell you that a stallion—in hip—is a stormy, stompin', difficult-to-handle young lady.

In late 1945 casting calls were going out for what would prove to be vaudeville's last hurrah, a revival called "The Passing Show." Buckley auditioned his tiring "Amos 'n' Andy" bit and was hired on the spot. While previewing the show in Boston in early 1946, one of the troupe's young dancers, a gorgeous, twenty-year-old blonde named Elizabeth Hanson, hailing from Detroit, caught the forty-year-old entertainer's eye.

After a few false starts, a whirlwind romance ensued and the two were married on July 23, 1946, by a J. T. Boddie (a "Minister of the Gospel" according to the marriage certificate, and probably a gentleman of African American heritage) while on the road with "The Passing Show" in Baltimore, Maryland. Some of the other historical subtleties revealed by the official document are Elizabeth's legal first name (Helen), Buckley's claim of Alameda, California, as his domicile, and the identification of his occupation: "artist." Even then, it seems, Buckley saw himself as something more than a mere entertainer.

Lady Elizabeth Buckley

We always loved music. I came from the big-band era and when I met His Lordship, the first thing he did was buy me twelve jazz records. I just had a wonderful time and I met all the beautiful musicians and soon it was very much a part of our life.

We had a very healthy relationship. We vied with one another in a wonderful manner. He was inspiring to be with. His Lordship spoke to everybody.

Now the formalization of Buckley's Royal Court could flower in earnest as Dick Buckley transformed himself into "Lord" Buckley and his new bride into "Lady" Elizabeth.

Elizabeth came from humble working-class roots in Detroit, Michigan. When her father, an electrician and carpenter, became ill, her mother went to work in order to support the family. Research by Lady Buckley revealed that a sixteenth-century relative on her father's side was a warrior for Queen Christina of Finland. After he demonstrated heroism in battle, the queen bequeathed land to him that is now the Helsinki airport. One way or another Elizabeth was destined for royalty.

It might be difficult to imagine that her family would welcome not only a suitor for their daughter so much her senior but one involved with the shadow world of show business to boot. But H.R.H. Lord Richard M. Buckley the First charmed them, and he was welcomed into the fold with open arms.

Larry Storch

I always thought he was very lucky to have a wife like Elizabeth. She was a beautiful lady: blond, ballet dancer. They had met in some show and it was love at first sight.

Charles Tacot

For a moment, let's turn to Elizabeth, his wife. Here was a woman who very deeply loved the man Lord Buckley, who bore him two children, and of whom I have only one outstanding impression whenever I think of her: she was dead game. Elizabeth had resigned herself to living with not a man but a royal court, and sometimes it seemed that she met this challenge with more fortitude than Richard himself. She was an extraordinary wife of an extraordinary man.

Mel Welles

She was a fabulous gal. Everybody thought she was an airhead and out in space. But in reality, she was a true lover of life.

Bobby Short

Bobby Short's name is synonymous not only with cabaret but also with intimacy, style, and class. His musical presentations have graced the lounge of New York City's Carlyle Hotel for decades.

I met Richard Buckley in the mid-1940s. I was playing at the Blue Angel in New York. My agent at the time was Bookie Levin, who was Buckley's agent. Buckley came with his wife to the Blue Angel one night and saved me because I was dying the death of a dog there. They sat in the audience and applauded very very very heartily for me and saved my show.

I knew that he was a successful entertainer then known as Dick Buckley. It was wonderful. I was pleased because my agent had a successful performer on his hands. Bookie talked about Dick Buckley quite often.

I didn't hear about Dick Buckley for a number of years and then it was by way of his recordings. But I never saw him again.

I will always be thankful for the generosity he showed that night for a young kid up there trying to make it. And he brought up the audience's applause, which was wonderful for me.

The program for "The Passing Show" was a gala affair complete with photos and bios of the principal performers. Next to a dashing portrait of Buckley ran the following résumé:

Dick Buckley has for many years been a featured entertainer with a great many name bands including Gene Krupa's and Woody Herman's. He is particularly well known to vaudeville patrons for an act which he conceived which scribes throughout the nation have been at a loss to label. He likes to call it Pantomimic Illusion. It consists of projecting an hilarious imitation of Amos & Andy through the medium of members of the audience chosen at random. Through a secret method—not ventriloquism—Buckley creates the illusion that it is his accomplices who are speaking and not himself. Buckley began to earn his living as a lumberjack in California—and drifted into vaudeville quite casually when a boardinghouse acquaintance who happened to be on the stage persuaded him to join his act.

Elizabeth, listed as Helen Hanson in the program as one of the show's dancing girls, is featured front and center in a photo collage of the dancers on the program's inside front cover.

According to the program notes, Richard Buckley appeared as the "Husband" in a sketch called "You Are the Jury" and as a "Customer" in another dubbed "Doughnuts" before engaging the audience in his then-famous Amos 'n' Andy–style "Pantomimic Illusion" as "The Projectionist."

Reviews of "The Passing Show" are hard to come by and barely mention Buckley. One Chicago daily paper reported that "Richard Buckley explained his points of view reasonably and was going into his hat trick when we were called away," while another reviewer complained that he bored them. So much for a rapt audience.

While in Chicago with "The Passing Show," Buckley moonlighted at New Frolics Theater-Restaurant in the city's Near North Side. Also on that after-hours bill were Beatrice Kay ("Famous 'Gay Nineties Girl' of Stage, Screen & Radio"), Perry Franks & Janyce, the Le Roy Brothers Marionettes, the Frolics Cover Girls, the Henri Lishon Orchestra, and Don Chiesta's Rhumba Band.

After "The Passing Show" passed into oblivion one last time, Buckley took his act back out on the road. *Variety* caught up with the comic twice in 1947 with two decidedly opposite (and genealogically inaccurate) notices. Of his spring show at New York City's Strand Theatre, the publication reported:

Times do change, and what was the family time act a few years ago now may be a Broadway deluxer click, without change of format. It's the result of the war and the new type of audiences the latter has given to theater. It's not only the free-spending, but the obvious intent of the customers to have fun and be entertained—in contrast to the 'I dare you to make me laugh' attitude that prevailed pre-Munich.

Buckley, an Englishman making his first appearance in N.Y., though he's played plentifully elsewhere in the U.S., is a perfect case in point. His act is corny and hokey, with little basis on talent, yet he gets howls. He gets four customers to come out of the audience and do the facial expression of the Amos 'n' Andy radio program characters while Buckley sits behind them and does the actual talking. And it's all unrehearsed and spontaneous, the volunteers do some self-embarrassing things. At show caught, Buckley got two youngsters, a soldier and sailor to play the parts, with the servicemen getting most of the laughs.

For a topper, Buckley works a hat-snatching bit with one of the volunteers, this time the soldier, and this also scored much stronger than it seems this type of bit is worth. The gag is an old juggling act routine.

One thing in Buckley's favor is his fast pace once he gets over the stage wait of picking the volunteers.

Variety's Miami correspondent seemed to have seen a different show when covering Buckley's July 30 performance at that city's Famous Door, perhaps the first public indication that Buckley was in the midst of a personal and aesthetic transformation:

Ops of this recently reopened spot seem to have hit the right combination to bring it back into favor with cafe patronage, lost when booking policy became fouled up last season. Then it was a case of too many partners.

In Dick Buckley, they've found a comic whose pseudo-British accentings and off-trail character delineations should attract a following via word-of-mouth. His stuff adds up to a howl. His unorthodox routines build slowly, but hit laugh jackpot as the payees catch up with his screwy approach. Switch from the Hollywood type of Britisher to a zingy takeoff on Louis Armstrong earns him top audience receptivity. Miming of an oldster sitting in the sun, colored preacher and old-fashioned lawyer are refreshing in their newness. Effectiveness is weakened at times by the too deliberate manner and those long pauses for the Barrymore glare at noisy ringsiders. Tops stint with his standard aud participation bit wherein he utilizes four stooges for live dummies while he voices Amos 'n' Andy characters from behind. Biz with hats adds to laugh potency of the sequence.

Lord Buckley

I came to be a Lord under the realization that *all* ladies and gentlemen are Lords and Ladies. It's a nobility of the gentility and the frame for that is this: if the sphere swings in its plumed height of all its garlanded beauty then it must have a fantastic basis, you see. So all ladies and gentlemen are Lords and Ladies, my dear. And from the caliber and the beauty and the sweet modern Americanized swing of this station and its projection and its reason and its meaning and its being, it is very very clear that I would safely say that ninety-nine and nine-tenths of the audience are Lords and Ladies, you see.

Exactly why, how, or when Buckley decided to confer on himself his particular grandiose title is somewhat open to debate. Certainly there is an implicit nod to the tradition of the era's jazz royalty: "King" Oliver and "King" Pleasure, Edward "Duke" Ellington and William "Count" Basie. By the same token Elvis "The King" Presley, Queen Latifah, and Prince can be seen as upholding this noble musical lineage. The veneer of royalty has even crept into the sports arena when "Sir Charles" Barkley strutted his stuff on the basketball courts of the N.B.A. from coast to coast.

Similarly, there is also the possibility that Buckley may have been influenced in his choice by the calypso stars of the era such as Lord Kitchener, who often employed the revered moniker. Even today, when Buckley's name is conjured, it is not uncommon for him to still be confused with the specialized music and artists associated with this Jamaican folk form.

One apocryphal story of how Buckley ascended to jazz royalty was floated by Donald Clarke who, in his *Encyclopedia of Popular Music,* suggested that Buckley won the title in a poker game.

Dan James

The following text were the liner notes from Way Out Humor, *Lord Buckley's 1959 LP on the World Pacific label, reprinted in the City Lights publication* Hiparama of the Classics *in 1960.*

Some men are born to their titles. Others win theirs. But Richard Buckley came into his title because a friend with the unlikely name of Midas, went to a bankrupt circus to buy his kids a pony. With a fine nose for bargains, Midas bought the circus. And phoned Buckley for help. (What do I do now, daddy?) . . . The watchman led them through the warehouse, marched them past the line of mighty elephant rumps, past the dark roaring cages with thick aromatic clouds hanging overhead. They halted before the wardrobe trunks. From the first trunk, Buckley pulls out a vast purple robe studded with emeralds, rubies, sapphires, all of fine solid glass. The robe is strangely shaped but he wraps it carefully around him, head to ankles. It leaves a broad trail in the dust as he steps over to the mirror. "Is he crazy?" the watchman asks. "That there's an elephant hanging. Belongs to the elephant!" But Buckley stares at his reflection. He bows. "Your excellency," he whispers.

Richard, now Lord Buckley, swept berobed from the warehouse and on through the streets of Chicago with people pretending not to stare, with the wind off the lake whipping his train sky-high, making a great clatter with the glass jewels. Arrived at his apartment, he set about celebrating his title, as nobility obliges. They came from everywhere, politicians, pimps and bankers, Negro musicians and Italian gangsters, chorus girls, policemen, pitchmen and hookers. And together they worked out the etiquette of the royal court. For Lord Buckley was not the man to keep all that nobility to himself. He knew that Lordship is no good unshared. So it was "Your Ladyship, this . . . Your Grace that . . . Will your highness please let go of my goddamn leg? . . ." They papered the kitchen with eviction notices. Everybody had a very fine time . . . and the party lasted three years.

David Amram

Even before he was recording, Lord Buckley had this incredibly original thing that he was doing that was more than comedy. He was really showing us the majesty and the dignity and the brilliance of a whole part of our culture that few people even knew about. It was street humor, it was wisdom, it was poetry that came just from the way people, everyday people, spoke. He was able, like a true artist, to take that beautiful material and develop it into classic tales, portraying all the characters he created like a one-man orchestra.

He was almost the triple whammy of humor by showing both a black American people's understanding of the British Empire and how stupid and silly all that pomposity could be. A lot of people from the West Indies used to do that too, to kind of try to imitate British royalty in a humorous way. Sometimes the musicians would dress up in these fantastic costumes with bowler hats and ascots, almost as if to just say there's not really anything fantastic about that, that's just clothes. True royalty comes from how you treat others, with respect and sharing.

A lot of musicians at the time used to talk about the idea that it seemed we were still colonialized. When the British would go into a country they would immediately make everyone speak English and give up their own language. They would teach that the sign of an intelligent or a learned or a valued person was if they could speak the King's English. Secondly, unless they could sound like the particular sound of the very upper classes, they were already doomed by the English class system to being total losers or being put in a slot that they could never get out of as soon as they opened their mouths. That's still the way it is in England to an extent, where you can tell where someone comes from as soon as he opens his mouth, and that dooms him to that lot he was born into.

Lord Buckley was making a tremendous comment about colonialism and our dependence on looking to a higher power to solve our problems in a humorous way. But he took it beyond having to have a king and a queen or an emperor. He took it all the way up to God, who he turned into the Nazz. After getting people into realizing that we still had that psychological need for a king and queen, he took it one step further and showed that we really needed to relate to God.

So, ultimately, he was using his humor to become this sort of fantastic preacher and minister. But if anyone said he was a highly spiritual person or a spiritual leader he would have been the first person to start laughing. But that's a big part of what he was because he brought a very spiritual quality to all the things that he did.

When I would see Duke Ellington or Count Basie, I would think of the idea of royalty in a much more refreshing way. I saw that true royalty, like Lord Buckley, is something that is not just passed along through marriage and is not something that you're born with. It's something that you acquire and earn by your conduct and your excellence of spirit and your humanity and your willingness to share what you have with others and the gift that you can bring to other people. That's a truly royal person—one who is generous and magnificent and enormous in spirit and achievement, which he was.

Curiously, surviving programs from "The Passing Show" might provide a clue to the mystery of why or when he began calling himself "Lord" Buckley. Across from Dick Buckley's picture and career description in the cast bios is an advertisement for Lord Calvert Scotch whiskey. The ads in their various forms display a distinguished, mustachioed, yet rugged-looking gentleman grasping a tumbler of the spirit who bears a striking resemblance to the entertainer. At any rate the title stuck, and for the remainder of his life Dick Buckley was known professionally as Lord Buckley or, among his growing solar system of acolytes, as "His Lordship."

Wavy Gravy

Clown Prince of the hippies and Holy See for the Phurst Church of Phun, Wavy Gravy (formerly Hugh Romney) has been committing acts of random kindness for decades. His spontaneous "Lord Buckley Memorial Sunset" in the mid-1960s helped lay the groundwork for the famous Acid Tests that followed.

The idea of an artistic mask or persona is interesting. Lord Buckley's choice to recast himself didn't influence my choice to transform myself from Hugh Romney to Wavy Gravy, at least not that I know of.

In my case, it's something that happened in 1969 in Louisville, Texas, with a blues guitarist named B. B. King. He suggested my name was Wavy Gravy and I said, "Yes, sir."

I was moving into my clown persona and, in this tradition, it's not unusual to take another name.

Ken Kesey

More than just the author of two twentieth-century American literary classics, One Flew Over the Cuckoo's Nest *and* Sometimes a Great Notion, *Ken Kesey helped spearhead the psychedelic movement of the 1960s with his band of Merry Pranksters. Though the last thirty years have mostly found him on his farm in Oregon, Kesey has continued to write. Lord Buckley is one of Kesey's great heroes.*

He was a sweet man. The whole notion of royalty was very important to him. "My lords and my ladies" . . . the way that he spoke that and lived that was sincere business.

Jon Hendricks

Lord Buckley lived what he believed and he believed that all men are equal: "Created level in front" as he said. He and his wife addressed everybody as

"Prince" and "Princess" or "Your Highness." He felt everybody was a king. There were no serfs or lower classes. *Everybody* was royal.

He was a very deep man. Very philosophical. He was showing the ridiculousness of racism, elitism and social stratification. He just wiped all that right out. People who are deeply embedded in that don't like to hear that at all and that's usually the establishment.

Steve Allen

Buckley and I weren't fishing buddies. I never got to hang out with him a lot. I always found it a little awkward to talk to Buckley as just a human being. Somehow he never seemed to get out of that fake Englishman character he did for a living. I think there must be something to the idea that, at a certain point, he became "Lord" Buckley for life. Ordinarily, whoever you are, whether you're one of the greats or just a run-of-the-mill performer, you are you and that's how you talk at Walgreen's lunch counter. But with Buckley it was always: "Ah yes, my dear Prince Allen." And for me it was hard to talk about what the Dodgers did that day with the guy always thinking and talking like that. So we never really got into any very interesting conversations.

Dr. Oscar Janiger

The late Dr. Oscar Janiger was a noted psychiatrist whose pioneering work with LSD has long been respected in medical circles. Some of his most noted LSD subjects were Cary Grant, Jack Nicholson, James Coburn, Anaïs Nin, and Lord Buckley.

He had this posture which had two facets. One was to point out the ludicrousness of the posture. The "Lord" thing was, in part, a kind of mockery of the whole notion of nobility. He was very subtly suggesting that everyone could be noble. That's why he conferred all of these titles on others. He wasn't elitist about it. He would be happy to give you a title.

The second thing was that he felt a sense of specialness about himself that was personified by using this costume or this symbol that he created to give himself a kind of stature and dignity. I'm a psychiatrist so I would see it that way.

I think the role was just lovely. If you heard about it you formed one opinion. But if you were with him you'd find that it was a totally different thing.

Robin Williams

I never saw him perform or even saw any old clips. The only images I have of him are from the album covers: that very regal bearing, wearing his pith helmet and bugging his eyes out—kind of looking like if Coleman Hawkins had a kid with Dali.

Calling himself "Lord" Buckley was self-elevating and, at the same time, self-mocking. Giving yourself status and simultaneously making fun of that status. He was saying, "Anybody can be royalty, check this out."

You can hear that persona on the records: "My lords and ladies, ladies and gentlemen, cats and kitties . . ." All of a sudden you're in the Royal Court.

There was a gentleness to it, making people members of the Royal Court and the "chosen few." In a gentle kind of jazz way, he was trying to bring people together.

There's nothing angry in him. If the anger's there, it's really buried underneath the language.

Judith Malina

Judith Malina and her husband, the late Julian Beck, cofounded the Living Theater in the 1950s and proceeded to break down the walls of Western dramatic tradition with such renowned presentations as The Connection.

It's a question of what the word *noble* really means. It's something that you are or something that you can become. It's a form of feeling, an obligation to your fellow human beings: being a steward of each other's happiness and serving each other on this higher level of noble behavior, which is never self-serving. The first sense of the word has become debauched into this hideous hierarchy. These people who could call themselves "*gentle*-men" though they were far from gentle. They carried swords and behaved like boors and cut off the heads of the peasants with no provocation when it pleased them. But what they aspired to be was something else. Buckley parodied the hideousness and came to this little secret strangeness of the English language.

Mel Welles

If you look for any real substantial foundation for Buckley you'll find that, other than the fact that he was a total one-off in terms of being an oddity and his own man and wild and crazy and bizarre, there's really no substance. I mean, this man is mostly a figment of our imagination. We attributed things to him that really were not true. One often gives people attributes out of love or hate or some emotion that they don't really have. The people around Buckley did this.

A demonstration of this is that I was working on a picture called *The Lion of St. Mark* in Italy with Feodor Chaliapin, who also played the old man in the film *Moonstruck*. In *The Lion of St. Mark* he played the doge of Venice and I played the general of his mercenary army. When he came out for the shot in this royal court wearing his robes, everybody was just standing around. He immediately yelled: "Cut!"

Everybody looked at him and he said, "Look, I cannot play the doge. You all have to play the doge. In those days people swooned, reacted when kings and princes entered a room. If you stand there like a bunch of props all I look like is a rabbi in pajamas."

And I remember that because that was quite true with Buckley. Buckley was what he was because of all the people around him and the attributes that they gave him.

Tubby Boots

You had to get into Buckley's clique. You couldn't *buy* your way in. Money didn't mean anything to Buckley. You had to be invited. Buckley picked and choosed. It didn't matter whether you were a big star or a little star. He had Sinatra there and Sinatra did something wrong and Buckley exonerated him because Buckley had a philosophy.

Sinatra always loved Buckley. You don't forget Buckley. Frank got the whole idea of the Rat Pack from Buckley and his Royal Court. But he didn't have Buckley's finesse. The Rat Pack was just a fun club. They were just fun people that wanted to be around each other. But it wasn't a way of living or a way of thinking. Frank had all the money and the others were just hangers-on. Frank was the big, major star and they were like his followers but you also had to be invited.

The first printed indication of Buckley's transformed mantle can be found in an odd source: the Manhattan telephone book. If someone wanted to get a hold of Dick Buckley in 1949 they had better look under "BUCKLEY, Lord" in the directory where they would find him listed as living at 212 W. 71st Street and reachable by dialing TRafalgar 3-6908.

Moving into this apartment on Manhattan's Upper West Side, Lord and Lady Buckley played host to an eclectic group of artists, jazz musicians, comics, dancers, socialites, bohemians, and street urchins. All were met with an open-door policy. The stunning hideaway, reportedly once a retreat for Big Apple Mayor Jimmy Walker in the 1920s and later a mortuary, included such attractive details as marble floors, skylights, and an indoor fountain.

When Lady Buckley gave birth to a daughter, Laurie (a name reportedly suggested by Ed Sullivan but perhaps chosen to honor Lord Buckley's mother Annie Laurie), on June 30, 1949, and a son, Richard Jr., on October 14, 1950, they became the most important members of the Buckleys' life party.

Lord Buckley

Recently, I had a hang-up on a bad hill in California with my two dwarves and my wife . . . I got children . . . I got them out of a schoolyard . . . they have them all over the place . . . you never see anyone out there counting them. You take two, if you like 'em, keep 'em, if you don't—vvrrrrpppttt—put 'em back, ya know.

As Laurie Buckley told *fROOTS (Folk Roots Magazine)* in the summer of 1999: "I was a princess born into a royal court, which existed only among those who agreed that it was so. The whole Royal Court was just a royal court of love, whether you were the millionaire or the alcoholic guy that dad brought home from the AA meeting. It was always a highly stimulating atmosphere, musicians, artists, actors, and actresses, always a collection of interesting, interesting people. He just had such tremendous insights into lives and souls, he had kindness and compassion and he never put people down. I might look over and say, 'What an asshole that guy is,' but he'd have said, 'Well, he's just not himself today'! He could identify the negative in people but he never used it against them.

"My brother and I were very well-behaved children; 'Yes ma'am, no ma'am, thank you,' very well mannered. They often say that we were so perfect that the people who met us would go home and beat their children, because they'd say, 'Why aren't you like those Buckley children?' It was required, simply because we traveled around in the business, up all hours, and you just couldn't be disorderly children and make the gig. So it was very important to my parents that we be well behaved as we were traveling constantly. We were so straight in such a wild world. When they smoked marijuana they never said what it was, not that we cared—we just knew that everybody was very happy.

"To show you how square we were as kids, I did not realize until I was in my early twenties at the first Renaissance Fair we had here in Las Vegas, and I heard these words that only my father would speak. I looked over and there's this hippie dude on bales of hay on a stage and he's doing 'Jonah and the Whale.' So I go over and I'm sitting there listening to him and it was only then that I realized what the great green vine Jonah was smoking was!"

In an interview published in the *Union Democrat* of Sonora County, California, in February of 1999, Laurie was equally eloquent when describing her father's legacy and unusual childhood: "You know him through Bill Cosby, George Carlin, Robin Williams, Whoopi Goldberg, even the Beatles. You hear his material so much in other people. When I listen to someone I can tell in a minute if they've heard my father.

"It's almost like a fairy tale when I look at it now . . . It never mattered whether we were in a one-room bungalow in Topanga Canyon or a thirteen-room mansion in Miami Beach. Home was for recharging. The great thing about family is that you go home to nurture. He loved to read, mostly newspapers but novels too, and he had these incredible conversations, and he could be very fun.

"The only way you know you're cool is if people are still talking about you."

Lady Elizabeth Buckley

When you got up in the morning you never could guess how many people His Lordship might invite over for dinner. It might've been five . . . or thirty.

Lord Buckley brought so many unusual people over to our apartment in New York. There was this one sweet little woman he found. The strangest little creature you ever did see. "Madam Pumpernickel" he called her. She must have been eighty years old if she was a day. A tiny, tiny dainty little thing with little red shoes, little red purse, little red hat! She visited us often, and she would sit there very demurely, never saying a thing. But then she'd get up and play the piano. And she was fantastic! Hands flying up and down the keyboard; but she'd only play Bach. Just Bach, and I never found out anything else about her. She hardly ever said a word.

Prince Booth was a sweet little child who, from the time he was fifteen and saw His Lordship perform at a theater in Baltimore, kept running away from home to follow him around. A short, roly-poly child who looked exactly like Charles Laughton. Somehow Lord Buckley finally got him a job in New York burlesque where he devised and regularly did this outrageous tassel dance dressed in a kind of red flannel nightie. Eventually he joined us as a baby-sitter and sort of handyman. I'll never forget that afternoon Prince Booth, with his tassel act, joined Madam Pumpernickel for an impromptu recital in our living room. It was very, very funny, but at the same time also quite sweet and beautiful.

Larry Storch

One night I was at a party at his house in the middle of winter. The place was on Seventy-first Street between Broadway and West End Avenue. This was where Elizabeth taught ballet. One huge room, stained-glass windows. It almost looked like a church. And he had everybody from the circus there. He invited the Fat Lady, the Bearded Lady, the Strong Man, the Tall Man—anybody you could think of. And, of course, a three-piece outfit: some musicians that we knew—both black and white. His Lordship dressed in Bermuda shorts, captain's hat, ascot tie.

At eleven o'clock at night some voices started coming out of the back yelling, "Quiet down there! We're working people! We gotta be up at seven o'clock in the morning! Quiet or we'll call the cops!"

Buckley, went out to the back into the yard and with his lungs like an animal yelled: "I'll never be quiet! Not while there's breath in my body! We're celebrating something here you should all appreciate: the hardworking people from the circus! Have you no feelings? No compassion? That's how we judge Man, by his compassion, by his pity, up the spiritual ladder. Don't you know that?!"

Sure enough, twelve o'clock: a knock on the door and two of New York's Finest came in huffing and puffing. Buckley, behind the door, slammed it shut as they entered. Heavy smoke filled the room and everybody had a glass of whiskey in his hand or wine or champagne. Buckley slammed the door, welcomed the two police officers and said, "We of New York City, we welcome you, the Finest in New York. You're not leaving here on a night like this without some sustenance."

"What do you mean by that?" they asked.

He gave a tumbler of whiskey to each officer, I saw it with my own eyes.

And His Lordship said, "You can't go back on duty without it in you to fortify yourself against Old Man Winter. Drink it down! Come on boys, cough it up!"

Well, they looked at each other. There was nothing they could do. They knew they weren't going to talk their way out of this one. They knocked off the whiskey and took off thanking Lord Buckley and glad to get out of there. That was the madness of Buckley.

Mel Welles

His one function was to conduct the bizarre. He was a conductor of the bizarre. I can remember once when he threw a party at his apartment in New York and he had a nude girl standing on a pedestal and everybody had to kiss her you-know-what on the way in. All these things were done not because of any belief in any system or ideology. They were simply done to get a reaction out of people —to do the oddest thing he could do.

Some of the bizarre things that he did would be considered scandalous if he were a senator or an evangelist. But he was *Lord Buckley*. All that kind of shit went on all the time. It was nonsense. It was a piece of cake. It was a bit of fluff. Everything was done just to have a good time. There was nothing serious about anything.

Red Rodney

I'd go to his house on West Seventy-first Street when he had a living room with a fountain in it. He had just married Elizabeth and she was very beautiful. I remember him saying that she was his ninth wife a few times. I remember one day at the place on Seventy-first Street she was carrying a tray of glasses with wine on it and held it up while posing in a ballet dancer's posture. He would kick her in the ass and she wouldn't move. And his remark was: "Sturdy wench, isn't she?"

I lived at the Shelton Hotel for a while on Lexington Avenue. They had a swimming pool there and Lord Buckley used to come and go swimming with me in the pool but he made so much noise that they threw him out. He would be singing or diving into the pool with a loud roar. He scared people: he was intimidating and imposing.

George Greif

He was always knighting people over at his place in West Seventy-first Street. The place had formally been a mortuary. You'd go in and Lenny Bruce would be sitting at his feet with Charlie Parker and his wife, Chan. Bird was in a cast and Elizabeth, Lord Buckley's wife, was giving him ballet lessons. It was so bizarre.

Buddy Jones

Buckley would call me "Lord Buddy" but Charlie Parker was "Prince Charles Parker." Lady Buckley gave ballet lessons to Bird. I was over there when Bird came in and he showed me what he had learned, going up on his toes and doing some other movements he had learned from Lady Buckley.

It was usually a pretty wild scene at that apartment. A lot of times it was so *embarrassing* and so heavy I would just have to disappear. He had this short guy who was a dwarf or something over there that made out like he was Buckley's slave. He would actually cuff him upside the head as though it was a medieval castle and he was royalty and this guy was a knave or something.

Chan Parker

The widow of Charlie Parker, the late Chan Parker held Bird's flame high after his death in 1955. Their relationship was poignantly documented in Clint Eastwood's 1988 film Bird.

I can't be of much help regarding Dick Buckley. I was never impressed by him although Bird was.

My one encounter was with Bird in Buckley's apartment. His wife was doing barre and I was asked to go into their kitchen and wash their dirty dishes.

Lady Elizabeth Buckley

Charles Parker was forever dropping by our place in New York to cool out. He'd double-park this big white Cadillac he had out in front of our apartment—even if he was going to stay overnight. I can't think of a single time he came to see us when he didn't get a parking ticket.

Tubby Boots

When the babies were born I was chief baby-sitter, cook, entertainer, and I was bringing money into the house with my gig at the Three Deuces on Fifty-second Street.

We didn't have television in those days. I think my favorite times were sitting around after dinner—and we ate for hours. We made a meal out of a meal out of a meal. We had leftovers made with leftover leftovers. Buckley would say, "Prince Charles, you do wonders with cooking." And I'd say, "I just throw in a few chives."

Despite throwing her hat in with a man as unpredictably flamboyant and effusive as Lord Buckley, Elizabeth was determined to evolve as an artist herself, refining and teaching her unique Balanchine-meets-bebop dance style she called "Ballet for Living" or "Ballet for Life."

Lady Elizabeth Buckley

I feel "Ballet for Living" is a new form of presentation. I always stress the posture. His Lordship stood so straight and so erect that you just automatically followed through. He just moved that way.

Larry Storch

I was one of Lady Buckley's pupils. She was very serious about it. She called it "Ballet for Life" at ten dollars a lesson. His Lordship would lie on the couch, a glass of Scotch in one hand and, more often than not, a reefer in the other, all the while extolling, "Smoke a thousand joints, Lord Storch, but never open up the bottle. No one ever won the war against John Barleycorn."

And he's sitting there with a glass of Scotch in his hand and drinking very royally and telling me, "Lord Storch, I've never seen such a clumsy article in my life. Elizabeth could give you a hundred lessons and you'll never get out of bed, never, never, never! You'll never make it, Lord Storch—not as a ballet dancer."

Bill Crow

A bass player and writer, Bill Crow's reminiscence of Lord Buckley appeared in his 1992 book From Birdland to Broadway.

One afternoon Dave Lambert steered me onto a baby-sitting job for Dick Buckley. Dave explained that Buckley was a nightclub comedian who billed himself as "Lord Buckley" and affected a British accent on and off stage. Buckley was no snob. He generously elevated all his friends to the peerage as well, addressing everyone as "Sir" or "Lady." I called the number Dave gave me, and Buckley asked me to come to his apartment at nine p.m.

Dave filled me in on Buckley's sense of humor and said he was fond of put-ons. Dave said he once threw open his front window and pushed his wife out over the sill, clutching her by the throat and waving a butcher knife in the air as he screamed, "I'll kill you, you bitch!"

When the police arrived, the door was open. Inside, they found the Buckleys dressed in evening clothes, listening rapturously to a recording of a Mozart quartet while sipping tea from Spode cups. They politely inquired, "What disturbance, officers?"

At the appointed hour I arrived at the Buckleys' ground-floor apartment in a brownstone building in the West Seventies. Lord Buckley, a slender man with a trim, waxed mustache, greeted me at the door.

"Welcome to the Castle!"

His bogus British accent and twinkling eyes gave him the air of a bunko artist. He led me down a hall past several small rooms and out into what had once been the backyard of the building.

A wide living room had been built there with a ceiling of opaque glass and a floor of red tile. In the center of the room was a small reflecting pool surrounded by ferns and philodendrons, with a stone cherub in the center, pouring water from an urn. Bookcases and paintings lined the walls, and pleasant indirect lighting gave the whole place a charming glow.

"Now, Sir Crow, come into the bedroom and meet Lady Buckley and the prince and princess."

I did so. The children, Richard and Laurie, were already in bed, and his wife, Elizabeth, was putting on her evening coat. Buckley performed courtly introductions and then led me back to the living room.

"Make yourself comfortable. The TV is in the cabinet in front of that easy chair, the record player is over on the sideboard, the records are in the bookshelf, and the pot is in the lacquer box above them. Help yourself to the bar, or to anything in the refrigerator. We'll be home by three."

I made myself a sandwich and spent a pleasant evening reading and listening to records. When they came home, Buckley slipped me my salary and bade me a formal farewell. After that, whenever I ran into him, he always greeted me as "Sir Crow," and promised to remember me to his family.

Ed Randolph

Knighted Prince Eagle Head in Lord Buckley's Royal Court, Ed Randolph is the world's oldest surfer. He moved to Hawaii in 1981 in order to, in his words, "surf properly before I die." Randolph also had a major hand in the production of The Parabolic REVELATIONS of the Late Lord Buckley.

In 1949 I first met Lord Buckley on West Fifty-seventh Street in New York City. I was with George Greif who took me up to somebody's office where I was introduced to His Lordship. Buckley took one look at me and said, "Prince Eagle Head," because I have a big hook nose and that inspired him.

Soon after, George took me up to the Royal Apartment on West Seventy-first Street. I was told before I went up there that I would have to do something, to perform something. It was my rites of acceptance. I think I sang an old English ditty from the war—something innocuous.

According to a 1981 cover story about Buckley in the *L.A. Reader,* Robert Mitchum was remembered to have been a guest at the convening of the Royal Court when Buckley had all the guests ensnared under chairs with a whip, not letting them out until they had performed and earned their way into the party.

Eddie Jefferson

The groundbreaking jazz singer and stylist Eddie Jefferson was a major force in exposing hip language to a mass audience. From the early 1940s Jefferson made a hobby of setting lyrics to previously recorded and well-known improvised jazz solos, pioneering the technique later adopted by King Pleasure and made nationally popular some years later by Lambert, Hendricks and Ross. The following transcript is excerpted from an interview conducted with Kirk Silsbee in 1976, three years before Jefferson's untimely and violent death at the age of sixty.

Oh, I knew Lord Buckley, yeah. I used to go to Lord Buckley's house. He lived on Seventy-first Street in New York. I remember he used to work on *The Ed Sullivan Show* all the time. There was another friend of mine named Little Buck who was a tap dancer, who introduced me to Lord Buckley. They were both on *The Ed Sullivan Show* together and they had just came from Alaska doin' the original Red Dog Saloon. They did a show from there, a "Face on the Barroom Floor" type of thing. This friend of mine, Little Buck, they had him as the piano player, he really was a dancer but they had him to play a little piano and then he did a little tap dance. Lord Buckley and he got very close and when he got back to New York, he took me to the Lord's house. Clever man. This was somewhere in the fifties—early fifties—I can't remember exactly when. Lord Buckley was a very clever man. He was one of the fathers of slang, bebop talk and whatnot. I used to see him, he'd come to the door and open the door with no clothes on. "Come right in, come right in . . ." and he's talkin' 'bout cabbages and all that stuff. Everything was slang.

I only went to his house about two or three times but there was always a lot of people of the arts: comics, singers and maybe a few producers or musicians. Always big parties, oh yeah. Very heavy man in the arts. And he loved people in the arts.

He just called me "the jazz cat." Clever man.

But if Buckley was living the high life, he was accomplishing it by his wits, the skin of his teeth . . . and a little help from his friends.

Charles Tacot

Dick could never hold onto money, or he never did, anyway. To know him was to have him owe you, but I don't think there is anyone who can really say that Lord Buckley was not worth whatever it was that he borrowed and, of course, never paid back. To have him visit you was to keep him, and his tastes, which sometimes were quite expensive . . . but few complained. Wherever he went, people seemed to pick up the tab, one way or the other, because Richard was always broke. However, if he had money, no matter how large the sum, he would spend it the same way. He did not treat his money any differently than he treated yours, and it seemed that the only thing he was concerned about was to get rid of it as quickly as possible. I have seen him buy dinner for thirty people with money he borrowed from me or anyone who happened to be there.

Tubby Boots

Buckley should have been born with money because I think he thought he had money.

He'd go out and tell the butcher, "My God, I'm having a party, Fred. And I'm having it in your honor. Every Hollywood star is going to be there. I know you're going to want to put the meat in the party." And he would invite the baker and say, "By God, Jules, I'm having a party in your honor because you've been in this neighborhood so long." And the guy would be so thrilled that he was going to a party with all these stars that he would donate all the bread. And before you knew it, Buckley had all the trimmings to give a party for a bunch of people. The fun came when the baker and the butcher showed up and thought they were the guests of honor. Buckley avoided 'em like the plague. But he did invite them.

He was in debt, always in debt. Bunch of bills. This bill. That bill. But people loved him because he only took advantage of his friends. That's one thing I always admired about Buckley. If he liked you, he'd con you. If he didn't like you, he avoided you.

One night I was soaking in the tub at Buckley's Seventy-first Street pad reading the *Journal-American*. I loosened the hot-water spigot with my foot when it suddenly became undone and scalded me bad enough to land me in Bellevue Hospital.

Now every day I received a telegram. Every day. "We miss your sunshine at the castle. Please get well, Prince Charles. Love, Lord Buckley, Lady Elizabeth and the children." And every day Buckley would come by and bring me a box of candy. And I'd say, "Isn't that nice. How thoughtful." I turned on the television one day and he was doing a quiz program called *Play Ball* and the sponsor was the same candy company.

Anyway, I didn't have any money or insurance, and I thought, "Oh God, what am I going to do about the hospital bill? When I was finally going to check out of the hospital, Buckley was doing the television show so he couldn't meet me at the hospital to take me home. So I got dressed, went to the front desk and said, "Well, I'm awfully sorry, but I can't pay you."

The person there said, "You don't have to worry about that. Your bill was paid by Lord Buckley."

I said, "It was?"

And they said, "Oh yes, he paid us in cash."

Tears came to my eyes. I said, "I don't believe this."

So I go home and I said, "Dick, you paid the hospital bill."

And he said, "Ah, anything for you, Prince Charles, a member of the Royal Family. And here, I've got a plane ticket for you to go down to Miami Beach, Florida, because you must rest for a couple of weeks. And here's five hundred dollars for your pocket. And I want you to go down there and have a vacation."

Well, I broke down and I cried. All the months he'd taken my salary at the Three Deuces and never let me have a penny. And now he's come through like a champion. And he takes me to the airport. And I go down to Florida.

Now once in Florida, I receive a notice from an insurance company which said, "Due to the fact that we've already given the twenty-five-thousand-dollar-claim to your uncle, we have to have you sign this waiver."

I said, "Twenty-five thousand dollars!"

Buckley and the insurance company had come to a quick out-of-court settlement. It wasn't the sum that bothered me but the fact that he had gone behind my back. If he had told me up front, I would have endorsed the scheme gladly. When I asked him why he did it, Buckley sweet-talked me and claimed he was "in hock to the government up to my ass."

I never resented any of it because I got more back than I gave. I learned about life. My whole worldview was formed in those days. Money was superfluous—

it was only what you could do with it. I was angry at the time because I would have rather he told me the truth. But I didn't hate him for it.

He died broke. Didn't have a dime, a pot to piss in or a window to toss it out of. Like a lot of women from that era, Lizbeth didn't know finances because Buckley kept all that shit from her. She knew they were broke but she didn't know why or how or when they got money or when they didn't have money or what was happening because he tried to shelter these things from her. He let her know up to a point.

Dick Zalud and Millie Vernon

Musician, composer, and conductor Dick Zalud and his wife, jazz chanteuse Millie Vernon, were respectively known as Prince Owl Head and Lady Renaissance in the Royal Court. Their careers in music and relationship with Lord Buckley ran deep. Lord Buckley introduced them to one another nearly fifty years ago, and they named their son David Buckley Zalud in His Lordship's honor. Additionally, Prince Owl Head collaborated with His Lordship on several of Buckley's best, including "Boston Tea Party."

Lord Buckley was once staying at the Chesterfield Hotel in downtown New York and we were living on Seventy-seventh Street and Amsterdam. One day we were just getting ready to go to work in the Catskills and the phone rings. I answered, "Hello?"

"Owl Head, come down here immediately with fifty dollars in your hand!"

I said, "Wait a minute, Buckley. Hold it. Stop right there. I don't have fifty dollars. I'm going to get paid. I don't have anything."

"Owl Head, you no-good dirty bastard! You son of a bitch!"

That was one of the few times I heard him curse. I said to Millie, "You know what he said to me? He called me a bastard."

She said, "Hang up on him!"

And I hung up.

So we take off and start driving upstate but I'm starting to have second thoughts. "God, maybe he's in some trouble. Maybe he really needs the money."

But we really didn't have the money. So I get paid and I wired him some money and I called him back the night after. He picked up the phone and said, "Aha! Conscience!"

Larry Storch

Some years ago, it must have been in 1948, he had a date up in Grossinger's, the very Jewish, very famous resort in the Borscht Belt. Really Jewish. I mean people in those days from the Eastern European countries used to pack the place. Lord Buckley's act was totally unsuited for them. And when he got up and said, "Good evening ladies and gentlemen," you could audibly hear people in the front row saying, "Oy, English!"

But he went ahead with his act: an outlandish and outrageous act for these people. They knew not one word of what he said and the act went right down the drain. And he was furious.

Afterward, we drove back to New York City in an open car, in my '48 Oldsmobile convertible. His Lordship sat in the back. He came dressed in tuxedo, never changed, and went back in his tuxedo. His wife, Elizabeth, dressed as a Chinese princess. His Lordship had finished half a bottle of Scotch and he was fuming all the way back.

As we passed a bar called the Never Sink Inn, he said, "Stop here, Lord Storch, I want to see what a man looks like who'd name a bar the Never Sink Inn."

So we stopped at the Never Sink Inn. As we were about to enter the door he said, "Hold it, everyone. Hold it, Elizabeth. Tell all of these peasants that I am going to make a speech tonight."

She said, "Of course, Richard. What is it going to be about?"

He said, "China."

"China?"

"Yes, China. Communist China is being gobbled up right now. The two culprits are Mao Tse-tung and Chou En-lai. Start them off with that Elizabeth and I'll think of something as I walk in."

She went in and said, "Quiet everyone," to all these apple pickers—all these guys with tattoos drinking boilermakers—the whole lot of 'em redneck transient workers.

And she came in and said, "Quiet everyone. Richard Buckley, His Lordship, is going to talk to you tonight about Communist China being gobbled up. The culprits are Chou En-lai and Mao Tse-tung. And remember, Richard earns more in one night than all of you do in a season of picking apples. Proceed ahead, Richard."

And His Lordship started discoursing about Communist China. Well, it was one of the most crazed performances you can possibly imagine. And at one point some woman said to him: "I don't understand a goddamned thing yer talkin' about there."

And he said to her, "Madam, you are an idiot!"

And with that her husband uncoiled.

Now Richard was six foot four and Richard's tough luck, the guy happened to be six foot six and he said, "My wife may be an idiot but no one's gonna tell her that except me."

Buckley said, "Easy, Lord Storch. We're not going to pay the bill on this one even though we've had our drinks . . . they're like sharks and monkeys: they can smell blood. Don't let them sense fear. Back out slowly . . . we'll have to kick our way out of this if need be."

As we burst out the front door, we could hear voices in the back, things like, "Get a rope! Get a rope!" We knew we were in a jam and we raced about the length of a football field toward the car, barely made it, jumped in and zoomed off to New York. That was the closest I came to bodily harm while in His Lordship's company.

A photo from that night of Lord and Lady Buckley, Storch, an unidentified woman, and an elderly Jewish man, all seated around a Grossinger's dinner table is revealing. Fittingly, it displays all the characters looking their respective parts. The older man appears miffed, the woman polite, a glazed-eyed Storch a tad inebriated, and Lady Buckley prim in her Chinese princess getup as His Lordship seems to let forth with a gleeful bellow.

Charles Tacot

Then there was the time Frank Sinatra was the headliner at the Copacabana. There was a comic who went on before Frank with Buckley set to go on after. And Buckley knew that nobody goes on after Frank—they'd fuckin' had it: he's taking you all the way around the block and dropping you back. It's "Good night" right there—they're all leaving. And suddenly—bam! "One more act, hold on everybody."

Half the people are getting up and Buckley walks out with a chair and a saw and he says, "Ladies and gentlemen of the Royal Court. It's hard to follow Frank but here's a little something to make you think."

And he starts sawing into his foot and the blood spurts out and the women start to faint and freak out. People threw up. And he cuts an artery at the edge of his foot and there's no bullshit about the man: he's sawing his fuckin' foot off . . . well, just enough to make it *really* bleed. And now it's all over the stage and it's spurting out and the people are screaming: "Ahhhhhh!"

And he says, "Thank you, now you know when you leave here that there's only one name on your lips and it's *mine!*"

And he turns around and walks out.

Frank came over to him afterward backstage and says, "Jesus Christ, man. That beats it."

And that's how they became friends.

Another time Buckley led sixteen nude people through the lobby of the Royal Hawaiian where Frank was performing. Sinatra had got him the job and when Frank got back to his hotel room the hotel manager called him up and told him about what had happened. So Sinatra called up Buckley and said, "It's the funniest thing I ever heard. Just don't ask me for any more favors."

Charlie Barnet

On one occasion Buckley was strolling through the lobby of the Waldorf-Astoria in New York in his usual royal manner when he heard loud music in the middle of a big rehearsal with various acts that were to appear at a benefit that night. Ed Sullivan was to be the emcee and Sammy Kaye the conductor.

During the lull in the proceedings, Buckley approached Sammy, introduced himself, and said his music had been delayed in transit. He needed a few cues that could easily be written down on a piece of paper. He then began to go through an imaginary routine. "That will require a drum roll followed by a cymbal crash," he would say. "Every time I raise my right hand, we'll have a chord in B-flat." After some forty minutes of this, the drummer had enough cues to fill a toilet roll, and everybody else had notations about that chord in B-flat, how long to hold it, et cetera, et cetera. At that point, Buckley thanked them profusely and made his exit.

That night at the benefit show, act after act appeared. Sammy and the boys had all their written notes ready for Buckley's performance but there was no sign of him. "What time is Dick Buckley to make his appearance?" Sammy Kaye finally asked Ed Sullivan. "Buckley, Buckley?" said Sullivan. "There's no Buckley in this show." Nor was there. It was just another of His Lordship's pranks.

Marvin Worth

Before the late bio-pic auteur and film producer Marvin Worth made his mark with such cinematic homages as Lenny, The Rose, *and* Malcolm X, *he consorted with and managed comedians and jazz musicians alike. The old Fifty-second Street denizen became Lenny Bruce's manager in the 1950s and got him his breakthrough booking on television's popular* Arthur Godfrey Show.

Many years ago I was taking a ride to Brooklyn in a cab with Buckley and a few other entertainers.

Buckley started making love to the cab driver, telling him: "What a cab driver you are. You drive so beautifully, man. Oooh, how you steer! Oooh look how he makes that right-hand turn, how he pushes down that signal!"

And he reached across the front seat and started stroking the cabby's hair and just doing all this stuff to the cab driver and the cab driver is sweating bullets because there's this cat with a tuxedo and this voice stroking him and making verbal love to him.

Buckley said, "Have you ever known the love one man can feel for another?"

By the time we get to where we were going, this cab driver was so fucking happy to get rid of this weird character.

But Buckley kept it going right up to the bitter end: "Ooohh baby! I have to hire you again. Give me your phone number. I need you to take me everywhere I have to go in Manhattan. I want you to come with me. I want to come with you!"

In 1949 Lord Buckley appeared on television's *Club 7,* a weekly half-hour variety show hosted by Johnny Thompson. First telecast in August 1948, *Club 7* was haphazardly broadcast for two years as an informal, low-budget musical variety program in the early days of the ABC network. It featured new talent, ranging from singers and dancers to acrobats and a recurring character named "Hank the Mule." After a hiatus in 1949–1950, the program returned as a nightly feature varying in length from ten minutes to half an hour since it was often truncated by short newscasts or other programs on either end.

An amazing cultural artifact in its own right, the lone known surviving kinescope of *Club 7* is, along with the early Sullivan show appearances, the best example we are likely to get of Lord Buckley in performance from this period. His extended slot in the middle of the show certainly must have come out of left field for the self-conscious New York studio audience, who look like they just stepped off a Kansas pumpkin patch rather than the F train from Queens.

Buckley, appearing without his false teeth, quickly wins them over with a charming and danceable rendition of "Put on Your Easter Bonnet" complete with expert Louis Armstrong vocal inflections before enlisting the band as cohorts in transforming the venue into a church by announcing that he is going into "preacher mode," at which a musician can clearly be heard intoning: "Amen!"

Flicking his cigarette aside with a stately flourish, an erect Buckley launches into a remarkable piece he calls "The Sinner." The setup and execution are simple enough: a Stepin Fetchit–modeled character nickel-and-diming the cash register at a pharmacy where he works is caught in the act by God. When questioned by the holy presence about his transgression, the Sinner graciously (and slyly) points out that if it wasn't for people like him, "What would you do all day?"

What makes the piece truly notable, however, is its place in the Buckley canon as a true missing link bridging Buckley's vaudevillian "Amos 'n' Andy" approach to a more rigorous invocation of the black linguistic muse and the hipsemantic. Several passages of "The Sinner," in fact, were grafted hook, line, and sinker (if they weren't there already) into Buckley's famous "Jonah and the Whale." Along with sharing identical openings ("The Great Lord was sitting in his rosy rocking chair one hallelujah morning when he spied a little mortal . . ."), the moment when God speaks is similarly experienced by the subjects of both stories ("I feel a crazy feeling all over my body! Make me want to spread my wings and . . . *good morning Lord!*").

After giving up the stage to a tap-dancing trio from Brooklyn, Buckley appears briefly near the program's conclusion, in which he plays a wild, knife-toting baker in a slapstick skit.

In an early example of what would become the tantalizingly elusive recorded legacy of Lord Buckley, the show's emcee alludes to both past and future appearances by His Lordship—appearances that seem never to have been preserved or are long lost.

Clearly Buckley was consciously making himself into a show business faith healer who could transform a nightclub, theater, or coffee shop into a shamanistic ritual.

The festivities wailed nonstop for almost a year when, despite a solid career in New York, His Lordship pulled up the family stakes and headed to Hollywood and the allure of the silver screen.

Lord Buckley

Let me hip you to something brothers and sisters . . . when you make love, *MAKE IT!*

Oh, some of you brothers and sisters . . . *HOLDOUTS!*

7 the nazz

Lord Buckley

Well I came by the language in association with the beauty of the American Beauty Negro and the sacred association with the field of music and its growing volume which has had a *fantastic* renaissance here in the United States during the years. In association with these people and, in their seeming rush, there isn't enough time—never enough time. They got themself a zig-zag way of talking and I think eventually became the intimate social language of the American Beauty Negro. It has a fantastic sense of renewal that'll take any old and revered movement and swing it right up to the pounce of the now and the meaning and it is sparkled with the magical beauty of the American Negro for which the United States should be tremendously grateful for many many other things: the brotherhood of the Negro race. Because, going up against the granite walls of stupidity, they have, as a consequence, at the other end of the pendulum, have dug out their wells of humor to such a point that it turned into a spring. It spread by a spring that is so deep because they had many many times to laugh at a number of things that weren't funny. But if they wanted to laugh, they selected some things that weren't funny and laughed at them anyway. And, as a consequence, in the law of conversation, they wound up with a very very deep sparkling humorous well of beauty.

By the late 1940s Buckley had fully developed the style he had been honing for nearly twenty years, taking the persona of "His Lordship" both on stage and off. At Lady Buckley's urging, the "Amos 'n' Andy" bit was de-emphasized in her husband's stage presentation. In its place were the classic Lord Buckley raps recasting incidents from history and mythology into a patois that cross-pollinated scat singing, black jive talk, and the King's English. This odd alchemy often yielded spectacular results, such as "The Nazz," three miracles from the life of Christ and his disciples in hip talk, which revealed Buckley's gifts and power in all their raging glory.

Lady Elizabeth Buckley

After we met and married in 1946, I immediately began to notice that when Lord Buckley worked clubs, the last set of the evening, when the place was pretty much empty except for the jazz musicians and hard-core fans, he was always much more adventurous than earlier in the evening when there were lots of customers. And since we were always lovingly competitive, I challenged him to begin using this more "artistic" and socially conscious material in the earlier sets. I suggested he tell some of the stories he told backstage when he was in front of the audience. And he did. And I think that was perhaps my major contribution to the Royal Court.

Larry Storch

"The Nazz," "Jonah and the Whale," and all the Shakespeare stuff were full-blown bits of material by the time I first saw Buckley in '46. He may have added on each show. He might do something or add something a little bit different to it.

Mel Welles

Around that time he went to Chicago and played the room in the Sherman Hotel. He did his "Amos 'n' Andy" bit, and he kind of died with it. And we talked until three o'clock in the morning about the future of his act and the content of his material. Just prior to his trip he had written "Hipsters, Flipsters and Finger-Poppin' Daddies" and "To Swing or Not to Swing" for the entertainment of his friends.

I told him, "Well, if you're going to go down, go down in a flame and do that routine."

And he did the routine the next night and he did go down in a flame. When he came back, however, he was so enchanted with the form that we began to write together.

The Nazz" is Lord Buckley's most famous piece. With a delivery firmly and undeniably rooted in the call-and-response "testifying" common in African American religious ritual, Buckley's attraction to the tale for its dramatic and historical resonance is easy to fathom. What's more, like many of the classics he chose to recast, there is more than a hint of autobiographical identification and empathy with the subject.

Lord Buckley

For instance, I have explained the three miracles I have on Our Savior, from the life of Jesus. The preachers tell me they're bringing hot-rodders into church with it, ya see. This work has been read by high ecclesiastical figures and they say that this unquestionably, absolutely and positively is a religious psalm. And, of course, it is.

> **THE NAZZ** Now look at all you cats and kitties out there whippin' and wailin' and jumpin' up and down and suckin' up all that juice and pattin' each other on the back and hippin' each other *who* the greatest cat in the world is! Mr. Malencoff, Mr. Dalencoff, Mr. Zalencoff, Mr. Eisenhower, Mr. Woosenwiser, Mr. Weisenwooser, Mr. Woodhill, Mr. Beachill and Mr. Churchill and all them Hills gonna get you straight. If they can't get you straight, they know a cat that *knows* a cat that'll straighten you.

But I'm gonna put a cat on you who was the *coolest, grooviest, sweetest, wailin'est,* strongest cat that ever stomped on this sweet, swingin' sphere. And they called this here cat: "The Nazz."

He was a carpenter kittie. Now The Nazz was a kind of a cat that came on so cool and so groovy and so *with it* that when he laid it down: "WHA-LAM!"—*It stayed there.*

Naturally, all the rest of the cats say: "Man look at that cat wail. He's wailin' up a storm over there!"

"Hey, I tell you he—"

"I dug that."

"Get off my back Jack! What's the matter with you? I'm trying to hear what the cat's puttin' down."

They're pushin' The Nazz to dig his miracle lick.

So The Nazz say, "Cool babies. Tell you what I'm gonna do. I ain't gonna take two, four, six eight of you cats, but I'm gonna take *all twelve of you studs* and straighten you all at the same time. You cats look like you pretty hip." He say, "You buddy with me."

So The Nazz and his buddies was goofin' off down the boulevard one day and they run into a little cat with a bent frame. So The Nazz look at this little cat with the bent frame and he say: "What's de matter wid you baby?"

And the little cat wid the bent frame, he say, "My frame is bent Nazz." He say, "It's been bent from in front."

So the Nazz looked at the little cat wid the bent frame. And he put the golden eyes of love on this here little kitty. And he looked right down into the window of the little cat's soul and say to the little cat, he say: "STRAIGH-*TEN!!*"

"Zoom-Boom!" Up went the cat like an arrow and everybody jumpin' up and down say, "Look what The Nazz put on that boy. You dug him before. Re-dig him now."

Everybody talking about The Nazz. What a great cat he was. How he swung with the glory of love. How he straighten out the squares. How he swung through the money changin' court and kicked all the short changers all over the place and he knockin' the corners off the squares. How he put it down for the cat, dug it: didn't dig it. Put it down twice, dug it: didn't dig it. Put it down a third time: Boom! Walked away with his eyes buggin' out of his head bumpin' into everybody.

And they pullin' on The Nazz's coattails. They wanted him to sign the autograph. They want him to do a gig here, do a gig there, play the radio, play the video. *He can't make all that jazz.* Like I esplained to you he's a carpenter kittie, got his own lick. But when he know he should go to blow and cannot go cause he got too much *strain* on him—*straightenin' out the squares*—he sends a couple of these cats to do his hippin'.

So came a little sixty-cent gig one day and The Nazz was in a bind and he put it on a couple of his boys.

"Say boys, take care of that for me would you?"

"Take it off your wig Nazz, we'll cool it."

And they started out to straighten it out for The Nazz and they came to a little old twenty-cent pool of water. And they got in the middle of the water with the boat and all of a sudden: "Wham-Boom!"—the lightnin' flashin' and the thunder roarin' and the boat is goin' up and down and these po' cats figurin' every minute gonna be the last when one cat look up and: *here come the Nazz* cool as anyone you ever seen, right across the water: *stompin'*.

And there's a little cat on board, I think his name was Jude. He say, "Hey Nazz, can I make it out there with ya?"

And The Nazz say, "*Make it Jude.*"

And ole Jude went stompin' off that boat, took about four steps, dropped his whole card and—*zoot*—Nazz had to stash him back on board again.

So The Nazz say, "What seem to be the trouble here boys? What's the matter with you babies now? You hittin' on that S.O.S.'n bell pretty hard. You gonna *bend* that bell knockin' on it like that."

One cat say, "What seems to be the trouble?! Can't you see the storm stormin' and the lightnin' flashin' and the thunder roarin'?!"

And The Nazz say, "I told you to stay *cool,* didn't I babies."

(To the people who don't know, that means to believe. To stay cool is to have the sweet fragments of serenity rock you away.)

So now everybody is talkin' about The Nazz. OOOOII this beautiful swingin' man. How he is settin' the country on fire with great sparks of great love like a swingin' non-stop satellites goin' through all the lanes and valleys and alleys and puttin' down the scene with such beauty and such power and such charm and now sparks seventy-five feet long shootin' out of the grapevine and they now got *five thousand* of these little cats and kitties in The Nazz's hometown where the cat live *lookin' to get straight!*

Well he knows he cain't straighten them there, it's too small a place, don't want to hang everybody up. So The Nazz backed away a little bit and he looked at these cats and kitties and he say, "Come on babies, let's cut out down the pike."

And there went The Nazz with these five thousand cats and kitties stompin' up a storm behind him. There's a great love river of joy is goin' like a great chain through these gorgeous cats and kitties as they swingin' along the great beat of The Nazz. And the birds are flyin' along on one side and singin' love songs to these cats and kitties and there's a great jubilee of love and The Nazz talkin' about, "How pretty the hour, how pretty the flower, how pretty you, how pretty me, how pretty the tree!" (Nazz had them pretty eyes. He wanted everybody to see through his eyes and see how pretty it was.)

And they havin' such a glorious, swingin' Mardi Gras time that before you know it, they were forty-two miles out of town and ain't nobody got the first biscuit.

So The Nazz look at all them cats and kitties he say, "You hongry, ain't you babies?"

And the one cat say, "Yeah Nazz, we's diggin' so hard what you puttin' down, we didn't *pre*-pare Nazz. We goofed."

So The Nazz say, "Well, we got to take it easy here. We wouldn't want to go ahead and order sumpin' you might not like, would we?"

And they say, "Sweet double hipness, you put it down and we'll pick it up."

And The Nazz step away a little bit and put a glorious sound of love on them. He said: *"Oh sweet swingin' flowers of the field!"*

And they said: *"Oh great non-stop singular sound of beauty!"*

And he said: *"Stomp upon the terra!"*

They did!

He said: *"Lift your miracle, the body!"*

The body went up!

He said: *"Lift your arms!"*

The arms went up!

He said: *"Higher!"*

They went *higher!*

He said: *"DIG INFINITY!"*

And they *dug it!*

And when they did—"Whamm!"—there was a great flash of thunder/lightnin' hit the scene. Cats looked down in one hand there was great big stuffed sweet smoked fish and in the other a long gone crazy loaf of that southern homemade honey tastin' ever-lovin' sweet bread.

Why these po' cats *flipped!*

Nazz never did nothing simple. When he laid it, *he laid it*!

In addition to Christ in "The Nazz," Buckley would employ his distinctive and compelling brogue to celebrate Gandhi ("The Hip Gahn"), Spanish explorer Alvar Núñez Cabeza de Vaca ("The Gasser"), Edgar Allen Poe ("The Raven" aka "The Bugbird"), Albert Einstein ("The Hip Einie"), William Shakespeare ("Willie the Shake," "Marc Antony's Funeral Oration," and others), Charles Dickens ("Scrooge"), Abraham Lincoln ("Gettysburg Address"), and the Marquis de Sade ("The Bad-Rapping of . . ."), to name just a few.

Buckley's choice to hippify the classics was more than a mere gimmick. By choosing tales familiar to the audience, he let the spirit and deeds of the old heroes and heels resonate anew, animating his yarns with visionary qualities and definite, if subtle, points of view.

Through the officially released and private recordings of "The Nazz" in circulation, it is possible to allow a telling study of Buckley's work and its evolution. Fortunately, there are six extant released and unreleased versions of "The Nazz" as well as a half-minute clip of him performing its peak moment in an obscure and forgotten film, *Chicago: First Impressions of a Great American City,* produced and directed by the late Denis Mitchell, a British documentarian.

The earliest-known version of "The Nazz" can be found on a rare demo release known informally and fondly as the *Turk Murphy Acetate.* Turk Murphy was a white jazz bassist and later a San Francisco club owner who made the jump from Dixieland to the big-band Swing Era to bebop and back again before he eventually helped lay the backbeat to the West Coast jazz "cool" revolution in the early 1950s. Murphy, a San Francisco Bay Area native, encountered and befriended Buckley in a Los Angeles jazz club shortly after His Lordship's 1950 landing in Southern California.

Charles Campbell

A fixture in the arts community of San Francisco, Charles Campbell befriended, photographed, and recorded Lord Buckley in the 1950s.

There was a musician in a band I managed named Turk Murphy. And Turk came up from Los Angeles with some 78 ten-inch records with titles written on the label in pencil. It was Lord Buckley. We were mad for the records and we tried to find out more about him. Turk didn't know anything about him. Later we heard all sorts of stories that he was from Jamaica and that he was black or wasn't black.

Later Buckley made some records with Turk, barroom ballads and things like Robert Service poems set to music. I don't think they were very interesting . . . they were pretty static. The material wasn't that interesting and I don't think ever commercially available.

An amateur recordist, Murphy set four of Buckley's live routines to some kind of posterity, probably on reel-to-reel tape. Most of the cuts included subtle piano backdrops. Along with an embryonic version of "The Nazz" (titled "Saints" on the eight-inch acetate's crude cardboard cover), Murphy captured Buckley's noir ode "Murder," "Myrtle the Turtle" (a smart-assed children's story written by Dick Zalud about the perils of doting parenthood) and "The Moronic Son and His Idiot Father" (a vaudevillian bomb about a mentally challenged boy who burns down a house that Buckley continued to interject into his performances as late as 1959).

Zalud, by the way, penned at least a couple of other unrecorded and rarely performed pieces for Buckley in a similar vein in the late 1950s ("Man in the Hole" and "The Pioneer") and claims major, if generally unacknowledged, credit for "Boston Tea Party," recorded for RCA in 1955.

Murphy then made a limited pressing of the results on acetate, which he distributed to select friends and some sympathetic record companies in hope of landing a contract for both himself and Buckley—a deal that never materialized. If the original acetates were of audio quality as poor as the surviving sources (not to mention the relative mediocrity of Buckley's performances and choice of material), it is no small wonder that they never found a place in the record bins. In addition, comedy and spoken-word records were virtually unknown at the time save for the odd pressing of Shakespeare or poetry.

It was going to take someone with Murphy's zeal and a larger bankroll to help spread Buckley's gospel via vinyl.

Lord Buckley

I am the only comic who brings the word of Christ into the nightclubs. And the more people who are exposed to that Message, no matter where they are, the better.

Paul Zaloom

Puppeteer, performance artist, star of the popular children's television show Beekman's World, *and early member of Peter Shuman's Bread and Puppet Theater, Paul Zaloom is a not-so-secret Lord Buckley admirer.*

I believe that Lord Buckley was one of the great American philosophers. I've always called him a theologian. His whole rap about people worshiping people would seem to put him in that category more than just about anything else.

He understood the idea of Jesus Christ probably better than any other human being that's ever lived. He's the best last hope for God that there ever was as far as I'm concerned.

Albert Goldman

You find the same amalgam of the fairy tale, the religious parable and the animated cartoon (with Dixieland soundtrack) in all of Lord Buckley's famous routines. In "The Nazz," he takes three miracles from the gospel and dips them in tar. Out comes a Jesus that is just as sweet and gentle and generous as the Hip Gahn, but who meets the challenges of the road—the encounter with the little cat who has a "bent frame," the storm on the Sea of Galilee, the demand for loaves and fish or at the wedding of Cana—with sublime power, with the thunder and the lightning and stentorian command to the cowering disciples: "DIG INFINITY!!!"

Tubby Boots

We had several paintings on the walls of the Castle. One was of Jesus Christ . . . autographed. "To Lord Buckley from your buddy cat, J. C." He had the painter autograph it because he said, "He would have been my buddy."

Capturing the post–World War II exuberance of bebop and the Beats, Buckley anticipated the civil-rights struggles by a decade and hippies by two. The essence embedded in Buckley's best both satirically condemn social ills and identifies enlightening solutions. Even today, if given the chance, Buckley could raise the hackles of both the Religious Right and the Politically Correct for all the wrong reasons.

It would be inaccurate to characterize Lord Buckley's work as based entirely on the classics, with his performance technique as solely derived from the African American stump preachers of the South or the disaffected hipster substratum. His influences are substantially more complex, and classifying his pieces is also a thorny matter. There are even distinct traces of Brooklynese in some of his pieces if one listens closely.

To be sure, the black delivery and sensibility Buckley adopted (that is, the syncopated bebopping scat song imbued with a moral subtext) can be found in most of his canon and it does, assuredly, mark most of his best work. But that body covers a wide range of categories. His entire output owes something to many different spheres and traditions. These include autobiography or identification, film and literature, sex, history, animal stories, political commentary, children's nursery rhymes and fairy tales, and atomic- or space-age concerns.

Alternately, Lord Buckley would craft other forms of expression that drew on Americana ("The Train"), pathology ("Murder"), psychology ("Subconscious Mind"), politics ("Governor Slugwell"), racial inequity ("Black Cross"), sexuality ("Chastity Belt"), and transcendence ("God's Own Drunk").

Joseph Jablonski

Joseph Jablonski's introduction to the City Lights edition of Hiparama of the Classics *was one of the first appraisals of Lord Buckley's artistic, social, cultural, and political depth. Excerpted here, the piece captures much of the energy of the 1960s generation's rediscovery of His Lordship.*

Lord Buckley's entire career was a continuing tribute to an exalted gift which, if it is not the same thing as the poetic marvelous sought by surrealism, is certainly a close cousin to it.

A final point about Lord Buckley concerns the question of sources. The humorist's affinity with Afro-America (which he himself acknowledged) is enormous. It is one that he developed on the entertainment and jazz circuits, as well as in his private experiences through association with blacks and exposure to their influence. It is palpable not only in his rhythmic oral style and street lingo; it is deeper than that, in the spirit of his work which shares the enthusiasm and aggressively impossibilist orientation of Afro-American art, culture and mythology.

It was the most ebullient vein of black existence mined for moral gold, so that his magic was directly inspired by the poetic values of that tradition. On this plane the question of a rip-off does not arise; for Buckley himself not only would acknowledge his debt but would actually proclaim it. To see his work side by side with its primary sources is to enjoy the signal illumination produced by the symbiosis.

Al Young

Al Young is the award-winning author of several screenplays and more than fifteen books of poetry, fiction, and nonfiction. Mingus/Mingus, *a memoir of the American composer and bassist coauthored with Janet Coleman, is an important collaborative effort. Mr. Young's impressions of Lord Buckley were collected by California writer Douglas Cruickshank.*

Buckley didn't rip anybody off. I remember something I once heard the late blues singer Big Bill Broonzy tell Studs Terkel. Broonzy said, "You can't steal something from somebody else. What you do is you take it and you do with it what you're going to do with it. But it's not the same." I think that's the process of making art. I'm not saying that, in the marketplace, people don't maliciously exploit such cullings or borrowings. I'm just saying that the spirit of Lord Buckley was not malicious, hostile or in any way exploitive. That was the language that was around in the world that he inhabited. Everybody talked like that. We talked like that when I was growing up in Detroit in the 1950s. We would study for a history test in those terms. We'd say, "George Washington went in and kicked the British's ass." It was a way of vividly reinterpreting the story so it seemed real. The old language just didn't say anything to us.

Of course Buckley was a storyteller. In that respect what he did was very close to black sermonizing—preaching—when you retell a chapter of the Bible in vernacular. But he was also a poet. His language was poetic, and the effects he achieved were poetic effects. And he had a sense of rhythmic development that not all monologists have. He also had the ear of a musician. He knew how to use repetition, he knew how to build a crescendo, he had a musical sense of dynamics. He was in the tradition of the folk storyteller that has been a part of America since the early nineteenth century. He did not do anything substantially different from what Mark Twain did. Lord Buckley was from that grassroots, populist, anarchist American tradition that was a force for so long in this country and, for a while there, made it great. Buckley reinforced my own inclinations as a writer. The vitality in the heart of storytelling and poetry resides in the spoken idiom, the vernacular. All the old guys knew that. Shakespeare knew that. You take the spoken word and you transform it.

Paul Zaloom

I remember buying some real dirty record by some black comedian that was recorded in the sixties and it was filthy—filthy, filthy, filthy. The shtick was called "The Signifying Monkey" but it sounded like a Buckley piece in a lot of ways, it was very much in that mode.

Obviously there's a black tradition of storytelling that Buckley was sort of copping from. I don't think that it was only that he was appropriating the hipster language at the time, but a certain oral tradition as well.

It's like you see an artist like Little Richard and you say, "God, the guy is so original." And then you see pictures of Billy Wright—the guy who Richard copped his stuff from—and you realize that nobody's original and that everybody draws from those different sources.

Is it politically correct to appropriate from other cultures? People have a hard time with Vanilla Ice and yet Buckley obviously took the English thing, he took the beat/hip thing, he took the black thing, and he took a lot of different sensibilities, combined it with his beautiful philosophy and his great ear. So I don't think it's fair to lay the politically incorrect thing on him. Nobody is saying a white guy *can't* draw on the black tradition. But what they may say is that here's another example of a white man ripping off black culture, which has happened in the past.

There are a couple of other reasons why Buckley may, mistakenly, be considered politically incorrect. He appropriated black culture and that's a very much discredited thing today. There's a lot of black resentment against the fact that that's been done. The argument that if Wynton Marsalis can play Bach why can't someone like Buckley celebrate the black storytelling idiom is countered by the argument that it's not like black people glommed onto something that a peripheral group of white people were nurturing and then propelled it into great popularity and generated a lot of money vis-à-vis Pat Boone's usurpation of Little Richard. I think that black people have a legitimate beef in this thing in terms of having their culture constantly ripped off.

What about Paul Butterfield? I've been listening to Butterfield lately. I remember listening to Butter over and over and over again as a kid. But then I heard Little Walter do "Yonder's Wall," I thought to myself, "Holy shit! What the fuck was I doing? What happened here?"

The other argument is that people like Butterfield were a doorway for people like me to check the deeper levels of this stuff out. Maybe we wouldn't have been as open to the deep blues had we not passed through him in the first place.

And then you have to take it beyond that, which is to say, "Forget what Butter did about opening doors. What was it about his art that was interesting and compelling?" And the Butterfield Blues Band with Mike Bloomfield and those guys were a great band.

Steve Allen

On one instance somewhere in the fifties I went to a club with him in New York for what I think was some sort of benefit. The audience was, to a significant extent, black. But I remember he got in trouble because of that fact. In performing he did some portion of the classic stories from the New Testament in hip talk. When he referred to Jesus Christ as "The Nazz" people were not laughing but were saying "What's this man talking about?" I don't know if it was they thought he was putting on blacks' speech or what because jazz talk is originally black.

Oddly enough I never ran into that kind of trouble. He and I apparently independently arrived at that same gimmick but we used it in very different ways. One of his ways was to just tell any given story in hip musicians' slang lingo. I got the idea, to do what we called "Bop Fables," from a child. One day Ernie Caceres, the guitar player from my show on CBS, was up at the house rehearsing something with me and he mentioned that the day before he had asked his son the eternal question that fathers often put to their children: "What did you study in school today, honey?" And the kid, not trying to be funny or hip at all, but just speaking the way his father and his father's friends spoke in his presence, said: "Oh, they taught us about some cat named George Washington."

Some of the hip phrases are still with us but there's new stuff that comes in every so often. It all gets mixed together now. There's a big media mix monster that mashes it all together. There's high school talk and "Valley" talk and it all gets mixed up with hip talk. It's just a dopey American way of communicating now. But there's a baseness and a desophistication to this approach now that does not necessarily elevate the mind.

Lord Buckley

The translation came through . . . It was first brought up out of the void of non-moving things to me by my application of the zig-zag talk that originates of course, from our beautiful Negro brothers and sisters. The zig-zag talk. And I found out that many times when I, in Chicago before, that I'd been living such a hectic life that I found many times that it was impossible to explain or project myself from my normal sense of projection. So I would slip out of that into the hip and say, "Well Jack, to hip you, to tell you the truth I, ya know that I'm not very cool today. I'm a little on the down and I'd like to get right and tight but I think I need a little more sleep. Dig?" So I would fall back to that particular type and kind of expression and it seemed to refresh me and then I would return to my normal vernacular. Soon I'm parlaying it and giving it flexibility and the use of it came to me that perhaps I could apply it to the classics such as Poe, Shakespeare, Our Savior, Mahatma Gandhi, Abraham Lincoln. And people who think that the "Gettysburg Address" to be . . . it would be satirical to employ this semantic against this revered work of Lincoln but it happened to the contrary. It even comes out stronger. For instance, allow me to address a little bit as "Solid sent upon the ace lick that all cats and kitties red, white or *blue* are created level in front," which means, in essence, that it was so before it was contended. That's some of the strange powers of the semantic.

David Amram

I think what Lord Buckley did was to see the poetry and genius and the majesty and the humor and the pathos of the African American ethos and he used it combining Shakespeare and the Bible. This was also done by black preachers whose eloquence mesmerized everyone who heard them including Lord Buckley.

Lord Buckley was the consummate performer, having total command of his instrument, which was his voice and his ability to be all the various people that inhabited the world he created for his memorable performances. He was one of the first to combine Shakespeare, the Bible and the poetry of the streets.

Like many of Buckley's well-known bits, "The Nazz" has found continued life in ways that may have surprised even the performer himself. John Sinclair, a British actor who starred in a 1983 one-man show titled "Lord Buckley's Finest Hour," covered "The Nazz" on a rare mock born-again Christian/gospel-styled 45 rpm release on Charisma, a division of Polydor, in 1979. Most significant was David Bowie's reference to the piece ("He was the Nazz/ With God-given ass") in the song "Ziggy Stardust" from his 1972 glitter-rock-defining album, *The Rise and Fall of Ziggy Stardust and the Spiders from Mars*.

More obscurely, a phrase from "The Nazz" ("Make it Jude!") seems to have slipped into one of the more impassioned refrains of the famous Beatles tune "Hey Jude."

Evidence of the Beatles' interest in Buckley is hardly limited to the possible reference in "Hey Jude." After forming their own Apple Records in 1969, the Fab Four launched Zapple records, intended as the home for experimental and spoken-word releases. It was named by John Lennon not, as Frank Zappa thought, for him, but in the spirit that the original name was chosen: "A is for Apple. Z is for Zapple"—the other end of the alphabet. Along with material from Allen Ginsberg, Charles Olson, Henry Miller, Charles Bukowski, and more than a dozen other envelope-pushing mind-breath artists, the Beatles considered reissuing the works of Lord Buckley and Lenny Bruce.

But contrary to popular rumor, Todd Rundgren's late-1960s band Nazz did not derive its name from the routine. Rather, Rundgren claimed to have incorporated a piece of old British blues slang into the band's moniker. According to Rundgren's comments in the liner notes from *Best of Nazz:* "The name came from the B-side of a Yardbirds single. I think it was 'Happening Ten Years Time Ago.' It was a song called 'The Nazz Are Blue.' It was an old blues term, but we just thought it made an interesting-sounding name."

Bill Crow

A few years went by during which our paths didn't cross. Then, one day when I was waiting to cross Sixth Avenue at West Third Street, along came Lord Buckley.

"Ah, Sir Crow!" he cried, and clasped my hand warmly. His clothes looked a little seedier than when I'd seen him last, but his regal bearing was intact. He beamed with enthusiasm.

"I've been on the West Coast, and I've developed a new routine that's going to knock everyone's arse off! Have you a moment to spare?"

"Come on up to my place and tell me about it. I'll make us some lunch." I had my own Village cold-water flat by then.

Buckley's new routine was the story of Jesus of Nazareth told in the argot of a hipster. He called it "The Nazz" and eventually recorded it. It was funny and, at the time (pre–Lenny Bruce), quite outrageous. I couldn't imagine where he'd be able to perform it without either puzzling or offending his audience, but I knew he'd break up the band. He gave me samples of other routines that he was developing in the same vein: a hipster's version of Shakespeare and of Roman history. We spent a pleasant afternoon lunching and laughing, and I noticed when he said good-bye that I had received a promotion. He shook my hand and said, "Farewell, Prince Crow."

Lord Buckley

Hip talk originated, of course, with the slaves when they wished to discuss things they didn't want the "Masters" to understand.

8 euphoria

Lord Buckley

I'll tell you what we have to do, you see. We have to spread love. We've got to. People of this nation have got to learn to be kinder, more gracious. They must rehearse kindness and graciousness with other people. They must do that. They must be more generous. The people who have things who are living next to people who haven't got things should give them some of the things that they have. We have to learn to give more. We have to learn to tighten, to magnetize this nation by love in this coming fight that we're in. We've *got* to do that. We *must* do it. We *absolutely* must. The government cannot do everything. The people must help. And they can help it by rehearsing love for each other.

New York's distinction as the world capital of jazz has been challenged only once over the past fifty years—during the 1950s, when California emerged with a splash on the jazz scene. The "West Coast sound," as it soon became known, was a breath of fresh air stirring both joy and debate in equal measure. However, one thing was evident: never before (or since) had so many jazz musicians from the "Left Coast" made such an impact on American music. Figures like Charles Mingus, Dave Brubeck, Dexter Gordon, Eric Dolphy, Ornette Coleman, Chet Baker, Art Pepper, Cal Tjader, Paul Desmond, Shelly Manne, and countless others shaped the jazz of this era and remain powerful influences today.

From its origins on Central Avenue in the heart of Los Angeles's postwar black culture, small clubs à la Fifty-second Street were spawned and, attracting the likes of Louis Armstrong, Charlie Parker, and Dizzy Gillespie, ignited California's love affair with jazz.

Though Lord Buckley blew into the sunny climes of Southern California in hope of making the Hollywood big-time, it was the world of music and musicians that he immediately inhabited.

It was fortunate that the L.A. jazz scene had blossomed to the point that it had: Buckley might have found himself flat on his face if not for the support system that the clubs provided. Economically or culturally, he couldn't have picked a worse time to make the move. Not only were the big studios struggling to compete with the meteoric rise of television (based back in New York), but the suffocating McCarthyist environment also discouraged movie execs from taking a chance on a man of Buckley's ilk and reputation.

As a result, Buckley had to scramble to make ends meet. At one point he moved his family to a hovel off Hyperion in the Silver Lake area of Los Angeles that he christened the "Crackerbox Palace."

Lady Elizabeth Buckley

He played this bravado character but inside was a sweet, very sensitive person who really didn't know how great an artist he was. I'll never forget when he invited Greer Garson to the Crackerbox Palace. It was a ramshackle place; she walked up all those rickety stairs—and I mean they were rickety—and she sat with us and had coffee and doughnuts, and she cried when Lord Buckley did "The Nazz" for her.

George Greif

Some years later I was at a dinner party for George Harrison. Somebody mentioned to George that I was Buckley's manager. We left the table, went up to my room and never went back. We stayed up and talked about Buckley all night. He even did some Buckley routines for me. I told him about when Buckley and his family were living in L.A. at a place he called the "Crackerbox Palace."

His whole life was desperate times. They were living hand-to-mouth there at the Crackerbox Palace. I wouldn't say it was abject poverty. That's where he got the name for Crackerbox Palace, because he could make a palace from nothing. It was a little house that looked like a crackerbox. Something about the story must have struck George.

George Harrison

Beatle emeritus George Harrison is such a huge Lord Buckley admirer that he even wrote a song, "Crackerbox Palace," dedicated to His Lordship. The following explanation of the song was given in an interview with Timothy White and appeared in an edited form in George's autobiography, I, Me, Mine.

Things serious and comical are like night and day. In a complete day you have the day and the night. You have both. You have black and white. So, therefore, in order to be comical you have to be serious and you have to be serious to be comical. You can't have one without the other. You can't have hot without cold because how do you measure hot if there's no cold to measure it by in relation? That is part of the dualities of the physical world. We have day/night, black/white, up/down, yes/no, yin/yang, good/bad, and that's it.

The third verse of "Crackerbox Palace" says: "Sometimes are good, sometimes are bad, that's all a part of life. And standing in between them all I met a Mr. Greif."

Now, Mr. Greif isn't just a clever rhyme with *life* as most people would think. There is a real person, and I met him in Southern France. He was talking to me, and the way he was talking really struck me. So I told him, "I don't know if this is an insult or not, but you remind me of Lord Buckley. He's my favorite comedian." He's dead now, but he was one of the first real hip comics. And the guy nearly fell over. He said, "Hey, I managed him for eighteen years!"

So we were talking about Lord Buckley, and Mr. Greif said he lived in a little shack, which he called Crackerbox Palace. I loved the way "Crackerbox Palace" sounded. I loved the whole idea of it, so I wrote a song and turned it from that shack into a phrase for the physical world. The world is very serious and at times such a very sad place. But at the same time, it's such a joke. It's *all* Crackerbox Palace.

As Harrison sings in the chorus: "I welcome you to Crackerbox Palace/Was not expecting you/Let's rap and tap at Crackerbox Palace/Know that the Lord is well and inside of you."

Except for a bit part in *We're Not Married*, the 20th Century–Fox romp starring Marilyn Monroe, Ginger Rogers, and Fred Allen in 1952, and a walk-on in Stanley Kubrick's *Spartacus* seven years later, Buckley's film career never did pan out. However, California proved to be the perfect locale for the free-spirited performer to fully forge his improvisational genius and mesmerizing stage presence.

Larry Storch

Typically, a Lord Buckley entrance featured the emcee introducing him with, "And now . . . Lord Buckley!"

From behind the curtain on stage right a perfect smoke ring billowed forth . . . but no Lord Buckley.

The emcee would again announce, "And now, ladies and gentlemen, here he is . . . Lord Buckley!"

Again, a perfect smoke ring billowed across the stage.

Once more, the emcee would intone, "And now, ladies and gentlemen, here he is, the one and only . . . Lord Buckley!"

Finally, Buckley would saunter out from the wings drawing sleekly on his cigarette to center stage where, in his best Claude Rains voice, he would say, "I'll bet you're all just dying for a smoke."

Buoyed by his growing reputation and sympathetic circle of admirers and acolytes, Buckley lit out on the jazz scene with messianic fervor. But despite the full flowering of his repertoire and performance skills, Buckley continued to be regarded as an entertainment curiosity and was primarily relegated to appearing in the gritty world of jazz clubs and strip joints—the "toilets" as Lenny Bruce often and accurately described them.

One simpatico came in the form of Jim Dickson, a young man with no experience in the record business who met Buckley by chance. As was Lord Buckley's custom, he immediately launched into a performance of "The Nazz" for Dickson, who was so moved that he immediately set out to introduce this man and his work to the universe at large. Dickson promptly rented a recording studio, hired a backup band, pushed the record button, and let Buckley wail.

The results were two albums released on Dickson's Vaya record label: *Euphoria* and *Euphoria Volume II*. These LPs were, along with the records of Spike Jones, arguably the first "concept" albums in modern popular culture, combining a unique artist with his one-of-a-kind-material—form and content deftly mixed and indistinguishable from each other. Even the title itself, *Euphoria,* is an immediate clue that some altered state of affairs is afoot, and the album jackets, with their quirky art and off-the-wall liner notes, give the impression of a handmade homebrew. *Vaya,* by the way, is a Sanskrit word meaning "life."

Visually, the designs of the album covers still stand out as striking and evocative period pieces of hipster folk art. Conceived by an artist identified only as "Andi," they feature a line drawing of a large-nosed man attired in a dinner jacket, a toga, a gladiator's helmet, and Roman Beatnik sandals while holding a dagger in one hand and a raised goblet in the other. The entire cover is geometrically segmented by oddly shaped blocks of red, black, and white (and green, black, and white on the sophomore affair). And as if to emphasize the royal nature of the outing, a king's crown is prominently displayed between the album title and the artist's name.

Jim Dickson

Jim Dickson launched his legendary career in the music industry with Lord Buckley. Dickson, the future manager of the revolutionary folk-rolk band The Byrds, founded Vaya Records in the early 1950s and produced two Lord Buckley albums that contained some of His Lordship's most influential grooves, including "The Nazz," "Jonah and the Whale," and "The Hip Gahn."

You could say that Lord Buckley put me in the record business.

I went over to meet him and he was living in a big place at Lake Malibu and when we took a walk out on the property he recited "The Nazz" to me, among other things. It was a minute or two before I had any idea of what he was even talking about.

So I looked in the Yellow Pages under "Recording," little knowing that all these years later I'd still be surviving based on the record industry. I didn't know what I was doing but I saw a place, C. P. MacGregor, in the Yellow Pages that had been in business twenty-five years. So I went down and talked to a guy named Jones who later became the head of the custom department at Capitol Records. He didn't have anything to do that afternoon so he explained the record business to me, which was the last straight answer anybody in the business ever gave me.

That was the beginning of Vaya Records.

After we recorded Buckley's first disc, I went to Music City, which was the largest retailer in town, and asked them who should distribute it. The guy there told me about a company that was currently distributing Miles Davis, Bo Diddley and people like that. And, as a strategy, that worked. I went down to meet with them and told them that their best customer had recommended them so they took us on. And from then on, we told everybody to go to Music City to buy the records and we started a small flow of the records going out.

Bit by bit people began to discover the record. There was a guy in New York named Mort Fega who played it on the radio and we sold a couple of thousand in New York over the next couple of years to Alpha distributors. And it went like that.

The record would go through cycles of popularity. Frank Sinatra discovered it and he knew Buckley and he gave them as Christmas gifts the following year. Sammy Davis Jr. gave them as Christmas gifts. Sammy Davis Jr. even used some of Buckley's material on occasion. They would find circles, you know. You'd get an order for three from Omaha, Nebraska, and then there'd be twelve orders and then twenty-four and then you wouldn't hear from Omaha again. Omaha would be saturated with thirty or forty records. It just went on like that for years and years.

When the first record came out the retailers didn't know where to put it in the store because there were no comedy records back then. The only spoken-word thing back then were things like "No Man Is an Island" by Orson Welles, Shakespearean material by John Carradine or something like that. There was no arena for Buckley. Sometimes the stores would file him with Tom Leherer and sometimes they'd file him under jazz.

What notoriety *Euphoria* and other Buckley releases garnered over the years was probably due to the misplaced notion of their irreverence. His albums often shared the reputation of his old friend Redd Foxx, whose raunchy "party records" were a rage in the mid- to late 1950s. Over two dozen "adults-only" Foxx discs were released on the small Dooto label and rarely found their way into white record stores. Gradually developing a crossover following, Redd also peppered his monologues with salty racial remarks: "It's not true that all Negroes carry knives—my uncle carried an ice pick for forty-five years."

Both Vaya albums (released variously as ten- and twelve-inch LPs—some on red vinyl) contained the following artist's biography printed on the back cover.

ABOUT RICHARD BUCKLEY Lord Buckley, as he is known by the entertainment world and his intimate friends, is more a way of life than just a personality. It has always been his philosophy that all people are in reality royalty; that is to say that they are truly Lords and Ladies, Dukes and Duchesses, Prince and Princess; and if each were to treat the other with the niceties and courtesies afforded members of a Royal Court, the world would be a better place in which to live. This philosophy is carried out in all he does in his professional and personal life.

Lord Richard Buckley, a philosophical humorist, has been associated with almost every phase of the theatrical world. He has appeared in the famous niteries and theatres across the continent including: the *Riviera, Roxy, Latin Quarter, Palace,* and *Strand* in New York; the *Oriental, Chez Paree,* and *Ball of Fire* in Chicago; the *Riverside Hotel,* Reno; *Chase Hotel,* St. Louis;

Chi Chi, Palm Springs; *El Rancho Vegas,* Las Vegas; *The Crescendo,* Hollywood, and innumerable clubs and theatres of varied sizes throughout the country. He has been seen in several movies, the last entitled *We're Not Married,* and his TV appearances are highlighted by his memorable performances on Ed Sullivan's *Toast of the Town* and *The Milton Berle Show.*

Lord Buckley, in his distaste for the usual stereotyped projection of humor, has gone far afield in search of humor with beauty, depth, and perception. We feel he has found it and on this record delivers it with great love and respect for the people about whom he paints his fascinating word pictures.

The rich color of dialects of the many groups of people in the world has long interested Lord Buckley, and has aided him in depicting a multitude of wonderful characters. This, his first recording effort, is done in the dialect and language of the modern hipsters. The intricate, lingual colloquialisms provide an interesting and gratifying challenge to the listener.

The *Euphoria* albums also included mini-descriptions of each piece written by Buckley and his Royal Court. Of "The Nazz," the liner notes say: "In reality this is the story of the Nazarene, an interpretation, by Richard Buckley, of the events in the life of Christ leading to each of the three miracles, starting with the selection of the twelve disciples and embracing the miracle of the healing of the cripple, Christ walking on the water, and the feeding of the multitudes."

While *Euphoria* was recorded in 1951 in a studio rented by Dickson, *Euphoria Vol. II* was done on the cheap in Mel Welles's living room in 1954.

Mel Welles

Euphoria II was not recorded in my living room because we intended to come out with an album. We just wanted to record all his material in case and we didn't have money for a studio. So we make shifted the whole thing.

Then we discovered that we had all these accolades from people like Henry Miller and so then we decided to come out with another album.

We did it in three nights. When he finished one session, we would listen to the results and do it all over again the next night.

The meat of these two efforts were combined on *The Best of Lord Buckley* on the Crestview and Elektra record labels in 1963 and 1969, respectively, and on *His Royal Hipness, Lord Buckley,* a Discovery Records CD released in 1992.

These repackagings, particularly the pressing by Elektra, were most responsible for keeping Buckley's legacy alive and rekindled interest in his work from the late 1960s through the mid-1970s, when it was not unusual to encounter the disc in the college dorm room of the cat with the good jazz collection or in the den of a friend's progressive parents.

The Elektra repackaging includes psychedelic album art at its purest, featuring a 1960 Jim Marshall photo of Buckley in midgrowl with a wild collage spewing forth comic-book-style from his mouth. Some of the peculiar iconography includes knights in armor slaying dragons, seashells, autumn leaves, and mushrooms. On the backside of the cover is a photo of Charles De Gaulle shot from the rear (looking very much like Buckley) at the ocean's edge, "digging infinity." From that abyss in front of him, Christ is resurrecting comic-book-style, with two oversized joints in each hand. The artwork is every bit the period piece of its predecessors, recalling the sensibility of the original Vayas.

The Elektra cover was created by writer Eve Babitz, then a young freelance artist who became a Buckley admirer as a teenager in the mid-1950s after her father had taken her to see His Lordship perform at a Hollywood movie theater between screenings of the afternoon's fare.

Looking at the combined Vaya output (many reportedly completed in a remarkable *one* take), we see an artist covering the full gamut of his expressive powers with loose ease and soulful passion.

Lord Buckley

When you start to fool with these classics, you have the tremulous stature of an amateur architect moving in the Taj Mahal. "Let me see now . . . must be something I can do here." So it's really dangerous work to begin with.

A new version of "The Nazz" led off the set. This is probably best known version of the hip gospel and finds Buckley leading a studio band in a gospel-inspired R&B jazz romp through "When the Saints Come Marching In" at key junctures in the performance—much as he would sometimes do live. This was edited for space purposes in later releases so that the musical accompaniment appeared only as a send-up addendum at the conclusion of the piece.

While the Vaya and subsequent re-releases of the material listed the piece on its jacket covers as "The Nazz" with two *Z*s, the 1959 World Pacific release spelled it "The Naz" with one *Z*, leading to confusion as to the correct spelling. Because it originally appeared with two *Z*s and because of its natural jazz alliterative qualities, "The Nazz" is the preferred usage.

Another Bible study from the *Euphoria* sessions also quite popular with the bohemian set of the 1950s (and subsequent generations of potheads) is Buckley's treatment of "Jonah and the Whale." Here we have another item that crosses into the several areas of Buckley's creative concerns. Primarily it is classical Buckley in which he reshapes a venerable tale. But it is also one of his many animal stories and contains autobiographical experience. Buckley, a renowned champion of marijuana, takes a not-too-subtle political stand with the first pro-cannabis stand-up routine; no doubt he was among the first twentieth-century recording artists to align spiritual awareness with pot smoking. Jonah, after all, smokes "the strange green vine" he had gathered earlier in his adventure to help him regain his composure inside the whale's belly and devise a means of escape.

More important, Buckley's ability to stylistically mimic and sincerely evoke the spirit of the stump preacher is what makes "Jonah" a keeper.

Robin Williams

The style and the roots of his style go back. I've been listening to gospel music recently and it strikes me that it goes back to the preachers, the old black preachers of the South. He softened it up. It's got that gospel preaching taken in jazz and mellowed through the smoke of a club. He's preaching still, but it's gentle and lyrical. He took the edges off and he really got to people. He was "testifying" like the old black preachers who didn't necessarily read from the Bible but, nonetheless, told the story.

Lord Buckley was hip enough to know that you can't preach *at* people but to get under the radar to use it in his own way. That's why he developed the style, the language, using those tools to preach "in the tongue" so people could be more accessible to it without him going, "Don't you *see* the beauty of it all?"

He just kind of let it slide in. And people, before they knew it, were laughing. But, still, he was getting through.

That Buckley was aware of the linguistic lineage of his vocation and aligned himself with the tradition's thematic and stylistic cornerstones should come as no surprise, surrounded as he was by the learned musical greats whose tradition sprang directly out of the black church and antebellum America. Certainly they sensitized him to the idea that the black preacher is *the* master storyteller in African American culture.

The black stump preacher's verbal artistry covers African American communal life like Brer Rabbit did the brier patch. And like Brer Rabbit, their trickster hero, African Americans have instinctively sought protection and reassurance from a hostile world and an uncertain life in the myriad stories told by their ministers. The black preacher generally employs three types of narrative style: personal narrative, biblical stories, and jokes.

In his personal narrative the black preacher fashions stories from his own life. In many ways these stories are a variant of the testimonies that members of his flock give in the traditional Wednesday-night payer meeting—definitively portrayed in the jazz idiom by Charles Mingus with his intense postbop composition "Wednesday Night Prayer Meeting." Duke Ellington's "Sacred Concerts" of the 1960s are probably worth a mention here, too, as they served as the maestro's none-too-subtle and beautifully rendered expression of his spiritual leanings as his final days approached. And let's not forget Duke's excruciatingly hip in-concert introductions to just about all of his music.

Dr. Martin Luther King Jr. was a skillful sower of the narrative seed planted by the stump preachers of yore. And how much in common do Buckley's oratorical peaks share with King's "I Had A Dream" speech or just about anything from the lips of Adam Clayton Powell Jr.?

Just as lawyers must learn the legal statutes of the states in which they practice, so, too, must the black preacher master the Bible "from Genesis to Revelation." The more familiar they become with the Word, the better able they are to improvise, weaving a biblical character, familiar verse, and/or story into their sermons. The late Reverend C. L. Franklin, the father of soul singer Aretha Franklin, was known as a master teller of these stories whose recordings continue to be sold. Even today a scan of the Sunday-morning AM radio dial will reveal any number of black preachers vigorously "testifying" in their home churches.

In 1927 the Reverend C. F. Weems of Chicago was captured on recording in mid-incantation and though, like Buckley, the full power and high dudgeon of his presentation, complete with supportive chatter from the pews, does not come off on the printed page, a quick read of the following excerpt from a sermon on "Jonah and the Whale" makes it difficult to deny its majesty or the probable influence this caste of spoken-word practitioners had on Lord Buckley:

> Dear Sisters and Brothers! Our text is found today in the Book of Jonah! In the First Chapter and the Seventeenth Verse. And reads like this:
>
> Now the Lord hath prepared a great fish to swallow up Jonah. And Jonah was in the belly of the fish for three days and three nights. Our subject is Jonah in the belly of the Whale. I tried to tell you how Brother Jonah got in the belly of the Whale.
>
> The Lord had told Brother Jonah to go to Niniveh and cry against that wicked city! Brother Jonah, like many preachers today, wasn't no beggared. So he went down to Jabot and got a ship goin' to Kashas. And while he was on that ship the Lord mooooved upon the weary Jonah!
>
> And the sea got tempestuous. And the seamen got afraid. And they cast lots to see what was the matter. So they found out that Brother Jonah was in troooouble! So Brother Jonah was down in the bottom of the ship. They went down there and got Brother Jonah out and made him cry unto his God!
>
> Brother Jonah told them that the thought was in him. And he told them to cast him overboard. And the Lord had prepared a great fish. And they cast him over . . .

Lord Buckley

Well see, I've been interested in doing these hipsemantics for quite some time. Primarily I became interested in them because of the tremendous advantage you have with the youth of the nation. The hip talk seems to be more or less their language. And, in translating the great classics of our time, I thought it would be a splendid way to bring the beautiful sounds, written sounds, to their attention, you see.

Like the stump preachers of yore, Buckley begins his religious fantasy of Jonah and the whale with an invocation: "The Great Lord was sitting in his rosy rockin' chair one hallelujah morning and he looked down and observed by a great body of water, a little mortal about five feet tall. And the Lord dug the mortal and he called for Gabe to put down his horn and swing with the book. And the Lord flipped the pages: A B C D E F G H I *J*. And it was Jonah getting his kicks on the beach."

After making contact with Jonah, God wails out his love for Jonah first by singing ("I dig you Jonah! I dig you Jonah! I dig you Jonah, 'cause Jonah is the Lord's sweeeeet boy!") and then by sending him on a mission across the Red Sea to "put the message on the Israelites" because "they're squarin' up over there."

Before Jonah departs, however, he visits a "great cathedral-like group of trees lifting their glorious arms up to Heaven in supplication of the master!" Down at the bottom of these giant sequoias Jonah saw growing "a strange green vine" beside which he sat, observed, rolled, sampled, and swung. Suitably fortified, he declares: "Man, where is that fool pool the Lord want me to dig? Look out: here come Jonah! He ready as the day is long."

Diving into the ocean and "cutting a gigantic V through the breast of waves," Jonah swims until hit with fatigue ("Morpheus was goofin' on his eyebrows"), whereupon he falls asleep. After dozing for twelve hours and fifteen seconds, he awakens to see the whale, who refuses to take him seriously: ". . . man, every time I stick my nose out of this fool pool I sure see some *crazy* jazz . . . heh heh heh . . . but *this* is the *bendin' end*."

Jonah, though, refuses to be intimidated and suggests to the whale, "It's a big pool. You groove your way. I'll groove mine. I'll swoop the scene and dig you later."

But the whale knows a free lunch when he sees one: "Lookie here, a little old bit of nothing a million miles from no place. He going to hip me, the King of the Dip what the lick is? Say, I got a good mind to *gobble* you up."

Jonah finally outwears his welcome with one last belligerent parting shot: "Don't you do that Mr. Whale cause if you *do* I am goin' to knock you in your most *delicate gear*."

Next thing you know, Jonah is swallowed by the whale, thrown onto the great sea mammal's blubbery rugs, slippin' and slidin' from one side of the sea creature to the other: "He couldn't go out the front end and he afraid to go out the back end!"

Almost all of Buckley's classics contain an element of appeal or prayer, when our hero (be it The Nazz, The Gasser, Marc Antony, Hip Gahn, or Scrooge) falls down on his knees and makes a sincere connection with the Almighty. And Jonah is no different: "Loorrdd! . . . Loooorrrrrdddd!!! Can you dig me in this here fish?"

But not only does this Lord have a sense of humor when he tells Jonah, "I got you covered," he gives him some very useful advice—reminding him to reach into his watertight pocket for the strange cigarettes he got from the great tree "and courage will return to you."

If there is any doubt about the combustible Jonah burns inside the whale, one only has to listen to the joint-toking, lung-clenching pyrotechnics Buckley employs and the cool change in Jonah's postinhalation attitude to determine what the "strange green vine" could possibly be.

Eventually the whale senses something is amiss, the intoxicating fumes having their desired effect: "I thought I was off the Hiberdy Islands, here I is two minutes from the Panama Canal. This jazz *got* to *go!*"

But it is too late. As Jonah tells him, "I ain't on the outside no more, Mr. Whale. I'm *inside* now."

Commandeering the mammal's steering wheel, full-speed-ahead lever, et cetera, Jonah steers the leviathan into the shallow water, pushes the mammal's gigantic "sneezer-meter," and is blown out onto the "cool, grooovy sands of serenity."

Buckley puts a little self-styled Confucian aphorism on the end of the riff with this famous piece of whimsical philosophy: "If you get to it and cannot do it, there you jolly well are—phew phew—aren't you?"

Albert Goldman

Buckley's monologues invariably concerned religious themes, like the life of Jesus or the story of Jonah and the whale. Far from burlesquing these sacred subjects, he exalted them anew by pouring into them all the enthusiasm and ebullience of his own extravagant temperament.

Like the old-time stump preachers and evangelists, Lord Buckley was possessed by the Spirit as soon as he spoke the Word. His eyes flashed, his muscular body rocked, his mighty voice—an organ of operatic range and power—swooped and soared like a drunken American eagle. When the theme really exercised him, as in his narrative of the miracles of Christ, he reached Shakespearean heights of eloquence and passion.

In "Jonah and the Whale," His Lordship associates sacred legend with dope. Thanks to the magic of marijuana, like Popeye's spinach, the hero defeats the mythic beast and escapes.

David Amram

Buckley's story "The Nazz" could be taught as a new parable of Christianity. Lord Buckley related to a lot of Jewish people like myself with his Old Testament stories like "Jonah and the Whale," which I tell my own children as a way of introducing them to the Bible (although I leave out the part about Jonah smoking pot inside the whale belly in my version). But the story itself is one of the great children's stories the way that Lord Buckley told it.

Regardless of its presentation in performance, it is quite astounding to realize that Buckley was thinly cloaking such risqué sentiments regarding what was then a very illegal substance nearly half a century ago. And he lived as dangerously as he spoke.

Tubby Boots

I saw him walk right up to a cop while smoking a joint of marijuana. "Officer," he said, "I want to report a dope addict. That gentleman," he'd whisper, gesturing to an innocent passerby. "Be very careful, he's watching us." As he warned him, Buckley drew a drag on his smoke and blew it in the lawman's face.

One time when I was very young we went out to lunch and he was explaining to me about pot. He was only educating—he never tried to turn me on. I would ask questions. He was discussing drugs with me because I asked him. You know how kids are: when you admire somebody you ask questions. He said he had trouble with alcohol and he told me never to drink.

Mel Welles

He was an alcoholic for about twenty years but I never knew him to go to an AA meeting because, by the time I met him in Hollywood, he had converted from liquor to pot. He was like an evangelist where marijuana was concerned. He thought it was the panacea for everything but he didn't believe in altering the mind with drugs.

Understand that Buckley was no dunce. He was a well-read person and, prior to his being drowned in alcohol, he was someone who was sensitive to what was going on in the world as well. I mean this in a political sense, a sociological sense and in a demographical sense. In fact, his alcoholism, in my opinion, was a direct result of the disillusionment he felt at how people stripped the dignity of their fellow man.

Les Thompson

Les Thompson's unique approach to his unique ax, the harmonica, has landed him in the grooves of recordings by the likes of Dexter Gordon and Al Jarreau as well as his own release, Mouth Organ Madness.

Lord Buckley smoked a lot of grass, I'll tell you that. I don't know that he saw it as a cure for society's ills, he just liked to stay loaded. But I never saw him drink. I was a pretty good drinker myself and he always came up to me and said, "Prince Les, don't touch that shit. Forget that."

As a matter of fact, he gave speeches at some AA meetings. I never went to them but he attended them.

Adam Keefe

As far as drugs went, whatever you got he took. He just seemed to have an enormous appetite for everything: food, drugs or drink. Aside from alcohol it was always pot and mescaline as far as I knew—nonaddictive psychotropic drugs. But I wouldn't be surprised at all if he had taken heroin or any of the hard stuff. You know, we were always smoking pot when we went up to see him. He always had pot around and everybody would sit around smoking it.

Pud Brown

In Chicago during the 1940s I worked with Lawrence Welk and Jimmy Dorsey. That's where I first met Dick Buckley. He came up on the stage and we're sitting there. It was about a twelve-piece band, a big band in a great big nightclub, one of the finest in town. And he appeared on the show. He came out on the stage and he turned around and he looked at the band and he turned around back to the audience and said, "I can't put a show on like this. I'm gonna take 'em downstairs and get 'em all high and we're gonna come back up here and do a show for all of you."

And we went downstairs and he got us all high on pot and we went back upstairs and did the show.

Ann Brooks

Ann Brooks (aka "Lady Bunny"/"Peter Pan") was one of the last members inducted into the Royal Court by Lord Buckley and claimed to be the last person to see him alive. Her reminiscences were drawn from a lengthy 1973 conversation taped with Del Close and musician Ray Watkins in Chicago.

He was frightened of hard drugs. Once he wasn't feeling too good and I went to get him some paregoric. I told him to take a tablespoon and he wouldn't go near the bottle.

Orson Bean

Wisecracking his way into millions of American living rooms as a panelist on TV's popular quiz show To Tell the Truth *in the 1960s and 1970s, Orson Bean is a man of many hats. Stand-up comic, actor, voice-over artist, television personality, and educator, Bean became acquainted with Lord Buckley in the late 1940s.*

I was breaking into the business in Boston as a comedy-magician to no discernible response and working in places like the Latin Quarter in Fall River and the Trocadero in Lawrence, Massachusetts.

I had just gotten out of the army so I guess I was around twenty years old. I was living in a theatrical boardinghouse in Boston even though I came from Cambridge, Mass. Every night we would go to a place called Dave's Delicatessen. "We" being the young performers who were lucky enough to be working. Even if we weren't working, we would stay up late and act as if we had been working and show up to have a corned beef sandwich.

Word spread around town that Lord Buckley was playing somewhere—no doubt at one of the slightly better places than where I was working.

One night that week, Lord Buckley came swaggering into Dave's Delicatessen and, of course, we recognized him and all clustered around. In retrospect, I believe he had kind of assumed the persona of George Saunders, the movie star. He had an elegance that kept the world at a safe distance. At the same time he was quite warm and he readily accepted the adulation that the young comedians and performers were offering him.

After a while he said, "Let's get out of here," and he took us on this tour of the city around midnight on a Friday or Saturday night, walking around Boston.

The first thing I remember him doing is taking a leak on the tire of a parked car. He then hopped up on the hood of the car he had pissed on and gave a great speech about capitalism, which was why he said he had pissed on the tire. A little crowd gathered around him and laughed at his stuff and loved him and he kind of led us like the Pied Piper.

Now there were maybe nine or ten people and he led us over to the Hayes-Bickford Cafeteria, which was the only thing that was open late, and he held court at a large table. He went on ruminating about life. He talked about his work, "The Nazz," and just about everything and we fell in love with him.

After a while most of the people left and he took the little group of maybe two or three of us young comedians back to where he was staying at the Touraine Hotel, which meant that he was making at least $250 a week, so that made him a big star in our eyes.

The Touraine Hotel had a kind of faded grandeur, but it had once been one of the finest hotels in Boston, probably around 1905. He took us up to his room and he rolled an enormous marijuana cigarette. I had heard of marijuana but never seen it and here was this cigar-sized stogie being passed around. I smoked it and it remains in my experience the finest pot I've ever smoked. I haven't smoked pot in years now but I remember that night with fondness: walking down the carpeted corridors of the Touraine Hotel and feeling I was about a foot off the floor . . . it was quite wonderful.

Eldon Setterholm

Eldon Setterholm was a young bohemian working in the film industry when he came under Lord Buckley's spell in the mid-1950s. He became a lifelong member-in-good-standing of the Royal Court as the Earl of Eldon and, on occasion, acted as Buckley's de facto agent. Eldon's reminiscences first appeared in a 1987 edition of Irregular Quarterly *magazine.*

He smoked Pall Malls while he did his act. He smoked on stage all the time. He'd be lighting and smoking while he did his thing.

He was the only guy I know who when O'Grady, the Hollywood vice fuzz, was trying to nail him when he was playing at Jazz City on Hollywood Boulevard, Buckley would put a joint under his foreskin. Then he'd go in the head and smoke it before he went on stage, because he liked to be stoned when he worked.

The Hollywood vice were tryin' to get on Buckley because he was upfront about smokin' it. But you know, guys like Sinatra were knowledgeable about pot and knew that most of the boys in the band liked it. And whether or not they do, they're not going to cop out. "Thou Shalt Not Cop Out!"—Buckley used to say that was the Eleventh Commandment. But *he* copped out all the time.

Lady Buckley was also reportedly instrumental in encouraging her husband to seek help for his long-standing drinking problem. She challenged him to do something about it in the same way she had previously done with his material, paving the way for his involvement in Alcoholics Anonymous.

Lady Elizabeth Buckley

I used to be scared out of my wits in the early years when he was drinking. He was so brilliant when he was drinking. He was so vital a person. He was like a cartoon—he *emanated.* We used to be out in public sometimes and you never knew what he was gong to do next. I'd just act like everything was normal.

He used to break my heart. But I could control him when he needed it. We used to have wonderful royal battles. I wouldn't give an inch.

We were always in a hurry. With Lord Buckley you traveled very fast. Things were done very quick.

If it hadn't been for the children I don't think I could have held on.

George Greif

When he was drinking he was in bad shape. But he would go for long periods without drinking. He loved to smoke pot and he smoked a lot of it. I saw him get a light on a joint from a cop and walk into Birdland smoking it. Charlie Ventura's band was playing and when Buckley came in puffing the whole place cleared out. In those days you'd go to jail for years if you got in trouble with pot.

When he was cruel he was *cruel,* but it was just the alcohol that would bring that on. I never really saw him act that way when he was sober. I never saw him drink that much. He was always advising me on how to live a clean, good life even though he didn't necessarily live one himself.

Robin Williams

His hard life probably fueled his darker pieces.

I've seen that with other comics. They change. The brain has a chemical reaction and they just go "Boom!" Their personality just switches. It's "Sybil de Sade." People who seem so gentle, all of a sudden the anger that fuels everything else just comes out.

Tubby Boots

He told me that he just woke up one morning and realized he had to stop drinking. He said, "I did it myself. I went to the meetings and straightened myself out. Didn't have to go that long because after a few tight spots of standing there and confessing, I realized how foolish I was."

He became a crusader against alcohol. He'd stop drinkers on the street and tell them, "Repent, baby, because I did it." He was mortally against alcohol afterwards because he saw how beautiful his life had become without it.

Buckley always did have a reputation for unreliability. This was based partially on his bingeing, as he demonstrated a remarkable propensity to shoot himself in the foot in acts of drunken self-sabotage that perennially held his career in check just as it seemed it was about to take off once more. But the cure was always only partially successful. On an arcane note, one of Buckley's reported comrades at the AA meetings he attended in California was none other than the state's chief executive, Governor Edmund Brown.

Lord Buckley

AA members are all kinds, sizes and designs. And everyone is an ex-flip—just one double shot away from takin' over the city.

Harry "The Hipster" Gibson

Late in the 1940s, General Artists booked me into the Five O'Clock Club in Miami Beach. While there I recorded several tapes with Lord Buckley. Later Buckley and I leased a club in a Beach hotel. He might have been one of the first members of Alcoholics Anonymous. Anyway, every once in a while, instead of doing his usual jazz-oriented act, he would give an AA sermon, telling the audience that booze is the tool of the devil and a destroyer of life and health. He was at one time a bad alcoholic. When Buckley drank booze, he just went completely out of his skull.

At the gigs, Buckley would all of a sudden get in the mood. He'd get up and he'd start into, "Why are you people drinkin' that vile devil's brew? Throw those drinks away, we don't want to see it!" He'd be out there ravin' away and I'm at the piano, I'm right in the back of him: "Yeah, get rid of that booze! Let's smoke some dope here, man! We don't need no booze!" Boom—I'd start lightin' up, take those big bottle of pills and I'd go around: "You don't need any booze! Here man, we don't want your money!" I'd be givin' out these bottles of bennies!

When the customers, who came in to be entertained while they drank, realized he really meant it, they walked out on him. Every time His Lordship emptied the joint that way, we would laugh hysterically.

Mel Welles

Buckley could sit on stage in a chair, not move and get you excited in his storytelling which, at the Club Renaissance in Hollywood, he used to do quite often because he was so stoned he *couldn't* stand up.

He used to come on to the stage erect and then he would sit thronelike in a chair and still excite hundreds of people with his storytelling because of his dynamics and his *love* for the subject he was talking of, the idiom that he was using and for the people who created the idiom: the musician, the black man, the hipster, the carney. So that combination of factors created a very powerful storyteller.

With bits like "Jonah," Lord Buckley was staking his claim as one of the premier World Beat storytellers, and his reliance upon the venerable oeuvre of the animal story, perhaps the most widespread of all folktale genres, is a strong testament to this.

To be sure, the animal story accounts, in some fashion, for more than a dozen of Buckley's seventy-odd surviving routines.

Lord Buckley

Dogs are people. Fish are people. Parakeets are people. Hummingbirds are people. "Never kick a dead dog" was the end bouquet of the patience of a great man who wanted to teach somebody the lesson to never kick *any* dog because dogs are people.

Les Thompson

He had a great friend in Santa Monica named Jay Kelleher who raised Redlington terriers. When he wasn't living in town but visiting, Kelleher would put him up and help him. As a matter of fact he gave Lord Buckley two of the Redlington terriers when Buckley was driving across the country. They were pups. Something happened—I don't know what the hell—but anyway he came back and Jay asked him how the dogs were and he said, "They got to be a pain in the ass so I threw the little beggars out the window."

Buckley's use of the animal tale is similar in many respects to the animal tales of all other lores. That is to say, they began as etiological stories that accrued meaning and resonance with the passage of time.

Along with "Jonah and the Whale," Buckley's fascination with animals receives wide treatment on *Euphoria Vol. II* as he interprets four *Aesop's Fables:* "The Dog and the Wolf," "The Mouse and the Lion," "The Grasshopper and the Ant," and "The Lion's Breath." Of this quartet of quirky minimalist gestures in hip, only "The Lion's Breath" stands up and roars. The piece is about an acid-breathed predator predictably dealing with other inhabitants of the jungle who have the bad sense to confirm his worst fears about his fetid exhalations. Like all good storytellers, Buckley never talks down to his audience and the Aesop material is no exception.

These animal stories were really compact allegories about human nature and the essence of people—always His Lordship's primary concern. "Jonah and the Whale" (both in the Bible and in the hipsemantic) is really about faith and man's constant battle with nature, while "The Lion's Breath" is a parable on how to deal with bullies.

Buckley had two young children at the time he made these recordings, and it is natural to assume that he wished to tailor his talents for their amusement.

Finally, the litany of animal stories associated with Lord Buckley seem to confirm a spiritual kinship with mammal, reptile, fish, and fowl.

Millie Vernon

Lord Buckley and Elizabeth were known characters. In the springtime he'd walk downtown to see all the agents. He wore this jungle hat and he walked with a cane. He'd say, "Elizabeth, dress the props!" which were the two kids, Laurie and Richie, who were five or six years old. She'd dress them up and he'd go down to see the agents with the kids.

Dick Zalud

He told a story about the time he saw an ad in a San Francisco paper from a man who was selling a baby lion. And Buckley went out to see this baby lion. The lion's name was "Baby" and Buckley would describe that this lion was so lovable and tame that it would lick you. His description of the whole scene was riveting. The lion licked his cheek and he said it felt like a piece of wet sandpaper. Buckley asked the owner if he could hold Baby's leash and the next thing he knew Baby was dragging him around the place.

When he told the story he would go through every room screaming, "Whoa Baby! Whoooaahh Baaabyy!" as he ran up the stairs and through all the rooms holding an imaginary leash. "Whoa Baby! Whooahh Baabyy! You're nice, Baby! Whooooahhh Baabyy! Whoooooooaahhhh Baaayyybbbyy!"

Dr. Oscar Janiger

I remember once he told a story about coming home in the early dawn in the bitter cold snow-covered Chicago morning. He was walking through the park dressed in his top hat and customary tails when he saw a squirrel. That began a dialogue between him and this squirrel that was absolutely astonishing. His objective was to get the squirrel under his top hat and bring him home. And finally, after a series of devices and marvelous repartee between him and the squirrel, he managed to get the hat on top of the squirrel. He reached under the hat to get at the squirrel and the squirrel just sank his teeth into his arm. He finally got the squirrel to his house and that began another sequence of the squirrel leaping around his apartment and tearing the drapes. This went on and on. The man was just plugged in.

Lady Elizabeth Buckley

Going shopping was like an expedition. The greengrocer, the butcher, everybody would wait for Lord Buckley to come in with his invisible dog. There was a restaurant in the West Forties just off Broadway where His Lordship would dine when he played the Palace or the Loew's State. And he'd go in and he would bark like he had a dog under the table. And all the waiters would smile and the people would look over wondering where the dog was. He made things fun in that way. It was really sweet and it brightened up everyone's day wherever he was. If you didn't know him well, you couldn't tell if he was rehearsing a bit of business or if he was creating it on the spot. He was always creating material. He was very serious about his work; he'd polish a piece until he was satisfied with it.

Buddy Jones

In the late 1940s we were both living in New York City. One time we were down in the Central Park Zoo. We'd go down there to smoke a joint of pot. The zoo was a good place because it was out in the open. We were getting high once around feeding time and there was a big crowd around a lion who was roaring and making a lot of noise.

After a few minutes of this all of a sudden I hear another roar behind me. I turn around and Dick Buckley is down on his hands and knees roaring. The people turned away from the lion to see this idiot that's down on his hands and knees impersonating a lion.

And so the lion would start roaring again and the people would turn around to watch the lion and then Dick would start throwing up dirt and acting like a lion until they turned back around to look at him until the lion started roaring again. Well, this went on for several minutes until he had *all* the attention and stole the crowd from the lion over to himself. If there was a crowd he wasn't going to take second billing.

Buckley infuses several pieces from the Vaya dates with political subtexts of varying subtleties. Most obvious among these is his take on Abraham Lincoln's crowning rhetorical glory, "The Gettysburg Address"—recorded for, but not appearing on the original Vaya vinyls. Buckley demonstrates his sincere but off-center appreciation for the Emancipation Proclamation.

Mel Welles

Nobody influenced him. No performer anyway. Abe Lincoln influenced him. Black musicians influenced him. I know of nobody with a keener perception and love for the black experience than him and I mean that sincerely. I know of nobody, black or white, that had a greater love for the black experience in its entirety, in its ugliness and in its beauty. And nobody understood the black amongst white people better than Dick Buckley.

The night that we wrote "Gettysburg Address," Benny Carter was over with a little combo and played "John Brown's Body" in the background. And I helped write most of the other stuff except that, at a certain point, he got so fluent with the idiom that he didn't need to write anything down. Like an instant translator at the United Nations, he could take any story and tell it in the hip and jazz idiom without any help.

Lord Buckley

Now there's different kind of cats, you see. Like this here cat sittin' over there, he probably a George Washington cat, you see, making it across the stream with the ice and stompin' soldiers and all that. And that cat over there he probably a Benny Franklin cat, he probably with Benny Franklin.

But myself, I'm a Lincoln cat. That's me. I dug sweet old swinging, non-stop, heavy-headed sweet Abe. Used to call him Lanky Linc. That's what they called him back in them days.

In what may be his cutest commencement of a hipsemantic translation, Buckley takes Lincoln's hallowed opening phrase ("Four score and seven years ago . . . ") and turns it into "Four big hits and seven licks ago" before launching into a spiel about how "our before daddies swung forth upon this sweet groovy land a swingin', jumpin', blowin', wailin' *new nation!*" Describing the war of the Union as "a king-sized main day civil drag," he wonders whether the United States "can stay with it *all the way*."

Acknowledging that his speech ("chop-beating session") is transpiring on the infamous battleground ("site of the worst jazz blown in the entire issue: Gettys-mother-boig"), he pays homage to the fallen from both the North and the South while trying to find a positive meaning for it all: ". . . so this jumpin' happy beat might blow *forever more*." With the horror of Gettysburg beginning to turn into a tragic memory ("digging it harder from afar"), Buckley reminds us to be humble ("we cannot take no wailin' bows"), vigilant ("we cannot mellow"), and ashamed ("we cannot put the stamp of the Nazz on this sweet sod"), because those who sacrificed their lives from both the Blue *and* the Grey ("the strong nonstop studs who both diggin' it and dug *under* it") did so in such a manner that defies comprehension ("we can hear it but . . . we can't touch it.").

Cognizant of the fact that foreign leaders viewed the Civil War with intense scrutiny (". . . the world cats will short dig"), he stresses the importance for the survivors ("us, the swingin'") to advance the cause of democracy and "pick up the dues of these fine studs who cut out here through to *Endsville*."

Arriving at the finale of the speech, Buckley orchestrates a fantastic verbal rave to crystallize his brand of patriotism with a powerful and dramatic flourish: "It is hipper for us to be signifying to the glorious gig that we can't miss with all these bulgin' eyes. That from these ace-stamped studs we double our love kick to that righteous ride for which these cats hard-sounded the last nth bong of the beat of their bell—that we here want it struck up straight, for *all* to dig that these departed studs shall not have split in vain. That this nation, under the great sweet swingin' Nazz, shall ring up a whopper of endless Mardi Gras and that the big law, of you straights by you studs and for your kitties, shall not be scratched from the big race! And that's why I'm a Lincoln cat."

Mel Welles

He considered "Gettysburg Address" to be his strongest piece. And everybody in the inner circle considered it to be his strongest piece.

The system of creation in his house was anecdotal and casual. All of the material was sort of open-ended: anybody could use it if they wanted. Nobody had the attitude of "That's mine!"

We were in the kitchen where we had been all night. Chuck Griffith and I were sitting at the table and Benny Carter had been there the night before. The thing took about eleven minutes to write. Buckley came out of the bathroom and I said, "Listen to this."

The only thing that I wrote for him was the "Gettysburg Address." The other things were not formal arrangements like where we sat down and composed. We would just start making up something and everybody there would put their two cents in. I was with him a lot—just he and I—so we were able to get a lot of stuff down.

"Jonah and the Whale," "The Gasser" and "Nero" were all done during that period. None of his work was done in a scholarly fashion. It was all done from recall and don't forget: we were all stoned at the time anyway.

He would lie in the bathtub with maybe fifteen people crowded in the bathroom and he would be on a pot trip. You can get some pretty absurd ideas when you're stoned and he would remember them later.

Something always disturbed me about Buckley historians. They talk about him as if he was an innovator and a creator of a lot of stuff. The fact is, other than a couple of pieces which he happened to make up as he went along, most of the hip stuff was written and created by other people which, when given to him, with his storytelling ability, allowed him to embellish upon it and make it his own.

The reason that, so far, nothing about Buckley has really been hugely successful is because basically—and I loved him deeply and still do—he was a loser not a winner. The idea that he was symbol of an era is fine but it really doesn't go very deep.

Underscoring his grasp of the primary source, a version of Buckley reciting Lincoln's authentic "Gettysburg Address" word for word was cut on the B-side of a rare 1956 single. This was released with a later recording of the hipsemantic translation and was released on the obscure Hip Records label, about which we will hear more later. Though a little stiff, the straight rendition (with the musical backing of a saccharine orchestral version of "The Battle Hymn of the Republic") augments the hip version nicely and indicates Buckley's familiarity with, connection with, and respect for Lincoln's original words, proving once and for all why he was "a Lincoln cat."

Buckley's hep translation of the most famous speech from Shakespeare's *Julius Caesar,* "Hipsters, Flipsters and Finger-Poppin' Daddies" (variously titled "Marc Antony's Funeral Oration," "Friends, Romans, Countrymen" or "Willie the Shake" in its different, officially released incarnations) is another quick but potent study of a revered monologue from classic literature and a fine introduction to the hipsemantic. It is also among his strongest.

Lord Buckley

This is a bouquet, m'Lords and m'Ladies, for your exquisite attention. We should like to do for you, in translation, some excerpts from William Shakespeare. We are going to do it in the hipsemantic which is the intimate social language of the

American Beauty Negro. Are you there? William Shakespeare—a dash of him in hip, in hip talk, ladies and gentlemen.

HIPSTERS, FLIPSTERS AND FINGER-POPPIN' DADDIES

Hipsters, Flipsters and Finger-Poppin' Daddies,
Knock me your lobes!
I came to lay Caesar out,
Not to hip you to him.
The bad jazz that a cat blows
Wails long after he's cut out.
The groovy is often stashed with their frames,
So don't put Caesar down.
The swinging Brutus hath laid a story on you
That Caesar was hungry for power.
If it was so it was a sad drag
And sadly hath this Caesar cat answered it
Here, with a pass from Brutus and the other brass,
For Brutus is worthy stud.
Yea, so are they all worthy studs,
Though their stallions never sleep.
I came to wail at Caesar's wake.
He was my buddy and he leveled with me.
Yet Brutus digs that he has eyes for power,
And Brutus is a solid cat.
It is true he hath returned with many freaks in chains,
And brought them home to Rome.
Yea, the looty was booty and hipped the treasury well.
Dost thou dig that this was Caesar's groove for the push
When the cats with the empty kicks hath copped out
Yea, Caesar hath copped out too and cried of a storm.
To be a world grabber, a stiffer riff must be blown.
Without bread a stud can't even rule an anthill.
Yet Brutus was swinging for the moon.
And yea, Brutus is a worthy stud.
And all you cats were gassed on the Lupercal,
When he came on like a king freak.
Three times I laid the kingly wig on him
And thrice did he put it down.
Was this the move of a greedy hipster?
Yet Brutus said he dug the lick,
And yes, a hipper cat hath never blown.
Some claim that Brutus' story was a gag
But I dug the story was solid.
I came here to blow, now stay cool while I blow.

You all dug him once because
You were hipped that he was solid.
How can you now come on so square
Now that he is tapped out of this world?
City Hall is flipped and swung to a drunken zoo,
And all you cats are goof to wig city.
Dig me hard, my ticker is in the coffin there with Caesar.
And Yea, I must stay cool 'til it flippeth back to me.

"Hipsters, Flipsters and Finger-Poppin' Daddies" is one of a handful of Buckley pieces to find life long after its initial pressing. Mark Murphy, a jazz vocalist with an international cult following, cut the bit on his 1989 Muse Records CD *Kerouac, Then and Now,* a musical homage to the Beats and their milieu. Retitling the piece as simply "Lord Buckley," Murphy picks up where Buckley left off, breathing new life into this paean of the hipsemantic with a cool jazz accompaniment.

Indeed, Buckley's work and legacy still evoke a lightning-rod reaction because of his hotly debated place as a stepping-stone between scat and rap.

Robin Williams

His Shakespearean bits are done in "hiptameter." It's almost like he was translating Shakespeare, Einstein and the Gospel into hip just to get to another group of people.

Scat is almost nonsensical in the sense of just that pure sound. Rap and poetry of rap are infused. And then there's Buckley.

It's preaching. It's signifying. It's rapping. It's nice marijuana rapping so that people kind of go: "Whoaaa . . ." It slips under. It gets in, doesn't smack you. That's one reason his work keeps coming back: it's in code, for time. People will go back to him and he'll keep coming back. He will always have that effect on people.

George Greif

Buckley was the first rapper. And his rapping, more than any of these rappers today who pick angry, bitter subjects, was really true satire. He took historical subjects and made them current. He made them into music.

Eric Bogosian

Actor, writer, and performance artist, Eric Bogosian's impact on the American underscape with such pieces as "Sex, Drugs and Rock 'n' Roll" will be felt for decades to come.

These days, the word *rap* means something specific, but as old as I am, I remember when *rapping* was a word the hippies stole from the hipsters. A kind of conscious ordering and steering of stream of consciousness. An attempt to take the very rational and ordered human mind and mouth and let those things get in touch with the (sur)real world.

James Taylor

It's hard to imagine a connection between Lord Buckley and the lilting-voiced folk-rock balladeer James Taylor, yet a strong one exists. Taylor has deftly incorporated Buckley phrases into several of his compositions over the years.

Buckley's approach has in common with rap that it was an oral verbal thing. But it was freer than rap and probably informed by a lot of different things. It is intellectual in that it refers to a cultural tradition. The cadence of it is a lot more open and freer. I think rap is great and exciting too but all these things get to marketplace and get ruined though some things shine through despite it.

Jon Hendricks

Some of my songs like "Gimme That Wine" or "Cloudburst" were rap. I made a rap record in 1957, *New York, New York*. That was pure rap but it was rap with a philosophy behind it. A lot of today's rap has no real philosophy behind it. It's mostly *against* something but it's not *for* anything.

Rap is the symbolic nadir of the decline of Western society. I'm a poet and I know where poetry comes from and it's not from your genitals and it's not from the sense of your own importance. It's from the spiritual force that's behind all life.

Steve Ben Israel

In the hip-hop community, kids would say: "Yo! Lord Buckley is representin' and blessin'."

You might ask what they mean by representin'. Telling the truth? Yeah . . . but something else. There's another element here . . . it's the soul. "Man that cat is *representin'!*"

If you're representin' out there, in life, then you're going to be representin' on the stage. What I've learned is that when you're working on a piece, between the idea and it becoming stardust is a very painful process. Sometimes you give up and you go back and you get it. But in the process of the craziness when you find that last line is what you go through to get that like a rock. Because if you really dig it, then people are going to really dig it. And I'm sure that Lord Buckley, being one of those personalities, was making sure every line was like Mozart. Every word was like Mozart. He knew that for what he was trying to do, what was required, in order to tell this shit that he told, he had to be somewhere the fuck else, man. And after that, you breathe, you pronounce the word and it is all there ready for you.

"The Hip Gahn," Buckley's homage in hep to the "All-Hip Mahatma Gandhi," is yet another example of His Lordship's political leanings as well as a brilliant demonstration of his innate musical prowess and sensibilities. Along with "The Hip Einie" and "James Dean's Message to the Teenagers" (later Buckley bows to Albert Einstein and the revered actor), "The Hip Gahn" stands out as one of his few celebrations of a twentieth-century figure—a man Buckley was fond calling the "Number Two Jesus Christ."

Structurally, "The Hip Gahn" (along with "The Hip Einie," "The Bad-Rapping of the Marquis de Sade," and several other of the wilder Buckley epics) is a couplet that includes a lengthy introduction, or setup, that bears only thematic resemblance to the heart and coda of the story. This form is not without precedent in the tradition of American storytelling, perhaps most successfully and popularly executed by Mark Twain in his cornerstone collection, *Roughing It.*

"The Hip Gahn," an "incident from the precious Mahatma Gandhi," begins with a symbolic description of the colonialized subcontinent:

> Now, you see, like I 'splained to you, see, they called this here cat "The Hip Gahn." That's what they called him. The Hip Gahn. The sweet, precious Hip Gahn. 'Cause he *swung* India. He *wailed* India. He *gassed* India. He *grooved* India. Now I'm gonna tell you why. Ya see India was bugged wid da Lion. Every time India gets a little extra scoff in the cupboard, WHAM! Here comes the Lion. Chomp! Swoop the scene and there stand the poor Indians, scoffless. Bugged them to death.
>
> That was before the Hip Gahn blew in on the scene, you see. And the day that the Hip Gahn blew in on the scene seem to be the Lion's big swingin' day, cause he was into the scoff patch up to his shoulders, scoffin' up an *insane* breeze.
>
> So the Hip Gahn back away about thirty or forty feet, and he holds out his arms cool-wise and he do a running broad jump—MAAP! Whapped on the Lion's tail so hard that the Lion *swooped* the scene and that gassed India—it gassed 'em. So, naturally, in return, they want to gas him back.

With the symbolic "Lion" (the authoritarian rule of the British crown) safely out of the way, Buckley establishes his scene and quickly focuses on what at first appears as a whimsical fantasy that has the Hip Gahn arranging a monster jazz-style jam session as a means of uniting his battered but hopeful new nation. Upon closer historical inspection, however, one of Gandhi's first acts as spiritual leader of his newly emancipated homeland was to invite musicians from all across India to partake in a mammoth concert of unification and love.

So as the Indians begin to fete the Gahn, Mr. Rabadee (the Hip Gahn's chief protocol cat) sends out notes to the Indian musicians—"the ribedee players, the dong-dong players, the RANG-RANG players, the reed heads, the lute heads, the bloop heads, the blowin' heads to come on in: we're gonna gas a big jam session from the Gahn."

After the processional epic entrance of the musicians, which gives Buckley yet another shot to jitterbug his tongue over all those cartoon names, moving up and down the scale like a harmonica, the mental camera swings around and you dig the entrance of The Man himself with his twenty-six chicks in horn-rim glasses, nineteen nanny goats, and two spinnin' wheels looking "so sharp an' so *fine* and so *groovy*—'cause he got a nice clean white *dow-dow* on—an' the lovelight is beamin' through his glasses and gassin' the whole scene."

And what a jam session it is! Buckley backs off vocally—like the Gahn winding up for his broad jump on the lion's tail—and starting off in a normal tone of voice, he gradually increases his volume, speed, and emotional intensity until he zooms up into a tremendous vocal crescendo:

> My lords and my ladies, I'm gonna hip you—you may've heard a lotta jam sessions blown off, you may heard of New Orleans licks, you may heard o' Chicago style, you may heard o' all kinds of jazz jumpin' the *wildest* and most *in*-sane trips—but you studs and you *stallions!* You cats and kitties! You never-before-dug any session like THESE CATS BLEW!!! They wailed so hard that the *snakes* in the *jungle* picked up on the lick and come stompin' in for the session. They had to send out the snake guards: "Ain't no dancin' tonight, boys—we just hippin' the Gahn."

Once the jam session of Buckley's fancy concludes, the Hip Gahn is asked by Mr. Rabadee which instrument blew the best. The Hip Gahn's response includes Buckley's invention and imitation of the accompanying instruments and their unique sounds, culminating in one of his most breathtaking moments on record:

> And the Hip Gahn say, "Baby, when I hear them rabadee players, the dong-dong players, and them blute-blute players, and the flipheads and the luteheads, and the reed heads, and all these boys wailin' up such an insane love breeze it brought to me the beauty, and the mysticism, and the wonder, and the gorgeous theme, and the gorgeous wising, and all the great wild non-stop etherea that is Mother India."

"The Hip Gahn" contains a comedic device found very rarely, if at all, in the Buckley lexicon—something that begins to approach the definition of an actual punch line. Near the end of the bit, when the Hip Gahn informs Mr. Rabadee that his favorite instrument is not present at the jam session, the Hip Gahn's answer comes in a long string of complicated ambidextrous jazz riffs, pure sound, and pure rhythm imitating the Gahn's favorite ax: "The spinning wheel, baby . . . I hope I didn't bring you *down."*

The lack of a normal punch line in Lord Buckley's work is significant in that it further supports the notion that if Buckley must be categorized as a comic, then it is a comedy quite apart from that containing the traditional Borscht Belt one-liner.

Albert Goldman

Probably the greatest of his routines is "The Hip Gahn," a chant-fable about Mahatma Gandhi that breathes love and joy through every pore as Lord Buckley imagines a great convocation of Indian musicians gathered in a feast of thanksgiving for their spiritual leader: he of the love-beaming spectacles and clean white dhoti. Reeling off the epic catalogues and processional scenes of this mad Mother Indian temple frieze, Buckley rhapsodizes up to the limits of language and then beyond as he swings into the spectrum of sound and music. The monologue's punch line is pure jazz.

More than the sunshiny humor of the jazzy virtuosity of this piece, what strikes one listening to it today is its amazing harmony with the spirit of love and joy and cosmic aspirations.

It's a sin to summarize a bit like this on paper because everything that's good about it gets lost in the translation. The timing, the phrasing, the irresistibly funny sound of Lord Buckley's voice—none of it comes across. Yet even such a crude sketch conveys some idea of what the man was putting down. The basic message is one of joy and ecstasy. His Lordship anticipates the Love Generation. He extolls a guru-hero: a gentle, loving, humble soul who returns only soft answers or speaks in Zen riffs.

The two final historical tracks on the *Euphoria* outings, "Nero" and "The Gasser," are studies from different times and places but with curiously related themes. Where "Nero" is Buckley's take on power abused, "The Gasser" demonstrates power's flowering positive possibilities when used, as Buckley says, "in immaculate purity."

In commencing a short study of Buckley's "Nero," the liner notes from *Euphoria* are revelatory here: "Again Lord Buckley uses the flexible language of the hipster in characterizing the famous Roman Emperor, his outrageous deeds, and the events leading to the crucifixion of the Christians as taken from *Quo Vadis.*"

Quo Vadis, the 1951 film starring Peter Ustinov as Nero and released just prior to Buckley's recording, is full-blown Hollywood cheese—a Technicolor stab at rekindling the spirit of the grand epics of D. W. Griffith with the Roman despot's megalomaniacal fancies as its vehicle. Buckley's take focuses specifically on the events following the aftermath of Nero's burning of Rome in a.d. 62, intended (according to unsubstantiated rumor) to serve as the backdrop for a recitation by Nero on the fall of Troy. Nero accused the Christians of starting the fire and he began the first Roman persecution.

Though "Nero" is a sometimes-overlooked piece in Buckley's body of work, it contains some unusual features. Lord Buckley's introduction is rather cute: two time-traveling hepcats find themselves at the foot of Nero's palace in the early a.d. One of the hipsters has no clue who Nero is and so his buddy clues him in Buckley-style:

> You don't know who Nero is? Let me hip *you!* Nero was one of the wildest, gonest, freakiest studs that ever stomped through the pages of history. He's the kind of a cat that balled every big, swingin', main day breeze, all the time everyday. And the chicks were jumpin' and the juice was flyin' and the band was blowin' and Nero havin' himself a fine time indeed. This cat balled Monday, Tuesday, Wednesday, Thursday, Friday, Saturday and Sunday, Monday, Tuesday, Wednesday, Thursday, Friday, Saturday and

> Sunday. In fact, he balled so crazy and so far out that occasionally he get his kick warehouse so full of kicks he can't stick no more kicks in. And when there ain't no place to put 'em, the po' cat gets hung.

Lord Buckley was keenly aware of the consequences of power abused. Much of his work pokes fun at and disparages the "greed heads": politicians or businessmen looking to stuff their pockets and fulfill their every whim and indulgence at the expense of others.

"Nero" is a dark, sprawling yarn that, however lively and graphic, never really finds an adequate closure. But it is chock-full of some of Buckley's best lines. For instance, his description of the persecuted Christians ranging in age "from two to toothless" is easily among his most poetic and profound. And Buckley had an easy time sinking his teeth into the dynamics of the piece, as it was reportedly one of his favorites to perform.

Mel Welles

He performed "Quo Vadis" in every live performance I ever saw. That was one of the pieces he performed that got the strongest reaction. When he worked at the Club Renaissance, I would say I saw him do "Quo Vadis" a minimum of a hundred times. And, if he didn't do it, you could rest assured that the crowd would start screaming for it.

His two favorite pieces were "Quo Vadis" and "The Nazz." He always felt he could do better on those two when we recorded them.

Particularly, I remember there was some question about whether he was right on with the "snatched them Christians" line. He was very particular about dynamics and "Quo Vadis" embodied his ability very clearly.

Just the way he handled lines like "knock a golden spike where that chick blew" was not so much the line itself but the way in which it was delivered that made it powerful.

Ken Kesey

When I first heard Lord Buckley I was at college, and I knew enough of his work to be able to use it when writing all my books. This ongoing Faulknerian dialogue came right out of Lord Buckley. I know all these records by heart. The rhythm in that! It's a thing where you're falling through space, grabbing words as you go, and building something as you fall, not sure if you're going to find them up there. It's the trip. Lord Buckley was more influential than anybody.

I think "The Nazz" has to be my favorite piece. The one I enjoy doing, though, is the one about Nero. When I was in college I wrote a play called *Status Quo Vadis* using that whole Nero thing. I played Nero dressed up as Elvis Presley with a great pompadour. We were to perform it at a big show that happened every year on campus. Each fraternity house entered a competition to see who would get their shows performed. Mine was ten times the best, and then I was informed a few days before the show that I couldn't do it because it was considered blasphemous. Buckley's rap about the Christians was enough to have some of the twits there at the sorority house tell me that I couldn't perform it. This was my first taste of right-wing, hardheaded craziness.

"The Gasser" is one of Lord Buckley's great achievements, containing all of the elements found in his best work: history, autobiography, charisma, and magic.

Magnificently translating one of the great though little-known stories in storydom, the epochal sixteenth-century adventure of Spanish explorer Alvar Núñez Cabeza de Vaca, Buckley celebrates an individual who was himself relegated to a mere historical footnote until the 1992 film *Cabeza de Vaca* chronicled his exploits. Actually Buckley does more in seven and half minutes to juice his subject than the film does in nearly two rather turgid hours. Until the film was released, Lord Buckley's treatment was probably the primary source of any popular recognition of Cabeza de Vaca's saga. As such, it deserves some explanation before Lord Buckley's exposition can be properly appreciated.

Overshadowed by the iron-fisted colonialist and missionary exploits of his contemporaries Columbus, Cortés, and Pizarro, Cabeza de Vaca's journey is the stuff of myth. Alvar Núñez Cabeza de Vaca was not, as Lord Buckley aptly put it, a "warrior cat for Ferdinand the First of Spain." Rather it was Charles V for whom de Vaca risked (and took) life and limb, a lieutenant in the elite corps who had heroically distinguished (or, depending one one's historical orientation, damned) himself during the Spanish Inquisition.

Cabeza de Vaca (literally translated as "cow's head") was not actually a surname but a hereditary title in his mother's family. He came to the New World as treasurer in the expedition of Panfilo de Navarez that left Spain in 1527 and reached Florida (probably Tampa Bay) in 1528, in hope of conquering the region north of the Gulf of Mexico.

Cabeza de Vaca, at thirty-eight years, was an adaptable man with some secret of spiritual growth in him. When hardship and Indian hostility caused the end of the expedition, Cabeza de Vaca was one of the survivors whose barges were shipwrecked on an island on the Texas coast. Scholars have argued extensively over the identification of that island, but Galveston Island and Mustang Island are popular choices as possibilities. The story that follows is one of the most remarkable in the annals of exploration and survival—right up there with Marco Polo, Lewis and Clark, and Ernest Shackleton's Antarctic voyage. After much suffering as slaves of the Indians inhabiting the island, Cabeza de Vaca and three other survivors escaped and started a long journey overland. His companions were Alonso del Castillo Maldonado, Andres Dorantes, and Estevanico (an Arab or possibly an African black—a "Moor" as described by Buckley).

In becoming the first Europeans to cross the North American continent, the party of four walked across Texas, New Mexico, Arizona, northern Mexico, and possibly (some argue) even California for the next eight years before turning south. In 1536 they arrived in Culiacán in Mexico and told their story to Spaniards there. In addition to being one of the great true adventure stories of all time, Cabeza de Vaca's account of their travels is an unparalleled source of firsthand information on the pre-European

Southwest—the variety of its climate, its flora and fauna, and the customs of its natives. They were almost certainly the first Europeans to see the opossum and the buffalo, the Mississippi and the Pecos Rivers, pine-nut mash and mesquite-bean flour. Their stories about the Pueblo Indians gave rise to the legend of the Seven Cities of Cibola (later magnified by Fray Marcos de Niza), and brought explorers in search of El Dorado. They gained great repute among the Indians as healers since remarkable cures were attributed to their Christian prayers.

It was then that he wrote a letter to his king, Charles V, relating what had befallen him—a letter that serves both as the primary document of the journey and the centerpiece of Buckley's amazing spiel. It begins as the usual story of a European adventurer who leaves home to exploit people. But little by little, he finds out that people are his brothers and sisters and feels genuine concern for them. Buckley credited Fanny Bandelier's twentieth-century translation, *The Power Within Us* (with an introduction by Henry Miller), as the source of his knowledge of Cabeza de Vaca's exploits. *The Power Within Us* was drawn from Cabeza de Vaca's own account, *Las Naufragios* ("the shipwrecked men"; 1542), describing the startling adventures of his party.

After returning to Spain, Cabeza de Vaca was appointed governor of the Rio de la Plata region and reached Asunción, Paraguay, after an overland journey from the Brazilian coast in 1542. His South American career was sadly different from that in North America. He got into much trouble with the popular Domingo Martinez de Irala. After he returned from an expedition up the Parana River to Bolivia, he was arrested, accused of high-handed practices, imprisoned for two years, and sent back to Spain. There he was found guilty but was pardoned by King Charles V.

Lord Buckley's dazzling performances of "The Gasser" bring forth the ecstatic faith-healing miracles Cabeza de Vaca performed by his own account.

Commencing with the Vaya release, four full-bodied versions of "The Gasser" can be found in the surviving Buckley catalogue: a 1957 studio recording, a 1959 radio broadcast, and the glorious 1959 Ivar Theater outing captured on the World Pacific LP *Lord Buckley: Blowing His Mind (and yours too).* The Ivar version finds Lord Buckley at the top of his game riffing the story with a loose, breezy passion as if he were merely and merrily entertaining guests at a cocktail party.

But the Vaya version is red-hot as well. Curiously, Buckley misidentifies Alvar Núñez Cabeza de Vaca in this premier version as "Cabenza de Gasca" and posits the story as pre-Columbian with the date 1410 rather than the later versions in which he inserts a more accurate but still incorrect date, "Fifteen Hundred and leapin' Ten." Why or if he chose to fictionalize the tale in its debut is, however, mysterious and unresolved. Perhaps Buckley was not fully aware of the details involving the true story so he decided to fudge and fantasticate it. Or maybe Buckley simply realized later that the truth was stranger than any fiction even he could manufacture.

Lord Buckley

Well you see, the hipsemantic has such a rhythm to it that you become attracted to it. I almost starved to death presenting this type of humor. Because most of the people I talk to at an audience of eighty, there would be about fifteen that understood what I was saying or else I might have been speaking in script of some kind. But I could not let go of it. The powers are great that come out of it.

Take a religious work like Alvar Núñez Cabeza de Vaca. He was a religious figure in the year 1500. He was a lieutenant for Ferdinand the First of Spain and he was a soldier. He knew nothing about the appeal of the powers of prayer.

And his story in the hipsemantic is very powerful and beautiful. The original story comes from *The Power Within*. It's a very, very tiny book called *The Power Within,* which is a record of his work and his adventure.

My hipsemantic retelling goes right down the line for line, scene for scene, theme for theme, meaning for meaning, go for go, groove for groove, swing for swing.

The scene of Alvar Nuñez Cabeza de Vaca. He was a soldier for Ferdinand the First of Spain and he was sent to the new world after bullion and he flipped.

And he said, "In order to know what it means to have nothing you must have *NOTHING!*"

And that's what he had in spades.

Through the story he gave me the knowledge of the healing of the hand. And I want ya to dig it deeply . . . I'm tellin' ya. Ha! He moved 'em. Well you see, the story, in hip goes down like this:

THE GASSER Now you all heard about Vasco de Gama the Island Bumper. He was a history cat with a big, fast press agent.

They say: "De Gama bump island number one, Boom! Put it in the book. De Gama bump island number two, Boom! Put it in the book."

But there was another cat jumpin' at about the same time that had a lean press agent that *cut* this first cat to *shreds!* And they called him: Alvar Núñez Cabeza de Vaca, *The Gasser!*

He was a warrior cat for Ferdinand the First of Spain. And Ferdinand the First of Spain was a ballin' king. He was a king that liked to see the chicks a-jumpin', and the juice a-flowin' and the good times a-goin'. He's a carryin'-on cat *all* the time.

He's the kind of a stud that stick his wig out of the castle window in the early bright and say: "Look at Princess Libadee this morning. She look pretty coo-coo today. Say, give that chick another castle!"

Say, "We ain't got no more castles, Your Majesty."

He say, "Well, build her one! Don't stand there like an id-git!"

As a consequence he's a little short of gold in the Treasury, see what I mean, and he had to send over a little expedition to the New World to knock up a little bullion.

So it was Alvar Núñez Cabaza de Vaca, *The Gasser's, mis*fortune to go with a *square* captain on a three-ship convoy, ran into *short* tilt on the *far* side and—vrrpppt!—blew the *whole* gig on the beach in Florida in Fifteen Hundred and Ten.

And Florida in Fifteen Hundred and Ten was Crocodile City. You couldn't sit, stoop or squat without them crocodiles snap snap snapping all *over* the place and every bug in the jungle is dive-bombing these po' cats and the ones that ain't dive-bombing was hitchhiking rides on 'em and their beat, bent, flapped, trapped and *de-gigged* . . . which is the worst thing that can happen to a cat. That mean they lose they job.

So it was Alvar Núñez Cabaza de Vaca, *The Gasser,* a Buddy Cat, a Moor and a Parrot. And the Parrot had the best go of the whole lick 'cause he had that feather overcoat. The other poor studs didn't even have a Union Oil map, but they went stompin' down the beach 'cause they didn't know where they was going but they knew where they was *wasn't it.*

So to show you how hung up they was they stomped all over Texas then they turned and stomped all the way to North Dakota in Fifteen Hundred and Ten. And then they turned around and stomped all the way to Mexico City. And when he got to Mexico City, Alvar Núñez Cabeza de Vaca, *The Gasser,* sat down to knock a note on Ferdinand the First to hip him where he had been goofin' all this time . . . it only took him *eight years:* a little Sunday afternoon flip, ya know.

Well, he's writing, he say: "Your Most Royal Swingin' Majesty. I have been on a lot of sad tours. I've been on a lot of mad, beat, bent-up, down-gradin' excursions. I've been on a lot of tilted picnics and a lot of double unhung parties."

He said, "I've suffered from pavement rash."

He said: "I been billed, willed and twilled."

He said: "I have been bashed, flashed and gashed."

He said, "I been flipped, ripped and tripped."

He said, "I've been flung, wanged, and loonged."

He said, "I been hung-up and jammed-up and framed-up and backed-up and stacked-up and macked-up and racked-up but I *never* dug no jazz like this last riff you put me on!"

He said, "My buddy cats and me was in such a sad bind we were breathin' in staccato just to keep the pilot light lit."

He said they were just about ready to give up the whole gig when they ran into an Indian village.

And The Gasser say, "Well I'll go in here and sound the Chief and get a couple of boxes of acorn." Say, "We might not find out *where* we is but we liable to find out *who* we is, that'll help a little bit."

He no sooner got that out and here come the Chief. He say: "Ugh. Me see you. You big God. Me hear you by Indian grapevine. See on ship. He no sail water. He got white wings. He fly sky. Me know me hear you. You plenty hip head. You got good miracle wig. Good thing you come. Me got buddy cat. He had little trouble seventeen crocodile. You straighten him out. You put magic lick on this boy, put him on he feet, me give you couple boxes of acorn maybe two or three squaw, OK?"

He ain't even slipped the cat a Nabisco up to now!

And here's the poor Gasser weavin' and wailin' and bent and spent. And he was up against a rough bind. He knew he had to do somethin'. He knew he had to wail someway. He knew that he had to go. He couldn't stop there.

And this poor cat that he suppose to wail on his feet is in *very delicate condition in-deed.*

He's *not* on the razor's flip, you see what I mean. He's on the theme of the beam of the invisible edge. He's on the *hone* of the *scone,* that's a wing-fittin' station. (Said, "Let me try that number seventeen again, will you? I think this is a little tight for me. I like that seventeen foot wing spread anyway much better. This is my first flight.") He was on his way out.

The Gasser, like I 'splained before, was a warrior cat: he'd been takin' them out, not bringing them in.

But they didn't call him Alvar Núñez Cabeza de Vaca *"The Gasser"* for nothing.

It was like asking a dying man to save a dying man. He fell down on his knees and he made a connection that shook the peninsula!

He said: "Lord! This is Alvar Núñez Cabeza de Vaca, The Gasser, soundin' to you Lord. No use in looking for me in the book Lord, you won't find me there, Lord. I've been blowin' for Ferdinand the First in another part of the field, Lord."

He said, "I know that you're busy, I can see your switch board is lit up with calls from all over the world. "'Help me here. Straighten me Lord. Do this for me Lord.'"

He said: "I wouldn't be soundin' you now Lord if I wasn't in such a serious bind, Lord. But if you do me this little favor Lord, and straighten out the chief's Buddy Cat, Lord, though I never blowed a note for you before in my life, Lord: *You got yourself a Boy!!!*"

At this The Gasser looked and he turned around the corner of his fingers and he see this cat was wailin' for stand up and say: "What time do we eat?"

Well that flipped the Indians and also knocked out The Gasser. And the Chief got out a couple of boxes of acorn and he straightened The Gasser and put a few on the Moor and cooled the Parrot.

It seemed like everywhere they went there was nothing to eat. Everybody was hungry but there was always cats who had heard about The Gasser and his great love connection, sitting in death's door with their backs to the street waitin' for The Gasser to appear. He cooled them all. Created about two hundred beautiful miracles right across the land. Even had one cat under a rug for two days, put The Gasser on him—honk—blew him up on his feet.

This is history. Dig this jazz . . . and it's beautful jazz.

And Alvar Núñez de Vaca, The Gasser said in the last page of his letter: "Your Majesty, I'm hipped you are a very groovy swingin' King with a fat book. But I'd like to knock a page on you."

He said: "I found out on this expedition that . . . there is a *Great . . . Power . . . Within*. That when used in beauty, in Immaculate Conception and complete purity can cure and heal and cause *miracles*." And he said: "When you use it, it *spreads* like a magic garden, and when you *DO NOT* use it, it *recedes* from you."

Alvar Núñez Cabeza de Vaca, The Gasser. Fifteen Hundred and Leapin' Ten.

Joseph Jablonski

Lord Buckley was capable of doing many things to get an audience to listen, to dig. The most astounding thing of all was what he said when he got their attention. An example is the "Gasser" routine. At the conclusion, Cabeza de Vaca, the lost explorer-soldier who became a famous healer among the Native Americans, writes a letter to the king of Spain to explain his unaccounted years in the New World. Buckley addresses the words of this letter to his audience, and the way he pronounces them evokes a most eloquent affirmation.

Lord Buckley's entire career was a continuing tribute to an exalted gift which, if it is not the same thing as the poetic marvelous sought by surrealism, is certainly a close cousin to it.

The *Euphoria Vol. II* liner notes mention Buckley's introduction to the Cabeza de Vaca tale: "This story of a pre-Columbus journey from Florida to Mexico was given to Lord Buckley by the noted author Henry Miller and the 'translation' is as you hear it."

The Lord Buckley/Henry Miller connection is definite, if a little fuzzy. Though the album jacket copy suggests a meeting between the two, there is other evidence (as will be seen later) indicating that this did not occur until some years hence. Miller seems to have been aware of Buckley and his work before their formal acquaintance commenced, as he alludes to His Lordship in the introduction to *Time of the Assassins*, his study of the French symbolist poet Rimbaud.

Jim Dickson

One of the people who discovered Buckley was the novelist Henry Miller. Henry Miller wrote me letters and had me send records to people over the years. One day I was driving through Big Sur and I thought I'd bring him some records. I had just gotten these twelve-inch versions of *Euphoria* which had a little picture of Lord Buckley up on the cover. When Henry Miller saw it and found out that Buckley was white he was outraged. He had apparently written about him in a couple of books thinking he was black. He could hardly control himself talking to me but he still took the records I brought. But he couldn't believe it. He had compared him to Rimbaud in the preface of a book. He mentioned Buckley in two different books. One I think was about Rimbaud who was a street poet in which he made comparisons between Rimbaud's language in his time and Buckley's language in the present time.

Henry Miller

Excerpted from Miller's introduction to The Time of the Assassins: A Study of Rimbaud, *published by New Directions in 1955.*

I should like to make it clear that this little study, written ten years ago, is the outcome of a failure to translate, in the fashion intended, *A Season in Hell.* I still nourish the hope of rendering this text in a language more proximate to Rimbaud's own "nigger" tongue. The authors of *Really the Blues,* or a man like Lord Buckley, are closer to Rimbaud, though they may not be aware of it, than the poets who have worshipped and imitated him.

The final track from the *Euphoria* sessions was Buckley's noir ode "Murder." On the jacket notes, Buckley wrote of the piece: "Murder follows a different vein entirely, and inasmuch as the enjoyment of this selection may be hindered by our explanation, we await your approval."

Although Buckley excused "Murder," his morbidly funny fantasy, as a "study in psychological humor," the rich, darkly Thurberesque bit owes much to the noir cinema of the 1940s. The hard-boiled minimalist bloodbath has scenes lifted right out of those sharp Nicholas Ray B-movie classics, dizzy with the woozy, moody grit of a 3 a.m. downtown police station. The confession, complete with the desk lamp shining in the accused killer's eyes, is a harrowing description of decapitation and dismemberment with a comic twist that anticipates Alfred Hitchcock's *Rear Window* by three years, Lina Wertmuller's *Seven Beauties* by twenty-five, and the passions raised during the O. J. Simpson spectacle by a light-year or two.

Buckley's account of the war between the genders (and "Murder" is very much a work with overtones of sexual politics—perhaps the last cogent equation of sex and death) indicates a certain personal affinity for the work and perhaps a streak of misogyny in the artist:

> **MURDER** M'Lords and M'Ladies of the Royal Court, we should like to do for you a portrait on the *wildest* most *fantastic* emotion since the first turn of the wheel on the axle. Ah, this emotion is so *frantic* and so *crazy* and so *insane* and such a *narcotic* that they get huge groups of people to play this game together. An emotion so *strong*, so *wild*—this whole thing is a portrait of Man's inability to completely control . . . WOMAN.
>
> This wild, wild, crazy, insane, far-out mother, non-stop, screamin' crazy mad emotion—and this emotion is . . . Murder! MURDER!!
>
> Murder . . . *very expensive* . . . murder.
>
> For there is no man—*No Man*—who has lived who has not said to himself at *one* time or *another*: "That woman. That woman. What is she doing to me? Lying to me. I know it. I know it. Cheating on me. Yes, yes, yes . . . talking while I'm talking. Leading me around by my nose . . . SPENDING MY MONEY!!!
>
> "Ohhhh, I'll murder her."

The scene is a walk-up flat in Greenwich Village. There are two characters in the scene. One is a man . . . and the other . . . a woman.

The woman's head . . . ohhh, ahhh . . . is not on her body.

In the man's hand is a long, lean, mean, keen . . . *bloody knife* . . . with the blood—ahhhh, ahh, ahh, ah—not yet congealed—ohhhhh ahhhh ohhhhh—just dripping, dripping, dripping, dripping . . . lightly . . . lightly . . . lightly . . . lightly . . .

The man's conscience speaks first: "Ahhh! Hoo! Hay! Oh! Oh! Ah, you brilliant mind! You great super-egotist genius. Look what you have done! Look at her lying there. Her head *cut* from her *beautiful* body. I know what you're thinking. You have plans. You have money. Run! Run! Run! Run! Run! Run! Run! Run! Run! Run!

"They'll pursue you. They'll bring you back. They'll put you under those hot lights. They will ask of you: the *motive*. And you best have the *motive*. The police want the *motive*. The papers want the *motive*. What is the *motive?*"

The man, himself, speaks: "So, they'll want a motive, eh? Well, I'll give them a motive. And I swear to you that I can see the look on their stupid, sweaty, sadistic faces staring down into mine when I tell them that I killed her because . . . *I LOVED HER*! Oh! Oh! Ohhh! Oh God help me I loved her. Everything she did. The way she walked. The way she talked—everything. I loved her so much I could think of nothing else. Day in day out. Year in year out. Oh God I loved her. Oh! When I tried to seek escape in sleep she'd come into my subconscious mind like she had a secret trap door. Come in like a little girl—like a tall one, like a thin girl. Oh God.

"And the . . . and the . . . and the . . . and the *rotten, vicious, monstrous* things she did were to me . . . *beautiful.* Beautiful! Beautiful, beautiful, beautiful . . .

"I loved her. I loved her. I loved her so—ahh ahh ahh ahh . . . I can still feel the—ahh ahh—exquisite pressure on my wrist when I grabbed her beautiful neck with a knife and the blood—Ohhh! Woah! Woah! Woah! Ha ha ha ha ha—the rich, red blood. Oh God! I did it! I did it. I'd do it again. I'd do it a thousand times. I told her . . . she wouldn't listen . . . I did it.

"Cut her up. Slice her up into little pieces. Cut her up. Slice her up—chop up her fingers. Ship her away. Ship her away. Ship her out. Put her in the car. Ship her, ship her, ship her. Cut her up. I told her . . . I'll do it a thousand times. Not he, not they—Me! Me! Me! I'll do it again. I'll do it again. I'll fix her. She can't show me. I'll show her—you bet your life. I'll do it again . . ."

"Henry?"

"I'll do it again."

"Henry?"

"Yes, yes, yes . . ."

"Henry."

"Huh?"

"Henry, I want you to go out out to the hen house and feed the hens before breakfast dear."

"Ah, oh, ahh yes dear . . . I was just putting my pants on . . . can't do anything until you've got your pants on . . ."

"Murder" is, perhaps somewhat surprisingly, Buckley's most recorded piece, appearing in seven nearly identical versions from different sources spanning the decade of his recorded legacy. Along with *Euphoria* and the previously mentioned *Turk Murphy Acetate,* Lord Buckley recorded the piece for official release on a rare 1952 Nonesuch disc, *The Parabolic REVELATIONS of the Late Lord Buckley,* and a somewhat truncated live version from the famed 1959 Ivar Theater concert appeared on the posthumously released World Pacific LP *Blowing His Mind (and yours too).* Additionally, there are three unreleased versions: a 1953 appearance at the Lighthouse in Hermosa Beach, California, a 1956 studio take for Hip Records, and a final live version probably dating from 1960.

Despite their general lack of variation, each version is splendid, attacked with just the right fever pitch and ghoulish relish as it walks the fine line, balancing the funny and frightening, that he took to even greater extremes with his later "Bad-Rapping of the Marquis de Sade"—a dizzying roller coaster of bile and tenderness. So passionately detailed and hateful are these performances that one wonders if Buckley wasn't speaking from actual experience.

The beauty of the misogynistic exercise in dark humor is that its conclusion reveals the homicidal act as just the product of a benign daydream, marvelously undercutting the truly horrible and graphic description and the schizophrenia of the dreamer.

Lord Buckley

I went to vaudeville and musical comedy and I did a picture with Fred Allen and Ginger Rogers called *We're Not Married,* a big, long interesting stinker.

It was precisely as *Euphoria* was released that Buckley landed a supporting role in *We're Not Married,* a gimmicky 20th Century–Fox comedy. The film, starring Ginger Rogers, Fred Allen, Zsa Zsa Gabor, and Marilyn Monroe, is quintessential early-1950s silliness: a justice of the peace performs marriage ceremonies a few days before his license is actually valid and is unaware of this mistake until two and a half years later, at which time letters are sent to the various couples. Thus five couples (in varying stages of marital bliss or misery) suddenly get the news that they are not, and never have been, legally married.

The segment involving Buckley concerns a popular "Mr. and Mrs." morning radio show in which Fred Allen and Ginger Rogers play the featured couple. This type of radio program was quite in vogue at the time, a kind of innocent but catty postwar version of the more recent blue hijinks of Howard Stern and Robin Quivers on the "shock jock's" nationally syndicated radio program. At any rate, by the time notice of their nonmarriage arrives, Ginger and Fred's relationship is in delicate condition indeed. At first the news is good for them—that is, until they realize that their very lucrative contract with the radio station requires that they actually be married. That things eventually work out for Allen, Rogers, and the rest of the couples is totally predictable. It's that kind of a picture.

Perhaps somewhat miscast, Buckley plays "Mr. Graves," a radio announcer at the station—a prissy middle-management type who is just asking for it. Not surprisingly, it is a role that Buckley appears to have a hard time sinking his teeth into, coming off stiff and workmanlike in his approach. At one point, while seated between the bickering couple, Buckley turns his head back and forth between Allen and Rogers with the weariness of a man who has endured one too many takes.

Buckley's fascination with cinema was long-standing and easy to fathom. Not only was it *the* form of popular entertainment during his rise in show business but, in working the movie-house vaudeville circuit during the 1930s and 1940s, he was forced to screen scores of two-reelers, often in quadruplicate, daily. As a result, he became a de facto student of the genre. Adapting a film for one of his routines was as natural as doing the same for Shakespeare, the Bible, or a jazz riff. His choice to draw on cinematic technique was timely considering the raison d'être of his move to Southern California in the first place: to gain a foothold in the movie biz.

Lord Buckley

The theater is a church and Hollywood is the Vatican of our theater.

George Greif

He was fairly reliable but there were times when he'd slip off the wagon or whatever. I remember I put him in his first film, *We're Not Married.* I believe Edmund Goulding, the director, had seen him and liked him and wanted to use him in the picture. But Richard wasn't good in it at all. He was drinking. He started to drink which he swore he wouldn't do. I got really PO'd because it was an important opportunity to be in a movie with Fred Allen, Ginger Rogers and Marilyn Monroe.

Mel Welles

There were a couple of beliefs that he had that I found very admirable. One was his belief that if everybody treated each other like Lords and Ladies of the Royal Court everything would be much rosier in life. He thought that too many people were insidious to each other rather than polite and respectful and he proved it once.

I got him to the job on a picture called *Marry Me Again,* which was later retitled *We're Not Married.* I was working at Fox at the same time so we drove to work together. I was working on a picture called *Soldier of Fortune* with Clark Gable and Susan Hayward.

So, when I broke for lunch I thought I'd go over and see how he was doing. I walked over to the stage where they were shooting and what I witnessed was fantastic. The grips and the electricians were all bowing to each other and saying things like "Your Lordship, would you mind throwing me that hammer?" or "Sir Hugo, would you please put another scrim on that light?"

In one morning he could turn an entire set into a fairy tale with people bowing to each other and addressing each other like they were Lords and Ladies of the Royal Court. So that was one belief that he had.

The other belief that he had was that people are really people and they're the most important thing in the world, that nature really sucks. He believed that people are important and that people should be good to each other. It doesn't matter what religion you are or the color of your skin or whether you are gay or not or anything like that.

Lord Buckley

My daughter asked me, she said to me, "Please do the character of the strange woman you did."

Now the strange woman I did for her was a character of a homosexual, which means, of course, a man of split gender. But what it means in actuality is a woman in a man's body. That's her home, that's her body. And the reason I say that it is her body is because of the fact that she cannot escape it. She's in that body. She has her own genitals. She has a phallic rather than a ueic, see. So that she is very, very, very, very insulted but she's not discouraged.

We're all in this together and I say this: of every so-called "fag" that you meet, every so-called person that's tilted in their gender, a woman in a man's body (a woman in a man's body means that this man can only love men cause she's a woman in the body). A man in a woman's body is just the opposite. So all of you be kind to them. You can laugh *with* them but not *at* them. Is that clear?

9 the church of the living swing

Lord Buckley

I don't give a damn what people say: love is love. That's the point I want to make to you. Never be unkind to anyone. Never join people in laughing *at* people. Join all the people laughing *with* people. Join them. See, when you're not informed through life you've got to carry a lot of remorse with you.

If the background scenery of Lord Buckley's professional life sometimes included the romantic ambience of a movie set, the trappings of his domestic life in Southern California during the early 1950s were usually anything but. The hard reality of raising a family on the salary afforded to struggling entertainers was crushing and forced His Lordship to shepherd his tribe through a variety of charming if pillar-to-post low-rent situations. As was his custom, each shelter acquired a name reflecting its attributes or shortcomings. There was "the Birdhouse," "the Chicken Coop," and the celebrated "Crackerbox Palace."

This desperation was certainly not apparent in an early photo of the Royal Family romping in Lake Malibu circa 1953 or 1954. Lady Elizabeth is frolicking in the water with her smiling blond tykes while Buckley, on the shore's edge, leans over them looking every bit the proud papa.

Lady Elizabeth Buckley

We were having fun having hard times. That was his secret. He knew how to turn anything around. Most people don't realize you have to work very hard to have good times.

Jimmy Gibson

The son of Harry "The Hipster" Gibson, Jimmy Gibson's childhood memory of his friends, Princess Laurie and Prince Richard Buckley, gives a youngster's perspective of life in the Royal Court and was included in Mike Zwerin's book, Close Enough for Jazz. *Lord Buckley was Jimmy's godfather.*

We never had a home. I was always in a hotel or backstage. I used to sleep under pianos. I learned right away that I was different from other kids. I had to make friends quickly and get something together because I wasn't going to be around that particular place too much longer. I learned how to make the best of the present, and to leave possessions.

Richie would be reciting Shakespeare or something and Laurie and I would be playing knights of the round table. I'd be Prince James. Growing up for me was like a long party. Buckley and Harry would be rapping and making up stories and they'd send us to bed but, you know, we'd be up all day and night sometimes.

Mel Welles

I used to have a photograph of him eating a hamburger at the Hollywood Ranch Market at four o'clock in the morning. That used to be his thing: he'd leave the club in his tails and his makeup and stand there with the bums on the street corner eating a hamburger at dawn.

Larry Storch

Once, when times were hard, he dressed his children up in their very best Little Lord Fauntleroy suits and with his wife Lizabeth dressed in her Chinese princess costume (she was really quite regal), he marched them all not to a fashionable restaurant but to an old White Tower hamburger joint. He sat them all down at the table and ordered hamburgers for his family and, indeed, everybody who was in there. And then, of course, when he couldn't pay the bill he talked his way out of *that.*

Sometime in 1952, about a year after the first Vaya tracks were cut, Buckley was in the recording studio again. Ed Randolph, whom Buckley knighted as Prince Eagle Head in the Royal Court, arranged a session at Radio Recorders in Hollywood with a studio audience consisting of Royal Court members to create a club atmosphere. Several takes of each presentation were made and carefully spliced to create a seamless performance that resulted in the rarest of all official Lord Buckley discs, *The Parabolic REVELATIONS of the Late Lord Buckley—A Collection of Six Lessons by the Hip Messiah.* Released posthumously on Pye Records, a British imprint of the Nonesuch label, this short workout covers familiar ground ("The Nazz," "Murder," and "Jonah and the Whale") and premieres several minor Buckley gems: "Governor Gulpwell," "Chastity Belt," and the legendary "Georgia, Sweet and Kind."

Jim Burns

The real essence of his style was not made known to us until Pye Records issued an LP made in 1952. On this it is possible to hear the range through which he worked: hip-talk versions of the classics, little non-sense songs, semi-surrealistic monologues on murder, all put over with a flair for words and speech rhythms which many a poet would be envious of. Above all there is the sincerity of the man as he tells the story of "The Nazz"—"the carpenter kitty" who was "turning these other kitties on through his eyes, so they could see everything pretty too." Like a jazz musician, Buckley keeps his performance fresh by improvisation on the basic theme. The other selections on the record range from an hilarious account of the discovery of the chastity belt to a mocking takeoff of Louis Armstrong singing "Georgia On My Mind," mocking because the lines about the joys of life in Georgia somehow get mixed up with the pleadings of a Negro who is about to be lynched.

The version of "Jonah and the Whale" appearing on *Parabolic REVELATIONS* drops any reference to the evil weed and begs the question of whether Buckley tempered his act for the recording session, if there was some tampering with the bit in the editing process or, most probably, that it hadn't been yet worked into the piece since the version of "Jonah and the Whale" on *Euphoria Vol. II* wasn't actually recorded until around 1954. For his part, Ed Randolph has no memory of editing the marijuana reference out of the *Parabolic REVELATIONS* version.

"Governor Gulpwell," an early rendition of the later, fully realized, better-performed, and more pointedly titled "Governor Slugwell," is one of several word paintings Buckley experimented with during his career. The pyrotechnical sketch is a tour-de-force portrayal of an integral slice of Americana: a Fourth of July–style political parade, rally, and speech. In the short routine Buckley at once voices the parts of a Negro fife and drum corps, cops, spectators, hawkers, gawkers, political hacks, and the good governor himself with sparkling color and verve.

The scene is grounded by a radio announcer who describes the scene before introducing Senator Gridley, the host of the event. An old-style smoky backroom political boss, Gridley takes the podium and speaks to the crowd with the kind of hot air we are all accustomed to: "My friends . . . I would like to say that *never* in my *political history* . . . have I ever enjoyed the privilege of presenting such a great beloved man. A *human being* not only *beloved* in this fair country . . . but *beloved* the world over. His name, a name that's imprinted on every heart in America . . . Governor Slingwell Slugwell!"

After a final salvo of trombone-blaring fanfare, Slugwell approaches the microphone: "My friends, I would like to say that, er, I have never before been greeted by such, uh, warmth, and, er, beauty. (I'll be there in a moment, Mary.) Now, I would like to say that things are going so well, and so, er, beautiful with me. My Rolls-Royces are running fine. Three more oil wells came in. I just bought the waterworks last week. I've had the gasworks for quite some time. And things are going at such a magnificent rate, that I believe that it is possible for *each* and *every* member of this great state, the employees association, shall receive a substantial raise in salary amounting to . . ." ("Trombone" fanfare) "Pam-pam, pam-pam. Roopety, boopety, boop, ba-boop, a roop, ba-boop, a roop, ba-boop. Roopety, boopety, boop" ("Trombone" fanfare) " . . . and seventy-five cents . . ."

The hidden revelation of Slugwell/Gulpwell's boozy bombast is his brazenly pitiless, in-your-face corruption: a Huey Long disguised as Norman Rockwell by way of

Frank Capra and/or Preston Sturgis. Both Robert Rossen's 1949 Oscar-winning film, *All the King's Men,* and Robert Penn Warren's Pulitzer Prize–winning novel on which the film was based (a thinly veiled account of the Kingfish's ascendancy and decline) were much-heralded works at that time. Buckley, with his keen interest in film and the specter of unbridled political power being a very recent international memory, may have been moved by its theme and flavor in concocting "Governor Gulpwell."

It is also possible that the very real threat of another megalomaniac power-grabbing tyrant, Senator Joseph McCarthy, who was just beginning his Hollywood witch hunt, may have inspired Lord Buckley's portrait of mass hysteria as well.

"Governor Gulpwell" is an excellent example of Lord Buckley's wildly inventive approach to presenting comedy. Listening to Governor Gulpwell greeting the masses before watching the evening news of the very early twenty-first century makes the piece ring with even greater authenticity. Both the dignitaries and the townsfolk may come off a little simpler than they do now, but the vacuousness and inherent deceit of today's electronic "talking head" politicians seem to make a little more sense.

Regardless of its roots and Buckley's agenda, "Governor Gulpwell" demonstrates both Buckley's incredible vocal virtuosity and his use of silence—one of the keys to understanding his innate musicality. Every great instrumental soloist either consciously or unconsciously employs silence to punctuate his notes, and Buckley expertly used both the music and drama this technique in his passion plays in miniature.

"Chastity Belt" is, along with the later "Bad-Rapping of the Marquis de Sade," one of the few outright bawdy routines in the surviving Buckley catalogue. This "study in fifteenth-century humor," as Buckley was wont to introduce it, is another two-part construction. The first phase is a straightforward social history of the title device, delivered in the formal language of English aristocracy:

> **CHASTITY BELT** As you know, between the Fourteenth and Fifteenth Century, there was a tremendous epidemic that swept the land. Everyone was going in search of the Holy Grail.
>
> Few of the beggars knew anything about it, and those that knew the least blew it up to such *fantastic* proportions: "You going, Fred?" "Yes." "You going, Harry?" "Yes." "Good, we all go together."
>
> The Duke of Cliftsford is standing in his courtyard. He's working his visor up and down. He doesn't want to get hung up in the middle of the fracas. There is much activity taking place in the courtyard. Various knaves and grooms are busy preparing the safari in search of the Holy Grail.
>
> There are three forges going, "Dang Dang Boom Boom Dong Dong."
>
> Finally, out of the thick smoke of the forges, comes a little blacksmith.
>
> He says: "Sire, may I have a word with you? I realize that I am taking my very head in my hands when I ask you for a few moments of your precious time, but I have conceived something in my fancy."
>
> "Very well."
>
> They opened the door—"Boom!"

> There on a table lay . . . a beautiful golden belt. It was Oriental gold, soft but hard. And all about it were phallic figurines *each* and *every* one of them engraved in *virgin pearls.*
>
> The Duke looks at this jeweler's fantasy and rather than being flattered, he flips: "How dare you bring me here to see this common, ordinary belt—busy man as I am! You know my mission! You know where I'm going! How dare you annoy me in this fashion! Before the sun rises, you will be singing soprano!"
>
> "But sire, it's not a common ordinary belt, it is a chastity belt."
>
> "A what?"
>
> "A chastity belt, your majesty, to preserve the honor of your Lady Faire while you, brave one, go in search of the Grail."
>
> The Duke looks at it again and says: "By Gad . . . *sheer genius.* Make me twelve at once."
>
> He had a few friends, ya know.

Part Two, however, is delivered entirely in the black voice and more akin to Buckley's "Amos 'n' Andy" bit than any of his latter compositions. The later scenario, describing a king's slyly disguised attempt to coax his queen into the anatomically protective gear, contains some of Buckley's most accessible and purely hilarious moments:

> The whole scene switches around. The Duke is a magnificent Negro Duke. He has the chastity belt behind his back. He's stacked up in armor and he is climbing the spiral staircase to the Queen's boudoir. While he is making the ascent, he is probing his brain for a piece of conversational putty whereby he may introduce this new and unusual affair to her Highness in *such* a manner as not to have to *chase her all over the blasted courtyard . . .* you know how the neighbors are.
>
> But, when he gets to the top, he has no answer. But being a creature of rhythm, he knocks anyway and a voice inside says: "Who's there?"
>
> "It's me baby, the King."
>
> "Is that my great and groovy lover and one of the greatest, stompin' studs that ever stomped through any Queen's boudoir and one of the greatest lovers in this here known world and that there world and all unknown worlds?"
>
> "Yes, Baby."
>
> "Fall in, Daddy. Look at that uniform on Daddy."
>
> "Yeah, they got me stacked in here pretty good, ain't they sugar? First they got to get me on a hoist to get me on a horse but when I'm on—vrrpptt—I'm gone."
>
> "I'm hip," she says. "What you got behind you Daddy?"
>
> "Well . . . ha ha ha ha ha . . . you ladies goin' to drive me crazy. 'What's this? What's that? Open this. Get that. Don't do this. Don't do that.'"

He sits her down. She go: "Ooooooooo."

He says: "What you 'Oooooooooooin' about woman?"

"I just say 'Ooooooooooo' was all I say—all I say was 'Oooooo.'"

He say: "Well, you been 'Ooooooooin' a little too much around here lately, you know that, don't you?"

Now she looks at it and, having never dreamed in the wildest dream the inspiration of a chastity belt, say to him with purest and high plum of naïveté, in the rich center of novitiate and expression say: "What is it Daddy, a jewel case?"

"Well," he says, "I suppose you could call it that, Sugar. Yeah, that's what it is, a jewel case."

He say: "You know that Grail?"

She say: "I'm hip, you goin' to pick up on it too, Daddy."

He say: "Well, you know there is a couple of cats around here sittin' up on top of the hill that aren't on the hook for the Grail. You know that too, baby?"

She say: "That's the livin', livin' truth, and some of them cats jump awful high and hard."

He say: "Just what I'm talking about, baby. Some night when my cats and kitties got that Grail in the corner, bout ready to Wwwhhaaaa-ppppm—I'm into the sack . . . say one of them cats gets jumping so high—Boom!—and so hard—Szzzzzz Bzzzzzz—right over that castle wall—pphh-hhhhh—right in your boudoir and this gadget is going to give them the *supreme* surprise of their natural born life."

He say: "Sugar baby, you gettin' yourself all bent 'bout a little thing like this. Sugar, it's just like a new pair of shoes, baby. You got to wear it a little while before you get used to it."

Buckley, it seems, was never above a little public bawdiness in his own life as well.

Bruce MacDonald

Pianist and composer Bruce MacDonald collaborated with many of the Swing Era greats, including Barney Bigard, Charlie Barnet, Roy Eldridge, Benny Carter, and Harry James.

I first met Dick Buckley, Lord Buckley, in Chicago. In 1947 a friend of mine and I were playing at the Aragon Ballroom in the James band. A bass player named Jimmy Stutts, who had been in California, came to see us with some other musicians we knew in Chicago. He said, "Hey I want you to meet a crazy guy—a good cat."

So he takes us to this swank hotel. We go up to his room, knock on the door, and Buckley greets us totally nude. There was a large divan in murky darkness behind him. He greets us all as "Prince" and says, "Come in gentlemen. The bar is over there. Fix yourselves a drink and make yourselves comfortable.

There's something I've got to finish." And he goes back over to the divan and continues the act of sex with this beautiful blonde chick. That's how I met Lord Buckley.

As a musician, I've been through a lot of things in my life but that was a strange way to meet someone.

Adam Keefe

He had a large and varied sexual appetite. He was rather public about his exploits as well—he didn't give a shit who knew what was happening. I mean he was "Lord Buckley" and that was that. It was not uncommon to be over there and have him start making it with some chick in the other room or right in front of you if he felt like it.

He liked to use his outrageousness as a way of testing those around him. You could stay or leave but if you left because you couldn't stand the heat, he'd admonish you: "You're a square!"

He'd test people with whatever drug he had handy, with the sex scene and with whatever else. If they didn't impress him or live up to his wacky standards, he'd yell: "You're a square, be gone!"

Two other versions of "Chastity Belt" have survived. A later, 1960 version of "Chastity Belt" released on the World Pacific label's *Bad-Rapping of the Marquis de Sade* LP is virtually identical in its delivery, dramatic humorous effect, and audience response to the performance from an unreleased recording at the Lighthouse in 1953.

The rare track on *Parabolic REVELATIONS* is "Georgia, Sweet and Kind," a bold example of Lord Buckley baring his sympathetic allegiance to black America. The concept of "Georgia" is simple enough: Buckley mournfully sings the famous Hoagy Carmichael tune "Georgia On My Mind" while augmenting it with frenetically frightful frames of accusation, mob law, and its dreadful consequences all culminating with more "strange fruit" hanging from a poplar tree.

Lady Elizabeth Buckley

The worst thing he did was to tell people the truth. Lots of times people don't like that. We had a man jump on stage in Florida with a knife who was going to kill him for some remark he made. Another night, I was sitting right in the middle of this club and he said to the audience, "You all have too much money and you don't know what to do with it." We left by the back door that night. One of the musicians said, "Now run and get in the car." I felt like I was living in a Humphrey Bogart movie.

Buckley's choice to perform this material in the infancy of the modern civil-rights movement often guaranteed him trouble. There were many occasions when his performance of "Georgia" and other related pieces or remarks that addressed racial inequity head-on resulted in confrontations of varying degrees of violence with less sympathetic audience members. He was often forced to flee a venue via bathroom window lest he face the wrath of angry patrons wishing to partake in the bloodletting of a "nigger lover."

Conversely, Buckley's use of the black vernacular was not always appreciated by African Americans themselves. This is, perhaps, the crux of his artistic and personal conflict: that he was at once seen as an unwelcome champion of civil rights by white racists and as a bigot by some blacks who felt he was, at best, misappropriating their culture.

Buddy Jones

I first met him in Washington, D.C., back in 1947 or 1948. There was an after-hours club called the Spotlight. I had a friend who knew Dick Buckley. I'm a bass player so he would take me, a piano player and a drummer to back him up at the Spotlight where he had been hired to do his act.

His compulsion to rip the skin off everybody's weaknesses might have prevented him from advancing more fully. I remember one night when we were working in Washington, D.C., there were a couple of guys from the South in the audience who were rednecks and drunks. They were the type of Southern rednecks that Lord Buckley didn't like.

And he would start singing "Georgia": "Georgia, Georgia, so sweet and kind . . ." And then he would say, "Oh, oh, don't Mr. MacGregor! You know I wouldn't do a thing like that!" He'd be singing "Georgia" so beautifully and augment it with this lynching scene until the guy in the act was saying, "Oh no! Don't tighten that rope around my neck . . . please don't . . . aaagghhh!!" And then the guy would be hung.

These two Southern guys sitting out there were now getting so mad that they were set to wait for him after the show to give him a licking. Buckley had to sneak out of the place to keep from getting hurt.

Dick Zalud

Sixty percent of the time he was his own worst enemy. I got him a gig with Florence Henderson's husband who owned a nightclub on Sunset Boulevard near Beverly Hills. Before the show I said to Buckley, "Look, do me a favor, don't do any of that far-out shit. Don't do 'Georgia.'"

"Georgia" was a bit where he sang that beautiful old slow romantic ballad "Georgia On My Mind" and intertwined that with a horrifying scenario involving the lynching of a black man in the South by a mob of rednecks. The irony was incredible.

I said, "Don't do any of that stuff. Don't do any of those horrifying things for these people because these people are all upper-crust Beverly Hills Hollywood movie types."

The first thing he did when he got up on the stage was "Georgia." He just scared the shit out of everybody.

Lord Buckley

Dig and thou shalt be dug. Drag not and shalt not be drug.

Of all the venues from which the new, cool West Coast jazz sound emanated, none epitomized the laid-back ethos better than the Lighthouse Café on 21 Pier Avenue in Hermosa Beach, California. Founded by bassist Howard Rumsey in 1949, the Lighthouse brought West Coast jazz as far west as it could geographically go. Even today, where the haunt still offers up the sounds that made it famous five decades ago, the sidewalk disappears near the end of a pier a few feet past the front door, its place taken by the beach, which gently slopes to the frosty froth of the Pacific Ocean.

Despite the romance of the locale and the name, the Lighthouse Café boasted no beacon for fogbound sailors, no towering turret, no crusty keeper. With its undistinguished facade and dank, claustrophobic interior, the club could well have passed for one of the decaying basements that featured jazz on New York's Fifty-second Street or any other East Coast city.

An unlikely locale to make jazz history, it was the picture-perfect postcard setting for Lord Buckley's 1953 sets that Rumsey captured and preserved on reel-to-reel tape. Rumsey, by then the club's proprietor and musical director, recorded just about all the acts passing through with a mike hung over the rafters and running to a tape machine under a table.

The surviving evidence of Buckley's appearance at the Lighthouse is extraordinary on several counts. The two forty-minute sets find the forty-seven-year-old Wordman from Wonderland dispensing his mixed bag of comedic weaponry that testifies to his wide-ranging performance gifts—from the delicate interplay with the house band and his own generally overlooked vocalese to stunning serenades of both his most famous and obscure bits, some of which the Lighthouse tape provide the only exposition.

The Lighthouse audience was a notoriously fluid crowd, as beachcombers and jazz freaks alike wandered in and out with a lack of reverence that patrons of the more traditional venues at points East would have found appalling. Their occasional lack of attentiveness and respect forced Buckley to employ both brusque and gentle devices to corral them into the Royal Court on this occasion, providing a fascinating study of the difficult arts of persuasion and conversion. At one point during the proceedings he singles out the most unruly perpetrator and, in defeating his noisy nemesis, slowly and effectively wins the crowd over.

The two sets from the Lighthouse are about as close as anything we are likely to get to an unedited evening with Lord Buckley in the flesh and in his prime. The one-hour-plus recording also features the Lighthouse All-Stars, led by pianist Hampton Hawes, and works as one of the best examples of musical accompaniment for the Beat Bard as he plays off them like a perfect cross between Louis Armstrong and a confident, fire-and-brimstone-spewing stump preacher. Buckley even commences the proceedings with a loving tribute to Pops before launching into an excellent Armstrong-inspired vocalese, "I Can't Give You Anything but Love," in the "key of G" as he notifies the band.

The early, mellow crowd is next tested with "The Neurotic Crocodile," an aging piece of burlesque about the title amphibian, then treated with perhaps the most diabolical version of "Murder" (his oral representation of the not-yet-congealed blood lightly dripping from the razor-sharp weapon is worth the price of admission alone), and finally rewarded with an unusual reading of "The Nazz" (complete with musical rave-ups of "When the Saints Go Marching In" perfectly punctuating the key pauses of his signature opus, à la the original Vaya pressing of the masterpiece) as Buckley leads the band through his favorite taste of gospel comedy.

Set two is not only a treasure of peak Buckley performances, but also the solitary extant example of His Lordship dealing with a sometimes-loutish peanut gallery. Though the believers greatly outnumber the heathen on this particular night, Lord Buckley's slick expertise in silencing even the most volubly obnoxious drunks with his stern "Are you there?" attention-getter peppering the proceedings is as nimble as it is bold as he wins the day in securing the soapbox and his acolytes' affections. "Are you there?" it should be mentioned, is a common Buckley koan and can be heard sprinkled through a few of his pieces and many an extemporaneous rap—a kind of Zen hipster's version of "What's the sound of one hand clapping?" or Ram Dass's fabled mantra, "Be Here Now." Needless to say, none of the double-square wannabes with their inane chatter (obviously fueled by suds and a long day at the beach) dare open their traps after Buckley has had his way with them.

And what a second set it is! After a similarly strong Armstrong-voiced vocal ("Sleepy Time Gal" this time) and a bit of warm-up cornpone ("The Judge"), Buckley wows the assembled with some red-hot rarities: "Pursuit of Morpheus," "Jonah and the Whale," "Georgia, Sweet and Kind," and "Chastity Belt."

Delivered in that corrupt old southern codger voice that would mark his later hillbilly comedy masterworks, "Governor Slugwell" and "God's Own Drunk," "The Judge" is essentially a successful courtroom plea by a respectable country lawyer making a case for his client's acquittal for an accidental shooting—a twelve-year-old boy who blew off a neighbor's face with some ill-aimed buckshot. Only in the end do we discover that the defendant is the blustery lawyer's son.

"Pursuit of Morpheus" is rendered as another, different type of approach to the black voice and legend. What a remarkable choice of subject matter: Morpheus, the lord of the dreamworld. Buckley, by the way, mentions Morpheus in some versions of "Jonah and the Whale," so he was evidently familiar with and impressed by the storytelling potential of the myth. Employing the cadence of his "Amos 'n' Andy" vocal approach, Buckley casts his story as an insomniac's plea to Morpheus for some shut-eye. The sleepless hero (a shy, diminutive fellow indeed) is part of the same recurring blackface Chaplinesque character found in several of Buckley's most famous and obscure bits as diverse as "The Nazz" and "The Sinner" from the 1949 *Club 7* television broadcast. This Stepin Fetchit character, unable to sleep, encounters the Sandman himself and, after some from-the-heart pleading, is finally whisked away into that somnambulistic netherworld. Despite the shamelessly cliché and hopelessly dated representation of the insomniac, the mood of "Pursuit of Morpheus" is distinctly gothic and points to the aesthetic Buckley would later demonstrate and "flesh out" in "The Bad-Rapping of the Marquis de Sade" a few years later.

A strong and unusual version of "Jonah and the Whale" follows and is accompanied, like the first-set "Nazz" before it, with the house band chiming in with "When the Saints Go Marching In" at just the right pauses on the piece.

Paradoxically, Buckley's antic yet devastating portrayal of the racial divide evidenced in "Georgia, Sweet and Kind" is met with guffaws typical of the pre–Politically Correct era. In trotting out this potentially inflammatory piece of business, Buckley showed that he wasn't afraid to confront an audience with, (what was then) his most pointedly political work, though he was probably guessing that the crowd's progressive sensibilities would help carry the day. That they heartily, if at times uncomfortably, laugh along with the piece seems a guiltless testimony to their personal allegiances.

Finishing his performance, Buckley leaves them laughing some more with "Chastity Belt" in what may be the best version of this ribald historical excursion—an obvious fan favorite that is met with an appropriate, knowing response.

All things considered, the Lighthouse tape is a full-blown example of a typical Lord Buckley performance from the mid-1950s.

Buckley found like-minded souls when he moved his flock to a ten-dollar-a-month shack north of Los Angeles in Topanga Canyon in 1954. Bob DeWitt, a local artist who managed the real estate and lived nearby, remembers that Buckley was "flat-ass broke" when he first appeared with his brood. DeWitt had already begun nurturing a bohemian scene in Topanga by staging art shows and folk concerts while renting properties to fellow leftist libertines such as Will Geer and Woody Guthrie. Buckley himself was soon bringing jazz buddies like Jimmy Giuffre, Shelly Manne, and Bud Shank up to Topanga to party and jam.

Eldon Setterholm

After the Crackerbox Palace, things started gettin' rough. When he lost that rental he moved out to Topanga Canyon. The Realtor up there was also an artist, an eccentric kind of a guy who never wore shoes and he went runnin' around the hills selling real estate and doing well. His name was Bob DeWitt and he sold parcels from the beach all the way to the top. He lived in this rancho up near the top with his wife and all his children, and they had goats.

One of Lord Buckley's favorite books was Whitman's *Leaves of Grass*. I remember out in Topanga Canyon one night, he got the oil light goin' and he was reading that and, I mean, he made those pages come alive, man. The entertainment at Buckley's house out there was conversation and reading. He had that tremendous ability to make the words live . . . yeah.

Buckley got right into the swing of things, performing at DeWitt's music and art presentations. DeWitt also operated a crude but groundbreaking light show while all the children took turns riding the DeWitt's family pony, pluckily named T.V., around the canyon. Confirming the notion that this was a prehippie culture spawning a good fifteen years ahead of schedule, DeWitt recalls Lady Buckley painting the word *Luv* on a pot and placing it at her husband's feet for appreciators to contribute donations for their well-being—usually about ten dollars an afternoon. In many ways things had not changed much for Buckley since his days as youngster busking the streets of Tuolumne.

Additionally, DeWitt remembers the powerful effect Buckley's raves had on the audience: "People would be pounding on the walls in hypnotic ecstasy."

Ira Westley

Veteran bassist Ira Westley worked with the great Jack Teagarden and Harry James bands of the 1950s. He was an original member of Herb Alpert's Tijuana Brass in the 1960s and produced the Hues Corporation in the 1970s.

Lord Buckley and I used to perform together. Every Sunday I'd take my family up to Topanga Canyon where there was a little art colony. I'd take my tuba and my string bass along and I would set 'em up so I could switch over from one to the other as I played behind Lord Buckley's recitations. We did this every Sunday for a whole summer and had a wonderful time. I also appeared with him several times at the Las Palmas Theater in Hollywood. Les McCann was the piano player with us.

The DeWitts' kids, my kids and Lord Buckley's kids all played with one another. The DeWitts, instead of buying a television set for the kids, bought a horse that they called T.V. And Buckley's kids used to ride T.V. along with our kids around the canyon.

There was a little art colony with little art exhibits on some of the DeWitts' property. So they set up these little Sunday afternoon meetings. People who came sat around on stumps and listened to Lord Buckley tell his story "The Nazz," various Bible stories and even some Shakespeare.

Lady Buckley was busy as well, transforming their modest shelter into another royal Buckley affair. She retrieved a roll of red velvet from the local dump and lined the shack with it, prompting Lord Buckley to dub their home "The Jewel Box" in an apparent reference to his blue bit "Chastity Belt."

When they installed a throne, the stage was properly set and the Royal Court was convened once again.

Lord Buckley

And under the well-known truth that our nation is so young, a wild, swinging dimple in the face of humanity, I should like to call your attention to the fact that we have not yet time to study, to appreciate, to grasp the volume and the beauty of our great artists and performers. And I should like to, in humility—in deep humility—dedicate this concert in this citadel, this swinging mountain-headed church, this religious meeting of the people, this peak-headed Americana, this ever-loving, non-stop, sweet, juicy, groovy swinger to end all swingers.

But, because the constraints of this venue proved too limiting, Lord Buckley simply opened his own club . . . with a twist. Not timid about dishing out his own brand of pixie dust, love juice, hellfire, and damnation, it was no surprise to the Royal Court when Buckley informally founded "the Church of the Living Swing" at the Topanga Canyon art gallery. Not quite John the Baptist territory but built on a solid rock, nonetheless.

Though the enterprise was short-lived (an early service was raided by the vice squad—some say on a tip by Buckley himself), the experience confirmed to Lord Buckley that his calling was an evangelical one.

Dick Zalud

He'd watch those television evangelists and say, "Man, religion is the greatest way in the world to make money."

Bruce MacDonald

Buckley had about a fifteen-year run as far as I'm concerned. He was bringing us a different approach to wit and humor. After World War II there was a certain naïveté and exuberance: a sense that anything was possible. And, along with that, new forms of expression were needed. I can't really think of him as a comedian at all. He was more like a visionary monologist. Here was something new. Here was a man telling us some things that we'd never heard before.

He was a success to all of us. Buckley wanted to be a guru and he became a guru in his own mind. He wanted to gather people around him and form a cult and he did—a very small, esoteric cult. I was never really a part of Buckley's cult because I'm something else—I'm my own man. I don't join cults. I never did. But that's what Buckley wanted and he became what he wanted to become. He had people around him and he impressed them. He created his own fifteen years. Buckley was on a mission. He wanted to convert people.

Viewing himself as a visionary leader of men, Lord Buckley threw himself into his art with missionary zeal. The Church of the Living Swing was a congregation that sprung Buckley's mind, which saw him preaching his gospel in a rented American Legion hall to a communion of musicians, belly dancers, derelicts, and camp followers.

Jim Dickson

One of the wilder Buckley experiences I had involved the Church of the Living Swing at Topanga Canyon. He hooked up with a Realtor named Bob DeWitt who gave him his office on Sundays, and he held what he called America's first jazz church and it would go on all day.

The most startling part about it was that the audience covered such a wide spectrum. You'd have jazz musicians in shades in the back, a gypsy woman on the floor nursing her baby, people from Malibu dressed for church who had received invitations, belly dancers, and light shows. Anything and everything.

He would do some of his material or he would just hold court because he could be extemporaneous and hold an audience for hours if he wanted to. He just went with his own interests. These raps didn't have any more or less of a spiritual, ethical or humorous slant than did his set pieces. He would precious tilt with lines like, "People haven't left the church but that church has left the people." Or he would do his hip versions of Aesop's Fables.

George Greif

Things like the Church of the Living Swing were states of mind for him. Like "House of Lords," a club he wanted to build once. Everybody would be Lords and Ladies in the House of Lords and he would do a Friar Tuck thing. He held court every night anyway, so why not do it in a club for money.

Mel Welles

The Church of the Living Swing—America's first jazz church. He opened this alleged church in Topanga Canyon. It was in a community hall. Everybody had been telling him that what he should have been was a minister or an evangelist, that he would have made a fortune.

That idea ticked off the Church of the Living Swing. Incidentally, some fifty people were busted for holding pot at the first service. Everybody came all dressed up in weird clothes. Lady Elizabeth looked like Gloria Swanson from *Sunset Boulevard* decked out in all kinds of blithe spirit. She would present her Ballet for Living at the services.

Lord Buckley

In order to salute this family of groovy, swinging, pretty chicks and solid stalwart studs, I'd like to blow a little scene on religion. Everyone is rubbing their wig to find out where religion lies: "Am I religious enough? Just exactly what do I do to hit that center beam—booooom—so I can ride down that beautiful swingin' stream of consciousness and keep right into the *flow* of the *go*."

How to do it. How to be it. How to be in there tight. How to be on the beat. How to give from the melon of life. How to swing. How to come on like a wild mother peacock—whoooooosh!

Buckley's scramble for a constant, legit paycheck led to ever-new devices for expression of his second greatest talent: the con.

Dick Zalud

They were living in, like, a chicken coop in Pasadena in the hills. Yeah, man, they scuffled—and with two kids! And yet he always managed to present a very immaculate image even when he was scuffling.

Millie Vernon

I think his whole existence was getting up in the morning and figuring out how they were going to make it that day—what he could do to get a job. Survive, but always live for the moment.

Ed Randolph

Once I was driving His Lordship to a recording session at Radio Recorders in George Greif's MG. His Lordship was seated next to me in the two-seater and I looked around to see if there was anything behind me so I could take a turn. And then, for some reason, I looked around again and, quite rightly, with wonderful logic, he said, "You only have to look once, Eagle." It was a kind of stern disciplining remark. You know, either you've looked or you haven't looked.

Another time he came up to me and said, "Eagle, I need fifty dollars for a new set of tires for the Fairyland Express," which was the name he gave his car. As his assistant manager I gave him the fifty to buy the tires so he could be mobile because if you're not mobile in L.A. it's catastrophic.

A few days later I saw him again, but he had the same old tires on his car, and I questioned him on this.

"I didn't get them," he said. "I spent the money on some grass instead."

"How could you do such a thing," I said.

"It's your fault, " he said. "You shouldn't have put the temptation in front of me."

Dr. Oscar Janiger

The best I can do is to call him a kind of troubadour. Like in the old-fashioned version of people who went from town to town with the news, the humor and music, often in a whimsical way.

Buckley had a sense that he could take from the world in the way that the troubadours of the past were paid and enjoy a certain kind of privilege. Some people may have felt that he was somewhat cavalier about that. But every time I took him to dinner, by God, I paid for him and was goddamned happy to do it. I could see myself giving him money and being glad of it—feeling that the man deserved it and was more than paying me back with his work. My guess is that he was spread out like Walt Whitman was spread out. Whitman, as you recall, said: "The world is my living room and everybody is my relative." I think Buckley felt that way, too.

Mel Welles

He never saw himself as a troubadour. He saw himself very clearly as a struggling entertainer who was not making it. See, I'm the only one that was privileged to see him when he was not "on." He never broke down to anybody else but me—not even Elizabeth. I have a Ph. D. in psychology and he knew that. So, whenever he needed to expound on his disappointment, bitterness or frustration he would do it to me. We had long three- and four-hour chats about it. But it never did any good because he never acted on anybody's advice. He always asked for it and he always listened to it but he never acted on it.

He was a mooch, a sponger. He would call you up and ask you to pick up lamb chops or veal chops on the way over but then never pay you for them. He was royalty on the one hand and then a small-time hustler on the other, in that he burdened all of his friends with his support.

It wasn't as if he felt that he was owed anything. That wouldn't have made him a nice guy if he thought that he was owed anything. The mooching was just a game that he felt that he was entitled to play because he was very generous with whatever he had. He shared his home and whatever he had there: his food, his good pot and all of that sort of stuff. He always had major name entertainers there for you to listen to. People like Miles Davis, Benny Carter, Della Reese, and Morganna Carter.

So the game that he played was that if he needed something, instead of asking you outright, you know, could you lend him a couple of dollars or could you bring some food, he would play this game. Sort of like asking you to help him save face.

Larry Storch

A great con man, someone once said about His Lordship that he was better at raising money for himself than anybody. But, when he finally did get ahold of some money, he really didn't know what to do with it. He wasn't very shrewd about holding onto it or passing it out.

Bruce MacDonald

Buckley was a hip con man. That's part of Buckley. He was witty and he lived by his wits. He was a good cat but he was a con man. He was an immoral moral man.

Huntz Hall

Best known as one of the Dead End Kids and for his role as Horace Debussy Jones (aka"Satch") in the marvelously campy Bowery Boys films of the 1930s and 1940s, the late Huntz Hall's career in the movies is mythic. He commenced a close friendship with Dick Buckley in Chicago during the late 1930s when the performer was traveling by hearse to his appearances at that infamous nightspot, the Suzy Q.

He looked like he never worried but he was a thoughtful man. He thought of people.

He never had any money. Richard lived day by day. One time he came to me for money and I was getting tired of always giving him money so I said, "You got to put up security. I have to have something Richard."

So he took his watch off which was worth like two thousand dollars. I didn't want to take it really but I thought I had to do this to see if he would actually pay me back. I told him I'd give him a week and if he didn't pay me I'd keep the watch. I never would have actually kept it but I just had to put in a little threat.

A week later he came into a bar I had a little piece of. I saw him and said, "Richard, you've only got about twelve more hours or it's mine."

I had two watches on my wrist, his and mine, and I showed it to him.

And he said, "Sir Hall, I have the money here in my pocket."

I was so happy. He gave me the money and I gave him the watch and said, "I love you Richard but I had to do this."

He said, "Ah, but it's the law of nature."

Then I said, "So Richard, ya need a hundred dollars?"

And he said, "Sir Hall, I don't beg."

Red Rodney

Once in California, I was beat and broke and my rent was due. He was beat and broke and owed rent and yet he went all around one night raising money for me to pay my rent. I'll never forget that. He took me everywhere with him and he borrowed money which he needed desperately for himself and he gave it to me to pay my debts. He took me to musicians so we were ahead of the game because they knew me or knew of me. Yeah, Dick was quite a guy.

He always had to go out and raise money for himself so he was already pretty good at it. But even when he got money, no matter how much, he'd blow it real fast. It meant nothing to him: you make it, you earn it, you get it, blow it and then start worrying about it again. It was always freewheeling around Buckley.

And like any charismatic worth his salt, Buckley's claims of healing powers were not without foundation.

Mort Fega

I witnessed him get rid of a headache I'd had for three days . . . over the telephone. Hard to believe. When I hung up the phone, my headache was gone. His contention was that when you're thinking all these beautiful thoughts, that out of the palm of your hand there emanates great therapeutic heat. Another time he put his hand up to my head. All of a sudden I felt this very hot heat on my forehead from his hand. He told me I could do the same thing. And I've done it.

Eldon Setterholm

He liked to consider himself a faith healer. If he'd catch somebody sick, boy, he'd take 'em by the hand and say, "You're getting better! Right here and now on the spot this sickness is LEAVING you!" And, sure enough, he would be so forceful that he'd make people get up out of sickbed.

Lord Buckley

And from this glorious man's adventure (Alvar Núñez Cabeza de Vaca, The Gasser) and from the association and translation of his works, it gave me the power of the laying on of the hands, the healing of the hand, which he says that we all have and which I found out to be true. Each and every one of us possess this.

I've cured arthritis . . . there was a little girl. I ran her down in Las Vegas recently and I heard she was paralyzed. And I ran her down—I found out where she lived. A little Negro girl by the way and she was so nervous that she wouldn't let me put the hand on her. But I explained to her that all over this world in the alleys and valleys, on the plains, on the mesa, and the mountain top on the plateaus to the sands to the Gulf through the whole scene of this world—black, green, blue, yellow, and pink—there's loaded with *beautiful* people that we never hear a thing about. We only hear about the winners and the losers and the others. But they're there. And those people are the protectors and progressers of the vaults of love which is known as "God." And when you appeal, when you go up a ladder, you go up the ladder and you go up so that you may get your vibrational points spread out so they go round-wise, electronic-wise, and you contact these people and you see their beauty and you hear the voices of the children and you see the sweet swing and the mighty power that's going ahead for greater perfection—for greater individual protection, for greater individual understanding, for greater presentation of the powers of the Garden of Love and contact with these people and—thack!—you could feel burning right in your hand. I've knocked out arthritis, anything that you're big enough to challenge.

10 finger-poppin' daddy

Lord Buckley

You know why they called this cat "Willie the Shake?" . . . because he . . . *SHOOK* everyone. They gave that cat five-cents worth of paper and a nickel's worth of ink and he sat down and wrote up such a breeze that when he got through—vrrppptt—*everybody got off.*

News of Buckley's on- and offstage exploits were spreading via word of mouth, and in early January of 1955 he again found himself in Radio Recorders, a studio on Santa Monica Boulevard, cutting grooves for RCA Victor, which were released later in the year as *Hipsters, Flipsters and Finger-Poppin' Daddies, Knock Me Your Lobes.* Aside from the title track, the cuts included "Boston Tea Party," "To Swing or Not to Swing," "Is This the Sticker?," and "Hip Hiawatha."

That Buckley landed a deal with a company as substantial as RCA Victor may strike some as being the anomaly that it was. It was also a rare instance of being at the right place at the right time.

Harry Geller

Harry Geller's big break in the music business came when he took Bunny Berigan's trumpet chair in the Benny Goodman band at Los Angeles's Palomar Ballroom in 1935. Geller went on to play with Artie Shaw, befriend both Spike Jones and Henry Miller, and find a second career as RCA Victor's West Coast A&R man.

I had seen Buckley a couple of times in Vegas and in L.A. and I thought he would be interesting to record. I tried to record as many different people doing as many different things as possible.

It was in late 1954 that I got his phone number, called him and introduced myself. He invited me to visit him at a little frame house he was renting in Venice near the beach.

I went over to his house and he introduced me to his wife and children. We went for a drive in my car to discuss his material and he brought along his son, Prince Richard. He introduced everybody in his family with a royal title.

As we drove we were talking about what kinds of material he had and what would be suitable for recording. Prince Richard was sitting on his father's lap and, at one point, Buckley asked his son to sing "Baa Baa Blacksheep" and he did. Buckley soon joined him in a duet and it was really quite charming. I later recorded that in the studio.

He came into my office the next day and we discussed the project further. He gave me the titles to the pieces he had been working on and he gave me a taste of nine or ten of them. So I set the record date for early 1955 and, on the appointed hour, he arrived at the studio with his son.

I let him handle the session pretty much himself. We recorded nine or ten of them and it occurred to me during the course of the session that some of these things would sound better with a small group of musicians backing him.

So, afterwards, I set up another date with Benny Carter, Red Callender and several other musicians.

I also thought that, aside from a jazz backing, his approach might be interesting if it were augmented by a string section. I had written a piece of orchestral music called "Release from Nervous Tension" which itself was inspired by a popular book of the time by the same title.

Buckley came back for the sessions and performed some of the material right along with the ensembles. It was very impressive how he could just mold himself to fit whatever situation was at hand.

He did everything from memory and he did it well so he rarely did more than two takes of anything. Sometimes I'd get him to do another take and ask him to slow a part down or change the inflection of a word.

I didn't get much response from New York after I sent them the master tapes. I don't think the RCA marketing people got behind it too well because it really didn't do that well. The New York executives made the decisions on what was to be included in the album and evidently decided to focus on the Shakespearean and American history routines with the classical orchestral backings.

I don't know how much Buckley would have been paid for the record. That really would have been an arrangement between his management and RCA's New York office.

The album's cover art, designed and rendered by the late, great James Flora, captures and rekindles the offbeat spirit of the Vaya productions. Dominated by an oversized Greek gladiator spewing the album's title out of his mouth comic-book-style, the cover features mytho-hipster satyrs and nymphs dancing amid the ruins of ancient architecture and modern jazz instruments.

Flora, whose long-overdue recognition as a contributor to mid-twentieth-century popular culture coincided with his passing in 1998, was a magazine art director and children's book author and illustrator who, in the early 1940s, became one of the first artists to design and illustrate record album covers, which helped transform the way records were marketed. As his ideas found their way onto album covers, he eventually became renowned for his distinctive drawing style. His lighthearted blend of surrealism and cartoon was notable for its comic juxtapositions of physically exaggerated characters, and his concept of design quickly helped define the look of record albums. In the words of Flora admirer Irwin Chusid: "Flora's manic illustrations featured bug-eyed jazz gremlins, totem-pole figureheads, geometric cityscapes and Mobius-strip

The earliest known photo of Lord Buckley (far right, in Boy Scout uniform), California, circa 1916. The other members of the Buckley clan are (left to right) Lester, Nell, Annie Laurie, Ben, and Jim. © Elaine Rains-Thomasen. Used with permission.

Dick Buckley: Master of Ceremonies, circa late 1920s or early 1930s. Billy Rose Theatre Collection. The New York Public Library for the Performing Arts. Astor, Lenox and Tilden Foundations.

Dick Buckley and Great Dane, circa mid-1930s. © Elaine Rains-Thomasen. Used with permission.

Buckley hams it up. *Fun for the Money* program, Hollywood, California, 1941. Billy Rose Theatre Collection. The New York Public Library for the Performing Arts. Astor, Lenox and Tilden Foundations.

A mid-1940s publicity photo of Dick Buckley during vaudeville's waning days. Photo: John E. Reed. Billy Rose Theatre Collection. The New York Public Library for the Performing Arts. Astor, Lenox and Tilden Foundations.

Two of the early Lord Buckley albums: *Euphoria* and *Hipsters, Flipsters and Finger-Poppin' Daddies Knock Me Your Lobes*
Author's collection.

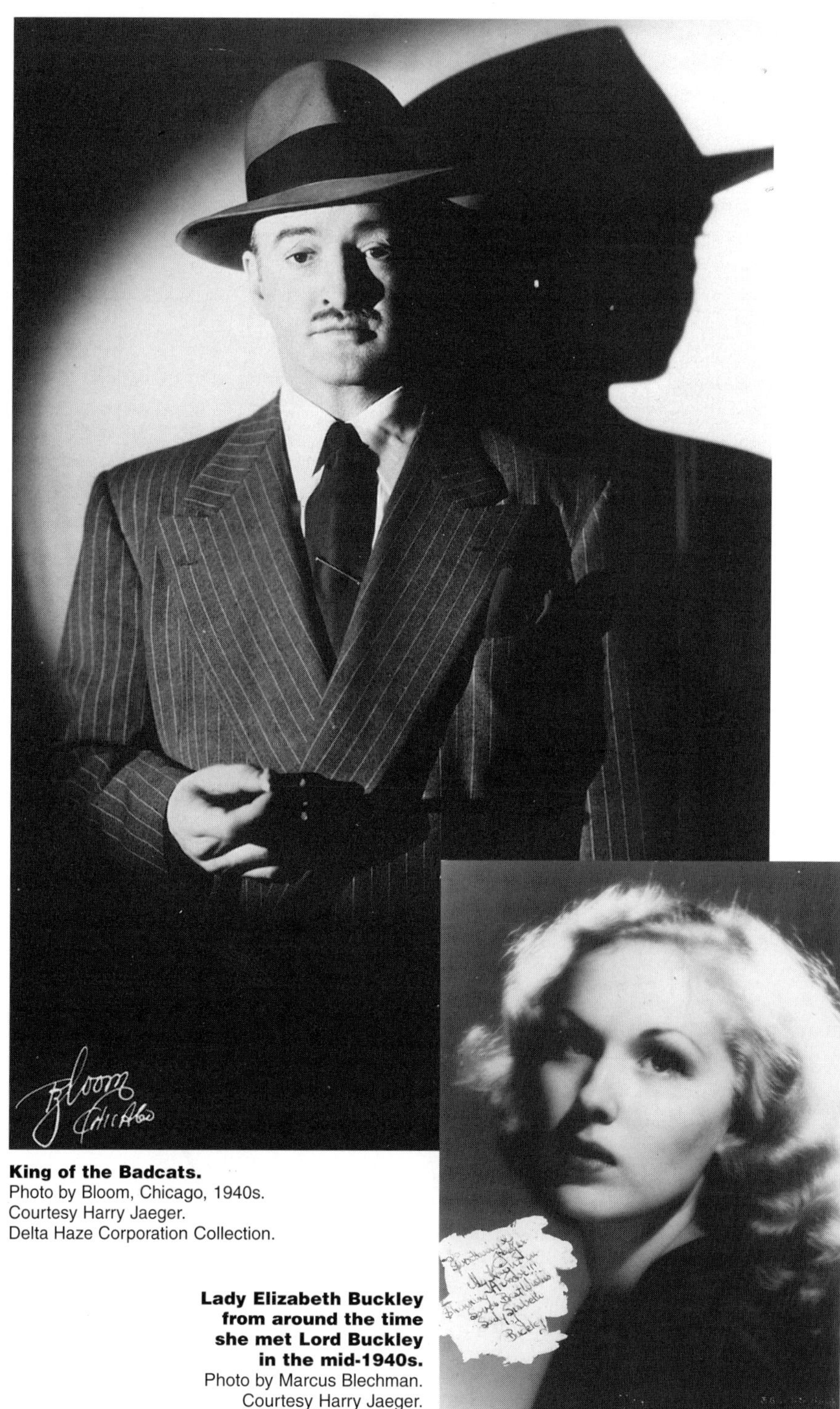

King of the Badcats.
Photo by Bloom, Chicago, 1940s.
Courtesy Harry Jaeger.
Delta Haze Corporation Collection.

Lady Elizabeth Buckley from around the time she met Lord Buckley in the mid-1940s.
Photo by Marcus Blechman.
Courtesy Harry Jaeger.
Delta Haze Corporation Collection.

The Lord of Flip Manor from a 1956 photo shoot in California. © Tom Heffernan/Roy Harte Jazz Archive.

Lord Buckley at Jazz City, Los Angeles, 1955. These photos were taken during His Lordship's lengthy run at the club where he met James Dean.
© Dave Pell/Roy Harte Jazz Archive.

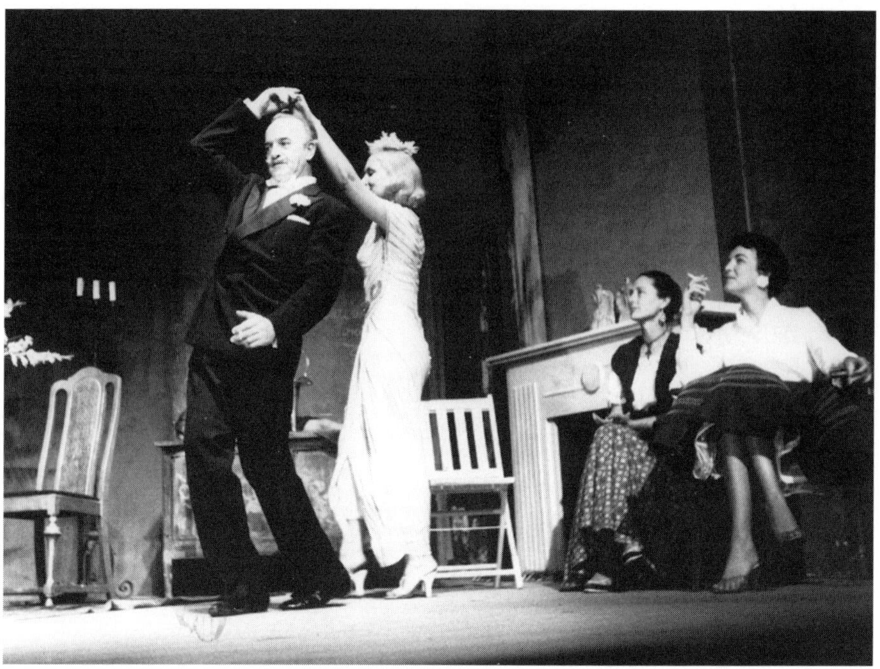

The most immaculately hip aristocrat waltzing with Lady Buckley on stage at the midnight Music Box gig, Hollywood, 1956. Photo: Ray Avery. Used with permission.

Bowing after at his command performance at the Music Box. The Roy Milton band (left), Lady Buckley, seated. Hollywood, 1956. Photo: Ray Avery. Used with permission.

Two of Buckley's later releases, *Way Out Humor* and *Blowing His Mind (and yours, too).* Photos: William Claxton. Courtesy of World Pacific, a division of Capitol Records, Inc.

Lord Richard Buckley

BUCKLEY DESCRIBES FIRST RIDE IN A JET!

Editors note: Lord Buckley goofs it up some, so I thought I should jump in here and hip you that the following is true. He actually took a panic ride in a two-seater jet plane. Here is what happened when the Lord somehow conned the Air Force into letting him make like a "spacehead."

I picked up the phone and a cat on the other end said, "This is Captain Shalleck, of the United States Air Force. I have been assigned to this project and I'll pick you up at 8:30 in the morning and we'll go to Palmdale for the jet ride . . . you *are* Lord Buckley aren't you?"

I said, "solid," and he said, "roger" and cut.

I said to myself, man, here's where I flip out into the wild blue yonder . . . I found out later why they call it *wild.*

The Captain hit my pad at 8:30 and by 10 we were there. We fell into the scene that was security city. Man, there was fuzz walking . . . fuzz riding . . . fuzz to the left . . . fuzz to the right . . . fuzz digging the fuzz and all of them putting the burn on me like I had personally cut out with the Statue of Liberty.

We cut upstairs where I was introduced to a tall cat with a face like a tanned hatchet. This was Captain Brown, *the cool.* He dug me with a "take" that said, *This man don't look like he's breathing too good at sea level.*

They put a pre-flight jazz book on me, that was a gasser. The opening lines were a hanger: "*It is a known fact that it is very difficult for the observer* (that's me!) *in an AT-33 aircraft to determine the state of an emergency should one arise, therefore all observers must rely on the actions and words of the pilot when unusual occurrences take place.*"

I began to suffer from a seizure of the flips . . . "*Extent of emergency . . . unusual occurrences*" They *must* have pulled a switch on me . . . this book is for the "test cats," *not me.*

While panicing on the cool words of advice in this little goodie, a cat comes up with a space hat and says, "Try this on for size." I tried it on and he took it off, squeezed it, and this time it felt like it was glued to my wig. Next he gave me a set of Churchill striders to put on my

38 DIG MAGAZINE

Preparing to take off into the wild blue yonder in the pages of *Dig* magazine. California, 1956. Author's collection.

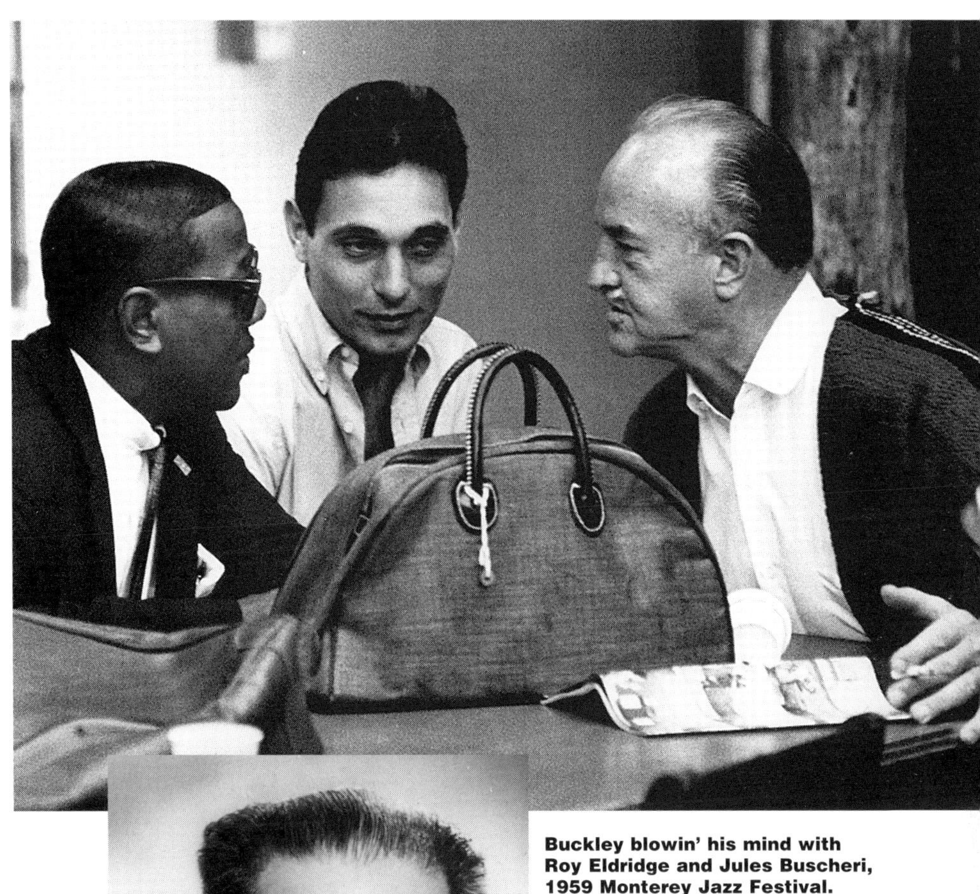

Buckley blowin' his mind with Roy Eldridge and Jules Buscheri, 1959 Monterey Jazz Festival. Photo: Jerry Stoll. Used with permission.

Cleveland poet and journalist, Joseph S. Newman, the author of "Black Cross." Photo courtesy of David C. Barnett. Used with permission.

American royalty: Lord Buckley and Ed Sullivan, New York City, 1959.
Courtesy of CBS Photo Archive.

A rare photo of Buckley performing his "Amos 'n' Andy" act. From left, Johnny Wayne, Frank Schuster, Lord Buckley, Trude Adams, and Ed Sullivan. New York City, 1959.
Courtesy of CBS Photo Archive.

"The Hip Messiah" and the beatniks. Sausalito, California, 1960.
Photos: Charles Campbell. Used with permission.

On his Cosmic Tour, Buckley preaches at a recording studio. Chicago, 1960.
Photo: Ed DePhoure. Courtesy of Dick "Prince Owl Head" Zalud. Used with permission.

Opening Night at the Jazz Gallery, New York City, October 4, 1960. From left, Joe Termini, Harold L. "Doc" Humes," Buckley, and Prince Lewis Foremaster.
Photo: Bob Parent/Archive Photos.

Dizzy Gillespie and Ornette Coleman blow an interstellar blues in His Lordship's honor at the Village Gate, New York City, December 1960. Photo: Bob Parent/Archive Photos.

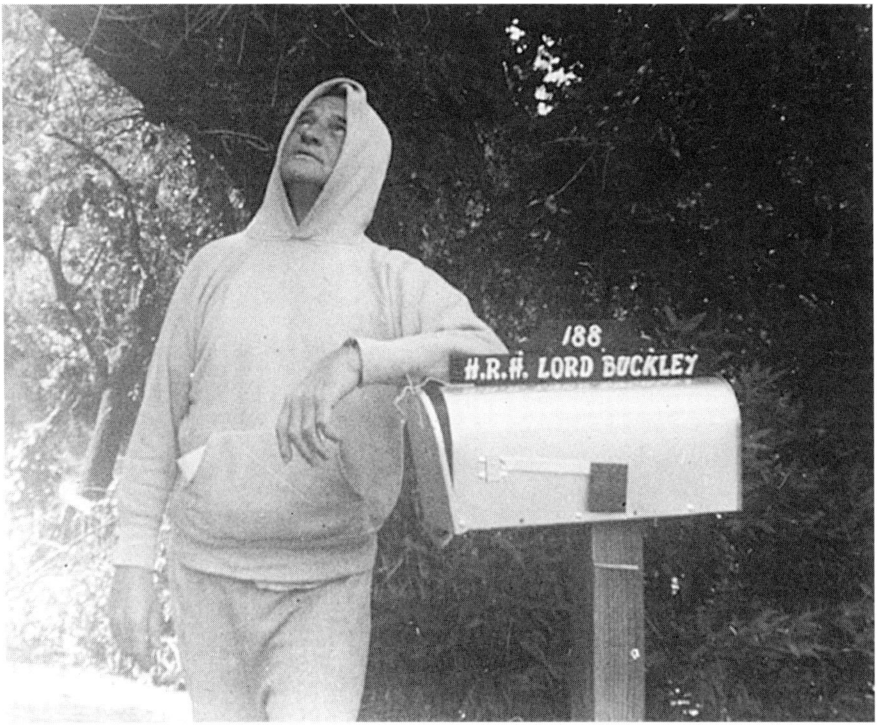

Contemplating the cosmos, Lord Buckley outside his home in San Rafael, California, 1960. Note the "H.R.H." on the mailbox. Photo: Charles Campbell. Used with permission.

The last known photo of Lord Buckley. Jazz Gallery, New York City, October 4, 1960.
Photo: Bob Parent/Archive Photos.

trumpets. Their two-dimensionality made them appear childlike, yet a sinister edge lent a tinge of sophistication."

For a variety of reasons, the RCA outing may be the least satisfying of Lord Buckley's official long-playing releases. No doubt Harry Geller's well-intentioned but sometimes stilted and schmaltzy symphonic arrangements (attributed on the album sleeve to "the Royal Court Orchestra under the direction of Sir Harry, M.G.") that accompany the renditions fall flat and, in the final wash, are a distracting factor. Charlie Parker could work with strings but, at least on this day, not Lord Buckley. Buckley seems a natural for musical backing but only rarely did it come off on recording, and then only in an informal jazz or spiritual setting. In this regard *Hipsters, Flipsters and Finger-Poppin' Daddies* was a gallant experiment but a noble failure nonetheless.

The larger problem with the RCA disc is the material itself, which lacks the free-wheeling dramatic range, nuance, insight, and verbal possibility of his earlier efforts. While the title track covers familiar ground less convincingly (despite the great alto saxophonist Benny Carter adding his velvety touch), there are two other Shakespeare soliloquies in hip to be found here. Hamlet's "To be or not to be?" becomes "To Swing or Not to Swing?" while "Is This the Sticker?" is a viper's translation of Macbeth's "Is this the dagger?" speech from Act Two, Scene One of the tragedy. A footnote to the album's title track is an alternate, jazzier, and better take of "Hipsters, Flipsters and Finger-Poppin' Daddies"—also including Carter on alto—which appeared on *The Golden Age of Comedy,* an RCA compilation released in 1972.

All of these were somewhat more successful performed in excerpted shorthand when Lord Buckley peppered them into other material during his live presentations in the years that followed.

In their favor, the three Shakespeare pieces are remarkable in that Buckley's narrative is done in graduate-level hipsemantic, perhaps as his ultimate tribute to the Bard. Unlike pieces such as "The Nazz" that can be appreciated and enjoyed without a grasp of the hipster lingo, even those sufficiently steeped in Shakespeare or the hipsemantic must translate the Buckley interpretations line by line in order to fully understand, as the following introduction to "To Swing or Not to Swing" shows:

> To *swing* or not to swing?
> That is the hanger!
> Is it hipper for the wig to dig
> The flips and drags of the wheel of fortune
> Or to come on like Kinsey
> Against this mass mess
> And by this stance cover the action.

With "Boston Tea Party" (cowritten by Dick Zalud) and "Hip Hiawatha," Buckley more convincingly renews the spirit of his earlier work and imbues it with a modern sensibility. Though this pair resonate more powerfully as political allegory than as spiritual histories such as "The Nazz" or "The Gasser," they do demonstrate Lord Buckley's firm grasp of history in their exposition of the colonialist uprising in

Revolutionary Massachusetts and the sixteenth-century unification of northeastern Native America. Buckley probably viewed himself as a gentle rebel or at least as an honorary Native American when choosing to hipsemantically recast these important chapters in North American history.

But with its overblown production values, *Hipsters, Flipsters and Finger-Poppin' Daddies* ultimately comes off as gimmicky and flat, lacking the cosmic love potion flavoring the balance of Lord Buckley's work. He does further succeed, however, in breaking out of the mold of "stand-up comic" on the album in his attempt to establish himself as a coolly insightful translator of classic literature and wise interpreter of American history.

For a classic jazz representation of Shakespeare following in Buckley's wake, *Such Sweet Thunder,* Duke Ellington's monumental 1957 album interpreting the Bard's work in a classic big-band context, is a must. It features titles such as "Lady Mac," "Sonnet for Caesar," and "Star Crossed Lovers."

Concurrent with the RCA outing, Buckley was crossing paths and trading fours with kindred spirits—the denizens of 1950s L.A. jazz club bohemia or those who showed up to party at "The Castle."

Relying on his old scamster skills, Buckley finagled a daffy widow into letting his family (and soon his entourage) inhabit her huge mansion in Whitley Terrace tucked away in the Hollywood Hills.

Dick Zalud

Buckley was looking for a house in Hollywood and found this little old lady in her eighties who owned this house, a gorgeous house in the Hollywood Hills. She was living at a Methodist home in a two-by-two room with a bath. He said, "Madam, you own a gorgeous house. Why are you living like this? You must come and live with us in your house and restructure your life and have some laughs and have some people around you and some joy!" He went on and on and on with this.

And sure enough he conned this old lady into moving into the house with him and his family. I don't know what the rent situation was or anything like that but I don't think they were paying any rent. She lived upstairs. She had a room and they were taking care of her. They were cooking her meals and that old lady was having a ball. But, in turn, they were using her house. And for some reason he nicknamed her the Witch and sometimes Lady Curl.

Cosmo was another character who hung around the Castle. Cosmo was a friend of Buckley's. He was a short, funny guy with a lisp who trained strippers. He actually trained strippers how to strip. He set the whole thing up for the stripper. Strip joints were big at that time. People were making a lot of money playing at Vegas. They were stars—big stars. Lili St. Cyr was one of the big ones then. Buckley played a lot of strip joints.

Nestled in the hills above Hollywood's neon-lit boulevards is a maze of diminutive, sharply curving streets with some of the city's most splendid architectural jewels. This landmark neighborhood of 163 houses and three small apartment buildings has been known since the end of World War I as Whitley Terrace in honor of its developer (and one of the city's most famous turn-of-the-century real estate moguls), Hobart Johnston Whitley.

Once the address of choice for Hollywood's most celebrated stars, producers, and screenwriters, Whitley Terrace remains an island of calm seldom found in the heart of a major metropolis and is, undoubtedly, the most beautiful piece of property Whitley ever developed. Created in the image of a Mediterranean hillside village complete with tile roofs, Whitley Terrace was conceived with such care and attention to detail that today the entire enclave boasts local, state, and national historical status.

The rise of Hollywood's movie industry coincided with the creation of Whitley Terrace, and the development's proximity to all the major studios prompted the silent screen's most illustrious stars to settle there. During the 1920s, 1930s, and 1940s, busloads of sightseers made regular circuits of the neighborhood to ogle at the homes of such celebrities as Rudolph Valentino, Harold Lloyd, and Charlie Chaplin, whose home gained fame as a prime party hangout.

But nothing jammed quite the way the former home of Barbara La Marr's did in the mid-1950s when the Royal Court of Lord Buckley moved into the nabe. Proclaiming the imposing structure, complete with towers and moat, "The Castle," Buckley set out to formalize his fluctuating flock with his own self-styled protocol. It was there that admirers of this Hollywood hepcat-in-residence (including Frank Sinatra, Sammy Davis Jr., Robert Mitchum, Tony Curtis, and Russ Tamblyn) stopped by midmorning or midnight. These were the halcyon days of the Royal Court, when Buckley refined his great works, everything was possible, anything could happen . . . and usually did.

Lady Elizabeth Buckley

The Castle had a magical effect on people.

We had beautiful salons where we would honor musical friends. For a while we lived in Barbara La Marr's old Spanish-style mansion in Los Angeles. We called it The Castle. There was a baby grand piano and velvet furniture, and a King Montezuma throne complete with a palm tree. We'd give concerts where we could do everything but applaud. Applauding disturbed the neighbors. The place was always polished. We had one fellow who worked for us and all he'd do was polish the chandeliers and soap the drawers so they'd open easily—he'd come over especially to do that. And a lady would bring a small sponge to church and take a little of the holy water to put in with our flowers at home. People used to have so much fun at the salons that they'd have to stop by the next day to see what happened after they left.

Lord Buckley never stopped. He rehearsed all the time. He took material from life, from whoever he met, from whatever it was he saw. That was the beauty of him.

Jim Dickson

I was at the Castle the evening Lord Buckley knighted Benny Carter, who didn't know if he was being put on or not but went through with it. Everything was done with great ceremony. Buckley made a parchment scroll, Lady Buckley drew it up with old English handwriting and they rolled it up with a ribbon around it. They even had a sword and had him kneel. The whole trip was held with about eighty people in the room watching. It was like a surprise party for his birthday.

Just living through the afternoon with Buckley was done with great ceremony with all sorts of people around. He gathered together a lot of interesting people who became friends with each other and have stayed friends. You'd go to Chicago and meet somebody who was friends with Buckley and you would become friends. People like him are catalysts.

Mel Welles

This was in the days when sex was not life-threatening like it is today. Group sex was common, particularly in Hollywood, and Buckley was a conductor of the bizarre and the weird. There weren't really orgies at the Castle. There was a lot of hanky panky, a lot of people ducking into the bathroom, people who had just met doing quick numbers. But there was never real flagrant group behavior. You've got to remember that Prince Richard and Princess Laurie were there at the Castle. So the Castle was his home with children and Lady Elizabeth was really and truly the apple of his eye. Even though he fucked everybody else that he could find that was willing, I guess he respected it.

All the "butlers" around the Castle were gay. They all had good taste. They were good with fabrics and good with their hands and they'd turn every place he was in into a veritable paradise. He always seemed to have a lot of free help. There was a little Italian guy from St. Louis there who was the funniest queen that I ever met. You don't have to be a queen to be gay but he was very queenie, very effeminate. And he had a permanent five o'clock shadow. He was a real small and a very dark, bushy-haired, hairy Italian. So, when he would greet you at the door in a mandarin robe it looked really absurd with his black hairy arms and five o'clock shadow in the morning just after he shaved. It was crazy.

Whenever we went sailing together Buckley would strip into the nude and stand out on the bow of the sailboat and bay at the moon like he was into primal screams and shouts.

Millie Vernon

He had no hang-up about nudity. He'd hold court in the bathtub in front of everybody. He'd get into the bathtub and scrub himself with this huge brush with hard bristles. He'd have a board across the bathtub and he'd be shaving, drinking coffee with everybody coming in and out. He'd hold court at all times—even naked in the tub.

Tubby Boots

He had to be the cleanest man I ever met in my life. He would sit in the bathtub all day long with a board over the tub and a phone on it so he could make phone calls. Never got out of the tub. When he did get out of the tub it was to walk around stark naked because he thought the body was beautiful. If he wasn't naked he was in tails.

Beulah Bondi, the great character actress who played Jimmy Stewart's mother in *It's a Wonderful Life,* lived right next door. She used to come out on her balcony in the morning and Lord Buckley would come there and start singing: "I dig Hollywood every moment, every moment I dig it. I dig Hollywood. Why do I dig Hollywood? Because all my friends are here." They'd greet each other and she thought nothing of him being stark naked on the balcony because that was Buckley. Even a person like Bondi was caught up in the aura of Buckley.

Stuart Whitman

As a young actor in the 1950s, Stuart Whitman became a de facto student of Lord Buckley's at His Lordship's Castle in Whitley Terrace.

Redd Foxx was around. So were Tony Curtis, Charlie Parker, Billie Holliday, and Miles Davis.

The Castle up in Whitley Heights was an amazing spot. I remember helping him move some stuff out to a treehouse there where we found boxes and boxes of early movie magazines which we sat around and read all day.

One on one with him was worth more than any of it. He was such a generous man with his knowledge and his experiences. I enjoyed him more one on one than at any other time and I was fortunate enough to have had quite a few hours alone with him.

Buckley was the first of the flower children.

Larry Storch

I know of some black musicians known as the Jones Brothers who had offended His Lordship. Clyde, Max and Herbie Jones out of Boston. So he sent them a telegram that read, "You're all busted out of the Kingdom! Don't ever bother to get in touch with me again!"

He called them that night and patched things up and, of course, they were all back in the Kingdom again.

Eldon Setterholm

I was working at Technicolor. A bunch of my buddies were working there too. One of them said, "Let's go down and hear Lord Buckley tonight at the Raven Bar on Melrose."

OK, I went with him. It was a regular bar, like any other, and when Buckley came on—I remember he was wearin' a gray suit—he got the mike—he was down at one end of the bar and I was at the other—and he went through his routines. I don't even remember what they were, but it wasn't my bag at all. I was interested in jazz music at the time and Buckley's shtick wasn't what I'd come to hear. It went over, under and around me. I didn't think much of it.

That holiday season, the Hollywood guys that I ran around with were sayin', "Whatchoo gonna do tonight? How you gonna bring in the New Year? Hey, well I hear Lord Buckley's havin' a party up at his house. Let's go up there."

So all my buddies (Dick Parisi, Stuart Whitman, Doug Deems, Bob Chamberlain, and Hank Lass)—a regular Hollywood clique of guys—decided to go to Lord Buckley's party. And we comprised most of the guests. Well, Buckley had no way of knowing that we all knew each other. It was up on Whitley Terrace. We always referred to it as the "castle pad" after that, and it was like a castle. From the back porch you could see that white-lighted cross at the top of Cahuenga Pass. It was a very castle-like place.

He finally made his appearance that night in his white tie and tails and he sat down at the grand piano. We liked that circumstance and we gathered around and he entertained us. We liked that.

Of course, a lot of us were juicing; we didn't know that he was in AA at that time. After he had entertained us for awhile, why he starts this trip goin', "All you lords and ladies are so beautiful this evening, except one nee-gate mother." And I'm thinkin', "Hmmmm, I wonder who could he mean." He kept on in that vein for awhile until finally I realized, "Hey, he's talking about *me!*" And I'm up on my feet and goin' to him nose-to-nose, sayin', "Hey, what do you mean, bringin' *me* down in front of all these people?!" And I'm ready to thump on him, you know. He pacified me real quick by saying, "Look at this rose, turned into a *LION!*" With words like that he was able to mollify me and get me to sit back down.

As the party wore on and as the dawn came, everybody had split except me and Doug Deems. We were sittin' in the coffee nook with Lord Buckley, and he's still rappin' away. I think he must have taken a lot of Dexies or Bennies or somethin' 'cause he stayed bright. That was always his style, to stay up late and sleep in.

Lady B had rented that place by rolling up to the front door dressed sharp. She had a flair about her. She just looked like she could be money. Lady B did. She went and rented that place by just saying, "His Lordship is in the East and I expect him any day now, and we'd love to have the castle all ready when he arrives. So, if you don't mind, he'll take care of the business end of it, but we *will* take the place." She laid somethin' to that effect on the old lady and got the pad.

It was the best pad they ever had. But I knew somethin' was amiss on that first night at the New Year's party because in looking over the house I saw that they had no fixtures in the kids' bedroom. They were like sleeping in drawers and very makeshift. I thought, 'Hey, somethin's not right here.' And, sure enough, they didn't last too long up there. But they had some great parties and I met a lot of celebs. He was very popular around Hollywood at that time.

To me (and Lady B would back me up, too) this was his best period in the last ten years of his life—the Whitley Terrace period. He was *in Hollywood* up in the hills in this castle; celebs would come and see and hear him. He was playin' the clubs around there too.

He had several little gay guys who were houseboys for him. Lady B would take care of all the guests—feed 'em and serve 'em coffee—and she had these two or three little gay guys runnin' around. And they did it for free, just to be on the scene. There were lots of young, handsome studs around so those little guys liked bein' there, y'know. One of 'em was working for that French actress Corrine Calvet and he wanted to leave her to work for free for Buckley, just to be on his scene.

But then he went from there over onto Griffith Park Boulevard and up the rickety, worn-out stairs to what he called the Crackerbox Palace. And that's what it was too. It was an old bat-and-board place that was fallin' apart. He moved the family in there. Of course me and my buddies kept visiting him there. It was open house and we went there frequently.

Once I went to court in Beverly Hills and while I was waitin' my turn, they brought in Edward G. Robinson Jr. Just as the judge was sayin' to him, "Mr. Robinson, how do you plead, guilty or not guilty?" he collapses, and they have to catch him. They bring one of these old wooden wheelchairs down, and they put Eddie G. Jr. in it, and they wheel him on out. That very night I was over at Lord Buckley's and there he was. Now isn't it a small world? Buckley was tryin' to get him off the juice.

Here's what would happen: the AA chapter would say, "Well, you should have a sponsor, Eddie G. Jr., cause you boozers are ruining your lives. But you need to have a sponsor." So Lord Buckley would catch that kind of person and be their sponsor and try to help 'em get off the booze.

When I got to know the guy after that New Year's Eve, I discovered that he was having a tough financial time of it. We were always tryin' to cook up some way to make money. I said, "Buck, let's go down to Santa Monica Beach where I hang out and see what you can do down there." So we went down by the volleyball court where Joel McRae and Peter Lawford spent time—where the up-and-coming young actor heads would go. And, sure enough, he started entertaining right out there on the crowded beach, and more people started gathering around him, and right when things started going good, Eldon passed the hat. He made some bucks for the grocery store on the way home.

Charles Tacot

As for the children, I have seldom seen any who were as well-behaved and well disciplined as Richy and Lori. It seemed to me sometimes almost as if Dick wanted to teach them what he had never learned. They were not disciplined in a threatened way, but with very real and obvious love. I remember Dick once asked the children to show me their room, which was downstairs in the Whitley Terrace house, and one of the ways of reaching it was a rickety staircase on the outside of the house. It was around 2 a.m., of course pitch-black, and the children started to go down the less hazardous route, but Papa would have none of it. He hustled all of us outside, and as Richy and Lori, who were only five and six at the time, were hurrying down the worn-out staircase, he kept saying, "Faster, children, faster, faster," until little Richy and Lori were just a blur of running arms and legs. Then Buckley turned back to me with his best maniacal look, and in a stage whisper said, "They are heavily insured."

Dick Zalud

One time we were sitting down in the little alcove there at about one or two in the morning when we hear a car pull up. There was a knock at the door. Buckley says, "Elizabeth, open the door." She did and in walks this very distinguished-looking man in a very square boxy suit with balding, gray hair.

Buckley got up an exclaimed, "By God, Luther!" And he grabs this man and he hugs him all the while eyeing the car out in the driveway. Luther had a brand-new Dodge. The wheels were always turning with Buckley.

"By God Luther," he said. "What a wonderful car. Maybe we could take a ride in it."

"Anything you want, Mr. Buckley." He didn't call him "Lord Buckley." It was "Mr. Buckley."

Buckley said, "Okay Elizabeth, wake up The Witch! She's been so good to us we're going to take her to Las Vegas. And Owl Head you're going to drive."

And we get in the car and take off to Vegas. The Witch is sitting in the backseat with Buckley. She's wearing a kimono nightgown and has all those little toilet paper twists in her hair. Luther was sitting in the passenger seat next to me and I'm driving a hundred miles per hour down that desert road to Las Vegas. That car was beautiful. The sun was coming up. It was beautiful and Buckley was singing and drinking coffee and having a wonderful time while The Witch slept.

We see a sign: "Nevada State Line ½ Mile."

All of a sudden Luther realizes something is wrong and yells: "Put on the brakes! Brakes! Brakes! Stop the car! Stop the car!"

I slammed on the brakes, the car went off the road, and it nearly turned over.

When the car finally stopped, Buckley asked, "What's the trouble my good man? What seems to be the problem?

Luther said, "Ask that lady to get out of the car, Mr. Buckley."

"My God Luther, its five o'clock in the morning. You want this woman to walk out on the road?"

"No, I want her to get out of the car and walk across the state line," he says.

She gets out of the car and he says, "Mr. Owl Head you drive real slow and she's gonna walk down the road next to us."

So she gets out of the car and walks down the road and across the state line. I pulled the car over to the side of the road and Luther said, "Okay, get her back in the car, let's go."

It turned out that Luther had just got out of Leavenworth for the Mann Act [consorting with underage women] and while he was there he'd saved enough money to buy his car. But he couldn't be in a car that was transporting a woman across state lines—any woman—even The Witch who was eighty or ninety years old. He didn't want to take any chances. He'd come straight from Leavenworth, Kansas to Buckley's house. I don't know what happened to him. I left them there in Vegas and went on my way. They went into the lobby men's room of some hotel, took a shave and she lay down and slept on one of the couches in the lobby.

Frank Speiser

Frank Speiser is an actor and performance artist who has staged brilliant one-man shows featuring the work of Lenny Bruce, Eric Bogosian, and Lord Buckley, respectively.

I heard a wonderful story years ago about Buckley's performance at the drug prison and rehab center in Lexington, Kentucky. At the time it was the biggest drug rehab center in the country. All the great jazz artists that were trying to kick would get sentenced to go down there and forcibly dry out.

And Buckley was doing a gig somewhere near Lexington and found out that the center was nearby and thought it would be a great idea to do a full production show for the inmates at the center. So he called up the warden and the warden, of course, didn't know who this guy was and thought that he was really this *Lord* Buckley character—maybe an actual British Lord or something. At any rate, Buckley, in the course of the conversation, convinced the warden that he should do a lecture for the inmates at the rehab center. So they set up a time with Buckley saying, "Don't worry about the money," and everything else like that.

The big day came and Buckley arrived at the center. He got backstage with the warden as all the inmates were filing into the auditorium. The warden began trying to explain to him that "this is a pretty surly crowd and you got to be very careful about what you say. If they get bored they can get really rowdy and embarrass you."

Buckley was taking it all in but assured the warden, "Don't worry about a thing, I've got it covered."

So, all right, the inmates have filled the auditorium, the lights dim down and a pin spot comes to the center of the stage. Buckley is about to be announced but he doesn't want the warden to announce him.

Instead, he starts walking on stage in the semidarkness casting a murky silhouette against the stage curtain. All of a sudden this rumbling starts coming from all these inmates, all these drug addicts, sitting in the audience. The rumbling starts building louder and louder and he's approaching the pin spot and coming more and more into the light.

And Buckley walks out into this pin spot and all five hundred of these drug-addict hepcat inmates just stand up on their feet and yell:

BUCKLEY!!!!!

Life at the Castle was something of a combination Dionysian bacchanal, nudist colony, and charm school where Buckley, at once jester king and Holy Fool, developed an etiquette and conferred his guests with an unlikely assortment of Runyonesque nicknames usually based on some physical characteristic or talent. There were Princes Hair Head, Owl Head, Cougar Head, and Eagle, Princess Merry Legs, and Lady Renaissance. There were Counts and Countesses, Barons and Baronesses, Vicars, Squires, Dukes, and Earls.

Mel Welles

He'd usually give everybody titles as part of his thing about the "Lords and Ladies of the Royal Court." So my title was "King Farouk" because I was and am a fat man with a mustache and because I had played King Farouk a couple of times on television and in films.

George Greif

He called me "Disraeli" probably because I was Jewish. Everybody had a title but I was the only one who was a prime minister because that's what Disraeli was.

Tubby Boots

He used to call me Princess Lily but Prince Charles of Booth was my title. Buckley used to say: "Lil! You had the misfortune to be born with the beautiful mind of a woman in the ridiculous body of a man."

Jonathan Winters

One of the most original and influential comedians in stand-up comedy, Jonathan Winters has dazzled and delighted audiences as a zany clown, a caustic comic, a Gatling-gun-tongued wizard of spontaneous humor, and sometimes all at the same time. His fifty-year career in show business includes nightclubs, television, and movies. Winters's memories and impressions of Lord Buckley appearing in this book were gathered by San Francisco writer Douglas Cruickshank.

When I first met Lord Buckley he started calling me "Prince Jon." And I asked him, "Why can't I be Lord Jon?"

"Because, my dear man, I am Lord . . . Lord Buckley."

And I said, "Yeah, I remember you in the forest. You were against the Black Knight and he all but dismembered you with some kind of medieval hand axe."

"Ahh, yes," Buckley said, smiling and taking a drag on his cigarette. "Yes, my friend, thank you for remembering."

Dick Zalud

I think he gave me the name "Owl Head" because he thought I was a wise person and owls are often associated with wisdom. Also, I looked a little owlish with my glasses on.

Millie Vernon

The nickname "Lady Renaissance" came from his head. He named people how he saw them. Cougar Head, Hair Head, whatever.

He also named objects. The Castle of course was his place in Hollywood. "The Fairyland Express" was a car. It was an Anglia, a little red English car—adorable.

Dick Zalud

Frank Eubank, a friend of ours, fixed up the car that Buckley tagged the "Fairyland Express." Eubank was an artist but he worked on cars to make money. He gave it white seats and put a big American flag on the aerial—a gigantic American flag. It was unbelievable how he nailed something with a nickname. If there was ever a "Fairyland Express," it was that car.

Millie Vernon

Honest to God! Eubank and I were with Buckley when he bought that car. Buckley had exactly two hundred dollars. We went to this used-car lot and he saw this car. "By God, I've got to get that but I'm only good for two hundred dollars," he said. "By God, that's it! 'The Fairyland Express'! Look at it. It's beautiful. I'm going to get that car, you see."

So we go inside this little office and these two young guys are there. You know . . . used-car salesmen. We sat down and Buckley starts working on these guys. He wants that car and they said, "Well, it's seven hundred dollars."

"Ah yes," he said and he started charming them, making them laugh and doing a whole number. Well it took about a half hour but he got it for one hundred dollars—not the two hundred dollars he had come in with—but one hundred dollars.

We got in the car and it was his. He had an absolutely hypnotic effect on people.

Tubby Boots

When he moved to the West Coast we began to drift apart. A few years passed since we'd been in contact and I made the mistake of calling him. I figured it had been a long time between. Why hold a grudge? What was done was done. So I called him. The minute he hears me it's: "Ah, Prince Charles, so beautiful to hear your voice. I felt so bad about what I did to you . . . with that thing with the insurance. I must make it up to you. I have a beautiful home in the Hollywood Hills; I just made a motion picture. Come out here and stay. Let me make it up to you."

So I give up my job, which was paying me $750 a week working in a nightclub and doing a radio show. And I get on a plane and I hop out to California, expecting to see a band greeting me and fans holding signs welcoming me to California and everything because Buckley did everything with a flair.

As I get off the plane and walk down the ramp, here's this black kid with paint all over him and Lady Buckley with her hair all disheveled, paint on her face and on her hands. "Come on, Prince Charles. Lord Buckley's waiting." And they scurry me off in a little sports car up to the Hollywood Hills.

And this is the exact scene that went on as I walked in the door. Buckley is on the phone saying, "I have an act for you. My God, he's fabulous." He turns to me. "What do you do now, Tubby? . . . Oh, he sings and dances and does comedy. He could open tonight. A hundred twenty-five? Sold!"

He was sitting on the phone, trying to sell me that night to open for a lousy $125 at a café on La Cienaga. Rather than come out there and work for $125 a week, I could have sent it to him. But in the same respect I got a lift out of living out there too. I got an experience you couldn't pay for.

I had just given up $750 a week to come to California to live in the lap of luxury and this bastard is on the phone selling me for $125. And meanwhile Buckley's got all these actors there. Larry Storch and his brother, Ray, and Russ Tamblyn. And everybody in the house is starving.

When the rent was due, the old lady he'd talked into letting him stay at the place—Lady Curl, he called her, or The Witch—would come and he'd con her out of the rent. I mean . . . well, he had a movement. Lady Elizabeth was a very good ballet dancer. So he would have this thing going, he called it "Swing for Life," where we would all get in ballet togs. If you could see us all in these stupid tights—all these comics who never knew the first thing about ballet. He would get us up the morning she was due and say, "Well, troops, Lady Curl, The Witch, is coming to collect the rent. And we must meet her at the fortress. So when she comes in, you'll all be gracious to Lady Curl . . ."

Well, the minute she hit the door, she'd say, "Lord Buckley, about the rent . . ." and he'd say, "Lady Curl, you are looking more beautiful every day. Get into your ballet costume, we're going to have the 'Swing for Life' movement . . . *now*." And he would get her into her ballet costume. And we would get there and we would do these ballet exercises. And then whatever food was left over, I would cook and throw chives in and make a special dinner in her honor. And he'd take a glass of wine and he'd say, "Well, I'll see you next month, Lady Curl, same time?" And put her out the door.

It got so bad Buckley took to selling the furniture in the house. And when Lady Curl asked about it, he'd tell her it was out to be cleaned. But Buckley had a thing about him. He could come out of anything on top. He was never upset by anything. And he was always at his best when he was broke. When he had money—working on a movie or in a nightclub or something—that's the time when he looked like he was in the most trouble of all. He didn't know who to pay first or how to get rid of it. In other words, if he was broke, he knew how to get it. But when he had it, he didn't know how to use it.

Dick Zalud

There was a guy in Las Vegas named Carl Cohen who was a mobster. Well, I don't know if he was actually a mobster but he was tied in. He was the pin boss at the Sands Hotel. He loved Buckley. He *loved* him. Used to give him money. I think that was a throwback from Buckley's Chicago days. He let Buckley stay wherever he wanted to stay. He even gave Buckley his apartment.

Lewis Foremaster

Prince Lewis is a Las Vegas native. He was Lord Buckley's aide-de-camp during His Lordship's later years, committing many of Buckley's performances to memory.

He was messing around all the time. That's the way show business is and that's what I liked about show business.

Carl Cohen was a Vegas mobster who owned the Sands. Cohen lent Lord Buckley seven thousand dollars and Buckley never paid him back. But he never paid anybody back. Still, he was basically an honest person. He wouldn't steal a newspaper off a newsstand.

In performance Lord Buckley had become a most immaculately hip aristocrat with a mischievous twinkle in his eyes as he twirled his Daliesque mustache and gracefully drew on his omnipresent cigarette, his massive frame cloaked in a tuxedo, a fresh carnation attached smartly to the lapel.

One can only imagine what the Buckley shows at Hollywood's Las Palmas Theater October 28–30, 1955, were like. The ad in *Variety* indicates that Buckley was wearing a producer's cap for the event:

LORD BUCKLEY
Imperial Peer of American Humor
Presents:
"HOUSE OF LORDS HALLOWEEN FIESTA"
FRI., SAT., SUN., OCT. 28, 29, 30
* 15 GREAT STARS *
* JACK COONS & ORCH *
2 BIG SHOWS

1st Show 8:30 to 11:30 P.M.
2nd Show Midnight till Dawn
$1.50 Admission
FREE PIZZA
Las Palmas Theater
1642 N. Las Palmas, Hlywd.
Reserv. HO 5-7191

As if to underline Buckley's scramble for greenbacks, new audiences, audiences of any classification, his appearance on several unlikely scenes can't go unobserved.

Eldon Setterholm

We stole a promotion once. "Bongomania" was on. That was a floating party where five or six hundred people would show up at the Preston Sturgis Players' Ring. They had leased it for this party. I didn't go with Buckley. I took June Blair who played on some of the *Ozzie and Harriet* shows. But Buckley was there that night and it was such a loosely run show that finally Buckley says, "Go down there, Prince, and introduce me to the house."

I had a few drinks in me, so I got the mike and said, "Ladies and gentlemen, we have in the house with us tonight, LORD BUCKLEY! Perhaps with a round of applause we can get him up for us."

And he came and took the mike and gassed everybody. He was hot. Then afterwards, when we were sittin' at our table, the promoters came to us and said that they wanted us to be their partners, because we gave the thing a little control from the mikes. We did some other concerts after that.

I always took him to where I was familiar. And so, after that, I took him down to the Los Angeles Community College campus at midday. Out there on the grass under the trees, he started doing some of his things and caused a big crowd to gather around. Finally some professor came out and said, "Here, here. This is against the procedure and rules of the campus."

And Lord Buckley says, "But this material of mine is immaculate. And it certainly has to do with the field of education." They got into a heated discussion over that.

I also promoted a thing down in Laguna—at Aldo's Europa Coffee House. Betty Davis and Gary Merrill were there. They came for the last set and sat right in the front. And Lord Buckley tried to slant the material their way . . . to show them that he was a good actor. Naturally he was figurin' that they might give him a break, to get a part so he could get a career going, and get some money. But it never happened.

Dr. Oscar Janiger

I always thought it was unfair to label him merely a comic. No, he wasn't that at all. In fact, one would almost have to invent a term for his genre. One could say he was the first performance artist, although performance art has gotten rather stereotyped in a way that he doesn't really fit into. It's hard to fit him into a classification.

Orson Bean

Buckley would go into these working-class clubs with real Archie and Edith Bunker types. And he did really sophisticated material and he made the people laugh. He had a way of reaching these people and kind of stretching them and making them come to him. He was quite amazing in that regard. He would never play down to them. And yet, I never saw him fail to win an audience over.

He did some of his classics and he did a lot of wonderful ad-libbing. He did some fairly dirty jokes but they were posed in a quite intellectual way. I think the audience felt it was worth their while to think the jokes through. He wasn't snotty.

I guess he always carried his cigarette in a holder that I later saw was an end of an enema tube and that was quite wonderful. I thought it was quite wonderful that he never mentioned that, he never called attention to it, he'd just have it. I don't know what kind of comment he was making about himself or about the kind of people that would use cigarette holders, but the enema tube cigarette holder kind of summed him up: that weird combination.

On August 8, 1955, Buckley made one of his more unusual television appearances on the fledgling *Tonight* show, then hosted by Steve Allen. Though Buckley performed one of his vaudevillian audience-participation show bits, "Steverino" introduced Buckley with appropriate befuddlement:

"Here's a fellow who has appeared in most of the nightspots around the country. He's a comedian but in a very different way. He doesn't come out and tell—I don't think I've ever heard this man tell a joke now that it occurs to me—but he sure does make people laugh. He is, as they say at Charlie's Tavern, a pretty flip character, and I can never tell how much of him is serious and how much of him is kidding but I always enjoy his work and I like him personally too. Here he is, Lord Buckley! What's gonna happen, I don't know."

Dressed to the gills, Buckley gracefully strutted on stage backed by a regal piano riff, flicking away his cig as he began his rap:

> My Lords and my Ladies of the television world. Flying in here from New York City on our rocket ship we were going a little too fast when presenting the Algerian acrobats this evening, my Lords and my Ladies, and coming in we got a little too much stratospheric speed aboard and—UUMMMPPP!—blew two of the Castle's affairs.

Unfortunately, the proceedings quickly devolve from there. Buckley gets a couple of college boys from the audience to join him, an NBC techie, *Tonight* show bandleader Skitch Henderson, and the singer Andy Williams (who was a singing guest on the broadcast that night) to partake in a wild group tumbling-and-handstand exhibition on some floor mats while the house musicians provide skittish circus music behind the antics. Actually, the bit is not without its moments as Buckley not only strips down from his formal evening attire to his skivvies in a matter of seconds, but manages to physically outperform men less than half his age as well.

Les Thompson

I worked a club with him. We opened the club and it was a dinner house in Inglewood. There was a wrought-iron bar around the stage and the band was set up in the back of the stage. There were people in ties and dinner jackets at the tables pressed right up against the front of the stage. There was some rich guy who owned the club. Buckley was something of an acrobat and his opener was that he just ran and did a flip and went over these peoples' tables and landed flat on his feet and started to do his act. And he was pushing fifty at the time!

Buckley's semiannual appearance on *The Ed Sullivan Show* in 1955 was also one of his best—it was certainly his most varied. After running through the "Amos 'n' Andy" bit with a quartet that included boxers Buddy Baer and Sandy Sadler (whose African American heritage gives the bit an added edge), a still-unidentified actress, and Sullivan himself, Buckley employs his old "hat routine" (also known as "The Jersey Switch") with Buddy Baer. A basic sight gag probably dating to his stint in the Walkathons, the act involved the two participants donning funky hats and exchanging them quickly with Buckley snatching the hat off Baer's head and placing it atop his own head as Baer simultaneously attempts the same. In this case the shtick doesn't really get on track, but is marked by the striking visual of the *immense* Baer towering over Buckley who, at some six feet two inches, was not exactly a shrimp.

All of his cool medium appearances beg the question: why didn't, wouldn't or couldn't Lord Buckley perform his hip material for the small screen?

Steve Allen

Definitely, in the fifties, I don't think he would have been allowed to do "The Nazz" or some of the other hip classics on television. In fact, I think I can say with some confidence, I'm sure he never discussed it with our people, but if anyone had gotten a whiff of it they would have said: "I'm sorry, man, I saw it the other night at Birdland and I loved it but you can't do it on TV."

Robin Williams

They weren't going to book him doing "The Nazz." "He's going to make fun of God on TV?!" They're still afraid of that. More recently, Bill Hicks had a routine on Right-to-Lifers and they wouldn't show that. They're still scared shitless of those people.

Lord Buckley

I'd appreciate if you'd quit filling each other's ears with inane vacuum and assemble your receiving sets to, shall I say, make room for the *large charge.*

11 king of the badcats

Lord Buckley

I knew the Marquis de Sade just like I knew Wild Lyle the While—sports car flip. Wild Lyle the While, Marquis de Sade both dug the same scene.

One of the most intriguing characters to enter Lord Buckley's royal realm was a minor bandleader and trombonist named Lyle Griffin—another wild white man cut out of Buckley's crazy cloth. Meeting in the jazz clubs, the two immediately took to each other and, at Griffin's urging, Buckley began actively developing and incorporating "atomic humor" more fully into his repertoire.

The first effort was a 1956 collaboration between Buckley and Griffin ("Wild Lyle the While," as he was tagged in the Royal Court) that resulted in "Flight of the Saucer," a single on Griffin's own Hip record label, also known briefly as Atomic Records. Partly an exercise in studio wizardry, partly another virtuosic display of Buckley's sound-effect prowess, "Flight of the Saucer" includes a simple plea to the people of Earth to carefully consider the consequences in opening the Pandora's box of nuclear energy.

The minor epic (with elements of both "The Train" and "The Hip Gahn") chronicles the journey by spaceship of "Space Correspondent" Lyle Griffin, Lord Richard Buckley ("Professor of Hipology"), and the Buckley-voiced Commander Abba-Dabba-Foo (a Jupiterian) on a trip through the solar system with stops on Mars and Jupiter during which they manage to just barely survive a storm of cosmic dust. Buckley provides the voices and language not only of a groovy Earthling but those of the inhabitants of the other planets as well. Each extraterrestrial is provided with a unique cosmic dialect, and Professor Buckley (as himself) translates each planet's language for the others as the message of interplanetary peace is put forth: "The satellite people would like to be buddy-buddy with us but they're real jumpy about the big blast—the big square blast—we're coming on with and hip us not to play the fool and lose the cool."

In the end all the characters seal the deal with a toast and imbibe with a special astral cocktail: "Jupiter Juleps."

One of the more amusing segments in the bit involves Buckley and Griffin marveling at the wonders of space. Griffin sees something that looks like whipped cream but Buckley responds by informing him, "That's the Milky Way, Jack: *Einstein's Playground.*"

Amazingly, the single's release garnered a small notice in the October 3, 1956, *Variety:*

Those recent headlines about an upcoming broadcast from a Martian flying saucer (as promised by saucer-ers in a London convention) may turn out to be a hefty plug for Hip Records' "Flight of the Saucer."

Disk features bandleader Lyle Griffin and Lord Buckley in what purports to be the narrative of a journey to Mars.

Complete with Griffin's All Star Jazz Band (from a 1946 Griffin track, "Flight of the Vout Bug," featuring Dodo Mamarosa on piano and Lucky Thompson on tenor sax) overdubbing the action, "Flight of the Saucer" recalls the work of the great jazz com-

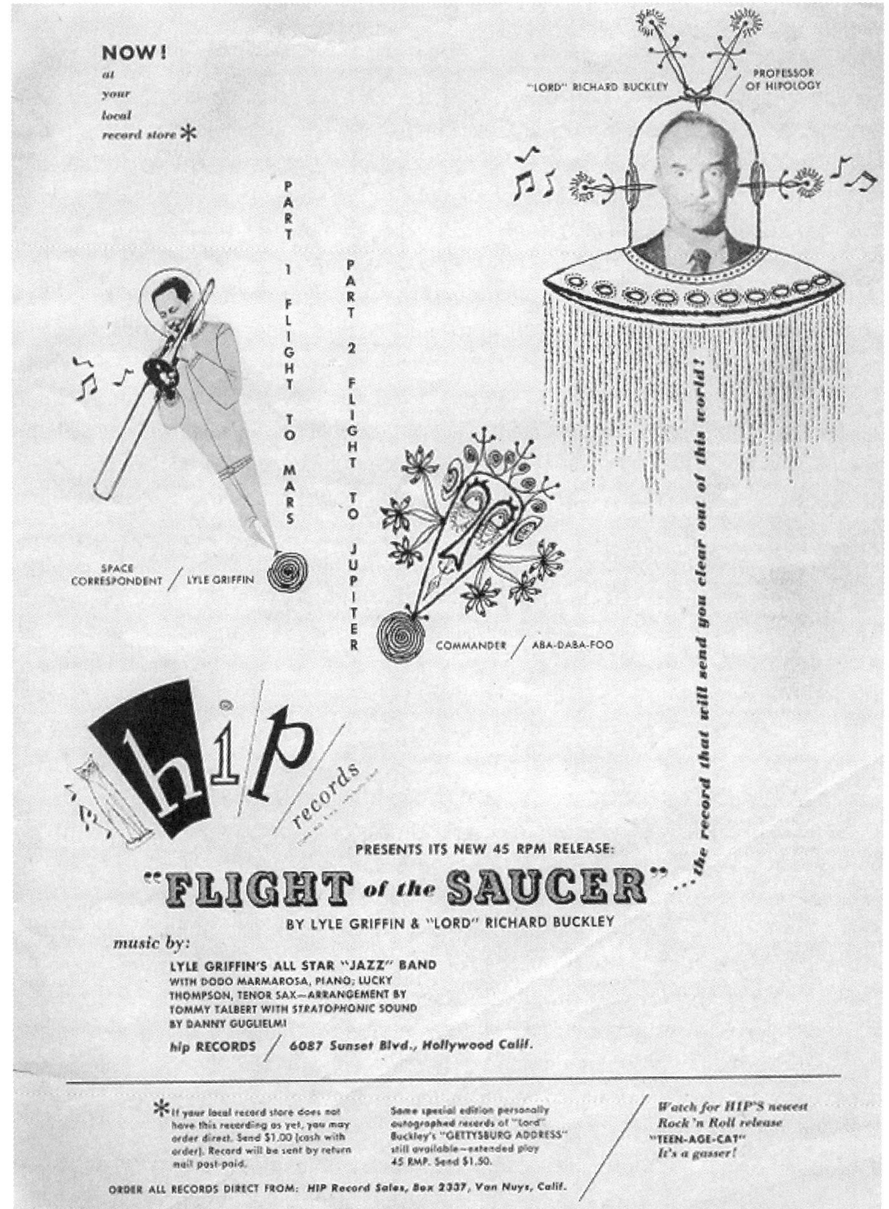

"Flight of the Saucer" ad from *Dig* magazine, 1956. Author's Collection.

poser and keyboard innovator Sun Ra, an old Club DeLisa alumnus who was just then also embarking on an creative journey with a similar message of universal harmony.

Much of Sun Ra's work as a bandleader and composer exists on some undefined astral plane. With his exotic incorporation of minstrelsy, melancholy, humor, hokum, apocalyptic brimstone, cacophony, whimsy, pan-planet rhythms, Egyptology, sci fi, and funk, Sun Ra left a legacy of thousands of tunes with such quizzical titles as "Rocket Number 9," "Have You Heard the Latest News from Neptune," "It's After the End of the World," and "Saturn." Ra himself lavishly boasted that the ringed planet was his cosmic point of origin.

The comparisons between Lord Buckley and Sun Ra don't stop with the odd, self-ordained monikers, the similarity of their expansive aesthetic, or their vision of a better "ominverse" for all. Coincidentally, both men took the step to produce and release their special material on their own independent record labels in 1956. Sun Ra's thirty-five-year endeavor with his own label, El Saturn, is one of the great little-told stories of modern jazz entrepreneurship on the cheap. It resulted in more than one hundred albums that the straight music industry wouldn't touch, though much of the music has gone on to directly and indirectly influence subsequent generations of artists from a variety of genres.

While certainly less prodigious than Sun Ra, Buckley was just as ambitious in founding the Hip label with Lyle Griffin. Though the enterprise never really got off the ground in a sustained commercial sense, Buckley did for a time succeed in taking greater control of his work in an undertaking that resulted in some of his rarest and most unusual pieces.

From the obscure to the arcane influence on the ridiculous, "Flight of the Saucer" may have found the ear of Don Van Vliet, known and pondered the cosmos over as Captain Beefheart. Beefheart's first Magic Band album, *Safe as Milk,* included a cut titled "Abba Zabba," speculated by some Buckleyologists as a very veiled reference to the good Commander Abba-Dabba-Foo of the Hip "Flight of the Saucer" track. For his part, Beefheart once claimed that the song title was derived from a brand of California-made toffee. There is also speculation that the commander's name may have also inspired Fred Flintstone's famous cartoon banzai: "Yabba Dabba Doo!"

Support of Buckley's inspiration on Frank Zappa (perhaps by way of Beefheart) can be found in Ben Watson's *Frank Zappa: The Negative Dialectics of Poodle Play,* an exhaustive exegis of the composer's work published by Quartet Books in 1994. According to the allegedly Zappa-approved study: "Lord Buckley's surrealist boptalk was a prime influence on both Frank Zappa and Captain Beefheart (who adopted a similar persona on *I Was a Teenage Meatshop*). Buckley takes you on a verbal trip, summoning forth a stream of images with illustrative mouth-noises and expostulations that precede events in the story, achieving utterly unexpected changes of tone and pace. He would work himself into a frenzy of excitement but keep his wit poised to deliver a hallucinogenic twist. Although Zappa learned a lot about tension and surprise from Edgar Varese, Lord Buckley taught him about the use of timing and imagery in speech, not just in his monologues *(Apostrophe ('), Greggery Peccary* and the introduction to 'Muffin Man' on *Bongo Fury)* but also in music, both via tape-slice *(We're*

Only in It for the Money) and scores ('Punky's Whips'). Toward the end of 'Help, I'm a Rock' someone says, 'No no no no no . . . man you guys are really safe, everything's cold,' verbal derailment straight out of a Lord Buckley routine."

And let's not fail to note that the Zappa title "Willie the Pimp" bears a striking resemblance to Lord Buckley's tag for the Bard, "Willie the Shake."

Though Griffin was never able to arrange adequate or widespread distribution, the Hip label discs were available by mail from their 6087 Sunset Boulevard offices in Hollywood. The Hip label releases were simple affairs: seven-inch, 45 rpm "extended-play" discs. Evidence of other artists having recorded on Hip Records is sketchy, but another jazz oralist and Buckley crony, Harry "The Hipster" Gibson, released at least one disc with the label around this time. Consistent with the quirky marketing endeavors of fringe record labels, some of the Hip label discs were manufactured on clear red vinyl.

An ad pushing "Flight of the Saucer" that ran in *Dig* magazine reinforces the down-home spirit of Buckley's earlier releases. Buckley is shown as a head suspended in a flying saucer floating over the words: ". . . the record that will send you clear out of this world." A trombone-wielding Griffin is pictured in a space helmet, and Commander Abba-Dabba-Foo is fancifully sketched as an elongated flower being of undetermined planetary origin. Along with a listing of the musical personnel, there is a message at the bottom of the ad inviting those interested to send one dollar for a personally autographed copy of Lord Buckley's "Gettysburg Address" record, available from Hip's Sunset Boulevard office. Naturally, these signed discs are among the most serious Buckley-related collector's items.

A seminal but forgotten underground teenage hipster rag, *Dig* magazine laid claim to that then-stil-undefined demographic market niche somewhere between *Tiger Beat* and *Down Beat,* though the magazine's very motto ("for teenagers only") would seem to have its audience firmly in mind. Despite its hep orientation, some of the magazine's old stringers recall its publisher, Trajen Underleigh, as a Nazi sympathizer who was later jailed.

There is some suggestion that Lyle Griffin and Hip Records were at least loosely associated with *Dig.* Hip label records were liberally advertised and generously reviewed throughout the magazine's pages, and Griffin is referenced by Buckley in "Flight of the Saucer" as "space correspondent for *Dig* the teenage magazine."

In addition to "Flight of the Saucer," Hip released a unique "Gettysburg Address" platter. While the B-side contained a new hipsemantic translation identical to that cut for Vaya, Buckley can be found giving Lincoln's hallowed testament a wonderful straight reading on the A-side over a saccharine-tinged string-quartet-type musical backdrop of "The Battle Hymn of the Republic."

Robin Williams

There is a kind of spirituality about Buckley. Just the fact that the people he talked about like "The Nazz" or doing the hipster's "Gettysburg Address" perhaps speaks to this the best. Lord Buckley doing the "Gettysburg Address" in straight talk is like Bessie Smith doing *Aida.*

Label from a rare Buckley EP on Hip Records, 1956. Author's Collection.

One of the most sought-after Hip label singles is a mismatched tandem of sides. Appearing on the A-side is "James Dean's Message to the Teenagers: Buckley Meets Jimmy at Jazz City," His Lordship's famous account of his introduction to and philosophical conversation with the "great swinger" himself. On the flip side is "Speak for Yourself, John," Buckley's minor take on the historically baseless romantic triangle of Plymouth Colony pilgrims Miles Standish, John Alden, and Priscilla Mullens as portrayed in "The Courtship of Miles Standish," Henry Wadsworth Longfellow's poem of 1858.

"James Dean," a relaxed monologue dubbed over a mellow jazz quintet, is an unusual piece in that it is Buckley's autobiographical straight-from-the-heart reminiscence of his 1955 encounter with the celluloid rebel. This meeting took place at Jazz City, an L.A. music joint located at the corner of Hollywood Boulevard and Western Avenue, where the comic was in the middle of a three-month run. At the time of the meeting, Buckley's reputation was widening, and his gig at Jazz City (he shared the bill with Conte Candoli, his tourmate from his days with Woody Herman's Thundering Herd) attracted celebrities as diverse as big-band leader Stan Kenton, singer Peggy

Lee, and actor Ben Alexander, the "great cat from *Dragnet*." As Buckley relates the meeting on record, he had just performed "The Nazz" when a waiter told him that James Dean was making the scene and had invited him to his table. Dean's rep had preceded him: Buckley had heard on the "vance grapevine" how strong and cool the great cat was coming on. But when he arrived at the table he was still unsure which one was the actor: ". . . with the blaring crash of jazz I couldn't dig the names, so I was not hip to which one in the group was the stud. So I played it cool—looking for that Hollywood type of category. This handsome cat with the glasses, hobnail jacket, no tie, one-day beard, I finally dug was The Dean."

Buckley's account of their conversation leaves no doubt as to how impressed he was with "The Dean" and demonstrates their shared concerns for the world situation and specifically the dawning of the atomic age. Buckley was quite taken with Dean, who, in his opinion, had none of the affectations of the stereotypical Hollywood star. According to Buckley, Dean thought the youth of America "the brightest, strongest and most intelligent of all the generations," but they were "looking for some kind of a cop-out in the face of the bad jazz of the atomic age," having "a ball before the blast," and that Buckley's hip translations of the works of Christ and Gandhi could help them understand the power of love.

The piece begins to wind down when one of Dean's cohorts reminds him that he is due for an early call on the set of *Rebel Without a Cause* in the morning. The group bid their farewells, leaving Buckley to remember: "I never saw James Dean again but I'll never, ever forget him."

Doug Boyd

Doug Boyd (pilot/educator/collector) lives in Southern California. He was a Lord Buckley camp follower in the 1950s. Mr. Boyd's reminiscences are drawn from his unpublished autobiography, Days of Joy.

It was sometime in the early 1950s when I first chanced upon His Lordship while I was shopping on Hollywood Boulevard. I think I had just left a little hole-in-the-wall record shop and was passing the entrance to what was then the newest bistro on the scene, Jazz City, when we literally bowled into each other headlong. The look of the old geezer who towered above me and who had just rushed onto the sidewalk out of the club was what was most startling to me. He was dressed in black swallowtails and, incongruously, was wearing a tan pith helmet right out of an African safari perched above his platinum white and sharply pointed waxed moustache. I found myself staring down at his feet in disbelief for his foot apparel was as unusual as that of his chapeau. Instead of shoes he wore a strange kind of slippers that turned up into points on which were sewn little silver bells.

I definitely caught the smell of booze as we backed off from each other though the sun was high and not yet over the yardarm. With a flourish that practically swept the sidewalk the tall, elegantly dressed man doffed his helmet with panache and, bowing to the waist, roared, "Begging your Lordship's pardon!"

Almost instantly he was off again proceeding at the same breakneck pace that had just caused our collision. Heads turned as his six-foot-plus frame strode down the wide Hollywood Boulevard sidewalk—tails flying out of his wild slipstream.

It was crazy. But, like The Pied Piper of Hamelin, I felt an urge to fall in behind and follow as if there had been some mystical, compelling connection. "Jesus Christ Chrysanthemum," I remember thinking. "Only in Lotus La La Land would you encounter such a character."

Looking up at the marquee over the doorway from whence the swift aberration had sprung I saw that it announced: "Conte Candoli Quartet plus the Hip and Way Out Humor of Lord Buckley Appearing Nightly."

Even though money was a bit tight for me then I vowed that I would have to return that night and take in this wily charismatic fellow. Besides, I really dug Conte's bebop trumpet. That was my first meeting with Lord Buckley.

Buckley and Griffin weren't through with each other quite yet. Later in 1956 Griffin invited Buckley to his home to record a series of tracks that would become the posthumously released, Frank Zappa–edited album, *a most immaculately hip aristocrat,* in 1970.

Though the album's low production values are evident (at one point a plane can be heard flying by), *hip aristocrat* premiered several of Buckley's best: "The Train," "The Raven," and "The Hip Einie." The taping also included the definitive version of "Governor Slugwell" and a rough but nonetheless harrowing first crack at what was to become one of Buckley's indisputable masterworks, "The Bad-Rapping of the Marquis de Sade—King of the Badcats."

Recalling the word paintings of "Governor Gulpwell/Slugwell," Buckley's breathtaking minor masterpiece "The Train" (complete with the master's array of amazing mammal and machine mimicries) is a bopster's celebration of what was then still America's primary mode of commercial transportation and is now a testament to a bygone era, operating as kind of Irwin Allen disaster flick in miniature. On both this and an unreleased studio take, Buckley introduces the two-and-a-half-minute rap (and it is debatably the closest thing to pure rap as we now define it that Lord Buckley comes to on recording) with a boarding call from the coolest conductor in the cosmos.

The essential musicality of Buckley's imagination is apparent in everything he does in this routine, from the vocalizations, fanfares, and run-ons to conveying the rhythms of the voices, the intonations of the speakers, and the gradually building madness of the conclusion that he orchestrates to a tremendous vocal rave-up.

The listener hears "The Train" make its everyday journey to an unexpected destination only to realize, perhaps, that it's really the most logical destination of all: calamity.

As the journey commences, Buckley includes a typical cast of characters: the conductor, the engineers, a candy vendor, passengers, and, most dramatically, the train itself as he punctuates the juggernaut with the most uncanny impression of a steaming, soon-to-be-out-of-control locomotive—its whistle shattering the black night.

Inevitably the situation slowly builds to its final, tragic climax. "The Train" is minimalist Buckley at its supercharged best. "The Train" introduces two minor but recurring characters in the Buckley lexicon, Fred and Charlie, the conductor and engineer respectively. Fred and Charlie are Lord Buckley's "Everyman," appearing either by name or inference in several of his bits and off-the-cuff philosophical raps.

Paul Zaloom

A colleague and friend of mine named Tom Calagna turned me on to Lord Buckley in 1973 or '74. We had a comedy group called the Oddvark. It was an improv group but one which did not take suggestions from the audience. We did Buckley's version of "Marc Antony's Funeral Oration" as a kind of four-part harmony piece.

At the same time I was still working with the Bread and Puppet Theater and I put together a one-man show in which I wanted to take the idea that *anything* can be a puppet. Anything that you put in your hands can be animated. I wanted to have a great oral tapestry that matched a visual one—very quick and hyperactive visually—but give it an oral dynamic that was equally as rich.

One of the things that really impressed me about Buckley from a standpoint of a puppeteer is the extreme right turns of his voices. Like "Murder" where his voices change on a dime—where he's doing one character and he changes the breath pattern and it's like two people doing it. Its just a bit of trickery that's very appealing to a puppeteer because that's what we do with dummy puppets, hand puppets or found objects that can have running conversations where the characters are absolutely nailed, absolutely tight and have a depthness of character and virtuosity. So I was inspired by Buckley in terms of his capability and his amazing verbal skills and the richness of the tapestry of the sound.

I did a puppet piece based on "The Train" where I created a prison riot in a birdcage using rubber bands as prisoners, screws as prison guards and a bottle of Mr. Clean for the parole board. The action builds up between all of these characters like a powder keg and I end it with the last line of Buckley's piece: "Seventeen dead and twenty-three injured . . ."

I've never copped material from anybody. I don't believe in it. I don't like to do it. But to take a little of Buckley and put it in there is a like a tribute. Nobody ever picked up on it.

Now there was also a philosophical element that he had going that influenced me later on. I did nine solo shows and, as the shows evolved over time, the themes drew on issues such as accidents involving nuclear weapons, the Department of Defense Dictionary of Military and Associated Terms, indoor pollution, Love Canal, Abscam, the S&L Scandal, the art wars, Jesse Helms, and the hypocrisy of religion—all these different themes fed into my shows. I began to realize that the problem isn't so much this little issue or that little issue . . . it's the whole civilization. It's not just the Western Hemisphere or capitalism or communism—the whole fuckin' thing is fucked and stinks. And I reached that through my two mentors and the natural progression of my own work. My two mentors being Peter Shumann (the director and creator of Bread and Puppet Theater) and Lord Buckley.

Simultaneous with their release on *hip aristocrat,* "The Train" and "Governor Slugwell" also appeared on *Zapped,* two identically titled but different sampler compilation albums put together by Frank Zappa on his own Bizarre label that featured a smorgasbord of "outside" artists.

Eric Bogosian

My first exposure to Lord Buckley's work was through a sampler album put out by Frank Zappa. He had his own label and had put out albums by all these weirdoes: Wildman Fisher and seminal Captain Beefheart. I've since lost the album but I am forever grateful to Mr. Zappa for the contact.

And of course, Lord Buckley doing "The Train." I loved the bit, played it again and again. The point was not so much the mimicry of an event (rather than people) but the attitude! Energy mixed with a very distanced, almost cinematic attitude toward a tragedy. I didn't know it at the time, but I was listening to a "hipster" or "cool" attitude. Later I would come to know the same attitude through Lenny Bruce or William Burroughs (and Zappa, of course). Very modern, very chilled, but ultimately more concerned than the usual Hallmark card sentiments so often expressed when we see tragedy in the media.

Buckley was an oddity when I first heard him. Years later, Richard Price played some vintage Buckley for me ("The Nazz," I think) and a door opened. That door was the pure synthesis of storytelling, humor, music . . . and social critique. A lot to get from one mouth, but Buckley did it. And of course, attitude. This is essential to the hipster. Attitude.

I guess the important thing for me was that he could do it. It was like a physics problem, "Well, we know it can be done in theory, but can anybody actually do this in the laboratory?" Lord Buckley could do what up to that point was theoretical in my mind. I think Bruce hit it in points, and I think I've been there once or twice, but Lord Buckley was pure. His work was always about those four things: vocalization, humor, storytelling and critique. "Governor Slugwell" is a perfect example: lots of sounds, funny, a good story and pissing on the self-important.

By comparison to "The Train," "The Hip Einie" is easily Lord Buckley's most convoluted piece, a hipsemantic history that falls into his "atomic" subgenus in both its celebration of Professor Albert Einstein's life and in the acknowledgment that his contribution to scientific advancement unleashed consequences of terrible beauty when manipulated by the masters of war.

Following his familiar formula for such extended pieces, Buckley breaks "The Hip Einie" into two sections: an introductory hip history sketching Einstein's early life, combined with a longer yarn chronicling the confirmation of his wild theories by the scientific community some years after he first expostulated them. In this second part of "The Hip Einie," Buckley essentially creates a hip-talking synthesis of the famous May 29, 1919, eclipse experiment supporting Einstein's 1905 Theory of Relativity. In the experiment English astronomer Arthur Eddington photographed a solar eclipse (the "unveiling of the Big Heater" in Buckley's parlance) on the island of Principe off West Africa. Einstein had insisted that his equations be verified by empirical observation and devised specific tests involving, among other things, the deflection of light rays toward the red end of the light spectrum by gravitational fields, which the 1919 eclipse experiment confirmed.

Despite the denseness of the ten-minute run, Buckley demonstrates at least a keen layman's grasp of the nuances of atomic and subatomic physics, and the scientific process of trial and error (a kind of "Physics for Poets" long before the term had been popularized as a gut course in the academy), encapsulating Einstein's cosmological vision in the hipsemantic this way:

> Now here was a cat who carried so much wiggage, he was gigless. He delegated his subconscious mind and proceeded to lay back into the longest goof in the history of the far out wig stretch. He goofed throughout the Zonesphere and the Vautesphere and the Rotesphere and the Hippisphere and the Flippisphere and the Zippisphere and the Gonesphere and the *Way-Gonesphere.* He was *way* out there.
>
> As a matter of fact, he was *so far gone,* he was *so far out,* that when he returned and cooled and dug what he brought back with him, he *flipped!*
>
> When his book hit the streets, it hit the Spaceheads pretty hard. No cat mentioned it for four years and no cat moved for *five years more.*

Robin Williams

He could explain Einstein in bebop—that's a great concept. It's like doing Stephen Hawking in a rap song.

Buckley describes the seemingly insurmountable obstacles Einstein had to overcome until he came to where he "laid back into the longest goof of the history of the far-out wig stretch" and became the "King of all Spaceheads." Buckley goes on to explain how this resulted in the Theory of Relativity, forever upping the ante for all concerned. But in dropping his science, Buckley could be speaking of the hardships and misunderstandings he had to face in presenting his artifice to the masses.

Mel Welles

You could ask him to tell you any story in that idiom and he could eventually do it, though not at the beginning. In the beginning everything had to be worked out and written down. Later, he wore the skin of that character so well—that wonderful hip-talking character—that he could simply translate any story or any poem into it.

When we were recording at my house I remember him doing "The Raven" right off the top of his head like one of those Cindy Miller–Donald O'Connor movies when they say, "I got it! I got it!," and play the whole tune with words and music. That's the way he did "The Raven"—right off the top of his head. He could perform magic.

Richmond Shepard

One day I'm in the alley behind the club and Buckley is smoking a joint back there. And he says: "Let me recite something for you, Prince." He said, "I just received it in the mail. And I want you tell me if I should put it in my wig." And I said, "Sure, go ahead, what is it?" And he recited Edgar Allen Poe's "The Raven" and he said, "What do you think, Prince, yes?" I said, "Sure, it's terrific, do it!" He said, "OK, I will."

Edgar Allen Poe and "The Raven" were naturals for Lord Buckley. Buckley's attraction to a character of such notable dissipated excess as Poe is not hard to fathom—and all the better that the protagonist of his most famous poem is an animal.

Buckley's translation of "The Raven" (aka "The Bugbird" or "Po' Eddie and the Bugbird") glows with the poetry of the outcast, the dropout, the artist, the black, and the young and takes the listener with him on Poe's journey into a tortured mind, unleashing the gloom and despair found there and to feel the mind's growing panic as it is being forced to the breaking point . . . by itself.

Lord Buckley

Poe's "Raven"—"The Bugbird." The Bugbird, of course, is a little something, an idea or a fear that you get caught in your mind and you throw it out the front door (honk) comes in the back. You throw it out the keyhole (honk) comes in the transom. You throw it left side (honk) it comes in right side. It's a Bugbird. And like I say, Poe—Eddie Allen Poe—was a swinger. He loved to *en*-joy that good whiskey and chase them little ladies all *over* the place, undstand what I mean? And he loved to carry on and *en*joy and he didn't want the bird. He didn't send for the bird. He didn't dig the bird. *He didn't even know what aviary the bird came from*. If they were to put the bird on him post*paid,* he wouldn't have dug it. But, just like I say, so many times, when you don't *need* the bird, when you don't *want* the bird, when you don't have the *first possible use for the bird*—honk—that's when you get it. And that's what happened to po' Eddie.

I want you to picture that cat: he's sitting in his pad, he's all spread out. He's flipped, he's flapped, he's had it, undastand what I mean? He can't make it. If he had it, he couldn't swing it so he's sitting there goofing the cool, ya see what I mean?

Buckley begins the piece by visiting Poe on that infamous "drug" midnight dreary where Poe was "goofing beat and weary" when he is interrupted by a tapping, "as if some cat were gently riffing, knocking rhythm" at his pad's door. Thinking that it was his witch of a landlady flying around on her broom to collect the rent, he ignores it thinking it the breeze . . ."and nothing more." But Po' Eddie slowly and painfully begins to sense that some dark visitation has come to settle the ultimate score. This is confirmed when "in stomped a king-size Bugbird, Jack, from way back days of yore."

Po' Eddie tries every way he can to communicate with this Bugbird visiting from the "night's Plutonian shore," even employing sympathy. But the Bugbird begins his "Nevermore" jag and Po' Eddie flips, goes out, drinks up a lot of "ignorant oil," and returns with a giant, king-sized hangover. Not wanting the bird to know he's feeling bad, he comes on lighthearted, asking the Bugbird all kinds of crazy questions ("The milkman been here yet?" "So who won the fifth race?"). But the Bugbird always has the same last word: "Nevermore!"

Lord Buckley

I think he laid one too many "nevermores" on Eddie. I don't know how much they weigh but it was just enough to snap that Eisenglass at the end of the fuse and *blow the whole gig.*

Po' Eddie's final hipsemantic harangue is one for the ages, as he tells the Bugbird in no uncertain terms what exactly it can do with his "black jazz," but to no avail.

Buckley was fond of invoking the image of the Bugbird in his life as well.

Dr. James Macy

Ophthalmologist and Buckley scholar, Dr. Jim Macy's professional background and personal friendship with Lord Buckley provide an unusual slant on His Lordship's legacy.

"The Bugbird" was a phrase that he commonly used both on stage and off. It appears most prominently in his version of Edgar Allen Poe's poem "The Raven." The Bugbird represented some kind of nemesis to him, some *betois:* the Black Beast.

The Bugbird," though one of Lord Buckley's darker works, is like the noonday sun when compared to his gothic opus "The Bad-Rapping of the Marquis de Sade—King of the Badcats."

Lord Buckley

The Marq was a *beautiful* man, a *beautiful* man. Oh, he was a big, bad, ballin', Mother jammin' stud of a *beautiful* man. Did you ever hear the Marq's dissertation on the human flesh? Well the old boy said, "A chicken is delicious, and pork is fine, and roast beef is divine, but how about a nice young girl done to a turn?"

The longest single piece in the Buckley canon at sixteen-plus minutes, his performances of "The Bad-Rapping" follow his tried-and-true two-section formula. Beginning with a sympathetic history of de Sade's exploits and subsequent persecution, Buckley soars into a fanciful tale involving one Prince Minski, a de Sade–inspired character, and the bizarre occurrences at his dungeonlike party pad. Ribald, bawdy, frightening, and downright ghoulish, it is in the Prince Minski episode that Buckley hits a peak of dark ecstasy that stands not merely in a class of its own, but in a whole mother university.

His Lordship's vast and uncensored imagination conjured up this giant of a man with a face like a "diamond hatchet" and an appetite that included everything from "chicks! . . . carefully woven together" to "rump of small boy." In his shadow-exploring epic, *L'Histoire de Juliette,* the real Marquis de Sade presented Minski as a Russian giant who eats the flesh of humans, which he generously offers to his guests. De Sade was said to have based his portrait of Minksi on a mythical personage from the murky waters of Russian folklore.

When Buckley begins the piece by explaining how the Marq's neighbors got green-eyed about him having a good time and all his carryings on and "how they bad-rapped the poor cat every step of the way," he is saying something about the calculi of good and evil and about how much (and how *little!*) difference there really is between them.

In the description of a cannibalistic dinner party later in the piece, Buckley gives the listener a chance to discover something about people who sell out openly and who are able to live with evil. In so doing, his concept of moral responsibility becomes less certain and more subtle. To be sure, the most maniacally funny parts of the story force us to face the possibility of evil within ourselves. Buckley's point in defending the man whose actions defined sadism is his claim that de Sade never forced his desires on anyone, yet "they bad-rapped the poor cat every step of the way."

THE BAD-RAPPING OF THE MARQUIS DE SADE I'd like to do one of the most unusual stories in storydom. It's about a hero in evil. A hero in evil called, "The Bad-Rapping of the Marquis de Sade."

The Marquis de Sade, as you know, was a very royal French nobleman, from a very wealthy family, that *dug the chicks.* He like to ball from the early bright right around the clock and then make it some more.

And this cat made Pass City—as a matter of fact, they named Pasadena after this stud.

When he said, "Marie, come here," and she didn't—Boom!—He didn't like no waitin' you understand what I mean?

He was a very interesting cat. As a matter of fact there was one time when he was wanted everywhere but he—brrrrrtt—*snuck in anyway.* He was a wild stud, a real wild stud.

He was sixty-four years old when he swooped off this satellite and he spent twenty-three years in the slammer, and if that ain't bad-rappin' you hip me!

And he went to all odds and ends to prove his philosophy. He said if you're cuttin' down a really crazy, wild country road on a cool, pretty day, and the breeze is comin' on and ricocheting the sweet perfume out of the wild flowers of life . . .

And you feel a hallelujah call in your soul . . .

And you swing around the corner, and there in front of the tree stands a pretty little chick with a lattice petty-coat . . .

And you never dug her before in your LIFE . . .

And you walk right up to her and you say: "*Baby . . . it's you and me . . . behind the tree!*"

And she say, "No," SHE'S GOIN' AGAINST NATURE!

And any cat you know you can't do that!

Now you take one look at my television face and you *got* to know I didn't get all these miles on my puss in one lifetime. So, you got to get hip to the fact that I'm a re-in-car-na-ted cat! And I knew The Marq real cool! Marq was one of them cats like to enjoy, you understand. He rent a small band, he get five or six chicks and a few gallons of juice and swing up a storm and the neighbors was gettin' green-eyed and blow the whistle on the poor cat and: BAD RAP 'EM EVERY STEP OF THE WAY!

Now you take the case of Ella Louise Louise Louise. This is case number 4229, Book Five, Chapter Eleven. She's that little chambermaid chick. It's in the history.

Now he knew this chick was sufferin' from gold shorts up front, so he pressed a fin in her palm, said, "Baby, let's split up to my pad, we'll suck up a little juice, and hear a little wax, and go a little CRAZY!"

She said, "Coo, coo!"

So she took his wing and—brrrrtt—they split toward the pad. And got halfway there and just *happened* to pass the Birch and Rod Store.

So the Marq said, "Scuze me a minute, Sugar."

He swung in and picked up on twelve miniature-styled, three-colored, silk-tasseled, circus day, children's pony, buggy whips. Put 'em under his wing—brrrrtt—and made the pad and: THEY BAD-RAPPED THE POOR CAT EVERY STEP OF THE WAY!

Now *why* did he pick up on those twelve long, mean, thin ones!?! He *knew* this chick was a square. He *knew* she was an octagon-head. He *knew* she was *not* with the *scene*.

And he *knew* it was the *wrong* thing to do to put such a *square* chick as she up against such a *tight* stud as he was on the bed of high sensuous consequence without alerting the chick a little bit in the first place and: THEY DONE BAD-RAPPED HIM EVERY STEP OF THE WAY!

I should like to give you, in hip, an example of the Marquis de Sade's sense of humor. This is one of the stories of his humorous shots.

You know, there's a lot of times when you hear something wild, something crazy, something insane, and you see the humorous thing will reach such a high altitude, that you say to yourself, "Man, that's, that's no longer funny." But, if it is humor, you'll find out there's a whole new *strata* up there. 'Cause humor goes in a complete circle, like the world. Humor is the oil of the soul.

Now, here it is: there were two chicks and two studs sittin' in the petticoats of Paris in a little gin joint, suckin' up a little juice and cuttin' up the Marquis de Sade's last gang bang.

One cat said to the other, "Man, that Marq is bad! He's a wild cat!"

"You hippin' *me?*"

He said, "I'm hippin' *you!*" He say, "What did you like in that last party?"

He say, "I dug the scene," he say, "Man, when them twelve naked chicks jumped out of that giant fish bowl and split up that cherry tree with the mad puppy dog! Yeah, I never saw chicks jump so fast in all my born days."

Other cat say, "Yeah, I like that one, but the one that really knocked me," he say, "was the one of, uh, in the big cage there with the *go*-rilla, with the *go*-rilla and the fonetailed blonde. And that little old fonetail blonde, she dancin' a ring-a-ding-ding and a dong-dong-dong. And the *go*-rilla, he's sittin' over there and ain't makin' a move. Ain't movin' a hair, see. And the little fonetail blonde she dig playin' the ignore for the *go*-rilla. But the *go*-rilla know the blonde know the *go*-rilla in there!"

And they cuttin' up and so on so forth . . . and all of a sudden—BAM!—the door swung open and in stomped a stud about nine-foot-two, built like a mortal anvil: a great big cat with a face like a diamond hatchet with rings on all fingers and money pouring out of his pockets. Looked like a cat with a steel rectum.

Come swingin' into the scene and he shook these studs up *so hard* that he hit their subconscious button *so strong* that they—vrrrrpptt—found themselves standing on their feet with a deep low bow to this cat, joined the table and they never dug him before in their born days!

Turned out to be Prince Minski!

Prince Minski was a cat that had been with it, he gave it away, he took it back, he put it down, he picked it up, he jumped it, he tumped it, he ripped it, he wrapped it, he tapped it, he papped it, he rigged it, he gigged it, he danged it, he donged it, he blanged, he jumped around, he split it . . . *he made every mother scene there was to make!*

And this cat is *not* spending his money! He's comin' on like *Vesuvius reachin' for Pompeii!* He's *BLOWIN'* his gold!

And the number six busboy that's waitin' on the number two waiter is pickin' up eleven-hundred-damn-two-ninety-six dollars a minute in short change, so you KNOW the joint is jumpin'!

And this big steel-tailed Minski, he's sitting there suckin' up all this juice and blowin' all this gold around and finally he turned to these two pretty little chicks and these two wild studs and say, "You know, I dig you two chicks and you two cats. You look like you with it all the way."

Say, "We dig you, too, sir, 'cause you know how to live. You know how to lay your gold out, man, live it up, that's what we say."

"Yeah," he said, "that's right." Said, "I got a big party pad over the hill here. Everything to have a good time with." He say, "How'd you like to join me out?"

They say, "How long can we stay?"

He say, "Long as you like!"

So they paid the tab and they split out of the joint and these two studs and two chicks, they expecting this wild stud to call a golden chariot and twelve horses and out-riders and all that jazz.

Instead of that he turns out to be a Mohicanhead and takes right off through the mother primeval and does about nineteen tail-breakin' miles over hill and dale. And if you turned 'em loose an hour after they started, they'd never found their way back so they're forced to go with the cat and finally come to a black lake with a blue boat on it.

And Minski say, "Get in."

Now these cats is all shook up. Their pants is ripped. They're sick. They're tired. They're hungry. They are SO HONGRY! They'd eat a caterpillar sandwich like you or I do ham 'n' eggs.

They are starvin' to death but they with this mad mother and they don't want to, you know, make no trouble with him.

So, they with him. And these two studs get in front of the boat, and Minski take the tiller: BOOM! The boat shoots out into the middle of the lake.

And the two cats sayin', "Man, I'm so hungry!"

"You hungry? Man, I'm about ready to die!"

"You body ache?"

"My body aches so bad, say, I don't know."

Say, "What, the cat's cool. He ain't made no bad move yet."

"No, he ain't made no bad move. No mad move. The cat's alright."

Say, "What's that out on the water? It looks like a cloud tied to the water."

The other cat says, "Man, can't you see?"

He say, "Whadda ya mean?"

He say, "That's a WALL!"

And it WAS a wall! It was a wall to stop all walls! It was a wall about eleven-hundred-damn-ninety-two foot high. A cloud-pushin' mother and God know how thick with a small uranium door in it, you know what I mean?

And the boat slide up to it and Minski take his big old long stock leg and he—ooonngg!—kick the brick button—vvrrrrppptt—and the door swung open, and—WHOOOOSH!—they go through and—KABANG!—that mother slammed like Doomsday's break!

And they finally come to another big deep underground—boom!—that one slammed. And they come to a drawbridge—BRRRTT—up and down they cross—vvrrrppptt—up back.

Now they come to a wall so tall it take seventeen French acrobats to see the top of this mother with a small arangadang door in it.

And they open that door and—BOOM!—they slipped through and—BOOM! BOOM!—that mother slammed. And the minute it did he turned to them and he said, "I'm the baddest cat in this world!

Said, "There ain't nothin' I ain't done."

He said, "I'm a cross-loader and a hanger-upper and a slip-slider and a double-dealer."

And he say, "I made every bad move there is to make."

He said, "I've done in my brother. I've done in my sister. I've done in my DONE-INS. I been all over this here world studying *scientifically* how to be a bad cat. I'm the King of the Bad Cats!"

"But," he say, "You my buddy cats. Sit down." Boom! They did.

And the minute they sit down they did a real wild take. 'Cause they found out that the chairs they was sittin' in was composed of skel-*e*-ton bones!

So they did a four-way take on him.

Say, "I ate them cats last week."

Then he say, "I suppose you cats is hungry."

They say, "If you ready, we ready, but if you ain't ready we ain't ready, but if you's ready, we's ready, but if you ain't ready we ain't READY!"

He said, "Well, I got a big feast prepared for you cats."

He said, "I know you hungry."

They say, "We is hungry, sir, there ain't no lyin' about that."

He said, "Well, I know you is gourmet heads."

They say, "We do enjoy good food."

"Well," he say, "We might as well go in an dine. Come with me."

So he open a big old door and there's a room about forty feet wide and eighty-five feet long in the middle of which stood a banquet table that was loaded with Goody City!

It had a hundred and twenty-two Japanese wing-ding dinners and hundred and twenty-seven Christmas dinners, and twenty-two Thanksgiving dinners, and Chinese lun-gow and chang-gow. And all them goodies just steamin' and these cats took a bang out of that and almost passed right out on the silver, and they were flippin'!

And about twenty-seven chicks naked as jays swingin' uranium trays and deranium trays and *who*-ranium trays and puttin' more goodies on this table.

So Minski, this big steel-tailed stud, he walked down to the end of the table. And he's standin' there. He standing over to the right hand side of the table about four feet away from the wall and in back of them was five chairs. So big old Minsky he look over and sees these five chairs and he say, "Chairs! Come here!"

And the chairs went: "Mmmmmmmmmmm!"

So he says, "Siddown!"

Boom! And they did.

And when they sat down they really did the take to end all takes, for they found out that the chairs they was sittin' on was composed of . . . *CHICKS!* . . . carefully woven together!

About this time Minski say, "Table! Come here!"

And the whole table—"MMMMMMMMMMMM."

And they look at this table and they find out the same gig is goin' there but by this time they are so hungry, they are so starved.

"We got to get something in our belly, make the brain work, that's all, get some fuel goin' there, make the wheels turn, don't worry about a thing. You got all this food. We're gonna eat. We'll talk it over later!"

So Minski sit down here and by this time he knocked out about nine bottles of juice. And he said, "Well, whatcha think of these goodies?"

And they say, "Crazy, sir, crazy. It is so *in*-sane crazy. I never smelled anything so aromatic in all my born days! Insane, crazy!"

And he say, "Well, I know you are gourmet heads. So I got somethin' prepared for you that's wild."

They say, "We know it, sir."

And he said, "Furthermore, let me hip you to this . . ."

"What's that, sir?"

He say, "You see all these goodies on this table?"

They say, "Yeah."

He say, "You see all these culinary effects, with smells and all these wild colors?"

And they say, "Yes, sir."

He said, "Well, I'm gonna hip you further that when you take your first bite you ain't gonna dig it. But surely enough, if you take that second bite—BAP!—you're hooked!"

They said, "We know it, sir."

He said, "Each and every piece of this great crazy food that you see on this table is *com*-posed of one thing and one thing only: *THE HUMAN FLESH!*"

Brbbdunnaadumadunnnnnnnaaaaaaa!!!!!!

"Well, I supposes it can't be no different than stuffed chicken!"

He say, "Pass me that rump of small boy over there!"

"The Bad-Rapping of the Marquis de Sade" is a true gothic opus, the yang to the yin of "The Nazz." Could there be one without the other? Buckley must have certainly realized both extremes within himself and therein lies perhaps the paradoxical, almost Buddhistic nature of the man's life and art. For every Nazz there is a de Sade, for every Nero a Hip Gahn, for every Gasser a Slugwell.

But despite the yarn's celebration of unabashed evil with a capital *E* (Minski's savage cannibalism couldn't be plainer), Buckley's treatment of de Sade is compassionate. Unlike the directed invective he reserves for flawed leaders like Nero or

Slugwell, Buckley himself was a heavyweight libertine, and the kinship he felt with de Sade and/or Minski is clearly evident. Freedom is, above all, what Lord Buckley strove for in his life, and his art is a necessary reflection of that ethos. To follow one's bliss, as mytho-historian Joseph Campbell wrote, despite the payback, was how Lord Buckley approached his entire existence.

Of all the tales told about Lord Buckley's hedonistic exploits, apocryphal or otherwise, perhaps the one about a party he threw in the 1940s while in Chicago is the best indication of an affinity he may have felt with "the Marq." Guests arrived to encounter Dick Buckley seated like a king on his throne while two voluptuous nude women attended to his *every* desire. In fact, if the desires of some of his male guests included the company of one of the "slave girls," that was perfectly acceptable as well. The only ground rule was that the woman the man brought to the party with him had to, at least temporarily, take the place of the "slave girl" in the host's harem.

Buckley's other preserved renditions of "The Bad-Rapping of the Marquis de Sade" can be found on two superior 1960 recordings: the World Pacific album of the same title recorded live at the Gold Nugget in Oakland, California, and a July 3 party tape made at the San Francisco home of his friend Charles Campbell. The World Pacific release in particular finds Buckley at the top of his game with a raucous but attuned audience that stays with him over every mad mile of this most hellbent of rides.

It is in these late versions of the piece that Buckley had chiseled the presentation like a sculptor's obsession on the exquisite detail of his finished verbal marble. All the thematic and performance elements of his work explode in the shimmering range of his influences. History, spirituality, autobiographical identification, the animal kingdom, literary reference, politics, and sex fuse with his expert musical cadence and pitch.

Jim Dickson

Pieces like "The Bad-Rapping of the Marquis de Sade" would pique the narrow window of his audience. The narrow window that he was playing to was a group of totally antiestablishment drug experimenters who were adverse to the law and who were individualistic, self-serving and even sociopathic in many ways.

Mel Welles

He knew he was playing to these kinds of people. So if he wanted to get a "Wow!" out of them, he had to make the Marquis de Sade look good. This was opposed to the other thing that he did for people which was to take someone like Jonah or Cabeza de Vaca or Gandhi or any of the sort of people that everybody would like to identify with and to show how wronged they were and how deep and how creative they were.

He had a dichotomy: to either make evil look okay, like when he says, "I killed her because I loved her" in "Murder," or to make the good look wronged—make the good look exceptionally good, repressed and suppressed by the great "they" out there.

George Greif

When he drank he could get evil. And when he was evil he was *evil*. To do a piece like "The Bad-Rapping of the Marquis de Sade" you had to be able to relate to that character and, when he was performing it, he was *it*. He used to do a thing with a fellow named Lord Jocko Crown Prince of Morocco where he'd whip him to death on stage with an imaginary whip. He'd pull back and make the sound of a whip cracking: "Whap!" And Jocko would fly over a table. It was acted out but it seemed very real.

Though Lord Buckley was not widely known himself, hip talk was beginning to be popularized through the medium of radio. The golden age of hepcat DJs was in full swing in the mid-1950s before the spread of the Top 40 concept made so many of them obsolete. Even before there was rock 'n' roll, occasional late-night rhythm-and-blues programs on stations in the South and Southwest were hosted by men and women who added a measure of verbal zest to the show, though few of them were African Americans.

Probably the best known of them was Lavada Durst of Texas, who hosted R&B shows on KVET in Austin from the mid-1940s to the 1960s. Durst, known to listeners as the one and only Dr. Hepcat, thrilled his audience with vocal pyrotechnics so extravagant that he once published a guide called *The Jives of Dr. Hepcat* to help his audience understand what he was saying. In his book *The Pied Pipers of Rock and Roll,* Wes Smith offers this sample of Dr. Hepcat lingo to describe how he would get a job, avoid the police, earn money, straighten his hair, buy some shoes, drive along the street, and make time with a pretty woman: "If I had a pony to ride, I'd domino the nabbers, cop some presidents, gas my moss, and maybe get togged with some beastly ground smashers. Then I'd mellow to puff down the stroll where I'd motivate my piece-chopper onto a fly delosis."

To distinguish their rock 'n' roll shows from the usual jazz and pop programs, which almost always featured hosts with measured, mellifluous voices, many early rock DJs developed a flashy patter (which in itself was one of the precursors of rap), delivered in a jivey voice like Dr. Hepcat's. Though John R. Richbourg of Nashville, Douglas "Jocko" Henderson of Baltimore, and Alan Freed of Cleveland and New York were the best known of these early cool-cat rock jocks, the airwaves in every mid-1950s American city featured such characters as the "Jet Pilot of Jive," "Daddy-O Hot Rod," "Poppa Stoppa," and even a female "Dizzy Lizzy" or two.

Wolfman Jack

Robert Weston Smith (aka "Wolfman Jack"), a street-talking jivester from Brooklyn, became the quintessential middle-of-the-night, all-knowing, and all-rapping radio swami during the 1960s and was immortalized in George Lucas's American Graffiti *with a poignant cameo. Wolfman's impressions of Lord Buckley were gathered just days before his death in 1995.*

When I first heard Lord Buckley I thought: "Oh my God! He knows everything."

I always thought Buckley was the guy who created the slang, the very hip language we still use today. I thought he was the man who came up with the original statement. I actually created my style from Buckley, in a sense. I'm a little bit of Buckley. I copied his style—I tried to get his voice down and everything. It was his hipness, it was his style, his timing.

You know, man, I think Lord Buckley came from the future.

Buckley laid down ten other tracks around this time (most likely for but never utilized by the Hip label) that never made it onto vinyl. Of the previously covered material that never officially surfaced, "The Hip Gahn" gets a slow but magical reworking and "Murder" gets its standard macabre treatment. This alternate version of "The Hip Gahn" is set up with a lengthy introduction describing both Lord Buckley's discovery and progressive implementation of the hipsemantic as well as a heartfelt homage to Mahatma Gandhi.

Lord Buckley

Ladies and gentlemen, we should like to do for you as an hors d'oeuvre in this miniature concert, a very short shot of the immortal, the fabulous, the divine, the precious, the beautiful, the gorgeous Mr. Louis Armstrong, an artist who is so beautiful and so profound that he is not even properly recognized by his own race. Are you there?

Attempting to pick up where "Georgia, Sweet and Kind" left off, Buckley gives two old blues bits, "Troubles" (performed to the tune of "Nobody Knows the Trouble I've Seen") and "Lonesome Road," his best Louis Armstrong–style vocalese with hip twists. But they are without the dramatic political irony of the former.

A pair of linked lyrics to a tune reminiscent of a "Seventy-six Trombones," a Gilbert and Sullivan composition, or a piece of John Philip Sousa–style fanfare results in "His Majesty, The Pedestrian" and "His Majesty, The Policeman"—two lighthearted odes to Joe Citizen and Our Protectors in Blue that Buckley would continue to cover and use as a downshift performance tool for the rest of his career.

Lord Buckley

Oh, yes. It's a love song. "The Pedestrian" is a love song to the people. And it happened one time we were driving down Hollywood Boulevard and we had a rather fashionable car and the Rolls Royces to the right and there were Jaguars to the left. And all of a sudden (honk) the whole line had to stop. So I looked down the corner to see what the hang-up was and saw one little pedestrian: "Doodly-do do-da do doodle da do." So I looked at this cat and I figured he must be a very important man to have stopped this whole parade. So I did a bit of research on him and I found out he built the buildings, he built the bridges, he built the airplanes, he built all the fine cooking recipes. He even built the automobiles trying to run him down. So I thought it would nice if we sang a little love song for him.

As for the Man in Blue, Buckley was his usual egalitarian self.

HIS MAJESTY, THE POLICEMAN I got to thinking about His Majesty, The Policeman, see. I figured that must be the draggiest job in the world. And what a drag it is going out on a good day. You're feeling really good. You're riding along and your squad car is all polished up, you know what I mean. And you're feeling real mellow. Along comes some poor stud with a car loaded with kids, like flower pots all over the place. Going a little too fast, you know what I mean. You've got to stop the cat. You've got to bring him down and lay one on him. It's a pretty tough job and when you walk up to him you don't know whether they're going to pull out a French seventy-five or a Walther. It's a drag. So I wrote a little thing called:

His Majesty, The Policeman,
He's the children's friend at every bend,
The Policeman
And you can bet your life,
He's hip to Mack the Knife
That's His Majesty, The Policeman

You should never trip a policeman
Or try to hip or even tip a policeman
Get a ticket to the ball
And you can't fight city hall
That's His Majesty, The Policeman

So remember their nobility
They're here, they're there, they're everywhere it's mobility
You can look near and far but they'll pin you by radar
That's Their Majesty, The Policeman

Here they come—hewbetty boop
The Man In Blue—hoobbit bop
The Sergeant's there—ribbetty bip
The Patrolman too—hahbetta bop
The Chief looks great—hahbetta bop
The Captain's straight—ribbetty bip
Hip Hip Hurray—da da da dah
The Royal Crew—Habetta bahbetta bah

You always try to swing with a policeman
And never ring-a-ding a policeman
And if you're really hip
You'll never make a slip
Against Their Majesties, The Policemen

"H-Bomb," the final cut from this session, is an important addition to Lord Buckley's "atomic" repertoire and one of his most outspoken political tracks and tracts —*years* ahead of its time both in its not-so-thinly disguised condemnation of atomic weaponry and profoundly insightful geopolitical prophesy:

H-BOMB Lord Boothby, the eminent British philosopher made the statement. He came along with a big, strong line. He said, "Humor is the *only* solvent of terror and tension."

Another great humorist Thurber, the beloved Thurber, came along and said that we as Americans must realize "that humor is one of our greatest allies."

And I, in humility, say, "It is the duty of the humor of any given nation in times of high crisis to *at*-tack the *ca*-tastrophe that faces it in *such* a manner as to cause the *people* to *laugh* at it in *such* a manner that they do not die *before* they get killed."

So I figure I'm going down to the bank tomorrow with a couple of trucks and take out a few bales of fifties—maybe a billion dollars—and I'm going to start a gigantic program over the television, over the radio, in the newspapers, in the funny papers, call the people who have anything to do with humor and I'm going to start a big, elongated eight-month campaign against the mother gasser of all time: THE BOMB.

A great spear of humor against the Bomb—rippity-tib zib zib and a ring ding ding against the Bomb. All kinds, all ways, all slides, all sides against the Bomb. A great, big elongated program through the air, by the billboards, by little ones, by big ones till eventually, you mention H-Bomb to someone say: "H-Bomb! Ha ha ha ho hooo hee heee—heard a story about an H-Bomb the other day—Ha ha ha—there was a couple of H-Bombs—ha ha heee—Missiles!—ha ha ha ho ho hee heeee—it's only a thistle, here comes a missile! Ha ha ha heee . . ."

And you hear songs like:

"Way down deep in the Ural Mountains
Far behind the I-ron curtain
I-van and the lads are flirtin'
With U-ran-I-um! U-ran-I-um
It's not geranium
I'm hip that you know
That when you lose your a-plomb

When the a-tomic bomb
Comes your way,
Ba bop be bop
Do you think you'll be gassed
When you hear that big blast
On the highway
Pom bomb pull lam bam
And everything goes up
Hoooooo vrrrppt, Boom!
And then comes down
And Fifty-second Street just can't be found
And Symphony Mother Sid is history?"

Now the next scene is the Kremlin. Kruschev has just returned from a very big visit shaking everyone up rattling the rocket and one thing and another. And they give him a big party in the Kremlin and what with Russian benzedrine and vodka and one thing and another he's smashed out—he's in the silk sacked out with a concrete wig—he's in *bad* shape.

And Moly comes in. He says, "Krusky!"

"Not now Moly! Some other time, please, not now! I'm a very sick man and I cannot talk now."

"But Krusky, something terrible has happened."

"Vat vat vat vat vat terrible could happen?! Vat terrible?!"

"But the Americans—"

"The Americans vat?!?!?!"

"The Americans are in the street *laughing* at the Bomb."

"Vat!?!? This is terrible news! If we cannot scare them to death we cannot beat them. Give me a double shot of vodka right away. Ve give them back Poland, see vat happens . . ."

The bit is simple enough, revolving around the Kremlin's reaction to the dire discovery that the American people are *laughing* at the prospect of nuclear annihilation. Though imbued with stereotypical but expert mimicries of Russian dialect and the Soviet brass's vodka-soaked leadership, the significance of Lord Buckley's stand against irradiated madness at the height of the Cold War should be not be lost. Buckley gets to have his babka and eat it too as he trashes the military-industrial complexes of *both* nations, thus avoiding any potential accusations of red-baiting or red-diapering.

Paul Zaloom

That quote introducing "H-Bomb" about the people dying before they are killed was my philosophy even before I heard it. When I finally heard it I said, "My God, that's what I've been doing. That's what my whole life has revolved around. That whole idea. I came out of Bread and Puppet Theater and did a show on the

Federal Emergency Management Agency's plan to evacuate 120 million people from risk areas to host areas. The government thinks they have all this stuff figured out like emergency change of address forms to make sure people get their mail forwarded from the place that got nuked to the new address. This kind of stuff was comedy that the government wrote. All I did was present it to the audience in some context. The work was done for me.

While the suggestion has arisen that Buckley's inability to break into Hollywood was a result of the aftershocks of blacklisting, there is no substantial evidence supporting this notion. Buckley was friends with the actor Lionel Stander, one of the blacklist's most controversial victims, but whether this caused the chilly winds of political repression to blow the comedian's way remain unsubstantiated. And while his outspoken opposition to the Bomb and his early support of civil rights may have alienated some of his audience, the jazz club bully pulpit of his professional domain was, in all likelihood, far too inconsequential to raise the eyebrows of those who could stymie his career. Freedom of Information Act requests made in Buckley's name for the purposes of this study revealed an absence of any documentation in the artist's files.

Red Rodney

He'd read the editorial pages of the *New York Daily News*. At that period we were very young and very ultra-liberal. I was reading *PM* and the *Star* and those kind of left-wing newspapers. Once he came into a nightclub and hollered: "Red Rodney is a communist!" He was just screaming it and that was a time when it wasn't necessarily cool to be called one either because it was in the McCarthy era.

Politically he was a Neanderthal really. He was very ultra-conservative. I don't think he realized that because I don't think he knew very much about politics. He was patriotic in a kind of gung-ho way. He was like Oliver North: my country right or wrong which is selling very big today.

Lord Buckley

Those dirty, lousy, miserable, rotten politicians! Those thieving monsters. Those greedheads. Look what they've done to this beautiful city! Look at these streets! Those rotten, foul-headed freaks! *Death to them . . .*

As if to confuse his political leanings even further, Buckley could be found hanging out with Marx, Groucho Marx that is—America's Number One Prime Time subversive—when he made two of his most unique media appearances on the radio and television broadcasts of *You Bet Your Life,* the famed Groucho-hosted game show, which aired Saturday, October 6, and Thursday, October 11, of 1956, respectively.

You Bet Your Life was played more for Groucho's comic conversations with his contestants than for the quiz segments. Groucho was obviously delighted and surprised by Buckley's freewheeling, as the show was usually heavily scripted, joke by clever joke.

Unfortunately Buckley's appearance on the show seems not to have been an exception, as he was not really given a chance to shine, speaking only in reply to questions and certainly not doing any bits, although his replies to Groucho's queries demonstrate a very brief glimpse of his style. Groucho does ask Buckley to sing, and His Lordship obliges with a taste of scat as Marx makes the obvious observation, "It's another Louis Armstrong," which amuses the audience. Though not screened by the author, there are other, equally reliable witnesses who insist that Buckley did perform at least a short section of "Hipsters, Flipsters and Finger-Poppin' Daddies," his hip *Julius Caesar* monologue, on the program.

According to Groucho experts, the "secret word" for that particular episode was *street.* Though episodes of *You Bet Your Life* are collected, the appearance by Buckley is hard to come by. The reason being may be in the following quote by Jay Hopkins, founder of the now-defunct Marx Brotherhood, a Marx Brothers fan association: "Unfortunately not every show in the series is currently in syndication. *All* TV prints from 10/05/50 to 9/23/54 were never syndicated due to a dispute with a writer who worked on those earlier programs. Originally, 250 shows were syndicated. In 1973, NBC destroyed some of these prints but was stopped by John Guedel (Producer) and Groucho Marx, who had the remaining 230 prints re-syndicated in 1974."

Buckley's appearance seems not to have been a plug for a new LP; the point apparently was just to be on a network show. Mark Petty, a Minneapolis-based Groucho expert, suggests that perhaps someone from Groucho's production staff saw Buckley at a club and decided to book him on the show. A standard type of guest was the oddball/eccentric, and Buckley was ready-made for the bill. Ernie Kovacs, another great American satirist, was also a guest on *You Bet Your Life,* and his appearance was similarly disappointing.

Richmond Shepard

I saw a rerun of Groucho's *You Bet Your Life* on television one night. And who's one of the contestants? Lord Richard Buckley. And he stood up straight and he had the same mustache and he actually answered questions. But some of the ordinary horseshit rigmarole that he carried with him had fallen aside a little bit. This was a gig, he was being paid.

A Buckley concert organized around this time transpired at L.A.'s Carmel Theatre on October 6, 1956, and was advertised in *Variety* with an endorsement from Frank Sinatra (". . . the most advanced & sensational comic of our times . . ."). Noting that the starring attraction was "HIP Recording Star—'Flight of the Saucer,'" the ad points out that the gig was set to commence at 2 a.m.: "In Person! For You! After Two!" Most striking was the general admission price of a ducat: $1.50.

Feeling the frustration at Southern California's dearth of appropriate or well-paying venues, the Royal Court began to expand its range and definition of performance. Perhaps the best visually documented of these happenings took place at the Music Box, a small theater in downtown Los Angeles. Renting the hall and promoting the

1956 show themselves, Buckley and company held forth in a midnight presentation that predated the spirit of the Fillmore West by a decade.

Ray Avery

In 1956 jazz lover and photographer Ray Avery snapped some of the best shots of His Lordship in performance.

I had heard a little about Lord Buckley and he was sort of an underground figure even then. I heard that he was doing a kind of little off-Broadway show at the Music Box and I went to see what it was like.

I didn't know it at the time but Mrs. Buckley was selling tickets at the front with long blond hair with a crown on. The stage situation was really quite interesting. The Buckley family, with his son dressed like Little Lord Fauntleroy in short little knickers, and entourage was sitting in a line on one side of the stage and the band (with Roy Milton and "Little" Willie Jackson) on the other side of the stage. The band would play and Buckley would do his monologues. And all the time during the performance there were people in the back of the stage painting the backdrop. I guess it was part of the performance but they were there painting the backdrop, adding to the free-form notion of it all. There was a very informal onstage quality to the whole affair and because of the painting of the backdrop on stage, it was like a dress rehearsal, like it wasn't really the show but it was.

I was interested in jazz at the time and really didn't know too much about him. Somebody told me that it might be something interesting to photograph. I really didn't know what to expect and it turned out to be quite surprising and interesting.

Avery's shots reveal a typical freewheeling scene. Picking up from where he left off from his days in Topanga Canyon, Buckley had invited Bob DeWitt to paint a huge canvas on which he featured obese Madonnas floating in the air at the rear of the stage while Roy Milton's combo warmed up the crowd and backed the main attraction. At the very least, it was remembered as a chaotic presentation.

"Little" Willie Jackson

Known for his collaborations with Stan Kenton's tenor man Vido Musso in his band "The Honeydrippers" during the 1940s and 1950s, the late alto saxophonist "Little" Willie Jackson was still going strong, playing the music he loved so much at various California venues until the early 1990s. Along with Musso and pianist Joe Liggins, Sir Willie backed up Lord Buckley at a series of Los Angeles performances in 1956, including the famous Music Box gig.

I met Buckley in California in the 1950s. He came into a club where our band with Vido Musso was working. He made himself known, got on the show and shot a few lines out at the audience. We just took to the man. He liked us too and invited us to do the theater thing—the whole king and queen thing. These were late shows after we'd get off from the club—like two or three in the morning.

His children were my escorts to the stage and were up on stage with him during the performance. We were all escorted up on stage like we were actually in a king's palace. They bowed and kissed my hand, put a cape around my shoulders and, with a scepter, knighted me "Sir Willie" like Prince Lancelot and the Knights of the Round Table. It was wonderful for me because I love children and they treated me like I was one of the family. It was one of these warm things, you know, like it was for real.

The show was very free-form. We played behind him while he did his act. We played Swing with a little bit of scat and complemented his material really well. We played out of the book: "Honeydripper," "I Got a Right to Cry," "The Peanut Vendor," and some other stuff that Joe Liggins wrote. His act was unique and was accepted by the public.

He was A-OK. When he first came on with his tone of voice, I couldn't dig it at first. I said, "What's he doing?" But the more I heard him the more I got it. He stayed in that character like a duke or a prince or spoke like a preacher. He called everyone "Your Royal Highness" or "Your Majesty." He had the kind of a voice where people shut up and listen. He turned on the house, let me tell you! I liked him very much. He was a fine cat, an aristocat!

Some of Avery's photos show members of the Royal Court on a flower-and-candelabra-bedecked stage, including a five-year-old Richard Jr. and Lady Elizabeth dressed in flowing white chiffon and wearing a flower tiara. Lord Buckley is resplendent in his evening clothes, replete with a white carnation on the lapel and a white bow tie around his neck. In some of the photos, however, he has stripped down to his shirtsleeves and can be seen using a straw hat as a prop for one of his bits.

Buckley was still making semiannual trips to New York City for his appearances on *The Ed Sullivan Show,* and his interest in alternative theatrical presentation led him to some peculiarly unique avant-garde quarters.

Judith Malina

I first met the great Lord Buckley around 1957 when the Living Theater had remodeled a department store on Fourteenth Street into a three-story theater plant. We had a big lobby and we worked very hard on it. We did all this immense schlepping ourselves and I learned how to lay bricks and mix mortar. We did a huge renovation job there with hundreds of good artists giving their elbow grease.

It was during that time that Lord Buckley used to appear in the midst of our labors and put on spectacular little events to inspire us on in our sweaty work. He came in and did little numbers about art and social justice, art and sexual justice which often entered into the question as well.

We would all lay down our sacks and our bricks and gather around. People would come down from the third floor, the plumbers came up from the basement and it was a great inspiration as he would do his inimitable shtick. Who could even say what they were about except they were all about everything and the here and now. He was in a certain sense a great inspiration to us about where the source of the new energy was. And in a way you can't say, in the long run, that hasn't even won out. The culture has changed from such sparks of inspiration that amounted to something by the Sixties.

He was a flashy dresser. He wore rather outrageous clothes and bright, light outrageous colors but always in some way representing the gentleman with a lot of humorous winks like "Dig this velvet jacket. Dig these threads." Today his fashion would fit right in with that downtown, hippie new wave pop art look.

The Connection was a piece in that genre of the belief that the true philosophy of our time was coming out of, shall we say, the brothels of New Orleans, the lofts of Harlem or wherever you want to say jazz found its beginnings, where a certain spirit of the truth was being spoken in a way that was a very different kind of philosophy of the schoolbooks and the university. It was in the same inspired tone that Lord Buckley took in his parody of the social structure that went from the clothes he wore to the accent that he adopted to the title in his name. It was a whole way of saying, "Look again at these structures and look what they really are and they, too, contain the truth and that truth is raunchy."

In *The Connection* we were inspired by that style and the general way in which Lord Buckley was part of a whole river of concept and sentiment that turned the world around and turned it into something more nitty-gritty and real and marvelous than the false poetics of the philosophers of tradition.

When we were doing *The Connection* he showed up again, sometimes even in rehearsal. But finally, when the opening came, there he was in the lobby of the Fourteenth Street theater. In *The Connection* the actors came out and panhandled the audience for money to buy dope during the intermission as part of the show. That part of the show and the way that each actor came out and did their little shtick was really inspired by the way that Lord Buckley did his shtick. The intermission of *The Connection* opened up the whole Pirandellian reality of what's real and what's performance for us in a very big way. Am I acting or am I spectator? Am I for real or am I pretending? Am I really a lord or am I a phony? Is the phony the reality or is the reality the phoniness and are they both holy?

The Living Theater was trying to break down and reassess those boundaries and concepts of traditional theater at that time and Buckley seemed to anticipate much of those ideas in his work. Of course there's always been the question and the question is a classical question. The Italian playwright Luigi Pirandello, whose work we had performed years before, was already dealing with that question.

Lord Buckley was a forerunner to the whole question of: what's formal, what's informal, what's phony, what's true, what's holy, what's real, who the hell am I? His combination of philosophical elegance with a kind of lowbrow, highbrow game that he played about which vocabulary he was using. The elegance of his ability to speak in a very highly modulated educated tone and at the same time to be able to be so truthful about the realities of this world and invoke the idiom of the streets no matter what streets he was walking.

That he was a bit older than most of us made us very happy: to see that we were not an isolated phenomenon but part of that spirit of cultural rebellion that had always been there.

I was around twenty-nine or thirty then and people were beginning to say: "Don't trust anybody over thirty." I thought: "Don't trust him? I'd trust him with my soul."

Being thirty then I didn't have to feel that I had to stop making revolution because I was going into another period of my life. And here I am: I'm seventy-five and I haven't given up on the beautiful, non-violent anarchist revolution one iota. I'm fighting it as much as ever with, if not with as much energy, certainly with a lot more smarts than I had then. I can look back on Lord Buckley's energy and say, "Hey, we aren't so bad." I hope I can still do what I do now when I'm eighty-eight and travel the world and say, "Don't give up on it! It's a static period but the pendulum is in the downswing and it will come up again!"

Stuart Whitman

We had many discussions on stage delivery. He used to go 600 miles per hour. If he had just pulled it up a little his audience would have *really* been with him.

He would come in to read for a part, but would read all the parts and drive the directors out of their socks. They were scared that he would dominate them. He just rocked everybody.

Lord Buckley

Yes. It's very religious work of complete dedication. It's dangerous work. If you're in the theater and you're not a star, you can't get credit anywhere.

The theater is actually a great, profound, pure, beautiful, multi-colored, non-stop, ever-swinging church. May I welcome the nobility to High Mass.

It's a little known truth that the theater is in itself a church, see. The theater is really a very religious institution because it presents life itself in all its beauty and in all its rhythm and it gives the people an opportunity to analyze life and to look at life and see it flowing before their very eyes. And it's a very, very profound and a very, very religious work.

I was in New York recently, I saw all the people running along at showtime: "Come on now and get a cab, Jack! Look out! Honk Honk! Ding Ding! Get your tickets! Watch it, Mary! Wait for me, Charles! Ring! Ding! Ding! Ding! Ding! Ding!" All running like mad. All running like mad for church and no one knows it.

When you walk into a theater you right away *feel*. You have a *feeling*. You have a feeling that it's a meeting with the people, it's a meeting of the people to receive a great reflection of the warm love of life through the talents and the arts of the individual.

12 lord and lenny

Lord Buckley

I'm not a sick humorist. I admire all kinds and types of humor and all of it is necessary. Evidently there wouldn't be sick humor if there weren't sick people.

Sick humor, to me, is humor off balance. The field of humor is wide open with plenty of material without resorting to such sadism.

No other person's name is invoked more consistently and reverentially in connection with Lord Buckley than Lenny Bruce. Though the jury is still out regarding the extent of their personal and artistic relationship, a serious case can be made for both. There were some close to Lenny who maintain that any appearance of kinship is purely coincidental—that they were of completely different worlds. However, the weight of testimony and artistic evidence shows their mutual respect and reciprocity.

One thing is for certain: Lenny Bruce remains the most controversial figure in the history of twentieth-century comedy.

Steve Allen

The name of Lenny Bruce should be introduced into the broad discussion at this point. I get really angry, literally angry, when people defend Andrew Dice Clay by saying: "After all, didn't Lenny Bruce do the same thing?"

I almost want to hit them at those moments. The answer is: "Hell no!" Lenny Bruce *didn't* do the same thing. First of all Lenny didn't use half as many offensive words, if you want to look at it on a pound-for-pound basis. And, even more importantly, when he did he was always making a philosophical point. He wasn't throwing in the word *fuck* just to get more laughter on a line. He was a philosopher and he was brilliant. To this day I don't know of any young comic out there who is as hip as he was.

I like to call it "concept humor." In fact, I still specialize in it to this day. If you can think in terms of concepts, it makes your work so much easier because it gets you away from having to come up with nineteen new jokes every few days. Now, I do write jokes—I've written thousands of them and I use them in my act. But I'll give you fifty jokes for one concept any time.

Buckley was a comedian but of a very unique type. Henny Youngman or Rodney Dangerfield can string forty-nine strong jokes together, do their act backwards and it wouldn't matter. But comedians who have some thought to their work, such as Buckley or Lenny, never seem to be standing in the same line of regular comedians like the Bob Hopes and Johnny Carsons.

Lenny was chiefly influenced by Joe Ansis. He sort of absorbed Ansis's personality. People used to say that Ansis was the funniest cat in the world if you're in a restaurant with him but he couldn't perform. If there were more than six people laughing he got nervous. But I think it was from Ansis that Lenny picked up the musician's lingo and then, later of course, he worked with a lot of musicians.

I loved everything Lenny ever did. He totally knocked me out. And we were buddies. He used to get a big kick out of my wife, Jayne Meadows, who is sort of a Katherine Hepburn type. She'd come from New England and her father was a clergyman. Lenny used to get a big kick out of her because they were from different planets altogether. When he would come to our place on Eighty-fifth Street and Park he would immediately go into a routine meant for her ears but apparently talking to me.

The question went something like, "What will we do on the show next Sunday?"

And he would say, "I have this funny bit about the two fag priests . . ." just to see what her reaction would be. She was hip enough to realize he was putting her on, but it took about five seconds before it hit her.

Buckley had that tough factor to him. Lenny was never tough. Lenny was delicate. He was very courageous but he was delicate in his work whereas Buckley had a toughness that was characteristic of the period of nightclub work from which he came.

Leonard Alfred Schneider was born on October 13, 1925, in Wantaugh, New York, on Long Island. A product of a broken home, Lenny grew up neurotic and starved for affection.

Increasingly he was drawn under the spell of his mother, Sally Marr, a sometime stand-up comic and entertainer who occasionally took him to burlesque shows. At the age of twenty-four Lenny found himself a winner in "Arthur Godfrey's Talent Scouts," a 1949 amateur contest.

Although Marr was mainly known for encouraging her son as a performer, she was herself a professional comic and talent spotter. Among those she helped discover were Sam Kinison, Pat Morita, and Cheech and Chong.

Sally Marr

Aside from promoting her son Lenny Bruce, the late Sally Marr was a fixture in show business since the 1930s. In 1994 Joan Rivers adapted Marr's life for a well-received Broadway show, Sally Marr . . . and Her Escorts.

I don't think Lenny was influenced by Lord Buckley at all. He did material that was nothing like Buckley's.

Lord Buckley and Lenny Bruce represented two different forms of comedy. But people have, for better or for worse, followed my son's direction and Buckley has fallen between the cracks. He's barely a footnote and that's a shame.

People know who Lenny Bruce is now but they hadn't until I did the Broadway show that became the film *Lenny*. That really put him on the map. I made it my business to do so because I knew he was someone who would go down in history as someone who helped redefine the First Amendment of the United States. I felt that he did something very important and people should know who he was.

Both Lord Buckley and Lenny were freedom fighters and Lenny won. But the shame of it all was when two weeks after Lenny died, he won all his cases. It was a paradox, ironic and tragic.

Lenny was friends with Buckley. He took me to that big mansion where Buckley was living in L.A. Everybody was on top of everybody else. It's a wonder no one smothered.

Nobody cared enough about Lord Buckley to push him and he didn't care enough about himself to go out there and do it. I saw him at a candy store in Marin County very late in his life and I asked him, "Why aren't you working more?"

He said, "I am."

And I said, "No you're not."

He was afraid to come out. He was chicken.

Mel Welles

Lenny Bruce, like Buckley, was one of a kind. Lenny's only influence was his mother, Sally Marr, who was a comedienne and was connected to all the subcultures of her time. That's another thing, a lot of this kind of wit is born out of connections to subcultures—not to the standard cultures but connected to subcultures.

Lenny and Buckley were friends, yes, and they had a lot of laughs from each other but they were different in a lot of ways. Lenny was a hard-drug user and Buckley disdained the use of hard drugs or anything that would alter you to the point of immobility. Lenny had his own very tight entourage and Buckley had his. But some of Lenny's entourage were persona non grata in Buckley's circles—certain people who Buckley felt were rotten on the inside.

You had to have a lot of nice for Buckley to like you. He might tolerate you if you didn't but if you wanted to be a friend of Buckley's—a huggin' and kissin' friend—you had to be basically a nice person.

Dick Zalud

I saw Buckley do a show in California with Lenny Bruce and Lenny's mother, Sally Marr, at a strip joint. That was the bill and in between the acts were the strippers. Strip joints used to be vogue in those days. A strip joint with a comic, acts and, of course, strippers.

Lenny began his career doing shtick, impressions, and master-of-ceremonies work in strip clubs. On this circuit he met and married Harriet Jolliff, a hot redheaded stripper known professionally as Honey Michel and Honey Harlowe.

Like Buckley, Bruce was an inveterate con artist, raising money any way he could. He was once arrested (and acquitted) for impersonating a priest soliciting funds for a leper colony.

In 1955 their daughter, Kitty, was born but, by the end of the decade, drug abuse and divorce shattered the family.

Honey Bruce

The widow of Lenny Bruce penned an autobiography, Honey: The Life and Loves of Lenny's Shady Lady, *from which the following reminiscence is excerpted.*

In order for a comic to stay in one city and work the clubs, he has to keep changing his routines or the customers don't come back. If you keep doing the same material, you have to stay on the road. That way, you're fresh in every town. While I was in Las Vegas, Lenny had gotten a job as an M.C. in a burlesque club on Pico and Western. Strip City (referred to by Lenny as one of his favorite "toilets") was located in a black and tan neighborhood. The caliber of customer (99.0 percent men) ranged from a bottom of unshaven and unkempt to a top of cheap and flashy. For Lenny, though, it was a steady job that paid ninety dollars a week. We didn't have to go out on the road again, and it forced him to continually change his material. It was at Strip City that Lenny started experimenting with comedy.

Strip City boasted six gorgeous strippers. The audience was not interested in anything going on in the club except what was happening with the strippers. Although Lenny complained about working a "burlesque striphouse," he continued there for a year and a half.

Lenny shared the comedy bill at Strip City with Lord Richard Buckley—great, swinging lord of Flip Manor, guardian of the gates to Groove City, and a genius whose influence on American comedy has never really been appreciated. I'm just a country girl, but I've been exposed (if you'll pardon the expression) to some of the finest comedy minds in America, something I'll always be grateful for, and Lord Buckley was tops.

Lord Buckley was always a legendary person among comedians and students of comedy. He was an absolutely immaculate dresser. Each night he would appear on the club stage decked out in tuxedo pants with a line of shiny satin down each leg and a white dinner jacket. His gray hair was always tightly slicked down so as not to distract from his Salvador Dali mustache, waxed and wicked, like two curious antennas scanning the air around him in search of the outrageous.

Lenny and Lord Buckley worked at Strip City on and off for a year. Strip City was a great place for a comic to break in material because no one would really notice if a comedy bit laid an egg. They also wouldn't notice if Bob Hope were on stage. This would sometimes frustrate Lenny, driving him to dream up bizarre stunts to relieve his boredom.

One particular night (when Joe Maini was also working), Lenny came in to introduce the strippers. The audience was the usual—a few drunks, a few about-to-be drunks, and the "crew" of owners, bartenders, and musicians. No one was paying attention.

"Good evening, everyone. It's a real pleasure to be working Arlington Cemetery tonight. *(Nothing. A chuckle from Joe Maini.)* You're gonna like our show because tonight we have ladies from *Science Fiction Review* performing for your pleasure. We'll be starting off with an acrobatic stripper known as the 'Upside-Down Girl,' a six-foot-two towering eyeful, and she'll be sharing star billing with a sensational newcomer, Miss Fifty-four D. If this little lady comes to your house to borrow some sugar, don't let her in! She's got the biggest cups in town." *(Joe Maini breaks up. The rest of the room is freeze-dried.)*

Now Lenny's mad. He decides to blow Lord Buckley's mind when he comes on. During the next band break, Lenny climbs up on top of an air vent hanging from the low ceiling directly over the stage. His plan is to lie in wait until Lord Buckley is about to lay out a punch line and then shout down through the air vent, "Hey, let's keep it quiet down there. I'm trying to get a little sleep!" Everything goes well and Lenny is tucked away out of sight. The band returns. Lord Buckley appears on stage and starts his routine. Then, just as Lenny shouts "Hey!" the ceiling gives way and Lenny comes crashing down, knocking the Lord to the stage, covering the two of them in a shower of dust and plaster.

Even this night's audience couldn't ignore the goings-on. At first, stunned silence, and then the sound of Joe Maini cracking up. Soon the band joined in; then Maynard Sloat, a crazy man and one of the owners (you'd have to be crazy to hire Lenny and Lord Buckley for the same bill!), decided the whole incident was cool.

Elegantly brushing at the plaster on his tuxedo, Lord Buckley took the mike. "Lord Leonard, you are the living end and the funniest person I've ever had the pleasure of meeting."

While the band played for Busty Brown, the debris was swept up and Lenny, Lord Buckley, and Joe Maini, three fugitives from a sane asylum, ducked out the stage door to smoke a quick joint. Lord Buckley, of course, was an outrageous "viper." Every puff was the last one he'd ever have, or so it seemed. He'd suck the smoke in and then hold it in his lungs as long as possible, all the time spouting a nonstop rap. His voice would go deeper and deeper, then turn guttural until it sounded as if he were talking from inside a whale that was buried in gravel. Finally, the looooong exhale out, and then, a joyful gleam in his eyes, he'd turn and exclaim, "No doubt about it, weed is a . . . *gasser!*"

I know Lenny learned a lot from working with Lord Buckley. Buckley was a master at changing his voice to create a comic scene that might have a cast of five or six. (If you've had the pleasure, and the belly laughs, too, of hearing Lord B's classic satire, "The Nazz," you'll know what I mean!) Prior to working with him, Lenny did vocal impressions of famous stars, but I believe he learned he could use his voice to create many comedy characters from his experiences with

Buckley. With Lenny's talents there was no problem in coming up with the voices, but it was the dear Lord Buckley who did it first.

During these years Lenny's comedy was in flux, turning hipper and "sicker." Audiences encouraged Lenny toward more free-form comedy and to follow his instincts to do fewer set bits and one-liners and more observational material drawn, like a jazz musician, from the sense and emotion of the moment. When some of his sexual or religious work garnered negative reviews, he was only challenged into pushing the envelope even farther.

Lenny Bruce didn't have all the answers and he didn't claim to. He did, however, think he had all the questions. But anti-Bruce forces were strong and getting stronger. The First Amendment protected him from the silencers in regard to his religious and political material, but when it came to his use of "dirty words," the law was clearly on their side. He was busted several times for obscenity, and in his struggle to free himself, while permanently changing attitudes and laws on obscenity, he found himself in a legal quagmire that drained first his money, and then his strength, away.

Lenny struggled on, his performances increasingly obsessed with dissecting law and language, trying to make sense of the nonsense. As a reflection of his declining popularity and drawing power, *Variety* reported that he made $108,000 in 1960 and only $6,000 in 1964. By 1965 he was belly-up financially, and by 1966 dead from an opiate-induced (and still somewhat suspicious) overdose. One sure thing remains: Lenny Bruce was just as controversial in death as he was in life.

Del Close

Legendary member of the Second City troupe, creator of several classic cult albums including How to Speak Hip, *and comedic guru to the likes of John Belushi and John Candy, the late Del Close was instrumental in developing the* The Return of the Hip Messiah, *a play based on his experiences with Lord Buckley that was produced by Chicago's Prop Theater and Second City shortly after his death in 1999. Close became associated with Lord Buckley and shared several bills with him in 1960. Del's final, and perhaps greatest, gesture in black humor was the bequeathment of his skull to the Goodman Theater in Chicago so he could finally play the role of Yorick in* Hamlet.

I feel that people like Buckley, Lenny Bruce and Antonin Artaud were men suicided by society because they were saying real stuff. Lenny was unfairly persecuted, because there were many comedians in the United States like B. S. Pulley and Redd Foxx that were far, far more obscene than Lenny was. But because Lenny would mix up the obscenity with cogent religious/political commentary he became unacceptable. Maybe I hallucinated this but I seem to recall reading a small article in a New York newspaper some years ago in which a member of the New York Police Department confessed to being part of a nationwide conspiracy to destroy the career of Lenny Bruce. Mort Sahl was blacklisted by the Kennedys because he was doing Kennedy material and talking about President Kennedy's sex life.

In some ways I think Buckley was dumped on because he was also dealing with issues. Whether blacks happened to like Buckley's characterization or not, he was dealing with racial issues and speaking out against lynching and prejudice. He was doing stuff like "Black Cross," "The Bad-Rapping of the Marquis de Sade" and talking about Gandhi and Cabeza de Vaca. Somehow or other when an American comedian takes on real issues, he sometimes seems to wind up dead or forgotten.

I used to kind of resent it and ask myself: "What am I doing alive?" I guess I just wasn't good enough to be killed by society. Now this is kind of a romantic view of it but Lenny Bruce, Mort Sahl and Buckley were the three great comedians of the late fifties and early sixties and they all disappeared in some way or another. You just have to start wondering what it is about this society and its comedians. Even today: Freddie Prinze is dead, Richard Pryor is sick, Andy Kaufman is dead. Maybe there's something terminal about the act of being that kind of comedian.

In the years since his passing, other comedians utilized elements of Lenny's style and teachings but with almost universally base results. In truth, only Richard Pryor, Robin Williams, George Carlin, Jonathan Winters, and a very small handful of others have artistically strolled through the pearly Gates of Eden Lenny opened, radically transforming the nature of stand-up.

Jonathan Winters

I *loved* Buckley's stuff. I thought he was one of the most gifted and one of the funniest guys I'd ever met, and I still do. Me, Lenny Bruce, the others—we were all out of the same magical pot, as it were. I think he rubbed off on all of us.

Probably the most apparent aesthetic similarity between Buckley and Bruce is in the idiosyncratic projection of the jazz persona and innate musicality in their stage delivery and manner. But where Buckley's verbal spirit and worldview were always hyperkinetically upbeat, the lion's share of Lenny's work is infused with an embittered cynicism. If one thinks of Buckley as the hipster that he was and Lenny as the consummate Beatnik, a cultural model can be derived: two traditionally linked but yet distinctly separate modes of expression and experience.

Jerry Garcia

Jerry Garcia, Grateful Dead lead guitarist and counterculture elder, became a Lord Buckley admirer after witnessing a performance by His Lordship in 1960.

Despite his appearances on the medium, Lord Buckley never was a television guy. So you don't get a chance to see what his classic performances were like. Lenny Bruce did do some TV so you could see his show. Lord Buckley was part of that whole coffeehouse, jazz club scene like the hungry i, the Outside at the

Inside and the Purple Onion. His classic work didn't penetrate into the Ed Sullivan reality.

Part of Lord Buckley's appeal is that basic humanness. With his bits there was always a little character who was like a verbal equivalent of Charlie Chaplin. There was some pathos in there. And you could sympathize with them. The characters always had their human side. I think that's something missing from Lenny Bruce who was happening on whole other levels but not that particular level. The heart chakra so to speak. Lord Buckley was the hipster of the heart.

Lenny's method of comic musicality is, perhaps, most present in his bit "The Sound," a hilariously poignant history of jazz chronicling the rise and fall of a white trumpeter that parodies the Kirk Douglas flick *Young Man with a Horn*. Similarly, "My Werewolf Mama," Bruce's jazzy send-up, demonstrates his R&B chops much in the way Buckley's numerous musical, Armstrongesque exhibitions do and particularly evident on "His Majesty, The Policeman," "His Majesty, The Pedestrian," and his interpretations of "When the Saints Come Marching In."

Robin Williams

Buckley and Lenny were both jazz. People used to say that Lenny Bruce was very musical, not just the routine, "Did ya come? Did ya come? Did ya come good?" But there are other ones that are very musical, too. Besides performing in those places, their work was jazz—verbal jazz.

Buckley, you might even say, was more lyrical or poetic. Something like "The Hip Gahn" or "The Nazz" he took in terms of the jazz world. It's almost like explaining it to white people in code. I don't know anybody doing that now.

Eric Bogosian

Buckley obviously influenced Bruce, but I'm not a biographer, I don't know how or where or when. The voice as weapon, the voice as musical instrument. I'd say that's the connection. Also, of course, elements like the jazz scene, the club scene, marijuana, and sex.

Ken Nordine

"Word Jazz" poet and voice-over deity, Ken Nordine's basso profundo has been regularly heard on Chicago radio for nearly four decades.

Buckley was much more of a wit that Lenny Bruce. Lenny Bruce dealt with the use of scatological material and four-letter words and tilting against sacred cows in our society. Actually, Lenny was more of a burlesque comedian from a strip joint like the Liberty Inn here in Chicago, a sort of fall-apart joint on Clark Street as I recall. A lot of Indians used to hang out there. But they'd have strippers there and he would talk the way people would talk at a sports bar. Doing his act as an emcee attracted a lot of heat: coppers were put on his case by the establishment of the city of Chicago even though they enjoyed what he was doing. He tilted against the Church, the Jews, the Gentiles, the copywriters . . . everybody he could jump on. And he did it with a sense of glee and a little bit of a sharp edge.

Now, on the other side of that, Lord Buckley was far more a legitimate talent in writing because he took the bopster language and translated things like Poe and Shakespeare and made it into his own.

Buckley would get into the language using it almost in a sprung poetic way of transubstantiation. He would, by changing the language, add certain things. He brought to the metaphor that he was using images and his own slant that was very much of his time. He was more interested in how he could play with the structures that he was in—how he could bend them to his own mind and in so doing he created his own rather unusual, unique style that nobody has approached since. He became, in a sense, possessed while he was doing his thing so he would string a whole line of images together in one breath and so, in that regard, he was most unusual.

Judith Malina

Lord Buckley's whole inspiration really created a language and created a vocabulary that not only became a way of speaking but of thinking as well. That form of thinking led to what Lenny Bruce did to liberate the prudery out of the language and performance and what a lot of people did was inspired right there from that spark of genius. And Lord Buckley was a genius.

Paul Zaloom

Lord Buckley's material is more difficult—I'm tempted to say more intellectual—than Lenny Bruce's. It's harder to understand. In terms of neglect, you could almost ask the same questions about Will Rogers. Why isn't Will Rogers more popular today? Will Rogers was probably the biggest star in American history and probably ever will be. Why aren't his movies more popular now? He was the biggest box office star in 1934—bigger than the Marx Brothers, bigger than W. C. Fields. Why doesn't anybody know who he is? Why are his movies never shown? Why isn't it known that he was the biggest Hollywood star of his era? The answer is simple: he did the country bumpkin shtick; there's no such thing as a country bumpkin anymore—case closed. He's irrelevant. He doesn't mean anything to us. Our innocence is so far gone, Will Rogers can't plug into the zeitgeist.

As far as Buckley is concerned, his material is very arcane. The hipster language requires paying attention. It requires sitting down and really listening and taking time. It's not as accessible as Bruce's stuff and Bruce was more sensational. Not that many people sit around and listen to Bruce but certainly more do than who sit around listening to Buckley.

When searching for evidence of Lord Buckley's mark in specific Lenny Bruce pieces, several routines spring to mind. "Religion Inc.," Bruce's full-blown condemnation of organized religions and those that front them, picks up where Buckley's political invective "Governor Slugwell" leaves off, right down to the fanfare of a small-town revival parade. It is classic satire on the concept, then new, that religion had become big business.

Not surprisingly, Buckley caught the same kind of flak as Lenny for some of his spiritually oriented pieces, particularly "The Nazz," from those who mistakenly perceived that he was mocking organized religion rather than reverentially reinterpreting its positive essence.

Jack Sheldon

Friend and bandstand mate with the likes of Lenny Bruce, Dexter Gordon, Art Pepper, and Wardell Gray, trumpeter Jack Sheldon helped spearhead the West Coast jazz movement of the 1950s. His group with saxophonist Joe Maini accompanied Lord Buckley on several Southern California engagements.

Buckley'd come and sit in with us at a place called Duffy's in Los Angeles. Joe Maini and I were working there with Lenny Bruce. Joe Maini was a friend of Lenny's and played alto sax. He shot himself to death when he was very young—thirty-six or something. He was drunk one time and he started playing with a .22 pistol that belonged to a friend of his and accidentally shot himself.

Buckley was like a Jesus to hear. Lenny Bruce identified with Jesus too. Lenny told me that himself. He said that he really identified most with Jesus. Strange thing coming from a Jewish junkie. Jesus was Jewish too, but it doesn't seem like it anymore, does it? That always dumbfounded me when Lenny said that. Lord Buckley was like Jesus too: just completely different from a human being.

When we worked with Lenny he was really funny. Toward the end of his career I don't think he was very funny anymore. He was studying law eight hours every day and he really got bogged down. He was taking so much methedrine because he loved Bela Lugosi so much. Bela Lugosi was strung out on methedrine and Lenny went to the same doctor as Bela Lugosi to cop drugs.

Lord Buckley was always encouraging—a supporter of music and young people. I was just a kid and hadn't made a name for myself but he treated me with a lot of respect. I always looked forward to seeing him because he always made me feel real good. He seemed to express love to me. A real positive, all-loving force.

He'd always come to the party after the gig with his wife. I always had the idea that he was very moralistic. I thought of him as being much different than us. We were wild. After the gig we would all be working on getting high and he would be at the parties. He always dressed impeccably, looking real sharp. He was always so gracious and polite. Elegant, always elegant. He was something that I'd never seen before or since.

These parties were pretty crazy and sordid when I look back on it. People would be shooting up in the kitchen while two guys with big dicks would be fucking some burlesque girl with everybody watching while a midget played a harmonica on the dresser. There'd be liquor and girls and it would just be wild going until dawn. Someone would always OD and we'd put them in the bathtub and turn the cold water on them while the rest of them were shooting up. We never lost one but Lenny finally did OD. We were people searching for an answer to life until I found that it wasn't at those parties. It took me years and years to discover that it wasn't there.

Lord Buckley would come to Lenny's house. He liked Lenny. We all admired Lord Buckley a great deal but he couldn't get a job. He didn't work very much at all but he was brilliant. There was just nobody that would hire him. I don't think people knew he was funny back then or something. They thought "The Nazz" would be almost sacrilegious. The cats in the band were the only ones laughing.

Ann Brooks

Booze and grass. That was Buckley's thing. Everybody thought he was a total dope addict but he had a fear of anything that smelt like smack. He didn't care for it too much. He was a dear beloved friend of Lenny's but he was very upset about Lenny's plight.

Lenny was much a student of Lord Buckley's. After Lord Buckley died I made the pilgrimage West and came back through Chicago. I wanted to go see Lenny and tell him about Buckley's death personally. I went looking for him at the Gate of Horn where he was performing, and when I couldn't find him, I got into a cab just as he got in on the other side. And from the Gate of Horn to the Maryland Hotel where he was staying, we started a running rap about Lord Buckley.

Amps [amphetamine ampules] were pretty heavy at the time and we got up to the room still talking two hundred miles an hour. The words were falling out of our mouths before we had a chance to think of where they were coming from. And we kept up a steady skit and never questioned each other until about seven o'clock that night when he had to go and do the show.

Lenny adored Lord Buckley but he didn't have a court name. Sammy Davis Jr. didn't either. Sammy loved His Grace as well. Lord Buckley had a lot of people that dug him but they weren't quite into the Royal Court scene. They dug him for his timing, for his diction and, of course, for his monologues.

Thematic elements of Buckley's rap "The Train" appear in several of Lenny's commentaries drawn from newspaper headlines, most notably in "Non Skeddo Flies Again," Lenny's demented modernist take on a *very* troubled airline.

Sensitivity to issues involving race and civil rights were central to the work of both humorists. But where Buckley's sympathy bared itself in his presentations of Joe Newman's "Black Cross" and his own twist on "Georgia, Sweet and Kind," Lenny turned the perversity of bigotry on its ear with such bits as "How to Relax Your Colored Friends at Parties" about a well-intentioned host who says *all* the wrong things.

Structurally, Lenny seems to have picked up a great deal from Buckley in regard to the art and craft of storytelling. He utilizes His Lordship's method of setting up a tale with two observers who become participants in his low-down routine "Hitler," a bit that gets almost as nasty as Buckley's diabolical "Bad-Rapping of the Marquis de Sade."

Further following in Buckley's wake, Lenny's "Hitler," "Thank You Masked Man," "Enchanting Transylvania," and "Father Flotski's Triumph" owe much to the art of the cinema.

And while we're at it, Lord B's "Martin's Horse" and the Bruce bit "Psychopathia Sexualis" share the same taboo subject: bestiality. Seems like they both had friends at Santa Anita Racetrack.

Ed Randolph

Lenny Bruce was a successful Lord Buckley. His Lordship was too much of an in thing and he never made the break that Lenny Bruce did in his lifetime. Don't forget that Lenny Bruce went to London and played The Establishment and got punched in the nose because he used four-letter words.

Would there have been a Lenny Bruce without a Lord Buckley? The question invites a thorny but ultimately fruitless exercise. Would there have been a Charlie Parker without a Lester Young? A Ginsberg without a Whitman? A Pollock without a Picasso? A Pynchon without a Joyce? A Dylan without a Guthrie? A Koufax without a Hubbell? Lenny was clearly an enormously talented and insightful individual who would have absorbed whatever was around him he found necessary to forge his particular vision and challenge the social boundaries that he deemed restrictive—which, in his eyes, just so happened to be practically all of them.

William Karl Thomas

"Media Maestro" William Karl Thomas was acquainted with Lord Buckley in the late 1950s. Some of his witness in this manuscript appeared in his memoir, Lenny Bruce: The Making of a Prophet, *published by Archon in 1989.*

Lenny Bruce, my collaborator on comedy material and screenplays at the time, and I had been dragged to the Ivar by Frank Ray Perelli, a fellow associate who had previously collaborated with me and was at the time coaching Lenny and grooming his career. Comedy records and concerts were relatively unheard of then. Frankie, who had the insight to recognize a rare talent in Lenny Bruce as no one else did at that time, also had the foresight to see comedy records and concerts as a more liberal platform for unusual comedy such as Lenny's, and potentially more profitable than the nightclub stages on which most comics depended. Frankie wanted us to see Lord Buckley who pioneered comedy records and concerts, and who dared to deal with the taboos of sex and religion.

Buckley worked with a small jazz ensemble who obviously knew his material well and maintained a rapport with his stream of consciousness, which vacillated from the profound to the profane and back again to the sublime. A handsome and charismatic man, he was the ultimate thespian whose face could contort almost as much as his phenomenal voice, which would glide from the thundering resonance of Shakespearean pomposity to the easy, warm, liquid smoothness of the 1930/1940 Negro jazz idiom, punctuated by loud, unlikely vocal sound effects, devastatingly funny in their shock effect and seemingly impossible to have been issued from a human larynx.

After the concert, Frankie introduced us and Buckley invited us to a bar on the corner for drinks, for which he borrowed ten dollars from Frankie. Buckley must have been in his early fifties, Lenny and Frankie in their early thirties, and I was a child of twenty-six, but a gifted and perceptive child. Lenny was reticent in his praise compared to Frankie, but I was eager to point out to Lenny that some of Buckley's Negro spiritual characterizations were what I had been unable to adequately describe to him from my past experience and to color that material on which we were collaborating. I found it ironic that even though Lenny shared so much in common with Buckley, being a comedian in the jazz/drug culture who dealt with sex and religion, he nonetheless seemed indifferent to the man and the magic of his particular brand of comedy. I eventually realized that Lenny's talent was to satirize what was negative in society, while Buckley primarily focused on what he perceived as positive, even if that included being drunk or high.

I saw Buckely a dozen or more times in the late 1950s when he would visit the clubs Lenny was working in. Buckley was "on stage" and "in character" almost every moment I saw him. The one exception was at a birthday party where, for the first time, I saw him in the company of his wife whom he appeared to badger and verbally abuse. His barbs were colored with courtly bandies ("Milords, mi'ladies, forgive this pitiful hag her shrewish ways"). His uncharacteristic treatment of her was either evidence of bad blood between them or a put-on in bad taste.

At one point I was working for Benny Shapiro who owned the Renaissance, a coffeehouse-cum-nightclub located in a private home on the south side of Sunset Strip across from the old Ciro's nightclub. Benny had tried to get me to influence Lenny to work the Renaissance, inasmuch as I had booked Lenny into the Sloate Brothers (where he made the front page of *Variety* for being fired the first night for blue material) and Cosmo Alley, the most successful coffeehouse at that time co-owned by Theo Bikel. Lenny's career had progressed to the point that he would only accept the most profitable bookings like the Crescendo a few blocks away on Sunset Strip. Instead, I talked Benny into booking Lord Buckley, whose price was still within reach and whose material was as appropriate to the revolutionary spirit of the time. We booked Paul Horn and his group to back him which was a beautiful blend of styles. Buckley was a smash hit, held over, and began to draw celebrities to the club such as James Mason, Terry Thomas, and many others.

Though I was not in the drug culture, and though I recognized Buckley as a flamboyant con man who like many religious and political leaders contrives the image of a benevolent father figure, I could not help but admire his consummate theatrical talents and whatever within him motivated him, with rare few exceptions, to always seek and champion that which was positive. I regard Lenny Bruce and Lord Buckley as the Yin and Yang of the sixties. Lenny's humor might be defined by his line, "If the world was perfect, I'd be out of a job," whereas Buckley's credo was in his line, "There ain't NO problem that LOVE can't solve, bebee."

Roseanne

Along with the following excerpt from her 1989 autobiography My Life as a Woman, *actress, comedienne, and media sensation Roseanne specifically thanks Lord Buckley in the book's preface.*

Lenny Bruce was perceived in the late part of the sixties as the future. The future that meant that the old way is dead, and passing. So he, like all people who remind other people of the future, have to either die, or be invalidated while they are alive, and then after, when they are dead, people can start worshipping them as a martyr, or great teacher, and pretend to themselves that if their heroes ever came back, in this time and age, they would listen, they would agree, they would be so fuckin' hip. They are so fucking hip they are busy censoring, invalidating, and fucking with the writers, artists, poets, that belong to them during their own lifetimes. It was no accident that Lenny had chosen comedy. It is the last "free speech" art form and, like my father said, it is mightier than the pen *and* the sword.

For years I thought it wasn't worthy of me, though I adored watching others do it. I aspired to be Gertrude Stein, or Dylan Thomas, or some poetess tragically and forlornly trying to scrape some piece of my misery off the sole of my soul and write some touching little fat girl shit about it. I thought fat girls had to write poetry until as a teenager I heard Lord Buckley, and Lenny Bruce, and understood the jazz of words alone, and that had a rhythm and a beat and a sensuous movement that you could get lost in. It is a place, perhaps the only place where a woman can speak as a woman, as a stranger in a strange land, as part of a group that defined itself in its own view, and with its own words, in a manner that seemed to heal, instead of wound.

Severn Darden

Stand-up philosopher, actor, and underground voyager, the late Severn Darden's offbeat take on the universe helped lay the foundation for Chicago's famed troupe, Second City. He shared a Windy City bill with Lord Buckley and Del Close at the famous "Seacoast of Bohemia" show in the summer of 1960.

Buckley was addressing a totally different audience than a comedian would today. He was really a top-flight entertainer from his vaudeville days. Even calling him a comedian is a somewhat limited definition. It's particularly limiting in reference to Lenny Bruce because his main force, if you relisten to his records, is reinforced with a sense of performing sociology. There are very few punch lines and very few jokes.

"Grampa" Al Lewis

Both Buckley and Lenny came out of the poetry and jazz thing. The funny thing is that I would say Lord Buckley influenced no one. Historically, I cannot find anyone whose material is derivative of Lord Buckley.

Dr. Oscar Janiger

I was also close to Lenny. He told me that Buckley was, in his mind, probably the finest comedian, or had the greatest comic spirit, of anyone he had ever known. The reason for that is because Lord Buckley was his own writer—he didn't have canned material. He'd take off and reach inside and pull out all this stuff.

Lord Buckley was the bellwether of that entire period. As is so often the case, both he and Lenny were ahead of their time and the things which we now take for granted were, in those days, on the cutting edge. They were "out there." I call them cultural heroes. They were people who broke the ground, broke the horizon so to speak. He was doing what he was compelled to do and I think he would have continued. He would have been acclaimed as one of the leaders. Lenny, posthumously, is regarded as such and Buckley is not, but he deserves to be. He would have been acclaimed as one of the great leaders of a movement and perhaps gone ahead and developed more and more of a style that would have been commensurate with the changes in society that were going on and moving in his direction.

I think if Lord Buckley had found a way of putting out his message, he could have been a very influential man. I could have seen him groomed by somebody to take on a particular role like Mort Sahl. He had a strong sense of social responsibility. And I think to some extent he was a social reformer. Much of what he wrote and talked about had that feeling about it. It's reminiscent of the works of Daniel Defoe or Jonathan Swift. He felt a true responsibility not only to the material and the audience but also to people in general.

Shelley Berman

A groundbreaking contemporary of Lenny Bruce and Mort Sahl, Shelley Berman was one of the handful of stand-up performers of the late 1950s labeled as "sick comics."

I never met Lord Buckley but I saw him perform one time and heard recordings of his work.

There's no comparison between what Buckley was doing and my own work. It was a totally different guise. I became a comedian in 1957 so my knowledge of him is mostly in reading quotes of his work. His work is legendary now because of his ability to take what we regarded as "classical" and bring it to another level altogether was great: these fairy tales being spoken in hip talk were marvelous. But I felt that musicians were more tuned into him than I.

The critics liked to lump anyone who wasn't doing the straight, one-line jokes or any other kind of performing style into a single category. As a result people like Lord Buckley, Lenny Bruce, Mort Sahl, and myself were labeled as "sick comedians," which is a very unfortunate part of being a performer. If you emerge at a certain time and are not doing what your predecessors did, well, then, according to the media, you must be doing something alike. But nobody was doing what Lord Buckley did. He emerged at a certain time and he was very distinctive but he was slaughtered in a time when others were getting more attention and I'm afraid the legacy of those others have tended to live on more than his.

One connection that Buckley and I might share is in the more formal presentation of our work. There was a certain degree of decorum that we felt would create a certain ambience. He was simply not a one-line artist. He was simply not a nightclub type. I don't know whether that worked to his benefit or worked against him. I'm sure it was hard for him because, indeed, many of us were trapped by these venues.

When I talked with others back then about Buckley, it wasn't like talking about a contemporary. He was so distinctive, so individual, one would refer to his work with a certain amount of admiration and joy. But we didn't speak of him as we spoke of each other. We could talk about Lenny much easier than we could talk about Lord Buckley. His career went back to the twenties so he was like some elder statesman as far as we were concerned but we had no specific knowledge of him. We didn't run across him. We didn't wind up in the same place.

When you break it down to the bottom line, Buckley seems to be remembered for a specific form of comedy and that's the hip talk. It's a very specific form. It's far different from, say, Norm Crosby's malapropisms. Norm Crosby is the comedian of my generation who uses malapropisms—just as another comedian might be known for a specific. And Lord Buckley was very specific in terms of our knowledge of him. It was specific. It was hip talk.

Lenny picked up on some of it but it wasn't like Lord Buckley. Bill Cosby took the classics too but it wasn't hip talk. It was the anachronistic reference to it. He modernized the story which is an old-fashioned comedy device: taking a biblical story, for instance, and bringing it down to Earth. Not only was Buckley one of the first to do that and institutionalize it, he did it with language. It wasn't necessarily conceptual. He stayed with the concept and brought it to another level. He was a language expert. He modernized only in terms of words, not the story itself. Thus the sense and the wisdom of the original stories remained intact. It wasn't the same as Bill Cosby's "Noah's Ark," which employed modern vernacular but not hip vernacular.

Buckley was something very splendid and special. He would thrill you with his original concepts and with the daring of delivering it. And with the fact that he was he and no one else. Now that mattered.

Lord Buckley

Humor should be used for beauty, not for ridicule or other cruel purposes.

13 it could be verse!

Lord Buckley

Comedy is the only thing I've been able to take seriously.

With her children a bit more manageable and with the household in need of supplemental income, Lady Elizabeth Buckley, encouraged by her husband to fulfill *her* creative impulses, auditioned for and landed a job as a dancer in the 1957 edition of the Ziegfeld Follies that toured the nation. When Lord Buckley was able to arrange engagements at clubs in cities that matched the Follies's itinerary, the whole family was off on the circuit during the fall of that year.

While in Cleveland, Ohio, Buckley was booked for a gig at the Black Angus Restaurant's El Toro Room by Bill Randle, a soon-to-be-renowned local disc jockey. Buckley's performances, advertised as "Word Jazz" in the local papers, drew not only Cleveland's budding hipster population but every cool hustler, hooker, pimp, and parolee as well.

Along with Alan Freed, Bill Randle is often credited with popularizing the term *rock 'n' roll* and for staging the first rock concert. It was Randle, not Ed Sullivan, who introduced the young Elvis Presley to a national television audience. After staging Elvis's pop concert debut at a Cleveland high school, Randle arranged for the singer's appearance on Jackie Gleason's *Stage Show* in 1956. He was also among the first disc jockeys to employ demographic techniques to program his show, talking to high school kids and clocking jukeboxes to find out what was popular.

Later he became a record producer. After recording Jack Kerouac for an album called *Readings on the Beat Generation,* Randle produced the last recording session of Chicago blues legend Big Bill Broonzy.

Randle also invited His Lordship to lay down some tracks in the studios of Cleveland's WERE-FM, the DJ's home-base radio station at the time.

On Sunday, October 6, 1957, Buckley recorded nearly an hour and a half of his latest act that included some never-before-or-since-heard works. The high-quality result exhibits definitive versions of "The Hip Einie," "The Gasser," "The Bugbird," "To Swing or Not to Swing," and "Swingin' Pied Piper." The latter was a hipsemantic translation of Robert Browning's "The Pied Piper of Hamelin" that Buckley was later to record on a few other occasions. Also included was a new history, "Hip Chris," his riff on Christopher Columbus's "discovery" of the New World, and the super-rare "Pursuit of Morpheus"—truncated here because the master tape ran out.

"Swingin' Pied Piper" is a dense Buckley piece, similar to his detailed line-for-line reworkings of Shakespeare, Lincoln, and Poe. With its implicit connections to his animal yarns, the piece is probably best viewed as Buckley autobiography. No doubt Buckley viewed himself as a kind of Swingin' Pied Piper leading his followers down a yellow brick road of his fancies to some undetermined Oz.

Lord Buckley

There's a magnificent pylon in this, there's a torch for the world: that life cannot be as beautiful as it should be. We have the blocks to make up the mosaic of life: the dream—a *beautiful, wonderful, warm,* unendingly delightful schematic of living. This is the truth. We have all these things to put them together. But the pylon that describes the torch of the world is Browning's "Pied Piper of Hamelin." The story of the broken promise . . .

"Swingin' Pied Piper" is a tour-de-force transmogrification of Browning's classic and a choice vehicle for Buckley's talents, encompassing the many elements of his artistic interest: autobiography, charisma, animals, myth, legend, music, and social improvement. At one point Buckley even likens the Pied Piper to Elvis Presley. Yet there is a melancholy tone to the entire piece that not only hints at Buckley's identification with the Pied Piper but also suggests that he felt the time had come for the piper to be paid, that is, himself. A complex yet tight hipsemantic, it is astounding that Buckley could continually reel this lengthy masterwork off the top of his exploding brain and tip of his ever-wiggling tongue like a true thespian adept, concluding the allegory with this fabulous, warmhearted moral: "So, Jack, let's you and me be wipers-out of scores with all men, especially pipers, whether they pipe us free from rats, rock and roll, or the blue suede shoes, let's solid keep our promises and we'll never blow the blues . . . no, we'll never blow the blues."

"Hip Chris" attempts to plow the same historical terrain and style as "The Gasser," but ultimately pales beside that masterpiece as the weak opening lines attest: "This is the tale of a Genoese called the 'Hip Chris.' This swingin' Portuguese cat used to sit on the dock and dig the aqua scene. The flippin', jumpin', stompin' billows of the realm of Neptunareni.

"The squares said the world was flat, dig? But the Hip Chris, as he used to sit there doing a long goof, decided it was *mellow*-size. They all put him down but he played the *ig*-nore for these doings and started making the rounds to dig some gold to pick up some ships to prove his wig was the straightest."

Interestingly, Buckley's "Hip Chris" is performed almost word for word by "J. I. Coleridge," a character played by John Drew Barrymore (of the Barrymore acting aristocracy) in *High School Confidential!,* a 1958 proto-Beat exploitation flick. In the movie Russ Tamblyn starred as a narc, while Mamie Van Doren displayed her vixenly virtues and Jackie (*The Kid* and "Uncle Fester") Coogan peddled dope. The supporting cast included an equally unlikely assortment of talent: Jerry Lee Lewis, Michael Landon, and Charlie Chaplin Jr.

Variety actually gave the movie a boffo review, as the following excerpt attests: "The screenplay by Lewis Meltzer and Robert Blees, from a story by Blees, is well constructed and faithfully told in the special language of today's juniors."

The similarity of the renditions of the Buckley and Barrymore raps has been long debated among Buckleyologists and B-movie freaks. Mel Welles, however, cleared up any confusion once and for all with some surprising insights.

Mel Welles

If you've seen the picture called *High School Confidential!*, you'll remember that John Drew Barrymore does a routine about Columbus in front of a history class. I wrote that piece of material and also the poetry and jazz piece that Phillpa Fallon does. Actually, I was the technical director on *High School Confidential!* for the "pot" language on that picture. But you can't consider "Hip Chris" to be one of Buckley's pieces because he never used it in his act.

There was another interesting picture called *Rock All Night* based on an Emmy Award–winning television show called *The Little Guy* that starred Dane Clark. Roger Corman bought the film rights, which I thought was very courageous of him, and he had Chuck Griffith write it into a rock script to emulate the success that *Rock Around the Clock* and all those pictures were having.

There's an interesting story about the character I play in the picture, "Sir Bop." Chuck, with my advice, wrote the part for Lord Buckley. I was an expert on grass, in my day. Anyway, that's the kind of stuff that Dick Buckley did, and Sir Bop was written for him. Then Buckley disappeared somewhere, so I played it myself—dyed my hair silver and tried to do him the best I could.

Because of the language in *Rock All Night*, Roger got really worried that nobody would understand the picture. So I wrote a dictionary called *Sir Bop's Unabridged Hiptionary: Lexicography for Hipsters of All Ages*. A couple of million of them were distributed with *Rock All Night* so that people would not get confused when the characters talked about their short [car] or their iron [motorcycle] or their kip [bed]. At that time, nobody knew anything except "groovy" and "dig," and they only knew *those* because Steve Allen and Frank Sinatra had used them on television. The rest of hip talk nobody knew except musicians, carnies and subculture people.

Pursuit of Morpheus" is an incomplete original from the session that cuts off before Buckley could really begin to sink his teeth into it—just as it seems to be developing into a tantalizing dark vision of Morpheus, the lord of dreams, similar in its gothic spirit to "The Bad-Rapping of the Marquis de Sade." Because this is all that remains of this version of the routine, Randle suspects that there is still at least one reel from the session that is unaccounted for and thinks it still must exist somewhere in a WERE storage locker or maybe in his hometown of Detroit. And thus the intangible Buckley legend continues.

The WERE performance repertoire is of primary significance to the Buckley lexicon because of its premier of three works penned by Joseph S. Newman, a nearly forgotten Cleveland poet. Newman's 1948 book of collected poems, *It Could Be Verse!*, evidently inspired the performing artist.

David C. Barnett

David C. Barnett is a Cleveland, Ohio, writer and radio producer who contributes pieces to the local National Public Radio station. The following radio essay he wrote about Joseph S. Newman solves the deep mystery Newman played in Lord Buckley's life and art.

If Joseph Newman never made much money from his poems, he certainly made his mark in Cleveland in many areas over the period of half a century.

While the world may be more familiar with Newman's nephew, actor Paul Newman, it was Joseph Simon Newman who has had the most enduring impact on Cleveland's history spanning such disciplines as business, science, politics and culture.

Nineteen ninety-eight marked the fiftieth anniversary of *It Could Be Verse!* and what would have been the 107th birthday of its author. In 1948, $2.75 cents bought this deceivingly thin volume of light verse packed with more humor and insight than many books of greater worth and girth. In the space of 180 pages, Newman elegantly expostulated on an eclectic collection of subjects including: anthropology, biology, comparative religion and the history of the world. From four line bits of doggerel to epic rewrites of *The Odyssey* and other classics, Joe Newman's poetic waxings knew no bounds.

Like his book, Joseph Newman had a thin body but broad interests. He was a businessman who started the first radio parts store in Cleveland and the largest sporting goods store in Ohio. He was a newspaperman who wrote popular columns for the *Plain Dealer* and the *Cleveland Press*. He was the author of five books. He was a political satirist who wrote hundreds of songs for the Cleveland City Club's "Anvil Review."

On a wall in the City Club's lunchroom hangs a relaxed portrait of the bespectacled Newman with a pipe in his mouth. "Baggy tweeds and a malodorous pipe," was the way one friend described him.

Though he started writing poems for fun when he was about ten years old, Joseph Newman's real passion was for science.

As the world entered the twentieth century, the country was in the midst of a technological upheaval that would thrust it into world dominance. The telephone, the phonograph and the radio were some of the fruits of the revolution. The new technology would link up what had previously been a scattering of isolated cities and towns. In these cities and towns, radio enthusiasts were deriving publications such as *QST* and *Wireless Age,* which instructed them in the construction of "cat's whisker" receivers. Newman had his own radio receiver and a sizable chemical laboratory in the basement. As a teenager he looked forward to college where he would major in science. He attended Case School of Applied Science but was unable to continue there because of financial problems.

This led Joe into being a vacuum cleaner salesman for a year and he eventually landed a job at the old Stearn & Company department store on Euclid

Avenue in Cleveland. There he became a toy buyer and PR man. He learned retailing and, because of his scientific bent, designed and patented some electrical toys and went into business as the Electroset Company. He went into the mail-order radio parts business and had a sizable catalogue of Galena crystals, cat's whiskers and all of the accoutrements that went to make up early crystal set radios and early radios because, at that time, a ready-made radio could not be bought. If you wanted a radio you built your own.

He decided that business was pretty good and convinced Arnold Stern to invest money for expansion as business was growing and the banks were leery about lending money to a new area like this. Stern, a bit of an entrepreneur, came in as a silent partner and they set up Newman, Stern & Company. However, when World War I came along the government stopped all amateur radio. They said the country needed all the airwaves and, besides, "those Germans might be using it to send messages to their country." So Newman and Stern were shut down. There was no relief from the government. They simply said, "You cannot sell these parts."

This was quite a blow to Newman as Stern got very worried and bowed out of the enterprise. Newman used a buyout settlement to invest in a line of sporting goods equipment that carried him through.

Joseph Newman was also a science teacher at heart. His talent for expressing complex ideas in light verse was equally effective in prose, be it humorous lectures under the guise of a slightly scatterbrained character named "Dr. Sy N. Tific" or designing science projects and regular columns for the *Plain Dealer* and *St. Nicholas Magazine for Boys.*

In 1913 Joe married his childhood sweetheart Babette Weidenthal. In examining her family tree, Babette once noted that the womenfolk were teachers and the menfolk were in the newspaper business. The Weidenthal name has been associated with Cleveland papers for many years starting with the old *Jewish Independent* and on up through the *Cleveland Press* and the *Plain Dealer.*

Playwright George S. Kauffman once said, "Satire is what closes on Saturday night." In an era where satire of sorts is seen on *Saturday Night Live* and a plethora of cable channels, it may be hard for us to appreciate the impact of Joseph Newman's lyrics for the City Club's "Anvil Review."

In those days the City Club was a very important place for everybody who was anybody who lived in the city of Cleveland, and the club had much to do with directing the city. They began to put on the "Anvil Review" just as skits and developed it into a larger proposition. Eventually, the entire script was front-page news published in its entirety in both the *Plain Dealer* and the *Cleveland News.*

The City Club's lunchtime discussion tables have always been an important part of the club's commitment to the free exchange of ideas. Members have traditionally sat at a variety of tables featuring topics such as the law, education and various sorts of politics. And Joe Newman was a fixture there for many years.

The "Anvil Review" started out as an annual members-only event but evolved into a grand theatrical display staged for the public at the city's Music Hall. Always, it poked fun at all of the big shots from the president of the United States on down.

In 1958 Newman bowed out of the "Anvil Review" after thirty-five years of involvement and nearly eight hundred songs.

A successful businessman, a science educator, a whimsical poet and beloved songwriter, Joseph Newman cast a large shadow in Cleveland.

During the inglorious days of the House of Un-American Activities, not even Joseph Newman was able to escape criticism. When a civil liberties group he had helped found fell apart over accusations of Communist influences, the *Cleveland Press* ran a condescending editorial calling Newman a "sucker" for leftist causes.

Social issues were important to Joe Newman. He often said that the wrong people have the power and that a way must be found of empowering the right people in society.

In the mid-1950s he had been hired by the *Cleveland Press* to write a column. He sold his interest in Newman, Stern & Company after his brother Art died in 1950. Powerful *Press* editor Louis Seltzer wasn't calling him a "sucker" anymore and Newman came on board with a weekly column that had a familiar title: "It Could Be Verse!"

Newman continued to churn out his columns and an occasional book until the day he died at age sixty-eight on November 10, 1960, cosmically and ironically just two days short of Buckley's passing.

During the WERE outing Buckley takes on two of Newman's poems that appear in *It Could Be Verse!* ("Jehovah and Finnegan" and "Leviathan") and another ("Shah's Embroidered Pants") that does not. His Lordship's decision to cover Newman was unusual not just because of the poet's obscurity, but also because Buckley's straight, nonhipsemantic readings change not one word of the original. Nary a dash of cool is applied to any of them, Buckley preferring to present the poems in his own dramatic voice, probably even close to how Newman imagined them read aloud. He didn't mess with Newman's words, letting sheer vocal dynamics fuel the performance.

How Buckley stumbled onto Newman's work in the first place is a matter of conjecture. But there is little doubt that being in Newman's hometown that October afternoon inspired the poet's somewhat top-heavy inclusion on this reel.

Lady Elizabeth Buckley

His Lordship was always moving about the territories so to speak and ended up finding so many different pieces of material and meeting people. The piece "Black Cross" has a very special significance. The author is a gentleman by the name of Joseph Newman. He was actually the uncle of the actor Paul Newman and a noted journalist for the *Cleveland Press*. And while we were touring with the Ziegfeld Follies, His Lordship called him up and started to say in his inimitable voice: "This is Hezikiah Jones." And the fellow thought, "Who in the world is this?"

Hezikiah Jones was the hero of Mr. Newman's most important poem, "Black Cross," which Lord Buckley would often perform.

But Mr. Newman did venture out to come and meet us. When he first met Lord and Lady Buckley he was a bit skeptical. We were a bit unusual seated in this hotel room but when the children came in after their nap, why he kind of melted and welcomed us. He was especially very kind to His Lordship and allowed him to use all of his material.

Perhaps it was at this meeting that Newman presented Buckley with "Shah's Embroidered Pants," which prompted His Lordship to perform it on the WERE aircheck.

In his choice of specific Newman poems, Buckley was also referencing his primary thematic concerns. "Shah's Embroidered Pants" pokes fun at hierarchical social structures and those who sit on the top of them à la "Nero," "Slugwell," or the venerable parable "The Emperor's New Clothes." "Jehovah and Finnegan" is a slice of the most American of Americana: baseball. More than merely a knockoff of "Casey at the Bat"—with which it shares metrical and dramatic similarities—"Jehovah and Finnegan" culminates with a punch line that should appeal to baseball mystics the world over: "Rain called on account of game."

"Leviathan," one of Newman's real masterpieces, is a madcap animal story—another whale tale in the spirit of Buckley's own "Jonah and the Whale" with a nod to Herman Melville's *Moby-Dick.* In his last years Buckley even dropped whole stanzas of "Leviathan" into his performances of "Jonah."

Mel Welles

Buckley could perform magic. As a storyteller he was incomparable. Still, to this day, there's nobody as dynamic. There have been many people who have done Buckley in an effort to re-create him but the dynamics are not the same. So he reigns supreme. I don't think anybody's equal to him. He did produce magic. "Leviathan" is a very rare piece—a kind of take on *Moby-Dick* involving a whale and is absolutely the wildest storytelling I've ever heard in my life.

The reason that he did some of Joe Newman's poems is *not* because he was impressed by Newman. Frankly, Dick wouldn't know a good poet from a bad poet if it fell on him. He was drawn to "Leviathan" because the piece suited his natural dynamics to a T.

Though not performed at the WERE aircheck, the last, most important Newman entry in the Buckley catalogue, "Black Cross," is, as will be seen later, a blast at the evil consequences of unchecked racism and perhaps Buckley's most outspoken political stand.

Finally, the WERE aircheck includes two additions to the "atomic Buckley" classification: "Wild Blue Yonder" and two nearly identical takes of an on-the-spot composition informally titled "Satellite Blips."

Autobiographical in origin, "Wild Blue Yonder" recounts the improbable but apparently true story of Lord Buckley's journey on a U.S. Air Force jet. By his own account, in this wild rap (and it is one of his most "out there") Buckley was performing at an air force luncheon in New Orleans during the mid-1950s when he was invited for a flight on an AT-33 aircraft. The resulting experience comprises the bulk of "Wild Blue Yonder," and if the mind's ear can envision the gonzo fever of *Dr. Strangelove* combined with the high-tech pluckiness of *The Right Stuff* as filtered through Buckley's machine-gun tongue, then some idea of the bit can be gleaned: "On goes the oxygen sniffer . . . the windshield is pulled down over my space hat . . . down goes the canopy . . . I feel like the top part of a ketchup bottle, under glass. Man, I am in like some strap spider flung a web on me . . . I felt like the low man on a fat man's totem pole. I was so down that my space helmet weighed 7 gillium pounds. If Marilyn Monroe was to walk by in her calendar suit, I'd have to take a rain check, 'cause man, I couldn't lift my head. Don't fight the ship . . . man, I'm fighting to get all these lead-tailed cats off my back . . . then we're upstairs again . . . before I could get my stomach out of my shoes we were coolin' in on the runway."

Not so coincidentally, "Wild Blue Yonder" was published almost verbatim in the December 1956 edition of *Dig* magazine as "Buckley Describes First Ride in a Jet!," which even includes a priceless photograph of Buckley, attired in flight helmet and suit, sitting in the cockpit of the aircraft.

A month before, in the November 1956 issue of *Dig*, the editors saw fit to print both versions of "The Gettysburg Address" alongside one another—Abe Lincoln's *and* Lord Buckley's. *Dig* also published "Hip Christopher Columbus" in its May 1956 issue, along with loony line drawings of the subject, which looked like they were lifted straight off the pages of *Mad* magazine.

There is a footnoted yarn regarding "Satellite Blips," the last bits on the WERE aircheck representing the final "space-age" entry in the Buckley canon. The weekend of Buckley's visit to WERE was a historically momentous one. The Soviet Union had just launched Sputnik and sent political shockwaves across the globe. WERE beat all of its competitors to the punch by broadcasting the first recordings of Sputnik's bugaboo blips as received via shortwave by staff engineer Joe Zelle. Zelle made national news that very weekend when he used his home shortwave setup to gather Sputnik's transmissions on tape, which he then quickly broadcast on the station. Accounts of Zelle's exploits were blasted across the front page of the *Cleveland Press* the day before Buckley's WERE visit.

As an homage to WERE and taking careful note of the profound significance of the event itself, Buckley rifled off an on-the-spot riff demonstrating the type of spontaneous creative combustion for which he was famous. Injecting a large dose of political commentary into the piece, Buckley considers the consequences of unchecked space and arms races by pointing out in the course of the "blip flip" that: ". . . what I don't dig is *even* if a man has the front door covered he's in bad shape with thousands of atomic-headed eagles at his side and backdoors and roosting in his trees so to hip. The Putnik sound has a bug-a-boo beat but any cat in the know *digs* it as a satellite king-sized gnat that can be slapped flat or topped as Father Time swings on. So let's all play the cool and relax a little already. Later . . ."

Plans between Buckley and Randle to release the WERE material with Mercury Records are evidenced by a letter written by the performer from New York when the Ziegfeld Follies were there in December 1957. While holed up at the Hotel Embassy on Broadway and Seventieth Street just around the corner from his old Upper West Side digs, His Lordship dashed off the following communiqué postmarked December 6 and addressed to "His Most Royal Highness Sir William of Randell Grand Duke of Maryland":

> Your Grace,
>
> I feel that something is terribly amiss with our plans with Mercury. What it is I do not know. I found out now that the $200 advance was out of your own pocket. This I did not know till now. Please forgive me. I have tried to get in touch with Mercury Records both here and in Chicago but I can get no satisfaction at all hopes of recording . . . will you please write me and inform me the true state of affairs.
>
> I am in a very Bad Financial Condition here in N.Y. The worst so I beg of you if the M. deal is off could you please forward a dub of what we have done so far that I may try to interest another company in recording it. Let me thank you for all your kindness to me & mine and from way down here to wish you a merry Xmas and a Happy New Year.
>
> Lord Buckley

Before hitting the road with the Ziegfeld troupe, the Buckleys had temporarily decamped in South Florida. Other than a February 8, 1957, gig at the San Marino Hotel's Carnivale Lounge in Palm Beach (in which he was advertised as "The Fabulous Lord Buckley—Monarch of Humor-In-Hip and His House of Lords"), Harry "The Hipster" Gibson's recollections of their shenanigans serve as virtually the only documentation of this short Florida period near the end of Buckley's career.

Harry "The Hipster" Gibson

The Miami scene. During the season, me and Buckley are stars down in Miami Beach. I'm talking about the jazz scene, they got these big Copacabana places where they got bars, the dancers, Jackie Gleason blowin' there. Jackie Gleason was one o' the cats that hung around us two. I mean this is a whole buncha guys, you see, the entertainers and musicians down there sorta hang out together 'cause it ain't like New York, not spread out or nothin'. Miami is just like a little town. We're workin' the season, ballin', both got good jobs. He's workin' a hotel, I'm workin' a big jazz club, and bam bam I'm in the bar of the Blackamoor Room, he's in somethin' like the Fountainebleu, no, we're both *livin'* at the Fountainebleu, the biggest hotel down there to live in—*everything* man. We're makin' big bread, we're spendin' big, we make it and spend it, we buy all the grass that's down there.

By this time I'm big-time in show business and Buckley had to change his act. Vaudeville had gone out of style but Buckley's got his new act goin' with "The Nazz" and all that jazz—he's got his gig goin', I got my gig goin'. We both have our families with us and my kid Jimmy is the same age as his boy and our wives are both dancers.

So we worked a whole season down there and we're blowin' in the best hotels, eatin' the best food, buyin' the best grass. So—boom—here comes the end of the season and you know us guys: we don't think too much about what's goin' on. So we're lookin' around and these kids are ready to go to school. We didn't realize they were school age! Well the law says a guy six years old has gotta go to school. Now this is the end of the season and the gigs are over, there's no gig. He ain't got a gig, I ain't got a gig and we got kids that supposed to go to school. Now whataya do? Where the hell we gonna send these kids? We worked downtown so the thing to do was find ourselves a neighborhood down there. So we went up to the Seventy-ninth Street Causeway that goes from Miami Beach to Miami proper. Well, at the end of the Causeway, right in Miami proper we look for somethin' that looks like a neighborhood. We already done spent all our money but I figure somethin' will turn up, I'll get a gig in a saloon somewhere. We ain't got no bread to get a high-class house or anything so we gotta look for cheap rent. So we go from the Fountainebleu, the biggest hotel in Miami Beach, to this beat-up old store with a window in it and a little beat-up house in the back. The whole thing was somethin' like twenty-five dollars a month—we could pick that up walkin' down the street, man! We got the twenty-five bucks a month, we got the "Cigar Box" in back. It was just a couple of little beat-up rooms, it wasn't even painted. It had a bathroom and a sink and bathtub. I took the store, he moved into the back with the two kids. The store had a bathroom in it so we had it made. It don't get that cold down in Miami—you don't even need heat. We moved in, none of us has furniture but there was furniture in the back.

As many years as I worked in Miami Beach, when the season was over, you split and go back to New York. So here were are. Miami Beach was a little small town. When the season was over, forget it. I knew it, he knew it, we knew it. So here we are, stuck with the kids. The reason why we picked that neighborhood, by the way, is that when we got over the Seventy-ninth Street Causeway there was a school. We saw the school and luckily we saw the "For Rent" sign. I said, "This has gotta be it, man. There's the sign . . ."

We go register the kids in school. The kids!! We done forgot all about the kids. You know in those days kids wore their hair *cut*. We never thought of that! Our kids have got *LONG HAIR!*

Now we ain't got no bread, little by little we're runnin' out o' bread. Finally, we get the paper. We gotta get jobs, we gotta get some bread here. We're walkin' along the street and there's a guy sellin' ice cream out of a freezer on one o' those big three-wheeler bycycles. This guy's a wino. I said, "Hey, man, where'd you get that gig? You can't have any references!" He says, "Oh man, you just go down to the ice cream place, walk in, they give you a bike and some ice cream and you go out and sell it."

So we go downtown the *next mornin'!* They said, "You guys got any experience?" I said, "Oh yeah, I used to sell ice cream up in the Bronx! This guy here's from Chicago, he used to sell ice cream at the ball game!"

So, first thing we do is we take the bikes and we ride 'em back to our pad and the kids are out there: "Hey, look at that!" "Yeah, we're ice cream men now." They thought it was really great—we're handin' it out. We're ridin' down the street and we come to a big construction site with guys all over the place. But when they come over they say, "There ain't no popsickle guys ever come around here! Smart guys carry wine—we buy wine from some of these guys for twenty-five cents." "*Ohhhh yeah?!*" "Yeah, you bring some wine around. Well, they're buyin' the ice cream 'cause it's hot. I said, "Man, what are we doin' sellin' ice cream?" Boom—we go to the store, we buy ourselves a couple o' big jugs of wine, stick it in the ice thing—boom—we come back, nice cold wine and some cups. Now we're sellin' wine for twenty-five cents a cup. The first thing you know, man, we're just rakin' in dollars, not a lot, a dollar here a dollar there. But what're we gonna do with the ice cream?

We're in a poor neighborhood—a black neighborhood—so we go down the street to get some more wine. You know when the black neighborhoods are poor down there, they are dirt poor. Thet got beat-up old shacks and kids runnin' around in the street, they ain't got *nothin'*. "Anybody want some ice cream here? Here it is *free!* We're gonna give it away!" We start givin' the ice cream away, we gotta get rid of it—boom boom boom—and we gave all the ice cream away. We go back to the construction site—bam—the guys are ready for some more wine. Boom—we sell 'em some more wine. We got ourselves a pocketful of bread. All of a sudden it's five o'clock, we suppose these guys gotta split.

We go back to the ice cream place. The boss comes out: "Hey, look at these guys. They sold all the ice cream! Hey, you guys must be some ice cream salemen!"

"Well, I was the best ice cream saleman in New York and this is the best ice cream man from Chicago here. Sure we're the best! How much we do owe?" Boom—we paid off the ice cream, we got bucks, we go back, we score. It ain't like show business!

We'd be ridin' along, some guy's come up, big Continental car, pull up and say, "Hey, ain't you 'The Hipster'? Is that Lord Buckley over there? What are you guys doin'?" I say, "We're retired—we don't work no more. We quit show business. Yeah, we quit! We're in business of our own now."

Everybody in town knew us. So this is what we do. There's the kids in school, we're sellin' ice cream. We're doin' this for a couple o' months. I was writin' a tune we used to sing: "Pop, Pop Pop, Here Comes the Popsickle Man." It just went on but, in the meantime, we're still lookin' for gigs. We're livin' in the Cigar Box and the beat-up front store. They finally got wise to us sellin' the wine. The guy who checks up on the ice cream people happened to come drivin' by: "Oh man, you can't do that! That's against the law!" He was afraid that *he* was gonna get put in jail for what we were doin', he ain't supposed to be sellin' wine out of his ice cream carts, so we said, "Oh, in that case we quit!"

One night we were having a little birthday party for Richie in the store and this is exactly the time when none of us has got a job. We had plenty of ice cream for the party. The kids thought, "Wow, this is the greatest." The kids thought we were the biggest shots that ever was. The kids are runnin' in the backyard and Richie runs smack dab into a plank with a nail stuck in it and the nail come right smack dab through his foot and we hear the kid screamin' out there. We all run out and there's Richie sittin' on the ground with a piece of wood and his foot stuck on the nail goin' through his foot. Everybody froze. I just went over to him, grabbed the nail, grabbed his foot, took it out. Then I put my hands on his foot. I'm standin', he's yellin'. What do we now? And all of a sudden the kid starts kinda gigglin'. Let's take a look at it. It was just a couple o' little dents on each side. The thing actually healed up. It went right through. It probably didn't hit anything.

Well you know Buckley: "Oh Hipster, you got the cure! You got the cure in your hands, man!"

Of course, he starts to spread the word: "The kid stepped on a nail and the Hipster cured him." When I began getting gigs, people'd come to me and say: "Hey man, can you cure me." One of the guys that owned an Italian restaurant heard about me doin' this thing and said: "Look, you come over to me place, you bring all your friends with you after hours, I'll give you all spaghetti on the house but see if you *cure my headaches!*" This guy's the spaghetti connection . . . I gotta cure this guy 'cause we gotta eat. I did the thing with the hands and the funny thing is, the guy did actually start gettin' better. It goes to show you the power of the mind. In fact, it was backstage at one of Buckley's gigs and the best part, of course, was the spiel we gave. Buckley was right there throwin' it back: "Yes Lord, yes! Get The Nazz! Contact The Nazz! Come on Nazz, come on down! You gotta help this boy!"

The word got all over Miami and Miami Beach: "The Hipster's got the cure, man."

One time I'm lookin' through the want ads and I see: "Piano Player Wanted for Spiritual Choir." So we call up and it's over there in Coconut Grove. Now, Coconut Grove was a huge black section of Miami back then. Buckley gets on the phone and he's doin' his Amos 'n' Andy thing—he's doin' the black talk and he's talkin' to this black lady. Those gospel people, they're very religious. Every other sentence they say "praise the Lord," "glory be," and Buckley's right in there givin' 'em Amos 'n' Andy. But he got me the gig.

So we go down to the church and it's a big black choir: they were real hot A Number One spiritual singers. We walk in and the guy said, "*YOU* the piano player? We thought you was black!" Buckley was talkin' black on the phone, everybody figures I'm black too. Man, they thought I was a black cat. They said,

"What we gonna do with a white cat? This is a black church here." The guy said, "Well, you're here, man, we ain't got a piano player, so you can play the rehearsal with us."

Well, you know me: anything I hear I can blow. They ain't got no music—boom—the guy hits the notes and here we go—boom—I start backin' up these cats on spirituals. Well, I'm good at that kinda stuff because whatever I hear comes right out of my fingers. So I'm backin' 'em up like crazy. They're singin'—boom—when I get through playin', the guy turned around and said, "We never had a piano player as good as that around here." And they're sayin', "Yeah, but he's white" or "But he sound good."

So this is the rehearsal and Buckley's there right next to me talkin' his black talk and they're lookin' at me: "How come he's white and he talk black?" I said, "That's the way he talks!" And Buckley comes on with a big story about how he came from the South: "My father had a plantation in Alabama y'all . . ."

What happened was they liked me so much, they said: "Oh, it don't make any difference. We gotta have a piano player and this guy can really blow." So they hire me—it was a gig.

So come Sunday, we're out there blowin' the scene. The place was jammed packed—boom—we're out there blowin' on the floor, the joint'd be rockin'. Buckley would come and stand next to me and every once in a while he'd jump up and down yellin': "Hallelujah! Yes, brother!" That's how they preach down there. Buckley'd be yellin' out all these wild funny things and the congregation would say: "Yes, you tell 'em brother."

Well, we did that, it lasted a couple o' months, but the neighborhood got up some kind of petition or somethin'—not the people in the church—but the neighborhood people didn't want white people comin' in there, they didn't want no white guy trailin' his manager. But I used to tell everybody: "This is my manager, wherever I go he goes." So they had to take him.

In fact, Buckley got so much material from just that alone. You heard the way he did his thing "Jonah and the Whale." That was the place where he picked up on a whole gang o' stuff.

At year's end Buckley pulled up the family stakes, such as they were, and moved to the show biz boomtown of Las Vegas where more consistent work was to be had on its dozens of high-paying casino stages. But because his engagement didn't exactly result in anything approaching the king's ransoms enjoyed by big-name acts, the fifty-year-old Buckley was forced to scuffle for menial labor.

George Greif

He was quite popular as a kind of curiosity. He played theaters and he played Reno and Las Vegas. He did that four-way act with the people and the hats. He would do the hip stuff in the living room but not on stage.

Vince Diaz

Musician and writer Vince Diaz was making the Vegas scene with Lenny Bruce's running buddy Joe Maini when he crossed paths with Lord Buckley. His reminiscences are drawn from a 1990 article in The L.A. Jazz Scene *and from personal correspondence.*

The legendary Lord Buckley came around a lot, sounding like a black preacher spitting fire and brimstone at the mike. Joe Maini had met Lord Buckley through Lenny Bruce who admired his original act. Joe and Lord Buckley stepped out into the Tropicana parking lot one night to invite the muse and I went along. Talk about hanging out with some far-out cats. Buckley looked like an English Lord wearing a monocle but he spoke like a gravel-voiced black man, spouting oobladee a mile a minute. It was the happiest I ever saw Joe and closest I ever came to seeing him laugh. The night air over Vegas turned into kaboom kaboom splang far-out poetry. Lord Buckley called Joe "a child of God" on that gig in Vegas.

He often came around to the Tropicana wearing work clothes (old faded denim overalls) and a funky navy blue jacket. The guys in the band said that he was working a night-shift job at the big cement plant in nearby Henderson. The dates for Ray Anthony's engagement at the Tropicana were approximately late November of 1958 through the first week of January 1959 (a six-week job). He was not working any lounge jobs at the time or I am sure it would have been our hangout. It seems to me that he may have worked two or three weeks. He was far-out for the Eisenhower-era public of that time.

I remember that although Ray Anthony was a strict disciplinarian he often allowed Buckley to wail at the mike for as long as fifteen or twenty minutes while the band howled with laughter. We would then finish the set with a flag-waver or two. As far as the bits Buckley did at the mike with us, I remember "The Nazz" and some funny things about the American people being "locked in" to Abraham Lincoln with all the monuments.

Sometime after arriving in Nevada, the Buckleys decamped in the desert on the outskirts of the Vegas city limits in a ranch house at 5000 Eldora Avenue that became known alternately as "The Mattress Factory," "The Mattress Farm" or "The Mattress Mine."

It seems that the U.S. Army had dumped scores of mattresses in a vacant lot across the road from the Buckley compound as either part of a kickback scheme or just plain bureaucratic incompetence. Never one to pass up a freebie, His Lordship commissioned members of the newly forming desert Royal Court to drag each and every one of them into and around his home.

Jonathan Winters

We went out in the desert where he had a mattress farm and everybody sat on those things, and he kind of held court.

Les Thompson

He had a house out in the desert near Vegas. It was a small house surrounded by 150 mattresses. He had all these mattresses around in case he had company both inside and outside the house. Since it never rained there, people could sleep wherever. And he had an iron horse in the living room that somebody had welded together for him.

Eldon Setterholm

Then Buckley went over to Vegas and he got a job at the El Rancho Vegas. I was seeing that he was always scuffling. That's why he went to live in Las Vegas—to be close to the Strip—the show capital of the world. And he made some good money and with that money he put down on this little two-bedroom house out in the desert. It had a little pump shed in the back for the water and generator.

There was also a shack next door, on the next property, sittin' out there in the desert, nothin' else around but just sand dunes and brush. He went over there and found that it was stored full of G.I. mattresses. Nobody would come around for months at a time. He called it his "mattress mine." He'd say "Richard! Go over to the mattress mine and get a couple of more, now. We want to make a walkway down to the pump shed, so that we can run down there and start the pump without having to walk on scorpions."

They built a great big U-shaped makeshift couch out of these mattresses around the fireplace out in the backyard which was the expanse of the desert. So the fire would be set at night and we'd all get comfortable under the stars and eat and carry on and he constantly entertaining. That's why he was so great—because he practiced on a daily basis. All he needed was an audience of one and away he'd go.

Somebody laid a big sculpture of Don Quixote on him. That thing was pretty big. How they got that thing in a Volkswagen, I don't know, but they did. They cruised around with that horse and rider in the back of a VW and they brought it home to the desert house. And it stood there on the porch for a long time.

He was always trying different voice sounds, using his voice to the fullest. And that's why, when he had this little pad out in the desert, miles from anybody, he could come out on his back porch and hit, at the top of his lungs, "EISENHOWER IS A FAG!!" and resound through the desert with it. Then he'd listen to it reverberate and he'd shout, ". . . AND MAMIE IS A LESBIAN!!!" He had great lung power and he exercised it like that.

One year he went back to New York to do the Sullivan show and he sent seven hundred dollars to Lady B. He told her to fix up the ranch with it, y'know. Well, at the time she knew this artist dude who convinced her they should have art classes. So she spent that money in trying to get these art classes going which they held in their little pad out in the desert. So they had to have a bunch of easels made . . . but it didn't work. They blew the money real quick and nothin' to show for it.

When Lord Buckley got home he was mad and jealous too. He wanted to know who she'd been foolin' around with. It was funny 'cause I was right in the middle of it. He's taking me aside and trying to find out information. He had jealous suspicions. He was a *bad* player himself, as far as females were concerned. He didn't restrict himself at all. He didn't try to play by any rules. The rules were for her.

A letter written by Lady Buckley on scorched paper to Dick Zalud and Millie Vernon gives some insight into what life was like at the Eldora Avenue digs:

> Hellow Hello, One last lonely sheet of our Fire Stationary personally burnt by us, takes only one house, 1/4 gl. of white gas and a bit of light—Presto—so decided to investigate and see for myself just what is happening at the Zalud Kingdom.
>
> Nothing but silence—ah these temperamental artists—success—fame—prestige—Well what can I say—Tell us what's doing & all the news—you know we've a right to know—After All—Your lucky I'm not suing you for a piece of the contract—After all—but we'll settle for a letter.
>
> We're a little flipped at this stage of our 'Pioneer Period' we're due for electricity in 3 weeks and we're preparing for the shock by giving a Lighted Party—Music again—t.v.—oh its too much—Out with the Colemans—We've really been lucky, our property has increased $3,000 since we've been here, $2,250.00 went into improvements from the fire—new paint and a grand for electricity—Good deal—
>
> Here's a kick story. We had a '46 Chevy and took it in for $50.00 worth of repairs—they ran it up to $140.00—we said keep it—got a '51 Convertible Imperial—a Gasser—as a power truck without brakes ran into it sitting in back of the repair shop—so we will get it for nothing—too Much—so we are once again a 2 car family—a Progress.
>
> The Sullivan show will be Sept. 7. Spoke with him here last week & he predicts Playhouse 90 etc.
>
> Please write soon—Hope you'll be wingin' out this way soon—or we might make the NYC scene—Still waiting for a few Zalud originals to grace the Castle Rancho walls.
>
> Much Love, Buckleys 4

The Las Vegas chapter in Buckley's life is also significant in that Buckley met and befriended a significant ally, Lewis Foremaster, a young man who would become his last aide-de-camp.

Lewis Foremaster

I met Lord Buckley in Las Vegas. I was a playboy and hung out at the hotels and casinos. I got involved with one of the showgirls, followed her out to California in my sports car and went to work for Milton Deutsch, a theatrical agent. That's when I first heard of Lord Buckley.

I came back to Vegas in 1957 after that scene, heard that he was in town and made myself available to him. I had a new Oldsmobile, plenty of money, and nice clothes so I took him on the road.

The thing that was mostly uptight with him was getting the money to Elizabeth to pay the rent on the Mattress Factory.

I had a little Sears & Roebuck tape recorder and I would tape him frequently. I have a suitcase full of tapes.

Lord Buckley set me on a spiritual path that I have been on ever since. He taught me the monologues and they will be with me forever.

Aside from his work in the casino's dinner clubs, Buckley was making his presence known in some other odd quarters of town.

Tom Constanten

Keyboardist for the Grateful Dead in the late 1960s and early 1970, the erstwhile "T. C." has charted an eclectic and broad career in music since boyhood. Many of those formative years were spent in Las Vegas, where he encountered Lord Buckley because of a shared passion: astronomy. The following remembrance is excerpted from T. C.'s 1992 tome, Between Rock and Hard Places: A Musical Audiobiodyssey, *published by Huolgos'i.*

At the old library building in downtown Las Vegas there was a meeting to start an astronomy club. Lord Buckley was there, his nattily waxed mustache glistening by the fire in his eyes. When the subject of picking a name for the group came up in the meeting, he suggested "Star Diggers," but, alas, they weren't ready for him at all.

Lord Buckley

The new philosophy of the Atomic Age is simply and merely this: that the steeples of the churches are too high for holes in the pants of the poor. And the drunk, the sickest and squarest of all, lies too long outside the closed doors without the arms of love to give him or her or it or they surcease, as it is written in every page of The Book.

So, therefore, it is said that the people have not left the church *but* the church has left the people. And if that is so, which it most certainly is, then it is only reasonable to assume, according to the study of the science of the cycle of design, that there must have been, and is working now, a whole new movement in great public beauty and therapy to take over the delinquencies of the church at *just* the propitious moment.

And I found that that is *music*, ladies and gentlemen . . . music.

14 

Lord Buckley

If you believe in something, stay on it! Because it belongs to you.

The hopelessly square Vegas clientele forced Buckley to once again fall back on his "Amos 'n' Andy" shtick and vaudeville material with its emphasis on audience-participatory parlor tricks. Except for the odd late show when he would unleash his hipsemantic classics on an unsuspecting and frequently unreceptive audience, the desert gig had a stifling effect on His Lordship.

Fortunately, there was always California, and Buckley made frequent trips back to Los Angeles and the Bay Area to flex his chops for more sensitive ears.

Buckley continued to perform in Southern California, and it was at a 1958 engagement at one of his favorite haunts, Club Renaissance (a Beatnik nightspot on Sunset Strip founded by a local free spirit named Ben Shapiro), that he found acceptance for his work.

The burgeoning scene at Club Renaissance attracted both the hard-core stratum of L.A. bohemia and a slicker clientele, with everyone from Rick Nelson to Ramblin' Jack Elliott stopping by to catch his sermons. Buckley even shared a bill one night with the great jump blues vocalist Jimmy Witherspoon and future film director Paul Mazursky, then a stand-up comic.

Jim Dickson

I saw him perform many times. I saw him perform at Strip City and Jazz City and the Club Renaissance, which held about three hundred people. His hip classics had more appeal but they didn't always make people laugh and that made club owners uncomfortable. "Where's the punch line?" they'd say. But the story was better than any punch line. Working in some kind of a punch line was always a strain for Buckley.

Sometimes when he had to work strip joints the people would become rowdy and ignore him and he got very abusive. Or there would be some heckling and interaction with the audience with some of them ready to punch him out. But when he worked places like the Club Renaissance or the coffeehouses near the end of his life he was different. People at these places loved him and understood him. It was the same thing that made those clubs successful for jazz and poetry readings. They had gospel music and they showed films there. It was that kind of coffeehouse—a more avant-garde artistic crowd. They could play Miles Davis without serving alcohol because the people listened.

These performance coffeehouses drew what would later become the Hollywood elite. They were sort of the Hollywood want-to-bes back in those days: the Sally Kellermans and the Jim Coburns. That world of people was in that coffeehouse era. That was the time for all the people that were in the beginning of the beatnik or hip movements. They all knew who Buckley was. But after he died that whole movement became not thousands but millions, but it was spread too thin. A lot of guys got lost when it got that big.

Nik Venet

The world is full of secret heroes, and the late Nik Venet was one of them. A founding force behind the Beach Boys, Venet cut his teeth in the music biz shepherding Buckley around L.A. in the late 1950s and went on to produce thousands of record dates, including those of Bobby Darin, Jim Croce, Les McCann, Lou Rawls, the Lettermen, Fred Neil, Sam Cooke, Gene Vincent, Rick Nelson, Linda Ronstadt, and Glen Campbell.

This was Hollywood before it became the sprawling metropolis that it is now—it was a lot smaller. Lord Buckley would leave my office at World Pacific, cross the street and go into the back door of Ben Pollack's Dixieland Bar and make himself a sandwich. And then he would walk down to the Renaissance and perform.

Phil Teretsky was the bookkeeper and associate of Richard Bock at World Pacific records who was also quite adept at equipment. He knew his stuff. Phil had moved all the portable Ampexes down to the Renaissance and recorded His Lordship for two weeks.

I don't know what ever happened to that stuff. And I know that there's a lot of stuff that hasn't been released because I sat there with the equipment, stopping and starting to save tape—today you could let the thing run for the whole show—but we used to stop when he would go offstage to get a drink. But that stuff never came out. He was trying out new material. And there were some remarkable things. They were all very new and very modern.

Perhaps the most significant chapter of Lord Buckley's California reign came as a result of a chance encounter at Club Renaissance with Dr. Oscar Janiger, a simpatico psychiatrist whose experiments with a then-obscure substance, lysergic acid diethylamide–25, were well underway.

Dr. Janiger was in the midst of a seven-year clinical research project exploring the potential medical use of LSD. At the same time that Janiger was spending his evenings at Club Renaissance, he was spending his days administering the yet-to-be-controversial psychedelic sacrament in a standardized natural setting to the likes of Anaïs Nin, André Previn, Cary Grant, and close to a thousand others from all walks of life. Janiger's research was aimed at studying the effects of LSD on a "demographic sample" cross section of the population. Apparently Lord Buckley needed little coaxing to define himself as a member of that particular control group.

Dr. Oscar Janiger

There was a club on Sunset Boulevard called the Renaissance Room in the late 1950s. It was run by a memorable man named Ben Shapiro. Ben ran the Renaissance Room. It was notable because in those days when guys got busted for marijuana, for example, they lost what's called their cabaret license. That was a very serious thing because it was a punishment that took away their livelihood. There were a number of people in that predicament who couldn't perform and Ben very generously allowed them to perform in his club in a sort of semi-clandestine way. Among that group was Wavy Gravy, Stan Getz, Jimmy Witherspoon and, of course, Lenny Bruce.

I was a psychiatrist in practice and I was connected to a medical school. And yet, I guess, I was sort of a hip guy, which was a unique combination. I would hang around the club, and got to know the performers and enjoyed the whole scene immensely. Sometimes I was pressed into service in the role of therapist-at-large. Lord Buckley was one of the guys. We hit it off and spent some fine times together. I found him to be a very literate and creative man and we became good friends.

Then, in 1958, when my investigation was going on with the various mind-altering substances, he volunteered as a candidate in them. LSD was legal then and I was conducting research through a grant I had received. That led to the occasion of Lord Buckley taking LSD and giving his extraordinary paean to the experience, of which he spoke with beautiful eloquence. It was one of the most extraordinary examples of extemporaneous humor and artistic use of language that I ever heard, filled with delicacy and sensitivity. It's amazingly good. He was speaking about the state that he was in after he'd taken it and acknowledging that fact. It was an extension of his way of looking at the bigger picture as it were: the larger sense of things.

I think the LSD might have changed his comedic orientation. More important, *he* said it did. He said that it gave him more freedom, more access to his creative inner self. He even embarrassed me somewhat by the generosity of his compliments such as saying that it had changed his life.

I had a special building that I was working in at the time. I had arranged it like a living room and included a garden to relax the subject and enhance the experience. The experiments are quite famous now. They were naturalistic studies of LSD and involved over a thousand people. Cary Grant was part of that experiment.

I've known a great many very, very interesting men but Lord Buckley was one of the most gifted—a most remarkably talented and expressive man.

The arrangement Dr. Janiger had with his subjects required that they write down their impressions of the experience shortly after having it. Lord Buckley's lengthy report of his soul excursion rhapsodizes in the inimitably jubilant Buckleyesque fashion. The result of the experience was that it seemed to break down even farther the barriers between his brain and tongue, if that were possible.

LSD: First Trip.

The following piece, a transcript of Buckley's LSD appraisal written for Dr. Oscar Janiger, was read and interpreted by John Hostedder, an actor and second-generation Buckley acolyte, in December 1988. It was broadcast by KRCW-FM as part of a three-part Lord Buckley special on The Roger Steffens Show *in Los Angeles. It appears with Dr. Janiger's permission.*

By Richard "Lord" Buckley, Ordinary Seaman on the Good Ship Lovely Soul Detonator under the Command of Fleet Admiral Oscar Janiger, Head Detonator and Head Head.

INTRODUCTION

I first felt a tenseness in my groin and chest, as if something big was there. Something I knew was going to rise up to break through to something new. My whole body was jingling with alert signals: "This is going to be one mother of a take-off. Hang on!"

It felt like a soul pressure. I felt strong. I felt words shooting out of me like projectiles. Acres of untapped sound were waiting to be put into the gun of expression and with the physical feelings of rising and breaking through came a great sense of expanding freedom.

I knew I was there when I saw the high fluorescence of vivid colors. As I talked, the knots on the pine ceiling grew larger. Not abnormally large—I mean, nothing to be alarmed about, you know what I mean—but four or five times larger. I took this calmly for I understood it to be the animation of the inanimate, ya dig.

Besides physical feelings of something big in my groin and chest and sights of pine balls growing before my eyes, I heard sounds of which triggered off new emotions. My ears were alert and pricked up like an intelligent dog. I heard a conversation on the divan—these people were interrupting me, making jokes and laughing rudely—irreverent towards the divine service being conducted in this holy cathedral. Their voices vibrated in my head like bells: "Ding! Dong! Ding! Dong!"

Why, normally I would have shouted them down, stomped upon the ground and silenced them. But I felt a strange patience for their clanging interruptions. Instead of straightening them with my blasting voice, I refrained, restrained by the new insight into beauty. I couldn't strike back at them. I didn't want to. My insight into beauty included them though I was annoyed by their lack of sensitivity. Yet, I saw that the tremulous beauty and sweet serenity which I saw included the air they breathed. I felt tolerance for them. They couldn't see what I saw. I was on a multicolored balloon swaying high above the motley crowd.

I found great extra-added pleasure in hearing old routines roll off my tongue as if a dam had broken loose—a golden river. They poured out, wrapped in the essence of love.

I looked down on these crows cawing on the couch and thought to myself, "I'm not mad at anybody. I have the patience of a rose."

Well, I knew I was at the top when I paused in my speech and looked at the light. One orange lamp came on in color with the power of a floodlight that was sired by the sun himself. White heat poured through red. Then some sweet guiding angel said, "Come outside and look at the light, baby."

I came outside and looked up through the trees. "Christmas," I said. "It's Christmas!"

Perfect reds, blues, greens, pinks—two absolutely white stars—purity stars. It was Christmas in Heaven. Heaven was hung with gorgeous light globes. I saw the tops of giant pines joined in union with the sky. I saw each star connected by an astral highway. Beams of light, not bold but clear, so clear—nice wispy clearness. The Dipper was connected by these same roads: the V in the diamond of the Dipper and all the stars seemed so close and friendly. I knew what they were. You knew what they were? I knew what they were: lovelights. That's right, lovelights.

The sky in its fullness showed a shifting, revealing infinity itself. A shifting to the left revealing depths of worlds beyond, a lifting of a curtain far beyond the first curtain: farms of Christmas trees as strong as those on the first curtain shining from infinite depths. Then the curtain would shift back and those beyond were lost. Then more curtains would shift. Curtain after curtain after curtain showing further back behind beyond the far stars, deeper yet. They were fluorescent jungle lights with a depth to them and a friendliness. They had a meaning as if they were shining not lights but messages.

One message, it came to me with great positivity: that there's only one way to live. That is, live in a house of love. That's right, the universe is a house of love. You can make every house a house of love. You can't walk out of a love house with a sword or a gun—there's none in there to come out with. You have to come with a flower. If attacked, defend yourself with a rose. There's no other way to live—the stars beamed it into me—except by love.

I walked back to the house under my own power but with a sense that the people with me were so beautiful. I would go anywhere they led me. The star-flashed message stayed with me and buoyed up my soul as I came down from the sky.

My conclusions: I was open to the beauty of people who had never seemed beautiful before.

You see, the next morning I went into a pancake house. I walked up and I bowed to four nuns. See, I'd never spoken to nuns before. I couldn't penetrate their cloak of reverence, you dig. I walked up to them and I loved them and they were sure I owned the place, you dig, and they gave me their orders for breakfast. When the waiter came and I sat down at my table, it shook 'em. But I spoke to them again and I told them I saw them as sisters of beauty and they tittered and giggled and blushed and they were very well pleased.

The love moment beat with a new tempo in me. It kept me from resting that day. It gave me further desire to perform, to salute the beauty of people.

LSD makes love for other people and its desired expression an immediate necessity. In coming over that Sunday morning to apologize, LSD made it mandatory. Before I would have said, "They are wrong! Make them wait! If they want to contact me, let them make the move!" But LSD made it a driving necessity that I see them now, immediately. It was: "Tell them that I love them."

Love must be shown at every moment! LSD tells me never to save up what I need to spend in my old age—spend your love now for I may not have the chance later on, dig? My unspent love draws no interest. Like an unused muscle, it goes slack. If LSD taught me one thing it taught me the immediate necessity of exercising the love muscle. Not tomorrow but now. Since this moment is now let me just say, to whoever's pretty eyes or ears pass over these words . . . I love you very much.

As might be expected, Buckley's psychedelic excursions were not limited to the clinical realm. According to *Acid Dreams: The CIA, LSD and the Sixties Rebellion* by Martin Lee and Bruce Shlain, Buckley was "a practitioner of yoga" who, at one point, "rented a yacht and threw mescaline parties in the San Francisco Bay with live jazz by Ben Webster and Johnny Puleo and the Harmonicats." Also, despite evidence to the contrary, Buckley allegedly claimed that he first tried psychedelics under government supervision in Chicago during the late 1940s.

Buckley's renewed verbal explosion was exhibited during a Thanksgiving weekend bash at the quirky Lake Arrowhead home of the equally quirky Thad Ashby a short while later. It was there that Buckley delivered a nonstop monologue that is said to have lasted at least a day.

Dr. Oscar Janiger

There was a party up at Lake Arrowhead in 1959 and Buckley was one of the people invited. We were all just having a good time. It was a lovely setting. Everyone was very bright and receptive. There was plenty of talent and plenty of things to talk about.

I had wanted to test the efficacy of LSD in a performance environment and this seemed like an excellent opportunity to make such an appraisal. I had discussed this with Buckley and he agreed to assist me in discovering whether it could be used as a stimulating creative catalyst in such a setting.

We prepared by administering the medicine and going out for a walk. When we returned, Buckley got up and just spontaneously took the floor. And when he did everybody immediately gravitated to him and we just sat there listening to him hour after hour. Nobody had a word to say because he was so extraordinarily entertaining. I eventually fell asleep from exhaustion and woke up and he was still going.

That was a virtuoso performance. Fresh, interesting material was just pouring out of him at every moment. We had a tape of it buried around here somewhere and I am told that it goes on for something like thirty-six hours.

What was perhaps most notable was that he did not use any of his standard routines. That's what made us immediately sit up and take notice. Here was a man who stepped aside of his prepared material and just pulled out magical, one-of-a-kind stuff.

I might have seen him perform after that but I never saw him in public often because I had him all to myself. It was redundant for me to see him perform. I had all his records and I had a command performance anytime I wanted.

He had a generosity about performing—a real class generosity, a real sharing of himself. He was a very serious man, a very profound man. When he wasn't "on," he was a very sensitive and aware guy. Despite his off-the-cuff spontaneity, he had a sober and reflective element to his character. He read a lot and he was well informed. We had a shared passion for literature and we would have great conversations. He had a remarkable intuition of the foibles of human nature.

Dr. James Macy

I was there for the Thanksgiving marathon at Lake Arrowhead in 1959. Buckley arrived following a gig in Las Vegas so he had to drive all the way there. He was kind of tired but once he got going he was terrific.

Believe it or not, we did not have a tape recorder. I called up a good friend of mine and said, "You've got to get a tape recorder up here. We got Lord Buckley here and he's going ninety miles per hour and this is too good. We've got to record all of this." So anyway he got Mort Sahl's tape machine, his Ampex, brought it up there and then we recorded him. It was the four-day Thanksgiving weekend so we got a couple of days of that. That's all we got out of it.

We gave him LSD that night. At one point during the night he went out and looked at the stars and said, "They told me it was a Christmas tree—and it was!" Meaning the effect of the LSD. Everything gets colored among other things.

After that it was just a nonstop weekend. He got going on anything you'd suggest to him. He'd start to weave it into things and then he also had his own routines that he had started to work out even though they weren't completed for professional performance. They were things that he probably couldn't perform on a public stage because perhaps they were a little too racy or something like that. So he went through a lot of things like that. He was just unbelievable.

Prince Foremaster had a suitcase full of tapes. These tapes were really something. One of them had Lord Buckley sort of jamming with Jonathan Winters.

They were friends. The way that they played off of each other was incredible—priceless stuff.

Doug Boyd

The party at Lake Arrowhead in the Sierra Mountains east of Los Angeles was *the* wildest non-stop swinging party and His Lordship performed for a three-day wild Thanksgiving weekend . . . and I wasn't even there.

Through my memory of the tapes though I can pretty much re-create the buzz of the affair, picturing the eighteen-foot semicircular couch facing Thad's great medieval fireplace before which His Lordship performed almost non-stop all those hours. Through those seven-inch reel-to-reel tapes it became the closest thing to having been there experiencing the whole thing firsthand. Besides, everyone kept relating things and details to me for months afterwards.

On those golden gem tapes while waiting for the acid to hit, Gloria Smyth—she was a Count Basie singer at the time—sang a stirring a cappella solo of the ancient WWI love song "Roses of Picardy." Then I vividly recall Buckley doing a stand-up rap about Abe Lincoln with the black singer. I was quite surprised when it turned heated in a kinda impromptu, black anger rehashing of the Civil War and the slavery thing. Gloria finally came right out and labeled Lincoln a hypocrite singing out, "ABE WAS A BIG HYPOCRITE!" in her rich, three-octave contralto voice which made Thad's doweled rafters tremble!

Buckley was more than a little taken aback by all the black rage and anger, the resentment she displayed in her improvised lyrics. Great Bugged Black Wombats! After all, hadn't ole Abe Lincoln freed her people from the bounds of slavery?!

Even though I wasn't actually sitting there, I felt apprehensive as to how His Lordship would handle this draggy racial anger. In all the things he'd ever done he had always shown a great genuine love and respect for black people. But Buckley held the cool ground though refusing to castigate or put down Abe. You could just feel the tension zapping between the two rappers up there but His Lordship, with patriotic zeal, wasn't about to trash the office of the sixteenth president of the United States. He was just too strong a patriot stud for THAT, daddy!

Gradually Lord Buckley began to feel the acid's effects, as he rose up from a chair at a new clear spot he had moved to near the kitchen's buffet counter, his voice rising to shouts as he became more and more agitated from the effects he was now feeling.

A little alarmed, Lady Elizabeth, a professional dancer of some worth, quickly took over the floor and, knowing her husband's vicissitudes, began to dance before him, executing some beautiful ballet steps that seemed to gradually calm His Lordship down. She continued her graceful performance much to the delight of the partygoers after her royal spouse had regained his composure.

"PHEW!! This joint is really jumpin'," he exclaimed looking around approvingly, "just full of lighted Christmas trees! Let's all go outside for a minute and get some fresh air."

Thad Ashby and James Macy led the way for His Lordship out through the aromatic pine and scented night air. It held the mountain chill, but was refreshing and delightful to experience. Everyone just huddled together making things even more of a gasser as they walked through the heavy forest tunnel. Then an opening in all the foliage as they broke out upon a clearing. Suddenly the heavens drowned them in stars. "God's Christmas trees!" Buckley intoned in an awed, squeezed voice as he bent his head up.

Then looking about at everyone in the party, he uttered what were to become for us the classic Buckley word talismans: "Would it embarrass you if I were to tell you that . . . I loved you?" Many cats and kitties found themselves involuntarily staring down with a self-conscious giggle at their nearly invisible feet, just as predicted.

Buckley the beautiful, chuckling with the understanding and humor of a true hip aristocrat he now had become for us all, intoned tenderly, "See . . . I told you it might embarrass and hang you babies up . . . " Now the crystal-clear forest air heard only soft murmurs and the gentle tinkle of joyous laughter.

Back inside, His Lordship, still visualizing the color-tinted heavens he had just experienced outside, couldn't keep from repeating "God's Christmas trees . . . they definitely were God's little Christmas trees . . . what a double gasser it is to be alive!"

Once settled again, Buckley launched into some skits and marvelous storytelling. He had several routines that he did on the military. One was "H-Bomb."

Buckley by this time was deep into the LSD trip, and gazing about the room, gasped, "PHEEW! I'm as high as a goose in full flight!"—one of his standard lines only this time HE WAS!

Next he did what, for me, was the greatest thing I ever heard him do. It wasn't a skit as much as great storytelling. I can't remember the name of the bit or if I ever heard a name. But it involved an old Confederate soldier trying to remember the name of his first old girlfriend while sitting on the porch of one of those antebellum mansions lying weathered and in disrepair on some old plantation in the deep South.

Before long you could just see and smell the old magnolias hanging around you, and even the old warped porch deck creaking in protest as he rocked in his old chair. He simply spoke those pictures. Pretty soon you were completely lost in the pathos of his story. He was "Old Folks," so poignant and beautifully described in those heartfelt and positive tenor sax notes played by Don Byas on the old Savoy 78 rpm record long ago: "Everyone just called him Old Folks / did he fight for the blue or the grey?"

You were sitting there with him, with his doddering despair of old age and fading memory. You were there as he struggled to remember her. Pretty soon you were lost completely in his story: you were there. He painted the goddamndest picture. The old Southerner getting the girls he had encountered or known mixed up and confused until he ended weeping in frustration. Just listening had me in about the same condition:

"Oh, let's see, was her name Mary Bell? No, I think it was Bonnie Bell, but wasn't she that little gal down by the creek who lifted my head an' gave me the drink of cool water when my mouth was so parched a-layin' there wounded all day after Gettysburg? Oh, but I'm not sure. Maybe that was Suzy . . . Suzy Mae? I can just see her with that lil' o' blue flower a-stuck in 'at pritty yeller' sweet smelling hair a-hers. It was right over her ear. But then? Oh no, ah thinks 'at was the little o' black-haired gal done the Virginnie reel wif me in Charlotte that afta'noon. She be a real vixen, that one was . . . with those scarlet ribbons tied roun' that shinny long black hair a-hangin' down here back an those flashin' dark eyes glitterin like pieces a-coal.

"Oh, well, ah can always 'member her hair 'least. Yes I can, it was long an' honey-colored in curls that hung past her lil' bitty shoulders." Now a chuckle of vivid rembrance and a smile. "Eh, eh . . . she would toss them about peeverish-like. An' they'd look 'xactly like spun gold in 'at Vir-ginnie sunlight whenever I teased her 'bout her skinny long neck. Wasn't it Lila Lee? Or was she that one I kissed down by the mill pond, maybe. I jus' can't seem ta remember her atall. What's matter wit me? I should be able ta remember her name 'least, damn it? But I'll think of it in a minute. Jus' you . . . sob, sob . . . wait . . ."

Buckley managed to convey all the sadness of growing old, useless, and forgetful in that one old vet's struggle to remember the name of his first love. He was the most remarkable storytelling Gasser of them all.

Lewis Foremaster

We took acid ten years before anybody else did. James Coburn was at Lake Arrowhead that night and Lord Buckley was pretty stoned and doing all his stuff and mixing up stuff like he never had before. His performance did go on for two days. It was a pretty wild scene. I've never been so high—I never came down.

I was there for the belly laughs. I was having the time of my life.

James Coburn

The actor and raconteur James Coburn, with films such as Affliction, The Great Escape, In Like Flint, *and* Pat Garrett and Billy the Kid *to his credit, was a young thespian making the boho L.A. scene when he first encountered Lord Buckley at Club Renaissance. Later he was present at the legendary Lake Arrowhead party.*

Club Renaissance was a place where anybody and everybody played. I don't like to put labels on things but it was that post-Beatnik, pre-hippie era when things were still fresh, new and fun.

Buckley sort of floated a little above everything. But he had never had acid until Lake Arrowhead and Thad Ashby had invited about thirty people to see this occurrence.

We knew that Oz, Dr. Oscar Janiger, was going to prepare him and give him some acid and everyone was curious to see how Buckley would respond under the acid experience. Most of the people there had done peyote or acid so they were intrigued how it would affect this unusual individual. Since Buckley was so off anyway we hoped that this was going to be some great alchemy in the sky. And, as it turned out it was.

I seem to remember that this gathering had been in the works for some time before it actually happened but Buckley kept postponing it for one reason or another. But, finally, it was set.

Many of us who had come to witness this great event also secretly hoped that there would be a little taste of the acid for all. This, however, was not the case.

We gathered in the main room of Thad's house while Oz prepared Buckley with the acid. Then they took a long walk in the woods before Buckley came back and performed.

He was on for about forty-five minutes and he talked about what he was experiencing. It was as accurate a description of the LSD experience that has ever been detailed.

I had seen Buckley perform before but the content of what he did at Lake Arrowhead was entirely different because of what it was about and why it was about, similar to the Mulla Nasrudin in the Sufi tales.

Jerry Garcia

I didn't know that Lord Buckley did acid but if he did I'm really glad. He was a seeker. I think of him as a seeker. A Holy Man. With that kind of power, it's an elemental experience. You recognize it immediately for what it is.

Lord Buckley invented his own kind of style too. What was it—"Gospel Comedy"? It was something very special. There are antecedents but there isn't anything exactly like it. So he's one of those guys that's an innovator but nobody followed through. He didn't create a school of comedy. But he certainly influenced the shit out of a whole generation of comedians, a lot of them without even knowing it. I really feel that Lord Buckley is an almost lost resource. He was on the track.

Stand-up comedy is like sleight-of-hand. It's a technique and there are technical comedians who know how to tell a joke and know how timing works and all the rest of that stuff. That's one kind of thing. Lord Buckley is being that guy that's not a stand-up comedian but instead is like a medicine man, a shaman.

Garcia's notion of Buckley as a shaman is close to the mark. Shamanism is primarily associated with Asian culture. Not a priest or a medicine man, the shaman's nearest parallel in the Western world is the artist—an artist who employs his talents for the well-being of his tribe. Lord Buckley's entire persona was pure shamanism: his bizarre appearance, the chants, the music, the drugs, the surrealistic visions. The club became his magical cave charged with tension as the audience sat hunched over and expectant, their eyes fixed on this fantastic figure in the center of the spirit circle wrestling with their fate . . . and his.

Lord Buckley

My Lords and Ladies of the Royal Court. Right here the time and now is the meaning of the word *religion.* It is a meeting of the people here, believe me . . . *and I'm the mother who authorized it all.* It was done in service to them these last thirty-five years. I am honored and privileged to swing in that natural church, the theater, let me hip thee.

15 straight to the road of love!

Lord Buckley

I think rhythm is the key to everything. Rhythm in attitude, rhythm in tension, rhythm in execution, rhythm in consummation. Rhythm, rhythm, rhythm—rhythm runs the whole swingin' gig.

Vegas had finally gotten to Buckley. By early 1959 he was spending as much time in L.A. as in Nevada, finding the time to make a very special studio date.

Moving in the substrata of the jazz universe, Buckley had always crossed paths with musicians and worked with many over the years, yet few of those unions were documented or preserved. His associations with the Herman and Krupa bands as well as the bop saints of Fifty-second Street are well noted. But along with the 1955 RCA sessions that included Benny Carter in a supporting ensemble role and the 1953 Lighthouse gig, only Buckley's unreleased January 6, 1959, gem of a studio date with vibraphone deity Lionel Hampton remains and must be regarded as the peak of his archived musical collaborations.

While the circumstances surrounding the impetus for the date (or even its precise location) are unknown, the stellar results are not. Hampton's light touch and obvious sensitivity to Buckley's material provide a definitive Buckley/jazz alchemy despite the frustrating and puzzling brevity of the session. For his part, Buckley's recognition of his company's strengths is evidenced by the pauses he takes between his verbal runs, giving the feeling of musicians "trading fours."

"Gettysburg Address" and "Swingin' Pied Piper" are the only two pieces known to have transpired at the session, but they are exceptional indeed—easily among the best and most unique versions of these two very different presentations. Each performer both anticipates and leads the other in what may be the perfect synthesis of jazz and "word jazz." Additionally, an extended Hampton solo between the routines creates the type of unified, thoughtful segue Miles Davis, John Coltrane, Roland Kirk, and rock bands like the Grateful Dead and the Allman Brothers employed with magical majesty within the coming decade.

Another Buckley recording of "Swingin' Pied Piper" transpired on September 25, 1958, several months before the Hampton session, when he ventured into an unknown studio to record a solo version of one of his most fully realized classic hipsemantic translations and allegorical portraits.

During the second week of February 1959 small ads began appearing in the entertainment pages of the Los Angeles newspapers advertising "An Evening With Lord

Buckley" at the Ivar Theater, a run-down burlesque house that had seen better days. The show honored Lincoln's birthday and ran from the 12th to 14th of the month; $2.50 would garner a good seat for what would be the pinnacle of the fifty-two-year-old entertainer's performance career.

The Ivar Theater, built in 1951 and once host to Hollywood's most celebrated stars, became best known for its presentation of X-rated films and live nude dancing between 1974 and 1989. The "Night Stalker," the notorious L.A. serial killer, is rumored to have been a frequent visitor. As a natural consequence of its activities during this period, the Ivar fell into disrepair—comfortable surroundings not being high on the priority list of the porn patrons. However, in 1989 the Inner City Cultural Center (a non-profit Los Angeles theater company) made the bold move of purchasing this historic site and, aided by friends, set out to renovate both the physical plant and the image of a venue that deserves to be one of the proudest members of L.A.'s family of theaters. During the author's 1995 site inspection, the troupe was deep in rehearsal for a Spanish-language presentation of Willie the Shake's *Antony and Cleopatra*—an irony His Lordship would have surely appreciated.

William Karl Thomas

The Ivar Theater, located in the block south of Hollywood Boulevard and two short blocks west of Vine Street, had evolved through a glorious history as a legitimate theater, became a movie house for a brief while and, in 1959, was desperate enough to book burlesque shows in order to survive. That's why there was a ramp extending out over the orchestra pit so Terpsichore's step sisters could prance out and cantilever their breasts and buttocks over a slobbering audience of males. Dick "Lord" Buckley made good use of that ramp when I first saw him there early that year.

Mel Welles

The performances at theaters such as the Ivar weren't exactly what I had in mind for Buckley. It was an okay compromise but it wasn't really what I thought he needed. What he needed was tone. He needed the counterpoint of surrounding himself with real tone: that feeling you get when the conductor shakes hands with the first violinist and the orchestra tunes up. He needed to be introduced as a man of substance and a wit of importance and that you can't get at the Ivar Theater. The Ivar was okay for Lenny Bruce because Lenny was an out-and-out comic. Lenny could play the worst kinds of toilets and get laughs but Buckley wasn't going for laughs. He was going for astonishment.

Nik Venet

We had originally planned for His Lordship to come out on a throne at the Ivar. But he wouldn't just come out and sit down on one. We were to build hand cranks—and we would lower him down on to the stage. We tried to figure out how to do it but we couldn't get the thing to work properly and we didn't have the budget or the money to do it right. What a racket! It sounded like you were lowering a load of lumber. It never did work.

Buckley's run at the Ivar was bankrolled by a Realtor and amateur guitarist named Earl Brown. The deal Buckley drew with Brown was pretty straightforward: Brown would lend Buckley fourteen hundred dollars for the sole purposes of producing the shows at the Ivar. Buckley would not be compensated but would not have to pay Brown back if the gate receipts fell short of the loan.

There are a couple of points to note here. That Buckley was not being paid for his production efforts or performing services for his involvement in the run is probably an indication that the entertainer may have been looking at the engagement as a showcase opportunity at a central and medium-profile venue.

Brown made an interesting home tape with Buckley about a week or two before the gig that finds the performing artist running through takes of a handful of never-before-heard, never-again-recorded, and difficult-to-classify oddities ("The Institution," "Young Girl," "Louise the Mouse," "King of Robins," "The Love Hook," and "Circus to the Lions") that sound like they could have come off the pages of one of Don Marquis's *archy and mehitabel* stories. Brown and Howard Hatmaier back up Buckley with guitars on several tracks.

Material from the first Ivar Theater concert on February 12 was recorded and released on World Pacific by producer Richard Bock and found long life after Buckley's short run. And if the house wasn't as packed as Buckley may have hoped, the recordings resulted in two of his finest albums: *Way Out Humor* (later retitled *Lord Buckley in Concert*) and side A of the posthumously released *Lord Buckley: Blowing His Mind (and yours too)*. The salient pieces from these records plus a previously unreleased Ivar track, "Martin's Horse," also appeared on another posthumous World Pacific collection, *Buckley's Best*.

The album cover art features pics of the artist as a middle-aged man at the peak of his days as Lord of Flip Manor. They stem from a shoot at which Buckley sat for two dozen photos by William Claxton, the noted jazz lensman. These shots, which display a pith-helmeted Buckley clad in a Mexican vest and mugging shamelessly for the occasion, also prominently display an imposing Victorian mansion looming like de Sade's party pad in the background. Contrary to common belief, the building was not Buckley's Whitley Terrace Castle but, ironically, a building that was later known as the noted Magic Castle—a famous L.A. dinner theater where magicians perform. With Buckley on his throne and looking every bit the Trickster/King of his legend, these photos appeared on the album covers of his World Pacific platters and stand as perhaps the best visual documentation of His Lordship in his late, relaxed prime.

These influential LPs spawned from the Ivar gigs find Buckley in top form, performing peak versions of "The Nazz," "The Gasser," and some Shakespearean gestures as well as a slew of new bits that cover his range of theatrical presentation and social concerns.

"My Own Railroad" is cut out of the same pyrotechnic vocal cloth as "The Train" and, though far less effective than its antecedent, is revelatory for its autobiographical account of the infamous drunken episode in Chicago when, during the 1940s, a soused Dick Buckley somehow managed to get his car wheels locked into the State Street trolley tracks on his way to the Club DeLisa. Backed by appropriately madcap drum, bass, and piano licks, Buckley invokes the lunacy of the evening with an excellent array of vocal mimicry and alcohol-soaked bravado.

Dick Zalud

"My Own Railroad" actually happened in Chicago. That was when they were digging up the streets in Chicago. He had this beautiful new car that he wrecked in Chicago by putting it out on the State Street trolley car tracks and driving it along the tracks without putting his hands on the wheel. The wheels fit right into the State Street trolley tracks and he didn't touch anything until he ran it right into a big ditch.

Subconscious Mind" describes a universal experience: the onset of a powerful sexual daydream while executing a mundane yet potentially fatal task—in this case, driving an automobile. Backed by his rhythm section, Buckley's evocation of the erotic flash recalls Molly Bloom's primal internal predawn ravings in James Joyce's *Ulysses*. In this regard "Subconscious Mind" might be seen as a kind of homage to Joyce's Molly in shorthand. New Wave choreographer Karole Armitage, by the way, presented a dancer's interpretation of "Subconscious Mind" during her collaborations with painter David Salle in the 1980s.

SUBCONSCIOUS MIND Play me some beautiful, dreamy music, dear Prince.

"Subconscious Mind," Mi Lords, Mi Ladies.

Gentlemen, have you ever swung along a beautiful country road with a gleam of sweet life in the air, *groovy* with gold in your pocket, ridin' a *wild* set of wheels at an easy pace?

Wheeewww!

Are you there?

Everything is smooth and cool. There's some traffic, but not too much traffic. It's all right, you see, because you've—brrrrtttt—got everything covered. Understand?

An' you're drivin' along and the feel of the sun and radio's swingin' a beautiful, crazy, wild tune and you're so good you—hah!—you're right in there tight. Can you feel it?

Yes.

And suddenly your mind—rrrrttttttt—goes over to Hippleyville and you start thinking about a beautiful girl that you met there *five years ago*. Whheeewww!

And what a gasser she was . . . Ho! Hah! Take me *now!!!* Wheeew! Beautiful!

Have your nose rubbed in the rose garden so many times that there are still petals up there? Indeed, indeed.

And you're thinking about how *charming* she was, how *gracious* her people were, what a *ball* you had, what a beautiful time, how how how sweet, how *gracious,* how *crazy,* how like a home in a home in a home HOME! *kick* it was.

An' you get t' thinkin' how you went out to the lake, an' you . . . cool, man!

Yes, yes, yeeesss, yes! Yes, yes, yes. Hewheeeeww!

An' you go many, many, many other places along that rosette of the reverie kick, an' all of a sudden you say—Rrrrtttt!—what am I doin'—wait, I—Is everything all right? I haven't hit anything I don't think, I don't know.

Those fenders all right?

"Yes."

Good. Excellent. Well . . . better watch what I'm doing here.

"Who do you think's been driving while you were gone?"

Much of the Ivar Theater production evokes the buoyant, helium-saturated stream-of-consciousness sensibility found in the work of Joyce. And like James Joyce, Buckley labored very hard on his material, obsessing over the inclusion and emphasis of each syllable. Both artists played with words, ultimately developing a language (and literary domain) that was theirs and theirs alone.

"Let It Down," an Ivar track that may have been a holdover from his vaudeville or Walkathon days, is a "commercial kick" about a farmer urging his reluctant cow to give milk. Not a "hip" piece, "Let It Down" recalls a couple of other Buckley bits containing hints of the country bumpkin, "Governor Slugwell" and, most famously, "God's Own Drunk."

Lord Buckley

The citizen is confused. He's tied to the machines: the washing machines, the television commercials, the time payments, the out-doing Charlie, the living better than Fred . . . the unhappiness.

Supermarket" is unusual Lord Buckley in that it finds him poking fun at the absurdity of modern society, the titled institution in question being his symbol of a world gone wrong when the simple act of procuring sustenance is a force toward the mechanization and thus dehumanization of the culture. Laden with subtle performance power, it is among the Buckley bits most infused with his unusual sound effects and musical cadence. The gist of the bit is that while the first supermarkets offered prices lower than those found at your friendly neighborhood grocer, the consumer, in time, paid the same and was "still pushin' that mother cart."

"Lions," a vague minimalist riff, comes off as the quickest of takes on the Old Testament tale of the Great Flood, though it could just as easily be a sketch of a couple of circus roustabouts discussing the foul-smelling animals in their care. Along with Buckley's earlier "Jonah and the Whale," "Lions" may have inspired Bill Cosby to put his cute, sanitized spin on what easily became his most popular early hit, "Noah," several years later.

Yet another animal sketch, "Martin's Horse," is a snappy Runyonesque riff involving a jockey's (Martin) saucy effort to coax his temperamental thoroughbred (Joey), a serious long shot, across the finish line first. With its overtones of bestiality, "Martin's Horse" can also be placed in the furtive realm of Buckley's lewdest sexual performance endeavors, breathing with the loose Americana of William Faulkner's *The Reivers* and moving with the hyperkinetic syncopation of Lord Buckley's jazzier work such as "The Train":

> You know, every jockey that rides a horse, besides having certain methods to expedite the speed of the horse, also has a certain way of talking to him. And you know what they talk about? . . . LOVE. What else, right? I'm talking in the essence and beauty of the sense, of course.
>
> So this nice little jock, this little man, got to the track early one morning and booked the favorite, Butterfly Nell. His manager got there a short time after and booked the dog, Joey. So he had to take his tight little buttocks off the favorite—*Parp!*—and put it on the dog.

Inevitably, the nag quickly falls off pace and is so far behind the pack that "no one knows whether she's last in this race or first in the next race." But Martin the jockey begins to plead:

> Baby, man, I've ridden a lot of horses in my life but I'm gonna tell you somethin'. UM this saddle—oh OHH . . . it feels so good, you've got such a nice rhythm, baby. It's so beautiful BUT A LITTLE BETTER BABY, A LITTLE BETTER!
>
> I'm gonna tell you somethin'—UMMM—I thought I'd ridden some horses before in my life but I'll tell you this true so help me God I'll never ride another horse but you as long as I race in the track—It's wonderful BUT A LITTLE BETTER BABY, A LITTLE BETTER!
>
> Ooh man! This is a great charge: How ignorant can a man be of the powers of horseflesh? I know that a jewel like you there in the stables with no name, no publicity and no nothing—you're beautiful baby BUT A LITTLE BETTER BABY, A LITTLE BETTER!

Joey begins responding to the jockey's seductive ministrations and overtakes the field as Buckley concludes:

> Baby, I don't care what they say. This'll be the first time. This'll crack every paper in the nation, baby. And I don't care what they say—so help me God—I mean this baby: if we win this race I can see you down the aisle with me arm-in-arm. I'LL MARRY YOU! BUT A LITTLE BETTER, BABY, A LITTLE BETTER!

One would assume by the title "Horse's Mouth" that the piece is another addition to the Buckley menagerie. Closer inspection, however, reveals that it is a short philosophical and gestured reference to Joyce Cary's wonderful eponymous 1944 novel and the nifty 1958 film adaptation, starring Sir Alec Guiness. Cary's wry book is a lyrical and whimsical portrait of Gulley Jimson, an eccentric, William Blake–inspired London artist who, when lack of funds prevent him from purchasing canvas, seeks oddball surfaces around his city to use for his ambitious paintings. Jimson, an inveterate con artist and aging lover, had just the right mix of vision and daring—constantly marching to the obtuse beat of his very own different drummer to attract the attention of Lord Buckley.

Without adapting a full-blown hipsemantic translation of Cary's book, Buckley limits himself to a paraphrase of the story's climax when a dying Jimson is visited by a nun. But the nun is startled to find the artist laughing.

"Mr. Jimson, at a very serious time like this, don't you think you should laugh a little less . . . and pray a little more?" asks the nun.

"But it's the same thing, mother," responds Jimson, uttering his final, smiling words. No doubt Lord Buckley shared Jimson's philosophy in such matters of the body and spirit and chose to celebrate it with this nod to him.

"Fire Chief" is a zippy but inconsequential wig bubble about a fireman who drops a woman he's trying to rescue. The bit is pure vaudeville and sounds like a reject sketch for an old Milton Berle show.

It seems no Lord Buckley record would be complete without some reference to Shakespeare. However, instead of a complete flip of a famous soliloquy, Buckley sounds slow, impassioned tastes of "Hipsters, Flipsters and Finger-Poppin' Daddies" and "To Swing or Not to Swing" for his audience after giving them Willie the Shake's lowdown on Antony and Cleopatra:

> And you remember when Marc and Cleo were swingin' on that velvet-covered barge, understand, out there on the Nile and the mooooon was shining and all that craaaaaazy Egyptian incense was jumping and Marc and Cleo was swingin' up a storm and in the meantime, Caesar had split to Rome like I 'splained to you before and got in that hassle and they sliced that poor cat up every which way. Well, that was Marc's buddy cat, you see. Well, Marc was a hip cat, he knows that every fox has got its box. But the only thing that was dragging him was they were bad-rapping Caesar, you see. Marc didn't dig that he had to put down Cleo which he didn't want to do cause Cleo was one of them early day Elizabeth Taylor chicks, undstand what I mean? But he had to put her down and go defend his line.

As evidence of the Ivar albums' resonance in the liturgy of the following generation of American minstrelsy, Joni Mitchell references Buckley's tag of the Bard in her song "Talk to Me" from her 1977 album *Don Juan's Reckless Daughter* when she sings, "I stole that from Willie the Shake, you know/Neither a borrower or a lender be/Romeo, Romeo talk to me."

Buckley's setup for "Hipsters, Flipsters and Finger-Poppin' Daddies" on this version includes the phrase "Well, naturally, the Roman Senate was jumpin' salty all over the place," a riff that James Taylor incorporated into "Let It All Fall Down," a song from his seminal 1974 album *Walking Man*.

James Taylor

I was fifteen or sixteen when I first heard Lord Buckley's records. I was in Chapel Hill, North Carolina, and someone down at the university suggested I listen to him. I had a friend down there and we got into Lord Buckley and began quoting him.

Some of his pieces were very earnest and very dark and he really departed from the humorous side of things. I got the impression that he was not only *not* about one-liners but that he was never out of character.

His stuff was delightful and inventive. His pieces speak from what was clearly an amazingly active imagination and mind. It was also taking on very important, meaningful stuff like Shakespeare and Christ, claiming it for a generation and expressing it in those terms. He was an interpreter and he made it fresh. I'm sorry I never saw him perform.

Lord Buckley was more like a storyteller or raconteur. He was a performance artist, too, in that he had this character that he assumed and that character was his life.

His stuff just became part of my internal dialogue after listening to it for such a long time at such an impressionable age. It was just in there. It wasn't like a conscious thing where I was hunting to put a Lord Buckley line in a song of mine. It's just quoted like any familiar thing would be that just fit it. It was really quite unconscious.

While the roots of Buckley's Uncle Remus–style yarn "God's Own Drunk" can probably be found deep in Buckley's past, its place on high in the Buckley oeuvre is set in stone. "God's Own Drunk," a shaggy-dog story told in the homespun vernacular of a southern country bumpkin, is the last inclusion of an animal story (in this case a bear) in Lord Buckley's canon and a testament to the ability of intoxicants to lift the soul to sublime stratospheric ecstasies. It also should not be lost on the nonlogomaniac that the first letter of each word in the title spell out the word "God."

Also known as "The Bear," Buckley would sometimes casually introduce "God's Own Drunk" as a story "in square," demonstrating an expansive interest in all forms and styles of comedic expression. In musical terms, if one thinks of some of Buckley's work as jazz-based, then pieces like "God's Own Drunk" or "Let It Down" are Buckley's nod to bluegrass.

Elaine Thomasen

Jim Buckley, Lord Buckley's older brother, told me the story about the time when, as teenagers, he and Dick were asked to watch a still while the owner went into town. And they started sipping away and got so drunk that Jim would never drink another drop of alcohol. They just wandered all over the mountain and they saw this and they saw that but Jim said he just about died. At one point they got so drunk they imagined they saw a giant bear. I'm sure that is where the story of "God's Own Drunk" came from because I heard it so much when I was growing up.

The story in question is fairly straightforward: the speaker, a "non-drinkin' man," is asked to check his brother-in-law's moonshine-frothing still hidden deep in the woods. When he finds it, temptation gets the better of him and he samples the goods in such quantity that he quickly becomes cosmically sloshed. One has to wonder if Lord Buckley's LSD experiences sparked a memory of or identification with the story and inspired its eventual presentation in performance, as there is no record of its display in concert until after his experiments with Dr. Janiger.

At the peak of his saturation he encounters a gigantic bear that he cajoles into sharing the white lightning with him. During the course of their carousal they become the best of friends before passing out. When the storyteller awakens he discovers that "the bear was gone. And you know what brothers and sisters . . . so was the still."

GOD'S OWN DRUNK I'd like to do a little creative wig bubble for you called "God's Own Drunk."

Said, eh, just like I say before: I, I'm a non-drinkin' man. Never drank for some reason or other. Didn't like it. But like I said, too, I promised to take care of my brother-in-law's still while he went in to vote.

Went up there and it was just where the map said it was. And I'm a gonna tell you something—it was no little old five or ten cent still. It was laid there like a *golden mountain opal,* with a kind of honey dew cry comin' from it.

I aren't a drinkin' man, like I 'splained to you, but that big old yellow moon was a hangin' up there, and God's lanterns was a hangin' in the sky, and that curiosity got the best of me, and I took a slash.

And I got a crazy, revolutionary feelin' in my body. That yellow whiskey went down my throat like honeydew vine water. Humph, it tasted mighty good!

I felt a revolution goin' through my body like there was great neon signs a goin' up an' sayin', "There's a Great Life a Comin'!"

Feelin' it talkin' to me, and I took another slash, and I got another jolt, and I took another slash, and I started to sing. I started to sing.

And that big old yellow moon a hangin' out there and God's sweet lanterns a hangin' in the sky, and I's a singin'. Never could sing a note in my life, but I's a singin' as fine and as pretty as you'd ever want to hear.

And I took another slash. And then I took a big full . . . That big old yellow moon a hangin' out there. God's lanterns a hangin' in the sky, and suddenly I got a tremendous revolution of emotion in my body like I was fallin' in love with everything in God's sweet world that moved, lived, didn't live, animate, inanimate, black, blue, green, pink, mountains, fountains.

I was in love with life, 'cause I was *DRUNK!!*

I wasn't fallin' down, slippin' slidin' drunk. I was GOD'S OWN DRUNK! . . . A fearless man.

And that' when I first saw the bear.

Big old Kodiak-lookin' fella, about sixteen foot tall. I walked right on up to that bear, cause I was God's Own Drunk and I loved everything in this world. Walked right up tight to him about four-and-a-half feet and I looked right up in his eyes and I want to tell you somethin' brothers and sisters: my eyes was redder than his was! Hung him up.

And he's a sniffin', he's a sniffin'. He's tryin' to smell some fear. He can't do 'cause I'm God's Own Drunk and I'm a fearless man.

He expects me to do two things: flip or fly. I don't do either. Hangs him up. I told him, I said, "Mr. Bear, I'm God's Own Drunk and I love every hair on your twenty-seven-acre body. I'm a fearless man!"

Said, "I want you to go . . . I know you got bear friends over the hill there. Harry Bear and Tim Bear and Jelly Bear and Tony Bear and Teddy Bear and Field Bear, Hazel Bear, John Bear, Pete Bear and Rare Bear! Go over and tell all of them that I'm God's Own Drunk tonight and I love everything in God's green creation. I love them like brothers. But if they give me any trouble, *I'm gonna run every Goddamn one of 'em off the hill!*"

I moved up two feet—don't you know he moved back three. I reached up and took the bear by the hand. I said, "Mr. Bear, we're both beasts when it comes right down to it."

He's a lookin' down at me. I said, "I want you to come with me. You're gonna be my buddy. Buddy Bear."

Took him right by his big, old, shaggy man-island sized paw, led him on over, sat him down by the still. Well, he's a sniffin'. He's a sniffin'. He knows there's honeydew around there, some kind of honey bear honeydew of some kind. He's a sniffin'. I know what he's a sniffin' at. I took a slash or two myself to taste 'er out and I filled him a bottle.

Did you ever see them bears, the silhouette of them bears at the circus, suckin' up that sarsaparilla? Ahhh, it's a fine lookin' sight! And he downed another bottle. And he downed another bottle. And I put two more in him and pretty soon he started to sniff and snort. Tapped his foot. And he got up and started to do the Bear Dance. Two sniffs, three snorts, a half a turn and one grunt.

And I'm tryin' to do it, but I couldn't do it 'cause it was just like a jitterbug dance: it was so simple it evaded me. But we was a dancin' and yellin'!

And God's sweet moon a hangin' in the sky, and God's sweet lanterns out there and there's jubilation and love on that hill. And finally, my love, it up and got so strong it overwhelmed my soul, and I laid back in the sweet green hill with that big, old Buddy Bear's paw right in mine and I went to sleep.

And I slept for four hours and dreamt me some tremulous dreams.

And when I woke up that old, yellow moon was a hangin' in the sky, and God's sweet lanterns is out there and my buddy the bear was a missin'.

And you know something else, brothers and sisters?

So was the still.

Henry Miller

One of the great, secret Lord Buckley fans and friends, novelist Henry Miller referenced Buckley in the introduction to Time of the Assassins, *his study of the French poet Arthur Rimbaud. More important, Miller wrote a dedication to Lord Buckley that was originally printed on the back cover of* Hiparama of the Classics, *a City Lights Books chapbook containing transcriptions of several of His Lordship's most famous raps.*

The one called "God's Own Drunk" is absolutely superb, a classic. It takes one back to the fountain of ecstasy buried in the wilds of Patagonia . . . You must have drunk from the Holy Bottle that Rabelais speaks of. I know you have drunk from many a bottle, but this one is the elixir, the eau de vie of the gods.

Though "God's Own Drunk" may initially appear to be a minor work in Lord Buckley's catalogue, it captured the attention of three modern minstrels. Jerry Garcia, for one, cited it as his favorite Buckley piece, and Jimmy Buffett used it as a cornerstone for many of his concerts in the 1970s and early 1980s. Of equal significance, James Taylor lifted a line from it ("God's sweet lanterns hangin' in the sky") and plugged it into "(I've Got to) Stop Thinkin' Bout That," a song from his 1991 album *New Moon Shine.*

James Taylor

"God's sweet lanterns hanging in the sky" is an ecstatic line and that particular piece, "God's Own Drunk," that has him falling in love with that family of bear and that trans-species ecstasy, is a truly sublime thing. That sends a jolt through me to this day. The thought of him drinking that moonshine up on the hill like that is a great image. The name of my album *New Moon Shine* even fits in with that a little bit.

No one ever picks up on the Lord Buckley influence in that song but I know, for instance, that my friend Jimmy Buffett used to recite "God's Own Drunk" in his show.

Not only did Jimmy Buffett perform the bit in concert, he released it on two albums: his 1974 LP *Living and Dying in 3/4 Time* and the live *You Had to Be There* disc in 1978. Set to the strains of a laid-back, honky-tonk groove, Buffett's 1974 version of "God's Own Drunk" isn't half bad. An in-studio audience has obviously needed little coaching (or coaxing) to party and they willingly oblige, helping to create an atmosphere of a turn-of-the-century roadhouse.

Buckley gained Buffett's attention during the 1960s, an era that should have cued His Lordship's comeback. "I been doing this particular song for about twelve years," Buffett told an Atlanta audience in 1978 when he performed a slightly raunchier version of "God's Own Drunk" for his *You Had to Be There* album. "I learned it from two friends of mine down when I first went to New Orleans . . . I was about eighteen years old. Got down to Bourbon Street . . . It was written by the late, great Lord Richard Buckley, who I heard it off of a record one night at a friend named Bob Cook and Brent

Webster's apartment. That song intrigued me to the point where I figured, 'Well, hell, this is really *great!'* Too many people have never heard of Lord Buckley, who was an old humorist and king of the jivers. So, with much respect to Lord Richard Buckley, this is 'God's Own Drunk.'"

Buffett's musical adaptations of "God's Own Drunk" recall the country genre of "comic drunk" monologues in which Johnny Bond ("Ten Little Bottles") reigned supreme.

In March 1978 John Rockwell wrote in the *New York Times:* "Mr. Buffett emerged as a sort of folkie Southern boogier, and his cult still seems to regard 'God's Own Drunk' as his theme . . ."

Buffett told Rockwell, a tad defensively, "People picked up on songs like 'God's Own Drunk,' which for me was almost like filler. I don't do that song anymore."

Perhaps not, but Buffett saw fit to tag two of his vehicles, an old pickup truck and a boat, respectively, with familiar Buckley references: "God's Own Truck" and "Euphoria II."

Buffett's artifice itself was once described by *Village Voice* critic Geoffrey Stokes as "John Wayne meets Xavier Cugat meets Boston Blackie meets Lord Buckley at a cocktail party in Buffett's head, and they all have a few drinks and go dancing with Carmen Miranda."

The hidden gem on the crown of the Ivar collection is Buckley's rendering of Joseph Newman's "Black Cross" from the poet's book *It Could Be Verse!* "Black Cross" is a haunting invective against the evil of racism and a companion piece to Buckley's own "Georgia, Sweet and Kind." Indeed, part of what makes this performance so successful is the eerie musical background accompaniment by vocalist Dorris Henderson on the old spiritual, "Koombaya." Ms. Henderson can also be heard moaning "Rock of Ages" in the background on the Ivar release of "The Nazz."

As Henderson recalled her involvement with the gig to Ian Anderson of *fROOTS* magazine in 1999, Lord and Lady Buckley were fans of folk music: "I was singing at the folk clubs like the Troubadour and the Ash Grove where they met me and invited me up to Bob DeWitt's Topanga Canyon colony. That's where I met Lord Buckley several times. He did a couple of concerts up there for Bob. Every Sunday they used to have folk people dropping in, and he heard me sing up there and asked me if I'd accompany him on these concerts he was doing at the Ivar Theater."

Later, after moving to England where she's lived since the early 1960s, her Ivar Theater records caught up with her one day when visiting Collett's, the famous book and music shop in London. "I wasn't aware at all that people in England knew of Lord Buckley until Gill Cook said, 'We've got some Lord Buckleys in, have you heard him?' I said, 'Yes, I've met him,' and so she played the album and I said, 'That's me!'"

The decidedly serious "Black Cross" was one of Lord Buckley's favorite pieces, a disturbing portrait he often performed late in his career even though the civil-rights movement was little more than a distant rumble to most whites at the time.

Lord Buckley

This is a beautiful thing by Paul Newman's beloved grandfather, a Cleveland poet. It's called the "Black Cross." It could be the "Red Cross," the "Blue Cross," the "White Cross," "The Pink Cross," "The Yellow Cross," "The Aquamarine Cross," "The Criss Cross," or the "Cross Cross." But we call it the "Black Cross."

BLACK CROSS

There was old Hezikiah Jones of Hog Back County
Lived on a hill in a weather-beaten hovel
And all that he owned was a two-acre plot
And a bed and some books and a hoe and a shovel.

Old Hezikiah, black as the soil he was hoeing,
Worked pretty hard to make both ends meet;
Raised what he ate, with a few cents over
To buy corn liquor which he knock down neat.

And a few cents more that he put in the cupboard
Against what he called "de rainy season,"
But he never got to save more'n two, three dollars
Till he spent it for this or that reason.

The white folk around knew old Hezikiah . . .
"Harmless enough, but the way that I figger
He better lay off'n them goddamn books,
'Cause reading ain't no good fer an ignorant nigger."

Reverend O'Green, of the white man's church,
Finally got to comin' ovah
To talk to him all about the Pearly Kingdom
An' to save his soul for the Lawd Jehovah!

"D'ya b'lieve in the Lawd?" asked the white man's preacher.
Old Hezikiah puckered his frosty brow,
"Well I can't say 'yes,' so I ain't going to say it,
Caze I've never seen de Lawd . . . nowhere . . . no how."

"Do you believe in the Church?" asked the white man's preacher.
Hezikiah said, "Well de Church is divided;
Ef *they* can't make up their minds, Ah can't either . . .
Ah'm just like them . . . I ain't decided."

"D'ya b'lieve in Heaven?" asked the white man's preacher,
"Where you go, if you're good, fer your last rewa'hd?"
"Ah'm good," said Hezikiah, "good as Ah'm able.
But Ah don't 'spect nothin' from Heaven *OR* the Lawd."

"You don't b'lieve in nothin'!" roared the white man's preacher.
"Oh yes Ah does," said old Hezikiah.

> "Ah b'lieve that a man should be beholding to his neighbah
> Widout the hope of Heaven or de fear o' Hell's fiah."
> "But you don't understand," said the white man's preacher,
> "There's a lot of good ways for a man to be wicked!"
> And they *hung* Hezikiah as *high* as a pigeon,
> And the nice folks around said, "Well, he had it comin' . . .
> 'Cause the the son-of-a-bitch didn't have no religion!"

"Black Cross" is an attempt to grasp the blind hatred of the lynch mob. Buckley speaks of Hezikiah Jones, "black as the soil he was hoeing," and slowly, eloquently builds up the picture of a dignified, self-educated man with noble principles, who, when accused of not believing in anything by "the white man's preacher," answers with the honesty that proves to be his epitaph.

Joan Baez

Singer, songwriter, musical interpreter, and social activist, Joan Baez's impact on American culture and world politics has been profound. She refers to Lord Buckley in her 1968 autobiography Daybreak, *and her son Gabe performed at the semiannual Lord Buckley Memorial Celebrations in California in the 1990s.*

I was on a Joan of Arc mission for nonviolence and folk songs and yet the man touched me because of his social depth. "Black Cross" was so deep. I'd be laughing one minute because he was so clever and witty but then he'd flip it over and I would have to leave the room because I'd be in tears. Lord Buckley reached way deep inside.

Ray Watkins

A longtime Chicago musician, Ray Watkins remembered his experiences as Lord Buckley's Gate of Horn lighting designer in a taped 1973 conversation with Del Close and Ann Brooks, from which the following testimony was drawn.

When I first met Lord Buckley I admired him but I didn't like him because he seemed very remote. Originally I was supposed to play piano for him at the Gate of Horn but we couldn't get together on the parts so he said, "Ray, just blow lights."

And so, I began working the lights.

Then one day, he tries out this piece of material, "Black Cross." I started hearing it and I did some rather interesting things with the lights, flashing on different colors. When the Deacon spoke in the piece I'd have red and blue coming at him from opposite angles so he would really burn. And when Hezikiah Jones himself was speaking, it would be a very soft pin spot and it would flash back and forth as he changed personalities.

That was the first time I ever really lit him and that was first time I ever really grew to like the man and love him.

Within two years of the release of "Black Cross" on Buckley's *Way Out Humor* album, Bob Dylan (then a young Jewish troubadour hailing from Hibbing, Minnesota) had transformed "Black Cross" into a dramatic talking blues in perhaps the one instance where a cover version of Buckley may well surpass the work of the master.

Dylanologists all agree that Lord Buckley helped fuel the singer-songwriter's inspiration and early aesthetic. Although the two never met, Buckley was important in Dylan's development.

A number of people are cited as having introduced Dylan to the Buckley magic, including comedian-turned-activist-clown Hugh Romney (now loved the galaxy over as Wavy Gravy) and New York stand-up shaman Steve Ben Israel, who was doing some Buckley riffs in his Greenwich Village nightclub engagements. Ben Israel also remembers a great night at the Cafe Wha? when Dylan shared the stage with Fred Neil, the Reverend John Hicken, and Dorris Henderson, who had supplied vocal support to Buckley's performance of "Black Cross" on the Ivar concert LP, so perhaps some connection was made then.

Another version of how Dylan may have gotten juiced on Buckley concerns the apartment he shared with Romney during the summer of 1961. When Romney brought home Buckley's album *Way Out Humor* that included "Black Cross," Dylan took to it immediately and studied it in the same way he had previously absorbed Woody Guthrie.

Mikki Isaacson

A friend of Bob Dylan's during his Greenwich Village coffeehouse days, Mikki Isaacson's recollection of Dylan's fascination with Lord Buckley is drawn from Dylan: An Intimate Biography *by Anthony Scaduto.*

He had collected a lot of material over the years, songs and things, and he asked me to take all these scraps of paper lying in his guitar case and type them out for him. One of the things he had me do was a routine off the Lord Buckley record, the one about the hanging of a black man. Bobby was so very anxious to learn it, and for me to type it for him. He was so excited about it, kept playing it on the phonograph over and over again 'til I was going out of my mind.

Jim Dickson

Albert Grossman was interested in distributing the Buckley material so we had a hot dog over it but nothing came of it. Albert had run the Gate of Horn, a club in Chicago, and I would imagine had his own experience with Buckley. He, undoubtedly, was the one who would have turned Bob Dylan on to Buckley.

To me, "Black Cross" was the most powerful piece that he did. When Buckley came back to California with that particular piece of material it knocked everybody's socks off. The civil-rights movement began post-Buckley. Buckley was out there by himself defending black people and getting black people's approval. But he made a lot of people nervous in those days.

The two extant recordings of Bob Dylan's interpretation of "Black Cross" (sometimes titled "Hezikiah Jones" or simply "Hezikiah" in Dylan discographies and on various bootleg releases) are phenomenal, but exist as a misidentified footnote in the singer-songwriter's own voluminous catalogue that warrants correction. The question at hand is the authorship of the piece, which has been indisputably established as Joseph S. Newman, not Richard M. "Lord" Buckley.

Some of the confusion surrounding the piece may have inadvertently been caused by Buckley himself who, on the Ivar recording, mistakenly introduces "Black Cross" either accidentally or on purpose, as written by "Paul Newman's beloved grandfather, a Cleveland poet." The offhand nature of the remark would naturally lead one into falsely believing that it was a merely another one of His Lordship's oddball, off-the-cuff put-ons. However, on other unreleased Buckley renditions of "Black Cross," he correctly identifies Joe Newman in the Cleveland clan's lineage.

Though there are only two surviving versions of Dylan performing "Black Cross," the budding singer-songwriter reportedly performed the song regularly over a period of about a year, starting in late 1961. His interpretations of it on the extant recordings are exceptional conjurings of the grizzled character of Hezikiah Jones and the bigoted deacon. Buckley was well into his fifties when he was performing it while Dylan was barely twenty, so hearing Dylan's voice break as he narrated how they "hung Hezikiah . . . high as a pigeon" is an astonishingly dramatic moment, highlighted by the tender age of the performer.

The monologue became a Dylan perennial of the period. Indeed, in a 1961 interview with Izzy Young (founder of the long-gone but fondly remembered Folklore Center in the Village), Dylan quoted whole chunks of "Black Cross" verbatim when asked about his views on religion: "Got no religion. Tried a bunch of different religions. The churches are divided, can't make up their minds and neither can I. Never saw a God, can't say until I see one."

It would appear that if Dylan was adapting Woody Guthrie's attire, mannerisms, and Okie twang at this time, he was working Lord Buckley into his neofolkie stew as well.

The earliest Dylan version of "Black Cross" was the last tune of an extended set recorded on December 22, 1961, on what is known among Dylanologists as the "Minnesota Hotel Tape." Actually it was performed at the home of his friend Bonnie Beecher (who later married Wavy Gravy) and captured for posterity by fellow musician and comrade-in-song Tony Glover. This first, somewhat weaker, take is an indication that Dylan was in the early stages of learning the piece. It is interesting to note, however, that all of the twenty-eight songs performed that night were covers, a reflection that Dylan, like his peers at the time, was mining the back eddies of the folk and blues tradition. Though it is top-heavy in its inclusion of Guthrie material, the "Minnesota Hotel Tape" features chestnuts from the likes of the Reverend Gary Davis, Big Joe

Williams, Brownie McGhee, and Blind Lemon Jefferson. Clearly Dylan was, at least unconsciously, lacing Buckley in this great lineage of American folk music by the inclusion of "Black Cross" into his repertoire.

By the fall of 1962, when the second Dylan version of "Black Cross" was recorded at the Gaslight Café in Greenwich Village, the young troubadour had learned his song well. The pacing and drama of the piece are perfectly nuanced, the unfolding horror of the story poignantly dark.

In this fashion Dylan tailored "Black Cross" into one of his finger-pointing protest songs similar to two originals he performed that autumn evening, "John Brown" and "Ballad of Hollis Brown"—sympathetic compositions that focused on the violent, martyred fate of its primary characters. The songsmith was to follow these up over the next couple of years with several others in the same vein, among them: "The Lonesome Death of Hattie Carroll," "Death of Emmett Till," and "Percy's Song."

Dylan encountered Lord Buckley at a crucial point in his emerging aesthetic and personal development. It was at this time that he was in the chameleonlike process of transforming himself from Bobby Zimmerman, middle-class son of a midwestern hardware store owner, into Dylan: the poet/prophet/waif who would change the times and music.

A Buckley reference appeared in a Dylan poem published in the December 1963 issue of *Hootenany,* the staunchly traditionalist songsters' pamphlet. Curiously titled "Blowin' in the Wind," the poem postdates that particularly famous Dylan classic and, along with mentions of Ray Charles, Julian Beck, Bertrand Russell, Marlon Brando, and Joan Baez, the fractalized bit of impressionism includes the following stanza:

> an Moondog's beatin his drum an sayin' his lines—
> an Lord Buckley's memory still movin'
> an Doc Watson's walkin'

Buckley also seems to have informed some of Dylan's later work. A close look at the atmospheric cover photograph of his 1965 album *Bringing It All Back Home* reveals another LP jacket, *The Best of Lord Buckley,* prominently displayed on the mantelpiece in the background amid the funky, but pointed, cultural detritus littering the portrait.

A couple of songs on that disc appear to show Dylan noting Buckley's teachings. The proto-rap "Subterranean Homesick Blues" bursts with harsh, black humorous syncopation and "Bob Dylan's 115th Dream" with obtuse history.

Additionally, "Mr. Tambourine Man," with its Pied Piper–like beckonings, contains the repetitive sound/phrase "jingle-jangle," echoing Buckley's "Scrooge," which includes the identical refrain. Similarly, a line from the later Dylan masterpiece "Like a Rolling Stone" ("when you got nothin' you got nothin' to lose") parallels Buckley's sentiments in "The Gasser": "To know what it means to have nothing you must have NOTHING!"

Within a year Dylan was utilizing Buckley's method of transforming legend into a postmodern sensibility with the title track of his next album, *Highway 61 Revisited:* "Oh God said to Abraham 'Kill me a son,'/Abe says, 'Man, you must be puttin' me on.'"

Dylan also populated a couple of other *Highway 61* songs, "Desolation Row" and "Tombstone Blues," with characters that either come straight out of Buckley's lexicon or could have. Those making cameos include Cinderella, Bette Davis, Ophelia, Einstein "disguised as Robin Hood," John the Baptist, the Commander in Chief, the King of the Philistines, Gypsy Davey, Cecil B. DeMille, Galileo, Delilah, Ma Rainey, and Beethoven.

And is it any accident that "Mr. Jones"—the man who knows something is happening but not quite what on *Highway 61*'s scathing "Ballad of a Thin Man"—shares a similar situation and the same surname as the doomed Hezikiah from "Black Cross"?

Concurrently, Dylan included the following reference in the "Electric Black Nite Crash" section of his murky novel/poem *Tarantula:* "nature has made the young West Virginia miners not want to be miners but rather get this '46 Chevy—no money down—take to Geneva . . . hunting for the likes of escape & Lord Buckley & Sherlock Holmes about to be his mother turning to Starhole the Biology Amazon saying 'i dont want to be my mother!'"

And others see a Buckley–"Black Cross" connection in "Sign on the Cross," one of the more intangibly weird songs from the intangibly weird American collaboration *The Basement Tapes.* Recorded informally in 1967 with The Band in upstate New York, *The Basement Tapes* feature a grab bag of genuine Dylan classics, genuine folk/pop classics, and genuinely inspired, off-the-wall lunacy. Built like a symphony, "Sign on the Cross" finds Dylan taking on a persona somewhere between a late-night radio preacher and an aged backwoods wise man, in a voice sounding alternately soothing and deranged.

Dylan shocked the music world in 1979 when he revealed that he was a born-again Christian and began performing a new, all-gospel repertoire—some of the most powerful (and unjustifiably maligned) music of his career. But, like Buckley before him, was he not merely celebrating the life and work of The Nazz in art and song?

In 1981, still later in Dylan's career, came the tune "Lenny Bruce" on his underappreciated *Shot of Love* album. Though there are again no Buckley-specific references in the song, it is reasonable to view the composition as Dylan's identification with and homage to the idiom Lenny and His Lordship transformed. And who knows, maybe when Dylan sang of hearing the "song of the clown who died in the alley" on "A Hard Rain's A-Gonna Fall" at the Gaslight that night way back in 1962, he had Lord Buckley in mind.

Perhaps more than the lyrics in many of these compositions themselves are the swirling, kaleidoscopic manner in which they flow singsong from Dylan's lips, defying rhyme and meter. Even the more straight-ahead rock and blues numbers have a raw angularity that reveals hidden facets with repeated listening.

To extend the idiom's lineage into the modern era (and Buckley's influence via Bob Dylan) are cover versions of two Dylan songs: Kurtis Blow's 1987 rap version of "Subterranean Homesick Blues" and a 1993 hip-hop rendition of "Like a Rolling Stone" by the Mystery Tramps, featuring the first-ever authorized sampling of the singer-songwriter's voice from the original cut in the dense but spunky high-tech mix.

Or maybe Buckley was, as some Dylanists suggest, little more than a footnote in the Bob Dylan story. Maybe Dylan, the living sponge, got hold of Buckley's records in 1961, spent a couple of weeks absorbing them inside out, and then moved on. Dylan often cannibalized people's record collections when crashing with them—the most famous example being when he devoured Harry Smith's *Anthology of American Folk Music*—and perhaps "Black Cross" was all that emerged from his binge. Maybe the Buckley album on the cover of *Bringing It All Back Home* is just an album on a shelf, where Dylan left him, resurrecting him possibly not again until the mid-1970s to draw on Buckley's hip "Dan McGroo" for "Lily, Rosemary and the Jack of Hearts."

"Black Cross" had a powerful, if opposite, effect on another composer/musician of renowned sound and round. When Buckley performed the piece in New York City in the fall of 1960, bassist Charles Mingus allegedly charged the stage with a knife in an attempt to stab His Lordship, whom he incorrectly felt was glorifying a lynching. It was only the quick action and soft words of Prince Lewis Foremaster that soothed Mingus and saved Lord Buckley on that occasion.

Though Buckley's Ivar gig is regarded on high, it did not have the same effect on everyone. *Los Angeles Times* reporter Geoffrey Warren's review of opening night was printed in the paper's February 13, 1959, edition.

LORD BUCKLEY PERFORMING AT THE IVAR

If the second half of "An Evening With Lord Buckley" is of the same caliber as the first, one could spend the same evening watching a program of fixed fights at a local smoker and derive approximately the same profit.

Lord Buckley is billed as an entertainer and, to a degree, this is true. If he were presented as the main attraction at a bar serving 40-cent highballs, tough popcorn and soft pretzels he would be worth the time spent in attendance. But, in a theater with a $3.25 top, this cat ain't worth the green.

His Lordship opens with a beat version of "a real incident in the life of Mahatma Gandhi" called "The All Hip Mahatma." This is followed by a rather tasteless "The Moronic Father and His Idiot Son."

'The Old Man'

One number shows some merit. It's "The Old Man," in which a certain amount of quality shows through. Another sketch, "The Nazz," could easily be viewed as profane, though the Cosmo Alley set seemed to enjoy it last night.

Among other numbers are "Don't Shoot Him, Fred. He's a Thoroughbred," "The Black Cross," "The Gasser," "15th-Century Humor" and "Lincoln's Gettysburg Address."

Lord Buckley will be presented at the Ivar Theater again this evening and tomorrow evening.

Two extended studio pieces, "Scrooge" and the convoluted "Maharaja," were recorded in the studio about a year after the Ivar gig and used to fill out the later *Blowing His Mind* Ivar disc, then added as bonus tracks to the 1996 re-release of *Bad-Rapping of the Marquis de Sade*.

With "Scrooge," Buckley takes a successful plunge into a classic with his dazzling translation of *A Christmas Carol* by Charles Dickens. All the elements of the original are present and incandescently soar through Buckley's verbal insight: Marley's appearance of warning, each ghostly visitation, Bob Cratchet's mousy humbleness, Tiny Tim's non-judgmental selflessness, and Scrooge's parsimoniousness, spiritual transformation, and ultimate revelation. "Scrooge" is Lord Buckley's last masterpiece, standing at the pinnacle of his achievements alongside "The Nazz," "The Gasser" and "The Bad-Rapping of the Marquis de Sade"—as the following excerpt from old Ebeneezer's midnight flight of fantasy demonstrates:

> All of a sudden—WHAM!!—Here comes another big spook. WHOOOOOO! He's a wild-lookin' spook. He's a crazy-lookin' spook. He's a far-out spook. He's a gaslight spook—he's got a gaslight right on the top of his wig—VRRRRRRRR!!—going around like one of them automatic satellites in a lighthouse. And he done gassed up the whole scene.
>
> He say, "Come with me, I am the ghost of Christmas present."
>
> And Scrooge looks around and he sees the joint is loaded with apples, bananas and oranges and crecladies and apple rots and rip-a-bits and all kinds of crazy wild grapes and crazy Christmas scenes and nuts and candy.
>
> And he say, "Come with me."
>
> VRRRRRRTTT!!—they done took off again.
>
> And he say, "I am the ghost of Christmas present." He said, "I want to show you what's going on in this world and how the people dig Christmas and how they all *en*joy."
>
> And he took him over to a little old outcast island. There, sittin' on a small beat-up rock was two studs chompin' up on a can of beans singin', "Merry Christmas with you, Merry Christmas with you, Merry Christmas to the whole world" and so on and so forth.
>
> And he showed the people jumpin' for joy here. And he show that the cats who ain't got nothing got something anyway and they're all jumpin' for joy, singin' "Merry Christmas" and the bells is ringin'!
>
> And he says, "Now you get yourself straight and see how things will jump. Come with me."
>
> So they fly over to Cratchet's place and there is little Tiny Tim. He's singin' over there in the corner diggin' a little crazy scene on his crutch fiddlin' around, you know what I mean. Playin' and carryin' on, see, and they're all takin' a look at this here goose. And they look down at this little goose about the size of a beat-up *re*-tarded sparrow and everybody is "Oooin' and Ahhin'" all over this goose and they say, "When are we going

to spread it?" And then Tiny Tim says, "God bless everyone even up and including old Scroogey Scrooge! God bless everyone!"

And old Scrooge got red eyes.

Vrrrrtttt—took him back again—Wheewwwww Boom!—the whole side of the building look bomb dong.

In came a long angular spook. He looked like seventeen gaslighter stove pipes come together with jingle jangle bells all over.

Scrooge takes a look at this cat and says, "Do I have to go with you?"

And he says, "You most certainly do because I am the Ghost of Christmas Future. Come with me!"

He says, "Where are we going?"

He says, "None of your business."

But he takes old Scrooge and they cut off down the pike and they're flyin' around the moonlight shinin' down at them.

Boom!—they are in a graveyard—wooooooo—a *wild*—woooooooo—*crazy* spooky graveyard. And old Scrooge is walkin' around and suddenly something stepped out at him like it was stuck in front of his eyes like with some sort of electronic pitch fork. And he reads one of them billboards in the graveyard. It says: "This is Scrooge, the baddest cat that ever lived. He ain't had nothin', he won't have nothin' and he ain't got nothing now. Period."

Owing just as much to the cinematic adaptations of the classic Dickensian tale as to the original text, Buckley's "Scrooge" is one of his most complete and fulfilling alchemicalizations, culminating with perhaps his entire worldview boiled down to a final testament: "You can get with it if you want to—there's only *one* way *straight* to the road of love!"

"Maharaja" is the story of a "cop out" with some strange homoerotic undertones. Wisely executed with a bongo drum backing, it fails, however, in its attempt to recall the glory of "The Hip Gahn" through subcontinent-specific allegory. The high point of the piece may be in Buckley's brief setup in which he defines a cop-out in takes-one-to-know-one style: "A cop out is the kind of a chap that you have around for awhile, sometimes for many years, that you want to KILL him . . . but you just can't quite get to it. 'Course everytime he gaslights you he comes around with such a wonderful story that he entertains you so strongly with his story that you forgive the accident or the catastrophe or the flip or the delinquency."

The rambling, energetic tale chronicles the plight of a double-dealer who has committed some outrageous and unforgivable sin yet manages to fast-talk his way back into the Maharaja's good graces. It is, in its favor, one of those mad Lord Buckley raves that takes you there and back. You may not know exactly where you've been but feel it was somewhere seemingly meaningful and exotic. Even subpar Buckley manages to sweep the listener away to another stratum altogether.

Nik Venet

In those days World Pacific was a skeleton operation. We used to be the engineer, the assistant, the producer and the photographer's assistant, and everything else. Sometimes Dick Bock would give me cameras. Remember I had no idea what the fuck I was doing, except that I had passion to be a producer.

Now that I look back on it it's quite funny because I knew about as much about producing as I did fixing a car. Richard Bock had a lot of faith in me and he trusted me. And he used to actually send me out with Lord Buckley on these functions so that nobody would steal the equipment because Lord Buckley would sell the equipment.

Dick Bock would say, "His Lordship's going to be in town for two weeks. Try to get him into the studio every night." So what he would do is put me with Lord Buckley. World Pacific had a room that contained the equipment, all portable Ampexes, these older mono- and two-track portable tape machines. And what we would do is—the main office for the secretary and the bookkeeper—we would move the tables and desks aside and that would become the studio. That's the way that operation was set up at that Sunset Boulevard address and I would try to drag him in every night after we made the rounds.

Now, it's interesting the way that he was recorded. We'd go in every night and he would do an hour but get tired. Plus there wasn't an audience.

So he would have to be pretty wired to come in to do it right after he did it at the Renaissance. It was walking distance. And he would try to put it down and we would do several things and then eventually Richard Bock would go through them and make some edits and pick what he wanted. But since we recorded Lord Buckley numerous times, there was lots of stuff that I've yet to see released. Now remember I wasn't thinking about the future then, so I don't know what happened to it. But I have a feeling it's buried deep in the bowels of World Pacific, which is now owned by EMI/Capitol.

I'll tell you where the pith helmet in the photos came from. Lord Buckley stole the pith helmet from the MGM prop department. I was with him that afternoon and I thought: "We're going to go to jail." His Lordship was so blatant about it. He went in and says, "My man!" to the guy in the prop room, the costume room. He says, "We are shooting on Stage Seventy-five hmmm harrr. And we need it." He did this whole routine and the guy comes out with a safari outfit and a pith helmet. He takes and tries on the jacket and it fits. And he said, "I need a lid. I need a lid." And the guy brings him the pith helmet. He puts the lid on and says, "Thank you." And the guy says, "Well, what, you know, you've got to give me the production codes and everything." And I don't know what he wrote on the paper. He walked out of the costume and prop department at MGM with a safari jacket, a pair of jodhpurs over his arm, and a pith helmet. That's how he got them.

I said, "By the time we get in the car, and get off this lot, we're going to get busted at the gate and—"

But he kept saying, “Drive on.”

And as he passed the guard, he stood up in my open convertible. He tipped his hat to the guards. They saluted him and we drove off the lot. He stood up in the car and he tipped his hat. The guards saluted him and we drove off the lot and he had pinched a goddamn jacket, jodhpurs and a hat.

Lord Buckley

I wish I had the nerve to be a thief. I know a fellow that can put seventeen sirloin steaks in his britches and you can’t see ’em. Gets a little chill before he gets out of there. Just loves to steal. I can understand that. Can’t you? Course . . .

16 Nepenthe

Lord Buckley

I should like to dedicate this to this great establishment, this modern church, this atomic chapel.

On Friday, February 20, 1959, a week after the Ivar Theater concert, Buckley began a seven-day stint at the Interlude, an intimate Los Angeles stage in a larger nightspot called the Crescendo near Sunset Boulevard, sharing an offbeat bill with the Ink Spots and Louis Jordan and his Tympany Five.

Run by local impresarios Maynard Sloate and Gene Norman, the club offered two tiers of entertainment. Downstairs, in the Crescendo, were the featured entertainers: top-flight cabaret stars and supporting acts. Upstairs, in the cozy Interlude, were the newcomers and the coterie performers such as Buckley.

Nineteen fifty-nine was also notable in the Buckley chronology for reasons other than stage performance, as it marked his final stab at the Hollywood big-time with his *Spartacus* walk-on.

Though it's appropriately (and not a little ironically) fitting that Lord Buckley appeared in a film with a story line from which he could have gained much hipsemantic mileage (and one that harked back to his earlier treatment of "Nero"), the *Spartacus* walk-on came about quite by accident.

Ira Westley

I used to do a lot of sideline work in the movies. At one point the contractor called me and said, "I need about twenty-two musicians to do sideline for a movie called *Spartacus*."

I sent out calls to a bunch of people, including Lord Buckley. There were several funny parts to the experience. One was that they fed us broiled half chickens sitting on picnic benches during our lunch break on the set. We're all in togas and I'm sitting there eating my chicken with Charles Laughton on one side of me, looking like Henry VIII, eating the chicken with his bare hands, and on the other side of me is Lord Buckley, eating with his impeccable table manners.

In doing these sideline things there's an awful lot of sitting around waiting. So I goaded Lord Buckley during one of our waiting periods to start telling some of his stories. Pretty soon he had the whole cast there listening to his stories when the director, Stanley Kubrick, came along and really raised hell: "What's going on here? What do you think we're paying you guys for!?"

Jack Coons

West Coast musician Jack Coons was tight with His Lordship in the late 1950s and is one of those responsible for securing His Lordship's Spartacus *walk-on.*

The musicians' union had split in Los Angeles at that time. The studio musicians were tired of picking up the bill for the union members that weren't working so they formed a musicians' guild. The type of work I did in the movies was called sideline work. That's when you have a horn in your hand but you don't play it. So they needed a hundred-piece band which they circled around the lot to make it look like it was much longer than it really was for *Spartacus*. So the contractor had called from the musicians' guild and told me to bring anybody I know who needs a job and can hold a horn. So I called Lord Buckley.

The scene in which we appeared was when Sir Laurence Olivier comes out of the Roman Senate and says, "Bring me Spartacus or bring me his head!"

While they were setting the scene up we were in this little room in the back of this huge Senate building and I got to chatting with Sir Laurence Olivier. I just mentioned Buckley's name and he said, "Oh, I've heard some of his stuff in England. He's completely charming."

And I said, "Well, he's right here on the set."

And he said, "Really? I'd love to talk to him."

So I went out and got Lord Buckley. Sir Laurence Olivier had just been knighted by the Queen of England and it was so funny to hear Lord Buckley saying, "Prince Olivier." They had quite a little chat.

But the big screen was not the only moving-image venue to engage His Lordship's services at this juncture.

Jim Dickson

When he came back from Las Vegas I got him a job at a cartoon company where I was working as the sound engineer. It was for *Beany and Cecil* and they had him do a character called "Go Man Van Gogh." But by the time the cartoon went out and received a positive response, Lord Buckley was dead. The character became very popular on the show but Buckley died. The producers had to get Scatman Crothers to imitate his voice and do the character. It seemed like it had gone full circle. I think Buckley would have liked that.

Created by Bob Clampett, the high-seas adventures of Cecil (the seasick sea serpent) and his friend Beany evolved from a daily fifteen-minute puppet show first broadcast in Los Angeles circa 1949 into a nationally syndicated, Emmy-winning weekly animated series by the early 1960s. But *Beany and Cecil* was more than an ordinary cartoon, utilizing broad slapstick gags, imaginative stories, and characters previously unseen in the medium.

Buckley's character, "Go Man Van Gogh," was the new Beatnik character on the popular series, which in its day enjoyed something of the same irreverent position that

The Simpsons does in contemporary popular culture. It became the favorite of many adults, including Lionel Barrymore, Jimmy Stewart, Albert Einstein, Joan Crawford, and Groucho Marx. And it was Groucho who once said that *Beany and Cecil* was "the only kids' show adult enough for my daughter Melinda to watch."

The surviving print of the *Beany and Cecil* episode in which Buckley's voice appeared, "The Wildman of Wildsville," has dated remarkably well. Beany and Cecil travel to a deserted island to track down and capture the Wildman (aka Go Man Van Gogh). While deftly working references to Lenny Bruce, Mort Sahl, and the hungry i jazz club into the script, the writers also manage to poke fun at Bugs Bunny and Freudian psychology. Buckley's parts are really quite funny both in content and delivery, and it appears as if the animation was rendered after he laid down some basic ad-libs.

Upon further consideration, a career in voice-over artistry may have made Lord Buckley a name as recognizable as Mel Blanc, the man behind the sounds of Bugs Bunny, Daffy Duck, and the rest of the Looney Tunes cartoons' crew. Though there is a great deal of diversity of styles and content, one never gets the sense that performers such as Blanc were just putting on funny voices. Even though the style of characterization could be ridiculously exaggerated, there's a sense of identification with the parts that brings these inspired characters to life.

If Buckley had any future aspirations for the big or small screen, they were probably dashed the day he went to read for another cartoon part. Unfortunately, the show's executives didn't share Buckley's sense of humor and free-spiritedness. The building where he auditioned was designed as a square with open ground at its center. On the open ground was a mound of dirt that Buckley retired to after his audition. There he rolled a joint and lit up, visible to the execs who, until they caught a glimpse of this, were seriously considering his possible employment.

By late 1959 the demands of the L.A. dives and Vegas gloss were wearing very thin for Lord Buckley. Frustrated in his efforts to bring his message to the chintzy crowds at the Vegas venues in which he performed and economically hindered by a dearth of L.A. dates, Buckley and clan were on the move again.

Attracted by the Bay Area's artistic community and mellow subcultures, the Buckleys landed in Marin County. Clubs like the Purple Onion and the hungry i were all the rage, headlining top-flight jazz acts and performers like Lenny Bruce, Mort Sahl, and Dick Gregory.

Charles Campbell

He almost got a job at the hungry i. We played the records for Enrico Banducci, the owner of the hungry i which was a place that he had been running for only a few months. Banducci liked his work and he said, "I just signed up a guy to work for a month so come back then."

It turned out the guy was Mort Sahl who stayed there for like nine hundred years.

So Buckley got weekend jobs at places like the Coffee Cantata and other little beat joints. He did all the stuff he became known for on his records but he also did a lot of stuff that was never recorded. He had a small hard-core following. Prince Lewis was always there acting like his acolyte. Buckley was his whole reason for living.

One time a friend of mine had a spare house in Stinson Beach. It just had a bed in it. Buckley came over to dinner at this guy's house one night and when the subject of the Nazis and Adolf Hitler came up he did like a one-hour performance of *The Rise and Fall of the Third Reich*. There were only the four of us there and he had us in hysterics as he marched up and down the room coming on like Hitler. It was just insane.

Del Close

The first time I encountered Lord Buckley: thereby hangs a tale. I was in the apartment of a young singer named Don Heller who I was in a Broadway show with called *The Nervous Set*. I was just about ready to get in a plane to go to San Francisco to play the hungry i and we were sitting around his apartment getting stoned and he asked me if I'd ever heard of Lord Buckley. "No," I said. "Is he some sort of calypso singer?"

"No," he said. "He's a comedian." He had one of Lord Buckley's records but his phonograph was broken. He was so desperate for me to hear this that he rigged the phonograph up with a Dixie Cup so I could hear it. That was the first I ever heard the likes of "Black Cross" and "The Nazz" and stuff like that. I was completely blown away. I thought that this was the best stuff I ever heard. I had heard Lenny Bruce in person but this was even wilder.

So, after a few more adventures, I wound up in San Francisco and met Enrico Banducci, who owned the hungry i, down in the basement of his club. He asked me if there was anybody that he could arrange for me to meet while I was in San Francisco. I told him that the only person I could think of besides Alan Watts was Lord Buckley.

He turned and said, "Well, here he comes now." And Buckley was walking down the stairs with his entourage. Buckley was wearing a complete tuxedo with a boiled shirt but his pants were about his six inches too short and he had on white socks and army shoes. And this was an apparition with a waxed moustache. I was not aware of the fact that he had outworn his welcome at the hungry i specifically, and the Bay Area in general, both because of the tiredness of his routine and the moochy qualities he was perceived to exhibit.

He had been performing in a club that was a convertible club: literally it had a roof that rolled back. He had this new material and so he went up and did "The Raven." I think it was one of the first times he performed it because he wasn't very good. The material was kind of stiff. He was kind of peculiar and a little tentative and a little too long.

I wanted to do a show to impress this guy who I was a fan of and I was just terrific, which is not to say I was a better comedian than Lord Buckley. He was, by some great distance, far better than I was or am. But that night I caught on and he didn't. And so it was like I cut the master that night.

But he wasn't at all put out. He said, "If anything goes wrong, give me a call. You can always come and stay with me in San Rafael."

So, about five weeks later, after a very undistinguished run at the hungry i, I did. I was a fairly green comedian. I'd only been doing it for about two and a half years and I didn't have enough material really. I had one good show and one really pale show. Anyway, whenever they got a chance to book Mort Sahl they did. They'd cancel whoever's there and book Mort. So they canceled the last three weeks of my second month there and put Mort on. So I called up His Royal Highness and he asked me if I wanted to do a show with him out in Concord, California.

The show happened to be on the same night as the second Patterson-Johansson heavyweight championship fight that meant that we didn't draw anybody. We drew like eight people in this civic auditorium that was like an overgrown bandshell.

The others on the bill that night were Ruth Price, the jazz singer, a jazz trio and a progressive tap dancer who we had to pick up at an AA meeting. We started driving out of town in the the "Fairyland Express"—the red VW van with the open roof that he drove all the way to New York—when the tap dancer said, "Hey man, I forgot my ax," which were his tap shoes. So we had to go back and pick those up at his house.

We had this big eight-foot-by-ten-foot American flag flying on top of the van—a great, big monstrous thing that we paraded around Concord attempting to drum up interest in the gig. But we couldn't work up any enthusiasm with this one-car parade.

When we got to this auditorium and there's like eight people there (three kids and four or five elderly citizens) sitting in the front row waiting kind of expectantly.

Buckley looked out and said, "I'll go on and warm them up."

And he was on for like two and a half hours, just out there doing stuff. Nobody else got on. Not the tap dancer, the jazz singer, the band, or me. He did the entire show himself. He went on and on, just tripping out with his material. I don't even think the audience was enjoying it particularly. It's possible that some of them might have left.

Then we packed it up and got back in the Fairyland Express. The house booker was with us and there was this long fifteen-minute silence on the way back. Finally, this house booker said, "You know, Your Royal Highness, we could have drawn more people if we'd done this in San Francisco."

And Buckley said, "We could have drawn more people if we'd done this on the moon."

Night had fallen and I had forgotten what the desert chill was like in Northern California. I didn't have the right kind of coat or anything so I had to wrap myself up in the American flag. And Buckley always used to say that that was his favorite image of me: wrapped up and shivering in the American flag, coming back from Concord.

With the flowering of the Beat Generation, California—specifically San Francisco—was the place to be. For an artist there was really no place that could have been quite like it, just at that time. Excitement in San Francisco at that point centered on Lawrence Ferlinghetti's City Lights bookshop, a favorite meeting place for local and wandering poets and bohemians. Housed in a narrow, crowded storefront between North Beach and Chinatown, City Lights functioned not only as a bookstore but also as a neo-Parisian café, where people could sit around at little tables to read, play chess, commune with its thoughtful inventory, and/or rant from ten in the morning to closing time at midnight. Buckley not only gravitated to this loose groove but arranged to have his mail delivered there for a spell as well.

There are surprisingly few references to Buckley in Beat literature. Perhaps the most significant nod to the man can be found in Jack Kerouac's 1961 opus *Desolation Angels,* in which he briefly mentions Buckley.

The particular passage in which Lord Buckley is mentioned, number eight in *Book Two, Passing Through Mexico,* is interesting because Kerouac departs from describing his and his friends' actions of 1956–1957, which the book is ostensibly about. He delivers a kind of Lord Buckley–style monologue about himself: "Take another look at me to get the story better . . ." he starts (admitting he's getting drunk).

Lucidly, with all his writing power, he deeply considers his purpose and talents. He muses with the reader about the most important things in his life, his "scribblings," his being an "Idealist," all of his "innocent go-ahead confessions," plus the church, his older brother, Gerard (whose death as a boy left Kerouac traumatized), life, "Light falling."

He tells us, "don't think of me as a simple character," but confesses that "I don't know what I am, some kind of fevered being different as a snowflake."

He summons his great visions into a strong finish, from Lord Buckley: "'Did I say all?' said Lord Richard Buckley before he died." Minimally referencing Buckley's "Swingin' Pied Piper," the passage begs the question of whether Kerouac is confronting death with his plaintive cry or affirming that, with his ambitious grabs for life and art, he got it all.

Lord Buckley

The beatniks are a very young sect and, like all babies, it's natural for them to dirty their pants once in a while.

From the cradle of the Beats to the glare of the cathode tube, Buckley did wing back to New York for a final appearance on the Sullivan show in May of 1959, this time including the great Canadian comedians Johnny Wayne and Frank Shuster, the actress Trude Adams, and Sullivan as his "Amos 'n' Andy" stooges. What made this last Sullivan show appearance particularly noteworthy was that the voice in which the routine is rendered eschews the dated "Amos 'n' Andy" presentation and sounds more akin to the weathered, whiskey-soaked cadence of his later, hipsemantic delivery. Buckley also manages to frame the discussion in which his dummies partake against the backdrop of the escalating U.S.-Soviet space race. A final Sullivan show note: Edith Piaf was one of the show's other performers that night, and Sullivan reran the show in the summer of 1961 as a posthumous tribute to Buckley.

Considering what a rich personality Lord Buckley barely contained, it is somewhat surprising that so few interviews with him have survived or were even, for that matter, conducted. It does, however, make perfect sense that he should have been invited to appear on the decade-old KPFA (the Pacifica Foundation's radio affiliate in Berkeley, California) for an interview-cum-performance on Bill Butler's September 16, 1959, program. Pacifica was just beginning its listener-supported, not-for-profit experiment in progressive, freedom-of-speech, free-form FM radio that continues to this day, and Lord Buckley was a natural for its early endeavors.

Perhaps more than any other single specific example, the Buckley KPFA appearance demonstrates that the mantle of "His Lordship" was a life commitment—not mere facile gimmickry and shtick. During the half-hour show, Buckley runs through excellent versions of "The Gasser," "Willie the Shake," "Hipsters, Flipsters and Finger-Poppin' Daddies," and "Swingin' Pied Piper" while peppering the broadcast appearance with that day's version of his life story, philosophy, claims of healing powers, and other whimsies. What makes the artifact even more fun is that Butler—who plays the perfect (unwitting?) straight man and is quite obviously amazed and somewhat at a loss as how to exactly deal with his most immaculately unusual guest—slowly becomes converted in the process.

By autumn Buckley had reestablished himself on the West Coast club circuit and ventured to the Monterey Jazz Festival on October 3, 4, and 5.

Photographer Jerry Stoll snapped a backstage photo of Buckley, looking something of a cross between gaucho and guru, cigarette burned to a butt in hand while earnestly rapping with trumpeter Roy Eldridge, his old friend from the Gene Krupa big-band days, and a young entrepreneur named Jules Buscheri. Buscheri was later misidentified as possibly being Lenny Bruce when City Lights published the photo in *Hiparama of the Classics*.

Things, however, didn't go as smoothly with some of the other participants at the Monterey soiree.

Grover Sales

Critic, manager, writer, and scholar, Grover Sales has been an important force in the West Coast jazz scene since the 1950s.

Mort Sahl was an emcee at the first year of the Monterey Jazz Festival in 1958. In 1959 Buckley showed up trying to get hired by the festival. He said, "You people need me here. I could really work this crowd."

Ralph Gleason, the writer and critic, came up to me and said, "Grover, he's your client, he's your friend, get rid of him. We don't want him around here."

Gleason just didn't understand his act. Gleason had a bug up his ass about this. We were very good friends but he could get very parochial.

There are also stories that Buckley got into an argument and then a fracas with another old acquaintance, scat master Dave Lambert, at the festival—a rhubarb that allegedly resulted in the singer being cold-cocked by the burly stand-up performer.

Being so close to Big Sur, Buckley couldn't resist the temptation to pay an impromptu house call on writer Henry Miller. Miller arranged a spontaneous command performance on September 12 at Nepenthe, the famed café and local cultural hub located at a beautiful point on the cliffs overlooking the Pacific Ocean.

According to Big Sur legend, the venue got its start when Orson Welles and Rita Hayworth, driving along Highway 1, fell in love with and bought a little log cabin on a ledge with spectacular views of ocean and mountain. They never found time to come back, and the cabin came into the hands of a man named Bill Fassett who had drifted across country from Tennessee. He would eventually expand it into a restaurant, which he called Nepenthe, a Greek word that can be translated into the vernacular as "no sorrow." Nepenthe would soon become, as it has remained ever since, the social and symbolic center of Big Sur country life.

How fitting that Buckley should perform at a venue named for the potion used by the ancients to dull pain or suffering—and one with a picture-perfect locale for one of the great Buckley gigs. A high-quality reel-to-reel tape has preserved about half an hour of the evening's program, filled with wall-to-wall classics and revealing Lord Buckley at his absolute coolest.

Introduced as a "meta-comic," Buckley loosened his larynx and vibed a reverentially "in" crowd with a touch of Willie the Shake's "Hipsters, Flipsters and Finger-Poppin' Daddies" and "Is This the Sticker?" before settling into definitive versions of "God's Own Drunk," "The Raven," "Black Cross," and an incomplete, tape-ending take of "Swingin' Pied Piper." "Black Cross," taken a pace or two slower than the Ivar Theater outing, is particularly powerful as Buckley steers the dark drama to its gnawing conclusion. Finally, and oddly, Buckley used the occasion to trot out his "Amos 'n' Andy" warhorse to the apparent delight of the assembled clique.

Acknowledging Miller's presence in the audience, Buckley is obviously loose and comfortable with his surroundings—at home with a group that is clearly sensitive to his medium and his message. His off-the-cuff (and wall) comments charm them, drawing performer and audience together in a spirit very much different from the jazz clubs, nightspots, and theaters of his performing norm. The presentation has, as Buckley notes, the feeling of "High Mass."

At one point during the concert (and demonstrating a definite understanding of who was on stage) someone in the audience calls out for "The Nazz," which Buckley promises to perform later in the evening, a rendition that, alas, was not preserved.

Lord Buckley

To the High Priest of the entire mountain scene, his most royal highness, Sir Henry Miller. I'd like a little sound for Sir Henry, a little love sound.

Henry Miller

To Lord Buckley, his most euphoric Lordship, greetings! What a treat to hear your new shatterbusting recording delivered like a true hipster with variations à la Paganini, Gilles de Rais and the Marquis of Queensbury! It seems to me that your Lordship opened a new vein, leading from the medulla oblongata (hold on to this one!) and the Cloaca Maxima. It's all so very alive and jumpin' and in the pauses one can hear the atoms exploding out there in the Milky Way where the grass comes up every once in ten billion years and there are no moth balls or frigidaires, no box office receipts, no railroads, no crucifixions rosy or otherwise . . . It is very far out, your Lordship . . .

Correspondence exchanged between the Royal Family and Miller's confidant, Emil White, shed some further light on His Lordship's relationship with Sir Henry but also suggest confusion in the chronology of their association.

Emil White

Henry Miller's confidant and Big Sur gatekeeper, Emil White's reminiscence of Lord Buckley appeared in his memoir Letters from Emil.

I'd like to tell you about Lord Buckley, an unusual, eccentric performer who originated "jive" talk and the "rap." He was very influential because of his ideas and use of language: Buckley was really the Father of Hip, the Daddy of the Beats. He came to see me because he wanted to visit Henry—people had to clear me first! Henry was scared of Lord Buckley from what he'd heard about the performer, so it was my job to assure Henry that Buckley was O.K., that he was someone worth meeting . . . Lord Buckley waited at Nepenthe while I hiked up to Henry's place, Buckley wasn't much of a hiker! It turned out fine: Lord Buckley performed his "Nazz" routine for Henry and Henry loved it. Buckley stayed on as a guest in my house. Several days later he performed at Nepenthe—the place was mobbed and everyone loved his show! Buckley wrote me a letter afterwards to thank me for his stay in Big Sur:

San Rafael, CA
May 31, 1960

His Most Royal Highness
Prince Emil of White
Big Sur, California

Your Grace,

Hope this letter finds you enjoying the happy vibrations of a swingin' life! After much too long an absence, silence from the Royal Court, we are at long last settled in our new Castle, much closer to the Golden Land of Big Sur. We would be honored should you travel this way to be at home here at home. Sending you a copy of His Grace's new album, which is moving nicely . . . Meeting you and His Majesty Miller after all these years of correspondence was the highlight of our entire trip, we left your lovely studio with such a superb feeling of love and love of humanity, we literally flew back on gilded wings. Your lovely luncheon and charming guests—you are a superb host, your Grace. I look at your picture of Nepenthe every day, a guaranteed smile even on those ROUGH mornings gave us a wonderful life of faith and genuine goodness, and we were pretty beat out characters, havin' a Ball continuous is hard work.

His Lordship is in his 22nd week at the "Outside at the Inside" in Palo Alto, a coffee house and theatre, working Thurs., Friday and Saturday. And Ella Daganova, dancer with the Pavlova company, is our house guest, and Lady Buckley is back at the barre every morning. Prince Lewis and the Troops and Grandmother Selma, our entire entourage, are contemplating a two day holiday at the mineral baths in Big Sur, perhaps at the end of this month. Some of that wonderful therapy of the waters, and the serenity of Big Sur and of course we can spend a few moments with you. In Meditation! Mardi Gras or two. How would or could we get in touch with the people at the Baths about our reservations, I'll look in the guide book. Right! Is Nepenthe open yet? Questions, questions, questions, I do hope you will have a moment to say hello, I know you're busy. Please convey our love to everyone at Big Sur, and whenever I get lethargic, I think of that hill to His Majesty's house—on foot—your warmth and graciousness and hospitality will always be treasured!

Love,
Lord Buckley (& Lady Buckley & Royal Court)

In December 1959 the Royal Family gathered in their desert digs on the outskirts of Vegas with Prince Lewis and other friends for what would be their final holiday season with one another. A surviving one-hour tape portrays an audio snapshot of life at the Buckley Ranch . . . Royal Court–style. Buckley holds court and forth on a variety of subjects while coaxing his excruciatingly well-behaved children and their chums to sing and perform for what seems to be a very conspicuous microphone.

What kind of father was Lord Buckley? The lifestyle described in this book begs the question quite naturally. Like his own father, Buckley was, due to the demands of his profession, somewhat absentee. And again like his father, he appears to have been somewhat of a disciplinarian. But there appears little doubt of the love, devotion, and responsibility he felt toward his family.

Relocating to a large, hillside house at 188 Prospect in San Rafael, California—then a sleepy blue-collar town on San Francisco Bay and not the developed shopping-mall suburb of the present day—the roving Royal Family quickly developed a new circle of friends and admirers.

Charles Campbell

He decided he'd live here in Marin County so he went to the bank. He had seen this house for sale that had been moved from one lot to another. It was a big house with practically a ballroom-like reception room when you first walked in. But it was on blocks and had been moved. He saw a "For Sale" sign on it but he had like fifty-two cents to his name.

He dressed up and walked into the Bank of America or Wells Fargo and told them, "I'm very interested in that house but I just can't buy it because I want to be sure I can possibly live in it so I'd like to stay there for a while and see what it would be like." And he conned himself into that house. He moved in and was there for like six months. I have a photo of him in front of that house with his name "Lord Buckley" on the mailbox.

I went there for the inauguration of the house. It was a great party.

Lewis Foremaster

There were lice in the San Rafael house and Buckley had to shave off his moustache to get rid of them.

Del Close

His place in San Rafael was amazing. It was falling into the canyon for one thing. It was not only on blocks, it was on stilts. It was built into the canyon and some of it was falling slightly into the canyon. There were these big cracks in the ballroom wall. But instead of papering them over or concealing them, he had Christmas tree lights strung in them so you could see the cracks at a distance as you were driving up to the place. It looked like the house was glowing from the inside like a jack-o-lantern.

When I was staying there, the first thing we'd do when we got up in the morning was do a ballet barre with Madame Dagonova, some Russian woman living with them.

Then we'd have Bible reading classes after that in which Buckley would point out where the jokes were in the New Testament and, actually, in some of the Old Testament as well. There was something about "The Wise and Foolish Virgins" and some of the jokes in the Gospel of Luke or John. One concerned Nathaniel the rabbi meeting Jesus on the road. I still know where they are.

He was holding court all the time. He was in character from morning to night. I never joined the Royal Court because joining the Royal Court meant getting involved with some sadomasochistic activities that I wanted none of. For instance, he once made Prince Lewis lick up the entire floor of a motel room because he'd spilled something. He was heavy into discipline and punishment. I don't know too much about it but I know about that.

With the Beat Generation going full tilt, Buckley came to the region at a very special and receptive time. The San Francisco Renaissance is usually described as a literary phenomenon hatched out of revolution in modern lifestyles. In truth, the heroes of the movement were not writers like Allen Ginsberg and Jack Kerouac but the hipster saints of jazz, Lester Young and Charlie Parker.

But perhaps the closest Beat poetry and jazz ever got to one another was in the city's North Beach district where San Francisco's special contribution to the anthology of American art forms crystallized. This hybrid was practiced by Kenneth Rexroth, the movement's respected elder, and it was displayed by scores of other poets, pseudopoets, and wannabe poets of every degree of talent and commitment who stood up in coffeehouses and bars and let forth, trying to match the jazz furor with the elliptical phrasing of a soloist.

Though this form of jazz and poetry may have betrayed itself by failing to commit itself to either, it did produce some classics such as Ginsberg's *Howl* (itself partly inspired by Lester Young's solo on a recording of "Lester Leaps In") and pointed vaguely forward to the day when pop music would abandon the witty lyrics of the Broadway show tune for the rhapsodic, surrealistic verbal pastiche of Bob Dylan.

Lord Buckley

I find ah . . . my experience with the Beat Generation . . . they turned out to be, in spite of their being maligned and used for publicity purposes and their dark spots pointed out and the wide angelic wings of their full beauty ignored, that they are a very, very strong and beautiful and honest and sincere renaissance in youthful Americana. I'm supposed to be a high sahib of the Beat Generation. I suppose I've been a beatnik all my life, I guess.

Steve Allen

There was that whole Mississippi-wide cultural stream in which both the Beat Generation and Lord Buckley's sphere were borne along. They were not clinging together. They were not that close but definitely in that stream. In the sixties a lot of things changed that did not necessarily originate in the sixties. Buckley is obviously chiefly of the fifties. But whatever is meant by the word *hip* was part of this large revolutionary culture. Unfortunately there was also a lot of bad stuff to it, but that's true of everything human. But Buckley and Kerouac were part of a new relaxation of the rhetoric of the street. Again you'd have to go back to black jazz musicians' urban culture where that language comes from. But there are a lot of fascinating threads that became interwoven here. It would be interesting to see if either one was conscious of the other. I think I could say with confidence that Kerouac would have loved Buckley's work. I knew Jack socially as well as just two celebrities staring at each other across a chasm. He was that hip that he would have liked what Buckley did very much. And perhaps he did.

Ken Kesey

The Beats had a deep appreciation for Lord Buckley. Neal, Jack and the rest just loved and respected him.

I have three heroes who I think of as the great tripsters: Lord Buckley, Neal Cassady and Roland Kirk. They could all take off and you'd follow 'em and they'd lead you to where you could never go without them taking you there—drawing you along with their minds—their minds moving too fast for you to deny it. Cassady was the best. He was the most spontaneous of them all by far. Buckley had a routine as did Roland Kirk. Buckley knew the piece he was playing and he could take off from it. But Cassady stepped off into the unknown and could keep his verbal syntax going in that unknown territory like nobody I've seen.

Jerry Garcia

Buckley's work was part of the whole bopster deal—the whole beatnik thing. It was the other side of the Neal Cassady/Jack Kerouac reality. Actually, it was the black side of it if you want to think about it that way. It had a little more of the black experience, which is an important part of the whole beatnik aesthetic. Lord Buckley was a more loving spirit. He would have fit in good with the hippies.

As I went along, I found out about people like Neal Cassady because of reading Kerouac. When I met these people it became that much more rich and three-dimensional.

Neal had a couple of Buckley raps but he could recite them all, I understand. All of the ones that had been out on record anyway. He had an incredible memory. Neal worked with obscure references and lots of numerical stuff so you'd catch little bits and pieces of Buckley if you listened to him carefully enough. You really had to pay attention to it.

Lord Buckley and Grateful Dead philosophy merge in a certain irony of viewpoint. It's not literal, it's indirect. But it fits in there in the way we actually do business and the way we relate to each other. It's kind of a sideways influence but it's definitely some part of it.

Wavy Gravy

Buckley was a freewheeling tongue-dancer. He was seminal to the Beat Generation. But his Beat rant was more entertaining. He certainly had a warm place in the jazz community and was Beat-identified at that time.

Buckley's appearance in San Rafael caught the attention of a local newspaper, the *Independent Journal,* which sent a young reporter, Don Keown, to check out this strange newcomer to town.

Keown's article, "His Humor's Both Hip and Healthy—Lord Buckley Doesn't Dig the Fad for Sick Comedy" ran on Saturday June 18, 1960, and took an upbeat, if bemused, look at his subject. It also featured a large photo of a casually dressed Buckley, omnipresent cigarette burnt to a familiar nub in hand, pontificating under the trees of his backyard. Including a thumbnail overview of Buckley's life and filled with quotes from his work and on-site interview, the article also makes mention of His Lordship's "conservative" claim of having given more than twenty thousand shows during his career and of his ongoing, twenty-something-week gig at Outside at the Inside, a popular Palo Alto coffee shop, each Thursday, Friday, and Saturday night.

Grover Sales

I did Buckley's publicity in 1959 and 1960. I did entertainment and theatrical promotion for everyone from Lord Buckley to the Budapest String Quartet and everything in between. But I specialized in jazz comedy. I did publicity for Lenny Bruce and Woody Allen. My association with Buckley began because I was doing publicity for two clubs he was appearing in. One in North Beach, the Coffee Gallery, and another in Palo Alto, Outside at the Inside, which was owned by Mike du Pont, an heir of the du Pont family.

Buckley did two different kinds of performances. For the Palo Alto group he toned down the performances considerably, focusing on his "Amos 'n' Andy" audience-participation material. He did stuff for the college crowd that wasn't all that hip. But when he played the Coffee Gallery in North Beach he did things like "The Nazz" and "The Bad-Rapping of the Marquis de Sade." He was very canny about tailoring his act for these two audiences.

He was a real cult comic because his comedy was limited to hipsters. He was a hipster's comic. Unless you were a hipster, a jazz musician or had a jazz orientation you wouldn't be able to understand what he was talking about. There were things like "God's Own Drunk" or "Martin's Horse" that would have an appeal to a broader audience. But "The Bad-Rapping of the Marquis de Sade" or "The Gasser" were just too specialized for most people.

It was when he opened at the Coffee Gallery that Ralph Gleason reviewed him as an Uncle Tom—a completely off-the-wall attack. Buckley just seemed to go right by him. Calling him an Uncle Tom is a rather bizarre way of looking at him.

Prince Lewis was on the scene imitating Lord Buckley's mode of dress at that moment which featured a bowtie made out of a multicolored straw.

Vaughn Marlowe

Already a Buckley fan when he arrived in Palo Alto, California, in February 1960 to attend graduate school, Vaughn Marlowe happily discovered that his hero was performing at Outside at the Inside, a popular local spot. Prince Vaughn is a playwright living in Oregon.

I opened the paper the night after I got there and saw that he was in town. I went down to the club that night but when I got there I was the only person there.

I asked one of the guys working there if Lord Buckley was going to be there that night and it turned out he was backstage right then. I asked him to tell Lord Buckley that a messenger had come from the Midwest bearing glad tidings. He went back and Lord Buckley came out. I didn't know he was white until he came out from backstage.

I introduced myself and told him I was a great fan of his. I had *Euphoria* with me and I asked him to autograph it which he kindly did, writing: "To Prince Vaughn, may you always swing in beauty."

Then he gave me *Way Out Humor,* his album that had just come out on World Pacific, and he autographed that too.

I caught his sets that night and we talked during the two breaks and then afterwards. We were standing outside at one point right by my Thunderbird convertible. This really excited him and he said, "God, look at you! You're young, you're handsome, you got a great set of wheels . . . You're the king of the Earth!"

He made me a member of the Royal Court so I became "Prince Vaughn."

I brought some friends one night who had no idea who he was. Lord Buckley came over between sets to sit with us. It was very noisy and he was riffing away. I asked him if he he'd ever worked on Part Two of "The Nazz" because his version only goes up to a certain point and there's some rich stuff after that.

And he started running a little riff about the Nazz at the Last Supper. One of the lines concerned Jesus talking about a "finger-poppin' fink who's gonna sell me out three times before dawn."

And one of my friends at the table who wasn't keeping up with the conversation too well thought Lord Buckley was talking about him and he got up and split. I had to go get him and explain that Lord Buckley wasn't talking about him, he was talking about "The Nazz."

Lord Buckley seemed to be into a pantheistic vision at the time. "Everything is alive. Everything is beautiful. Everything is God. Everything is you."

The night in front of the Thunderbird he was talking about a trip he had made through the redwoods and how the forest was the "Great Cathedral of Man."

Two radio broadcasts documenting the doings at the Outside at the Inside in Palo Alto venue were recorded and have survived. It seems KPUP, a San Francisco station on the emerging FM band, sent roving reporter John Taylor around the Bay Area to scout out and present some of the odder cultural happenings in the environs for his program *Taylor at Large.* Along with Buckley, the half-hour broadcasts showcase a variety of talent at the club, including some cool jazz (the Morris Hubbard Trio), a torch singer

(Jean Arnold), and (paradoxically) a tap dancer (Tommy Conine)—except for Buckley, not exactly acts shown to their best advantage on radio.

Despite falling back on his less compelling material, Lord Buckley is briefly but effectively featured as the centerpiece to the shows dating from February 12, 1960 (exactly a year after his debut at the Ivar), and February 19, a week later. On the first outing Buckley chooses an odd pair to share: "His Majesty, The Pedestrian" and a solid send-up of hip Shakespeare, "To Swing or Not to Swing." The latter broadcast again finds Buckley in top form in the only preserved live portrayal of Joseph Newman's "Leviathan."

Concurrent with his Outside at the Inside job, Buckley was sandwiching in performances at the Coffee Gallery in San Francisco and the Gold Nugget, a hip dive in North Oakland. However, Buckley's appearances seem to have stirred up very little interest in the local press. The only apparent mention in the *San Francisco Chronicle* was in Ralph J. Gleason's January 10, 1960, roundup of upcoming events: ". . . Lord Buckley is giving a 'reading' tomorrow night at the Coffee Gallery . . ."

Lord Buckley

It's small, but they really listen. They understand and they follow what I am saying.

Photogapher Jim Marshall did the best job of documenting Buckley's Coffee Gallery gig, showing up at a couple of performances and snapping close to one hundred images that capture Buckley at his leonine peak. Standing up on the podium and amid a practically clichéd vision of a bohemian San Francisco café, a dressed-down Buckley displays the gamut of facial expressions and physical postures in a show that simply must have overpowered the tiny room.

Ken Kesey

I saw Lord Buckley at the Coffee Gallery in San Francisco not long before he died. He'd been in a fight and his arm was broken and in a cast. He kept making a lot of statements about it. He did "The Bad-Rapping of the Marquis de Sade" ("Just dropping by the rod and birch store"). Oh yeah, he was great.

Jerry Garcia

I didn't know him. I couldn't say that. But he was certainly a famous person when I was growing up.

For me he was this large mythical figure and I was lucky enough to actually have seen him perform before I knew who he was. And from there it was a matter of discovery: "Who is this guy?"

I saw him perform someplace in North Beach when I was about sixteen or seventeen, at the Coffee Gallery or someplace like that. It was hilariously funny. That may have been the first time I even heard of him. I had no idea who he was when I went to see him. And I loved him by the end of the show. You couldn't tell what race he was by looking at him. He could have been anybody. He looked like a generic Third Worlder. He could have been from any continent.

The way he did his show was very dramatic. It would start off like a regular stand-up routine but he had lights and the whole deal. I don't know if he had them cued. I was just caught up. He did those spooky things like "The Bad-Rapping of the Marquis de Sade" and it would get really dark. I love "God's Own Drunk." That's about my favorite and, of course, "The Nazz." That was his show-stopper.

It was like sitting around a campfire with a guy telling a story. It really turned into kind of a primal experience. A very powerful style with a lot of magic. Real magic. You can't act it. You have to think of yourself as "Lord Buckley." That's one of the things that made him really special. This wasn't a guy just doing shtick.

But after that I immediately started making connections with others who were into him. It was one of those things like when you discover gold—suddenly it's everywhere. After I'd seen him perform, more or less accidentally, all of a sudden everybody I ran into knew all this stuff about Lord Buckley and knew all of his routines. It was everywhere maybe because the records were widely circulated at that time. My friends and the guys in the Grateful Dead knew about Lord Buckley. Pigpen [the late vocalist and organist Ron McKernan], one of our early guys, used to do Lord Buckley routines. Phil [Grateful Dead bassist Phil Lesh] was really into Lord Buckley as well.

He provided an aspect to the sense of humor, a certain coloration and a kind of colorful use of language. He used language like a musician uses notes—that kind of riffing. Old hippie friends of mine used to call it riffing, really when you're talkin', you know, talkin' shit. It's something that's been around for a long time.

I see all this stuff in the folkloric vein 'cause that's one of my handles. Lord Buckley's routines had a little of that formalness you get in the rhyming recitations of prisoners, street rap stuff or playing the dozens. All of these things that are part of the black language experience. Like Joseph Campbell, the mytho-historian, Buckley was into putting the new clothes on the old horse.

It's all part of the same thing. At that time, I was starting to discover the richness and whole total experience of American music: black music, white music, country music, city music. So, for me, seeing Lord Buckley was just throwing another set of doors open. That's what I was looking for and that's what I was finding. If you put yourself on a path like that eventually you're going to find out what you're looking for. And Lord Buckley was part of that process of discovery. And for me it was just as exciting as everything else was.

Harry "The Hipster" Gibson

In the late fifties, me and Buckley are workin' up in Frisco, right? The "beatnik" era. I'm workin' at a big jazz club with the Modern Jazz Quartet. Every night after the jazz club, I go over to Buckley's gig.

Number one, it's after hours because after hours they don't sell booze in there. It's a coffeehouse—they're sellin' coffee. It's right on the sidewalk, the whole front was open so the tables are not only sittin' inside, half of 'em are comin' outside. You walked in through this big entranceway and there was Buckley in the back of the joint onstage in the middle of the floor, doin' his show.

Once Keenan Wynn rode up on his motorcycle from L.A. to see my show. Afterwards, I jump on his motorcycle, we shoot around, go down a couple of blocks and there's the joint right there. He jumps the curb—boop—up the curb and we drive *right into the club! Buckley's out on the middle of the floor talkin' and we drive right up on the floor, man!*

Buckley just continued as though nothing unusual had happened: "Oh 'The Hipster' just flew in! Who's that cat with you." I said, "That's the grass connection."

We're out there and we're doin' a wild show. "Hey man," I said, "Buckley, for the finale, let's get on the motorcycle and ride around on the floor?" Buckley says, "Yeah." He gets on the back, I get on the front and Keenan Wynn's in the middle. I said, "Go man!" Zings around the floor, comes around the entrance and zings right out there and right down to the beach . . . three guys on a motorcycle.

During its heyday in the late 1950s and early 1960s, the Gold Nugget in Oakland, California was one of the Bay Area's best-kept secrets. Started by Don Mupo and Bob Frohn, a pair of local jazz lovers who threw out the jukebox and started spinning hep discs from their own extensive collections, the L-shaped room catered to an unlikely but egalitarian assortment of patrons that included college kids, Ph.D.'s, cops, Beatniks, businessmen, night owls, and nefarious nocturnals.

The joint really jumped when a live-jazz policy was instituted on weekends. For the dollar cover charge, patrons could check out such greats as Dexter Gordon, Stan Getz, Zoot Sims, Shelly Manne, Joe Pass, Maynard Ferguson, Conte Candoli, and Stan Kenton up close and personal. Mupo and Frohn were also the first to hire Art Pepper after he was sprung from San Quentin.

Buckley had developed a strong local following, and it seems that practically all of them showed up at the Gold Nugget the night Don "Marquis de" Mupo taped the evening's late set at His Lordship's request, a recording that resulted in Buckley's *The Bad-Rapping of the Marquis de Sade* LP.

Mupo recalls that since the hangout had no stage, Buckley, usually dressed in khakis with an open shirt, would perform on a small platform comprised of eight beer bottle cases stacked two high. For his services, Buckley received seventy-five dollars a night, considered a nice piece of change in those days for a venue as small and off the beaten path as the Gold Nugget.

Though not of superior fidelity, the posthumous 1969 World Pacific LP is the culmination of a lifetime of work. The club ambience is intimate and Buckley is at his loosest, totally at one with his audience. He raps about his favorite subjects: history, literature, the outrageous, and social concerns, all the while philosophizing about religion and the nature of humor and humans. That woozy Buckley voice is omnipresent, sometimes singing, sometimes imitating musical instruments, sometimes stentorian, sometimes whispering, always seductive and stimulating.

The album is significant for both the inclusion of a new Buckley bit, "The Ballad of Dan McGroo" (Buckley's hipsemantic translation of the Robert W. Service poem, "The Shooting of Dan McGrew") and the *ultimate* performance of the title track. Also containing smart, definitive versions of "H-Bomb," "Chastity Belt," and "His Majesty, The Policeman," the album evokes Buckley's late-night tribe who are with him every mad mother step of the way. Even during a piece as deep, dark, and dense as "The Bad-Rapping of the Marquis de Sade," they respond with the spirited reverence of inured subterranean denizens.

"Dan McGroo" may well be the most overlooked chunk of officially released Lord Buckley. But like "The Bugbird" and "Swingin' Pied Piper," it is a long, rambling, paintstakingly detailed hipsemantic spin of a classic poem with lines that hook you immediately: "A bunch of the studs was swingin' it up at the old Red Dog Saloon. And a cat he was rockin' the eighty-eight and blowin' 'How High the Moon.'"

An interesting sidebar to the inclusion of "Dan McGroo" regards the surfacing of a strange black-and-white film clip of Buckley performing Service's poem in its original form possibly around this time. While the date, source, and purpose of the footage still seem unclear (it almost looks as if it were drawn from a longer film), its relatively elaborate production values suggest that someone with high aspirations for Buckley may have bankrolled the project as a kind of promotional clip. At least one source has indicated that Ed Sullivan may have been behind the project—allegedly as part of the first network show broadcast from Alaska. Though this seems a bit far-fetched, the set created for the recitation does a decent if B-movie job of re-creating a turn-of-the-century North Country saloon, complete with at least a dozen actors portraying card players, hard drinkers, a black piano player, and a couple of working girls, one of whom initiates a conversation with Buckley (dressed as a kind of western dandy under a bowler hat) that inspires the straight recitation of the Service epic as the room quiets in overdramatized, hushed awe.

Four additional cuts from the Gold Nugget surfaced in 1995 as part of the Dick Zalud collection. Included is a rare live version of "Nero," an unusual reading of "God's Own Drunk," another expert but truncated rendering of the difficult "Swingin' Pied Piper," and a never-otherwise-recorded or -documented curio, "Return of the Stranger."

Four more Gold Nugget pieces, apparently liberated from the United Artists archive sometime back in the 1970s, found their way into collectors' paws in 1999 and included equally stellar versions of "Gettysburg Address," "His Majesty, The Pedestrian," "Jonah and the Whale," and "Nero."

As these represent some of the last extant examples of Lord Buckley in performance, they once again underline the prevailing sentiment of what his friends and admirers still contend: that the man was on the top of his game as his end days drew nigh. Taken together, these reels provide a treasured glimpse of a twilight-year gig.

Lord Buckley

I should like to ask your opinion. I have a very provocative movement called "The Return of the Stranger" or "The Sacred Fix."

I asked a profound, charming friend of mine where he thought I should produce this play—it's in three acts—and he told me, in all sincerity: on a bulletproof theater boat beyond the twelve-mile limit. That's an amazing thing to say about a script that's immaculate. But this movement is heated with truth. And the only way we can figure out truth is with a little calculi: two mother times two . . . right? *If it was good enough for the Hip Einie it oughta be good enough for us.* So I want to do this for you in beauty—I want to do it in beauty and clarity and I want it to be please be understood that if any one of the listeners feel the lightest vibration of the *ne*-gate, please look high . . . *and I'll be waiting up there.*

Anticipating Lenny Bruce's scathing "Religion Inc." by at least a couple of years, "Return of the Stranger" casts the Second Coming in a corrupt phantasm of the middle future, which crests in a rare and wonderful Buckley punch line: "Jesus Christ! It's Jesus Christ!"

An energetic "Nero" follows, aided by the Gold Nugget crowd, who seem to spur His Lordship to rarely equaled performance heights as Buckley wails at a peak on par with his "Marquis de Sade" presentation. This rare live recording of the piece demonstrates it has matured in fluidity and power since its early-1950s vinyl release.

Switching gears, Buckley barrels through a rousing version of "God's Own Drunk," bookending the transcendent yarn with the hillbilly storyteller settling down in a country store next to a hot stove, all the while complaining about the proprietor's sharp-toothed canine—thus ironically juxtaposing the interspecies ecstasy portrayed in the soused story. This would seem to be the source of that bit of Buckley doggerel that spices several of his official and unofficial releases: "By God if I see that damn dog again, I'm going to drill 'im."/"Don't shoot him, Fred, he's a thoroughbred."

Rounding out the date is the most complete live version of "Swingin' Pied Piper"—further evidence that Buckley was enamored with this composition in the last years of his life.

The Zalud collection also revealed an undated reel-to-reel Ampex undoubtedly recorded around the same time—probably at a Sausalito gig with bassist Bill Loughborough adding some choice backing. With an unidentified bongo player intermittently and subtly covering the action, Buckley again plows familiar terrain with passionate renderings of "The Raven," a rare "My Own Railroad," another harrowing "Black Cross," a devastating "Murder," another unique casting of the flexible "Jonah and the Whale," and a rare presentation of "Gettysburg Address" done up passionate-style. Buckley, incidentally, can be heard ordering a Scotch between numbers—an indication that his commitment to sobriety—alcoholwise—was loosening.

Of the classic material presented here, "Jonah" is worthy of special note, as Buckley deftly weaves in an extended stanza from Joe Newman's whale-chasing "Leviathan" to complement the mammal-specific setting.

The jewel in the crown of this reel, however, is nearly a one-of-a-kind treatment of "Lucius," drawn from a chapter of Apuleius's *The Golden Ass,* one of the earliest novels of Western civilization, dating from Rome of second century a.d.

The tale of Lucius, or the Golden Ass, has been a favorite one for nearly two millennia, and its fame is near to that of the *Decameron* or *Don Quixote*. T. E. Lawrence carried it, in its original Latin, in his saddlebags with him all through the Arab Revolt, and it was Lawrence who first introduced the book to his friend Robert Graves, whose English-language translation stands on high. Lucius, a carefree and virile young man, goes to stay in a strange town and has an affair with his host's beautiful maidservant. His hostess is said to be a witch, and Lucius, overcome with fatal curiosity, watches her turn herself into a bird. Wishing to do the same, he rubs himself with the magic ointment, but to his horror he is transformed into an ass and stolen by thieves before he can get hold of the antidote: a rose. In his ass form he has a long series of adventures: comical, satirical, dangerous, amorous, and always entertaining. He is often beaten and ill treated and is several times in danger of being killed. To his embarrassment, a wealthy lady falls in love with him and proves to have greater appetites than even an ass. Finally, with the aid of a goddess or (depending on the translation) Isis, he succeeds in eating a wreath of roses and becomes human again.

Spliced from the chapter in which Lucius is transformed into the ass, Buckley's translation would, on the face of it, seem an unlikely choice for hipsemantic exploitation, primarily because of its relative obscurity when veiled against the more historically familiar bulk of his creative omniverse. The results are anything but arcane, however, as Buckley rises to a performance pinnacle, at one point verging on the frenetic tongue-speaking hallucinating Pentecostal snake-handling incantations common among various backwoods spiritualist sects.

The gothic Hansel and Gretel–like mood of the routine suits Buckley to a T, allowing him to employ his powerful, inarticulate vocalese to amazing heights of scat musicality and depth.

The Sausalito gig was also captured for visual posterity by Charles Campbell, who snapped about a dozen grainy but energetic photos that find Buckley donning his gaucho apparel for the evening and commandeering center stage of the dingy basement as if it were the bully pulpit of his favorite parish.

A final unreleased recording from this period finds Buckley reuniting with Turk Murphy and his house band in a San Francisco studio for an unusual and strangely compelling Dixieland-style accompaniment to superior versions of "The Shooting of Dan McGroo" and "The Hip Gahn." One of the participants, tuba player Al Conger, contributed a reading of the Service epic in its original form at the end of the reel, augmenting Buckley's swinging version rather nicely.

Buckley's friendship with poet, publisher, and City Lights bookstore owner, Lawrence Ferlinghetti, turned into a business relationship—a union resulting in a legendary underground artifact: *Hiparama of the Classics*.

The City Lights–published book contained seven somewhat crude and sometimes truncated transcriptions from Buckley's library: "The Hip Gahn," "The Nazz,"

"Gettysburg Address," "Hipsters, Flipsters and Finger-Poppin' Daddies," "Nero," "The Gasser," and "The Bad-Rapping of the Marquis de Sade." Graced with a fiery Jim Marshall cover photo of Buckley (the first published photo by the man who would go on to define jazz, rock, and folk photography) with his arm in a cast, *Hiparama of the Classics* included a decent, if incomplete, discography and a reprint of Dan James's *Way Out Humor* liner notes. A second printing included an informed introduction by Joseph Jablonski in which Buckley is cast as a surrealist of the highest order. During the 1970s and early 1980s, when Buckley's recorded works were hard to come by, this book served as one of the few sources of information about the man, the myth, and his work.

When the chapbook was reprinted in the early 1980s, noted reviewer Christopher Lehmann-Haupt of the *New York Times* chose to note its publication with the following review from the paper's November 28, 1983, edition:

Richard (Lord) Buckley, the bop comedian who got his start in Chicago speakeasies during the 1920s, became famous in the 1960s and is said to have influenced Lenny Bruce. It's not easy to convey Mr. Buckley's peculiar appeal to anyone who hasn't heard him live or recorded, but with this little volume in hand, fans can finally figure out what he was saying in some of his manic passages.

Lewis Foremaster remembers the incidents leading up to Buckley's broken arm.

Lewis Foremaster

Sometimes he smoked a lot of pot before he went on stage. He didn't drink because he was AA but when he did drink he was scary.

One time in Las Vegas, we were at the Sands in Las Vegas and Dean Martin was paying homage to him when Lord Buckley noticed Tony Curtis gambling at one of the tables. He sent me over to borrow fifty dollars. But Curtis refused and Lord Buckley stormed over to the pit and threw a silver dollar at Curtis, prompting the security guards to throw us out on our butts.

We went over to a joint known as the Nevada Club where Lord Buckley attempted to take over the show by doing one of his famous jumping-over-the-stage bits. But a guy grabbed his leg and Lord Buckley fell over and broke his arm.

A still-unresolved and far more underground and suspect Buckley publishing venture involves an item that turned up in the Main Branch of the New York Public Library. The book, *Pot: How to Plant, Cultivate, Harvest, Cure, Prepare . . . Enjoy,* appears to be one of the earliest published lessons in the tender loving care and nurturing of *Cannabis sativa*—certainly a subject near and dear to His Lordship's heart. Consistent with the possibility of Buckley's authorship is that the title is listed under the name "Richard M. Buckley 1906–(1960)" in the Library of Congress card catalogue. The book, according to that information, is 196 pages long with 20 pages of illustrations. More significantly, both the card and the back cover of the book describe it as "A Lord Buckley Publication."

The mystery deepens, however, because the covers of the book are all that remain in the library's celebrated stacks. The pages were literally ripped from the spine. A stamp on the inside covers indicates the library noted the "mutilation" on December 2, 1974. What seems to give the evidence away as a tongue-in-cheek ruse or front for an expert on the subject who, intelligently, wished to remain anonymous is that both the cover art and utilized typefaces have a distinct late-1960s/early-1970s "mod" sensibility.

There is some indication that Buckley was a master marijuana cultivator. Guests of the Royal Court at The Castle in Whitley Terrace several years earlier recall Buckley giving them a grand tour of the grounds, which included a stop at his pot patch in the backyard. More incredibly, there is other reliable suggestion that Dick Buckley was putting his green thumb to good use during his Chicago days in the late 1930s.

Lady Buckley returned to Detroit with the children for a period in early 1960 to attend to matters following her father's death. During this period Lord Buckley and Prince Lewis became a familiar sight around the Sausalito houseboat community, where they befriended a scruffy circle of sympathetic souls.

One of those Buckley encountered in Sausalito was a sound engineer named Sandy Jacobs. When the balance of the Royal Family returned from Michigan, Buckley brought young Richard Jr. into Jacobs's makeshift houseboat studio and laid down "Baa Baa Blacksheep." The sketch is the allegorical tale of a large family of sheep, one pink (the mother), one blue (the father), nine white, and one black. The black sheep is scoffed at until the day he helps out a small boy and girl in trouble by giving them not one, but three pounds of wool ("he turned out to be whiter than the rest of them," says Buckley). In the story the title song is sung by Richard Jr., adding a spritely air of innocence to the outing.

On July 3, 1960, His Lordship made a sojourn with young Richard to a pre-Independence Day party at the San Francisco home of Charles Campbell. Easily coaxed by his host into performing for his skeptical guests and an open-minded reel-to-reel tape recorder, Buckley soon won them over with some audience-participatory vocal antics (the hippest "Hip-Hip Hooray" this side of the Fargoneisphere) and cute collaborations with his son on several of the warm-up presentations: the aforementioned "Baa Baa Blacksheep," "Sheepherder" (a ribald parable with allusions of bestiality), and "Myrtle the Turtle," the vaudevillian dud he clung to in performance.

Suitably prepared, Lord Buckley then launched into a surprising and strong rendition of "The Bad-Rapping of the Marquis de Sade" before winding down with his populist ode, "His Majesty, The Pedestrian."

Charles Campbell

I once gave a party that Buckley performed at. He wanted to do the party so I invited about twenty-five friends. It was not a big house and it got pretty crowded. Most of them knew of him if they hadn't actually seen him. One guy was a very prissy cat. I told him to just come over without any preconceptions and he loved it—he was in hysterics. Buckley did "The Bad-Rapping of the Marquis de Sade" and variations of his other material that was never recorded on disc.

Lord Buckley

The problem of humanity, of progress, is to be beautiful, to be more gracious, more sweet, more divine. And, when you balance yourself, the international truth that the world is a family—love will hit you. And love is swinging.

17 cosmic tour

Lord Buckley

A hip good-bye is to all the solid Cats and Kitties that swing this precious cherry-land of America: may you always put it down solid and in great truth and in great beauty. And it is the prayer of the hipsters that the hip gangs, the Cobras and all the gangs: quit squarin' up and get hip, which means to be wise and make the people that love them, proud of them.

According to subterranean myth, Lord Buckley set off with his aide-de-camp Prince Lewis Foremaster during late July or early August of 1960 in the Fairyland Express (in this incarnation, a red Volkswagen microbus) on what he dubbed his "Cosmic Tour." Contrary to that popular Buckley legend, the Cosmic Tour was not quite the cross-country whistle-stop escapade often recounted. Prince Lewis did, in fact, drive across the continent, but he met and picked up Lord Buckley in Cincinnati, Ohio, where the maestro, who had flown in from the coast, performed a gig at a forgotten jazz club.

Next stop was Chicago, where an extended decampment included the legendary "Seacoast of Bohemia" gig with Del Close and Severn Darden (members of the newly formed Second City troupe), an interview with a curious Studs Terkel, and an extended, *very* late-night, pass-the-hat type engagement at the famed Gate of Horn nightclub.

A high-quality tape documenting about half an hour of one of Buckley's Second City sets was preserved by Lew Foremaster. As nice a slice of very late-period Lord Buckley as there is, the reel includes the only full version of "Lucius" and a wonderfully bizarre audience-participation bit in which the Lord simulates the sounds of sexual ecstasy and proceeds to get nearly everyone in attendance to then join him in what he calls "moaning in pleasure." As a yogic exercise or a kind of hipster's primal scream therapy, Buckley achieves the desired effect in at least making the crowd totally sympathetic to his powers.

Lord Buckley

I found out a peculiar thing: if it's alright to moan in pain, it's legitimate to moan in pleasure. So if you feel good, you can moan. But it sounds so wild because it's a mystic sound.

Del Close

The night he was to arrive a whole bunch of people waited for him in the Second City beer garden where the methedrine ampules crunched like cicada shells underfoot. And so, when the Fairyland Express pulled up, I had like a line of twenty people all kneeling as His Royal Highness stepped out of the van and walked into the beer garden. It was literally a triumphant entrance into Chicago, with people calling him "Your Royal Highness" right and left.

He picked up a whole bunch of old friends later on from his days in Chicago back in the thirties and forties. A lot of them turned up—certainly a gang of them turned up at "Seacoast of Bohemia."

"Seacoast of Bohemia" was a bill consisting of me, Severn Darden and Lord Buckley. It was three stand-up acts: two shows. It was not a three-way collaboration by any stretch of the imagination. And since I was supposedly the closest to reality, the least far-out of the three, I would open. Then Severn would do his lecture on metaphysics, a short talk on the universe. And then Buckley would do whatever he wanted to do. And then we were to do it again.

"Seacoast of Bohemia" is a setting from the Shakespeare play *A Winter's Tale*. It also includes the stage direction: "exit—pursuit by a bear," which I believe was the title of the other show playing at Second City at the time. So we picked up another quote from the same Shakespearean play and called it "Seacoast of Bohemia." It was the perfect Second City generic show title, which has been continued through the years all the way down to the present time. See, there is no Seacoast of Bohemia—it's landlocked.

This was the first Monday night show Second City had ever done. This was in August of 1960 around the time that Severn and I and like thirty beatniks infiltrated the Republican National Convention to mount a demonstration for Stevenson. We wanted the Independent Republicans to draft Stevenson. We got on national television for about a minute and a half and eight years later, of course, was the Democratic Convention in which we would have gotten killed for doing what we did.

Anyway we did the show and we had very serious difficulty in getting Buckley off the stage. Like he did his "Amos 'n' Andy" routine where he'd take people up on stage and he had like a Chicago alderman and a black hooker doing this love scene, with him providing the dialogue. He was killing 'em—everybody loved him but we couldn't get him off the stage. We were supposed to do the show again—that was the thing he just couldn't get through his head. We'd turn the lights on and off. Finally I walked out and literally dragged him off.

But then we finally managed to do the show again and we just let him stay on as long as he wanted.

He was doing all the great stuff but he couldn't remember "My Own Railroad," which was one of the things we all loved from the record.

Alan Ribback came to the show and he fell in love with Buckley and he booked Buckley into the Gate of Horn where he played until he went to work in New York at the Jazz Gallery. And he played the late show at the Gate of Horn every night for a while. He wasn't like the main attraction. It was like ". . . and Lord Buckley." But there again he began to wear people out—he'd start to wear out his welcome but not before he generated a huge mass of tape.

Buckley was staying at an apartment house behind Second City that had many, many cockroaches in it. The walls were crawling with them. And I remember that Barbara Harris and I went up one time to buy some pot from Prince Lewis. Both Barbara and I were sitting in the kitchen with Lewis and Buckley getting off on the pot. The conversation was always very formal around Buckley, at least for us because we liked playing the game.

Barbara said, "Prince Lewis, it appears that you have many cockroaches."

Prince Lewis says, "Yes, many insects inhabit this place, Lady Barbara."

Buckley would sometimes turn up at our door and hoot. He'd make that train sound he did on various routines. Instead of knocking, we'd hear this "Hoot!" And we'd say, "Ah, His Royal Highness just wants to bum some marijuana."

There were various weird things that happened. Like I remember we went down to this fraternity house on the South Side. This was in the early days of the black consciousness movement or whatever you want to call that and there were a bunch of black students that had dressed up in African garb and had done this tribal dance. Buckley had insisted that I arrange a concert for him there. And I demurred, saying "No, they don't want you, Your Highness. They really don't."

But he prevailed and we went to this fraternity house. On the way over there Prince Lewis couldn't find the place and kept turning down the wrong street. Prince Lewis said, "I apologize, Your Royal Highness, but we seem to be on the wrong street."

"Nonsense! Every street is a beautiful street. Drive on!"

When we got there and it was time for him to go on he started in but he began by doing the "Amos 'n' Andy" routine with all these black students around who just fucking didn't want to hear it. I forget exactly how it ended but it came close to physical violence.

I guess you could make an argument that he had a thirties liberal attitude toward blacks that didn't play too well even in the early sixties.

In retrospect people claim to have seen his death coming: that he was behaving in such an unpredictable way with bursts of irrationality and anger. For instance, one time he hit Severn out of the blue for no reason. Severn claimed that anybody who hits him dies. Apparently he'd been hit by people that died and Buckley was one of them.

Severn Darden

I knew Buckley through Del Close. Buckley was in Chicago to do a Gate of Horn job. He came over to Second City one night and he and Del and I each did a single show twice during the evening. It was possibly the most successful evening I've been involved in the theater either to watch or to perform in.

It was simply the three of us doing our separate acts which were quite different and the audience just went crazy. It was just that that particular combination of three people somehow worked.

It was the most remarkable evening I've ever seen happen in the theater. The audience cheered and laughed throughout all of it. And afterward, they wouldn't leave, but sat around basking in the glow of what had happened. At the end of the second show there were still people left over from the first show standing out in the street talking about it.

Buckley was an amazing performer and he was wonderful that night. He was an extremely bright and sweet man, with extraordinary powers. For the month or so he was in Chicago he was always hanging out with, I mean, some real strange low-life types. Perhaps they were cronies from the old days. I mean hookers and like that. And he was drinking quite a lot. Still, he could manage to turn around and go out to dinner with me and my parents, who were *very* conservative and southern, and totally and utterly charm them. He had impeccable table manners.

I must say that he was capable of meanness too. But it really wasn't his fault. I think he'd recently suffered a mild stroke, and sometimes he completely lost control of what he was doing and became violent.

Lord Buckley and I got into a fight once. In a few minutes he became like a hated enemy. We were hanging out with this woman who worked for Second City. She only weighed seventy or eighty pounds and he started twisting her arm and hurting her. So I started twisting his and one thing led to another, words were exchanged and he hit me.

I heard him one night very late at the Gate of Horn and he was onto something I had never heard before. It was his piece "The Bad-Rapping of the Marquis de Sade" and he scared the bejesus out of the audience. There wasn't a single laugh.

Lewis Foremaster

I remember that he had a minor stroke on stage at the Gate of Horn in Chicago. He just kind of blacked out for a moment. It takes so much energy to do the monologues. There was also some tension with the Black Panthers after the Studs Terkel radio show. They didn't like the way he was doing the black stuff.

Located on Clark and Dearborn in Chicago's Near North Side, the Gate of Horn was a hot cave, euphemistically labeled a nightclub, with all the charm of a Montmartre dive. There, his regal features bathed in the bright yellow glare of the spotlight, Lord Buckley held court nightly for anywhere from half an hour to well over three hours, all the time hiking back and forth across the stage, talking, smoking, sipping, talking, lighting cigarette after cigarette, puffing, talking, using the floor as a giant ashtray, dropping still-lit cigarettes here, there, everywhere, talking, talking, talking, talking.

Del Close

He used to bring that microbus right in front of the Gate of Horn and park in an illegal parking zone for which he strangely never got a ticket. And he would hold court right in that bus if the Gate was too crowded and you'd be expected to pay homage.

It is with prophetic irony that one of Buckley's last gigs would be at a club named for a signpost drawn from Greek mythology. The Gate of Horn of legend was, after all, the portal in the Underworld through which true dreams came to men from the cave of Hypnos, the god of sleep, and stood in opposition to the Gate of Ivory, through which deceitful dreams came to men. Together, the Gates of Horn and Ivory formed the Gate of Dreams and can be seen as an early Western conceptualization of heaven and hell. Hypnos lived in the Underworld and never set eyes on the sun. At night, however, he changed into a bird and brought sweet rest to mortals. That he was the father of Morpheus who brought dreams to humans and of whom Buckley wove one of his more fancifully obscure tales further feeds into the Joseph Campbell–esque notion that Buckley's "hero's journey" was the real deal.

Judy Collins

In the summer of 1960 folk songstress Judy Collins ventured to Chicago for an engagement at the Gate of Horn. There she encountered Lord Buckley in the midst of his Cosmic Tour. The following is excerpted from an April 1970 article she penned for McCall's *magazine.*

In 1960, we drove across the Great Plains from Denver in our funky little English Anglia and moved into a huge apartment on the South Side of the Windy City, near Hyde Park. One block north was Forty-seventh Street, an immense arm of the black ghetto, and one block south, the slightly liberalized and integrated community of the University of Chicago.

I was hired to sing at the Gate of Horn because of a tape I made which included a song called "The Great Silkie of Shule Skerry." I sent the tape to Alan Ribback, the owner. He liked it and hired me to come and sing. And there I was, dressed in my nicest, with my guitar around my neck and my leg in a cast up to my waist. I had broken it skiing in the mountains the past winter. I sang, and after that first night the cast was forgotten by all except one reviewer who commented about the second act at the Gate of Horn: "a girl who hails from Aspen (which I don't: I guess he thought that was the only place they have snow in the West) and has a cast to prove it."

The Gate of Horn was eulogized years ago by Shel Silverstein, on the liner notes of an album that Bob Gibson and Hamilton Camp made there. Shel really captured the feeling of that place. The bar was separate from the clubroom. There I always found someone to talk to, to sip a drink with, to share the long night between the performances. Bob Gibson was there, leading this vague, disconnected life of love and music, and when he sang he was magic, and when he and Hamilton Camp sang together, double magic, too. Hamilton Camp and I would sit in the bar and sing old Irish songs, the sweet harmonies, our voices wafting out into the street at the corner of Dearborn and Chicago. There is nothing there now but the old Rice Hotel. People from the Second City company were friendly with the Gate of Horn crowd, and Severn Darden, the actor, was around some nights with his dark suits and tennis shoes, benignly making the rounds of the full bar.

Alan Ribback was sailing his boat on Lake Michigan one afternoon, and ran into another boat with some friendly people on it. They started talking and before long, Alan discovered that Lord Buckley was among them. Alan asked him to work at the club. And soon, after Gibson and Camp and I had done our singing and the evening was waning into the easiness of the Chicago nights, Lord Buckley would do the late last show. Most of us around the club would huddle with a beer or Pernod and water in the dark recesses of the clubroom and go on Lord Buckley's charted trips. He was a teller of allegories—a white man who spoke in the idiom and slang of black jazz musicians. His stories were full of beauty and soul and humanity. We became drunk on the visions of this dreamlike and tragic man who was called a comedian by some people in those days. Lord Buckley would come in at night, dressed in an old beautiful suit, a fresh flower in his lapel, gracious to all, with hugs, with deep laughs and strange sighs, always gentle, always uneven in the rambling levels of his midnight confrontation with demons and saints. He was vulnerable to near perfection. A quiet legend even before his time was over, he died of starvation and thoughtlessness during the attempt by the city police of New York to prevent people without cabaret cards from making a living, from working at the only thing they knew how to do. This brutality of spirit, inherent in red tape and in the affairs of the state, was the very thing he could not cope with. It is the antithesis of love. And Lord Buckley's life was full of love.

Francis Newton

Francis Newton is a British writer. His witness here first appeared in the December 31, 1960, edition of the New Statesman *and later in the liner notes of* The Parabolic REVELATIONS of the Late Lord Buckley *under the title "Death of a Peer."*

When I saw him he came on at the Gate of Horn, Chicago, at 2:30 A.M. to a public of artists and night people; for at this time even the habitual cabaret audience is elsewhere. He looked like a colonel cashiered from the Indian army in 1930, or rather like somebody imitating one: spruce, elderly, smoothly attired (no other word will do) in evening dress and vaguely unconvincingly; oozing a bonhomie which was not wholly false and a cynicism which was not true. He began in the age-old style of the cabaret ham, plummy and hoarse, the eye magnetic, the smile fixed. And then suddenly, within a sentence or two, we were in a wholly different world of controlled satirical growls, imitation trombone phrases and the mock simple baroque of Negro hip talk interspersed with attacks on the H-bomb, little nonsense songs and dreamlike surrealist conversations. Then back to the hip talk versions of the miracles of Christ and the Marquis de Sade.

Rex Benson

Actor Rex Benson was working in public relations when he became Buckley's last manager du jour during His Lordship's 1960 Gate of Horn run.

The first time I met Lord Buckley I was hired to do publicity for Frank Sinatra, Dean Martin, Joey Bishop, and Sammy Davis Jr.—the clan—who were coming in to Chicago for a special NAACP show at Comiskey Park, the home of the Chicago White Sox. And Lord Buckley was in the audience.

The show was set up in the center of the field and I was standing near him and heard him making comments, remarks, and being a smart-ass. And he had everybody laughing around him.

I asked, "Who are you?"

He says, "I'm Dick Buckley."

And his aide Lewis Foremaster started telling me about him and that he was working at the Gate of Horn.

I first saw him appear at the Gate of Horn and he was working after the regular show was done at like one o'clock in the morning. He was brilliant that night—a complete revolution from a performer's point of view. For the times, his use of the language—the vernacular—was extraordinarily radical in a nightclub . . . even by 1960.

The hippie flippers in the crowd were the results of the people from Bughouse Square, a park in Chicago where people used to get up on soapboxes on the weekends and just rattle off their feelings about things.

And he would pass the hat—he didn't make much money. He ended up making twenty bucks a night and that was barely enough to feed them. They were living in a flophouse apartment that somebody let them use.

After the show we went out for coffee and I asked him what he was doing in Chicago. He said he was just passing through looking for money. I said, "What do you mean?" He said, "I'm looking for friends to borrow money from." He was a shameless beggar.

Steve Ben Israel

I think about the fact that Lord Buckley was playing in Chicago at like one o'clock in the morning. Huh?! Somebody that fantastic. Somebody so great—probably him and Chaplin in the twentieth century, Buster Keaton and maybe a couple of others—with that level of humanity and compassion. This guy is like *the cat* blowin' on the *planet!* There's revolutionaries in Guatemala, there's Martin Luther King, there's all these great people coming up in the fifties, and the Beats, Murray Bookchin writing the first book that mentions ecology, and there's all this stuff coming up. And the guy who's culturally speaking for all these people, synthesizing all the things he had learned about black America, jazz, and the theater enacting the collective impulses of the time at the highest level . . . and he's passing the hat at one o'clock in the morning in 1960?

The Gate of Horn engagement proved momentous in an improbable area. Denis Mitchell, a British film documentarian, was in town with his BBC crew at the time shooting *Chicago: First Impressions of a Great American City*. The progressive noir verité was eventually broadcast on British television, produced in its final cut as a kind of midnight-to-midnight "day in the life" of Chi Town.

With Studs Terkel acting as Virgil to his Dante as he stepped into Chicago's nether realms, Mitchell and his crew happened onto Buckley's act when they were shooting some of the city's after-hours nightlife, and a clip of His Lordship performing the peak moment of "The Nazz" is featured early in the reel. As such, it represents the only known moving and sound image of Buckley doing what he is most famous for.

For students of Buckley who never saw the man but imagined how he presented himself on stage, the extant thirty-six seconds of footage used in the film confirm everything about his performance that emanates from vinyl, magnetic tape, or encoded disc. Indeed, it is all one could fantasize about and more. Dressed in his nifty gray tweeds, replete with the de rigueur carnation on his lapel and cigarette in hand, Lord Buckley struts his stuff with the calculated grace and persuasion of a ronin. Each motion and verbal nuance carries with it the experiential weight of nearly forty years under the spotlight. His eyes burn with the passion of a man on a mission as dancer and dance become one and "DIG INFINITY!!"

Mitchell died in the early 1990s but his widow and collaborator, Linda Mitchell, confirms that though she remembers all of Buckley's set being filmed that night, it has long since been swept from the cutting-room floor.

Buckley's Gate of Horn gig made a big splash in the local press, garnering at least a half-dozen supportive notices. The Saturday August 27, 1960, edition of the *Chicago Daily News* ran a photo of a bow-tied, tweedy Lord Buckley under a Bavarian chapeau with the following PR:

"His Royal Highness" Lord Buckley, "King of the San Francisco Renaissance," is being introduced at a special show at 1 a.m. nightly and at 2:30 a.m. Fridays and Saturdays in the Gate of Horn.

The next day the *Chicago Tribune* ran a more lengthy review:

That old saw, "If you can't convince 'em, confuse 'em," readily applies to the performance Lord Richard Buckley presents once each night in Alan Ribback's Gate of Horn, Chicago Avenue and Dearborn Street.

This Lord Buckley is the same Dick Buckley whose comedy eccentricities amazed—and delighted—Chicago's informal cafegoers of many years ago.

In those early, hectic and exciting nights of Buckley's theatrical career, he worked without script, or formula . . . excepting for a favored sketch in which he voiced all characters of the Amos 'n' Andy show in which volunteers from the audience acted the roles.

Now, in his once-a-night show in the Gate of Horn, he is amply prepared with a large collection of original characterizations, which include poetry, dramatics, surprising comedy lines, and hip stuff. Among the many sketches are "Mother India," "Cleopatra," "Jonah and the Whale," "Pedestrian," "Pied Piper," "Millionaire," and "God's Own Drunk." All these we saw and enjoyed—and he has a lot of other comedy-drama-hip stuff he hasn't unpacked.

Over at the *Chicago Sun-Times* that same day Gabriel Favoino devoted his entire column to the Gate of Horn doings:

HIPSTERS AND FLIPSTERS

Every business, every trade has its own special language.

And because of its constant use in entertainment, the trade jargon most familiar to laymen is probably the hippy argot of the music business. To most of us now, square is more than just a geometric figure, to pick the most obvious example.

As with all trade jargon, the language of the hip is the product of unique conditions existing in the business.

Trade jargon is a device used to divide the knowing from the unknowing, and it seems from a certain pride of vocation.

So the construction men have their "cats" (caterpillar tractors), the power men their "hot lines" (high tension wires) and the railroad men their "high balls" (fast freights).

Inevitably, a cat had to come down the pike and do his whole act in hip.

Such a one is Lord Richard Buckley, farthest out of the way out comedians and forerunner of them all. Buckley returned to Chicago this week after a 20-year absence and is currently appearing at the Gate of Horn.

The veteran comic does one show nightly at 1 a.m., for the delectation of "hippies" and those who wish to give that appearance.

At times a little obscure, Buckley does hit the mark when he jazzes up Shakespeare.

His version of Mark Antony's speech from "Julius Caesar," begins, "Hipsters, flipsters, and finger-poppin' daddies, knock me your lobes" (Friends, Romans, countrymen, lend me your ears).

And, "To be or not to be," becomes "To swing or not swing."

The humor of this brand of Shakespeare of course stems from the actual contrast between the dignity of the original and the flippancy of the hip derivative.

For those who want to dig, Buckley has a World Pacific album on the market entitled, "Way Out Humor." Now in orbit.

Two weeks later, *Chicago Sun-Times* columnist Irv Kupcinet reported that "'Lord' Richard Buckley, the sharp-tongued comic at the Gate of Horn, joins the Marty Faye show (Channel 7) once a week. He'll try to do for Faye what Alexander King does for Jack Paar."

Rex Benson

I called Marty Faye who had a nightly television show and told him about Lord Buckley's hip version of the news. Marty was interested and we met him the next day. Buckley gave him a little extemporaneous example of his bit. Marty told us that although they didn't have a big budget, he could hire Buckley three nights a week for the next few weeks. Buckley agreed. So that was $150 a week which took him off the nut.

Buckley said to me, "You're a fox! Prince Fox!" And that became my nickname in the Royal Court. Later I also acquired the name Prince Squirrel because I was able to get things done quickly.

On the Marty Faye show, the regular newscaster would deliver the news and then Buckley would follow up with five minutes of his version of that same news.

While in Chicago, Buckley and Lewis added another member to their mobile Royal Court. Ann Brooks, an itinerant stripper in her late thirties, was promptly dubbed Lady Bunny, though Buckley was also fond of calling her Peter Pan because of her closely cropped blond hair and spritely manner. Lady Bunny had been on the road since her teens, when she ran away with a circus and became an acrobat. The circus was a hard-traveling affair that, at one point, landed her in Batista's infamously decadent Havana. Lord Buckley taught Bunny many of his monologues, which she continued to share with whomever she could, including her daughter, Bambi, until her passing in the mid-1970s at about age fifty.

Ann Brooks

I went into single stripping and I was a little brought down. I wasn't too turned on. I was just making money but I wasn't too happy with it.

One time after the show, I went into the Corner House, a pancake house on Rush Street. Everybody went there at the time. I was sitting there alone, having a very solitary blue breakfast about at six o'clock in the morning with the stage makeup still on, of course. It was kind of a mark of honor to walk in with your stage makeup on. You just didn't bother taking it off.

I slowly became aware of a fantastic conversation going on in the booth behind me so I turned around and said, "I sure would like to join your party."

It was Lord Buckley and Prince Lewis. Prince Lewis had been Lord Buckley's faithful retainer for about two years at that point. He had sold his trailer camp and insurance policies to become a member of the Royal Court. I think he was in his early twenties—the rest of us were a little older.

After a while Lord Buckley said, "Prince Lewis, kiss that lady's feet."

And Prince Lewis got on his hands and knees and said, "Yes your Grace," and proceeded to lick my feet in the restaurant. I was completely turned on. I stayed with him from the time I met him until the time he died. I never left his side.

So, at that moment, I became a member of the Royal Court with the titled name of Lady Bunny at first until he changed it later to Peter Pan. But it was just Lady Bunny in the beginning. Once in a while he'd call me "The General."

I wasn't quite an aide-de-camp. He gave me all the monologues whereas Prince Lewis was an aide-de-camp. He was there to lick feet, kiss hands, and do anything Lord Buckley asked him to. Obviously an authority seeker. Boy, did he need somebody to push him around. You could ride on his back like a horse and he'd "nay."

Lord Buckley didn't care how many people used his material. He figured the more people who used his material the more people would get the message that he was trying to put down as the Hip Messiah.

One of Lord Buckley's homilies was "Action is the timing of love." If he were to ask me or anybody else that was present at the time to do something it was an automatic thing to jump and say, "Yes, your Grace." There was no waiting or hesitating because it didn't show any love if one dawdled.

Buckley, Lewis, and Bunny were holed up at the Hotel Maryland, one of the more popular hideaways for the theatrical crowd, a well-known skyscraper nestled deep in the heart of Chicago's glittering and garish Near North Side.

Rex Benson

He invited me up to see his cockroach haven. When I saw that I flipped. On the side of the refrigerator were probably 2,000 baby cockroaches just crawling everywhere while their parents were out courting. To him it was just a place to live. "They keep us warm," he said. That was pretty typical of his attitude.

I saw this vulnerable situation. It was just very distasteful and disgraceful. I had a room at the Maryland Hotel which had been given to me in exchange for some advertising I was able to arrange. So I told Buckley, "Shake out all your clothes. Shake all the cockroaches out of your suitcase. Tomorrow we're moving you into the Maryland Hotel." And that's where they lived for the next six or seven weeks—free.

Ironically, the most comprehensive and revealing printed documentation of Buckley's visit to Chicago appeared posthumously in *Fling Festival,* a little-known and mostly forgotten risqué rag reminiscent of a low-rent *Ramparts* or *Evergreen Review.* The six-page article ("The Lord Was a Swinger: Fling Records the Last Days of Lord Buckley—Hippest of the Hip!" by Bob Ellison) displays ten of the most madcap photos of Buckley ever snapped, including several of a liberally lathered Lordship mugging in the bath-tub. Another features Buckley, legs akimbo like some Eastern swami clad only in a pair of briefs garnished with hearts inscribed, "My heart pants for you," about to suck on a suspiciously thick "cigarette." One photo shows Buckley displaying a very moderne wire sculpture over his head, while still another pose has him crouching and waving, pith helmet in hand, at the feet of a lion statue outside Chicago's Art Institute.

Indeed, the described proceedings in Buckley's hotel room have a poorly disguised stoned ambience as Ellison chills with Buckley, Prince Lewis, Lady Bunny, and Ted Travers—an old friend of the comedian's from his days as Dick Buckley a generation earlier. At one point Lady Bunny decides to change, stripping bare, then staying that way.

The bulk of the piece is devoted to a Q&A session in which Buckley is freely quoted (and probably misquoted) on an array of subjects.

On heaven: "Thank God everything's legal in Heaven. Errol Flynn—a really *beautiful* man—is up there, you know, and he's flippin'. He wouldn't leave Heaven for no amount of money, cuz he's got 422 fourteen-year-old angels all his own. And they're really swingin'."

On a recent misadventure with Prince Lewis: "We were on our way to California and we happened to pass a graveyard near Vegas. Well, I began wondering philosophically why all this beauty was lying in a graveyard. Such *beautiful* statues. No one there loves them. No one to look at them but the worms. So the prince and I borrowed a hoist truck. Together we resurrected a truly beautiful angel. It's in my living room in California now. I don't consider that thievery. I consider that intelligent action put down against antedated ideas. After all, those *beautiful* statues get lonesome out there."

On celibacy: "It is very fine and very good in a way, but it's also a selfish thing because you refuse to get in with the people and celebrate with them and do the things that a normal human does."

On polygamy: "I approve of the Mormons. My aide is a Mormon. His great-great-grandfather had 122 wives. And I wish I were his great-great-grandfather."

In early August, Buckley was invited to visit the studios of WFMT by Studs Terkel to participate in his famous *Wax Museum* radio show. The resulting session, similar to Buckley's Pacifica radio appearance a year earlier, differs primarily in host Terkel's ability to not only keep up with his guest but augment his presentations as well.

Along with relaxed, if truncated, recitations of "Hipsters, Flipsters and Finger-Poppin' Daddies," "The Bugbird," and "Swingin' Pied Piper," Buckley was equally effective with particularly hot versions of his "His Majesty, The Pedestrian" and "His Majesty, The Policeman," all the while earnestly bending Terkel's ear with a volley of philosophical musings and meanderings.

Studs Terkel

His approach was remarkable. His complete mastery of hip. People thought he was black. At the Gate of Horn I got a kick out of those young, heavy-lidded hipsters who thought they were "It." They saw this gray-haired, distinguished-looking guy with a well-trimmed and manicured mustache looking like Dean Acheson with his elegant air, addressing all the "Lords and Ladies" in the audience and suddenly going into the hip. That threw them for a loop—they didn't know what hit them.

Lord Buckley

I have the greatest appreciation for this audience and for any of the millions of audiences in my hundred thousand years in the business that I've worked to.

I know it's very difficult when you're in your High Temple of Happiness to give complete concentration to new material. I appreciate that point. I would like to do one more structure for you but I will not do it in the face of the froth of your verbal diarrhea. There are many things to wade through and some of them are very difficult. But verbal diarrhea is a monstrous stream to broach.

18 the hip messiah

Lord Buckley

It has been a most precious pleasure to have temporarily strolled in the garden of your affection.

Partly on the strength of his Gate of Horn reception, partly based on the "vance grapevine," and partly due to a few not-so-secret admirers, Buckley was able to secure a monthlong gig at the Jazz Gallery, a new club on 80 St. Mark's Place in New York City's East Village once aptly described as "a cold, concrete cave that could be an abandoned subway station." This was to be His Lordship's first nightclub presentation in New York in more than a decade, and the city was primed for him. And Buckley was priming his wallet for the gig's greenbacks, reported to be upward of seven hundred dollars a week in exchange for his verbal services.

Rex Benson

I told him I had a connection in New York who was very wealthy and asked him, "Would you be willing to sell a piece of yourself to somebody for cash?" And he said, "You are my manager from now on. Do what you think is right."

So I called this guy, Harold Humes, and he said, "Oh yes, we love Lord Buckley. We love his album. In fact, we play it all the time." And he eventually bought 30 percent of Buckley for three thousand bucks and arranged the gig at the Jazz Gallery.

We drove the VW van to New York but he wanted to stop off in Cleveland and borrow some money from a disc jockey friend of his. I said, "No, we're not going to do that. Be prepared: we're going to start you off and get you famous again."

This was like the worst time of his life. But he did that to himself. He alienated himself from the mainstream of show business. Like van Gogh. Nobody bought Van Gogh's paintings. The only person who bought van Gogh's paintings was his brother and now they sell for forty-three million dollars.

So we get to New York and the first person we meet is Harold Humes who took us out to dinner and got us in a nice little, inexpensive hotel for which he footed the bill until we got our first week's pay from the club. He agreed to give us the three thousand. He drew up the contract which I still have in my possession.

Without me having to ask, Buckley said, "Being my manager, you get one-third, we get two-thirds." I said fine and immediately sent my money home because I had five children.

The next day I got on the phone and looked in the ads and we got an apartment from this woman who was going to Florida for six or seven weeks, which we rented at 39 Gramercy Park for a month and a half for five hundred dollars and fifty dollars security. He sent five hundred dollars home to Elizabeth and we had five hundred dollars to live on until the first week's six-hundred-dollar check, which I made him send home to Elizabeth. And I had Prince Lewis promise me that he would have Buckley send half his check back home because I had to return to Chicago.

Doc Humes

It must have been 1955 when I first heard Lord Richard M. Buckley's recording of "The Boston Tea Party." It was the first thing of his I ever heard and still remains one of my all-time favorites. I have collected two extant versions of "The Nazz" as well as all the other products of his fantastic imagination only to have them repeatedly slip through my fingers into the hands of beggars, borrowers and thieves. Somehow I never regretted losing a Buckley record because I knew most of them by heart, and besides, they were made to be stolen. So what the hell.

(There is absolutely no way to get the juice out of Buckley's work except to hear it, although if you have a passable ear for oral rhythms you may be able to reconstruct some of his verbal handsprings from close reading of the text. But text is to sound as a roadmap is to landscape, it tells you how to get there but not what you're going to see.)

In any event, Buckley remained for me sort of a legend. I didn't know whether he was black or white, straight or stoned, dead or alive, until I tracked him down to do the voice-over soundtrack on a film I was doing. It took several cross-continent telephone calls but we finally found him working in the Gate of Horn in Chicago. He agreed to do the soundtrack and arrangements were made for him to come East. Coincidentally, he was booked into the Jazz Gallery in New York City at the beginning of October.

A few days after these arrangements were made he arrived in New York on a Sunday midnight. He arrived in a red Volkswagen microbus with his aide-de-camp, Lew Foremaster, a remarkable guy in his own right, and Rex Benson, his business manager from Chicago. I was pleased and rather honored that before they checked into their hotel, they came directly to my place where my wife set out a midnight spread for us. I was immediately struck by Buckley's immense personal dynamism and charm, and he kept us up into the wee hours with bits and routines he'd recently invented. Meeting Buckley in the flesh was an experience.

Mort Fega

I was an admirer of Buckley's recordings and became very enamored of what he did. I appreciated his particular talent. I use the word sparingly but I believed that Buckley had a special touch of genius. Consequently, I used to play his records on the air with some regularity.

One night around in 1959, he stormed into my studio wearing an ankle-length lavender suede coat as only he could do. He was a most flamboyant personality. At the top of lungs he introduced himself, embraced me and said that my message had reached him in the desert and that he came to let me know that he appreciated my efforts on his behalf. He sat down and proceeded to recite "The Pied Piper of Hamelin" in rhyme. One of the great regrets in my life is that I didn't have my engineer record this.

The consequence of this encounter and my playing his records was that my interest in Buckley precipitated an engagement at the Jazz Gallery.

Joe Termini

Along with his brother Iggy, Joe Termini owned and managed two of America's most famous jazz clubs: the Five Spot and the Jazz Gallery. It was while performing at the Jazz Gallery in October 1960 that Lord Buckley was pulled from the stage over an alleged cabaret card violation.

Originally my brother Iggy and I opened the Five Spot on Cooper Square between Fourth and Fifth Streets. The name Five Spot came from the address of the original bar which was at Five Cooper Square. The old customers used to call it "Number Five." Prior to that it was just a neighborhood bar, something our father owned before us. We took it over after World War II and got very bored with the whole thing. Some of the neighborhood guys talked us into having jazz and I guess we were pretty good at it because the Five Spot ran from about 1956 to 1975.

After a while we moved to a bigger location on the corner of St. Mark's Place and the Bowery. Thelonious Monk liked the place so much that for seven years it was the only club in New York he'd work. Most of the original customers were painters and writers and we wanted to keep them so I never raised the prices too much. We never had a cover charge.

One of the customers, Doc Humes, talked me into hiring Lord Buckley. Doc said, "He's really funny. You should take a crack at him."

At that point I was ready to try something different because we mostly presented jazz. So I took his advice and hired him. Doc was a very exuberant fan. He loved the music and would come down often. He really loved the whole scene.

We were probably paying Buckley about seven hundred dollars a week. The money in those days was nothing compared to today. When Aretha Franklin performed she got about five hundred dollars a week but she was a kid just starting out. This was big money to me at the time. It's probably equivalent to about two thousand dollars a week today. One of the reasons Buckley got as much as he did was because he was from out of town and I figured he had to check into a hotel. If he had been local he probably would have been paid four hundred dollars.

Presenting him was something different for the Jazz Gallery or the Five Spot. We ran both clubs at the same time for a while, but the Jazz Gallery lasted for about two years. It was a financial disaster so we got out of it. But in the meantime we tried everything: the Basie band, Joe Williams, and Aretha Franklin when she was a kid.

We took a chance with Lord Buckley. He was a very likable gentleman and I thought he was funny too. But he did nothing for us financially. He really wasn't drawing in that much of a crowd.

When he came in the first time I gave him a big hello. Everything with him was "Your Eminence." I, as the owner of the Jazz Gallery, was "Your Eminence" but everybody had a title. It was "Sir This" and "Prince That." And, of course, the Jazz Gallery to him was a "Cathedral of Joy." He was half kidding. He was very florid.

The Hip Messiah" (as Buckley was now billing himself) began holding court nightly at the Jazz Gallery and was warmly received by the city's night people. A word on the "Hip Messiah" monicker is probably in order here, as it suggests either that the mantle of spiritual royalty had truly gone to Buckley's head or that he was taking the grand put-on to its ultimate extreme. Either way, even in a city as liberal as New York was circa 1960, it was bound to attract the kind of attention he probably would have been wise to shy away from.

And Doc Humes had other ideas for Buckley as well.

Doc Humes

Don Peyote was a movie I began making. I was down on Macdougal Street and saw a lad named Ojo ride by on a bicycle. He reminded me of Don Quixote. I went to the Café Figaro with some other people and we cooked up a modern film version of Quixote, calling it *Don Peyote.*

A few days later we started improvising scenes. But I needed a narrator. I'd been collecting Lord Buckley's records for years so I helped get him a New York job and planned to use him on the film. Then we started having trouble obtaining shooting permits.

The movie was to be improvisational, like jazz. Sometimes scenes would have no background continuity. We might start in a vacant lot and wind up in an excavation without explaining the shift. I put down the idea that art has to communicate. It's basically an effort to impose order on chaos: you have to explain things first. Then it can communicate.

On Tuesday night, October 4, Buckley arrived at the Jazz Gallery with Humes for opening night in a chauffer-driven Rolls-Royce with an open sunroof. *Life* magazine photographer Bob Parent was there and snapped pictures of Buckley's arrival. He also photographed him with Humes, Prince Lewis, Mort Fega, and Joe Termini in the Rolls and in front of the club. Buckley, looking healthy and stout in his carnation-lapeled black evening suit, does not appear to be a man for whom the final pages were about to turn.

Later that night Parent captured the last-known photo of Lord Buckley ever taken: on stage in front of a microphone, floating in the inky pool of nightclub noir, those all-seeing and all-loving whiskey eyes gazing wisely into space, holding out his arm as if blessing the audience, his flock, for eternity.

Lord Buckley did not disappoint. For more than two weeks he held forth with fiery fetes that wowed the traditionally hard-to-please New York nightclub crowd. The entertainment underground was humming with news of Buckley's renaissance, and he slowly began drawing new acolytes to the Jazz Gallery, where he was sharing the bill with another Swing Era saint, the trumpeter Harry "Sweets" Edison.

But Buckley's old predilections died hard.

Rex Benson

I had a friend in the advertising business who was looking for a British character to be a salesperson for Coca-Cola. It was going to be a hundred-thousand-dollars-a-year contract for two or three years. So I told Buckley that I had an audition set up for him. I told him to be at the offices of BBDO at ten o'clock the next morning. I said, "Richard, please don't go out tonight. I'll be here to pick you up in the morning."

Well, I left him about 11 p.m. I called him back at twelve and they were just getting to sleep. I said, "Good. I'll see you in the morning." I told him to just take a cab and meet me there at ten.

I got there at nine-thirty. At ten the executives came in. The bird dog on this was that one of the executives had seen Buckley perform, loved him and thought he'd be perfect for this character.

So ten-fifteen, ten-twenty, ten-twenty-five, ten-thirty. Finally, Buckley walks into the boardroom with two hookers—gorgeous ladies. He was introduced to everybody and he introduced the women: "These are my beautiful princesses. Darling ladies, take off your clothes and give all these men a blow job."

The girls started to disrobe and the men yelled, "No! Stop! Stop! We don't want this! This is not what we're here for!"

And Lord Buckley said, "But gentlemen, there's no charge."

Then, for reasons that to this day remain shrouded in controversy and mystery, things soured for the fifty-four-year-old entertainer. On Thursday, October 20, he was, depending on who's doing the reporting, either prevented from going on or actually dragged from the Jazz Gallery stage by plainclothes undercover members of the New York City Police Department's vice squad, who revoked his cabaret card for violating its often-suspect and -vague strictures.

Rex Benson

After the first week he wasn't drawing any people. In the middle of the second week, the guys called me in and laid it on the line. They said: "Listen, you got to cut his deal in half."

I said, "I don't think he's gonna do that."

They said, "Then you better make him do it or you're both gonna end up in trouble."

I said, "What do you mean by that? Is that a threat?"

He said, "You can take it for whatever you want."

I said, "I'll relay that information."

I went to Buckley that night in the apartment and told him that they wanted to cut his money. He said, "I'm not going to do that."

I said, "You better because these guys are bad guys and they threatened me and they threatened you and they're gonna do something about it."

He said, "Well I'm not going to do anything about it. Nobody can push me around. They know who I am."

"They know who you are," I said. "But you're not drawing. Let's face that fact. You're not drawing."

So I told him I had to leave and that he better make some deal with them.

Joe Termini

He was there a couple of weeks when, in the middle of a show, the vice squad cops came in and said that Buckley couldn't work there because he didn't have a cabaret card and they pulled him off the stage. I tried to get them to wait until the end of the set but they made me stop the show and pull him off the stand right then and there. There was really no need for it. The cops were just showing their power. They could have waited twenty minutes for the set to finish. There wasn't much anybody could do. They shut us right down. You didn't yell at the cops in those days.

Apparently he had gone down to get a cabaret card and they checked him out and they found that years before he had got into a fight when he was drunk.

Lord Buckley was pretty downcast about the whole thing. There was no confrontation between him and the cops.

The next day I was watching the news and Doc Humes and then Police Commissioner Kennedy, who was a hard-nosed, no-nonsense guy, were going at it toe to toe. Doc Humes was waving his finger in the Commissioner's nose and saying, "You mean to say that because this man got drunk and had a fight fifteen years ago that he can never work in this city?"

I was shocked. I thought that all hell was going to break loose and it did. The cabaret card commission went on a rampage throughout the entire city closing down any and every restaurant and club in town that had any violation, above and beyond the legality of the performers working there.

Lewis Foremaster

I don't remember the cops pulling Lord Buckley off stage but I do remember them telling him not go on.

The cabaret card law was an antiquated statute that prevented not only performers but *any* restaurant and club employee from working if they had been convicted of a crime, however minor. This included bartenders, waiters, waitresses, diswashers, hat-check girls, and doormen. Buckley had been busted but, according to him, not convicted for public drunkenness nineteen years earlier in Reno—and there were those Chicago and Indianapolis busts still on record. Buckley, apparently because of a misunderstanding, failed to report this on his cabaret card application and this was used as the excuse to confiscate his license and shut down his show. Charlie Parker, Thelonious Monk, Billie Holiday, and Lenny Bruce were some of the more notable artists who also suffered at the hands of the cabaret card licensing bureau. For an under-the-table price, of course, one's card was usually returned—no questions asked.

Under a department ruling in 1941, all nightclub employees, including star performers, had to apply for police identification or cabaret cards before they were allowed to work. They had to be fingerprinted, "mugged" (photographed), and pay a two-dollar fee for a card that had to be renewed every two years. Some entertainers felt the practice was illegal and virtually all knew it to be humiliating, discriminatory, and an inducement to corruption. Under police rules a cabaret could be closed if the owner was discovered allowing an employee to work without a card.

Doc Humes

Lord Buckley was a beautiful nut. He believed we should all treat each other like royalty. I can say he was a decent, generous man, and I liked him. After he was gone it was evident to everyone who had wanted to help him that something had to be done about the cabaret bureau. Their card system is a real cancer. I think the police have arrogated tremendous power to themselves in the past two decades. And that's how the committee got started.

That whole period around November 1960 has to be looked at in terms of pathology. It was crazy beyond belief—the cabaret card scandal centering on Lord Buckley, the trouble the Village coffeehouses were having and, of course, the big folksingers' riot in Washington Square Park, which was the first anyone saw the T.P.F., the Tactical Police Force, in fatigues instead of uniform. I was chairman of the Citizen's Emergency Committee which was attempting to deal with the repressiveness being brought down on Buckley. Since the days of Prohibition the New York police had been mugging and fingerprinting artists before they could do club work. Thelonious Monk had to pay ten thousand dollars to get his card back. It was a real racket—out-and-out harassment.

That's when the cabaret card thing blew up. Actually it was Buckley's trip east that blew the cabaret card scam sky-high. When Nina Simone burned her card everybody else decided they would burn theirs and a lot of stuff in the newspapers came out about the cabaret cards and the scandal that went on around them.

The cabaret card scandal was a scandal that went back to the twenties and Prohibition days. If nothing else they should have put that on Lord Buckley's tombstone: "The guy that blew the cabaret card scam sky-high." That was a major achievement.

Joe Termini

The ironic thing is that they had a good reason for originally instituting the cabaret card laws. During Prohibition they had these bust-out joints where girls worked nude or semi-nude. When a tourist walked in a nice-looking girl would come over, sit down and say, "Do you want to buy me a drink?" And the next thing you know she's ordering champagne and the guy is getting hit with a bill of fifty dollars which is the equivalent of three hundred dollars today. If there was any complaint the bouncer would come over and beat the hell out of the guy. There was no use in calling the cops because they were in on the deal and they might give the guy a second whacking to boot. It was such an abusive thing and, with the racket guys who were running those businesses, the cabaret card laws were instituted in the hopes that it might keep out some of the fringe criminal elements.

So the cabaret card laws started out as a good thing but it turned bad. A guy like Buckley was faced either with paying a lawyer who specialized in those cases five thousand dollars to work for him or slipping a few hundred dollars under the table to the cops downtown. Either way he was taking his chances.

In those days the police were very poorly paid. If the guy in charge of the chicken coop is hungry all the time you know what's going to happen. In fact, shortly after the cabaret card law was rescinded, they gave the police a nice raise which is what they should have done in the first place. When you got a man in a responsible position like that he's got to be well paid. If he loses a job like that he's going to lose a real good job.

Red Rodney

The system was so corrupt back then it was ridiculous. All of us had problems with that. It was terrible. But even though I had a police record I could pay twenty-five hundred dollars and get one. It was a bribe. The inspector got the twenty-five hundred dollars. It was a law allowing the police to put money in their pockets.

Ann Brooks

The night I arrived was the night the police pulled him off the stage right in the middle of his performance at the Jazz Gallery. They walked right on stage and asked him if he had his police card and he said, "No."

Well, the next night we were uptight because he wasn't working. He couldn't go back on stage until he got his police card back. All you had to do to have trouble with your card was to have been arrested, not even convicted, and Lord Buckley had been arrested on the most insignificant of trifles. They hated Lord

Buckley because they thought he was a threat to their sanity or something.

We needed some money and Sir Laurence Olivier was at the St. James Theater doing *Beckett*. Prince Lewis and I went down there with a note that Lord Buckley had written him. The note was an invitation for Olivier to appear at the Royal Court that night and pleaded with him to come over after the show and grace us with his presence. And, if he couldn't grace us with his presence, could he please give Lord Buckley a hundred dollars.

When we got there we just walked right through the stage door like we owned the place and ran right into Olivier and handed him the note. He read it and he roared—he absolutely roared. He immediately called Lord Buckley and while he was talking with Lord Buckley, he began roaring all over again. I don't know what the other end of the conversation was but we got a one-hundred-dollar bill.

But when we got back Lord Buckley was very disappointed that Olivier hadn't come over. He called Olivier back late that night and said: "Sir Laurence, you're backsliding. How come you're not here at the Royal Court?" But Sir Laurence never did make it over.

There was just a tremendous amount of melancholia after he lost the police card. He felt the police were harassing him and, in fact, they would come up to the apartment every day and search the place. The harassment was truly terrible. And, naturally, he was very brought down by the whole thing. He was very upset. It was his renaissance and they just cut it right in the middle. He was doing so well at the Jazz Gallery.

The events of the following three weeks are murky and convoluted at best. Friends and associates of Buckley alternately report wild partying, despondency, and/or both. But from the many personal reminiscences and press reports in the New York newspapers following Buckley's death, it is possible to piece together some outline of his movements in those last days.

Championing Buckley's cause, Doc Humes quickly organized an outfit calling itself the Citizen's Emergency Committee, a loose-knit group comprised of many of the city's literary, musical, and socially progressive intelligentsia including George Plimpton, Norman Mailer, David Amram, and Norman Podhoretz. The high-powered personalities, counting on Buckley to testify, forced the issue, garnering front-page headlines and an official investigation of the cabaret card bureau's questionable modus operandi. The group charged that the cabaret licensing bureau had deteriorated into an institutionalized shakedown operation conducted by a shadowy wing of the New York Police Department.

On October 21, 1960, the day after Lord Buckley's cabaret card was lifted by the New York police, Buckley and Doc Humes went to the license bureau and talked to Sergeant Frank Nolan. Unknown to the sergeant, Humes carried a Mohawk 500 tape recorder in a shoulder holster and a microphone in his sleeve and recorded the conversation. Humes's tape offers insight into the administration of the cabaret cards for entertainers in New York City at the time. The entire transcript, the so-called "Secret

Tape," originally appeared in the January 5, 1961, issue of *Down Beat* magazine and, as the following short excerpt demonstrates, shows a surprisingly subdued Buckley letting Humes do most of the talking and hints at the low regard with which the police department held nightclub performers:

Humes: How long will it be? He's not able to work without that card, according to you.
Sgt. Nolan: That's right.
Humes: What happens if he works without the card?
Sgt. Nolan: Then we give the premises a violation and we close them.
Humes: You close down the premises? Pretty rough way to treat people, don't you think?
Sgt. Nolan: It depends on the people.
Humes: Depriving a man of his livelihood without due process of law?
Sgt. Nolan: There are some people when they're selling narcotics say we're depriving them of their livelihood.
Humes: This is a different thing; he's an entertainer.
Sgt. Nolan: It's not a different thing.
Humes: You don't lift a taxi driver's license before you . . .
Sgt. Nolan: We'd lift it more quicker than we would ever lift an entertainer's.
Humes: How many years ago was this?
Sgt. Nolan: The last one, the (unintelligible) tax act was 1946. The 1956 is minor. Six traffic misdemeanors—whatever they are.
Humes: Well those aren't criminal. I mean, a traffic offense is not criminal, when you speak of a criminal record. Are there any convictions on these?
Sgt. Nolan: This is what we are sending to find out—to ascertain.
Buckley: What shall we do? Call you back on it?
Sgt. Nolan: We asked him the question, "Were you ever arrested?"
Buckley: I said, "No," because (unintelligible).
Sgt. Nolan: We are lifting on the false statement on the application.

And still later in the conversation:

Humes: This is liable to jeopardize his entire future livelihood.
Sgt. Nolan: Could be.
Humes: *Could be.* My God! Suppose someone did this to you?
Sgt. Nolan: We have the attitude we would like to keep a certain type of element out of this field. That's our purpose.
Humes: When you say "a certain type of element," you made a statement which is prejudicial . . .

But Humes was the first to leap to Buckley's aid, accompanying His Lordship to a hearing several days after the cabaret card confiscation. At the hearing before Deputy Chief Inspector Lent, Buckley was accused of having falsely stated in his application that he had never been arrested or summoned for anything more than a traffic offense. Buckley had been arrested several times but again claimed that he misunderstood the question on the application, thinking it to mean had he ever been convicted of a crime, which, to his mind, he had not.

Doc Humes

It just seemed unfair. Everybody that knew the man liked him. He wasn't hurting anybody. He was building bridges between black and white. That was one of the reasons why some people got on his case. After eventually abolishing the cabaret card system, the Citizen's Emergency Committee went on to do things like make it possible for the folksingers to continue singing in Washington Square Park. The Citizen's Emergency Committee did an awful lot to keep freedom in this country.

Maxwell Cohen

Prominent New York City attorney Maxwell Cohen was a key member of the Citizen's Emergency Committee, which rallied to Lord Buckley's defense after his cabaret card was revoked. Cohen fought on after Lord Buckley's death to eliminate the antiquated restrictions that thwarted His Lordship. His following discussion originally appeared in Michael Ullman's Jazz Lives.

I learned that the system got started accidentally. There was around 1939 a Presidential Directive to the FBI instructing them to prepare a list of those whose presence might be adverse to the security of the United States. It was thought that many of the unions were dominated by Communists, particularly the waiters' union. The list was prepared. Later when the police department was helping in an attempt to break a strike, they became involved in passing on the qualifications of waiters and chefs to work in restaurants. If they had any previous criminal offense, even as minors, they could not work. This was seen as a way of weakening the unions. In the course of time, like any other uninhibited authority, this began to stretch horizontally, and in the process it began to take in musicians and performers. And so a "law" never passed by legislation (and so never intended to restrict musicians and artists) became a tremendous factor in their lives. There was one decision in 1941 that sustained the law and said that the police had the right to such an authority because of the number of cabaret robberies, none of which was committed by musicians or performers. It was an outrageous decision, but it gave some degree of legal coloration to what the police department was doing.

I knew some of the musicians who were suffering because of the law. The very distinguished J. J. Johnson was denied a card. He had committed an offense as a juvenile delinquent. The law was, and is, very firm that delinquency can never be a legal disqualification against a man after he became of age. Johnson's was the first test case. It was successful to the extent that the court directed the police department to give him a card. The court avoided the issue of whether the police department had any rights in respect to the establishment of the card as a criterion for employment, but the very fact that the police department had been challenged successfully was important. There were several test cases after that.

Lord Buckley was managed by a well-known novelist and former editor of *The Paris Review* by the name of Doc Humes, Harold Humes. Harold went down to the police department with a tape machine hoping that in the course of arguing for Lord Buckley's card someone would approach him for a bribe. No one did, but the policeman in charge referred to the fact that there was very little difference between a performer and a criminal anyway. That brilliant observation was taped and I made much of it later. Humes introduced me to Buckley at the suggestion of Dorothy Schiff, publisher of the *New York Post,* and I asked the police department for a hearing. Now these hearings were usually before an inspector who was sympathetic. They were simple hearings. I would produce the applicant and he would testify that he was married and that he had not committed an offense for a number of years. In other words, that he was rehabilitated. And that would have been the routine in Lord Buckley's case except Doc Humes was a very effervescent individual with a tremendous amount of energy and a sense of drama. So instead of one witness he came with eight noted writers and with reporters from the New York papers. It was a Friday afternoon. We didn't finish the testimony, and the hearing was postponed for two weeks. Lord Buckley died one week later. He died on a Saturday night. Then an amazing thing happened—seventy-eight of the foremost writers and publishers in New York formed a citizen's committee to fight the police department on this issue. The New York papers made this front page news.

At the scheduled hearing, at which I planned to ask for a card, even posthumously, at the Buckley family's request, I appeared with one witness. When I came to headquarters I was surprised to see a number of television cameras, reporters and high officials in the police department. I was told by the officer in charge [Officer Lent] that the Police Commissioner, Stephen Kennedy, was going to sit in. He was a feared political power, a man who would throw his weight around in the city. During the hearing, which was very simple, the Commissioner handed the Inspector in charge a note. I asked to see it, but the note was torn up. We knew from the Inspector's apologetic demeanor that it instructed the Inspector to deny the card. Then Commissioner Kennedy took over, and began harassing my witness. He asked his name, and then whether the witness was known by any other names. I pounced on the Commissioner. "You don't have the right to offend a witness by that question." And then we went at each other as the cameras began to grind. The Commissioner had made a tactical mistake: a powerful individual should not start up with a small man. Later Doc Humes came in and it became a shouting match between the two of them. Finally at about three o'clock we finished.

That was the beginning of the end of the police card.

George Plimpton

Author, essayist, Paris Review *publisher, television personality, and fireworks connoisseur, George Plimpton has carved a unique niche for himself in American letters.*

Lord Buckley was a legendary bohemian to all of us. There was something about him. He became a sort of mythological figure even though I don't think many of us had been down there to see him or hear him at the Jazz Gallery. We appreciated him as a real pioneer. Mort Sahl, Lenny Bruce came after him. Bruce, who had many more troubles than Buckley, to put it mildly, was the most highly regarded comic of that iconoclastic tradition.

The Citizen's Emergency Committee was part of the big attempt to change things. And it was all through the arm-twisting of Doc Humes as I recall that they came together. Doc had chattered a lot about a film he was working on, *Don Peyote,* in which he said he planned to use Lord Buckley, though I don't know what happened to it.

Perhaps because Doc was a novelist, he got the bit in his teeth about the confiscation of Buckley's cabaret card because the performance had to do with words rather than music. Thelonious Monk and Charlie Parker were musicians whereas Buckley was a monologist. He dealt with words. Doc himself was a writer—the author of two novels, *The Underground City* and *Men Die.*

The thing I always thought was so remarkable about the Citizen's Emergency Committee was that Doc had pulled together quite a high-powered group of people. It was quite an eclectic conglomeration. Mark Lane, Robert Silvers, who was then an editor at *Harper's,* Daniel Ogden Stewart of *The New Yorker,* the Grove Press's Barney Rossett, Norman Podhoretz of *Commentary,* and the composer David Amram, to name some of the members of the group when they first formed.

The funny thing about the Citizen's Emergency Committee was that it seemed to be mostly social. There used to be meetings but I don't recall any petitions. I don't recall what the force of the thing was. It was a Citizen's Emergency Committee but how much power it had I really don't know. I think it just voiced a lot of complaints and tried to get the press involved. There were a lot of news stories that came out during the cabaret card investigation. John F. Kennedy had been elected president just a week before Buckley's death so the times were rife with controversy and change. But the committee did succeed on bringing the issue before the public. Eventually, the cabaret card licensing ceded. It was, by edict, eventually done away with, and I like to think the Citizen's Emergency Committee (what a grand-sounding name!) had something to do with it.

I remember nothing of the specifics of Lord Buckley's death and though Doc and other members of the Citizen's Emergency Committee suggested that it was hastened by the police harassment, I tend to doubt it.

Not surprsingly, the *Village Voice* stepped into the fray and offered the first of three in-depth reports of the controversy in its November 3, 1960, edition.

'HIP MESSIAH' LOSES CABARET CARD TO FUZZ HE LOVES

by Mary Perot Nichols

It was an exciting day for the "fuzz" last Thursday when a whole slew of reporters and a couple of novelists showed up at a hearing at the Police Department Division of Licenses. The ink-stained contingent appeared on the scene to find out why the police had lifted the cabaret card of Lord Buckley, the "Hip Messiah."

Buckley, who had been playing at the Jazz Gallery as a "mass pantomimist," had been relieved of his card earlier in the week, without prior notice or hearing.

The police claimed that Buckley had falsified a statement on his application for a card when he denied he had ever been arrested. Buckley later told the police that he was confused in his mind as to whether the question had meant "arrested" or "convicted."

DANGEROUS EXTENSION

Maxwell T. Cohen, Buckley's attorney, told Deputy Chief Inspector Francis W. Lent that the question of arrest was "inherently prohibitive in any court," and that it was a dangerous extension of power for the Police Department to be able to ask such a question.

The Police Department produced an FBI file at the hearing which showed that Buckley had been convicted for being drunk in Reno 19 years ago, and that he had been arrested in Indianapolis 17 years ago for assault and possession of marijuana. There was no record of conviction in the latter case.

Cohen argued that Buckley's record "was too remote in time to have a bearing on his character," and that his cabaret card had been removed without prior notice—a violation of Police Department rules.

The high point in the hearing occurred, however, when Cohen informed Inspector Lent that the defense had a tape recording an interview involving Police Sergeant Frank Nolan, novelist Harold Humes (author of "Underground City"), and Lord Buckley.

Cohen began to read a transcript of the interview with Nolan and to question the officer on what he had said at the time. Humes, Cohen pointed out, had, at the interview, charged the Police Department of "depriving a man of his livelihood without due process of law." To this Sergeant Nolan had allegedly replied: "There are some people who say we are depriving them of their livelihood when they are selling narcotics." Humes then said: "This is a different thing—he's an entertainer." According to the transcript Nolan replied: "It's not a different thing."

Inspector Lent called a hasty recess in the hearing at this juncture.

At one point in the hearing, the court reporter seemed unable to believe his ears and asked Lord Buckley to sit closer to him. Buckley switched seats obligingly with novelist Norman Mailer and the stenographer said: "You mentioned Jesus Christ."

Buckley proceeded to explain his form of entertainment. "I teach the words of Christ" in night clubs, he explained coolly. Buckley has appeared on nine Ed Sullivan shows, and his lawyer elicited from him the fact that he had been seen by possibly 100 million viewers "without any complaint from any municipal or state authority."

It was later brought out in court that he had been an entertainer at the Police Department Honor Legion's dinner the previous Monday night—and without a cabaret card. "It was a work of love," Buckley told the hearing. "Love for the Police Department?" his lawyer asked. "Yes," Buckley replied.

Later, Lord Buckley, whose name is Richard M., explained: "I believe all ladies and gentlemen are Lords and Ladies." He told The Voice that his act for the Police Department had been "mass pantomimicism" (a word he coined himself). "I got four policemen to stand up and I projected four voices through them in sequence," he said. Did the fuzz like the act? "They were really swinging," Buckley replied.

Some of the people Buckley brings into his act are Jesus Christ, Mahatma Gandhi, Confucius, and the Marquis de Sade "translated into hip talk."

At the beginning of this week Buckley was still without a cabaret card, and still unable to go back to work at the Jazz Gallery.

On Thursday, November 10 (other sources suggest dates as early as October 24), Buckley and Humes found themselves at a Police Honor Legion dinner held at the Park Sheraton Hotel. The entertainer had (suspiciously and ironically) been asked to "donate" a performance as the first step in regaining his card. The Police Honor League, not officially connected with the police department, was, and continues to be, a social organization to which both policemen and ordinary citizens belong. It was at the dinner, Humes later charged under oath, that Buckley was offered an opportunity to "buy" back his confiscated card by a guest whom Humes said identified himself as "Mr. Winters."

According to Humes, Winters offered to introduce Buckley to "a deputy police commissioner" who would see that the cabaret card was restored for a consideration of "not less than one hundred dollars." Winters pointed to a table, said Humes, "but to my regret now, I didn't look."

For his part Buckley seemed to have dug the gig, telling the *New York Post:* "Maybe I can entertain the police again. I enjoyed performing for them the other night. I really love the Police Department. What would we do without the police?"

It was later determined that "Mr. Winters" was one Albert Wintner, a theatrical booking agent. According to Humes, Wintner had offered himself as a liaison between Buckley and the men in blue, arranged Buckley's gig at the Honor League dinner, and set up the alleged bribe designating himself as the delivery boy. Wintner, for his part, denied any wrongdoing in the matter under oath in the heated aftermath of Buckley's death.

Another ally of Buckley's who stepped forward in the days following his passing was Phil Kerness, also a theatrical agent. Kerness charged that, at the Honor League function, he had delivered Buckley's hundred dollars to Wintner, who was to pass it on to a top cop.

No record of the dinner exists in the Police Honor League archive, but it would be more than ironically fitting and not at all surprising if His Lordship had performed "His Majesty, The Policeman" on their behalf. In retrospect, it's hard to believe he didn't.

None of the cloak-and-dagger mechanizations seemed to have done Buckley any good. His card was not reinstated, as Humes pushed for a hearing the following Monday. But Lord Buckley never made it—his last missed gig.

There is variant testimony from several who claimed to be with Lord Buckley during the last two days of his life. He was either drinking mescaline-spiked vodka while making nonstop love to an underage mulatto woman, having a violent falling-out with some Greenwich Village engravers over a jewel heist or counterfeiting scheme gone south, having a voodoo curse put on him by some unspecified acquaintances, gracefully charming the city's cultural crème de la crème at one of George Plimpton's famous literary parties, being beaten to death by black militants who were unhappy with his act, being harassed hourly by the cops at his Gramercy Park pad, or some combination of the above.

Speculation surrounds (and continues to surround) the circumstances and official version of Buckley's passing, with every theory from foul play to a broken heart cited as the cause. Perhaps, as one friend suggested: "Lord Buckley was so heavy, Jake, he just *fell* off the planet."

Though Doc Humes was, especially in his later, hyperbolically prone years, wont to claim that Buckley was given something at a party identified to him as mescaline and died several hours later coughing up blood, he took a somewhat more subdued stand on Buckley's passing in "His Lordship's Last Days," the May 1961 article he penned for *Swank,* the girlie mag that, for a short spell in the early 1960s, devoted several pages in each issue to higher-browed literary aspirations.

Doc Humes

I took him to his opening in a Rolls. A week and a half later, without notice or hearing, without even giving a reason, the police picked up Lord Buckley's so-called Cabaret Identification Card. Three weeks later, after living through the exquisite Chinese torture that passes for the standard operating procedure of the Police Cabaret Bureau, Lord Buckley was dead. According to the two doctors who attended him in the last hours of his life, he died of a stroke; and this was the cause of death noted on his hospital chart at the time of his death. The police, however, after hurried consultation with the autopist, said he died of an old "kidney ailment."

The last conversation I had with His Lordship was on the telephone at two o'clock in the morning on the day of his death. He called me to chew me out for not being with him—almost as though he had a clear premonition of what was coming. I remember the conversation vividly because it was the first time I ever heard Lord Buckley talk about the fear that must have been in him those last weeks of grinding anxiety when each day he called the cabaret bureau and each day was told to "call tomorrow." (He once said that a performer who couldn't perform might as well be dead.) Toward the end of that last conversation between us he told me that they'd been living on spaghetti all week and that he needed five or ten dollars to buy food. I was so shook that I immediately called Art D'Lugoff at the Village Gate and asked him if he could get some money to Buckley right away, since he was in his neighborhood. To his eternal credit, D'Lugoff asked no questions, but immediately sent money over.

The last thing Buckley said to me over the telephone before he hung up forever was: "I'm sorry, I've got to find help somewhere, they're bugging me to death. In fact I got the Bugbird in me right now."

The Bugbird, as anyone who has heard his version of Poe's poem knows, is the Raven, symbol of impending death. The last thing he was working on before he died was a wall plaque; I have it in my possession. He was hand-lettering a quotation from Mencken, but he didn't get to finish it. Only half the letters are colored in. It reads as follows: "The best and clearest thinking of the world is done, and the finest art is produced, not by those who are hungry, nagged and harassed, but by those who are well-fed, warm and easy in mind. It is the artist's first duty to his art to achieve that tranquility for himself."

But it's useless to carry on this way. I'm still sore that he's dead, because he should have died laughing. He was a religious man in his orbital way, and he believed deeply in what he was doing. He called the cabarets where he worked "atomic age cathedrals," and he meant it. In an age of insanity he carried grace with him wherever he went, and had the knack of conferring it on whomever he met. He believed that if everyone treated each other as sovereigns, as lords and ladies, the world could be made livable again. He carried this out in his personal life to the extent that I have seen him make a lady out of a three-wheeled cadmium-plated bitch merely by punctiliously kissing her hand as he left her. And it was completely typical of him to tell the police—this was during his first hearing after losing his livelihood—that he thought the police needed more love. This was a deadly truth. For this man there is no choice but death.

In a last-ditch attempt to publicize Buckley's plight, Humes made a bold, grandstanding move: he threw a party.

David Amram

In 1960 I was invited to this party at George Plimpton's house. I had known George from Paris in the early 1950s when he was starting up the *Paris Review*.

When I moved to New York and wasn't working I would go over and play piano at these literary parties George gave at his apartment on East Seventy-second Street. This was before he was on television or anything like that. He was a wonderful host and party-giver. He liked to hang out with different people so he'd just have a book party for someone, and then enjoy himself and make everybody feel at home.

The thing is, no one would know whose book it was. It was so low-key that you never knew who the author was. Everybody tried to be so low-key when they were there since the parties were always presented in this kind of subdued style. Even people who were there on the hustle were trying to pretend that they weren't because they wanted to be invited back again so they could then hustle again in that low-key way. But many people like myself were there to party, look for romance, enjoy a wild assortment of people . . . and see George.

I'd sit there and play the piano and I met a lot of people I'm still friendly with. I met all these fantastic writers, professional athletes and could, since I was single at the time, meet all these real intelligent women who were mostly interested in writers and not in struggling musicians. But still, it was stimulating being there. And George was always friendly and fun to be with.

I got to the party and saw Lord Buckley. He said, "Prince David, welcome to the Royal Court of hip New York happening. You can hippify these cats with some sacred sounds. You're Oscar's French horn player."

I was writing music for Shakespeare in Central Park when I was at Birdland with Oscar Pettiford, the great bassist. Oscar used to tell everybody, "My man, Dave, my French horn player is writing Shakespeare in the Park," meaning that I was writing the music. He knew that Shakespeare had written the plays.

So when Lord Buckley mentioned Oscar and the music I'd written for Shakespeare, I said, "That's right," and told him how much I enjoyed everything that he'd done over the years, how he gave me a new insight into Shakespeare, and how Dizzy and Dick Leith and so many other musicians had introduced me to him.

Since Shakespeare in the Park was free, a lot of people who didn't go to the theater would go to see the performances. So there were a lot of beboppers there as well as Shakespeare fans.

Lord Buckley had seen some of the plays I had written the music for and he said, "Play me some Shakespeare in the Park and we'll turn these cats on to the sweet sounds of the groovy bard."

So I began playing a kind of Elizabethan piano and he went over in the corner and was just standing there. He was such an incredible-looking person that some of the people who were there didn't know if he was a famous author or maybe some eccentric multimillionaire. No one was sure. He had such a strong presence that some of the literary types actually stopped talking to one another and began eyeballing him.

The room quieted down and George Plimpton said, "We have a very special guest this evening who we'd really like you to hear. He's a wonderful protagonist of spontaneous prose and he's quite original. I think you all will really enjoy hearing Lord Buckley."

So Lord Buckley looked at everyone and got that gleam in his eye and said, "My Lords and Ladies, welcome to the royal court of his holiness George Plimpton."

All the guests looked dumbfounded and didn't know what to do because they'd never heard anything like this before. He gave me a nod to play some more and raised his hands like Moses recieving the Ten Commandments.

Buckley then started going into this fantastic improvised routine about Harvard Yard and the ghetto. He was kind of summing up everything in the room interspersed with some stuff that I'd never heard him do before. The people in the room were spellbound, and he launched into a new version of *Julius Caesar* done in street style.

Just in the middle of it a loud, garrulous voice said, "Is this supposed to be humor? Doesn't sound very spontaneous to me and it doesn't sound like prose."

It was Norman Mailer who was at the party and imbibing heavily at that time. In retrospect he was obviously in the throes of some personal difficulty. It was odd because Norman was usually the first person who would take the side of anybody who was considered off the track and defend them and go out of his way to try make everyone else appreciate them and even start a fight to quiet people down if they were bothering anybody.

So Lord Buckley said, "My Lord, that was a beautiful thought," and he continued rapping away and about every other minute Norman, who was really blasted out, would start heckling him. This made it even better for Lord Buckley who was really a master at dealing with hecklers, including people who were gangsters and people with murder raps and everything. He did it in such a humorous way that Norman really got into and became part of the program.

We continued for about forty-five minutes. But what I didn't know was that George Plimpton and novelist Doc Humes had invited some people who worked in television who they thought could help Lord Buckley out. See, I wasn't aware of the cabaret card troubles that Lord Buckley was having. I knew about the cabaret card law and that Billie Holliday couldn't get a card and all the troubles that Lenny Bruce had. But I didn't know that it was such a terrible thing for Lord Buckley. As a result he couldn't work any clubs in New York. George and Doc Humes hoped perhaps he might get booked on TV, where you didn't need a cabaret card.

And we kept on going, not knowing that most of the guests were expecting to hear five minutes. Once Lord Buckley got started he could do five or six hours and go over to someone's house and do another five or six hours because he was really into what he was doing.

Doc Humes came over to me while I was playing and said, "Man, he's going on too long. He's going to lose the TV execs."

And I said, "I don't think he cares about that."

Lord Buckley then asked me to play some blues and then he just started making up all kinds of wild poetry and scat—incredible material. And then I saw he was just going to have some fun. He'd done his performing and he was just going to perform for himself like a jazz musician in the traditional sense, as if to say, "I'm really doing this 'cause I want to do it and you're welcome to enjoy it."

Well, at that point, I think he expected people to just wander around and two or three people to hang out by the piano that wanted to hear. But they all stayed there because they were all people who I guess were trained to show that they had good manners. It was still a literary-type scene where everybody wanted to act proper. But they had been standing for over an hour.

So, after about an hour and a half Doc Humes finally came over and said, "That was Lord Buckley—isn't he fabulous!" And everybody applauded and immediately refilled their drinks and went back into their socializing and literateuring.

And Doc never really got a chance to tell all the guests about the cabaret card law because Lord Buckley had gone on so long—he was having such a good time and, being a guy who lived for the moment, he really wasn't concerned about the gathering being some sort of a benefit for him or some kind of literary showcase for his talents. So they never really got around to explaining to the people who were there that he was a man who couldn't perform in New York because of an antiquated law.

And I think at that point Doc wanted to take him home. But Lord Buckley was having too a good a time to leave. He went over afterwards and he was talking to Norman Mailer and kind of cheered him up giving him a big hug to show that he didn't mind—that he enjoyed the heckling.

I would always stay at the parties till George was ready to go to bed because I didn't want to miss anything. Since I hadn't written a book at the time I really had nothing to sell. I just wanted to hang out and have a good time. And Lord Buckley was the same—he was just hanging out and enjoying himself. So we were drinking and eating up everything in sight—all the canapés, little sandwiches, the cheese and all the stuff that was there. After we scarfed up everything and had a few drinks, we played some music and then he called out different tunes. Duke Ellington tunes and Charlie Parker tunes. We started talking about music, all the great jazz literature and the structure of music too. Almost all the guests had gone, and Lord Buckley was still wailing.

And, finally, he said, "Well, let's go down to my pad and hang out. I think His Lordship George should cop some Zs."

So I left with Lord Buckley and Doc Humes. There was also a young man from the Southwest whose name I don't remember. He was kind of a fan and disciple of Lord Buckley's. He was a very nice, young guy not more than twenty years old and he drove us all downtown.

So we got in this little Volkswagen mini-van and started driving. George's place was over by the East River on Seventy-second Street and we drove over to and down Second Avenue to the place Lord Buckley was staying on Gramercy Park. As we started going down Second Avenue Lord Buckley started this fantastic rap—like an incredible saga and, as he was rising to a crescendo, we were going through these staggered traffic lights. The driver was going faster and faster so, finally, since the lights were timed at twenty-three miles an hour, we went through the yellow lights and then the red lights with Lord Buckley maniacally urging him on: "Go on, man! Get it! Go! Wail! Go! Go! Drive the chariot faster, my son. The Holy Grail is nearing!"

The young man kept going through the red lights, with Lord Buckley driving him on: "Go on, man! Go! We're going to hit the greens again! Go! Beautiful! Beautiful!" Meaning that we would eventually catch up with the green lights again.

So we were roaring through all the red lights while I'm thinking we're going to get hit by a car except it was about two in the morning so there wasn't much traffic coming crosstown.

Well, just as we were about to catch up to the green lights, I saw those flashing red lights from behind and I looked around and there was a police car.

I yelled, "Oh my God, man, we're all going to get busted!"

And he said, "Go on, man! Go on! Go! Don't worry about that cat! Go! Go!"

So the driver kept going faster.

Finally, the police car veered over to the side of the van and looked like he was going to force us off the road and I moaned, "Oh boy, we're all going to spend the night in jail!" I had just finished writing the music for the film *Splendor in the Grass* that summer. I was thinking that I was going to get a chance to do some really great stuff and now I wouldn't be able to go to the preview because I was going to be in jail.

Anyway, the driver stopped the van and both the policemen came over with their hands right next to their guns and these huge flashlights shining in the windows.

But Lord Buckley said, "Don't worry. Everything is cool. Everything is beautiful. God loves us. Everything is cool. Don't get upset. Everything is beautiful. Just stay cool."

They came around to the driver's side of the van and said, "Let me see your license and registration. Don't move your hands. Go into your pocket very slowly."

So this young driver went very slowly into his pocket. The cop flashed his light around the car and he saw Lord Buckley and the most incredible thing happened. The cop said, "Oh." Then they turned from the side of the van, got into the police car and drove off.

That was all the cop said: ". . . Oh."

Now, I never understood whether or not he was a bigger Lord Buckley fan than anybody or Lord Buckley had put some kind of cosmic whammy on him. I believe he had the power to do stuff like that. I had the impression that he didn't even know Lord Buckley. On the other hand, being a professional policeman and all that we'd done . . . well, I've never to this day been able to figure out why he didn't bust us right on the spot. Not that Lord Buckley ever said anything like that, it's just that I never experienced such a situation like that in my life—especially with a policeman. Anyway, the policemen walked back in front of the van, got into the car and drove off. They didn't say anything but "Oh."

Doc Humes and I didn't even say a thing because we were afraid they might come back again.

After the cops drove off Lord Buckley said, "Come on, let's get up to the pad," and urged the young driver to start racing the lights again. "Go man! You got it! Beautiful! We're free!"

This time the driver was as terrified as we were and wouldn't go through another red light.

So we got down to Gramercy Park, parked the van and went up to this place where Lord Buckley was staying and the four of us just sat around talking until dawn.

He started telling us about the cabaret card problem and what a tremendous strain it was because all he really wanted to do was to be free to do what he was doing. New York was one of the places especially where he was really appreciated and accepted by everybody that knew about him. There were an enormous number of people that appreciated him and a tremendous number of black people that appreciated him in New York.

Most white people thought that Lord Buckley was black from listening to his records. Black people didn't really care if he was black or white—it didn't make any difference to them. That was just a technicality because in his spirit and his soul and his delivery and his life he had so much love and appreciation and reverence and respect for that tradition that he just transcended all the racial barriers because what he did wasn't done in a racist way. It was done in a loving way, in a cultural way. Just like anybody can play Beethoven regardless of what their background is. You don't have to be German to play Beethoven if you devote your whole life to it. And if you devote your whole life to jazz or what Lord Buckley did, eventually you can learn that and it can become a part of you if you do it with humility and reverence. And he talked about that too.

I always felt I loved Shakespeare as much as Lord Buckley did and I loved the English language and respected all that but I also felt that there were other traditions that were just as equally valuable and equally important. Lord Buckley was that way just as Dizzy and Charlie Parker had been in the respect that they were multicultural people. They all encouraged any musicians or people I knew to try to learn and glean to the beautifulness of the world's people and the world's culture. And Lord Buckley was talking about that too. The whole idea of the global concept was very important to him. He thought that comedy was a way to get people thinking and feeling and to see the humanness in themselves that they share with other people.

He said, "It's just like blowing, man." Just like when you're improvising or playing—you're free but you're dealing from a cultural perspective or a style that comes, in the case of jazz, from African procedures that have gone back thousands and thousands of years combined with European techniques and stuff that is specifically American and then being able to improvise on the spot and combine everything.

He said, "We do the same thing in comedy you do when you're playing. We play off the cash register too."

That was an old expression because in the little clubs that he used to play, what Lenny Bruce called the "toilets," there was always a cash register with a big ring. So in the middle of some gorgeous ballad or some great joke of his you'd hear the cash register ring. The other side of that coin is that when the cash register hit or somebody flushed a toilet or a gun shot went off you, as a performer, had a chance to do something to relate to that—use that as part of the arrangement. He said he would use that as part of the comedy. So, when a heckler came like Norman Mailer, he enjoyed that because that became a whole new vista, a new whole new cast of dramatic characters that he would put into whatever he was doing. Because he was so amazing he could do so many different characters and voices that if someone was heckling, that just added a character to expand the ones he already had.

He talked about playing in the Capone-owned clubs back in the Chicago of the thirties. That was part of his routine too and he had a lot of fans, of course, who were gangsters—everybody did. When I played with Charles Mingus at the Bohemia, some of the people that used to come down there were pretty wild. I don't think they were big figures but the interesting thing was that the Mob-connected people always were the nicest to the musicians, the most respectful, and treated you very well as long as you didn't make any outrageous demands. But Lord Buckley had a lot of fans who were in that . . . everybody did at that time. That's who owned the clubs.

I finally left, went home and crashed. A few hours later, Doc called and told me that he had died. That always stayed in my mind. I always had a special place in my heart for him since then. Whenever I would hear Shakespeare or hear jazz, not just hear his records. Whenever I would meet people from any of those places that would talk about leaders or meeting world leaders I would think of him. When I would see Duke Ellington or Count Basie I would think of the idea of royalty in a much more refreshing way. I saw that true royalty, like Lord Buckley, is something that is not just passed along through marriage and is not something that you're born with. It's something that you acquire and earn by your conduct and your excellence of spirit and your humanity and your willingness to share what you have with others and the gift that you can bring to other people. That's a truly royal person—one who is generous and magnificent and enormous in spirit and achievement which he was.

Concurrently, certain quarters of the black community were said to be disturbed by Buckley's shtick, which they regarded as outdated at the very least.

Adam Keefe

I was with Buckley the day before he died or a couple of days before he died. I was up at his place at his invitation. And he had some underage mulatto chick up there running around naked. He had a bottle of vodka into which he was dropping mescaline tablets from time to time. They were dissolving the mescaline into the vodka and he was swigging this bottle. He offered me a swig and at first I said, "No, no, that's a little scary to me." So finally, on his dare, I took one little sip of the goddamned thing and I was up for three days and nights seeing everything in Technicolor.

I really think that's what kicked off his heart. He had this chick running naked around the joint and the both of them were swigging this vodka. Supposedly, the semiofficial version was that he had had a heart attack while making it with her.

But there's another story that went around. Somebody that was with him when he died said that the last thing he said was, "Spo-Dee-O-Dee," and then he died.

Spo-Dee-O-Dee was a black comedian who I think was based in Chicago. And the story is that a lot of Buckley's material or his approach to material was taken from Spo-Dee-O-Dee. It's also said that a lot of the black musicians hated Buckley because they felt he was ripping off Spo-Dee-O-Dee. I never saw Spo-Dee-O-Dee perform myself.

Spo-Dee-O-Dee was in the black entertainment world when there was a color line. There were places that whites worked and places that blacks worked like the Cotton Club. They were in other cities, too, like Chicago. I think Spo-Dee-O-Dee worked in clubs like that but he might have also worked in clubs that white people wouldn't go near.

There was some suspicion that he was murdered by Spo-Dee-O-Dee or by people who were close to Spo-Dee-O-Dee. My understanding was that some of the musicians, or some of the patrons of the club he was working in before he died, were threatening him and had a thing going against Buckley because they felt he had ripped off the black man in general and Spo-Dee-O-Dee in particular.

I was shocked by his death. The man seemed indestructible, invincible somehow. He was like one of those people that inspired you to believe he was going to live to 160. Because he was a powerful man, a big man. There was so much energy coming from him that you couldn't believe it could all of a sudden get shut off like that.

Dr. Oscar Janiger

There are several theories about his death. One was that he tangled with some Black Muslims who beat him up very badly. The other, and the one that I subscribe to, was that after he had his cabaret card taken from him the cops started harassing him in shifts night and day. They wanted five hundred bucks for the card and Buckley would not pay it. They wouldn't let him get any sleep and it put a terrible and, ultimately, fatal strain on him.

Mort Fega

He came to my house in New Rochelle for dinner on the Thursday night before his death, accompanied by two members of his court, Prince Lewis and Lady Bunny.

On Saturday morning Bunny called me up in an absolute panic saying that he was sick. I told her to call a doctor in their apartment building but apparently they didn't get much satisfaction. They ended up taking him to Columbus Hospital where I suppose they didn't have a lot of ancillary equipment to take care of him properly.

There was always a cloud over the circumstances of his passing. It has been said that in his apartment the night before his passing there was a heated discussion between Buckley and some militant blacks. There was also a rumor about a bottle of tainted wine found under a sofa in Buckley's apartment.

Harry "The Hipster" Gibson

All I know is that the cops took him off his gig and put him in the back of a police car and a couple of guys back there just whacked him around, punchin' him in the belly, bangin' him where you can't see. Yeah and they drove him home! They do something like that where they don't leave too many marks, whatever it is, but they just beat the shit out o' ya like that and they took him and like dropped him off at his place and he went up there and went to bed and he never woke. That was it. Aced out. He sure didn't deserve to go out that way. That's a royal bring-down.

Lewis Foremaster

There are a lot of stories about Lord Buckley's last days and although there was some strange stuff going on, I think he probably died of natural causes.

He was shacked up with a black chick for about a week before he died. In addition, he had a falling-out over something with these people who had an engraving place in the Village. I remember they left in a huff. There was tension.

Doc Humes

It was a martyrdom. That was one of the sad things about the whole thing. This country has a way of making martyrs out of its best people. The aged seer is a revered figure in folklore. They didn't go putting them out in the cold.

He got poisoned and that's that. There's not much else to say. It was a group that played in-between. That's neither here nor there: everybody knows he was done in.

Eldon Setterholm

He did get back to sipping wine and that might have hurt his liver. It might have been some sort of an attack that gave him paralysis that he died from. Others have said that it could be . . . special karate-type blows to the vital organs that would render him paralyzed and unable to express himself.

Dick Zalud

We saw him perform at the Jazz Gallery right before he died. It was really something to see. He was electrifying. I never saw him that good. But then he had his cabaret card taken from him.

That last night at the Jazz Gallery he put a joint on me. I put it in my pocket and I forgot all about it.

A couple of days later an owl flew right in front of our car. I'd never seen an owl fly but those two big eyes stared at me for half a second. It nearly hit the windshield of the car.

When we got home I found the joint. We decided to invite him for breakfast, smoke it and then he'd be in rare form.

Sure enough, the next morning I woke up and I called Buckley. This guy Prince Lewis answered the phone and told me, "His Lordship passed during the night."

Jon Hendricks

When they took away his ability to work in New York they killed him. He just died from a broken heart.

Ed Sullivan

He was a wonderful, decent man. During the war he was part of my troupe that entertained in hospitals all over the country. Nobody found it necessary to screen him then or have him carry a police card.

Larry Storch

You know, we never really thought Lord Buckley would die. We thought he had it from his mouth to God's ear.

Elaine Thomasen

When I heard he had passed on, I thought: "There is a man who's lived seven lifetimes in this one experience." He had a strong self-image. He was a rare, gifted man who had an individual brilliance—an aura about him. He could enjoy paupers or kings and be equally at ease.

Whatever truth or partial truth any of these tales may hold, it is clear that sometime on Saturday, November 12, Lord Buckley suffered some kind of seizure—probably a stroke, since paralysis seems to have been involved. After a delay of undetermined length, he was rushed to the charity ward at Columbus Hospital where he passed away soon after, officially pronounced dead by attending physician Dr. Younis Kao at 7:20 p.m. But the confusion continues even as to the exact cause of death. Newspaper accounts variously reported it as a stroke, a heart attack, a long-standing kidney disease, or uremic poisoning.

Buckley's death certificate sheds little light on the ultimate cause of death, indicating only that it was due to "natural causes." This document, partially filled out by Lady Buckley several days later, contains several interesting details, including, perhaps most poignantly, her description of her late husband's occupation: "artist."

Dr. James Macy

He died in character. His death was ironic.

Prince Foremaster told me that he had a heart attack while they were in a taxicab in Manhattan. Buckley always called the shots and said, "Take me back to the apartment." He said he didn't want to go to a hospital. So they went back to the apartment. He lay there complaining: "The Bugbird is eating my heart." This went on for a few hours and then he died.

Anyway, that's what he told me. People can judge it any way they want. So to me, being a physician, that was the great tragedy because he might have possibly been saved.

Ann Brooks

Sometimes when I think about his death I burst into tears right on the street and hang on to a parking meter. It still gets me.

It just happened so fast. He was waiting for the hearing where he was going to plead his case to get the police card back so he could go back to work and he died the night before we were to go to court.

I had been away for a night or two doing a photo shoot and I got a call from Prince Lewis who told me that some people from the Village Church were over to visit Lord Buckley. Lord Buckley had a very mystical thing about these people coming from the Village Church to visit him. But Prince Lewis said they kind of put him down. They also brought Lord Buckley some whiskey which had made him ill. He had gone to sleep but when he woke up he couldn't move.

When I got there Lord Buckley was in his bed stretched out stiff. At first I thought he was dead. But when I went up to him I could see that his eyes were moving, that he was breathing and still alive. He couldn't talk, he just uttered a few sounds.

Lord Buckley was desperately ill and we had to get him to a hospital immediately. We didn't want to take him to Bellevue—he was very upset with the thought of going to Bellevue because I could see the reaction in his eyes when I mentioned Bellevue.

But we did call Bellevue because we had no money and no choice. Somehow, though, we got magically mixed up and had called Columbus Hospital instead, which was about four blocks from where we were living.

And then something very strange happened. Along with the two ambulance doctors came the ambulance driver who was a magical little man. He was the size of an elf, about three foot six, and he looked like one too. He was charming but absolutely ridiculous looking in his ambulance hat with the little red cross on it. They put Lord Buckley on the stretcher and all the time I'm admonishing them: "Be careful with this royal man. He's a beautiful, talented, loving gentleman."

I sat in the back with Lord Buckley and held his hand. When we got to the hospital I looked around for this elf to thank him but he wasn't there—he just disappeared.

In the emergency room I was still warning everybody to be careful with Lord Buckley and instantly there were about ten doctors and surgeons around him putting tubes and things in his arm and mouth. We got him up to his room and I said, "Hang on. Hang on Lord Buckley. Please hang on."

I began recalling his thing about Gulley Jimson from *The Horse's Mouth* when Gulley Jimson was dying and commented that laughing and praying were the same thing. And Lord Buckley began to laugh. I was holding his hand and I told him, "Well, I've got all the monologues, everything you've done. Now all I need is a little help."

And the one hand that he used was in mine. Somehow he managed to take his hand out of mine and wrap it around mine. I held on to it and I felt a little tingle going through his body to mine. And that was it. He flipped out. He just left.

Buckley's obituaries were bicoastal. The November 13, 1960, edition of the *New York Times* ran the following notice:

RICHARD BUCKLEY DIES

Entertainer, 54, Was Known as the Hip Messiah

Richard M. Buckley, an entertainer known as Lord Buckley, died last night in Columbus Hospital. He had suffered a stroke earlier in the day at his apartment, 39 Gramercy Park West. He was 54 years old.

Mr. Buckley, who was known as the Hip Messiah, often had appeared on the Ed Sullivan television show. His only cafe appearance here in many years, at the Jazz Gallery, 80 St. Marks Place, was halted last month.

His license was suspended by the police, who said he had falsified information on his license.

Mr. Buckley, who sometimes performed wearing tails and sometimes wearing a sweater, often recited Biblical stories in the rhythmical jargon of hip, a purer form of the semi-secret language identified with the so-called Beat Generation. His stage name was derived from his height and regal bearing. During World War II he performed extensively before armed services audiences.

Mr. Buckley is survived by his widow, Elizabeth; a daughter Laurie, and two sons, Richard Jr. and Frederick.

The following day the *San Francisco Chronicle* ran its obit:

COMEDIAN LORD BUCKLEY DIES IN N.Y.

Richard (Lord) Buckley, the San Francisco comedian who rose to prominence on his "hip" version of the classics, died last night in New York City.

Mr. Buckley, 55, was in the East on a series of nightclub engagements. Until about two months ago, he and his wife and children had made their home in San Rafael.

A native of Tuolumne, Mr. Buckley had an entertainment career for more than three decades. He was at one time a Shakespearean actor and during World War II, toured extensively as a vaudeville performer.

He appeared with Fred Allen and Ginger Rogers in the movie "We're Not Married" and was in the Broadway musical "Passing Parade" in 1946.

Recently, he had appeared on the Ed Sullivan, Groucho Marx and Steve Allen television shows and was seen with Don Sherwood on his local program.

Mr. Buckley became best known for his "bop talk" renditions of Biblical, Shakespearean and other tales. He had recorded albums of these performances for RCA Victor and World Pacific.

City Lights bookstore had recently published a collection of these performances titled "Hiporama."

In addition to his wife, a daughter and two sons survive.

Locally, the *Village Voice* led the charge with its take in a long article, which appeared in its November 17, 1960, edition under the provocative head: "Graft Charged—Cabaret Card Fight Set Off by 'Lord' Buckley Death." Buckley's death received its widest national exposure when *Life* magazine ran a sympathetic spread on the cabaret card brouhaha in its December 5, 1960, issue. Along with one of Bob Parent's photos of Buckley and Humes arriving at the Jazz Gallery in a Rolls, the *Life* article featured pics of Joey Adams (baring his ink-smudged digits to a nightclub audience from a fingerprinting earlier in the day to obtain his new cabaret card) and one of a timely lineup of chorus girls at the International Club in full, top-hatted costume, waving their cards at the customers in a telling sign of anti-cabaret-card solidarity.

The show, however, went on without Buckley. Humes and members of his Citizen's Emergency Committee showed up at city hall for a hearing with the N.Y.P.D.'s brass on Monday, November 14, in what turned out to be an apparently unsuccessful bid to have Buckley's card posthumously reinstated—though there are some who claim it was returned "posthumorously." Meanwhile, Lady Buckley was quoted in the November 18 *New York Daily News* as saying: "My husband was going hot three weeks ago when they took away his card. To deny him the right to work was a terrible thing to do. You should have the right to work in show business like any other business. There shouldn't be this licensing."

The publicity scandal following Buckley's death was huge. And because it involved celebrities, the New York press kept it on the front pages for weeks. Entertainment unions called on Governor Nelson Rockefeller to investigate and he, in turn, asked Mayor Wagner for a report. Police Commissioner Stephen Kennedy ordered an intensive sweep of all cabarets, in order—repeating the too-often-employed bureaucratic mantra—"to prevent their becoming a rendezvous for criminals and persons of questionable character."

One thousand cops inspected 2,478 places just before Thanksgiving, when the raid's impact upon holiday business was at a peak. What they uncovered was a mass evasion of the regulations. The famous torch singer Sophie Tucker and her accompanist were working without cards at the International Club on Broadway. In every major establishment people were found to be working without them. The Citizen's Emergency Committee thought that the N.Y.P.D.'s outcry about lax enforcement was beside the point, as what they sought was no enforcement.

Most sensationally, it turned out that none other than Frank Sinatra, Old Blue Eyes himself, had worked New York clubs in the late 1950s without a cabaret card. Police Commissioner Kennedy, after first rashly denying that it was possible, discovered that Sinatra had repeatedly worked at the Copacabana without his license. Sinatra was even quoted as saying, "I will not seek a cabaret card in New York because of the indignity of being fingerprinted, mugged and quizzed about my past."

Finally, the cops, in an obvious case of harassment, also went after Humes, branding him as a traffic scofflaw, charging that he had ignored twelve tickets since 1958.

At the end of November Maxwell Cohen began another lawsuit in the state supreme court against the cabaret card system, this one brought on by singer Nina Simone, composer/arranger/musician Quincy Jones, the Village Gate nightclub, and some dissidents in the musicians' union. But when pushed, the N.Y.P.D. pushed back in the form of another crackdown. The licenses for the premium clubs, including the Copacabana, the Stork Club, and El Morocco, were suspended. Joey Adams, who, like Sinatra, had refused to apply for a card, was forced to get one but said, "Why should we have to get police permission to work any more than the guys in the dress business or newspaper reporters? If even an ex-convict has paid his debt to society and is law-abiding, I don't see why he has to pay a bribe to somebody in order to be allowed to play a horn or dance in a nightclub."

The implication of the practice at large was that those with power and money did not have to comply with the rules while perceived fringe characters like Lord Buckley, an anonymous jazz musician, or a club employee would be forced to comply and face the low regard in which they and their haunts were held. Continuing its coverage of the scandal, the *Village Voice* ran an article in its December 22, 1960, issue alleging that members of the Citizen's Emergency Committee were subjected to subtle police harrassment.

The immediate results of this publicity avalanche were pathetically paltry. The fancy clubs got their licenses back through legal remedy, and Mayor Wagner reported no substantial evidence of corruption. At the beginning of 1961 the mayor announced that the cabaret cards of musicians and entertainers would be made permanent, rather than renewable, and that the administration of the cards would be transferred to the Department of Licenses. Police Commissioner Kennedy declared himself overjoyed as he had never much enjoyed the task of policing the cabarets, perhaps because he realized the potential of corruption. Nina Simone's case was dismissed on an ancient legal precedent as the court reinforced the policy of using the cabaret cards to control corrupting influences.

But the seed was planted within the hearts and minds of New York's liberal Democratic political establishment, and by the end of 1967 the battle that Lord Buckley unintentionally started was won when the cabaret card system was finally abolished in the city.

All of this was much too late for Lord Buckley. His funeral on November 16 at the Frank E. Campbell Chapel on Eighty-first Street and Madison Avenue (just a block east of where Charlie Parker died nearly six years earlier) was attended by about fifty mourners, including Lady Elizabeth, who had flown in from the coast. Fittingly, Ed Sullivan (who reportedly made the arrangements for and picked up the tab for the funeral), Mort Fega, and Father John Gensel, the jazz pastor, are remembered as having delivered poignant eulogies. Later that day Lord Buckley's remains were cremated at the Ferncliff Crematory in Hartsdale, New York. The ashes were later scattered on a mountain outside Las Vegas, though there are a few who claim that he was buried in an unmarked Potter's Field grave.

Richmond Shepard

The coffin was open from the waist up as far as I could see and he was wearing his white tie and tails. But it was propped up a little bit and he was just lying there, looked like Lord Buckley asleep. You know he was only fifty-four years old but he died of old age.

Mort Fega

J. Fred Coots, composer of such great American standards as "You Go to My Head," a man who was held in very high esteem in the popular music domain, was supposed to deliver a eulogy. At the last minute, Elizabeth came up to me and said he couldn't do it, would I? Christ . . . every hipster in town was there.

He was laid out stiff and stark virtually at my feet as I was talking. There was a quote on the back of one of his Vaya albums, the one about people being flowers, which I thought was particularly appropriate to the occasion and which The Great Architect in His infinite sympathy allowed me to remember.

There was a great bond between us even though I knew him a for a comparatively short time. And I feel really privileged to have had the opportunity to speak at his funeral. I'd had no time to prepare my remarks, so I'm convinced that Lord Buckley was whispering in my ear as I concluded my homage with this wonderfully appropriate quote of his, "The flowers, the gorgeous, mystic, multicolored flowers are not the flowers of life, but people, yes people, are the true flowers of life. And it has been a most precious privilege to have temporarily strolled in your garden."

Tubby Boots

I hadn't seen His Lordship or Lady Lizbeth for some years when I walked into Campbell's Funeral Home. I'm sitting there thinking to myself, "How is Elizabeth going to come in? Is she going to come in mourning wearing black? Or is she going to remember what Buckley told her: "Always wear colors like flowers." She came in through the door wearing the brightest red Chinese dress with yellow and red palms in her hair. She came over to me and said, "Prince Charles, His Lordship is waiting." And we walked in.

And if anybody looked like they were ready to get up and do a performance, it was Lord Buckley. He looked so majestic in death, just as he did in life. I expected him to sit up and say, "Lily! Good God, you came!"

Cannonball Adderly and his band played at the ceremony.

And I watched one of the most touching things. A comedian named Sid Gould walked over to the casket, bent down, stuck a joint in Buckley's breast pocket, kissed him, and said, "When you get there, here's a little thing for you."

Afterwards, a few of us drove in a limo out to the crematorium with a supply of joints. All the way out there we smoked reefer, including the driver of the limo. And we talked about all the beautiful things that had happened in our life with Lord Buckley.

Lady Buckley looked up and said, "He's here in the car with us, you know. He's enjoying this."

And you could feel that he hadn't left yet. He wasn't about to go anywhere. He was still digging the scene.

In early December many of Lord Buckley's friends and admirers mourned his passing with a memorial service to benefit the Royal Family at the Village Gate several weeks after his death. Eulogies were given, stories told, and glasses raised as Dizzy Gillespie and Ornette Coleman blew a cosmic blues deep into the mystic night.

Lord Buckley

Love is the international understanding that each and every one of us have exactly the same problems to fight.

19 stompin' the sweet swingin' sphere

Lord Buckley

What a great thing it is to be alive. My Lords my Ladies . . . would it embarrass you very much if I were to tell you that . . . I love you?

It embarrasses you, doesn't it?

As with most underground geniuses, Lord Buckley's reputation and artistic contributions have gained in power in the years since his passing. No graffiti appeared on the New York subway walls or subterranean commode stalls across America sounding a phoenixlike rise from the ashes as the message "Bird Lives" had done in 1955. But like Charlie Parker, Lord Buckley had boldly crossed the ill-defined frontier from icon to myth. He had taken the language of his art from dross and cliché, and invested it with new intensity, color, and significance.

Buckley's name and routines have been magically invoked since the 1960s like some sorcerer's talisman. Titles like "The Nazz" acquired a cabalistic power for succeeding generations of Buckley admirers. Just as Mississippi Delta bluesman Robert Johnson was secretly revered by the guitar heroes of rock music, Lord Buckley became a code word for the modern hipnoscente. The process was much like the chameleon artisic evolutions of W. B. Yeats, Picasso, Miles Davis, or Bob Dylan; it was sensed that Buckley had similarly and deftly transformed himself from tent show roustabout to dance marathon emcee to nightclub shill to vaudeville comic to hip comic to metacomic to poet to healer to visionary mystic.

Almost exactly nine years after *Life*'s coverage of Buckley's death, the magazine began to fan the flames for his renaissance with a glowing full-page article extolling the virtues of the man's legacy in Albert Goldman's December 19, 1969, article. Coinciding with both the release of World Pacific's *Bad-Rapping of the Marquis de Sade* and the re-release of the Vaya material on Elektra's *The Best of Lord Buckley,* Goldman's celebratory prose helped ignite the mini–Buckley revival of the late 1960s and early 1970s, hipping the hippies to the cosmic comic's love vision.

Others have also attempted to wave Buckley's flag high. In 1983 C. P. Lee, a British actor/writer, launched a successful one-man show delivering some of Buckley's monologues at London's Red Lion Theatre.

That same year British actor John Sinclair and producer/director Richmond Shepard cowrote and launched "*Lord Buckley's Finest Hour*" in Los Angeles, a well-received one-man show mixing biography and shtick. Shepard joined forces with actor Tom Calagna for a rousing New York City revival of the show from 1996 through 1998.

Seeing Calagna work the room is to behold not merely a performer at the top of his game, but a Buckley oracle as well. With lungs like a lion and radiating a robust stage presence to boot, Calagna's meaty sets sampled a fine mix of His Lordship's most famous and obscure bits. Squint your eyes a little and you could easily believe that Lord B was in the room as well. A lot of the fun was Calagna's interplay with his sharp backing band led by drummer Joe Piazza. Jazz and poetry can be a dicey mix at best, but this alchemy was a match made in Valhalla as sound and sensibility merged in rare harmony.

Tom Calagna

Actor, comedian, orthopedic shoe specialist, baseball mystic, and wannabe scratch golfer Tom Calagna first learned of Lord Buckley from his late brother John as a youngster in the 1960s. A Lord Buckley channeler, he is among the finest imitators and interpreters of His Lordship's craft.

I was beyond amazed when I first heard Buckley. To me it wasn't comedy. It was hip philosophy. And his use of language just blew me away. It inspired me to do theater and comedy. I liked his use of hip talk. I liked his turning historical and religious themes into a beatnik vein of humanism. I've always described Lord Buckley as a "verbalist." He'd take terms and give them multiple meanings. I thought his cleverness, his speed of delivery and his use of black speech idioms were impressive. The two things I wanted to portray in my shows were his humanity and his nobility.

Don McCaslin, a Santa Cruz musician and composer, picked up where Sinclair and Shepard left off with *The Naz: A Bebop Drama,* which carefully wove Buckley's life, work, and times into first a series of performances and then a popular radio play.

In the mid-1990s Frank Speiser, a Cuban-born, Brooklyn-bred actor, was equally successful with his Buckley show titled *Are You There? (A Hip History Lesson).* Concurrently Jason Eisenberg, a Groton, Massachusetts–based home builder and visual artist, began reinventing his life as an ace Buckley channeler as he blanketed New England with his show *The Pounce of the Now.*

In a rare case of Lord Buckley gender-bending, Martha Cinader, a New York City poet, storyteller, and performing artist in the Buckley tradition, draws from his style of hipsemantics with an added feminine twist. Martha began exhibiting not only a kick bag full of Buckley riffs in her live presentations as the millennium drew to a close but some choice Buckley-inspired tales as well, particularly "Teslavision," her very cool take on the life and work of scientist/inventor Nikola Tesla.

Finally, the author has gathered many of the above-mentioned artists—Tom Calagna, Mikhail Horowitz, Richmond Shepard, Steve Ben Israel, and others—in various forms and configurations for *Dig and Thou Shall Be Dug,* semiannual group performances of Buckley's material in New York City.

In 1999 Charles Pike, an Aztec, New Mexico–based playwright and actor, collaborated with the author on *The Return of the Hip Messiah,* a stage play based on Buckley's Cosmic Tour and relationship with members of Second City, specifically Del Close. Produced by Chicago's Prop Theater and staged at Second City as part of the famed troupe's fortieth-anniversary celebration season in November 1999, *The Return of the Hip Messiah* featured Windy City thespian Richard Henzel in the title role of a lifetime and one in which he rose to the occasion, drawing raves in the Chicago press.

In literary quarters Buckley's influence is surprisingly paltry, with only *Been Down So Long It Looks Like Up to Me,* Richard Fariña's proto–Beat/hippie crossover novel published two days before his death in 1966, mentioning "Lord Buckley out doing the Gauguin," though Ken Kesey's Alaskan novel *Sailor Song* is laced with Buckleyisms.

Popular music, as we have seen, has been an altogether completely different story. By the 1970s Bob Dylan had incorporated Buckley's approach into his own vision; Joni Mitchell, David Bowie, and James Taylor had referenced Buckley in their work; Jimmy Buffett was covering Buckley's "God's Own Drunk" in concert; George Harrison had released "Crackerbox Palace" in tribute to the Hip Messiah; Frank Zappa had overseen the release of unearthed Buckley material and loosely incorporated His Lordship's absurdist ethos into some of his work; and Tom Waites freely acknowledged His Lordship's influence on his unique repertoire. To bring the rock music connection fuller circle, the late, influential critic Lester Bangs is known to have treasured no less than three Buckley discs: *Bad-Rapping*, *hip aristocrat,* and *Blowing His Mind.*

One of the more intriguing and successful attempts to reinvigorate Buckley's legacy can be found in the work of flutist/composer/arranger Robert Dick. Dick, who has virtually invented a new language for his instruments, has composed three very different pieces, all of which incorporate Buckley riffs into his aesthetic. "Digging It Harder from Afar" (named with a line from "Gettysburg Address" in mind) from Dick's 1994 CD of the same title is the most accessible of the trio—a driving, jazz-infused foray incorporating a hard-bop edge. "A Black Lake with a Blue Boat on It" (named for a line from "The Bad-Rapping of the Marquis de Sade") is, as one might expect from the source of the title, a much darker instrumental with Oriental overtones and can be found on Dick's 1991 CD *Venturi Shadows.* Undoubtedly Dick's most fully realized venture into all things Buckley can be found on an ambitious, unreleased composition titled "My Own Railroad" in which he avants the garde by performing over a vocoded sampling of short Buckley riffs drawn from the Buckley bit of the same name and "The Nazz."

Robert Dick

A brilliant and very adventurous flutist pushing the limits of his instrument, Robert Dick is perhaps the most unusual artistic disciple of Lord Buckley's. Dick, who graduated from the Yale School of Music, has played with a who's who of "new music," including Steve Lacy, Evan Parker, George Lewis, John Zorn, Marty Ehrlich, New Winds, and Tambastics.

I've been into Lord Buckley since playing a cassette found in an apartment in Paris (sublet from an Australian opera singer, a soprano no less) in 1978. Thought Lord Buckley was Lord Sutch, a lead-throated heriditary Early of the wrong Court—a genetic sneeze really—with the loot to hire oveerdrugged rock stars to indulge his abcessed talents. Desperate for a non-opera tape I, a professional musician, a creative artist of young, but growing repute, was ready to settle for the sludge of "Lord Sutch and His Heavy Friends." I was driven to this lower case compromise by the lonliness of the instant—a magic combo of isolation from the flood-tide of humanity streaming Frenchily about, and a stupid, crashed affair with a not-so-great jazz singer—and, salting the wounds were all those *God-Damned Opera Cassettes* cluttering the crib! Verily, it was a depressed soul who depressing the play button, certain that a snort of an early-Seventies fart was momentarily to ensue. And then, ssshhhhhhBAM! A MIRACLE!! With a titanic bong, fate's gong announced the dissolution of the dismal, for at that moment Lord Buckley issued himself forth from the unknown (the swinging, whopping, wailing unknown that was unknown to *me,* that was) and rolled out the red carpet to the Court of Joy.

Buckley is the greatest storyteller I've ever heard and the hundreds of hours spent grooving in the Court have clearly effected my art. Buckley shows in my phrasing and inflections on the flute and I've made two pieces directly influenced by him. The title "A Black Lake with a Blue Boat on It" does of course came from "Bad-Rapping." And the music is definitely about a ride into the not-so-comfy unknown. A very recent piece, "My Own Railroad," uses small snippets of Buckley's voice to vocode musical textures created by the flute with delay devices.

311, a California-based techno-pop band cut out of the same cloth as the Red Hot Chili Peppers, released a tune called "Brodels" on its eponymous 1995 CD that referenced Lord Buckley, the Nazz, and Trevor Cole (Lord Buckley's grandson, who roadied for the band and turned them onto Lord B)—sampling snippets of Buckley and including lines like: "The Brodels is the Nazz and the Nazz knows where it's at." The cut would fit right into the audio fabric of an all-night acid house rave.

Working in a similar vein, Trans-Global Underground, a British techno-pop conglomerate, invoked Buckley's "Hipsters, Flipsters" mantra on its 1998 CD and on stage as well. According to band member Alex Kasiek: "Lord Buckley records were the sort of mysterious obscurities you'd find in British junk shops many years ago (and may well still be). I think I bought one because there was a blurb on the back about how he was the only person to have started a church to have been raided by the Vice Squad. Don't know if this is true . . . anyway, it came in useful when I started DJing. I've long had a habit of mixing Lord Buckley stuff into the middle of other people's records while working as a DJ, and the 'Mark Anthony Funeral Oration' was always a favourite. The song 'Nile Delta Disco' was originally an instrumental and I used to spin that piece over it; so Tuup, the vocalist, naturally chucked it into the stew of lyrics he was creating. (We did wonder where the 'Hipsters, Flipsters . . .' phrase came from . . . the first time I heard it was on a song by British-based American soul singer Geno Washington.)

The song itself is really a collection of random ideas, impulses and musical improvisations by a whole bunch of disparate people, some of whom have never met each other. So a little Lord Buckley tribute does seems very fitting. Incidentally, when DJing to a particularly difficult crowd, a blast of the 'Bad-Rapping of the Marquis de Sade' often does the trick."

Buckley's work showed up in some not-so-surprising quarters as well. Jazz singer and Grammy-nominated wunderkind Kurt Elling included "It's Just a Thing," a marvellously fanciful story and hilariously warped never-fade-away insider's tribute to His Lordship with no fewer than a half-dozen references to the Master's Voice, on his 1997 CD *The Messenger.*

David Amram beat them all to the punch with his unique orchestral composition "Ode to Lord Buckley" in 1980. A stirring synthesis of jazz, classical, and court music as filtered through Amram's broad sensibility, it continues to be performed as the millennium flips.

But recorded sound and the traditional spoken-word presentation were by no means the last outpost disseminating Lord Buckley's work. *Crap,* a spunky, punky New Wave comic produced by J. R. Williams, a Pacific Northwest graphic artist following in the valiant footsteps of R. Crumb and *Zap Comix,* quoted Buckley in the mandate of his first issue ("It is the duty of any given nation in time of high crisis to attack the catastrophe that faces it in such a manner as to cause the people to laugh at it in such a way that they do not die before they get killed") and included the odd visual representation of Lord Buckley in his comic. In 1997 Williams created "Dig," a set of collector cards that, along with Lord Buckley, included such spoken-word recording artists as Rudy Ray Moore, Kenneth Patchen, Captain Beefheart, Brother Theodore, and Lenny Bruce. Speaking of R. Crumb, his son Jesse's 1995 collaboration with Erica Detlefsen produced the colorful "Beat Characters," a nouveau weirdo trading card set with a card representing a pith-helmeted Lord Buckley. "Oddballs & Visionaries," a 1992 card set produced by WFMU (the must-hear free-form radio station sending signals from its base in Jersey City, New Jersey) featured a colorfully subterranean Doug Allen pen-and-ink rendition of the hip aristocrat in all his noir, tuxedoed glory. Additionally, *Nowheresville,* a noirish comic evoking the ethos of the Beats and B-movies, published a glossary of hip Buckleyisms in 1996.

An image from a 1997 trading card.
Artist: J.R. Williams. Used with permission.

In the realm of the moving image a surprising dearth of expression has been attempted. An ample chunk from "Nero" (the "he come swangin' down doin' a Mexican Tailspin and the Japanese a bab-a-dap" section) showed up as part of a Lee Marvin monologue in *Pocket Money,* a 1972 comical modern-day western. Based on a book by J. K. S. Brown, the film depicts an impoverished and deeply indebted cowboy (Paul Newman) and his con artist pal (Marvin) who find themselves hopelessly engaged with an outlaw rancher (Strother Martin)—a *Cat Ballou* meets *Butch Cassidy and the Sundance Kid* with a dash of *The Sting* kind of thing.

In 1996 poets Joshua Blum and Bob Holman included the introduction to Buckley's "The Train" as a voice-over in a shot of a steaming locomotive in *The United States of Poetry,* a five-part series celebrating the tapestry of American lyric that was broadcast on PBS.

More significantly and aesthetically successful (though far less publicly), Oakland, California, videographer Ian Moore created several distinct visual environments for Buckley's work: a straight-ahead actor's re-creation of Buckley's club act with "The Nazz" as the obvious designated rave of choice; a surrealist/dadaist collage of "Supermarket"; a cute switch of the original soundtrack in the Marlon Brando "Friends, Romans, Countrymen" soliloquiy in the film of *Julius Caesar* with Buckley's hipsemantic translation; and a most interesting re-rendering of Buckley's "Scrooge" employing still shots of exotic African masks doing the talking if not the walking.

In the realm of philosophy, a group of surrealists led by Joseph Jablonski, author of the introduction to the City Lights reprint of *Hiparama of the Classics,* cofounded the first and only journal devoted the art and life of Lord Buckley, *The Hipsomantic Times,* a 1990 one-shot effort featuring poetry, interviews, tract, and treatise.

Even during his lifetime Buckley was a natural for late-night, free-form, all-frantic radio—a tradition kept up most notably by Vin Scelsa, a beloved New York City DJ who traditionally spins Buckley's "Scrooge" at Yuletide on his tangentially formatted program *Idiot's Delight.* Additionally, Bob Fass has been spinning Buckley discs since the early 1960s on his program, "Radio Unnameable," emanating on New York City's WBAI.

Bringing things up to the pounce of the cybernetic now, Michael Monteleone, a Puget Sound artist, has created "Lord Buckley Online," an Internet site: www.industrialhaiku.com/Lord_Buckley_Online.html. For even more information on and fun with Lord B, tune into a computer near you.

Maybe the greatest stride Buckley's legacy made toward some kind of acceptance in the academy was his inclusion, albeit a small one, in the Whitney Museum of American Art's 1996 retrospective, *Beat Culture and the New America, 1950–1965,* in which a Bill Claxton photo of His Lordship hung on a wall beside the likes of Jack Kerouac, Neal Cassady, Allen Ginsberg, and Gary Snyder while a sampling of his verbal artistry was available along with the grooves of Pres, Bird, Diz, and Trane at an audio installation adjacent to the exhibit.

It has taken more than three decades, but the Buckley legacy is finally being properly acknowledged. Not only is much of his catalogue of haphazardly released commercial recordings now in distribution, but the art form he helped pioneer, rap, is the most prevalent and controversial form of current popular American expression.

Additionally *His Royal Hipness,* a 1992 repackaging of the Vaya material, was named the number one comedy CD of the year by Tower Records' *Pulse* magazine.

On the bizarre end of the spectrum, the nuttiest tribute to Lord Buckley can be found at the grassroots radio station WJFF in Jeffersonville, New York, a short hike over the mountain from the site of the original Woodstock Music and Arts Festival at Yasgur's Farm. The progressive station, the work of a wizened pixie by the name of Malcom Brown, is often hydropowered by a sweet nonstop spinning vintage 1918 waterwheel that Brown named "Lord Buckley" because its syncopated rhythm is reminscent of Buckley's vocal technique on "The Hip Gahn."

Perhaps the most compelling testament to Buckley's alive and jumping staying power were the semiannual Lord Buckley Memorial Celebrations held in Southern California in the late 1980s and early 1990s. To an outsider, the event appeared to be something of a cross between a meeting of the Brontë Society and a Grateful Dead concert as a wild gumbo of gonzo revelers decked out in tie-dyes and pith helmets (and sometimes nothing at all) remembered His Lordship with a bash he would have appreciated.

Punctuating the event was a smorgasbord of musical entertainment with Buckley imitators performing his lost classics and appearances by the Royal Family: Lady Elizabeth, Princess Laurie, Prince Richard, Prince Fred, Laurie's children Prince Trevor and Princess Nicolette, and an assortment of regal canines.

Originally conceived as a way to bring together the forward-thinking and -acting elements of the area in a forum of dialogue and good times, the celebration's founders, Mark Schecter and Fred Zingeser, decided to focus the event on the spirit of Lord Buckley's love, warmth, and humor. What money the not-for-profit gathering garnered was earmarked for environmental and humanitarian groups like Greenpeace and Amnesty International.

The highlight of the event was Lady Buckley's demonstration of "Ballet for Living," the original choreography she developed during the heyday of the Royal Court. On stage she resembled a medieval squire or a wood sprite from *A Midsummer Night's Dream.* As she floated across the stage, all present became members in good standing of the Royal Court, while somewhere above the dusty hills in the rich blue sky Lord Buckley was smiling.

Lord Buckley

Make the most of all that comes. Make the least of all that goes.

Lady Elizabeth Buckley

When I lost him, when the family lost him, all my friends were as kind and generous and as beautiful as he was. They looked after me but we talked all we could talk and I still couldn't sleep—I still couldn't let go because I had been so terribly angry. I couldn't understand how they could take this man out. Why him? I went through all of those different scenes.

After His Lordship died we were pressed for money. And since I had two children to raise, it was very difficult for me. I struggled with getting certain record companies to pay royalties that were owed to us. But mostly I was never able to get them to come across. I had to go out and find a straight job and totally change my way of life which was . . . amusing.

I'm convinced that if His Lordship had lived another two years he'd have become a rock star. His and Charles Parker's deaths at such early ages were a terrible blow to the arts of this country. They were close friends. Imagine the magnificent things they could have created working together.

Paul Zaloom

Buckley's whole philosophy about God being those two guys on the San Berdoo Freeway that change his tire for him was an idea I had in my head. But hearing Buckley talk about it like that made it gel. So in the end of one of my pieces about religion, I hold up a mirror to the audience showing them to be God. That was inspired by Buckley's idea and I believe that. It's influenced the way I behave towards my child. But at the same time I believe that the way you worship God is by loving your children. I'm an agnostic—I don't believe in God but I believe in Buckley's God.

The way he articulated these things with such tremendous beauty and conviction became terribly important to me.

Doc Humes

Lord Buckley's stuff was very popular during the late 1950s. You used to hear it all the time on the late-night jazz shows. I was into listening to late-night jazz formats. There were a number of them who sort of started replaying Buckley's work. And Buckley is one of those people who just comes out every few years or so. He catches on again and there's another spate of interest in his work and then it falls in abeyance and then it catches on again. He's been like that for years. Every generation sort of discovers Buckley on their own and then they branch out into the rest of his stuff. It's a pretty interesting phenomenon actually.

Buckley's idea was that great ideas survived best in the vernacular. And he pointed to Dante and Cervantes as artists before him who were both praised and put down for writing in the vital vulgar rather than in the dead issue. There were two kinds of people who didn't like this man: those for whom the status wasn't quo enough, and those for whom the status was too damned quo to bear.

Revolutionaries didn't like him because he dug that it made no difference who be in the driver's seat since, no matter who, he be bound to square up—since square be the shape of all driver's seats. Nice people didn't like him because he talked about freedom as though he meant it (and he did), and he was even hurt in the last weeks of his life by musicians whose work he loved, who put him down for talking like a downhome Negro when he wasn't. He was hit hard by the cracker attack from *both* sides of the shadow line. But that's the way the corn shucks, I suppose. Nobody looks to motives anymore, just labels. And there are not many easy riders around to keep things level, either. But there you go. Everybody's got to have something to care about. And Buckley cared about Gandhi, who got more done in a few decades than perhaps any single man in recent history. He told me once that, "It's the greedheads that will destroy this country, the greedheads." And he's right. Any other kind of head gets busted.

James Taylor

I think people may well rediscover Buckley. But if he were alive today trying to make it, I don't know how he would fare. Now, if you make it, you have to make it on TV and you basically have to interface with corporate information and show business in order to progress into a career. I think that would have been too much to ask of him.

He was a real artist and for that reason there was an impossibility to his being in the world. My guess is that he was too genuine, too out there to come to market in an acceptable way.

In his day you could find a subculture, an alternative culture that would support you. You didn't rely on being on TV. But television now has permeated the global mass media farther and farther so there are very few things that can exist without having a television identity. Some people handle it well and some things handle it well but that would not have been my guess about Lord Buckley.

Studs Terkel

We have all these new kids of the moment, to use Lillian Hellman's phrase. "The Kid of the Moment," "The New Star," et cetera. We're so accustomed to that Andy Warhol celebrity "Fifteen Minutes" that there's no span of attention or remembrance. We suffer from a national Alzheimer's disease, politically, socially and culturally. There is no yesterday. But Lord Buckley is still so warm and rich. He was all-enveloping.

Albert Goldman

Is Lord Buckley due for a revival? Can *nostalgie de la boogie-woogie* rehabilitate this long-gone and I do mean gone Hipster Saint? Can you imagine a comic getting his break nearly twenty years after his death? Not as a once-famous performer coming back from the grave, mind you—like W. C. Fields or Lenny Bruce—but as a complete unknown coming out of nowhere to posthumous fame? Can you picture this Great Unknown, this man without a face, without a legend or even without a crown of thorns becoming a byword as this generation's superfunny grandfather figure? If you can't handle this mental overload, you obviously aren't ready for the Lord Buckley Trip.

Buckley appears to have vaulted over his own and the intervening age to land smack down the middle of these Aquarian times. Too healthy for sick humor, too Western for New York humor, too gentile for Jewish humor, too generous for sarcasm and too ebullient for satire, a total anachronism in the old days, Lord

Buckley is today the only comic perfectly in tune with what is happening.

Whether you look at the man as a master mixer of the media, a pop-eyed bard of blackness or the first great surfer on that sea of Eastern mysticism that is engulfing our youth, Buckley checks out as beautiful and contemporary. Everything that once might have seemed forced or false in his art suddenly rings true. Now you want to be with him, digging the man's indomitable gusto, his wild and whirling words, his vocal bops and beats—digging everything right down to his low boozy chuckle and ripely flatulent Bronx cheer. What is there left to say? The only good comic is a dead comic!

Francis Newton

Nightclub satire is a golden activity in America these days. Bob Newhart ("the man with the button-down mind") outsells Presley on LP. Mort Sahl, his poisoned fangs smothered in the embrace of *Time* magazine, clocks up grosses which inspire *Variety* to its hippest headlines ("Mort Sahl Boffo at Blinstrubs in Boston"). Norman Granz, the jazz impresario—jazz and nightclub satire go together like rugby and beer—has just sold his Verve record label for over two and a half million dollars, largely on the strength of his foresight in signing up Shelley Berman, Sahl and other nighttime gravediggers of Nixon's U.S. If Lord Buckley (the title reflected a persistent strain of anglomania in this very American artist) had lived, perhaps he too would have earned a lot of money. Now he will never be tempted to conciliate the squares.

The few who knew him classified him wrongly with the 'far-out' comedians of the 1950s, probably because he also breathed out jazz as Spanish shepherds exhale garlic. He was older. His technique was that of a glorified amateur; he timed his act like a striking rattler. Sahl is not thinkable in a Montmartre cabaret of the Toulouse-Lautrec period. Buckley was, which is, perhaps why he was not the better act. Above all, he was not a critic but a preacher, "the Hip Messiah" as he told the puzzled New York nuns from his deathbed. He dreamed of a big rock candy world where cats and chicks have a perpetual ball, bathed in the rays of equality and love; Gandhi's and Jesus's as well as Venus's. It is a sentimental utopia, but then both America and show biz have soft centers. Nevertheless, it is a genuine utopia.

He had a stroke in November, on the verge of success, when the New York police withdrew his cabaret card, a well-known device for shaking down artists. (His death produced a public campaign against the police.) He leaves behind a Volkswagen mini-bus, a few numbers played in his honor by Monk and Gillespie, a record or two, and a lot of tape which ought to be issued. May he have a ball wherever he is.

Judith Malina

It's people like Lord Buckley that inspire us to feel that the energetic active hot form of life isn't really over with when you get your first gray hair and after that you're a has-been and over the hill. Buckley's vision was so clear and so strong and will always be with us because it forms rings upon rings with the generations. It was a seed that not only came to fruit in the 1960s but is still coming to fruit. It's still happening. We're still fighting that revolution.

The other day all of us theaters that get a little something from the government got this directive that we had to sign promising that we say nothing obscene on stage including not mentioning the subject of homosexuality. So we're still fighting about that kind of liberatory behavior that says: "I am the revolution!" Lord Buckley brought that to us.

I think he thought the social structure was vicious and that what he felt he was showing us was a way to battle it with the best which is in us rather than with the worst in us which is the violence that exists in all of us. He was saying: "Here's the best in us which is humor and love. Rise above the situation with aplomb and imagination and bursts of energy!"

Joseph Jablonski

On the way to Eldorado you will meet, if you travel far enough, the wandering shade described in Edgar Allan Poe's haunting poem of the name; then you may even chance to meet the utopian legions of American Fourierism, lost but still searching; and then, farther along than these or any other aspirants of the impossible, you will certainly espy the frontier's hip Paracelsus himself—none other than Alvar Núñez Cabeza de Vaca (The Gasser), who once upon a time was reincarnated as Lord Buckley.

No doubt can exist about this: if the spirit of the sixties was in vibrant life anywhere prior to December 31, 1959, all of it (if not more) was concentrated in Lord Buckley's aggressive, optimistic humor. And *optimism* is a colorless word indeed with which to describe the brilliant dialectical gold rays the one and only Lord of Swing could direct to the blind apostles of the fifties-style miserablism. No American entertainer or humorist had ever done what Buckley did in the sense of bringing a great reality and immediacy to the notions of genius and inspiration (freedom, really), and at the same time demystifying the "greats" themselves. Lenny Bruce, who is said to have been influenced by Buckley, could hit very hard; but he lacked Buckley's extravagant generosity and his instinct to transcend malice with moral miracles.

At the time of his death, in the early sixties, he was the most noted of the "hip" or "bop" comedians who performed their routines in jive slang. At one juncture or another he had been obscure, ignored, imitated, and applauded.

If Buckley's fame has slipped during the "slipped-disc seventies," that of his imitators has vanished. They were the drunken pallbearers who quickly fell on their faces in the mud, while the royal coffin floated away to the strains of the Hallelujah Chorus. But apart from the imitators, the image of "pallbearers" seems to arise here specifically to remind us of Ishmael Reed, who has captured some of the spirit of Lord Buckley in his books, such as *The Free-lance Pallbearers*.

In any case, Buckley's legend has a built-in resistance to facile adulation. The moment anyone begins to revere or eulogize him, one hears in response the creaking of an insidious laughter. It appears to emanate from the pores of a creature half-sphinx and half-pomegranate. Suddenly, in a flash, Sun Ra approaches in a chariot from the direction of his ancestral star, and Apache warriors in terrible garb line the horizon. Inflamatory spectacles of Umor attend the thought or mention of Lord Buckley. Posthumous fame of the conventional order is completely irrelevant.

Fourier, because of his extravagant good will which wreaked havoc on the acknowledged principles of rationality, has a special place in Andre Breton's *Anthology of Black Humor* alongside Lautreamont, Peret, Roussel and the other exemplars of mad laughter. Perhaps there is no fitter comparison by which to gauge the extremes of Lord Buckleyism than Fourier himself. An appalling and ruinous generosity pervades both men, begetting a kind of *white* humor serving the same subversive function as the black. The key to Lord Buckley's alchemy was undoubtedly his "umorous" technique of inflation that allowed him to both valorize and satirize Great Men like Gandhi (The Hip Ghan), Jesus (The Naz) and Cabeza de Vaca (The Gasser), while contriving somehow to diffuse their mythical, miraculous gifts within a spirit of bop egalitarianism and universal aristocracy of the free.

Like many of his routines, Lord Buckley's own life was a hectic and chaotic parody of grandiosity. He held court constantly and he had willing courtiers because he was, for many admirers, the Living Presence of Swing. Ironic as it may seem to some, Lord Buckley in his humor took up the sword of the many lay prophets through history who fought to free man's inner gifts from the repressive and authoritarian deformation of them contained in religious ideology. His boisterous hedonism, challenging bourgeois morality at every turn, fits the same context. It is the pleasure principle allied to poetry, which fights against the reality principle, allied to the religious "truth": "There's someone bigger than you on the block, boy, so kneel." Lord Buckley gave proof of an immense awareness of the grandeur that existed outside of him, but he did not think it would represent any tribute to that grandeur if he groveled in front of an altar. "People should worship people," was his reply.

Jim Burns

It is always a great disapointment when one finds out about something good taking place, after it has actually happened. In a way, that is how it has be with "Lord" Buckley; the proof of his artistry only became available to us after his death.

The great point in Buckley's favor is that, unlike some of the other satirists, his work does not date; in any case, as has been pointed out, he was not a critic but a preacher. The problems he dealt with were, on the whole, the ever-present ones which have occupied the attention of preachers, philosophers, and thinkers since time immemorial. The humor and comment in his work will still be relevant in the future, and his use of slang was skillful enough to ensure it being understood by his audience. He believed that great ideas survive best in vernacular and he was sincere enough to put his beliefs into practice, even to the extent of making things hard for himself by doing so.

Buckley called the cabarets where he worked "atomic age cathedrals" and he believed deeply in what he was doing. In his own way he was a religious man. Like The Nazz, he was trying to make other people see everything pretty too, and it was typical of him that at the time when his cabaret licence was seized, he told the police he thought they needed more love. It was once said of him that he wasn't willing to spout banalities to earn a dollar. Perhaps that is why we didn't hear of him when he was alive.

Dr. James Macy

Before Buckley there was silence. After Buckley there was a great rainbow of laughter. Laughter illuminated the great window to the cat's soul.

Jonathan Winters

Lord Buckley painted such great verbal portraits. I've never been able to single out many people who really put me on the floor. Buckley was one of them. I think he is going to last forever. I've got everything he ever did. On rainy days and chilly nights, summertime or whenever, I pull out one of his records and listen to it. People are going to rediscover Lord Buckley. He was a far-out dude. If you're a fan of his, you're a fan for life.

Charles Tacot

Sir Richard Buckley—Lord of Flip Manor, Royal Holiness of the Far Out, and Prophet of the Hip—has gone to his reward. It probably won't be as swinging as his life, but Valhalla will have a hard time keeping him down.

I think it is terribly difficult for anyone who really knew Richard Buckley to think of him as dead. It is more like he has been on an extended engagement in Reno and can't get back to town—I still expect a 4 a.m. phone call from him, trying to borrow money, and tendering an invitation to visit the new Castle, which is inevitably on top of a mountain or just inside the gates of Disneyland.

He was that rare breed of quixotic non-conformist who tolerates nothing short of a full-tilt charge at life—no shrinking beatnik mumbling poetry in a corner, but a heads-up, belly-in, screaming blaster in a red-faced rage, who never took "no" for an answer. His windmills were all marked "you can't" and he demolished a lot more than the dictators of social behavior would like to admit. He marched sixteen nude people through the lobby of the Royal Hawaiian Hotel, organized his own brand of religion (The Church of the Living Swing, America's first Jazz church) starring himself and a pair of belly-dancers on a split bill, which had the distinction of being the only church performance ever raided by the vice squad. The bizarre incidents would (and undoubtedly will) fill a book.

His humble birth gave no hint of the riotous life to come, or his future influence on American comedy, but his presence is felt strongly in the Mort Sahls and Lenny Bruces of today.

To go on the road with Lord Buckley was another experience you would never forget, and I once had this honor bestowed upon me, with the result that Dick and I didn't speak for about a year. But despite his disorganization you would find people in every major city who knew and really loved Lord Buckley, and when he came to town they dropped whatever they were doing and took care of him. He was that type of person. Dick could not be ignored or put aside. To have him in your company was to yield to whatever happened to pop out of his head, and I was always amazed at the number and types of people who would, for a few days, quite joyously put their whole life aside and jump into the royal court to lead Buckley's existence for the time that he was there.

He believed in life more deeply than anyone I have ever known. He extended himself more in that direction than anyone I have ever known, and he got his wife to go along with it. He made no compensations for anything. He went straight over or straight up or straight down, whatever it happened to be, with apologies to no one and love for all.

Doug Boyd

Richard "Lord" Buckley was a true American original. A poet and patriot with a strong sense of justice without prejudice. To really dig his words was to love him completely. Just to have been around his presence was something almost akin to being in a holy presence. I was with him. I was in the canvas.

Lewis Foremaster

He was always on time and never late for a gig. He was shunned by many top stars even when he was alive. There was some kind of professional jealousy. There was some kind of genius there that you don't see today.

Jim Dickson

The times had sort of caught up to where he could have benefited from what he had pioneered. If he had lived he would have had an enormous cult following. Even so there were rock groups named "Nazz" and "Euphoria." When I met David Carradine he told me, "I used to learn dynamics from those Lord Buckley albums. I used to put that record on loud and then try to match it to give myself some depth and dynamics."

Dick Zalud

You know, in show business you're always searching for the formula. You search years and years and years and years for it, that formula—especially if you're a comedian. And Buckley finally found the formula.

He started it in San Francisco and he killed them in San Francisco. They drove to Chicago and he killed them in Chicago. Then he came to New York and he was about to kill them in New York and the cabaret card thing went down and he died.

But you know, he had the formula. He knew then and there at that late age what to do for the people. And if he had had the health and the endurance to continue he would have been a *giant*.

"Grampa" Al Lewis

Buckley was like Baudelaire—a junkie gone intellectually berserk. Flying so high that people laughed and applauded out of curiosity not out of understanding. It's like Baudelaire's poem about the albatross the sailors nail to the deck of the ship and laugh at it while it wildly tries to get away.

Lord Buckley was also like the alcoholic poet Dylan Thomas who all the college boys used to ply with alcohol and get him drunk in all the bars and then challenge him when he wanted another drink to take off his clothes and run down the street. He ran down the streets intellectually. And God punishes intellectuals that way. He did to Lord Buckley, Lenny Bruce, Dylan Thomas, Baudelaire . . . all of them.

David Amram

I believe he's probably one of the last people that has yet to be acknowledged as a tremendous force in that whole period of the forties and fifties who influenced the sixties, seventies and everything that has happened since then.

Now that there's been acknowledgement of Charlie Parker and Monk with the great film, *Straight, No Chaser,* and Kerouac's now being acknowledged as the great writer that he was, I think it's Lord Buckley's turn to finally be acknowledged in his own right. He was much more than he was supposed to be. He was supposed to be a club-date nightclub comic. He was much more than that.

One of Charlie Parker's classics is "Now's the Time." Now I think it is Lord Buckley's time.

Richmond Shepard

Sometime between five and ten years after Buckley died, my life was in the bottom of a trough, in terms of what was happening financially. And I had young children at that time, and we had no money and no work. And everything was devastated. And I felt Buckley come to me in a dream one night and he said,

"Have courage, great warrior!" And I've since then always hooked onto that a little bit. It felt like a spiritual essence touched me and Buckley was important in my life so it maybe came through the filter of my imagination or what I saw in my subconcious as somebody who would say something like that. But the message was clear and it was a Buckleyesque message: "Have courage, great warrior!" And it's sort of been my motto and it's been a long time now since then. So I have a very warm place in my heart for His Majesty.

Del Close

Buckley sure as hell had a big influence on me and Severn Darden. The seriousness and the poetry of comedy that he exemplified were just fucking amazing.

Ed Randolph

The last time I saw Lord Buckley was in Florida in 1957. It was a wonderful goodbye. I remember driving away, waving to the family under the sunny Miami palm trees. I remember thinking: "I hope I see him again." But I didn't. I remember it sharply because he gave me a doobie and said, "This is one toke shit Eagle, trust me."

I trusted him and it was. I mean that sucker took me from that morning all the way through that day.

Wavy Gravy

Buckley's work was hidden from me until I finished my album for World Pacific entitled *Hugh Romney's 3rd Stream Humor* which was produced and engineered by Jim Dickson who produced the early Buckley material.

As soon as the record was in the can he sat me down in the studio and played some Lord Buckley for me. He hadn't wanted Buckley to influence my work at the time because he saw in my work a lot of Buckley indeed. He thought it would be startling for me and it was. I thought, "My God, this guy is inside me somewhere." Buckley validated stuff that had just been pouring out of me.

Recently I collaborated with guitarist Henry Kaiser for a tribute album to Joseph Spence, the great musician from the Bahamas. I sang a piece about a crow and after the song I went into a rant for Joseph Spence which was totally improvised in the studio. It sounds more like Buckley than anything I've done in my life. It was like Lord Buckley tipping his pith helmet to Joseph Spence. I didn't realize it at the time, of course, it was a strictly out-of-the-body experience.

I still like to perform "The Nazz" around Easter and I do the "All-Hip Mahatma" with a band called Zero from time to time.

Dick Gregory

My respect for him came from other folks. I never saw him perform live but friends of mine played me his records and I thought they were hilarious.

I think, God, had he lived, the course of comedy would have changed faster than it did. Now you have people who just shock but have no substance.

He was out there. People say he was ahead of himself. I don't believe someone can be ahead of themselves. But with the information on television today, he would have been one of the foremost names in the world if he were still alive.

Remember, television news was in its infancy when he was performing and his big thing was current—what was happening socially, economically and politically.

The fact that Americans have such a swift means of getting news today, he would have had a field day. You can judge the value of what some people might contribute to these times if they were still alive but with him you could never judge the value. Because as swift as the news is, he was always ahead of the news. He was always ahead of what was about to happen.

Ken Kesey

He was an artist who was like Jackson Pollock. He was splattering and making sense of those splatters. And all of us who were into that kind of art were quite taken by it . . . beyond Dada.

Lord Buckley is kind of a secret thing that people pass under the table. I don't think Lord Buckley was ever meant to be really popular. It's like Samuel Beckett. You ask writers who they think's the best writer and they all mention someone above them. Gradually you get up to the top and you get to Beckett and not many people have read him. But a lot of people were influenced by Beckett. They might not have read him but they had read others who had read him and were influenced by them and so they, in turn, without realizing it, were influenced by him. And I think the same was true with Lord Buckley. There were a lot of people influenced by Lord Buckley that have never heard his material or heard of him.

I always think about one particular night in 1961 or 1962 as some kind of night of holy comedy. Me and a guy named Vik Lovell (who *Cuckoo's Nest* was dedicated to) and Sally Dema, the first teenybopper, had taken peyote and gone up to San Francisco to see Lenny Bruce. And we were walking along the street there on Broadway and I saw this guy bustling along with real big broad shoulders and a cowboy hat and kind of a cowboy outfit. "Look over there," I said. "It's Jonathan Winters."

He heard me say his name and, when he turned around to look at me, I threw an imaginary ball across the street at him. He snagged it out of the air and threw it back to me. And we walked down the street throwing this imaginary ball from each side of the street. And we get on down the street and turned the corner and by then we were kind of friends and so he said, "Who are you?"

I said, "I'm just a college student down at Stanford but I'm a great admirer."

He said, "Where are you going?"

"I'm going down here to see Lenny Bruce."

He said, "Ah Lenny! God love ya!"

It turned out he was going to see Lenny too. We got down to the club, the Off-Broadway, and we were all standing there when Shelley Berman and Mort Sahl came out from seeing Lenny Bruce. And we're all standing around there and talking and these comedians are talking about Lenny and this girl who was with Jonathan Winters is saying, "Oh yeah, he's the greatest."

I said, "Yeah, I guess he is now that the greatest is dead."

And Jonathan Winters turned immediately and said, "Who? Who are you talking about?"

I said, "Lord Buckley."

He said, "Lord Buckley was the Stan Kenton of comedy. He had more influence on real comics than anybody else in this century."

Lord Buckley was neglected all his life and after his death too. He wasn't what anybody thought he was. You have to be really somebody special to appreciate Lord Buckley.

Jerry Garcia

I wish I could have made music with Lord Buckley. Oh God, I'd leap at it. I think it would be really, really sparse with just a little teeny bit of percussion. For me it sounds right to go back into that coffeehouse space. So I'd have some bongos and little wind chimes and things that make hollow, rattling sounds—an ethereal glassy sound. Then maybe a flute—very sparse—and a little bit of something that sounds like something between a sarod and a banjo. Something that has that sensual Eastern quality but has that happy thing of a banjo. I can hear it in my mind's ear. If I had twenty minutes with Lord Buckley I could do it really nice.

Sun Ra is another one of those guys who is like a Twilight Zone performer. It's tough when you're somebody who invents another reality. You invent it and you can't define it outside of those terms. Sun Ra invented his own place in music—he invented his own music and along with it a whole lifestyle that goes along with it. And that's an incredible thing to have done in one's life.

Dr. Oscar Janiger

The way he combined things is almost as if he were a folk hero in a certain way. He gathered together material that resembled the language and the sort of feeling that you got when you read about Uncle Remus, Davey Crockett and all those imaginary encounters. He carried along the same tradition as Mark Twain.

He took the role of court jester and trickster. That's what came through. And every once in a while, when you thought you had him cornered, he would just puncture his own balloon and leave you there with it.

Robin Williams

Lord Buckley still works for people.

The spirit lives on anytime people are more accessible to his kind of work. He's obviously back if people are doing his stuff again.

He's influenced me and a lot of different people. His is almost a subliminal influence with me. I've never tried to do anything like Buckley as a full character. I've never tried to pull out a monologue like he did but he's always been in the back of my mind—not just that voice.

There are Buckleyesque elements to the Genie in *Aladdin.* But again, it was subconscious. I did one version that was even hipper than what they ended up with. In the end they went for the safer way. I gave them thirty hours of stuff, so they had a lot to choose from. There was William F. Buckley in there, I did some De Niro. I tried some things and just went off. I said to myself, "Well, let's just 'morph' it." It started out as more of generic falafal genie and I said to myself, "Let's kick this out a little bit."

But hey, you can kick out and expand *anything.*

I sometimes enjoy quoting Lord Buckley's piece "People," about how "people are like flowers and it's been a privilege walking in your garden." It's that thing in the back—almost more of a philosophical route than a comedic.

I don't think he's a footnote. He's not some kind of archaic thing like George Jessell. You don't listen to it and say, "Oh, that's quaint." Anytime people find out about him he hits again. He comes back. Once you hear him you're hooked. If you're open to music and to that kind of lyricism and poetry and comedy, you can't hear it and not be moved. It hits you on those levels and it comes back.

His stuff gets ingrained in your psyche. That's why it's subliminal—it's there. The tone comes back again. [in Lord Buckley's voice] "To have that voice comin back at ya."

And you go, "Oh wow! I know that voice. It's Buckley."

Tubby Boots

Like a painter, Buckley had to die to be discovered. And his stuff is fresh now because they are works of art. They are things that people should know but don't know.

Steve Ben Israel

When I did Buckley for the Gowana tribe in Morocco they didn't understand one word of English. But you know what? When I finished, they looked at me, put their hand over their heart and said "La Bes."

I've done him for Indians in Brazil and peasants in a cave in France near Avignon.

So, like I told my story like everybody has their story. I called Symphony Sid: "Whaddya want? Whaddya want?"

"Sid what was that?"

"What was what?"

"What was *that?*"

It was like one of the major keys of the universe was made at my disposal. You know, you can keep kosher, but it's better if you keep continuity.

Ed Sullivan

Sir Laurence Olivier, in *The Entertainer,* plays the part of Archie Rice. The role would have offered even greater opportunity for Olivier if it had been modeled on 'Lord' Richard Buckley. Buckley was an entertainer known to us all in the profession. During WWII, he was with us on all of our hospital treks to Army, Navy, Air Force and Marine installations, and just how many wounded roared at his special brand of humor will never be estimated. Grandiloquent in manner and possessed of great vitality and authority, he was a 'take charge' performer. Off stage, he was impractical as many of his profession are, but the vivid Buckley will long be remembered by all of us.

Lady Elizabeth Buckley

I loved the man and I loved the artist too. I was just happy that he passed my way because he looked at life differently than anyone else. We always ate well and we were always warm and we always had shelter. We lived in palaces and we lived in tiny places like the Crackerbox Palace. It never seemed to make any difference—we were happy together.

You must understand—the two of us were both *very serious* about show business.

Lord Buckley

Yes. Well, I would like to say that in my feelings for the people everywhere I've worked, that their wonderful attention, their divine concentration, their precious presence and their attitude to *each* and *every* performer on the stage only goes to prove more and more: that the flowers, the beautiful, beautiful magical flowers are *not* the flowers of life. That *people . . . people* are the true and wonderful flowers of life and it is always a great honor and a great privilege and a rare pleasure to even temporarily stroll into the gardens of their attentions. God swing them and God love them.

appendix a: the lord buckley discography, videography, and filmography

BY WALT STEMPEK AND OLIVER TRAGER

EUPHORIA LP—*Vaya Records, 1954 (recorded 1951); #:CPM 10-1715, a 10″ mono red vinyl LP, and as Euphoria Vol. I, a 12″ mono LP; #:VLP-101/102 in 1957. Produced by Jim Dickson and Peter Grant. Directed by Mel Welles and Dick Zalud. Music under the direction of Dick Smith, assisted by Larry Kinnamon and Bill Richmond. Liner notes by Lord Buckley. Artwork by Andi. Recorded in Los Angeles, California.* "The Nazz," "Mark Antony's Funeral Oration," "Nero," "Murder"

EUPHORIA VOL. II LP—*Vaya Records, 1956 (recorded 1954); #:VLP-107/108. Produced by Jim Dickson. Directed by Mel Welles. Liner notes by Lord Buckley. Artwork by Andi. Recorded in Los Angeles, California.* "Jonah and the Whale," "Cabenza de Gasca (The Gasser)," "The Hip Gahn," "The Dog and the Wolf," "The Grasshopper and the Ant," "The Mouse and the Lion," "The Lion's Breath"

HIPSTERS, FLIPSTERS, AND FINGER-POPPIN' DADDIES, KNOCK ME YOUR LOBES LP & EP—*RCA Victor, 1955; #:LPM-3246 (10″ 33 rpm LP), #:EPB-3256 (7″ 45 rpm LP). Sir Harry M. G. (Harry Geller) musical director. Album design by James Flora. Liner notes by Lord Buckley.* "Friends, Romans, Countrymen," "Hip Hiawatha," "To Swing or Not to Swing?," "Boston Tea Party," "Is This the Sticker?"

WAY OUT HUMOR LP—*World Pacific, 1959; #:WP-1279. Recorded live at the Ivar Theater in Los Angeles, California, February 12, 1959. Re-released by World Pacific in 1964 as* LORD BUCKLEY IN CONCERT: *#:WP-1815. Released in Great Britain as* LORD BUCKLEY IN CONCERT *on Fontana: #:68801022, 1966 in Great Britain. Re-released in Great Britain by Demon Verbals, Demon Records Ltd. in 1985 as* LORD BUCKLEY IN CONCERT*: #:Verb 4. Produced by Richard Bock. Photography by William Claxton. Re-release photography by William Claxton and Ray Avery. Liner notes by Dan James. Reissue liner notes by C. P. Lee.* "Supermarket," "Horse's Mouth," "Black Cross," "Lions," "The Naz," "My Own Railroad," "Willie the Shake," "God's Own Drunk"

THE BEST OF LORD BUCKLEY LP—*Crestview, 1963; #:CRV-801 (mono) & #:CRV7-801 (stereo). Material previouly issued on Vaya Records with the addition of "Gettysburg Address." Re-released in stereo by Elektra, 1969; #:EKS-74047 in United States and #:2410 002 in Great Britain. Produced by Jim Dickson. Engineering by Charles Tacot. Cover design of Crestview release by William H. Harvey. Cover design of Elektra release by Robert Heimall. Collage by Eve Babitz. Liner notes by Charles Tacot. Photography by Jim Marshall.* "The Nazz," "Gettysburg Address," "The Hip Gahn," "Jonah and the Whale," "Marc Antony's Funeral Oration," "Nero"

THE PARABOLIC REVELATIONS OF THE LATE LORD BUCKLEY: A COLLECTION OF SIX LESSONS BY THE 'HIP MESSIAH' LP—*Pye Records/Nonesuch, 1963; #:PPL 208. Originally recorded in Hollywood, California, 1952. Edited under the supervision of*

Denis Preston by Vic Keary with direction by Ed Randolph. Liner notes by Francis Newton and Ed Randolph. "Jonah and the Whale," "Georgia, Sweet and Kind," "The Nazz," "Chastity Belt," "Governor Gulpwell," "Murder"

LORD BUCKLEY: BLOWING HIS MIND (AND YOURS TOO) LP—*World Pacific, 1966; #:WP-1849. Recorded live at the Ivar Theater in Los Angeles, California, February 12, 1959, except "Maharaja" and "Scrooge" which were recorded in 1960 at Pacific Recorder studios. Re-released in Great Britain as* LORD BUCKLEY: BLOWING HIS MIND (AND YOURS TOO) *by Fontana, 1966; #:TL5396. Re-released in Great Britain as* LORD BUCKLEY: BLOWING HIS MIND (AND YOURS TOO) *by Demon Verbals, Demon Verbals Ltd., 1985; #:Verb 3. Produced by Richard Bock. Photography by William Claxton. Reissue photography by William Claxton and Ray Avery. Liner notes by Jim Dickson. Reissue liner notes by Jim Dickson and C. P. Lee.* "Subconscious Mind," "Fire Chief," "Let It Down," "Murder," "The Gasser," "Maharaja," "Scrooge"

BUCKLEY'S BEST LP—*World Pacific, 1968; #:WPS-21879; Liberty Records, 1969; #:LBS 83191E in Great Britain. Live performances culled from World Pacific's previous 1959 Ivar Theater releases plus a previously unreleased Ivar track, "Martin's Horse." Produced by Richard Bock. Art direction by Woody Woodward. Design by Gabor Halmos. Photography by William Claxton. Liner notes by Fred Buckley.* "Supermarket," "The Naz," "The Gasser," "Subconscious Mind," "Willie the Shake," "Martin's Horse," "God's Own Drunk"

BAD-RAPPING OF THE MARQUIS DE SADE LP—*World Pacific, 1969; #:WPS-21889. Originally recorded in early 1960 at the Gold Nugget in Oakland, California. Re-released in Great Britain by Demon Verbals, Demon Records 1986; #:Verb 6. Produced by Don Mupo (uncredited). Reissue photography by Ray Avery. Front cover design by Roger Chouinard and Ron Wolin. Liner notes by John Carpenter. Reissue liner notes by John Carpenter and C. P. Lee.* "Bad-Rapping of the Marquis de Sade," "H-Bomb," "Chastity Belt," "The Ballad of Dan McGroo," "His Majesty, The Policeman"

A MOST IMMACULATELY HIP ARISTOCRAT LP, CD, Cassette Tape—*Straight LP, 1970; #:STS-1054. Reprise LP, 1970; #:RS-6389. Re-released on LP as* A MOST IMMACULATELY HIP ARISTOCRAT *in Great Britain by Demon Verbals, Demon Verbals Ltd. in 1989; #:Verb 8. Enigma Cassette Tape, 1989; #:7 73398-4. Rhino-Bizarre/Straight & Enigma CD, 1989; #:7 73398-2. Produced and engineered by Lyle Griffin. Executive producer: Herb Cohen. Edited by Frank Zappa. Written by Lord Buckley. Cover by Cal Schenkel. Cover photography by Ed Caraef. Interior photo by Ray Avery. Liner notes by Richard Selnikoff. Originally recorded in 1956, Los Angeles, California.* "Bad-Rapping of the Marquis de Sade—King of the Badcats," "Governor Slugwell," "The Raven (The Bugbird)," "The Train," "The Hip Einie"

THE LEGENDARY LORD BUCKLEY LIVE IN CONCERT Cassette Tape—*A Bruce Mitchell Ignition got Paranoid Plastics Production, 1982. Produced by C. P. Lee. A re-release of material found on Buckley's previously issued World Pacific recordings.*

"The Nazz," "Horse's Mouth," Black Cross," "H-Bomb," "God's Own Drunk," "Willie the Shake," "His Majesty, The Policeman," "The Gasser"

LORD BUCKLEY LIVE: THE TALES OF LORD BUCKLEY Cassette Tape—*Shambhala, 1991; #:SLE 20. A compilation from various sources. "The Hip Gahn," "The Gettysburg Address," "Murder," "Trouble," and "James Dean" are drawn from Lord Buckley's released and probable unreleased output for Hip Records in 1956. "God's Own Drunk," "The Nazz," "The Gasser," and a totally remastered "Scrooge" are drawn from Lord Buckley's World Pacific releases. "Is This the Sticker?" is drawn from Lord Buckley's 1955 RCA Victor release,* HIPSTERS, FLIPSTERS AND FINGER-POPPIN' DADDIES, KNOCK ME YOUR LOBES. *Finally, "Baa Baa Blacksheep" is a previously unissued track, an outtake probably from the 1955 RCA Victor sessions. Executive producer: Dan Barrett. Produced by Richard Buckley Jr. Photography by George Jerman.* "The Hip Gahn," "The Gettysburg Address," "God's Own Drunk," "Is This the Sticker?," "The Nazz," "Trouble," "Murder," "Baa Baa Blacksheep," "Scrooge," "James Dean," "The Gasser"

HIS ROYAL HIPNESS, LORD BUCKLEY CD—*Discovery Records, 1992; #:71001. Material originally released on* EUPHORIA *and* EUPHORIA VOL. II *on Vaya Records and subsequently re-released on Crestview (1963) and Elektra (1969) as* THE BEST OF LORD BUCKLEY *with the addition of "Cabenza de Gasca (The Gasser)" and the previously unissued "People (Epilogue)." Produced by Jim Dickson. Liner notes by Charles Tacot. Photography by Ray Avery.* "The Nazz," "Gettysburg Address," "The Hip Gahn," "Cabenza de Gasca (The Gasser)," "Jonah and the Whale," "Marc Antony's Funeral Oration," "Nero," "People (Epilogue)"

BAD-RAPPING OF THE MARQUIS DE SADE CD—*World Pacific/Capital Records, 1996; #:CDP 7243 8 52676 28. Re-release of* BAD-RAPPING OF THE MARQUIS DE SADE *(WPS-21889) and partial re-release of* LORD BUCKLEY: BLOWING HIS MIND (AND YOURS TOO) *(WP-1849). The bulk of the material was originally recorded in early 1960 at the Gold Nugget in Oakland, California. The balance of the material ("Maharaja" and "Scrooge") was drawn from World Pacific's* LORD BUCKLEY: BLOWING HIS MIND (AND YOURS TOO) *in 1960 at Pacific Recorder. Produced by Don Mupo (uncredited) and Richard Bock. Reissue produced by Michael Cuscuna. Front cover design by Roger Chouinard and Ron Wolin. Liner notes by Oliver Trager.* "Bad-Rapping of the Marquis de Sade," "H-Bomb," "Chastity Belt," "The Ballad of Dan McGroo," "His Majesty, The Policeman," "Maharja," "Scrooge"

Singles (7″ 45 rpm EPs)

FLIGHT OF THE SAUCER *(Parts 1 & 2)—Hip Records, 1956. #:HI-270-1/270-2. By Lyle Griffin and "Lord" Richard Buckley. Music by Lyle Griffin's All Star "Jazz" Band with Dodo Maramarosa, piano; Lucky Thompson, tenor sax; arrangement by Tommy Talbert; with stratosphonic sound by Danny Gugliemi.*

THE GETTYSBURG ADDRESS (straight and hipsemantic versions)—*Hip Records, 1956. #:HI-301-1/301-2.*

JAMES DEAN'S (MESSAGE TO THE TEENAGERS)/ SPEAK FOR YOURSELF, JOHN—*Hip Records, 1956. #:HI-302-1/302-2.*

Compilation Albums

ZAPPED LP—*Bizarre Records, 1970. #:PRO-368.* "The Train" from the 1956 Lyle Griffin Hip Records sessions that produced A MOST IMMACULATELY HIP ARISTOCRAT.

ZAPPED (BIZARRE)/STRAIGHT SAMPLER LP—*Bizarre/Straight Records, 1970. #:PRO 2-9086.* "Governor Slugwell" from the 1956 Lyle Griffin Hip Records sessions that produced A MOST IMMACULATELY HIP ARISTOCRAT.

THE GOLDEN AGE OF COMEDY LP—*RCA Victor, 1972. #:LPV-580.* "Friends, Roman, Countrymen." Outtake from RCA Victor's 1955 LP/EP releases of HIPSTERS, FLIPSTERS AND FINGER-POPPIN' DADDIES.

GARDEN OF DELIGHTS LP—*Elektra, 1969; #:S3-10.* "The Nazz" from Vaya's original 1951 recording appearing on EUPHORIA, EUPHORIA VOL. 1, THE BEST OF LORD BUCKLEY, and HIS ROYAL HIPNESS can be found on this rare, three-record set.

BIZARRE/STRAIGHT SAMPLER CD—Rhino Records, 1991. #:PRO2 90086. "The Train" from A MOST IMMACULATELY HIP ARISTOCRAT.

THE BEAT GENERATION CD—*Rhino Records—Word Beat Series, 1992; #:R2 70281.* "The Hip Gahn" from Vaya's original 1954 EUPHORIA VOL. II, THE BEST OF LORD BUCKLEY, and HIS ROYAL HIPNESS can be found on this popular three-CD set.

Unreleased Lord Buckley Recordings

TURK MURPHY ACETATE. *Los Angeles, California, 1950. Produced by Turk Murphy.* "The Moronic Father and the Idiot Son," "Myrtle the Turtle," "The Nazz," "Murder"

THE LIGHTHOUSE. *Hermosa Beach, California, 1953. Produced by Howard Rumsey.* Buckley is backed by the house band, The Lighthouse All-Stars with pianist Hampton Hawes, throughout his performances. "Jonah and the Whale" and "The Nazz" are both augmented with backing musical rave-ups from the house band of "When the Saints Go Marching In." "Sleepy Time Gal" and "I Can't Give You Anything but Love" are Louis Armstrong–inspired Buckley vocalese presentations. First Set: "Louis Armstrong," "I Can't Give You Anything but Love," "The Neurotic Crocodile," "Murder," "The Nazz." Second Set: "Sleepy Time Gal," "The Judge," "Pursuit of Morpheus," "Jonah and the Whale," "Georgia, Sweet and Kind," "Chastity Belt"

RCA VICTOR OUTTAKES. *Los Angeles, California. Early January, 1955. Produced by Harry Geller.* Benny Carter—alto saxophone, Maury Harris—trumpet, Milt Burnhart—trombone, Ted Nash—tenor saxophone, Edwin "Buddy" Cole—piano, Red Callender—bass, Lou Singer—drums. "Baa Baa Blacksheep," "Pursuit of Morpheus," "Jonah and the Whale," "Speak for Yourself, John," "Ace in the

Hole," "Meeting of Marc Antony and Cleopatra," "Leviathan," "Swingin' Dan McGroo," "The Raven"

POSSIBLE HIP RECORDS OUTTAKES. *Los Angeles, California. Recorded in mid-to late 1950s or 1960.* "His Majesty, The Pedestrian," "His Majesty, The Policeman," "The Train," "Murder," "H-Bomb," "Trouble," "Lonesome Road," "Hip Talk Rap," "The Hip Gahn," "MG Commercial"

WERE-FM AIRCHECK. *Cleveland, Ohio. October 6, 1957. Produced by Bill Randle.* "Hip Chris," "To Swing or Not to Swing," "Wild Blue Yonder (Lord Buckley Describes Jet Ride)," "Shah's Embroidered Pants," "Jehovah & Finnegan," "The Hip Einie," "Leviathan," "Pursuit of Morpheus" (partial), "The Gasser," "The Raven," "Swingin' Pied Piper," "Satellite Blips" (two takes)

LOST STUDIO SESSION. *September 25, 1958. Location unknown.* "Swingin' Pied Piper"

LIONEL HAMPTON SESSION. *January 6, 1959. Studio location unknown. Recorded with an unidentifed drummer, these two selections segue into one another.* "Gettysburg Address," "Swingin' Pied Piper"

EARL BROWN TAPES. *Recorded at Earl Brown's home in Beverly Hills, California. February 1959. The cuts identified with an asterisk (*) were probably recorded at the Gold Nugget in Oakland, California in 1960. Guitarists Earl Brown and Howard Hatmaier accompany Buckley on several tracks.* "The Institution," "Young Girl," "Louise the Mouse," "King of Robins," "Lions," "Swingin' Pied Piper" (two versions), "The Love Hook," "Black Cross" (three versions), "People Worshipper," "Big Dog" (two versions), "Lucius (The Golden Ass)" (two versions), "The Cow," "Lanky Linc," "Circus to the Lions," "Scrooge," "The Raven,"* "The Whistle Cord,"* "God's Own Drunk" (three versions)

IVAR THEATER OUTTAKES. *Ivar Theater, Los Angeles, California. February 12, 13, 14, 1959. Produced by Earl Brown. Peppy Romero plays guitar on "The Nazz," "Black Cross," the second take of "Swingin' Pied Piper," and "Jonah and the Whale."* "Dogs," "Lions on Boat," "High Mass," "The Hip Gahn" (two versions), "The Moronic Father and his Idiot Son," "Swingin' Pied Piper" (two versions), "The Gasser," "Willie the Shake," "The Chickens," "The Shooting of Dan McGroo," "The Old Man," "The Nazz," "Big Dog," "Black Cross," "Supermarket," "Gettysburg Address," "The Train," "The Raven," "Lucius (The Golden Ass)," "Nero," "Bad-Rapping of the Marquis de Sade," "Jonah and the Whale"

PERFORMANCE FOR SIR HENRY MILLER. *Nepenthe, Big Sur, California. September 12, 1959. Recorded by Gary Larsen.* "Hipsters, Flipsters and Finger-Poppin' Daddies," "Is This the Sticker?" "God's Own Drunk," "The Raven," "Black Cross," "Swingin' Pied Piper" (partial), "Amos 'n' Andy" (partial)

KPFA-FM PACIFICA INTERVIEW WITH BILL BUTLER. *Berkeley, California. September 16, 1959.* "The Gasser," "People," "Willie the Shake," "Hipsters, Flipsters and Finger-Poppin Daddies," "To Swing or Not to Swing," "Swingin' Pied Piper"

TURK MURPHY STUDIO TAPE. *San Francisco, California, 1959.* Musicians: Turk Murphy—trombone, Al Conger—tuba and vocals, Larry Conger—trumpet, Bon Helm—clarinet, Pete Clute—piano(?), Lammie—banjo, Hal McIntyre—drummer/engineer. Al Conger also reads Robert Service's "The Ballad of Dan McGroo" in its original form. "The Ballad of Dan McGroo," "The Hip Gahn"

HANGIN' AT HOME. *Las Vegas, Nevada. December 1959.* Lord Buckley holds court with friends and family.

SCOTT BRADY'S HOUSE. *Los Angeles, California, 1960. Lord Buckley, Scott Brady, Prince Lewis, and others discuss life. Buckley performs "Nobody Knows the Trouble I've Seen" with Dorris Henderson. Buckley leads the room in a ragged version of "His Majesty, The Pedestrian." Performance highlight is Henderson's solo rendition of an old, unidentified folk/blues chestnut.* "Nobody Knows the Trouble I've Seen," "Folk/Blues," "His Majesty, The Pedestrian"

KPUP AIRCHECK #1. *Recorded at Outside at the Inside, Palo Alto, California, February 12, 1960.* "His Majesty, The Pedestrian," "To Swing or Not to Swing"

KPUP AIRCHECK #2. *Recorded at Outside at the Inside, Palo Alto, California, February 19, 1960.* "Leviathan"

LOST GOLD NUGGET TAPE #1. *Recorded at the Gold Nugget, Oakland, California, 1960.* "Return of the Stranger," "Nero," "God's Own Drunk," "Swingin' Pied Piper"

LOST GOLD NUGGET TAPE #2. *Recorded at the Gold Nugget, Oakland, California, 1960.* "Black Cross," "The Bugbird," "God's Own Drunk," "Swingin' Pied Piper"

UNITED ARTISTS ARCHIVE. *Probably recorded at the Gold Nugget, Oakland, California, 1960.* "Gettysburg Address" (partial), "His Majesty, The Pedestrian," "Jonah and the Whale," "Nero"

FROM THE COSMOS. *Date and location unknown but probably recorded in Sausalito, California, 1960.* "The Raven," "Lucius (The Golden Ass)," "My Own Railroad," "Black Cross," "Murder," "Jonah and the Whale," "Gettysburg Address." Note: performed with unidentifed bass and bongo players. The first parts of both "The Raven" and "Lucius" are missing.

CHARLES CAMPBELL PARTY TAPE. *San Francisco, California. July 3, 1960.* "Blacksheep," "Sheepherder," "Myrtle the Turtle," "Bad-Rapping of the Marquis de Sade," "His Majesty, The Pedestrian"

SECOND CITY. *Chicago, Illinois. August 1960.* "Introduction," "Black Cross," "God's Own Drunk," "Lucius (The Golden Ass)," "Gettyburg Address"

STUDS TERKEL WFMT-FM INTERVIEW. *Chicago, Illinois. August 1960.* "Gettysburg Address," "Hipsters, Flipsters and Finger-Poppin' Daddies," "Willie the Shake," "Swingin' Pied Piper," "His Majesty, The Pedestrian," "People," "The Raven"

FROM A VANILLA QUARK. *Location and date unknown. Probably 1960.* "Jonah and the Whale," "Murder," "Chastity Belt," "The Nazz"

PRINCE LEWIS FOREMASTER ARCHIVE. *California–New York. 1959–1960.* Along with several of the above-mentioned recordings *(Hangin' at Home, Scott Brady's House,* and *Second City),* Lewis Foremaster haphazardly archived Buckley in a variety of informal settings over the course of the last year or so of Lord Buckley's life.

Television & Film

THE ED SULLIVAN SHOW/TALK OF THE TOWN (television)
1949: "Amos 'n' Andy"
1949: "Amos 'n' Andy"
1955: "Amos 'n' Andy," "Hat Routine"
1959: "Amos 'n' Andy"

CLUB 7 (television) 1949. "Put on Your Easter Bonnet," "The Sinner"

WE'RE NOT MARRIED (film) 1955. Buckley plays a radio station manager and announcer in a scene with Fred Allen and Ginger Rogers midway through this film.

TONIGHT SHOW Steve Allen (television) 1955. Brief hip rap and tumbling act with Skitch Henderson, Andy Williams, and several others.

THE SHOOTING OF DAN MCGREW Unknown date and source, probably mid-to late 1950s. Buckley performs Robert Service's poem in an Old West barroom setting.

SPARTACUS (film) 1960. Directed by Stanley Kubrick. Very brief walk-on in a scene featuring a cast of thousands.

CHICAGO: 1ST IMPRESSIONS OF A GREAT AMERICAN CITY (film) 1960. Directed by Denis Mitchell. Buckley performs climax of "The Nazz" at the Gate of Horn nightclub in this unusual documentary film.

BEANIE AND CECIL (cartoon) 1960. Produced by Bob Clampett. Buckley lent vocal talents to Go Man Van Go, a beatnik character in the "Wildman of Wildsville" episode of this quirky cartoon.

THE SOURCE (film) 1999. Directed by Chuck Workman. Buckley appears via photograph and loose audio reference in this impressionistic documentary about the Beat Generation.

appendix b: bibliography and sources

Books

Aesop. *Fables of Aesop*. New York, London, Penguin Books, 1954, 1964.

Allen, Steve. *Funny People*. New York, Stein and Day, 1976.

Amram, David. *Vibrations*. New York, The Viking Press, 1968.

Baez, Joan. *Daybreak: An Autobiography*. New York, Avon Books, 1966, 1968/Dial Books, 1968.

Bane, Michael. *Who's Who in Rock*. New York, Facts On File, Inc., 1983.

Barnet, Charlie. *Those Swinging Years: The Autobiography of Charlie Barnet*. Baton Rouge, Louisiana, Louisiana State University Press, 1984; New York, Da Capo Press, 1992.

Berger, Phil. *The Last Laugh*. New York, Morrow Publishers, 1975; New York, Limelight Editions, 1985.

Barr, Roseanne. *My Life as a Woman*. New York, Harper & Row Publishers, 1989.

Bishop, Morris. *The Odyssey of Cabeza de Vaca*. New York/London, The Century Co., 1933.

Blum, Joshua, Bob Holman, and Mark Pellington. *The United States of Poetry*. New York, Harry M. Abrams, Inc., Publishers, 1996.

Bogle, Donald. *Toms, Coons, Mulattoes, Mammies, & Bucks: An Interpretive History of Blacks in American Films*. New York, The Viking Press, 1974.

Brooks, Tim, and Earle Marsh. *The Complete Guide to Prime Time Network TV Shows, 1946–Present* (revised edition). New York, Ballantine Books, 1981.

Browning, Robert. *Selected Poetry*. London, England, Penguin Books, 1989.

Bruce, Honey. *Honey: The Life and Loves of Lenny's Shady Lady*. Chicago, Illinois, A Playboy Press Book, 1976.

Bruce, Kitty. *The (almost) Unpublished Lenny Bruce*. Philadelphia, Running Press, 1981.

Bruce, Lenny. *How to Talk Dirty and Influence People*. New York, Fireside Books/Simon & Schuster, 1992.

Bruce, Lenny. *Stamp Help Out and Other Short Stories*. Los Angeles, self-published, 1964.

Buckley, Lord. *Hiparama of the Classics*. San Francisco, City Lights Books, 1960, 1980.

Buckley, Lord Richard. *Pot—How To: Plant-Cultivate-Harvest-Cure-Prepare . . . Enjoy*. A Lord Buckley Publication, No city, year.

Cabeza de Vaca, Alvar Núñez. *Adventures in the Unknown Interior of America*. Albuquerque, University of New Mexico Press, 1961, 1983, 1992.

Carr, Roy, Brian Case, and Fred Dellar. *The Hip*. London, England; Boston, Massachusetts, Faber and Faber, 1986.

Cary, Joyce. *Horse's Mouth*. New York, HarperCollins, 1957.

Chase, Allan S. *Sun Ra: Musical Change and Musical Meaning in the Life and Work of a Jazz Composer*. Unpublished thesis, 1992.

Chevigny, Paul. *Gigs: Jazz and the Cabaret Card Laws in New York City*. New York, Routledge, 1991.

Cinader, Martha. *Dreamscape: Real Dreams Really Make a Difference*. New York, Tenth Avenue Editions, 1995.

Clancy, William D., and Audrey Coke Kenton. *Woody Herman: Chronicles of the Herds*. New York, Schirmer Books, 1995.

Crosby, David, and Carl Gottlieb. *Long Time Gone: The Autobiography of David Crosby*. New York, Dell Publishing, 1990.

Crow, Bill. *From Birdland to Broadway: Scenes from a Jazz Life*. New York, Oxford University Press, 1992.

Cruickshank, Ben. *Bob Dylan: Blottingpaper Man*. Andover, England, Agenda Books, 1995.

Dalzell, Tom. *Flappers 2 Rappers.* Springfield, Massachusetts, Merriam-Webster, 1996.

Davis, Miles. *Miles: The Autobiography.* New York, Simon & Schuster, 1991.

Dearborn, Mary V. *Mailer.* New York, Houghton Mifflin, 1999.

Debenham, Rev. Warren. *Laughter on Record.* Metuchen, New Jersey, and London, England, The Scarecrow Press, 1988.

Durst, Lavada (Dr. Hepcat). *The Jives of Dr. Hepcat.* Self-published, Dallas, Texas, 1953. Reprinted by Alan B. Govenar in association with Documentary Arts, Inc. Dallas, Texas, 1989.

Dylan, Bob. *Tarantula.* New York City, St. Martin's Press, 1994.

Ely, Melvin Patrick. *The Adventures of Amos 'n' Andy.* New York, The Free Press, 1991.

Eng, Steve. *Jimmy Buffett: The Man from Margaritaville Revealed.* New York, St. Martin's Press, 1996.

Fariña, Richard. *Been Down So Long It Looks Like Up to Me.* New York, Penguin, 1966/1997.

Fernandez-Shaw, Carlos. *The Hispanic Presence in North America.* New York, Facts On File, Inc., 1991.

Firestone, Ross. *Breaking It Up!: The Best Routines of the Stand-Up Comics.* New York, Bantam Books, 1975.

Gibson, Bob, and Carole Bender. *I Come for to Sing—The Stops Along the Way of a Folk Music Legend.* Naperville, Illinois, Kingston Korner, Inc./Folk Era Productions, Inc., 1999.

Gioia, Ted. *West Coast Jazz.* New York, Oxford University Press, 1992.

Giuliano, Geoffrey. *Dark Horse: The Private Life of George Harrison.* New York, Dutton Publishers, 1990.

Goldman, Albert. *Freak Show: the rock soul blues jazz rock jew black culture humor sex poppsych gig and other scenes from the counter-culture.* New York, Atheneum Books, 1971.

Goldman, Albert. *Ladies and Gentlemen Lenny Bruce!!* New York, Ballantine Books, 1974.

Gordon, Robert. *It Came from Memphis.* Boston, Faber and Faber, 1996.

Goss, Linda, and Marian E. Barnes, (eds.). *Talk That Talk.* New York, Touchstone Books/Simon & Schuster, 1989.

Gravy, Wavy. *Something Good for a Change.* New York, St. Martin's Press, 1992.

Gray, Michael. *Mother! The Frank Zappa Story.* London, Plexus, 1993.

Harper, Laurie. *Don Sherwood: The Life and Times of "The World's Greatest Disc Jockey."* Rocklin, California, Prima Publishing & Communications, 1989.

Harrison, George. *I Me Mine.* New York, Simon & Schuster, 1980.

Helm, Levon. *This Wheel's on Fire: Levon Helm and the Story of the Band.* New York, William Morrow & Company, 1993.

Heylin, Clinton. *Bob Dylan: Stolen Moments.* London, England, Wanted Man Publications, 1988.

Heylin, Clinton. *Bob Dylan: Behind the Shades.* New York, Summit Books, 1991.

Heylin, Clinton. *Bob Dylan: A Life in Stolen Moments.* New York Schirmer Books, 1996.

Humphrey, Mark. *The Jimmy Buffett Scrapbook.* New York, Citadel Press, 1993.

Humphries, Patrick. *Small Change: A Life of Tom Waites.* London, Omnibus Press, 1989.

Humphries, Patrick, and John Bauldie. *Oh No! Not Another Bob Dylan Book.* London, Square One Books Ltd., 1991.

Jackson, Blair. *Garcia: An American Life.* New York, Viking Press, 1999.

Jenkins, Ron. *Acrobats of the Soul: Comedy and Virtuosity in Contemporary American Theater.* New York, Theater Communications Group, 1988.

Kenney, William Howland. *Chicago Jazz: A Cultural History, 1904–1930.* New York, Oxford University Press, 1993.

Kohler, Eric. *In the Groove: Vintage Record Graphics, 1940–1960*. San Francisco, California, Chronicle Books, 1999.

Kopka, Mathew, and Iris Brooks. *Jali Kunda: Griots of West Africa & Beyond*. Roslyn, New York, Ellipses Arts, 1997.

Krassner, Paul. *Confessions of a Raving, Unconfined Nut: Misadventures in the Counter-Culture*. New York, Simon & Schuster, 1993.

Krogsgaard, Michael. *Twenty Years of Recording: The Bob Dylan Reference Book*. Stockholm, Sweden, Scandinavian Institute for Rock Research, 1980.

Krogsgaard, Michael. *Positively Bob Dylan: A Thirty-Year Discography, Concert & Recording Session Guide, 1960–1991*. Ann Arbor, Michigan, Popular Culture, Ink., 1991.

Kruth, John. *Bright Moments: The Life & Legacy of Rahsaan Roland Kirk*. New York, Welcome Rain Publishers, 2000.

Lawrence, Larry. *The Life of Honest Abe Done Up Brown in Jazzistory*. The Milwaukee Journal, 1929.

Leary, Timothy. *Flashbacks*. New York, St. Martin's Press, 1983, 1990.

Lee, C. P. *Like the Night: Bob Dylan and the Road to the Manchester Free Trade Hall*. London, England, Helter Skelter Publishing, 1998.

Lee, Martin, and Bruce Shlain. *Acid Dreams: The CIA, LSD and the Sixties Rebellion*. New York, Grove Press, 1985.

Lees, Gene. *Leader of the Band: The Life of Woody Herman*. New York, Oxford University Press, 1995.

Lenburg, Jeff. *The Encyclopedia of Animated Cartoons*. New York, Facts On File, Inc., 1991.

Lit, Hy. *Hy Lit Dictionary*. Philadelphia, Pennsylvania, Hyski Press, Inc., 1968.

Litweiler, John. *Ornette Coleman: A Harmolodic Life*. New York, William Morrow and Company, 1992.

Long, Haniel. *The Power Within Us: Cabeza de Vaca's Relation of His Journey from Florida to the Pacific—1528–1546*. Nevada City, California, Harold Berliner, 1975.

Manso, Peter. *Mailer: His Life and Times*. New York, Random House, 1985.

Martin, Carol. *Dance Marathons: Performing American Culture in the 1920 and 1930s*. Jackson, Mississippi, University Press of Mississippi, 1994.

Mazursky, Paul. *Show Me the Magic*. New York, Simon & Schuster, 1999.

Mezzrow, Mezz, and Bernard Wolfe. *Really the Blues*. New York, Random House, 1946; Citadel Underground, 1990.

Miller, Henry. *The Time of the Assassins*. New York, New Directions Publishing Corp., 1946, 1956.

Newman, Joseph S. *It Could Be Verse!* Cleveland, The World Publishing Company, 1948.

New York Telephone Book. Manhattan, 1949.

New York Times, The. *Index—1960*. New York, New York Times Publishing Company, 1961.

O'Day, Anita. *High Times Hard Times*. New York, G. P. Putnam and Sons, 1981; Limelight Editions, 1989.

Oliver, Paul. *Songsters & Saints*. Cambridge, England, Cambridge University Press, 1983.

Petty, Mark. *Tell 'em Groucho Sent You*. Minneapolis, Minnesota, Wide Angle [4534 Nicollet Avenue, Minneapolis, Minnesota, 55409-2037, (612) 827-4902], 1997.

Phillips, Julia. *You'll Never Eat Lunch in This Town Again*. New York, Penguin, 1992.

Phillips, Lisa, et al. *Beat Culture and the New America 1950–1965*. New York, Whitney Museum/Flammarion, 1996.

Porter, Lewis, ed. *A Lester Young Reader*. Washington, D.C., Smithsonian Institution Press, 1991.

Ragan, David. *Who's Who in Hollywood: The Largest Cast of Film Personalities Ever Assembled*. New York, Facts On File, Inc., 1992.

Rexroth, Kenneth. *An Autobiographical Novel*. New York, Doubleday, 1964.

Robert, James. *Ghosts and Angels in Hollywood*. Jefferson, North Carolina, Parish/McFarland & Co., 1994.

Rowley, Chris. *Blood on the Tracks: The Story of Bob Dylan*. New York, Proteus Books, 1984.

Russell, Ross. *Bird Lives!* New York, Charterhouse, 1973.

Sade, Marquis de. *The 120 Nights of Sodom and Other Writings*. New York, Grove Press, 1987.

Sade, Marquis de. *The Passionate Philosopher: A Marquis de Sade Reader*. Selected and translated from the French by Margaret Crosland. London, England, P. Owen, 1991.

Scadutto, Anthony. *Bob Dylan: An Intimate Biography*. New York, Grossett & Dunlap, 1971, 1973.

Schwartz, David, Steve Ryan, and Fred Wostbrock. *The Encyclopedia of TV Game Shows*. New York, Facts On File, Inc., 1986.

Sculatti, Gene (ed.). *The Catalog of Cool*. New York, Warner Books, 1982.

Sculatti, Gene (ed.). *Too Cool*. New York, St. Martin's Press, 1993.

Shaw, Arnold. *The Street That Never Slept*. New York, Coward, McCann & Geoghegan, Inc., 1971.

Shelton, Robert. *No Direction Home: The Life and Music of Bob Dylan*. New York, Birch Tree Books/ William Morrow & Co., 1986.

Shenk, David and Steve Silberman. *Skeleton Key: A Dictionary for Deadheads*. New York, A Main Street Book published by Doubleday, 1994.

Smith, Ronald L. *The Stars of Stand-Up Comedy*. New York & London, Garland Publishing, 1986.

Smith, Ronald L. *Who's Who in Comedy*. New York, Facts On File, Inc., 1992.

Smith, Ronald L. *Goldmine Comedy Record Price Guide*. Chicago, Illinois, Krause Publications, 1997.

Stern, Jane and Michael. *Encyclopedia of Pop Culture*. New York, HarperCollins Publishers, 1987.

Talese, Gay, et al. *Smiling Through the Apocalypse/"Looking For Hemingway."* New York, A Delta Book/Dell Publishing Co., Inc./Esquire Magazine, 1969.

Thomas, William Karl. *Lenny Bruce: The Making of a Prophet*. Hamden, Connecticut, Archon Books/Shoe String Press, 1989.

Thompson, Frank. *Robert Wise—A Bio-Bibliography*. Westport, Connecticut, Greenwood Press, 1995.

Travis, Dempsey. *An Autobiography of Black Jazz*. Chicago, Illinois, Urban Research Institute, 1983.

Tytell, John and Mellon. *Paradise Outlaws: Remembering the Beats*. New York, William Morrow & Co., Inc., 1999.

Ullman, Michael. *Jazz Lives*. New York, New Republic Books, 1980.

Vale, V., and Andrea Juno. *Incredibly Strange Music Volume II*. San Francisco, California, Re/Search Publications, 1994.

Various editors. *The Harmony Illustrated Encyclopedia of Rock*. New York, Harmony Books, 1988.

Various editors. *The Rolling Stone Guide to Alternative Rock*. New York, Rolling Stone Press, 1996.

Watkins, Mel. *On the Real Side*. New York, Simon & Schuster, 1994.

Watson, Ben. *Frank Zappa: The Negative Dialectics of Poodle Play*. London, England, Quartet Books, 1994.

Williams, Paul. *Performing Artist: The Music of Bob Dylan, Volume One, 1960–1973*. Novato, California/ Lancaster, Pennsylvania, Underwood-Miller, 1990.

White, Emil. *Letters from Emil*. Big Sur, California, self-published, 1980s.

Zwerin, Mike. *Close Enough for Jazz*. London, England, Quartet Books, 1983.

Articles

Ableman, Lester. "Probe Performer License Graft, Mayor Orders." *New York Daily News,* November 15, 1960.

Alvey, Ted. "Please Mr. Postman: Letters to the Editor" *Goldmine,* April 12, 1996.

Amram, David. "David Amram Remembers." *Evergreen Review,* January 1970.

Anderson, Ernie. "The Hipster Story." *Jazz Beat,* Spring 1991.

Anderson, Ian. "Tongue Dancer." *fROOTS/Folk Roots Magazine,* August/September 1999, Nos. 194–195.

Anderson, Jack. "Dance: Karole Armitage." *The New York Times,* January 22, 1987.

Armstrong, David. "Record Labels Going for Comic Release." *San Francisco Examiner,* April 26, 1992.

B., L. E. "Untitled Review." *Springfield Morning-Union,* July 20, 1943.

Bambarger, Bradley. "Gray, Bogosian Speak Up." *Billboard,* June 6, 1998.

Barber, Lynden. "Straight Swinger." *The Weekend Australian,* September 12–13, 1998.

Batchelder, Edward. "Oh Lord." *The Resident,* September 25, 1998.

Batchelder, Edward. "Hipsters & Flipsters, Your Lord Returneth." *Jazziz,* February 1999, Volume 16, No. 2.

Bell, Nelson B. "Untitled Review." *Washington Post,* November 3, 1944.

Bellamy, Peter. "Untitled Review." *Cleveland Plain-Dealer,* October 7, 1944.

Bennett, Charles G. "Cabaret-Card Use Ended by Council." *The New York Times,* September 13, 1967.

Bernheimer, Martin. "Armitage Ballet in Debut." *Los Angeles Times,* September 12, 1987.

Bloom, Michael. "Frank Speiser: Lord Buckley Reincarnated." *Boston Phoenix,* May 12, 1995.

Blouin, Denny. "Celebration: 'To Have the Sweet Fragments of Serenity Rock Your Wig.'" *Shambhala Sun,* May 1994.

Bonney, Jo. "Fragments from the Age of the Self." *American Theatre,* Volume 16, Number 10, December 1999.

Broadhurst, Judith. "Call from Uptairs." *Monterey Bay,* November–December 1991.

Brower, Millicent. "Anti-Cabaret Card Group Interrogated by Police." *The Village Voice,* December 22, 1960.

Brown, Geoff. "Lord Buckley 'Live in Concert.'" *Time Out,* January 28–February 3, 1983.

Buckley, Lord Richard. "The Discovery of America" *Dig Magazine,* May 1956.

Buckley, Lord Richard. "Lincoln's Gettysburg Address" *Dig Magazine,* November 1956.

Buckley, Lord Richard. "Buckley Describes First Ride in a Jet!" *Dig Magazine,* December 1956.

Buckley, Lord Richard, and Larry Sloman. "A Hip Christmas Carol." *National Lampoon,* December 1987.

Burns, Jim. "The Hip Messiah." *The Guardian,* August 12, 1963.

Burns, Jim. "Lord Buckley." *Jazz Monthly,* September 1970.

Burns, Jim. "The Hip Messiah." *Altrincham,* 1976.

Burns, Jim. "Central Avenue Breakdown." *Blues & Rhythm,* July 1986.

Burns, Jim. "Far Out with Lord Buckley." *Beat Scene,* No. 19, 1994.

Burns, Joe. "'50s Jive Comes Alive in Speiser Show." *Cape Cod Times,* August 10, 1994.

Calloway, Cab. "Cab Calloway's 'Hepster's Dictionary.'" *Dance Band Album,* 1946.

Carr, Patrick. "Creaky Beauty: Ramblin' Jack Elliott." *The Village Voice,* April 7, 1998.

Carr, William H. A. "Performs for Cops—Without Cabaret Card." *New York Post,* October 27, 1960.

Carr, William H. A. "Death Voids Cabaret Card, Brings Fight on Cop Graft." *New York Post,* November 14, 1960.

Carr, William H. A. "Probe of Police." *New York Post,* November 15, 1960.

Carr, William H. A. "Agent Called on Police 'Fix' Story." *New York Post,* November 16, 1960.

Carr, William H. A. "City Pressing Inquiry in Cabaret Card 'Fix.'" *New York Post,* November 17, 1960.

Case, Brian. "The Hiparama, Jack." *Wire Magazine,* June 1987.

Cassidy, Claudia. "Ancient but Not Venerable Hodgepodge, 'Passing Show' Brings Willie Howard to Erlanger." *Chicago Tribune,* January 28, 1946.

Chinyelu, Mamadou. "The Medium Is the Messenger." *The Village Voice,* February 27, 1990.

Christon, Lawrence. "'Buckley's Finest Hour' Is One." *Los Angeles Times,* August 12, 1983.

Christon, Lawrence. "Buckley: High Lord of the Hip, Cool Groove." *Los Angeles Times,* September 18, 1983.

Christon, Lawrence. "Olivier's Son Gets Charge from 'Battery.'" *Los Angeles Times,* March 23, 1986.

Christon, Lawrence. "Comedy Award to Mazursky." *Los Angeles Times,* October 1, 1986.

Chusid, Irwin. "Flora in Twilight: An Old Master of Album Covers." *New York Press,* July 15–21, 1998.

Collins, Judy. "My Early Days." *McCall's,* April, 1970.

Collins-Harper, Laura. "Zig-Zag Language: New Play a Tribute to Lord Buckley." *The Cape Codder,* August 5, 1994.

Connor, Laurie. "Mr. Whitley's Neighborhood." *Angeles,* March 1991.

Crowther, Bosley. "We're Not Married." *The New York Times,* July 12, 1952.

Cruickshank, Douglas. "All Hail Lord Buckley." *San Francisco Examiner Image Magazine,* September 6, 1992.

Cruickshank, Douglas. "The Resurrection of the Exalted Wizard of Words." *Salon* #5 (www.salon1999.com), November 1995.

D., J. D. "Untitled Review." *Springfield Daily News,* July 20, 1943.

Deford, Frank. "The Blond Bomer." *The New York Times Magazine,* January 4, 1997.

Delatiner, Barbara. "It'll Be a Weekend for Festivals." *The New York Times,* August 28, 1983.

Dieckmann, Katherine. "Past Tense." *The Village Voice,* January 14, 1992.

Dieckmann, Katherine. "Eric the Rad." *The Village Voice,* February 20, 1990.

Dylan, Bob. "Blowin' in the Wind." *Hootenany,* December 1963.

E., R. F. Jr. "Untitled Review." *Boston Herald,* September 3, 1943.

Eck. "The Passing Show." *Variety,* November 14, 1945.

Ellison, Bob. "The Lord Was a Swinger: Fling Records the Last Days of Lord Buckley—Hippest of the Hip!" *Fling Festival,* 1961.

Evett, Marianne. "Offbeat One-Man Shows Diverting." *Cleveland Plain Dealer,* October 20, 1995.

Favoino, Gabriel. "Hipsters and Flipsters." *Chicago Sun-Times,* August 28, 1960.

Federici, William, and Sidney Kline. "Our Boss Cop Turns Heat on City's 1,100 Hot Spots." *New York Daily News,* November 19, 1960.

Federici, William. "Police Uncover Violations in Town's Top Night Spots." *New York Daily News,* November 22, 1960.

Federici, William, and Henry Lee. "Citizen-Author-Scofflaw Humes Snorts, Stomps, Rages, Fumes." *New York Daily News,* November 24, 1960.

Federici, William, and Henry Lee. "Copa Gals Got 'n' Forgot Cards." *New York Daily News,* November 26, 1960.

Federici, William. "Act to Alleviate Joints Where They Deviate." *New York Daily News,* December 1, 1960.

Federman, Don. "Radnofsky Shows Off with 'Lord Buckley.'" *Portland Press Herald,* March 18, 1981.

Fiorillo, Michael. "It's the Trivial Paranoia Quiz & Contest." *Apocalypso,* No. 2, March 1986.

Fisher, Al. "Who the Hell Was 'Lord' Buckley?" *Sabin's Radio Free Jazz! USA,* Vol. 4, No. 4, April 1974.

Freeman, Ira Henry. "Café Drive Turns to Homosexuals." *The New York Times,* December 1, 1960.

Fremer, Michael. "The Unexpurgated Jim Marshall: Interview with Michael Fermer." *The Tracking Angle,* Winter 1998.

Friedwald, Will. "The Wayoutsphere." *The Village Voice,* June 3, 1997.

Fulbright, Newton H. "Police Head Asks Proof of Cabaret License Graft." *New York Herald Tribune,* November 15, 1960.

Fulbright, Newton H. "Actor's Agent Is Located in Cabaret Graft Probe." *New York Herald Tribune,* November 16, 1960.

Fulbright, Newton H. "Police Probe Open, to Call Sinatra." *New York Herald Tribune,* November 17, 1960.

Gavin, James. "When I'm 64: Mark Murphy Stays on the Road." *The Village Voice,* January 28, 1997.

Gelb, Arthur. "Charges of Police Corruption Made by Citizens' Group Here." *The New York Times,* November 14, 1960.

Gelb, Arthur. "City Will Study Cabaret Charges." *The New York Times,* November 15, 1960.

Gill, Andy. "Judas Christ Superstar." *Mojo,* November 1998.

Gitler, Ira. "Lord Buckley Benefit." *Down Beat,* February 16, 1961.

Gleason, Ralph J. "On and Off the Record." *San Francisco Chronicle,* January 10, 1960.

Goddard, J. R. "Cry of 'Corruption' Brings Crackdown on Cabarets." *The Village Voice,* November 24, 1960.

Goddard, J. R. "Humes vs. the Cards: 'Don Peyote' Tilts with Police Cabaret Bureau." *The Village Voice,* December 8, 1960.

Goldman, Albert. "Posthumous Stardom for a Once and Future Lord: The Lord Buckley Phenomenon." *Life,* December 9, 1969.

Goldman, Albert. "Heah's Yo Ole Daddy, Lord Buckley!" *High Times,* January 1978.

Goodman, Walter. "Vaudeville: Ed Sullivan Before Ed Sullivan." *The New York Times,* November 25, 1997.

Grant, Steve. "Sweet Lord Above" *Time Out*, January 28–February 3, 1983.

Gravy, Wavy. "What Makes Wavy Run" *Whole Earth Review*, Spring 1991.

Gregory, Sophfronia Scott. "'Diss' Is the Word of the Lord." *Time,* July 26, 1993.

Gurley, George. "An Oral History of George Plimpton: The Man Does Everything Rather Well." *The New York Observer,* December 22, 1997.

Gustafson, Klas. "Lorden Som Bildad Skola For Manga Artister." *Dagens Nyheter* (Stockholm, Sweden), January 10, 1987.

Hamlin, Jesse. "Mark Murphy Likes It Underground." *The San Francisco Chronicle,* November 2, 1989.

Hardy, Owen. "Concerto for Saxophone Blends Musical Styles." *Louisville Courier-Journal,* April 7, 1982.

Haun, Harry. "'Vaca' Takes the Scenic Route." *New York Daily News,* May 15, 1992.

Hebert, James. "The Unfiltered Truth." *San Diego Union,* October 24, 1999.

Heller, Steven. "James Flora, 84, Author Cover Illustrator, Dies." *The New York Times,* July 18, 1998.

Helbig, Jack. "Lord Almighty: A New Play Resurrects a Master." *Chicago Reader,* April 8, 1999.

Henriques, Kevin. "Inner Thoughts of a Keyboard Giant." *The Financial Times,* April 27, 1985.

Hentoff, Nat. "The Onliest Lenny Bruce." *The Village Voice,* February 5, 1991.

Hentoff, Nat. "How the FCC Saves You from Indecency." *The Village Voice,* May 25, 1993.

Herder, June. "'Passing Show' Is Revived at Shubert." *Philadelphia Record,* November 21, 1945.

Herszenhorn, David M. "Wolfman Jack, 57, Raspy Voice of Rock-and-Roll on the Radio." *The New York Times,* July 3, 1995.

Hicks, Robert. "Satirist and Storyteller: Lord Buckley Is 'Resurrected.'" *The Villager,* February 28, 1998.

Hinckley, David. "Black Humor—Too Many Don't Get It." *New York Daily News,* October 22, 1991.

Hinckley, David. "For Beat's Sake." *New York Daily News,* December 22, 1992.

Hinckley, David. "Let's Kill All the Comedians?" *New York Daily News,* July 13, 1993.

Hochman, Steve. "Nik Venet, Record Producer for the Beach Boys." *Los Angeles Times,* January 6, 1998.

Hogg, Brian. "The Lenny Bruce Story." *Beat Scene,* 1991.

Holden, Stephen. "It's Comedy! From Skit to Song to Satire." *The New York Times,* October 27, 1980.

Honan, William H. "Harold Louis Humes, 66, Novelist and a Paris Review Co-Founder." *The New York Times,* September 12, 1992.

Humes, Harold L. (Doc). "His Lordship's Last Days." *Swank,* May 1961.

Jablonski, Joseph. "Swinging Stirrups: Announcing the Formation of the Knights & Ladies of Lord Buckley." *Arsenal,* No. 4, 1992.

Jacobs, Laura A. "Armitage Ballet." *The New Leader,* February 9, 1987.

Jackson, Blair. "Pigpen Forever: The Life and Times of Ron McKernan." *Golden Road,* 1993 Annual.

Jones, Chris. "Prop Presents 'Hip' View of Alternative Comedy's Role." *Chicago Tribune,* November 18, 1999.

Joyce, Mike. "Murphy Marches to Different Beat." *The Washington Post,* February 16, 1990.

Judge, Joseph. "Between Columbus and Jamestown: Exploring Our Forgotten Century." *National Geographic,* March 1988.

Judge, Mark Gauvreau. "Bring in 'da Class." *New York Press,* March 11–17, 1998.

Kanter, Nathan, and Sidney Kline. "Charge Quota Set on Cabarets, Too." *New York Daily News,* November 30, 1960.

Kaplan, Mike. "Clef Dwellers." *Variety,* October 3, 1956.

Kart, Larry. "It's Not Funny! American Humor Hasn't Been Well Preserved." *Chicago Tribune,* March 22, 1987.

Kart, Larry. "Laughter, Change and Those Smothers Brothers." *Chicago Tribune,* September 17, 1987.

Kart, Larry. "Second City's Brilliant New Revue Pokes at the Silly Side of Reality." *Chicago Tribune,* October 23, 1987.

Katz, Leonard, and Gene Grove. "Norman's Mailer's Wife on 'Critical' List." *New York Post,* November 22, 1960.

Kernis, Mark. "Odd Couple: Redbone and Waits." *Washington Post,* November 17, 1978.

Kelp, Thurston. "Don't Cut This Class: A Wild, Jubilant Tribute to Lord Buckley with Great Bebop Jazz." *The Cape Codder,* August 12, 1994.

Keown, Don. "His Humor's Both Hip and Healthy." *San Rafael Independent Journal,* June 18, 1960.

Kirk. "John Sinclair." *Variety,* December 28, 1983.

Kirkman, Edward, and Sidney Kline. "Big Club Wins a Stay with All the Stuffin's." *New York Daily News,* November 24, 1960.

King, Loren. "One-Man Show Recreates Satirist Lord Buckley." *The Advocate,* August 25, 1994.

Kissel, Howard. "'Lord' Works in Strange Ways." *New York Daily News,* May 30, 1997.

Kisselgoff, Anna. "Stretch Your Arms No Higher than Your Sleeve." *The New York Times,* November 20, 1987.

Krim, Seymour. "For My Brothers and Sisters . . ." From *The Art of the Personal Essay.* Selected by Phillip Lopate, New York, Anchor Books, 1998.

Kupcinet, Irv. "Kup's Column." *Chicago Sun-Times,* September 11, 1960.

Lary. "Famous Door, Miami." *Variety,* August 13, 1947.

Lee, C. P. "The Day Dylan Came to Didsbury." *Mojo,* February 1998.

Lehmann-Haupt, Christopher. "Books of the Times." *The New York Times,* November 28, 1983.

Linehan, Gary. "'Lord Buckley': Native Son Still a Comic Force." *The Union Democrat, Sonora,* February 12, 1999.

Long, Doug. "The Process of a New Play." *PerformInk,* July 4, 1999.

Luce, Betsy. "Copa Owner Faces 2d Quiz on Sinatra." *New York Post,* November 23, 1960.

Luce, Betsy. "Cabaret Takes Top Cop to Court." *New York Post,* November 23, 1960.

Luce, Betsy. "Resume Fight in Court over Club Licenses." *New York Post,* November 25, 1960.

Luce, Betsy. "Mayor Holds Cabaret Card Reform Talks." *New York Post,* November 28, 1960.

Lustig, Jay. "Radio Rebel." *Newark Star-Ledger,* January 4, 1998.

MacBeath, Rod. "Looking Up Dylan's Sleeves: Part One." *The Telegraph,* No. 50, Winter 1994.

Marks, Peter. "When a Lone Voice Can Fill a Stage." *The New York Times,* April 10, 1998.

Marriott, Michael. "Upbeat Farewell For a 'Jazz Pastor': Musicians' Minister Retires." *The New York Times,* January 3, 1994.

Marsh, Ward. "Untitled Review." *Boston Herald,* October 27, 1944.

Martin, Carol. "Life on the Floor—Art, Sport and Scam: Dance Marathons of the Twenties and Thirties." *New Observations,* No. 39, 1986.

Martin, Douglas. "Village Gate Struggling to Avoid Its Last Chorus." *The New York Times,* March 9, 1993.

Martin, Mildred. "Untitled Review." *Philadelphia Inquirer,* March 4, 1944.

Mead, Rebecca. "The Beats Are Back." *New York Magazine,* May 3, 1993.

Michaels, Kevin. "David Amram on Poetry & Jazz." *Spoken Word Journal,* Spring 1996.

Miller, David. "Rockefeller Called on to Probe 'Widespread Police Corruption.'" *New York Herald Tribune,* November 15, 1960.

Moberley, Leeds. "Wife Stabbed, Novelist Held: Norman Mailer Seized at Hospital." *New York Daily News,* November 22, 1960.

Moore, Dave. "Letters to the Editor." *The Telegraph,* No. 51, 1995.

Morgenstern, Dan. "Ornette Meets Dizzy." *Metronome,* March 1961.

Musto, Michael. "How to Take 'America' with a Grain of Salt." *New York Post,* April 5, 1997.

Newton, Francis. "Lord Buckley." *New Statesman,* December 31, 1960.

Neugerbauer, William, and Sidney Kline. "Mystery Man Denies Police License Bribe." *New York Daily News,* November 16, 1960.

Nichols, Mary Perot. "Lord Buckley: 'Hip Messiah' Loses Cabaret Card to Fuzz He Loves." *The Village Voice,* November 4, 1960.

Noble, Arthur, and Jack Smith. "Cops Nip 2 Cabarets (and Sophie Tucker)." *New York Daily News,* November 21, 1960.

O'Connor, John J. "Poetry in Motion, Read Aloud or Simply Imagined." *The New York Times,* February 1, 1996.

O'Neill, Edward, and Sidney Kline. "Bribe Show Gets Bigger Stage and Frankie Sinatra." *New York Daily News,* November 17, 1960.

O'Neill, Edward, and Sidney Kline. "Copa: on the Carpet: How Did Sinatra Sing License?" *New York Daily News,* November 18, 1960.

Osofsky, Dale. "The Resacralization of American Culture: Lord Buckley and the Grateful Dead." Unpublished, 1999.

Ostlere, Hilary. "Stepping into the Past with a Quickstep." *The New York Times,* April 20, 1997.

J. P. "Lord Buckley: His Royal Hipness." *Utne Reader,* January/February 1993.

Palmer, Robert. "The Pop Life." *The New York Times,* August 25, 1982.

Patner, Andrew. "The Return of the Hip Messiah." *Chicago Sun-Times,* December 9, 1999.

Pearl, Ralph. "Vegas Days and Nites." *Las Vegas Sun,* November 13, 1960.

Peluso, Dominick, and Henry Lee. "Big Night Spot Fights Suspension of Permit." *New York Daily News,* November 23, 1960.

Peluso, Dominick, and Loren Craft. "Bob Pledges Reform on Entertainer Cards." *New York Daily News,* November 29, 1960.

Perlman, Ken. "Bryan Bowers: Autoharp Master." *Sing Out!,* Vol. 43, No. 1, Summer 1998.

Perlmutter, Emanuel. "Police to Step Up Vigil on Cabarets." *The New York Times,* November 20, 1960.

Poirer, Normand. "Lord Buckley Steals His Last Show." *New York Post,* December 6, 1960.

Powell, Kevin. "The Beat Generation." *Rolling Stone,* February 4, 1993.

Powr. "High School Confidential." *Variety,* May 28, 1958.

Pouncey, Edwin. "Invisible Jukebox: Ken Kesey." *The Wire,* September 1998.

R., J. W. "Untitled Review." *Boston Daily Globe,* September 3, 1943.

Ravo, Nick. "Redd Foxx, Cantankerous Master of Bawdy Humor, Is Dead at 68." *The New York Times,* October 13, 1991.

Reed, Bill. "Lord of the Hepcats." *L.A. Reader,* November 27, 1981.

Reiter, Susan. "A Punk Princess with a Taste for Ballet Classicism." *Dance Magazine,* September 9, 1987.

Reiner, Jay. "Wigged-Out Lord Buckley Honored with One-Man Show." *Los Angeles Herald Examiner,* August 19, 1983.

Riesel, Victor. "Seek Peace Parley with Cops." *New York Mirror,* November 27, 1960.

Robertson, Nan. "1,000 Policemen Check Cabarets." *The New York Times,* November 21, 1960.

Robinson, Layland. "City to Bid Sinatra Testify on Cabarets." *The New York Times,* November 17, 1960.

Robinson, Richard. "Humor in the Rock Environment." *Hit Parader,* May 1970.

Robins, Natalie. "The Secret War Against American Writers." *Esquire,* March 1992.

Ross, Earl, and Gerald Duncan. "Accused Confronted by Accuser of Bribe." *New York Mirror,* November 17, 1960.

Saxon, Wolfgang. "Marvin Worth, Film Producer and Writer for TV, Dies at 72." *The New York Times,* May 3, 1998.

Scho. "Dick Buckley." *Variety,* 1947.

Schuller, Billie Henderson. "The Endurance Shows in the Middle West." *Repertoire Theatre History Seminar,* April 19, 1997.

Seymour, Gene. "A Conquistador Turned Healer." *New York Newsday,* May 15, 1992.

Severo, Richard. "Red Skelton, Knockabout Comic and Clown Prince of the Airwaves, Is Dead at 84." *The New York Times,* September 7, 1997.

Shepard, Richard F. "Going Out Guide." *The New York Times,* Janaury 20, 1987.

Silsbee, Kirk. "A Ray of Hope at This Week's Grammy Awards: Singer Kirk Elling." *New Times,* February 19-25, 1998.

Patricia Simmons. "Untitled Review." *Washington Star,* November 3, 1944.

Smith, Ronald L. "Comedy." *Pulse,* December 1992.

Sprague, David. "Divine Styler." *Beatz,* May 1992.

Stegner, Bentley. "Folk Song and Jive." *Chicago Sun-Times,* August 28, 1960.

Stempek, Walter. "Lord Buckley: A Most Immaculately Hip Aristocrat." *Goldmine,* March 1, 1996.

Sullivan, Rob. "Doctor of Drums." *L.A. Style,* March 1989.

Sullivan, Ronald. "Severn Darden, 65, a Master of Improvisation." *The New York Times,* May 27, 1995.

Suzuki, Dean. "The Rudy Scwartz Project: Gunther Packs a Stiffy." *Option,* July–August 1995.

Tosches, Nick. "Mr. Sunday Night." *Vanity Fair,* July 1997.

Trager, Oliver. "Stompin' the Sweet Swingin' Sphere: Celebrating Lord Buckley in Southern California." *Organica,* Summer 1992.

Trager, Oliver, and David C. Barnett. "Black Cross: Lord Buckley, Joseph S. Newman and the Bob Dylan Connection." *On the Tracks,* Vol. 6, No. 3, Fall 1998.

Unknown. "Buckley Supplies Arcadia Laughs." *Chicago American,* February 6, 1935.

Unknown. "Special Events at Walkathons." *Chicago American,* February 19, 1935.

Unknown. "Nudists to Be Walkathon Stars." *Chicago American,* March, 12, 1935.

Unknown. "Walkathoners for Movies." *Chicago American,* March 23, 1935.

Unknown. "Untitled Review." *Washington Post,* July 25, 1943.

Unknown. "Untitled Review." *Boston Globe,* October 27, 1944.

Unknown. "diggin' DIG." *Dig Magazine,* May 1956.

Unknown. "Clef Dwellers." *Variety,* October 3, 1956.

Unknown. *Chicago Daily News,* August 27, 1960.

Unknown. *Chicago American,* August 27, 1960.

Unknown. "Lagniappe." *Chicago Sunday Tribune,* August 28, 1960.

Unknown. "Richard Buckley Dies." *The New York Times,* November 13, 1960.

Unknown. "Richard Buckley." *New York Daily News,* November 14, 1960.

Unknown. "Comedian Lord Buckley Dies in N.Y." *San Francisco Chronicle,* November 14, 1960.

Unknown. "Richard Buckley TV Entertainer." *New York Herald Tribune,* November 15, 1960.

Unknown. "Lord Buckley." *Variety,* November 16, 1960.

Unknown. "Light on Licenses." *New York Daily News,* November 16, 1960.

Unknown. "Cabaret-Card Fight Set Off by 'Lord' Buckley's Death." *The Village Voice,* November 17, 1960.

Unknown. "Cabaret Bureau Hit; Action Against Village Gate Put Off." *The Village Voice,* November 17, 1960.

Unknown. "Frankie Unkown to Cops." *New York Daily News,* November 18, 1960.

Unknown. "Hotspot Zone, Quiet—by PD Order." *New York Daily News,* November 20, 1960.

Unknown. "'Lord' Buckley Was on AGVA'S 'Unfair List.'" *Variety,* November 23, 1960.

Unknown. "A New Twist on Cabaret Cards." *Down Beat,* November 24, 1960.

Unknown. "Wagner Parley Aimed to Ease Cabaret Rule." *New York Daily News,* November 28, 1960.

Unknown. "A Card Game with the Cops." *Life,* December 5, 1960.

Unknown. "A Memorial in Jazz for Lord Buckley." *New York Daily News,* December 6, 1960.

Unknown. "The Cabaret Cards—Have They Killed a Man?" *Down Beat,* December 22, 1960.

Unknown. "Cabaret Card Situation Simmers." *Down Beat,* January 5, 1961.

Unknown. "The Secret Tape." *Down Beat,* January 5, 1961.

Unknown. "Karole Armitage." *Dance Magazine,* May 1986.

Unknown. "The Clown Prince of Pot." *High Times,* June 1993.

Unknown. "Sally Marr, 91, the Mother of Lenny Bruce." *The New York Times,* December 20, 1997.

Unknown. "Obituary: Nik Venet, 1936–1998." *Mojo,* March 1998.

Unknown. "Café Bringing '50s Scene Back to Life." *The Union Democrat, Sonora,* February 27, 1998.

Vernon, Paul. "'Blowing His Mind (And Yours, Too)'—Lord Buckley." *Blues & Rhythm,* July 1985.

Vincent, Sarah G. "Listening to the Maestro: Composer/Multi-instrumentalist David Amram." *Fifteen Minutes,* December 7, 1995.

Voce, Steve. "It Down Mean a Thing." *Jazz Journal International,* January 1983.

Wagenheim, Jeff. "Books On Tape." *New Age Journal,* June 1992.

Wald, Elijah. "For David Amram, the Music Is in the Mix." *Boston Globe,* November 29, 1995.

Waller, Don. "Tom Waites Shines His Lamp on Sleazy Underside of Life." *Los Angeles Times,* November 9, 1987.

Warren, Geoffrey. "Lord Buckley Performing at the Ivar." *Los Angeles Times,* February 12, 1959.

Weeden, Phil. "Lord Buckley—'In Concert.'" *Blues & Rhythm,* November 1985.

Wernick, Robert. "Big Sur." *Smithsonian,* November 1999.

Whalen, John. "The Trip: Cary Grant on Acid, and Other Stories from the LSD Studies of Dr. Oscar Janiger." *L.A. Weekly,* July 4, 1998.

White, Ken. "Lord of Hip." *Las Vegas Review-Journal,* February 5, 1996.

White, Timothy "George Harrison Reconsidered." *Musician Magazine,* November 1987.

Willen, Liz. "I'd Rather Do Radio than Sex: Wolfman Jack Wild to the End." *New York Newsday,* July 4, 1995.

Williams, Albert. "The Return of the Hip Messiah." *Chicago Reader,* November 19, 1999.

Williams, Martin. "Cabaret Bill Deplored: Lindsay, Isaacs Attack City's Anti-Intellectualism." *The Village Voice,* May 18, 1961.

Wolmuth, Roger. "Hoist 'Em High Pards, Lash Is Back." *People,* April 1, 1985.

Wright, Carol Von Pressentin. "Exploring the Mother Lode." *The New York Times,* May 16, 1993.

Wright, Dion. "IQ Interview: Eldon Setterholm Recalls Lord Buckley." *Irregular Quarterly,* Vol. 3, No. 3, 1987.

Young, Bob. "Wacko Comic Lives Again in Bio-Tribute." *Boston Globe,* November 14, 1995.

Magazine and Newspaper Notices/Reviews

Variety: December 8, 1934; "Seltzer Chi Shows Setting Fast Pace" January 12, 1935; February 2, 1935; February 9, 1935; April 13, 1935; June 1, 1935; June 22, 1935; July 6, 1935; July 13, 1935; July 20, 1935; August 3, 1935; August 31, 1935; September 14, 1935; September 28, 1935; October 10, 1935; December 4, 1935; May 5, 1943; February 14, 1945.

Billboard (routes): July 3, 1943; July 24, 1943; July 31, 1943; August 7, 1943; August 14, 1943; August 21, 1943; August 28, 1943; September 11, 1943; September 23, 1943; November 20, 1943; December 11, 1943; December 25, 1943; January 1, 1944; January 8, 1944; January 15, 1944; January 22, 1944; January 29, 1944; February 5, 1944; March 11, 1944; April 15, 1944; April 22, 1944; August 12, 1944; August 19, 1944; August 26, 1944; September 9, 1944; October 14, 1944; November 11, 1944; November 18, 1944; November 25, 1944; January 6, 1945; February 17, 1945.

Advertisements

Variety. June 22, 1935; December 21, 1935–October 31, 1936; October 28, 1955; October 5, 1956.

Springfield Daily News. July 18–21, 1943.

Springfield Morning-Union. July 18–21, 1943.

Washington Post. July 23–25, 1943; November 2–8, 1944.

Boston Daily Globe. September 2–9, 1943; October 25–30, 1944.

Boston Herald. September 2–9, 1943; October 26, 1944.

Philadelphia Inquirer. March 3–9, 1944; November 16, 1944.

Cleveland Plain-Dealer. October 5–7, 1944.

Washington Star. November 2–8, 1944.

Chicago Daily News. November 30–December 2, 1944.

Dig Magazine. November 1956.

Dig Magazine. April 1957.

Los Angeles Mirror News. February 20, 1959.

The Village Voice. October 9, 1960; September 18, 1990.

Berkeley Barb. October 18, 1968.

Liner Notes

Alfonso, Barry. *The Beat Generation* 1992
Amram, David. *Ode to Lord Buckley* 1981, 1985
Buckley, Fred. *Buckley's Best* 1968
Dickson, Jim. *Lord Buckley—Blowing His Mind (and yours too)* 1985
Gibson, Harry. *Harry "The Hipster" Gibson: Everybody's Crazy but Me* 1986.
Gleason, Ralph. *The Real Lenny Bruce* 1974
James, Dan. *Way Out Humor* 1959
Lee, C. P. *Lord Buckley Concert* 1985
Lee, C. P. *Lord Buckley—Blowing His Mind (and yours too)* 1985
Marill, Alvin H. *The Golden Age of Comedy* 1972
Newton, Francis. *The Parabolic REVELATIONS of the Late Lord Buckley* 1952
Pekar, Harvey. *Lord Buckley Live* (unpublished reissue), 1994
Selnikof, Richard. *a most immaculately hip aristocrat* 1970
Tacot, Charles. *The Best of Lord Buckley* 1963, 1969
Tesser, Neil. *Kurt Elling: The Messenger* 1997
Trager, Oliver. *Bad-Rapping of the Marquis de Sade* 1996
White, Timothy. *Lord Kitchener: Klassic Kitchener, Volume One* 1972
Unknown. *Euphoria* 1951
Unknown. *Euphoria Vol. 2* 1954
Unknown. *Lord Buckley LIVE* 1991

Albums

Joni Mitchell. *Don Juan's Reckless Daughter*
James Taylor. *Walking Man, New Moonshine*
George Harrison. *33 1/3*
Jimmy Buffett. *Living and Dying in 3/4 Time, You Had to Be There*
David Bowie. *The Rise and Fall of Ziggy Stardust*
Bob Dylan. *Bringing It All Back Home, Highway 61 Revisited, Blonde on Blonde, Blood on the Tracks*
Madeleine Eastman. *Art Attack*
Kurt Elling. *The Messenger*
311. *311*
Robert Dick. *Digging It Harder from Afar, Venturi Shadows*
Mark Murphy. *Mark Murphy: Kerouac, Then and Now*

Miscellaneous Recordings

"Jonah in the Belly of the Whale" Rev. C. F. Weems, Chicago, 1927.
"Black Cross" Bob Dylan, Minneapolis, Minnesota, December 21, 1961, and Gaslight Café, New York City, Fall 1962.
"Joe Newman's Rhymes and Reason" Producer: David C. Barnett, WCPN-FM, Cleveland, Ohio. Aired: September 1, 1993.
"Lord Buckley" Producer: David C. Barnett, WCPN-FM, Cleveland, Ohio. Aired: October 25, 1995.
"My Own Railroad" Robert Dick, 1996.
"Liberties Taken: With Prince Minsky" Jason Eisenberg, 1997.
"Dead to the World" Producer: David Gans, KPFA-FM, Berkeley, California. Aired: February 25, 1998.
"Hipsters, Flipsters and Finger-Poppin' Daddies, Knock Me Your Lobes: Klaus Gustafson Discovers Lord Buckley" Producer: Klaus Gustafson Sveriges Radio P1, Stockholm, Sweden. Aired: December 28, 1999.

Programs

Fun for the Money. Hollywood, California, 1941.
The Passing Show. Nixon Theatre, Boston, Massachusetts, December 10, 1945.
The Passing Show. *The Playgoer: A Magazine for the Cass Theatre*, December 23, 1945.
The Passing Show. Erlanger Theatre, Chicago, Illinois, January 7, 1946.
Lord Buckley's Finest Hour by Richmond Shepard and John Sinclair. Starring John Sinclair. Presented by Frederick Buckley. Richmond Shepard Theatre Studios, Hollywood, California, 1983.

"The Sixth Annual Lord Buckley Memorial Celebration" Spring 1994.

Are You There? A Hip History Lesson on the Life of Lord Buckley by Frank Speiser, Cleveland Public Theater, October 1995.

Lord Buckley's Finest Hour by Richmond Shepard and John Sinclair. Directed by Richmond Shepard. Starring Tom Calagna, Don't Tell Mama, New York City 1997.

Trading Cards

Allen, Doug, and Oliver Trager. *WFMU Crackpots and Visionaries* 1994

Crumb, Jesse, and Erica Detlefsen. *Beat Characters* 1997

Williams, J. R. *Dig* 1997

Comix

Crap #1, J. R. Williams, 1993

Crap #7, J. R. Williams, May 1995

Nowheresville #2, 1996

Interviews by Author

Berle Adams. *November 25, 1991.*

Steve Allen. *May 22, 1992.*

David Amram. *June 15, 1991.*

Buddy Arnold. *October 21, 1992.*

Ray Avery. *September 15, 1991.*

Eve Babitz. *April 21, 1994.*

Joan Baez. *April 6, 1993; April 29, 1993.*

Orson Bean. *April 16, 1991.*

Steve Ben Israel. *February 23, 1994.*

Milton Berle. *October 21, 1992.*

Shelley Berman. *March 31, 1991.*

Charles "Tubby" Boots. *October 9, 1991; November 24, 1991.*

Chris Brooks. *June 1993.*

Doug Boyd. *October 9, 1991.*

Albert "Pud" Brown. *January 30, 1992.*

Lady Elizabeth Buckley. *May 12, 1992; August 31, 1992; October 3, 1992.*

Charles Campbell. *September 30, 1991.*

Conte Candoli. *September 14, 1992.*

Bill Claxton. *September 15, 1991.*

Richard Clayton. *June 3, 1992.*

Del Close. *September 30, 1991; October 23, 1991.*

James Coburn. *March 4, 1994.*

Herb Cohen. *November 12, 1991.*

Jack Coons. *November 11, 1991.*

Prof. Irwin Corey. *April 1, 1993.*

Tom Dahl. *March 4, 1992.*

Faith Dane. *September 28, 1992; February 10, 1993.*

Severn Darden. *October 29, 1991.*

Edward Dephoure. *September 1, 1994.*

Bob DeWitt. *July 1992; September 30, 1992.*

Jim Dickson. *October 28, 1991.*

Jerry Douglas. *February 10, 1993.*

Harry "Sweets" Edison. *June 17, 1992.*

Dan Einstein. *August 9, 1993.*

Herb Ellis. *January 22, 1992.*

Art Farmer. *April 21, 1991.*

Mort Fega. *May 18, 1992.*

Lawrence Ferlinghetti. *April 30, 1994.*

Prince Lewis Foremaster. *May 9, 1994.*

Larry Foster. *May 7, 1993.*

Jerry Garcia. *February 18, 1992.*

Harry Geller. *September 13, 1994; September 22, 1994.*

Garry Goodrow. *April 8, 1992.*

Wavy Gravy. *September 1, 1994.*

Dick Gregory. *May 1, 1993.*

George Greif. *November 21, 1991.*

Eddie Hall. *May 7, 1993.*

Huntz Hall. *May 7, 1993.*

Jon Hendricks. *March 12, 1993.*

Milt Hinton. *April 30, 1994.*

Wally Holmes. *November 20, 1991.*

John Hostedder. *October 9, 1991; June 27, 1992.*

Bill Hodge. *March 4, 1992.*

Wolfman Jack. *February 6, 1995.*

Little Willie Jackson. *September 9, 1991.*

Sandy Jacobs. *October 30, 1991.*

Dr. Oscar Janiger. *October 2, 1991.*

Buddy Jones. *November 18, 1991.*

Harold Jovian. *July 24, 1992.*

Stacey Keach. *October 5, 1994.*

Adam Keefe. *May 10, 1991.*

Ken Kesey. *July 25, 1991.*

Dave Keown. *March 21, 1993.*

Dr. Muarry Korngold. *September 15, 1992.*

Mark Lane. *April 1, 1991; May 7, 1993.*

Bertha Larsen. *May 10, 1992.*

C. P. Lee. *July 2, 1992.*

Al Lewis. *August 7, 1991.*

Sally Marr. *June 30, 1993.*

Bruce MacDonald. *November 12, 1991.*
James Macy. *October 12, 1992.*
Judith Malina. *April 21, 1992.*
Vaughn Marlowe. *September 13, 1992.*
Don McAslin. *May 17, 1992.*
Robert Mitchum. *January 30, 1993; February 3, 1993.*
John Montgomery. *September 29, 1991.*
Jerry Moran. *August 2, 1993.*
Larry Moyer. *September 15, 1992.*
Mark Murphy. *May 27, 1993.*
Don Mupo. *September 29, 1993; October 4, 1993.*
Fayard Nicholas. *February 8, 1993.*
Harold Nicholas. *February 10, 1993.*
Chuck Niles. *August 9, 1994.*
Ken Nordine. *January 22, 1992.*
Dave Pell. *September 30, 1991.*
Jim Philbrook. *July 27, 1993.*
George Plimpton. *May 3, 1991.*
Bill Randle. *December 29, 1993.*
Ed Randolph. *October 31, 1991.*
Charles Richards. *September 28, 1991.*
Red Rodney. *May 18, 1992.*
Jimmy Rowles. *November 14, 1991.*
Marie Rozier. *March 4, 1992.*
Grover Sales. *September 14, 1992.*
Phil Schaap. *March 27, 1993; May 18, 1999.*
Jack Sheldon. *October 3, 1991.*
Bobby Short. *September 15, 1992.*
John Sinclair. *November 1993.*
Bob Smith. *December 1, 1993.*
Herb Snitzer. *March 23, 1993.*
Frank Speiser. *May 11, 1994; June 7, 1994.*
Gus Statiras. *September 29, 1993.*
Roger Steffens. *October 2, 1992.*
Sleepy Stein. *January 16, 1996.*
Walt Stempek. *September 11, 1992.*
Larry Storch. *June 18, 1991.*
Charles Tacot. *October 22, 1991.*
Dr. Billy Taylor. *May 10, 1993.*
James Taylor. *April 25, 1993.*
Rip Taylor. *February 3, 1993.*
Studs Terkel. *April 2, 1993.*
Joe Termini. *February 5, 1992.*
Elaine Thomasen. *February 11, 1993; June 22, 1993; January 27, 1994; September 14, 1999.*
Les Thomson. *November 20, 1991.*
Nik Venet. *September 15, 1995.*
Millie Vernon. *October 7, 1991; October 20, 1991; May 10, 1992; September 22, 1992.*
Ira Westley. *November 13, 1991.*
Marvin Worth. *May 5, 1994.*
Mel Welles. *May 4, 1991; October 22, 1991.*
Robin Williams. *July 14, 1994.*
Stuart Whitman. *July 7, 1992.*
Harry Woodward. *February 1, 1992.*
Paul Zaloom. *January 16, 1996.*
Dick Zalud. *October 7, 1991; October 20, 1991; May 10, 1992; September 22, 1992.*

Interviews by Kirk Silsbee

Eddie Jefferson. *1976.*
Harry "The Hipster" Gibson. *1983.*

Interviews by Douglas Cruickshank

Al Young. *December 21, 1990.*
Dan Barrett. *March 24, 1992.*
Jonathan Winters. *April 14, 1992.*
Dr. Oscar Janiger. *April 10, 1992.*

Interviews by Del Close

Ann Brooks. *May 10, 1974.*
Ray Watkins. *May 10, 1974.*
Del Close. *May 10, 1974; May 17, 1974.*

Interview by Jason Eisenberg

Mort Sahl. *May 21, 1997.*

Interviews by David C. Barnett

Dizzy Gillespie. *circa 1991–1992.*
Mose Allison. *circa 1991–1992.*
Studs Terkel. *circa 1991–1992.*

Interview by Walt Stempek

Ken Kesey. *September 1992.*

Letters to Author

Adams, Berle. *December 14, 1994; March 3, 1995.*
Baraka, Amiri. *April 30, 1993.*
Barks, Nicholas J. *September 23, 1995; October 25, 1995; March 12, 1996.*
Barnett, David C. *January 16, 1993; February 26, 1993; June 13, 1993; May 20, 1994.*
Bogosian, Eric. *July 30, 1992; September 4, 1992; April 4, 1993.*
Boyd, Doug. *December 29, 1994.*

Buckley, Lady Elizabeth. *June 24, 1992*; *October 22, 1992*; *October 27, 1992*; *December 8, 1992.*
Burns, Jim. *March 2, 1993.*
Campbell, Charles. *February 15, 1992.*
Cassady, Carolyn. *February 16, 1993.*
Catanzaro, Brian. *January 1, 1993*; *January 13, 1993.*
Chase, Allan S. *June 20, 1993.*
Clarke, Donald. *March 1, 1996.*
Cohan, Alan. *December 16, 1993.*
Constanten, Tom. *October 1992.*
Crow, Bill. *March 27, 1993*; *May 26, 1998.*
Cruickshank, Douglas. *September 6, 1992.*
Crumb, R. *May 17, 1997.*
Dalzell, Tom. *July 8, 1996*; *July 30, 1996*; *December 11, 1996.*
Diaz, Vince. *August 21, 1996.*
Dick, Robert. *May 18, 1996*; *June 11, 1996.*
Drew, James. *February 2, 1997.*
Dunton, David. *April 22, 1992.*
Eisenberg, Jason. *May 7, 1997*; *September 6, 1997.*
Firestone, Ross. *October 13, 1996.*
Forematser, Lewis. *March 5, 1993*; *January 24, 1994*; *September 5, 1996.*
Gilford, Sam. *August 8, 1994.*
Ginter, Thomas S. (U.S. Department of Justice/Federal Bureau of Investigation). *May 25, 1993*; *June 17, 1993.*
Grady, John. *May 9, 1996.*
Griffin, William D. (U.S. Department of Justice/Federal Bureau of Investigation). *May 17, 1993.*
Harrod, James A. *January 4, 1995*; *October 24, 1995*; *October 25, 1998.*
Hayes, Martha. *April 24, 1998.*
Holland, Orrin. *April 16, 1998.*
Horowitz, Mikhail. *July 26, 1996*; *January 29, 1997.*
Huff, Richard L. (U.S. Department of Justice). *June 2, 1993*; *August 31, 1993.*
Jablonski, Joseph. *November 10, 1995.*
Jackson, Blair. *December 1992.*
Jordan, Linda. *May 6, 1996; May 29, 1996.*
Keever, Tom Dale. *May 14, 1993*; *July 20, 1993.*
Kenney, Bill. *August 7, 1993.*
Krassner, Paul. *February 26, 1993.*
Martin, Carol. *May 26, 1997.*
McCaslin, Don. *May 2, 1992.*
Monteleone, Michael. *April 16, 1995.*
Moore, Dave. *January 24, 1996.*
Moore, Ian. *March 21, 1997.*
Newman, Paul, and Darice O'Mara. *January 26, 1995.*
O'Brien, Kevin (U.S. Department of Justice/Federal Bureau of Investigation). *June 15, 1993.*
Ostlere, Hilary. *May 2, 1997.*
Parker, Chan. *October 3, 1994*; *November 16, 1994.*
Pettet, Roger. *December 18, 1992*; *January 28, 1993*; *February 22, 1993.*
Petty, Mark. *November 18, 1997.*
Prillman, Randolph G. (U.S. Department of Justice/Federal Bureau of Investigation). *May 18, 1993.*
Roth, James J. (U.S. Department of Justice/Federal Bureau of Ivestigation). *April 21, 1992*; *March 29, 1993*; *July 27, 1993.*
Savlov, John. *February 18, 1993.*
Scialli, Dr. John V. *May 23, 1994*; *June 11, 1994*; *June 22, 1994*; *July 6, 1994*; *March 18, 1995*; *March 20, 1995*; *August 25, 1996.*
Sculatti, Gene. *October 12, 1995.*
Silsbee, Kirk. *January 30, 1992; April 1, 1992*; *November 11, 1994*; *January 14, 1995*; *March 12, 1996.*
Stempek, Walt. *October 26, 1992*; *February 8, 1994*; *November 1, 1994*; *July 23, 1995.*
Thomas, William Karl. *June 5, 1992.*
Thomasen, Elaine. *July 29, 1993*; *December 16, 1993.*
Williams, J. R. *July 12, 1995*; *August 4, 1995*; *February 5, 1996*; *September 17, 1997.*
Wright, John H. (Central Intelligence Agency). *September 30, 1993*; *January 27, 1994.*
Young, Israel G. *September 9, 1999.*

To David Amram

Buckley, Lady Lisbette. *October 22, 1988; January 8, 1989.*

To David C. Barnett

Burns, Jim. *March 3, 1992.*

To Douglas Cruickshank

Pettet, Roger. *December 18, 1992.*
Thomasen, Elaine *February 10, 1993.*

To Charles Campbell

Buckley, Lady Elizabeth. *November 24, 1960.*

To Bill Randle

Buckley, Lord. *December 6, 1957.*

To Lord Buckley

Miller, Henry. *November 18, 1959.*

To Lawrence Ferlinghetti

Buckley, Lord & Lady. *June 20, 1960.*
James, Dan. *July 19, 1960.*
Bock, Richard. *July 20, 1960.*
Buckley, Lady Lisbeth. *July 30, 1968*; *September 2, 1974*; *August 5, 1975*; *December 20, 1977*; *June 21, 1981*; *October 28, 1987.*
Griffin, Lyle. *May 6, 1969*; *June 25, 1969.*
Cullman, Brian. *February 16, 1981.*

To Dick Zalud and Millie Vernon

Buckley, Lord. No date.
Buckley, Lord & Lisbeth. *November 28, 1958.*

Ephemera

Marriage License, Richard M. Buckley –Helen E. Hanson, State of Maryland, July 23, 1946.
Poster, Carnivale Lounge, San Marino Hotel, Palm Beach, Florida, February 8, 1957.
Legal Agreement Between Lord Buckley and Earl Brown, February 10, 1959.
Legal Agreement Between Lord Buckley and Richard Zalud, July 6, 1959.
Press Release KFAX Newsradio, November 1, 1960.
Certificate of Death: Richard Buckley, November 13, 1960.
Flyer for Lord Buckley's Finest Hour, 1984.
Flyer for The Fifth Annual Lord Buckley Memorial Celebration, 1993.
Flyer for The Sixth Annual Lord Buckley Memorial Celebration 1994.
Flyer for Jason Eisenberg Performs Lord Buckley's Greatest Hits, January 1997.

cast of characters

The following list will provide the reader with a quick-access reference to the page numbers where the witnesses in the oral historical element of *Dig Infinity!* can first be found.

acknowledgments

An old Japanese proverb suggests that there seven ways to say "thank you" and all of them are insults. But if any book deserves a companion tome just to say "thank you" to all the selfless souls who aided its birth, this would be it.

First, last and always, I have to put my wife, Elaine, and son, Cole, at the top of the list. Elaine, without your patience, suggestions, inspiration, and love, *Dig Infinity!* would not exist. Thank you from my heart and soul—I'll try to pick an easier subject next time around. Cole, your rendition of "Jonah and the Whale" would not only make Lord Buckley proud, it's one of a million things that make me proud too.

My family is really sick of hearing about Lord Buckley so I gotta thank my mom and dad, sister and brother, stepfather and stepmother, for not daring to derail this runaway train.

On the bureaucratic front, special kudos need to be given to my manager Stephen Smith for nurturing the project at a critical time (and for sealing the real deal, natch). Stephen appeared like an angel to urge, spur, inspire me and is one of the main reasons you are now holding this book. John Weber is the publisher of Welcome Rain so since these words are being printed on his dime and time I must bow in humble supplication of the master for taking the greatest of all leaps of faith. Thank you also to the nimble-minded Chuck Kim and the intrepid Karyn Slutsky of Welcome Rain, as well. Mike Golden had been trying to jump on the caboose of this locomotive for quite a while and finally made it by hooking me up with John. My lawyer, Alan Bomser, has always regarded me and this project with an air of bemused incredulity. Still, he can say "no" like no one I've ever met—that's what I pay him for. Thank goodness he says "yes" sometimes as well. Also a heartfelt thanks to Doveen Schecter and her mom, Leona, for their work in promoting the book in publishing circles some years back and for selling them on a couple of others.

Certain individuals stand above the fray for the excellence of spirit and gonzo willingness to share their time and materials with me. Mark Miller was the guy who first turned me onto to Lord B back in 1976 and, for this alone, should receive instant karma. Walt Stempek shared his voluminous Buckley archive with me and really helped me flesh out some of the missing pieces of the puzzle. Radio journalist David C. Barnett for all kinds of recorded and printed matter specifically (and not so specifically) relating to Lord Buckley's 1957 visit to Cleveland and His Lordship's relationship with Joseph S. Newman. Bay Area writer Doug Cruickshank, an early supporter who generously allowed me to use interviews he conducted in this book, has always been there with his shoulder to cry on. Kirk Silsbee was one of my greatest champions—he's an L.A. writer who sent scads of materials, interviews, interviewees, clips, dips, mips, and bits my way. Kirk, U D MAN!

There are a passel of Lord Buckley interpreters who have done much to spread the gospel of the Royal Court via their stage presentations. Their generosity and openness have been one of the joys of working on this project, allowing me to glimpse shades of Buckley's genius that had escaped me via vinyl.

Tom Calagna was selling orthopedic shoes when I met him in 1996 (still does, in fact). As the greatest living channeler of Lord Buckley, Tom has been following that intangible Buckley muse since he was a kid . . . and it shows. Besides, he's a Yankee fan so how bad can he be? After getting his chops back together, Tom has taken center stage with the Buckley Ouiji Board act to end all acts: "Lord Buckley Alive!!!!"

Steve Ben Israel is a wandering New York City shaman and I have been honored and blessed to become associated with this important artist. Steve does some great send-ups of Buckley and his piece "The Spinning Wheel, Baby" takes Lord Buckley's work up to and beyond the pounce of the now. If you don't bump into him at Veselka, you can catch his piece "Non-Violent Executions" around town . . . if you're blessed.

Martha Cinader, a poet and performer, does a mean version of "Jonah and the Whale" and some wonderful Buckley-inspired material—especially "Tesla-vision," a hipsemantic take on the life and work of Nikola Tesla, the overlooked twentieth-century inventor. Jason Eisenberg is a home builder by day and a Buckleyologist by night who worked up a fine one-man show featuring a tour through Buckley's hip classics. Actor Frank Speiser did a notorious one-man Buckley show, "Are You There? A Hip History Lesson" up and down the East Coast a few years back but he also provided many valuable insights into Buckley's nuanced craft. Theater rat extraordinaire Tom Dale Keever was the first person I ever saw perform Lord Buckley's material when he and his saxophone accompanist numbered more on stage than the lone me in the CBGB audience.

The photographers whose work helps populate this work deserve a shout-out here. Ray Avery, William Claxton, Bob Parent, and Tom Heffernon . . . get up and take a bow!

I have a bunch of freinds who really indulged me. Thank you to the *Apocalypso* crew (Michael Fiorillo, Peter Polshek, Steven Skollar, and Rick Weisfeld). Thanks to Jim and Ellyn Polshek. Thank you Marc Greene, Ken Rosenberg, Ben Miller, Jo Stein, Jeff Golick, Jeff Jackson, James Johnson, Ray Hill, Richard Lewis, John Savlov, Tom Foster, David Ostiller, and John Sullivan (most of all).

Judy Aley for help with EMI and for clarifying Karole Armitage's invovlement with Buckley's work. Jon Altschuler for his legal ear. David Amram for early and constant support and access to materials. David Armstrong of the *San Francisco Examiner* for tracking down Bay Area leads and for taking a good-natured pass as Buckley's erstwile Boswell.

Eve Babitz for California bushwhacking. Ross Baker for historical information on Tuolumne, California. The people at Archive Photo (particularly Michael Shulman and Mitch Blank) for enthusiasm and pop-cult wisdom. Win Bottum for hipsemantic insights. Linda Elleman and Bread and Puppet Theater for leading me Zaloom's way. Chris Brooks for background on Club Renaissance. Murray Bruce for his thoughts and support.

Ray Carlucci for being a mensch. Charles Campbell for providing photos of Buckley in Marin County circa 1960 and the rare Fourth of July party tape. The late Del Close for tapes and patience (even when I called a little too early in the a.m.). Carolyn Cassady for writing back. Rick Castro and Soledad Brown for preserving the Earl Brown archive. Brian Catanzaro for turning me on to the Joni Mitchell connection. Harold Channer for documenting "Dig and Thou Shall Be Dug," the 1996 Lord Buckley performance celebration in Greenwich Village. Alan Chase for providing background on the Club DeLisa. Richard Clayton, Lord Buckley's nephew, for providing family background history. Herb Cohen and Martin Cohen and their assistant Diane at Third Storey Productions. Fred Cohen at the Jazz Record Center for giving me a "deal" on some rare Buckley platters. Janet Coleman for hosting a couple of Lord Buckley specials on WBAI-FM radio in New York City. Brian Cullman for pointing me in some right directions and sending me some great tapes. Michael Cuscuna for producing the 1996 re-release of *Bad-Rapping of the Marquis de Sade* and the throwing the liner notes gig my way.

Steve Dalchinsky (poet/wise man/Beatnik/visionary sort of cat who can also be found hawking the coolest books, LPs, and tapes on the streets of Soho) was always there with just right bit of sage advice. John Dalton at Capital/Blue Note for finally returning my calls. Tom Dalzell wrote an unusually cool book about slang *(Flappers 2 Rappers)* and included some of my research in his book so he should be thanking me . . . but I learned a heckuva lot from him too. John Dellgatto greased the Steve Allen wheels for me but also sent some sensational tapes of the Kentucky Colonels. One of the best things about this trip was meeting so many of the heppest of the hep and Joel Dorn (who worked and hung with everybody from Mingus to Debbie Harry to Doc Pomus) can outhep 'em all. Alan Douglas for being in the right place at the right time. Madeleine Eastman, a Bay Area scatress, for doing her thang. Dan Einstein for discovering the super ultra mega rare *Club 7* kine.

My old employee David Eisichovits for helping with a bunch of tasks when I could not muster the mustard. All the cats and kitties at EMI: Buckley Hugo, Joel Swaine, David Wolfson, Dag Sandsmark, and Rose Marie Gawelko. Arnie Engleman and his band of Merry Pranksters at the Westbeth Theatre Center for doing such a great job with "Dig and Thou Shall Be Dug." Tom Evered at Capitol/Blue Note for pushing the papers through corporate and having the check checkers checked check.

Art Farmer for trying to remember. Bob Fass for spinning Lord B on BAI on many a late-night, all-night "Radio Unnameable" broadcast. Ross Firestone for playing the role of the most ultimate middleman. Dan Flesses for acting as Buckley pointman in Portland, Oregon. Michael Ford for introducing me to Kirk Silsbee. Prince Lewis Foremaster, Buckley's last aide-de-camp, for keeping the monologues alive and for the most unusual postal communiqués one could ever hope to receive.

Sam Gilford, old friend and self-styled "Revolutionary Cultural Evangelist" for teaching and sharing. John Grady for his expertise on the Beat Generation. John Guedel for trying to track down Buckley's appearance on Groucho's "You Bet Your Life." Allison Guss at A&E for leading me to the Nicholas Brothers. Klaus Gustafson for spreading the Buckley gospel in Sweden.

Jim Harrod, erstwile chronicler of Pacific Jazz Records, for tracking down the Jazz City photos of His Lordship and more. Bob Holman for insights into the poetry of Lord Buckley and for using Buckley's material in his film *The United States of Poetry.* John Hostedder for leading the charge. Jeff Hughson for leading me points north, south, east, and west.

C. Bernard Jackson for giving me a V.I.P. tour of the Ivar Theater. Blair Jackson is my oldest friend whom I finally met—he provided me with background documentation on minstrelsy. Linda Jordan at the Bancroft Library at U.C. Berkeley for unearthing the Ferlinghetti collection.

Citizen Kafka for for his secret museum. Ron Kolm for knowing all. KPFA Pacifica radio in Berkeley for getting that 9/16/59 interview Bill Butler conducted with Lord Buckley. Nancy Kriegle for all kinds of feedback. Gary Krebs for all kinds of suggestions and questions.

Gary Lambert for opening the Grateful Dead doors of perception. Lisa Law for hooking me up with Wavy Gravy. Arthur Levine for a copyright law citation freebie. Lisa Lieberman for assisting in the Robin Williams interview. Michael Liebert for insights into both Alvar Núñez Cabeza de Vaca "The Gasser" and Henry Miller.

Campbell MacLaren for a lunch or three. Neal McCabe for vital e-mails and his book *Baseball's Golden Age.* Paul McIsaac for leading me to Mel Welles. Dennis McNally for incredible patience and for setting up my interview with Jerry Garcia. Barry Mitchell for archival video leads. Linda Mitchell for her recollections on the making of *Chicago: First Impressions of a Great American City.* Bill Morgan for his help in procuring the printing boards for *Hiparama of the Classics.* Michael Momm for putting me up in L.A. Don Mupo for his reminscences of Oakland's Gold Nugget.

Chuck Niles for leading me to the Lord Buckley's Lighthouse recordings. Nina at Whitley Terrace for a special tour of the neighborhood.

The late Don Parent for turning up and sharing his late brother's (Bob Parent) 1960 photos of Lord Buckley. Ken Pastore for pointing out the strains of Buckley in the work of Joni Mitchell and James Taylor. Dr. Francesco Patricolo for a gestalt whammy and for his insights into Lord Buckley's place in the grand oral tradition. Alan Penchanski for his connections in the world of public relations. Jim Philbrook for sharing tapes of his Buckley rarities, for selling off the cream of his collection to me, for his connection in the world of Buckley collecting, and for leading me to both the Lighthouse tapes and the RCA outtakes. Ken Poston for his hand in uncovering the 1953 Lighthouse reels.

Andy Reichsman for business and soul counseling. Reno for carrying the torch. David Rubin for encouraging me to build it so that they could come.

Tony Sampas for riding "The Train." Vin Scelsa for spinning "Scrooge" on Big Apple airwaves each Nazzmas. Phil Schaap for a being a role model—"Bird Lives!" Mark Schecter is one of the world's great not-so-secret heroes in the Lord Buckley universe, as his weekend celebrations attested: no one who attended will ever forget them! Doug Schulkind is an old friend, fellow baseball mystic, and jazzbeaux comrade-in-arms who has a must-hear-now Friday-morning radio program, *Give the Drummer Some,* on WFMU out of Jersey City—not only did Doug oversee the dubbing of some fragile Buckley reel-to-reels, but he invited me me up to the station for a couple of Buckleythons too. Dr. John V. Scialli for helping me track down the Buckley/Zappa/Beefheart connection. Gene Sculatti for research ideas and for witing his books, *Cool* and *Too Cool.* Joel Selvin for his attempts at putting me in touch with San Francisco's bohemian old guard. David Segal for backing me up on piano at "Dig and Thou Shall Be Dug" in 1994—and for being an incisive raconteur. Michael and Gil Segal for their confidence. Don Siovatti, formerly of the Museum of Broadcasting and Communication in Chicago, helped uncover Denis Mitchell's documentary *Chicago: First Impressions of a Great American City.* Lance Slom of New Orleans for putting me in touch with Jon Sinclair, taking Elaine and me to Ugelich's (the best restaurant in the Crescent City), and some great ideas. Ron Smith for sharing his collection of moving-image Buckley. Kim Spurlock (author of the hopefully to-be-published biography of Neal Cassady) for commiserating. David Stanford for urging. Roger Steffens for sharing his collection of Buckley and Marley and for introducing me to his circle of Lordophiles.

Ron Taft for early legal advice (and for sensing BS even when he didn't smell it). Lady Elaine Thomasen for invaluable information regarding Lord Buckley's roots and youth. Residents of Tuolumne, California (Bill Hodge, Ross Baker, and Barbara and Tom MacDonald), for their essential background knowledge and experience in the region. John Tytell for being impressed by my mother's knowledge of Lord Buckley.

Dr. Sherwood Waldron for an unguided tour into the realm of Oedipus. Ray Watkins wherever you are. Robert Weide for showing that a documentary film about a societal scourge can be done right and tight. Stacey Wescott for turning Pearl Jam on to the Lord.

Jeff Zinn for his involvement with Frank Speiser's 1995 New York City run.

permissions

Quotations from *High Times Hard Times* by Anita O'Day reprinted with permission by Limelight Editions.

Quotations from *Those Swinging Years: The Autobiography of Charlie Barnet* by Charlie Barnet reprinted with permission from Louisiana State University Press.

Quotations from *Honey: The Life and Loves of Lenny's Shady Lady* by Honey Bruce and Dana Berenson reprinted with permission by IMG Literary.

Quotations from *Jazz Lives* by Michael Ullman reprinted with permission from New Republic Books.

Quotations from *My Life as a Woman* by Roseanne reprinted with permission from Harper & Row.

Quotations from *From Birdland to Broadway* by Bill Crow reprinted with permission from Oxford University Press.

Quotations from "Posthumous Stardom for a Once and Future Lord: The Lord Buckley Phenomenon" and "Heah's Yo Daddy, Lord Buckley!" by Albert Goldman reprinted with the permission of Shpritzgun Productions, Inc.

Quotations from *Time of the Assassins* by Henry Miller reprinted with permission from New Directions Book.

Quotations from "Death of a Peer" by Francis Newton reprinted with permission from Francis Newton.

Quotations from *Hiparama of the Classics* "Introduction" by Joseph Jablonsky reprinted with permission from Joseph Jablonsky.

Quotations from *Way Out Humor* liner notes by Dan James reprinted with permission from Blue Note/Capitol Records.

Quotations from *The Best of Lord Buckley* liner notes by Charles Tacot reprinted with permission from Charles Tacot.

Quotations from Lord Buckley's routines reprinted with permission by Warner Bros. Publications U.S. Inc.

Quotations from Lord Buckley's L.S.D. transcript reprinted with the permission of Dr. Oscar Janiger.

Lord Buckley quotations from his 1960 WFMT interview with Studs Terkel used with the permission of Studs Terkel.

Lord Buckley quotations from his 1959 KPFA interview with Bill Butler (BB1089 Noblesse Obliging: Lord Buckley interviewed by Bill Butler) used with the permission of the Pacifica Radio Archives, North Hollywood, California.

Transcript Permissions

"Bad Rapping of the Marquis De Sade," by Lord Buckley © 1969 (Renewed) EMI U Catalog Inc. All Rights Reserved. Used by Permission. Warner Bros. Publications U.S. Inc., Miami, Fl. 33014

"Black Cross," by Lord Buckley © 1959 (Renewed) EMI U Catalog Inc. All Rights Reserved. Used by Permission. Warner Bros. Publications U.S. Inc., Miami, Fl. 33014

"The Chastity Belt," by Lord Buckley © 1969 (Renewed) EMI U Catalog Inc. All Rights Reserved. Used by Permission. Warner Bros. Publications U.S. Inc., Miami, Fl. 33014

"Gettysburg Address," by Lord Buckley © 1960 (Renewed) EMI U Catalog Inc. All Rights Reserved. Used by Permission. Warner Bros. Publications U.S. Inc., Miami, Fl. 33014

"God's Own Drunk," by Lord Buckley © 1959 (Renewed) EMI U Catalog Inc. All Rights Reserved. Used by Permission. Warner Bros. Publications U.S. Inc., Miami, Fl. 33014

"The H-Bomb," by Lord Buckley © 1969 (Renewed) EMI U Catalog Inc. All Rights Reserved. Used by Permission. Warner Bros. Publications U.S. Inc., Miami, Fl. 33014

"The Hip Gahn," by Lord Buckley © EMI U Catalog Inc. © Renewed. All Rights Reserved. Used by Permission. Warner Bros. Publications U.S. Inc., Miami, Fl. 33014

"His Majesty The Policeman," by Lord Buckley © 1969 (Renewed) EMI U Catalog Inc. All Rights Reserved. Used by Permission. Warner Bros. Publications U.S. Inc., Miami, Fl. 33014

"Jonah And The Whale," Lord Buckley © EMI U Catalog Inc. © Renewed. All Rights Reserved. Used by Permission. Warner Bros. Publications U.S. Inc., Miami, Fl. 33014

"Let It Down," Lord Buckley © 1960 (Renewed) EMI U Catalog Inc. All Rights Reserved. Used by Permission. Warner Bros. Publications U.S. Inc., Miami, Fl. 33014

"Maharaja," by Lord Buckley © 1960 (Renewed) EMI U Catalog Inc. All Rights Reserved. Used by Permission. Warner Bros. Publications U.S. Inc., Miami, Fl. 33014

"Marc Antony's Funeral Oration," by Lord Buckley © EMI U Catalog Inc. © Renewed. All Rights Reserved. Used by Permission. Warner Bros. Publications U.S. Inc., Miami, Fl. 33014

"Martin's Horse," by Lord Buckley © 1959 (Renewed) EMI U Catalog Inc. All Rights Reserved. Used by Permission. Warner Bros. Publications U.S. Inc., Miami, Fl. 33014

"Murder," by Lord Buckley © EMI U Catalog Inc. © Renewed. All Rights Reserved. Used by Permission. Warner Bros. Publications U.S. Inc., Miami, Fl. 33014

"The Naz," by Lord Buckley © 1959 (Renewed) EMI U Catalog Inc. All Rights Reserved. Used by Permission. Warner Bros. Publications U.S. Inc., Miami, Fl. 33014

"Nero," by Lord Buckley © EMI U Catalog Inc. © Renewed. All Rights Reserved. Used by Permission. Warner Bros. Publications U.S. Inc., Miami, Fl. 33014

"Scrooge," by Lord Buckley © 1960 (Renewed) EMI U Catalog Inc. All Rights Reserved. Used by Permission. Warner Bros. Publications U.S. Inc., Miami, Fl. 33014

"Subconscious Mind," by Lord Buckley © 1960 (Renewed) EMI U Catalog Inc. All Rights Reserved. Used by Permission. Warner Bros. Publications U.S. Inc., Miami, Fl. 33014

"Willie The Shake," by Lord Buckley © 1959 (Renewed) EMI U Catalog Inc. All Rights Reserved. Used by Permission. Warner Bros. Publications U.S. Inc., Miami, Fl. 33014

Audio Permissions

Lord Buckley interview with Studs Terkel used with the permission of Studs Terkel, WFMT-FM in Chicago and the Chicago Historical Society.

Mechanical recording rights for Lord Buckley's routines on CD ("Subconscious Mind," "Black Cross," "Willie the Shake," "The Nazz," "Murder," "His Majesty, The Policeman") used with the permission of the Harry Fox Agency.

Master recording rights for Lord Buckley's routines on CD ("Subconscious Mind," "Black Cross," "Willie the Shake," "The Nazz," "Murder," "His Majesty, The Policeman") used with the permission of Blue Note/Captiol Records.

CD on reverse side of page